Αmerica Past and Present

Robert A. Divine

University of Texas

T. H. Breen

Northwestern University

George M. Fredrickson

Stanford University

R. Hal Williams

Southern Methodist University

HarperCollins*CollegePublishers*

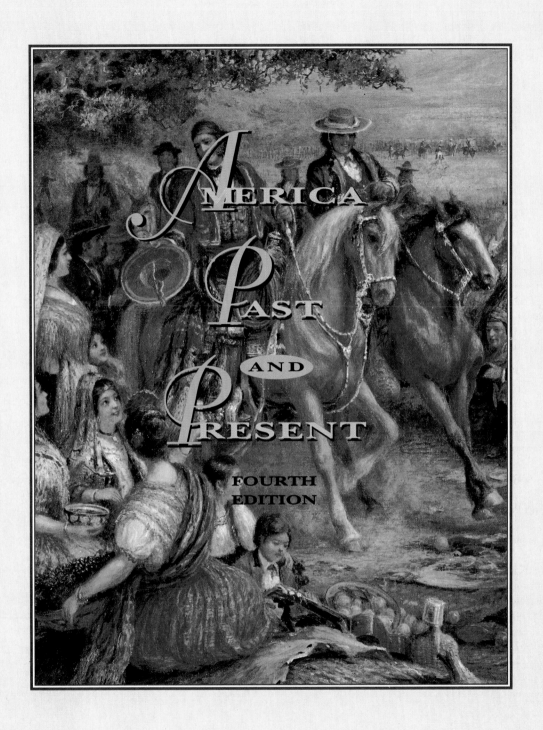

America Past and Present

FOURTH EDITION

Volume One to 1877

Executive Editor: *Bruce Borland*
Director of Development: *Betty Slack*
Project Editors: *Steven Pisano and Shuli Traub*
Design Manager: *Jill Little*
Cover Designer: *Kay Petronio*
Art Studio: *Mapping Specialists Limited*
Photo Researchers: *Leslie Coopersmith and Mary Goljenboom*
Electronic Production Manager: *Mike Kemper*
Manufacturing Manager: *Joseph Campanella*
Electronic Page Makeup: *RR Donnelley Barbados*
Printer and Binder: *R.R. Donnelly & Sons Company*
Cover Printer: *Coral Graphics Services, Inc.*

America Past and Present, Volume One to 1877, Fourth Edition

ISBN 0-673-99193-8 (Volume One)
ISBN 0-673-99194-6 (Volume Two)

94 95 96 97 9 8 7 6 5 4 3 2 1

Brief Contents

Detailed Contents

CHAPTER 1

New World Encounters   1

CHAPTER 2

Competing Visions: English Colonization in the Seventeenth Century   31

Maps

Charts, Tables, and Graphs

Preface

The fourth edition of *America Past and Present* is a major revision that strives to achieve the shared goal of the previous editions: to present a clear, relevant, and balanced history of the United States as an unfolding story of national development, from the days of the earliest inhabitants to the present. We emphasize the *story* because we strongly believe in the value of historical narrative in providing a vivid sense of the past. In each chapter, we sought to blend the excitement and drama of the American experience with insights about the social, economic, and cultural issues that underlie it.

REVISIONS FOR THE FOURTH EDITION

In this edition, we have reviewed each chapter carefully to take account of recent scholarly work, to offer new perspectives, and to sharpen the analysis and the prose. In many cases we have adopted the suggestions offered by those who used the previous editions in their classrooms.

Throughout this revised edition, we devote increased attention to discussion of the ethnic diversity of the United States. New material has been added on Native Americans, African Americans, Hispanic Americans, and Asian Americans. They appear throughout the text, not as witnesses to the historical narrative, but as principals in its development. The opening vignette in Chapter 1 deals with the encounter between Columbus and the Taínos Indians of Hispaniola; Chapter 4 has increased material on settlement in the Spanish borderlands of the eighteenth century as well as on the encounters between Native Americans and European settlers in the "Middle Ground" between the Appalachian Mountains and the Mississippi River. The opening vignette in Chapter 16 discusses the career of Robert Smalls, one of the most famous southern black leaders of the Civil War and Reconstruction era. Material on immi-

gration from China and Japan during the early twentieth century has been added in Chapter 23, and Chapter 33 includes extensive discussion of the ethnic diversity of the United States in the period from the late 1970s to the 1990s.

Another focus of this revision is expanded discussion of the "frontier" in American history. For example, in Chapter 4, material has been added on settlement in the backcountry during the eighteenth century. Chapter 17 now includes discussion of the thesis of the new western historians on the continuing migration to and development and exploitation of the American West.

The final three chapters have been completely rewritten. Chapter 31 discusses politics and diplomacy from the mid-1960s to 1980, the social upheavals of the 1960s, and the energy crisis and inflation of the 1970s. Chapter 32 covers the major political and economic developments of the Reagan-Bush era, the presidential campaign of 1992 and the return of the Democrats to the White House with the election of Bill Clinton, and the momentous political changes of the late 1980s and early 1990s with the collapse of communism in eastern Europe, the dismantling of the Soviet Union, and the end of the Cold War. Chapter 33 is an entirely new chapter covering the social, demographic, ethnic, cultural, and economic changes in American life from the 1970s to the present.

APPROACH AND THEMES

As the title suggests, our book is a blend of the traditional and the new. The strong narrative emphasis and chronological organization are traditional; the incorporation of the many fresh insights that historians have gained from social sciences in the past quarter century is new. We have used significant incidents and episodes to reflect the dilemmas, the choices, and the decisions made by the people as well as by their leaders. After discussion of the colonial period, most of the chapters examine shorter time periods, usually about a decade, permitting us to view these major political and public events as points of reference and orientation around which social themes are integrated. This approach gives unity and direction to the text.

In recounting the story of the American past, we see a nation in flux. The early Africans and Europeans developed complex agrarian folkways that blended Old World customs and New World experiences; as cultural identities evolved, the idea of political independence became more acceptable. People who had been subjects of the British Crown created a system of government that challenged later Americans to work out the full implications of theories of social and economic equality.

The growing sectional rift between the North and South, revolving around divergent models of economic growth and conflicting social values, culminated in civil war. In the post–Civil War period, the development of a more industrialized economy severely tested the values of an agrarian society, engendering a Populist reform movement. In the early twentieth century, Progressive reformers sought to infuse the industrial order with social justice. World War I demonstrated the extent of American power in the world. The resiliency of the maturing American nation was tested by the Great Depression and World War II. The Cold War ushered in an era of crises, foreign and domestic, that revealed both the strengths and the weaknesses of modern America.

The impact of change on human lives adds a vital dimension to our understanding of history. We need to comprehend the way the Revolution affected the lives of ordinary citizens; what it was like for both blacks and whites to live in a plantation society; how men and women fared in the shift from an agrarian to an industrial economy; and what impact technology, in the form of the automobile and the computer, has had on patterns of life in the twentieth century.

Our commitment is not to any particular ideology or point of view; rather, we hope to challenge our readers to rediscover the fascination of the American past and reach their own conclusions about its significance in their lives. At the same time, we have not avoided controversial issues; instead, we have tried to offer reasoned judgments on such morally charged subjects as the nature of slavery and the advent of nuclear weapons. We believe that while history rarely repeats itself, the story of the American past is relevant to the problems and dilemmas facing the nation today, and we have therefore sought to stress themes and ideas that continue to shape our national culture.

STRUCTURE AND FEATURES

The structure and features of the book are intended to stimulate student interest and to reinforce learning. Chapters begin with **vignettes** or incidents, many of them new, that establish direction for chapter themes stated in the introductory sections (which also serve as overviews to the topics covered) and with **expanded summaries**. Each chapter has a **chronology, recommended readings, bibliography** (revised and updated for this revision), and two-page **special feature essay** on a topic that combines high interest and instructional value. Three of the special feature essays are new in this edition: Chapter 4, on etiquette and manners in the eighteenth century; Chapter 13, on the life and experiences of women—black and white, slave and free—on the plantations of the Old South; and Chapter 33, on political, economic, and cultural relations between the United States and Mexico.

New in this edition are the four **four-page essays on "Law and Society."** Each of the essays covers a significant legal case in American history and includes a discussion of the background of the case, excerpts from the trial transcript, and coverage of the case in the news media of the period. Questions at the end of each essay invite students to explore the legal contest from the perspective of social/cultural historians. The cases featured in the essays are the Salem witch trials, the Beecher-Tilton adultery trial of 1875, *Muller* v. *Oregon*, and *Bakke* v. *Regents of the University of California*.

The extensive **full-color map program** has been expanded to provide more information on the ethnic diversity of the United States and more integration of information and action. **New charts, graphs, and tables**—many with a capsulized format for convenient review of factual information—relate to social and economic change. See, for example, the new table in Chapter 26, "Major New Deal Legislation and Agencies," which lists the principal agencies of the New Deal and summarizes the purposes of each. The rich **full-color illustration program**, bearing directly on the narrative, advances and expands the themes, provides elaboration and contrast, tells more of the story, and generally adds another dimension of learning. The illustrations also present a mini survey of American painting styles. The **"Growth of the United States" series** at the front of the book combines maps, narrative, and a time line of parallel events. The augmented **Appendix** includes the Articles of Confederation (in addition to the Declaration of Independence and the Constitution of the United States and its Amendments). Charts, tables, and graphs present a demographic profile of the American people.

Although this book is a joint effort, each author took primary responsibility for writing one section. T. H. Breen contributed the first eight chapters from the earliest Native American period to the second decade of the nineteenth century. George M. Fredrickson wrote Chapters 9 through 16, carrying the narrative through the Reconstruction era. R. Hal Williams is responsible for Chapters 17 through 24, focusing on the industrial transformation and urbanization, and the events culminating in World War I. Robert A. Divine wrote Chapters 25 through 33, bringing the story through the Great Depression, World War II, and the Cold War from its beginning to its end. Each contributor reviewed and revised the work of his colleagues and helped shape the material into its final form.

SUPPLEMENTS

For Instructors

Instructor's Resource Manual
Prepared by James P. Walsh of Central Connecticut State University, each chapter of this important resource manual contains interpretative essays, anecdotes and references to biographical or primary sources, and a comprehensive summary of the text.

America Through the Eyes of Its People: A Collection of Primary Sources
Prepared by Carol Brown of Houston Community College, this one-volume collection of primary documents portraying the rich and varied tapestry of American life contains documents of women, Native Americans, African Americans, Hispanics, and others who helped to shape the course of U.S. history. Designed to be duplicated by instructors for student use, the documents also have accompanying student exercises.

Discovering American History Through Maps and Views
Created by Gerald Danzer, University of Illinois at Chicago, the recipient of the AHA's 1990 James Harvey Robinson Prize for his work in the development of map transparencies, this set of 140 four-color acetates is a unique instructional tool. It contains an introduction on teaching history through maps and a detailed commentary on each transparency. The collection includes cartographic and pictorial maps, views and photos, urban plans, building diagrams, and works of art.

A Guide to Teaching American History Through Film
Created by Randy Roberts of Purdue University, this guide provides instructors with a creative and practical tool for stimulating classroom discussion. The sections include "American Films: A Historian's Perspective," a listing of "Films for Specific Periods of American History," "Practical Suggestions," and "Bibliography." The film listing is presented in a narrative form, developing the connection between each film and the topics being studied.

Visual Archives of American History, 2/e
This two-sided video laserdisc explores history from a meeting of three cultures to the present and is an encyclopedic chronology of U.S. history offering hundreds of photographs and illustrations, a variety of source and reference maps—several of which are animated—plus approximately 50 minutes of video clips. For ease in planning lectures, a manual listing barcodes for scanning and frame numbers for all the content will be provided.

American Impressions: A CD-ROM for U.S. History
This unique, ground-breaking product for the Introduction to U.S. history course is organized in a topical/thermatic framework, which allows an in-depth coverage for each topic with a media-centered focus. Hundreds of photos, maps, pieces of art, graphics, and historical film clips are organized into narrated vignettes and interactive activ-

ities to create a tool for both professors and students. This first volume of a series includes: When Three Cultures Meet, The Constitution, Labor and Reform, and Democracy and Diversity: The History of Civil Rights. Each topic is explored through three major themes: Politics, Culture and Society, and Science and Health. Available for Macintosh and Windows formats.

Video Lecture Launchers

Prepared by Mark Newman, University of Illinois at Chicago, these video lecture launchers (each 2 to 5 minutes in duration) cover key issues in American history from 1877 to the present. The launchers are accompanied by an Instructor's Manual.

Test Bank

Prepared by Carol Brown and Michael McCormick, Houston Community College, and James S. Olson, Sam Houston State University, this test bank contains over 1,200 multiple-choice, true/false, matching, and completion questions.

TestMaster Computerized Testing System

This flexible, easy-to-master computer test bank includes all the test items in the printed test bank. The TestMaster software allows you to edit existing questions and add your own items. Tests can be printed in several different formats and can include figures such as graphs and tables. Available for IBM and Macintosh computers.

QuizMaster

The new program enables you to design TestMaster generated tests that your students can take on a computer rather than in printed form. QuizMaster is available separate from TestMaster and can be obtained free through your sales representative.

Grades

A grade-keeping and classroom management software program that maintains data for up to 200 students.

For Students

Study Guide and Practice Tests

This two-volume study guide was created by Donald L. Smith, Houston Community College; Richard Bailey, San Jacinto College; Charles M.

Cook, Texas Higher Education Coordinating Board, Community and Technical Colleges; and Jon V. Garrett, Houston Community College. Each volume begins with an introductory essay, "Skills for Studying and Learning History." Each chapter contains a summary, learning objectives, identification list, map exercises, glossary, and multiple-choice, completion, and essay questions.

Learning to Think Critically: Films and Myths about American History

Randy Roberts and Robert May of Purdue University use well-known films such as Gone with the Wind and Casablanca to explore some common myths about America and its past. Many widely held assumptions about our country's past come from or are perpetuated by popular films. Which are true? Which are patently not true? And how does a student of history approach documents, sources, and textbooks with a critical and discerning eye? This short handbook subjects some popular beliefs to historical scrutiny to help students develop a method of inquiry for approaching the subject of history in general.

SuperShell II Computerized Tutorial

Prepared by Ron Petrin, Oklahoma State University, this interactive program for IBM computers helps students learn the major facts and concepts through drill and practice exercises and diagnostic feedback. SuperShell II, which provides immediate correct answers and the text page number on which the material is discussed, maintains a running score of the student's performance on the screen throughout the session. This free student supplement is available to instructors through their sales representatives.

Mapping American History: Student Activities

Written by Gerald Danzer of the University of Illinois at Chicago, this free map workbook for students features exercises designed to teach students to interpret and analyze cartographic materials as historical documents. The instructor is entitled to a free copy of the workbook for each copy of the text that is purchased from HarperCollins.

TimeLink Computer Atlas of American History

This atlas, compiled by William Hamblin of Brigham Young University, is an introductory software tutorial and textbook companion. This

Macintosh program presents the historical geography of the continental United States from colonial times to the settling of the West and the admission of the last continental state in 1912. The program covers territories in different time periods, provides quizzes, and includes a special Civil War module.

ACKNOWLEDGMENTS

We are most grateful to our consultants and critiquers whose thoughtful and constructive work contributed greatly to this edition. Their many helpful suggestions led to significant improvements in the final product.

Joseph L. Adams
Meramec Community College

Frank Alduino
Anne Arundel Community College

James D. Border
Berkshire Community College

James E. Fell, Jr.
University of Colorado, Denver

Don R. Gerlach
University of Akron

August W. Giebelhaus
Georgia Institute of Technology

Anne Hickling
San Jose City College

I. E. Kirkpatrick
Tyler Junior College

Fred Koestler
Tarleton State University

Robert C. McMath, Jr.
Georgia Institute of Technology

T. Ronald Melton
Brewton-Parker College

Elliot Pasternack
Middlesex County College

J'Nell L. Pate
Tarrant County Junior College

Douglas W. Richmond
University of Texas, Arlington

George G. Suggs, Jr.
Southeast Missouri State University

Clyde D. Tyson
Niagara County Community College

Nancy C. Unger
San Francisco State University

Daniel C. Vogt
Jackson State University

James M. Woods
Georgia Southern University

A large number of instructors, too many to name individually, who used the previous editions were most helpful in reporting on the success of the text in the classroom. We heartily thank them all.

The staff at HarperCollins continued its generous support and assistance for our efforts. We appreciate the thoughtful guidance of Bruce Borland, who was instrumental in initiating the project; developmental editor Betty Slack who helped us augment and enhance the appeal of the text. Project editors Steve Pisano and Shuli Traub and design supervisor Jill Little deftly guided the new edition through the many phases of production. Others of the HarperCollins staff who gave valuable assistance include photo researchers Leslie Coopersmith and Mary Goljenboom.

Finally, each author received aid and encouragement from many colleagues, friends, and family members.

The Authors

About the Authors

ROBERT A. DIVINE

Robert A. Divine, George W. Littlefield Professor in American History at the University of Texas at Austin, received his Ph.D. from Yale University in 1954. A specialist in American diplomatic history, he has taught at the University of Texas since 1954, where he has been honored by the Student Association for teaching excellence. His extensive published work includes *The Illusion of Neutrality* (1962), *Second Chance: The Triumphs of Internationalism in America During World War II* (1967), and *Blowing on the Wind* (1978). He is also the author of *Eisenhower and the Cold War* (1981), and editor of *Exploring the Johnson Years* (1981) and *The Johnson Years*, Vol. II (1987). He has been a fellow at the Center for Advanced Study in the Behavioral Sciences and has given the Albert Shaw Lectures in Diplomatic History at Johns Hopkins University.

T. H. BREEN

T.H. Breen, William Smith Mason Professor of American History at Northwestern University, received his Ph.D. from Yale University in 1968. He has taught at Northwestern since 1970. Breen's major books include *The Character of the Good Ruler: A Study of Puritan Political Ideas in New England* (1974), *Puritans and Adventurers: Change and Persistence in Early America* (1980), *Tobacco Culture: The Mentality of the Great Tidewater Planters on the Eve of Revolution* (1985), and with S. Innes of the University of Virginia, *"Myne Owne Ground": Race and Freedom on Virginia's Eastern Shore* (1980). His *Imagining the Past* won the 1990 Historic Preservation Book Award. In addition to receiving an award for outstanding teaching at Northwestern, Breen has been the recipient of research grants from the American Council of Learned Societies, the Guggenheim Foundation, the Institute for Advanced Study (Princeton), and the National Humanities Center. For his article "Narrative of Commercial Life: Consumption, Ideology, and Community on the Eve of the American Revolution," which appeared in the July 1993 issue of *William and Mary Quarterly*, Breen received an award from the National Society, Daughters of Colonial Wars, for best article published in the quarterly in 1993, and the Douglass Adair Memorial Prize for best article published in the quarterly during the 1988–1993 period. He has served as the Fowler Hamilton Fellow at Christ Church, Oxford University (1987–1988), and the Pitt Professor of American History and Institutions, Cambridge University (1990–1991).

GEORGE M. FREDRICKSON

George M. Fredrickson is Edgar E. Robinson Professor of United States History at Stanford University. He is the author or editor of several books, including the *Inner Civil War* (1965), *The Black Image in the White Mind* (1971), and *White Supremacy: A Comparative Study in American and South African History* (1981), which won both the Ralph Waldo Emerson Award from Phi Beta Kappa and the Merle Curti Award from the Organization of American Historians. His most recent work is *The Arrogance of Race: Historical Perspectives on Slavery, Racism, and Social Inequality* (1988). He received both the A.B. and Ph.D. degrees from Harvard and has been the recipient of a Guggenheim Fellowship, two National Endowment for the Humanities Senior Fellowships, and a Fellowship from the Center for Advanced Studies in the Behavioral Sciences. Before coming to Stanford in 1984, he taught at Northwestern. He has also served as Fulbright lecturer in American History at Moscow University and as Harmsworth Professor of American History at Oxford.

R. HAL WILLIAMS

R. Hal Williams is Professor of History at Southern Methodist University. He received his A.B. degree from Princeton University (1963) and his Ph.D. degree from Yale University (1968). His books include *The Democratic Party and California Politics, 1880–1896* (1973), *Years of Decision: American Politics in the 1890s* (1978), and *The Manhattan Project: A Documentary Introduction to the Atomic Age* (1990). A specialist in American political history, he taught at Yale University from 1968 to 1975 and came to SMU in 1975 as chair of the Department of History. From 1980 to 1988, he served as dean of Dedman College, the school of humanities and sciences, at SMU. In 1980, he was a visiting professor at University College, Oxford University. Williams has received grants from the American Philosophical Society and the National Endowment for the Humanities, and he has served on the Texas Committee for the Humanities. He is currently at work on a biography of James G. Blaine, the late-nineteenth-century Speaker of the House, secretary of state, and Republican presidential candidate.

MAP SERIES

The Growth of the United States

Routes of the First Americans
xxv

1600 to the Present
xxvi–xxxiii

Routes of the First Americans

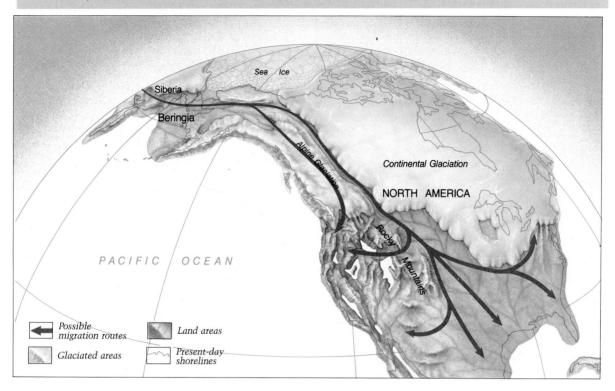

The peopling of North America began about 30,000 years ago, during the Ice Age, and continued for many millennia. Land bridges created by lower sea levels during glaciation formed a tundra coastal plain over what is now the Bering Strait, between Asia and North America. In the postglacial era, the warmer climate supported the domestication and, later, the cultivation of plants. By the first century A.D., intensive farming was established from the southwest to the east coast of what is now the United States. (Ch. 1)

Except for an abortive attempt by Norsemen in the tenth century to settle the New World, contact between North America and Europe was not established until the Age of Exploration at the end of the 1400s. Settlements were founded in Mexico and Florida by Spain in the 1500s, and along the Atlantic littoral by France, England, Sweden, and Holland in the early 1600s.

From the founding of the first colonies along the Atlantic coast to the current involvement of the United States in global affairs, the dominant theme in American life has been growth. The pages that follow chronicle the growth of the United States from its colonial origins to the present in fifty-year intervals, using maps, narrative, and a chronology of major and parallel events.

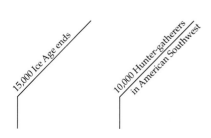

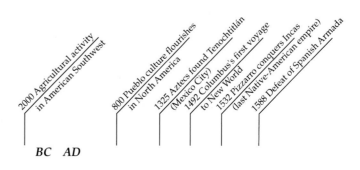

BC AD

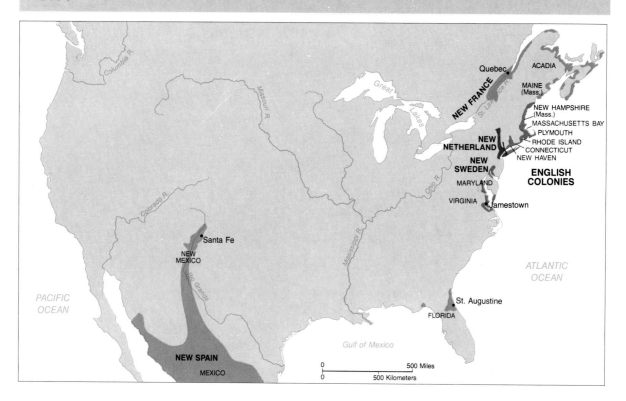

Following up on Columbus's New World discoveries, the Spanish set sail for America and conquered the Native American Aztecs and Incas in the sixteenth century, establishing a vast colonial empire stretching from Mexico to Peru. The search for gold and silver brought Spanish explorers into the present-day American Southwest, where they established outposts in New Mexico in the early 1600s. Even earlier, Spain had begun the settlement of Florida with the founding of St. Augustine in 1565. Far to the north the French, attracted by the profits of the fur trade with the Indians, began settling the St. Lawrence valley in the early part of the seventeenth century.

Between the Spanish to the south and the French to the north, English colonists founded a series of scattered settlements along the Atlantic coast. Driven by the desire for economic gain, religious freedom, or both, colonists in Virginia and Massachusetts Bay endured severe weather and periods of starvation to establish small but permanent colonies. By mid-century, settlements had sprung up in New Hampshire, Connecticut, and Rhode Island. Along Chesapeake Bay, Maryland was founded as a place of refuge for persecuted Catholics. In the midst of these English colonies, the Dutch established New Netherland and took over a small Swedish settlement. By the middle of the century, the seeds had been planted for a future United States.

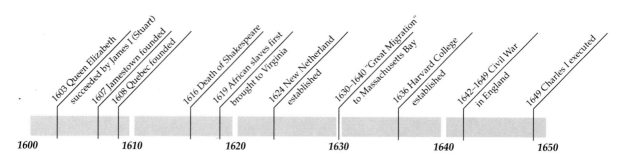

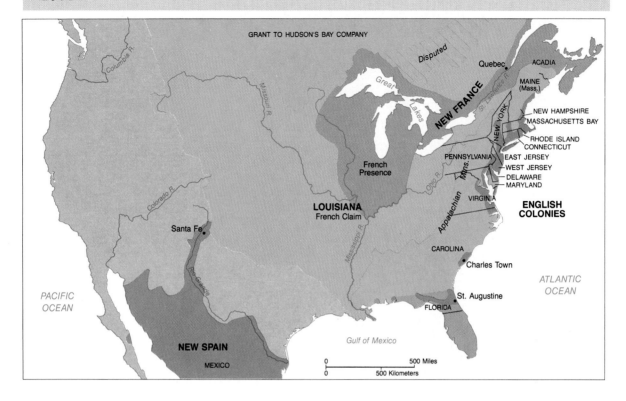

Having established a precarious foothold, the English settlements slowly began to grow and prosper. The later New England colonies received royal charters, separate from the original Massachusetts Bay charter. William Penn established Pennsylvania as a place of refuge for Quakers, welcoming French, Dutch, German, and Swedish settlers, as well as English and Scotch-Irish. Nearby New Jersey became the home for an equally diverse population. Under English rule, New Netherland became New York. In the south, English aristocrats founded Carolina as a plantation society populated in great part by settlers from the Caribbean island of Barbados. What was most remarkable about these English colonies was not their similarities but the differences between them. Bound together only by ties to the mother country, each developed its own character and culture.

Meanwhile, intrepid French explorers based in Quebec penetrated deep into the interior of the continent, driven on by the imperatives of the fur trade. Père Jacques Marquette navigated the Mississippi River and Sieur de La Salle journeyed to the Gulf of Mexico, laying claim for the King of France to a vast territory—all the lands drained by the Mississippi and its tributaries. This French initiative alarmed colonists along the Atlantic coast, many of whom believed that France planned to block English settlement on the lands beyond the Appalachian Mountains. About the same time, Spain established missions in Texas as a token presence. (Ch. 1, 2)

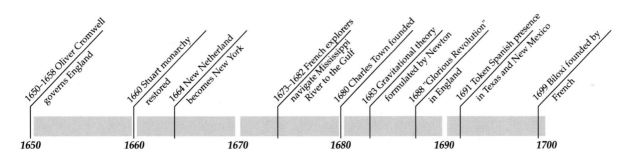

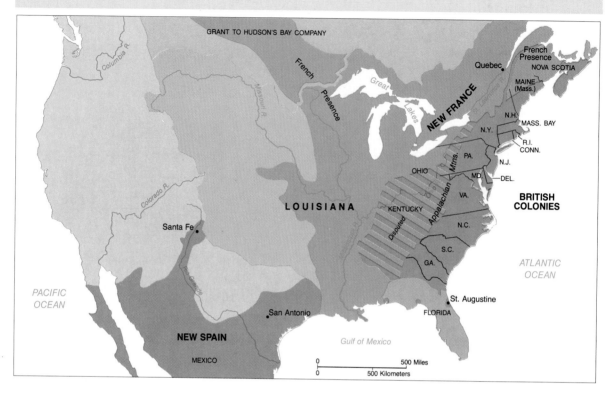

A century-long European struggle for empire between the French and the British led to military confrontation on this side of the Atlantic. Britain's victory in Queen Anne's War changed the map of North America. It gave the British control of the land bordering on Hudson Bay, as well as Newfoundland and Nova Scotia. The French redoubled their efforts to develop Louisiana as a buffer against the westward expansion of the seaboard colonies. Concerned with the Spanish presence in Florida, the British founded the colony of Georgia in 1732 to guard the Carolinas, which had been divided in 1729 into the separate royal colonies of North and South Carolina.

By the middle of the eighteenth century, the American colonists were rapidly moving onto the lands between the Atlantic coast and the foothills of the Appalachian Mountains. Descendents of the original settlers, along with newcomers from England, Northern Ireland, and Germany, filtered into the Shenandoah Valley to settle the backcountry of Virginia and the Carolinas. Other Americans contemplated crossing the mountains to occupy the fertile lands of Kentucky and Ohio. The French, fearful of a floodtide of American settlers, made important alliances with Indian tribes of the Ohio country to strengthen their position, and built a chain of forts to defend the area. Imperial rivalry for control of North America was approaching its climax. (Ch. 4)

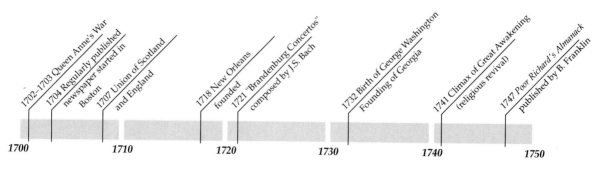

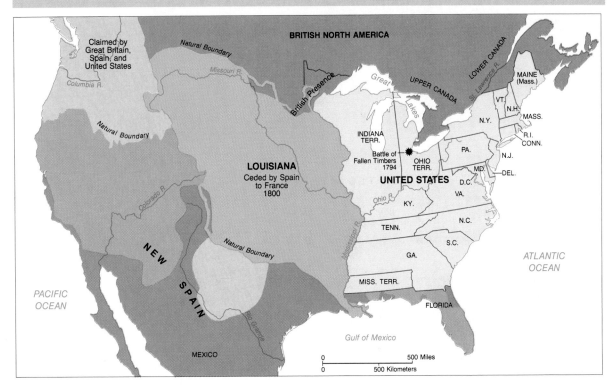

In the half century between 1750 and 1800, the map of North America underwent extensive political change. First, the British defeated the French and drove them from the mainland of the continent. The Peace of Paris in 1763 called for the French to surrender Canada to Great Britain and transfer Louisiana to Spain. The subsequent British Proclamation Line of 1763, designed to preserve a fur trade with the Indians by blocking settlement west of the mountains, angered the colonists and contributed to the unrest that culminated in the Revolutionary War.

Independence stimulated the westward expansion of the American people. Even while the fighting was in progress, pioneers like Daniel Boone began opening up Kentucky and Tennessee to frontier settlement. In the 1783 treaty that ended the war, Britain granted the United States generous boundaries, stretching from the Great Lakes and the St. Lawrence River on the north to Florida on the south, and the Mississippi on the west. But the young nation found it difficult to make good its claims to this new territory. Indians tried to hold on to their land, with British and Spanish encouragement. In the mid-1790s, however, diplomatic agreements with both nations and a crushing defeat of the Indians at Fallen Timbers opened the way to American settlement of the land beyond the mountains. Kentucky and Tennessee became states in the union before the end of the century, and Ohio would follow just a few years later. (Ch. 4, 5, 6, 7)

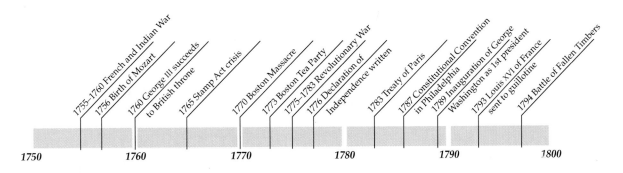

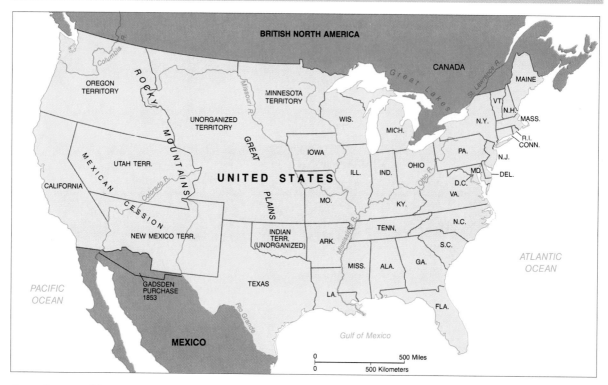

Over the next fifty years, the territory of the United States more than doubled. The purchase of Louisiana from France brought in the vast trans-Mississippi West, stretching across the Great Plains to the Rocky Mountains. From 1804 to 1806, William Lewis and Meriwether Clark and their expedition crossed the continent. Distance, fierce Indian resistance, and an arid climate delayed the settlement of the trans-Mississippi West, but American settlers poured into the area east of the Mississippi. The eastern Indians, their power broken in the War of 1812, were no longer able to resist the tide of settlement; they agreed to evacuate their ancestral homelands and in 1835 the last holdouts, the Cherokees, were forcibly removed to Oklahoma.

The climax of western expansionism came in the 1840s, when the United States extended its boundaries to the Pacific. Proclaiming the nation's "manifest destiny" to occupy the continent, American settlers leapfrogged over the inhospitable Great Plains and rugged Rockies to settle in California and Oregon. Diplomacy with Great Britain secured Oregon to the 49th parallel. Americans moved into Texas in the 1820s, broke away from Mexico in 1836, and joined the union in 1845—a move that led to war with Mexico in 1846. The American victory two years later gave the United States California and the New Mexico territory. The purchase in 1853 of a small strip of southern Arizona from Mexico rounded out the nation's present-day continental boundaries. (Ch. 8, 9, 10, 12)

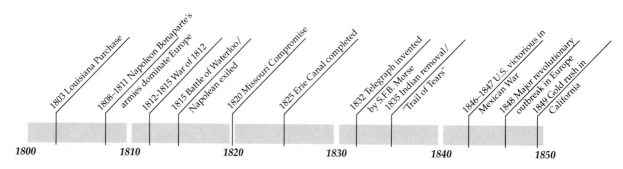

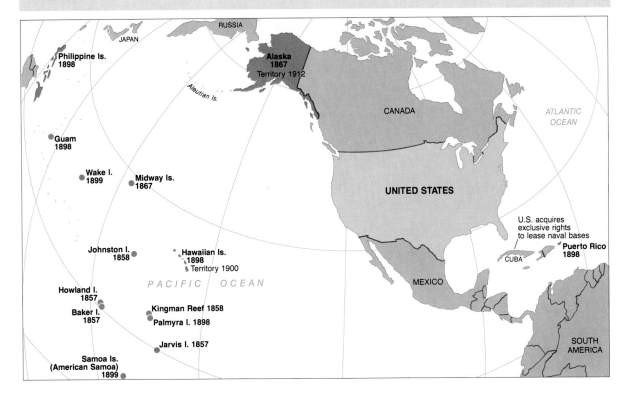

Newly acquired territories brought great opportunities and bitter sectional quarrels. The discovery of gold in California at mid-century was followed by a rush to the Pacific, but the question of extending slavery into the new areas set North against South. That controversy contributed to the outbreak of civil war and the end of slavery. In the three decades following the Civil War, Americans finally settled the last frontier: the Rockies and the Great Plains.

Railroads linked widely separated regions when the first transcontinental line was completed in Utah in 1869. Prospectors flocked to the Rockies, drawn by the bonanza of mineral wealth; ranchers drove cattle through the grasslands of the great open range from the Texas Panhandle to Montana; farmers, using new technology and methods to meet the semiarid conditions, increased the fertility of the soil of the Great Plains. In 1893 historian Frederick Jackson Turner proclaimed the American frontier was disappearing, signaling the end of an era.

With the continent settled, expansionists looked overseas. William Seward added Alaska to the nation's territory in 1867. Three decades later, victory in the Spanish-American War led to an outburst of enthusiasm for empire. The United States acquired Puerto Rico and the Philippines from Spain, and annexed the Hawaiian Islands. (Ch. 14, 15, 17, 21)

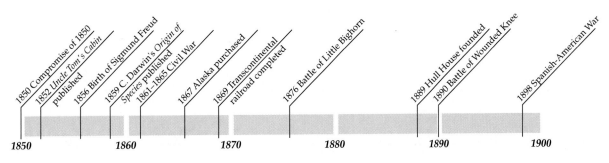

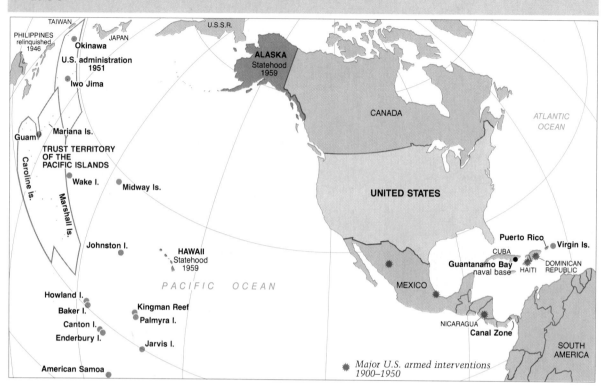

Major U.S. armed interventions 1900–1950

Taking an active role in world affairs led to recurring armed interventions by the United States in distant lands. In 1900, American troops took part in the international effort to put down the antiforeign Boxer Rebellion in China. Over the next decade and a half, the United States intervened in several Latin American countries with armed force, most notably in Panama, where the United States acquired the Canal Zone in 1903, and in Mexico, with the six-month occupation of Veracruz in 1914.

America remained neutral for the first three years of World War I in Europe but finally entered the war against the Central Powers (Germany, Austria-Hungary, and Turkey) in 1917, eventually sending more than two million men to fight in France. At the war's end, President Wilson played an active role in

negotiating the Treaty of Versailles, even though the United States did not join the League of Nations created by the treaty.

Despite attempts in the 1920s and 1930s to limit American involvement in the world, the 1940s found Americans fighting Germany and Japan around the globe. American forces waged World War II in North Africa, on many Pacific islands, and in Europe. Although the United States took the lead in forming the United Nations, the end of the war did not usher in an era of lasting peace. To the contrary, the United States and the Soviet Union faced off in a Cold War that led to the permanent stationing of American troops from West Germany to the Pacific Trust Territory. The Philippines gained their independence in 1946. (Ch. 21, 24, 27, 28)

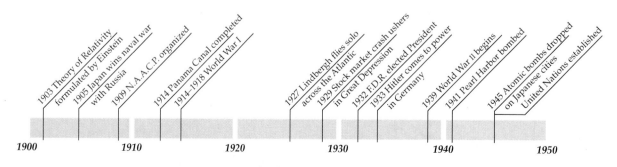

The United States took part in two Asian wars after 1950: a stalemate in Korea and a long, frustrating, losing struggle in Vietnam in the 1960s and 1970s. Closer to home, Russian ties to Fidel Castro led to a dangerous showdown during the Cuban missile crisis in 1962. In the Middle East, European dependence on Persian Gulf oil and American support for Israel made and continue to make this region an area of vital concern for U.S. foreign policy.

There have been changes in the status of America's territorial possessions: Hawaii and Alaska became the forty-ninth and fiftieth states in the late 1950s; and Puerto Rico was granted commonwealth status in 1952. A new frontier—outer space—was opened up with the Soviet launch of *Sputnik* in 1957. In 1969 came the world's most spectacular space achievement to date when American astronauts landed on the moon. Rockets now launch unmanned probes into the farthest reaches of the solar system, gathering invaluable scientific data. America's space shuttle program—despite setbacks—continues the investigation of space. American horizons, once limited to the confines of thirteen struggling colonies, have expanded over four centuries to embrace the entire world and the nearer reaches of outer space. (Ch. 28, 29, 30, 31; 32, 33)

The greatest changes have come in Europe. The wave of liberation that swept across central and eastern Europe in the summer and fall of 1989 was fittingly exemplified by the crumbling of the Berlin Wall. Germany was reunited, and Communist regimes throughout eastern Europe collapsed. The disintegration of the Soviet Union in 1991 marked the end of the Cold War.

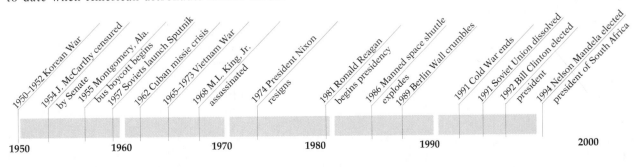

New World Encounters

single dramatic moment altered the course of history for peoples living on three continents. On October 12, 1492, the Taínos, American Indians living in the Bahamas, encountered Europeans and perhaps a few Africans for the first time. How the Taínos regarded the Spanish invaders will never be known. They left no written records. Only the impressions of Admiral Christopher Columbus and his lieutenants have survived. Columbus's journals describe how a group of Europeans rowed to the beach, unfurled a royal standard, raised colorful banners, and, as the natives watched, took possession of territory that generations of Taínos had always called their own.

For contemporary Europeans, Columbus provided a compelling interpretation of the event's historic significance. The discovery of unknown lands and peoples across the seas brought glory to Christianity, to the Spanish monarchs, and not least, to Columbus himself. In a letter circulated throughout Europe upon his return to Spain, Columbus announced, "As I know that you will be pleased at the great victory with which Our Lord has crowned my voyage, I write this to you, from which you will learn how in thirty-three days, I passed from the Canary Islands to the Indies. . . . And there I found very many islands filled with people innumerable, and of them all I have taken possession for their highnesses [King Ferdinand and Queen Isabella]."

Columbus and the adventurers who sailed in his wake wove a narrative of discovery that survived long after the Taínos had become extinct— a fate that befell them in the mid-sixteenth century. The story recounted first in Europe and then in the United States depicted heroic captains, missionaries, and settlers carrying civilization to the peoples of the New World and opening a vast virgin land to economic development. This familiar tale celebrated progress, the inevitable spread of European values, the pushing back of frontiers. It was a history crafted by the victors—usually males—and by the children of the victors to explain how they had come to control the modern world.

This story no longer seems an adequate explanation for European conquest and colonization. It is not so much wrong as incomplete. History from Columbus's perspective inevitably silences the voices of the victims, the peoples who, in this view, resisted economic and technological progress. Heroic tales of the advance of Western civilization fail to acknowledge the millions of Indians who died following conquest or the huge numbers of Africans brought to America as slaves.

By placing these complex, often unsettling events within a framework of *encounters,* we recapture the full human dimensions of conquest and resistance. The New World demanded extraordinary creative energies from the men and women of different cultures who found themselves dealing with one another in unprecedented situations. While the New World was often the scene of tragic violence and systematic exploitation, it allowed ordinary people opportunities to shape their own lives; neither the Indians nor the Africans were passive victims of European colonization. Within their own families and communities they made choices, sometimes rebelling, sometimes accommodating, but always trying to make sense in their own terms out of what was happening to them. Although they occasionally failed to preserve dignity and independence, their efforts poignantly reveal that the history of the New World—be it from the perspective of the Indian, the African American, or the European— is above all else an intensely human drama.

NATIVE AMERICAN CULTURES

As the Taínos well knew, the peopling of America did not begin in 1492. In fact, although the Spanish invaders proclaimed the discovery of a "New World," they really brought into contact three worlds that in the fifteenth century were already old. The first migrants entered North America approximately thirty thousand years ago.

Some archaeologists maintain that human settlement actually occurred much earlier, but the evidence in support of this thesis remains highly controversial. All agree, however, that at the time of the initial migration, the earth's climate was considerably colder than it is today, and that huge glaciers, often more than a mile thick, pushed as far south as the present states of Illinois and Ohio. Much of the world's moisture was transformed into ice, and the oceans dropped

Published in Barcelona in 1493, the first edition of the Carta a Santángel, in which this illustration appeared, announced the news of Columbus's arrival in the New World.

hundreds of feet below their current level. The receding waters created a land bridge between Asia and America, an area now submerged beneath the Bering Sea.

This northern region was largely free from glacial ice, and small bands of spear-throwing Siberian hunters chased giant mammals—woolly mammoths and mastadons, all now extinct—across the open tundra that covered the land bridge. These hunters were the first human beings to set foot on a vast, uninhabited continent. The migrations continued for thousands of years, interrupted only by changing water levels that occasionally flooded the land bridge.

Because these movements took place over such a long period of time and involved small, independent bands of nomadic people, the migrants never developed a sense of themselves as representatives of a single group. Each band pursued its own interests, adjusting to the opportunities presented by various microenvironments. Some groups, presumably those who had first crossed the land bridge, migrated the greatest distances, settling South and Central America. Newer arrivals probably remained in North America.

Whatever their histories, no two groups had precisely the same experience, which helps explain the strikingly different cultures that developed in the New World. Over the centuries, relatively isolated lineage groups—people claiming a common ancestry—developed distinct languages. Anthropologists estimate that, at the time of European conquest, the Native Americans who settled north of Mexico spoke between 300 and 350 separate languages.

Native hunter-gatherer cultures changed substantially during the long period prior to the European colonization. The early Indians developed many of the same technologies that appeared in other parts of the world. Take, for example, the introduction of agriculture in Native American societies. No one knows precisely when people first cultivated plants for food in North America, but archaeologists working in the Southwest have uncovered evidence suggesting that some groups were farming as early as 2000 B.C. These early cultivators depended on maize (corn), beans, and squash. Knowledge of the domestication of these crops spread slowly north and east, and by 800 B.C., cultivation of squash had reached present-day Michigan.

The Agricultural Revolution helps explain obvious differences among the North American Indian communities. Groups living in the Northeast who knew little about the domestication of plants or who learned of it comparatively late relied more heavily on hunting and gathering than did the cultivators of Mexico or the Southwest.

Wherever agriculture developed, it transformed Indian societies. The availability of a more reliable food source helped liberate women and men from some insecurities of a nomadic existence based on hunting and gathering. The vegetable harvest made it possible to establish permanent villages, and as the supply of food increased, the Native American population expanded. It is estimated that approximately four million Indians lived north of Mexico at the time of first contact with Europeans.

Greater population densities in some areas led to the development of a more urban style of life. Mississippian groups who dominated the Southeast around A.D. 1200 constructed large moundlike ceremonial centers and lived in populous towns, at least one of which, Cahokia, near the site of the modern city of St. Louis, contained as many people as did medieval London.

Aztec Society

The stability resulting from the Agricultural Revolution allowed the Indians of Mexico and Central America to structure their societies in different ways. Like the Incas who lived in what is now known as Peru, the Mayan and Toltec peoples of the Valley of Mexico built vast cities, formed complex government bureaucracies that dominated large tributary populations, and developed hieroglyphic writing as well as an accurate solar calendar. Their cities, which housed several thousand people, greatly impressed the Spanish conquerors. Bernal Diaz del Castillo reported, "When we saw all those [Aztec] towns and villages built in the water, and other great towns on dry land, and that straight and level causeway leading to Mexico, we were astounded. . . . Indeed, some of our soldiers asked whether it was not all a dream."

The rise and fall of some Native American civilizations predated the European conquest. Not long before Columbus began his first voyage across the Atlantic, the Aztecs, an aggressive, warlike people, swept through the Valley of Mexico, conquering the great cities that their enemies had constructed. Aztec warriors ruled by force, reducing defeated rivals to tributary status. In 1519, the Aztec's main ceremonial center, Tenochtitlán, contained as many as 250,000 people as compared with only 50,000 in Seville, the port from which the early Spaniards had sailed. Elaborate human sacrifice associated with Huitzilopochtli, the Aztec sun god, horrified Europeans, who apparently did not find the savagery of their own civilization so objectionable. These Aztec ritual killings were connected to the agricultural cycle, and the Indians believed the blood of their victims possessed extraordinary fertility powers. A fragment of an Aztec song-poem captures the indomitable spirit that once pervaded this militant culture.

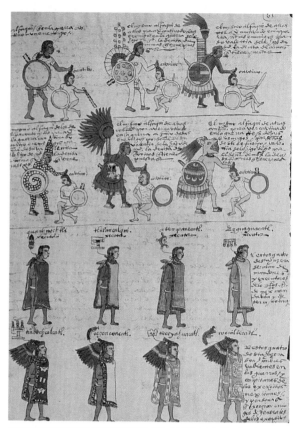

Aztec warriors were organized into regiments and groups distinguished by their distinctive dress. Warriors gained rank—and the right to wear more elaborate attire—by taking captives.

Proud of itself
is the city of Mexico-Tenochtitlán.
Here no one fears to die in war.
This is our glory. . . .

Who could conquer Tenochtitlán?
Who could shake the foundation of heaven?

Eastern Woodland Cultures

In the region along the Atlantic coast claimed by England, the Indians did not practice intensive agriculture. These peoples, numbering less than a million at the time of conquest, generally supplemented mixed farming with seasonal hunting and gathering. Most belonged to what ethnographers term the Eastern Woodland Cultures. Small bands formed villages during the warm summer months. The women cultivated maize and other crops while the men hunted and fished. During

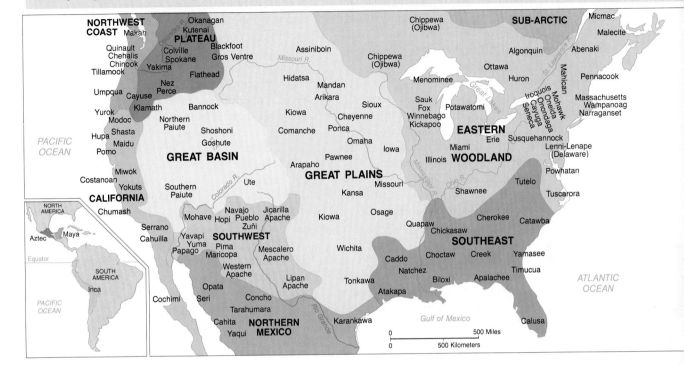

The First Americans:
Location of Major Indian Groups and Culture Areas in the 1600s

Native Americans had complex social structures and religious systems and a well-developed agricultural technology when they came into initial contact with Europeans.

the winter, difficulties associated with feeding so many people forced these communities to disperse. Each family lived off the land as best it could.

Seventeenth-century English settlers were most likely to have encountered the Algonquian-speaking peoples who occupied much of the territory along the Atlantic coast from North Carolina to Maine. Included in this large linguistic family were the Powhatans of Tidewater Virginia, the Narragansetts of Rhode Island, and the Abenakis of northern New England.

Despite common linguistic roots, however, these scattered Algonquian communities would have found communication extremely difficult. In their separate, often isolated environments, they had developed very different dialects. A sixteenth-century Narragansett, for example, would have found it hard to comprehend a Powhatan. The major groups of the Southeast, such as the Creeks, belonged to a separate language group (Muskogean); the Indians of the eastern Great Lakes region and upper St. Lawrence Valley generally spoke Iroquoian dialects.

Linguistic ties had little effect on Indian politics. Algonquian groups who lived in different regions, exploited different resources, and spoke different dialects did not develop strong ties of mutual identity, and when their own interests were involved, they were more than willing to ally themselves with Europeans or "foreign" Indians against other Algonquian speakers. Divisions among Indian groups would in time facilitate European conquest. Local Native American peoples greatly outnumbered the first settlers, and had the Europeans not forged alliances with the Indians, they could not so easily have gained a foothold on the continent.

However divided the Indians of eastern North America may have been, they shared many cultural values and assumptions. Most Native Americans, for example, defined their place in society through kinship. These personal bonds determined the character of economic and political relations. As historian James Axtell explains, "The basic unit of social membership in all tribes was the exogamous clan, a lineal descent group determined through one parent." The farming bands living in areas eventually claimed by England were often matrilineal, which meant in effect that the women owned the planting fields and houses, maintained tribal customs, and had a role in tribal government. Among the native communities of Canada and the northern Great Lakes, patrilineal forms were much more common. In these groups, the men owned the hunting grounds that the family needed to survive.

Eastern Woodland communities organized diplomacy, trade, and war around reciprocal relationships that impressed Europeans as being extraordinarily egalitarian, even democratic. Chains of native authority were loosely structured. Native leaders were such renowned public speakers because persuasive rhetoric was often their only effective source of power. It required considerable oratorical skills for an Indian leader to persuade independent-minded warriors to support a certain policy.

Before the arrival of the white settlers, Indian wars were seldom very lethal. Young warriors attacked neighboring bands largely to exact revenge for a previous insult or the death of a relative, or to secure captives. Fatalities, when they did occur, sparked cycles of revenge. Some captives were tortured to death; others were adopted into the community as replacements for fallen relatives.

THE INDIANS' NEW WORLD

Arrival of large numbers of white men and women on the North American continent profoundly altered Native American cultures. Change did not occur at the same rates of speed in all places. Indian villages located on the Atlantic Coast came under severe pressure almost immediately; inland groups had more time to adjust. Wherever they lived, however, Indians discovered that conquest strained traditional ways of life, and as daily patterns of experience changed almost beyond recognition, native peoples had to devise new answers, new responses, new ways to survive in physical and social environments that mocked tradition. Historian James Merrell reminds us the Indians found themselves living in a world that from their perspective was just as "new" as that which greeted the European invaders.

Native Americans were not passive victims of geopolitical forces beyond their control. So long as they remained healthy, they held their own in the early exchanges, and although they eagerly accepted certain trade goods, they generally resisted other aspects of European cultures. The earliest recorded contacts between Indians and explorers suggest curiosity and surprise rather than hostility. A Southeastern Indian who encountered Hernando de Soto in 1540 expressed awe: "The things that seldom happen bring astonishment. Think, then, what must be the effect on me and mine, the sight of you and your people, whom we have at no time seen . . . things so altogether new, as to strike awe and terror to our hearts."

What Indians desired most was peaceful trade. The earliest French explorers reported that natives waved from shore, urging the Europeans to exchange metal items for beaver skins. In fact, the Indians did not perceive themselves at a disadvantage in these dealings. They could readily see the technological advantage of guns over bows and arrows. Knives made daily tasks a lot easier. And to acquire these goods they gave up pelts, which to them seemed in abundant supply. "The English have no sense," one Indian informed a French priest. "They give us twenty knives like this for one Beaver skin." Another native announced that "the Beaver does everything perfectly well: it makes kettles, hatchets, swords, knives, bread . . . in short, it makes everything." The man who recorded these observations reminded French readers—in case they had missed the point—that the Indian was "making sport of us Europeans."

Trading sessions along the eastern frontier were really cultural seminars. The Europeans tried to make sense out of Indian customs, and although they may have called the natives "savages," they quickly discovered that the Indians drove hard bargains. They demanded gifts; they set the time and place of trade.

The Indians used these occasions to study the newcomers. They formed opinions about the Europeans, some flattering, some less so, but they never concluded from these observations that Indian culture was inferior to that of the colonizers. They regarded the beards worn by European men as particularly revolting. As an eighteenth-century Englishman said of the Iroquois, "They seem always to have Looked upon themselves as far Superior to the rest of Mankind and accordingly Call themselves *Ongwehoenwe*, i.e. Men Surpassing all other men."

For Europeans, communicating with the Indians was always an ordeal. The invaders reported having gained deep insight into Native American cultures through sign languages. How much accurate information explorers and traders took from these crude improvised exchanges is a matter of conjecture. In a letter written in 1493 Columbus expressed frustration: "I did not understand those people nor they me, except for what common sense dictated, although they were saddened and I much more so, because I wanted to have good information concerning everything."

In the absence of meaningful conversation, Europeans often concluded that the Indians held them in high regard, perhaps seeing the newcomers as gods. Such one-sided encounters involved a good deal of projection, a mental process of translating alien sounds and gestures into messages that Europeans wanted to hear. Sometimes the adventurers did not even try to communicate, assuming from superficial observation—as did the sixteenth-century explorer Giovanni da Verrazzano—"that they have no religion, and that they live in absolute freedom, and that everything they do proceeds from Ignorance."

Ethnocentric Europeans tried repeatedly to "civilize" the Indians. In practice that meant persuading natives to dress like the colonists, attend white schools, live in permanent structures, and, most important, accept Christianity. The Indians listened more or less patiently, but in the end, they usually rejected European values. One South Carolina trader explained that when Indians were asked to become more English, they said no, "for they thought it hard, that we should desire them to change their manners and customs, since they did not desire us to turn Indians."

To be sure, some Indians were strongly attracted to Christianity, but most paid it lip service or found it irrelevant to their needs. As one Huron told a French priest, "It would be useless for me to repent having sinned, seeing that I never have sinned." Another Huron announced that he did not fear punishment after death since "we cannot tell whether everything that appears faulty to Men, is so in the Eyes of God."

Among some Indian groups, gender figured significantly in a person's willingness to convert to Christianity. Native men who traded animal skins for European goods had more frequent contact with the whites, and they proved more receptive to the arguments of missionaries. But native women jealously guarded traditional culture, a system that often sanctioned polygamy—a husband having several wives—and gave women substantial authority over the distribution of food within the village. French Jesuits seemed especially eager to undermine the independence of Native American women. Among other demands, missionaries insisted on monogamous marriages, an institution based on Christian values but that made little sense in Indian societies where constant warfare killed off large numbers of young males and increasingly left native women without sufficient marriage partners.

The white settlers' educational system proved no more successful than their religion was in winning cultural converts. Young Indian scholars deserted stuffy classrooms at the first chance. In 1744, Virginia offered several Iroquois boys a free education at the College of William and Mary. The Iroquois leaders rejected the invitation because they found that boys who had gone to college "were absolutely good for nothing being neither acquainted with the true methods of killing deer, catching Beaver, or surprising an enemy."

Even matrimony seldom eroded the Indians' attachment to their own customs. When Native

On the walls of the Canyon del Muerto in present-day Arizona, an Indian artist carved this petroglyph of Spanish conquistadores, whose arrival in the New World so profoundly changed Native American life.

Americans and whites married—unions the English found less desirable than did the French or Spanish—the European partner usually elected to live among the Indians. Impatient settlers who regarded the Indians simply as an obstruction to progress sometimes developed more coercive methods, such as enslavement, to achieve cultural conversion. Again, from the white perspective, the results were disappointing. Indian slaves ran away or died. In either case, they did not become Europeans.

Disease and Dependency

Over time, cooperative encounters between the two peoples became less frequent. The Europeans found it almost impossible to understand the Indians' relation to the land and other natural resources. English planters cleared the forests and fenced the fields and, in the process, radically altered the ecological systems on which the Indians depended. The European system of land use inevitably reduced the supply of deer and other animals essential to traditional native cultures.

Dependency also came in more subtle forms. The Indians welcomed European commerce, but like so many consumers throughout recorded history, they discovered that the things they most coveted inevitably brought them into debt. To pay for the trade goods, the Indians hunted more aggressively and even further reduced the population of fur-bearing mammals.

Commerce eroded Indian independence in other ways. After several disastrous wars—the Yamasee War in South Carolina (1715), for example—the natives learned that demonstrations of force usually resulted in the suspension of normal trade, on which the Indians had grown quite dependent for guns and ammunition, among other things. A hardened English businessman made the point quite bluntly. When asked if the Catawbas would harm his traders, he responded that "the danger would be . . . little from them, because they are too fond of our trade to lose it for the pleasure of shedding a little English blood."

It was disease, however, that ultimately destroyed the cultural integrity of many North American tribes. European adventurers exposed the Indians to germs and viruses against which they possessed no natural immunity. Smallpox, measles, and influenza decimated the Native American population. Other diseases such as alcoholism took a terrible toll.

Within a generation of initial contact with Europeans, the Caribs, who gave the Caribbean its name, were virtually extinct. The Algonquian communities of New England experienced appalling rates of death. One Massachusetts colonist reported in 1630 that the Indian peoples of his region "above twelve yeares since were swept away by a great & grievous Plague . . . so that there are verie few left to inhabit the Country." Settlers who possessed no knowledge of germ theory—which was not formulated until the mid-nineteenth century—speculated that a Christian God had providentially cleared the wilderness of heathens.

Historical demographers now estimate that some tribes suffered a 90 to 95 percent population loss within the first century of European contact. The death of so many Indians decreased the supply of indigenous laborers needed by the Europeans to work the mines and to grow staple crops such as sugar and tobacco. The decimation of native populations may have persuaded colonists throughout the New World to seek a substitute labor force in Africa. Indeed, the enslavement of blacks has been described as an effort by Europeans to "repopulate" the New World.

Indians who survived the epidemics often found that the fabric of traditional culture had come unraveled. The enormity of the death toll and the agony that accompanied it called traditional religious beliefs and practices into question. These survivors lost not only members of their families, but also elders who might have told them how properly to bury the dead and give spiritual comfort to the living.

Some native peoples, such as the Iroquois, who lived some distance away from the coast and thus had more time to adjust to the challenge, withstood the crisis better than did those who immediately confronted the Europeans and Africans. Refugee Indians from the hardest hit eastern communities were absorbed into healthier western groups. Nonetheless, the cultural and physical shock that the dwindling Native American population experienced is beyond the historian's power ever fully to comprehend.

WEST AFRICA: PEOPLES AND HISTORY

During the era of the European slave trade, a number of enduring myths about sub-Saharan West Africa were propagated. Even today, commentators claim that the people who inhabited this region four hundred years ago were isolated from the rest of the world and had a simple, self-sufficient economy. Indeed, some scholars still depict this vast region stretching from the Senegal River south to modern Angola as a single cultural unit, as if at one time all the men and women living there must have shared a common set of political, religious, and social values.

Sub-Saharan West Africa defies such easy generalizations. The first Portuguese who explored the African coast during the fifteenth century encountered a great variety of political and religious cultures. Many hundreds of years earlier, Africans living in this region had come into contact with Islam, the religion founded by the Prophet Muhammad during the seventh century. Islam spread slowly from Arabia into black Africa. Not until A.D. 1030 did a kingdom located in the Senegal Valley accept the Muslim religion. Many other West Africans, such as those in ancient Ghana, resisted Islam and continued to observe traditional religions.

Muslim traders from North Africa and the Middle East brought a new religion to parts of West Africa, while they expanded sophisticated trade networks that linked the villagers of Senegambia with urban centers in northwest Africa, Morocco, Tunisia, and Cyrenaica. Great camel caravans regularly crossed the Sahara Desert carrying trade goods that were exchanged for gold and slaves. Sub-Saharan Africa's well-developed links with Islam surprised a French priest who in 1686 observed African pilgrims going "to visit Mecca to visit Mahomet's tomb, although they are eleven or twelve hundred leagues distance from it."

West Africans spoke many different languages and organized themselves into diverse political systems. Several populous states, sometimes termed "empires," exercised loose control over large areas. Ancient African empires such as Ghana were vulnerable to external attack as well as internal rebellion, and the oral and written histories of this region record the rise and fall of sev-

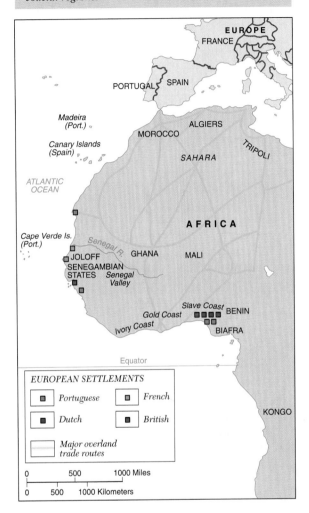

Trade Routes in Africa
African trade routes were well established by the late 1600s. Trade restrictions—and a deadly disease environment—confined European settlements primarily to coastal regions.

eral large kingdoms. When European traders first arrived, the list of major states would have included Mali, Benin, and Kongo. Many other Africans lived in what are known as stateless societies, really largely autonomous communities organized around lineage structures. In these respects, African and Native American cultures had much in common.

Whatever the form of government, men and women found their primary social identity within well-defined lineage groups, which consisted of persons claiming descent from a common ancestor. Disputes among members of lineage groups

Ecological Revolution

Sudden and sweeping disruptions of the environment are now almost commonplace, but an even greater ecological revolution than that witnessed following the end of World War II occurred in the century after Columbus's voyages. European explorers, African slaves, and Native Americans brought together three remarkably different worlds, physically separated for millennia. The exchange of plants, animals, and diseases transformed the social history of the Old World as well as the New.

Differences in the forms of life in the two hemispheres astonished the first explorers. They had expected America to be an extension of Europe, a place inhabited by familiar plants and animals. They were surprised. The exotic flora of the New World, sketched here from sixteenth-century drawings, included the food staple maize and the succulent pineapple. Equally strange to European eyes were buffalo, rattlesnakes, catfish, and the peculiar absence of horses and cattle. No domestic animal was common to both sides of the Atlantic except the dog. And perhaps the most striking difference was between the people themselves. Both Native Americans and Europeans found each other to be the most exotic people they had ever encountered.

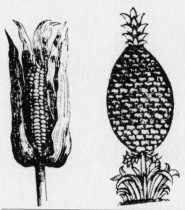

New World plants, including maize and the pineapple, expanded and enriched the European diet.

The most immediate biological consequence of contact between the people of these three startlingly dissimilar continents was the transfer of disease. Within a year of Columbus's return from the Caribbean, syphilis appeared in Europe for the first time and became known as the "American" disease. By 1505, it had spread all the way to China.

The effect of Old World diseases in the Americas was catastrophic. Native Americans had little natural immunity to common African and European diseases because America remained biologically isolated after the reimmersion of the Bering Land Bridge. When they were exposed to influenza, typhus, measles, and especially to smallpox, they died by the millions. Indeed,

European exploration of America set off the worst demographic disaster in world history. Within fifty years of the first contact, epidemics had virtually exterminated the native population of Santo Domingo/Haiti and devastated the densely populated Valley of Mexico.

Also unsettling but by no means as destructive was the transfer of plants and animals from the Old World to the New. Spanish colonizers carried sugar and bananas across the Atlantic, and in time these crops transformed the economies of Latin America. Even more spectacular was the success of European animals in America. During the sixteenth century, pigs, sheep, and cattle arrived as passengers on European ships, and in the fertile New World environment, they multiplied more rapidly than they had in Europe. Some animals survived shipwrecks. On Sable Island, a small, desolate island off the coast of Nova Scotia, one can still see the small, long-haired cattle, the successors of the earliest cattle transported to America. Other animals escaped from the ranches of New Spain, generating new wild breeds, like the fabled Texas longhorn.

No European animal more profoundly affected Native American life than the horse. Once common in North

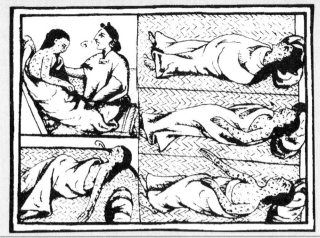

As Native Americans were exposed to common Old World diseases, particularly smallpox, they died by the millions.

European settlers brought plants and animals such as the long-haired steer to the New World, adding to the large variety of flora and fauna that had so amazed the first explorers.

European and African societies. From his first trip to the New World, Columbus brought back a plant that revolutionized the diets of both humans and animals—maize. During the next century, American beans, squash, and sweet potatoes appeared on European tables. The pepper and tomato, other New World discoveries, added a distinctive flavor to Mediterranean cooking. Despite strong prohibitions on the use of tobacco (in Russia, a user might have his nose amputated), European demand for tobacco grew astronomically during the seventeenth century. The potato caught on more slowly in Europe because of a widespread fear that root crops caused disease. The most rapid acceptance of the white potato came in Ireland, where it became a diet staple in the 1600s. Irish immigrants—unaware of the geneology of this native American crop—reintroduced the potato into Massachusetts Bay in 1718. And in West Africa, corn gradually replaced traditional animal feeds of low yield.

These sweeping changes in agriculture and diet helped reshape the Old World economies. Partly because of the rich new sources of nutrition from America, the population of Europe, which had long been relatively stable, nearly doubled in the eighteenth century. Even as cities swelled and industries flourished, European farmers were able to feed the growing population. In many ways, the seeds and plants of the New World were far more valuable in Western economic development than all the silver of Mexico and Peru.

America, the horse mysteriously disappeared from the continent sometime during the last Ice Age. The early Spanish explorers reintroduced the horse to North America, and the sight of this large, powerful animal at first terrified the Indians. Mounted conquistadores discovered that if they could not frighten Indian foes into submission, they could simply outmaneuver them on horseback. The Native Americans of the Southwest quickly adapted the horse to their own use. Sedentary farmers acquired new hunting skills, and soon the Indians were riding across the Great Plains in pursuit of buffalo. The Comanche, Apache Sioux, and Blackfoot tribes—just to name a few—became dependent on the horse. Mounted Indian warriors galloped into battle, unaware that it was their white adversaries who had brought the horse to America.

Equally dramatic was the effect of American crops on

were generally settled by clan elders. These senior leaders allocated economic and human resources. They determined who received land and who might take a wife—critical decisions because within the villages of West Africa, women and children cultivated the fields. These communities were economically self-sufficient. Not only were they able to produce enough food to feed themselves, they also produced trade goods, such as iron, kola, and gum.

The first Europeans to reach the West African coast by sail were the Portuguese. Strong winds and currents along the Atlantic coast moved southward, which meant a ship could sail with the wind from Portugal to West Africa without difficulty. The problem was returning. Advances in maritime technology allowed the Portuguese to overcome these difficulties. By constructing a new type of ship, one uniting European hull design with lateen (triangular) sails from the Middle East, Portuguese caravels were able to navigate successfully against African winds and currents. During the fifteenth century, Portuguese sailors discovered that by sailing far to the west, often as far as the Azores, they could, on their return trips to Europe, catch a reliable westerly wind. Columbus was evidently familiar with this technique. Before attempting to cross the Atlantic Ocean, he sailed to the Gold Coast, and on the way, he undoubtedly studied the wind patterns that would carry his famed caravels to the New World and back again.

The Portuguese journeyed to Africa in search of gold and slaves. Mali and Joloff officials were willing partners in this commerce, but insisted that Europeans respect trade regulations established by Africans. They required the Europeans to pay tolls and other fees and restricted the foreign traders to conducting their business in small forts or castles located at the mouths of the major rivers. Local merchants acquired some slaves and gold in the interior and transported them to the coast where they were exchanged for European manufactures. Transactions were calculated in terms of local African currencies: a slave would be offered to a European trader for so many bars of iron or ounces of gold.

The slave traders accepted these terms largely because they had no other choice. The African states fielded formidable armies, and the Europeans soon discovered they could not impose their will on this region simply by shows of force. Moreover, local diseases proved so lethal for Europeans—six out of ten of whom would die within a single year's stay in Africa—that they were happy to avoid dangerous trips to the interior. The slaves were usually men and women taken captive during wars; others were victims of judicial practices designed specifically to supply the growing American market. By 1650, most West-African slaves were destined for the New World rather than the Middle East.

Even before Europeans colonized the New World, the Portuguese were purchasing almost a thousand slaves a year on the West African coast. The slaves were frequently forced to work on the sugar plantations of Madeira (Portuguese) and the Canaries (Spanish), Atlantic islands on which Europeans experimented with forms of unfree labor that would later be more fully and more ruthlessly established in the American colonies. It is currently estimated that approximately 10.7 million Africans were taken to the New World as slaves. The figure for the eighteenth century alone is about 5.5 million, of which more than one-third came from West-Central Africa. The Bight of Benin, the Bight of Biafra, and the Gold Coast supplied most of the others.

The peopling of the New World is usually seen as a story of European migrations. But in fact, during every year between 1650 and 1831, more Africans than Europeans came to the Americas. As historian Davis Eltis writes, "In terms of immigration alone . . . America was an extension of Africa rather than Europe until late in the nineteenth century."

EUROPE ON THE EVE OF CONQUEST

In ancient times, the West possessed a mythical appeal to people living along the shores of the Mediterranean Sea. Classical writers speculated about the fate of Atlantis, a fabled Western civilization that was said to have sunk beneath the ocean. Fallen Greek heroes allegedly spent eternity in an uncharted western paradise. But because the ships of Greece and Rome were ill designed to sail the open ocean, the lands to the west remained the stuff of legend and fantasy. In the fifth century, an intrepid Irish monk, Saint Brendan, reported finding enchanted islands far out in the

European traders built compounds along the African coast for the sole purpose of expediting the slave trade. Each compound within these "slave factories" served a different European country.

Atlantic. He even claimed to have met a talking whale named Jasconius, who allowed the famished voyager to cook a meal on his back.

In the tenth century, Scandinavian seafarers known as Norsemen or Vikings actually established settlements in the New World, but almost one thousand years passed before they received credit for their accomplishment. In the year 984, a band of Vikings led by Eric the Red sailed west from Iceland to a large island in the North Atlantic. Eric, who possessed a fine sense of public relations, named the island Greenland, reasoning that others would more willingly colonize this icebound region "if the country had a good name." A few years later, Eric's son Leif founded a small settlement he named Vinland at a location in northern Newfoundland now called L'Anse aux Meadows. At the time, the Norse voyages went unnoticed by other Europeans. Soon the hostility of Native Americans, poor lines of communication, and political upheavals in Scandinavia made maintenance of these distant outposts impossible. At the time of his first voyage in 1492, Columbus seemed to have been unaware of these earlier exploits.

European Nation-States

At the time of the Viking settlement, other Europeans were unprepared to sponsor transatlantic exploration. Nor would they be in a position to do so for several more centuries. Medieval kingdoms were loosely organized, and until the early fifteenth century, fierce provincial loyalties, widespread ignorance of classical learning, and dreadful plagues such as the Black Death discouraged people from thinking expansively about the world beyond their own immediate communities.

In the fifteenth century, however, these conditions began to change. Europe became more prosperous, political authority was more centralized, and the Renaissance fostered a more expansive outlook among literate people. A central element in this shift was the slow but steady growth of population after 1450. Historians are uncertain about the cause of this increase—after all, neither the quality of medicine nor sanitation improved much—but the result was a substantial rise in the price of land, since there were more mouths to feed. Landlords profited from these trends, and as their income expanded, they demanded more of the luxury items, such as spices, silks, and jewels, that came from distant ports. Economic prosperity created powerful new incentives for exploration and trade.

This period also witnessed the centralization of political authority under a group of rulers whom historians refer to collectively as the "New Monarchs." Before the mid-fifteenth century, feudal nobles dominated small districts throughout Europe. Conceding only nominal allegiance to larger territorial leaders, these local barons taxed the peasants and waged war pretty much as they pleased. They also dispensed what passed for justice. The New Monarchs challenged the nobles' autonomy. The changes that accompanied these challenges came slowly, and in many areas violently, but the results altered traditional political relationships between the nobility and the Crown, and between the citizen and the state. The New Monarchs of Europe recruited armies and supported these expensive organizations with revenues from national taxes. They created effective national courts. While these monarchs were often despotic, they personified the emergent nation-states of Europe and brought a measure of peace to local communities weary of chronic feudal war.

The story was the same throughout most of western Europe. The Tudors of England, represented by Henry VII (1485–1509), ended a long civil war known as the Wars of the Roses. Louis XI, the French monarch (1461–1483), strengthened royal authority by reorganizing state finances. The political unification of Spain began in 1469 with the marriage of Ferdinand of Aragon and Isabella of Castile. These strong-willed monarchs forged nations out of groups of independent kingdoms. If political centralization had not occurred, the major European countries could not possibly have generated the financial and military resources necessary for worldwide exploration.

A final prerequisite to exploration was solid technical knowledge. Ptolemy (A.D. second century) and other ancient geographers had mapped the known world and had even demonstrated that the world was round. During the Middle Ages, however, Europeans lost effective contact with classical tradition. Within Arab societies, the old learning had survived, indeed flourished, and when Europeans eventually rediscovered the classical texts, in a period known as the Renaissance, they

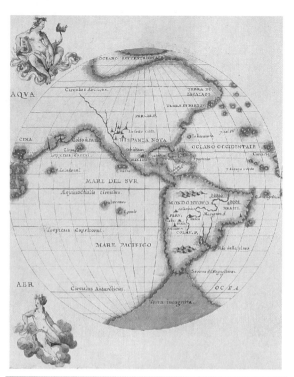

Early sixteenth-century mapmakers thought the New World was really an extension of Asia. Note that on this map of the Western Hemisphere, China appears to be connected to North America.

drew heavily on the work of Arab scholars. This "new" learning generated great intellectual curiosity about the globe and about the possibility of the world that existed beyond the Mediterranean.

The invention of printing from movable type by Johann Gutenberg in the 1440s greatly facilitated the spread of this technical knowledge. Sea captains published their findings as quickly as they could engage a printer, and by the beginning of the sixteenth century, a small, though growing, body of educated readers throughout Europe were well informed about the exploration of the New World. The printing press opened the European mind to exciting prospects that had been hardly perceived when the Vikings sailed the North Atlantic.

EUROPEANS' NEW WORLD

By 1500, centralization of authority and advances in geographic knowledge brought Spain to the first rank as a world power. In the early fifteenth century, though, Spain consisted of several autonomous kingdoms. It lacked rich natural

Improved printing methods in the 1440s allowed navigators to share their geographical findings more easily, spawning a new wave of exploration in the early 1500s.

fact, there was little about this land to suggest its people would take the lead in conquering and colonizing the New World.

By the end of the century, however, Spain suddenly came alive with creative energy. The union of Ferdinand and Isabella sparked a drive for political consolidation that, because of the monarchs' fervid Catholicism, took on the characteristics of a religious crusade. Spurred by the militant faith of its monarchs, the armies of Castile and Aragon waged holy war—known as the *Reconquista*—against the independent states in southern Spain that earlier had been captured by Muslims. In 1492, the Moorish (Islamic) kingdom of Granada fell, and, for the first time in centuries, the entire Iberian peninsula was united under Christian rulers. Spanish authorities showed no tolerance for people who rejected the Catholic faith.

During the Reconquista, thousands of Jews and Moors were driven from the country. Indeed, Columbus undoubtedly encountered such refugees as he was preparing for his famous voyage. From this volatile social and political environment came the *conquistadores*, men eager for personal glory and material gain, uncompromising in matters of religion, and unswerving in their loyalty to the Crown. They were prepared to employ fire and sword in any cause sanctioned by God and king, and these adventurers carried European culture to the most populous regions of the New World.

Long before Spaniards ever reached the West Indies, they conquered the indigenous peoples of the Canary Islands, a strategically located archipelago in the eastern Atlantic. These expeditions, leading eventually to colonization, provided a kind of rehearsal for the invasion of the New World. The harsh lessons the Spanish learned on the Canaries served as models of subjugation in America. Indeed, the Spanish experience paralleled that of the English in Ireland (see "English Colonization in Ireland," pp. 25–26). An early fifteenth-century Spanish chronicle described the Canary natives as "miscreants . . . [who] do not acknowledge their creator and live in part like beasts." Many islanders quickly died of disease; others were killed in battle or enslaved. The new Spanish landholders introduced sugar to the islands, an intensive plantation crop requiring a large labor force. The workers came from Africa, slaves in a place that may truly have been the first American frontier.

Admiral of the Ocean Sea

If it had not been for Christopher Columbus (Cristoforo Colombo), of course, Spain might never have gained an American empire. Little is known about his early life. Born in Genoa in 1451 of humble parentage, Columbus soon devoured the classical learning that had so recently been rediscovered and made available in printed form. He mastered geography and—perhaps while sailing the coast of West Africa—he became obsessed with the idea of voyaging west across the Atlantic Ocean to reach Cathay, as China was then known.

In 1484, Columbus presented his plan to the king of Portugal. However, while the Portuguese were just as interested as Columbus in reaching Cathay, they elected to voyage around the continent of Africa instead of following the route

Indian Slaves Working at a Spanish Sugar Plantation on the Island of Hispaniola *(1595) by Theodore de Bry. Spanish treatment of the Native Americans was often brutal.*

suggested by Columbus. They suspected Columbus had substantially underestimated the circumference of the earth and that for all his enthusiasm, he would almost certainly starve before reaching Asia. The Portuguese decision eventually paid off quite handsomely. In 1498, one of their captains, Vasco da Gama, returned from the coast of India carrying a fortune in spices and other luxury goods.

Undaunted by rejection, Columbus petitioned Isabella and Ferdinand for financial backing. They were initially no more interested in his grand design than the Portuguese had been. But time was on Columbus's side. Spain's aggressive New Monarchs envied the success of their neighbor, Portugal. Columbus boldly played on the rivalry between these countries, talking of wealth and empire. Indeed, for a person with little success or apparent support, he was supremely confident. One contemporary reported that when Columbus "made up his mind, he was as sure he would discover what he did discover, and find what he did find, as if he held it in a chamber under lock and key."

Columbus's stubborn lobbying on behalf of the "Enterprise of the Indies" gradually wore down opposition in the Spanish court, and the two sovereigns provided him with a small fleet that contained two of the most famous caravels ever constructed, the *Niña* and *Pinta,* as well as the square-rigged *nao Santa Maria.* The indomitable admiral set sail for Cathay in August 1492, the year of Spain's unification.

Educated Europeans of the fifteenth century knew the world was round. No one seriously believed Columbus and his crew would tumble off the edge of the earth. The concern was with size, not shape. Columbus estimated the distance to the mainland of Asia to be about 3,000 nautical miles, a voyage his small ships would have no difficulty completing. The actual distance is 10,600 nautical miles, however, and had the New World not been in his way, he and his crew would have run out of food and water long before they reached China, as the Portuguese had predicted.

After stopping in the Canary Islands to refit the ships, Columbus continued his westward voyage in early September. When the tiny Spanish fleet sighted an island in the Bahamas after only thirty-three days at sea, the admiral concluded he had reached Asia. Since his mathematical calculations had obviously been correct, he assumed he would soon encounter the Chinese. It never occurred to Columbus he had stumbled upon a new world. He assured his men, his patrons, and perhaps himself that these islands were indeed part of the fabled "Indies." Or if not the Indies themselves, then they were surely an extension of the great Asian landmass. He searched for the splendid cities Marco Polo had described, but instead of meeting wealthy Chinese, Columbus encountered Native Americans, whom he appropriately, if mistakenly, called "Indians."

After his first voyage of discovery, Columbus returned to the New World three more times. But despite his considerable courage and ingenuity, he could never find the wealth his financial supporters in Spain angrily demanded. Columbus died in 1506 a frustrated but wealthy dreamer, unaware he had reached a previously unknown continent separating Asia from Europe. The final disgrace came in December 1500 when an ambitious falsifier, Amerigo Vespucci, published a sensational account of his travels across the Atlantic that convinced German mapmakers he had proven America was distinct from Asia. Before the misconception could be corrected, the name "America" gained general acceptance throughout Europe.

Only two years after Columbus's first voyage, Spain and Portugal almost went to war over the

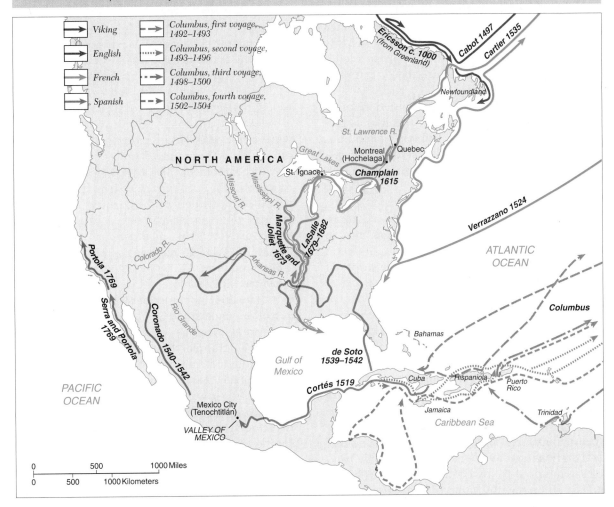

Voyages of Exploration

Routes of the major voyages to the New World. Early explorers and navigators established land claims for the European nations.

anticipated treasure of Asia. Pope Alexander VI negotiated a settlement that pleased both kingdoms. Portugal wanted to exclude the Spanish from the west coast of Africa and, what was more important, from Columbus's new route to "India." Spain insisted on maintaining complete control over lands discovered by Columbus, then still regarded as an extension of China. The Treaty of Tordesillas (1494) divided the entire world along a line located 270 leagues west of the Azores. Any new lands discovered west of the line belonged to Spain. At the time, no European had ever seen Brazil, which turned out to be on Portugal's side of the line. (To this day Brazilians speak Portuguese.) The treaty failed to discourage future English, Dutch, and French adventurers from trying their luck in the New World.

The Conquistadores

Spain's new discoveries unleashed a horde of conquistadores on the Caribbean. These independent adventurers carved out small settlements on Cuba, Hispaniola, Jamaica, and Puerto Rico in the 1490s and early 1500s. They were not interested in creating a permanent society in the New World. Rather, they came for instant wealth, preferably in gold, and were not squeamish about the means they used to obtain it. Bernal Díaz, one of the first Spaniards to migrate to this region, explained he had traveled to America "to serve God and His Majesty, to give light to those who were in darkness, and to grow rich, as all men desire to do." In less than two decades, the Indians who had inhabited the Caribbean islands had been virtually exterminated, victims of exploitation and disease.

For a quarter century, the conquistadores concentrated their energies on the major islands that Columbus had discovered. Rumors of fabulous wealth in Mexico, however, aroused the interest of many Spaniards, including Hernán Cortés, a minor government functionary in Cuba. Like so many members of his class, he dreamed of glory, military adventure, and riches that would transform him from an ambitious court clerk into an honored *hildago.* On November 18, 1518, Cortés and a small army left Cuba to verify the stories of Mexico's treasure. Events soon demonstrated that Cortés was a leader of extraordinary ability.

His adversary was the legendary Aztec emperor, Montezuma. The confrontation between these two powerful personalities is one of the more exciting of early American history. A fear of competition from rival conquistadores coupled with a burning desire to conquer a vast new empire drove Cortés forward. He was determined to push his men through any obstacle, preventing them from retreating by scuttling the ships that had carried them to Mexico. Cortés led his band of six hundred followers across rugged mountains, and on the way gathered allies from among the Tlaxcalans, a tributary people eager to free themselves from Aztec domination.

In matters of war, Cortés possessed obvious technological superiority over the Aztecs. The sound of gunfire frightened the Indians. Moreover, Aztec troops had never seen horses, much less armored horses carrying sword-wielding Spaniards. But these elements would have counted for little had Cortés not also gained a psychological advantage over his opponents. At first Montezuma thought that the Spaniards were gods, representatives of the fearful plumed serpent, Quetzalcoatl. Instead of resisting immediately, the emperor hesitated. When Montezuma's resolve hardened, it was too late. Cortés's victory in Mexico, coupled with other conquests in South America, transformed Spain into the wealthiest state in Europe.

Managing an Empire

Following the conquest of Mexico, renamed New Spain, the Spanish Crown confronted a difficult problem. Ambitious conquistadores, interested chiefly in their own wealth and glory, had to be brought effectively under royal authority, a task easier said than done. Adventurers like Cortés were stubbornly independent, quick to take offense, and thousands of miles away from the seat of government. The Crown found a partial solution in the *encomíenda* system. The monarch rewarded the leaders of the conquest with Indian villages. The people who lived in these settlements provided the *encomenderos* with labor tribute in exchange for legal protection and religious guidance. The system, of course, cruelly exploited Indian laborers. One historian concluded, "The first encomenderos, without known exception, understood Spanish authority as provision for unlimited personal opportunism." Cortés alone was granted the services of over twenty-three thousand Indian workers. The encomíenda system made the colonizers more dependent on the king, for it was he who legitimized their title. In the words of one scholar, the new economic structure helped to transform "a frontier of plunder into a frontier of settlement."

Spain's rulers attempted to maintain tight personal control over their American possessions. The volume of correspondence between the two continents, much of it concerning mundane matters, was staggering. (All documents were duplicated several times by hand.) Because the trip to Madrid took many months, a year often passed before receipt of an answer to a simple request. But somehow the cumbersome system worked. In Mexico, officials appointed in Spain established a rigid hierarchical order, directing the affairs of the countryside from urban centers. Persons born in the New World, even those of Spanish parentage *(criollos),* were regarded as socially inferior to natives of the mother country *(peninsulares).*

The Spanish also brought Catholicism to the New World. The Dominicans and Franciscans, the two largest religious orders, established Indian missions throughout New Spain. Some barefoot friars

Spanish priests sought to convert Native Americans to Catholicism. Although the priests and friars could not stop the economic exploitation of the Indians, they frequently condemned the conquistadores' excessive cruelty. In this seventeenth-century work by an anonymous artist, a Spanish friar baptizes a Mexican Indian.

tried to protect the Native Americans from the worst forms of exploitation. One courageous Dominican, Fra Bartolomé de la Casas, published an eloquent defense of Indian rights, *Historia de las Indias,* which among other things questioned the legitimacy of European conquest of the New World. Las Casas's work provoked heated debate in Spain, and while the king had no intention of repudiating his vast American empire, he did initiate certain reforms designed to bring greater "love and moderation" to Spanish-Indian relations. It is impossible to ascertain how many converts these friars made. In 1531, however, a newly converted Christian reported a vision of the Virgin, a dark-skinned woman of obvious Indian ancestry, who became known throughout the region as the Virgin of Guadalupe. This figure—the result of a creative blending of Indian and European cultures—served as a powerful symbol of Mexican nationalism in the wars for independence fought against Spain almost three centuries later.

About 250,000 Spaniards migrated to the New World during the sixteenth century. Another 200,000 made the journey between 1600 and 1650. Most of the colonists were impoverished, single males in their late twenties seeking economic opportunities. They generally came from the poorest agricultural regions of southern Spain—almost 40 percent migrating from Andalusia. Since so few Spanish women migrated, especially in the sixteenth century, the men often married Indians and blacks, unions which produced *mestizos* and *mulattos.* The frequency of interracial marriage indicated that, among other things, the people of New Spain were more tolerant of racial differences than were the English who settled in North America. For the people of New Spain social standing was affected as much, or more, by economic worth, as it was by color.

Spain claimed far more of the New World than it could possibly manage. After the era of the conquistadores, Spain's rulers regarded the American colonies primarily as a source of precious metal, and between 1500 and 1650, an estimated 200 tons of gold and 16,000 tons of silver were shipped back to the Spanish treasury in

Madrid. This great wealth, however, proved a mixed blessing. The sudden acquisition of so much money stimulated a horrendous inflation that hurt ordinary Spaniards. They were hurt further by long, debilitating wars funded by American gold and silver. Moreover, instead of developing its own industry, Spain became dependent on the annual shipment of bullion from America, and, in 1603, one insightful Spaniard declared, "The New World conquered by you, has conquered you in its turn."

FRENCH EXPLORATION AND SETTLEMENT

French interest in the New World developed more slowly. More than three decades after Columbus's discovery, King Francis I sponsored the unsuccessful efforts of Giovanni da Verrazzano to find a short water route to China, via a northwest passage around or through North America. In 1534, the king sent Jacques Cartier on a similar quest. The rocky, barren coast of Labrador depressed the explorer. He grumbled, "I am rather inclined to believe that this is the land God gave to Cain."

Discovery of a large promising waterway the following year raised Cartier's spirits. He reconnoitered the Gulf of Saint Lawrence, traveling up the magnificent river as far as modern Montreal. Despite his high expectations, however, Cartier got no closer to China, and discouraged by the harsh winters, he headed home in 1542. Not until sixty-five years later did Samuel de Champlain resettle this region for France. He founded Quebec in 1608.

As was the case with other colonial powers, the French declared they had migrated to the New World in search of wealth as well as in hopes of converting the Indians to Christianity. As it turned out, these economic and spiritual goals required full cooperation between the French and the Native Americans. In contrast to English settlers who established independent farms and who regarded the Indians at best as obstacles in the path of civilization, the French viewed the natives as necessary economic partners. Furs were Canada's most valuable export, and to obtain the pelts of beaver and other animals, the French were absolutely dependent on Indian hunters and trappers. French traders lived among the Indians, often taking native wives and studying local cultures.

Frenchmen known as *coureurs de bois* (forest runners), following Canada's great river networks, paddled deep into the heart of the continent in search of fresh sources of furs. Some intrepid traders penetrated beyond the Great Lakes into the Mississippi Valley. In 1673, Père Jacques Marquette journeyed down the Mississippi River, and nine years later, Sieur de La Salle traveled all the way to the Gulf of Mexico. In the early eighteenth century, the French established small settlements in Louisiana, the most important being New Orleans. The spreading French influence worried English colonists living along the Atlantic coast, for it appeared the French were about to cut them off from the trans-Appalachian west.

Catholic missionaries also depended on Indian cooperation. Canadian priests were drawn from two orders, the Jesuits and the Recollects, and although measuring their success in the New World is difficult, it seems they converted more Indians to Christianity than did their English counterparts to the south. Like the fur traders, the missionaries lived among the Indians and learned to speak their languages.

The French dream of a vast American empire suffered from serious flaws. The Crown remained largely indifferent to Canadian affairs. Royal officials stationed in New France received limited and sporadic support from the mother country. An even greater problem was the decision to settle what seemed to many rural peasants and urban artisans a cold, inhospitable land. Throughout the colonial period, Canada's European population remained small. A census of 1663 recorded a mere 3,035 French residents. By 1700, the figure had reached only fifteen thousand. Moreover, because of the colony's geography, all exports and imports had to go through Quebec. It was relatively easy, therefore, for crown officials to control that traffic, usually by awarding fur-trading monopolies to court favorites. Such practices created political tensions and hindered economic growth.

THE ENGLISH NEW WORLD

The first English visit to North America remains shrouded in mystery. Fishermen working out of

In the dead of winter, the streams of New France turned to ice. French voyageurs built sledges, placed their canoes and supplies on them, and proceeded down the frozen course into the heart of the continent.

Bristol and other western English ports may have landed in Nova Scotia and Newfoundland as early as the 1480s. The codfish of the Grand Banks undoubtedly drew vessels of all nations, and during the summer months some sailors probably dried and salted their catches on Canada's convenient shores. John Cabot (Giovanni Caboto), a Venetian sea captain, completed the first recorded transatlantic voyage by an English vessel in 1497, while attempting to find a northwest passage to Asia.

Cabot died during a second attempt to find a direct route to Cathay in 1498. Although Sebastian Cabot continued his father's explorations in the Hudson Bay region in 1508–1509, England's interest in the New World waned. For the next three-quarters of a century, the English people were preoccupied with more pressing domestic and religious concerns. When curiosity about the New World revived, however, Cabot's voyages established England's belated claim to American territory.

Religious Turmoil

At the time of Cabot's death, England was not prepared to compete with Spain and Portugal for the riches of the Orient. Although Henry VII, the first Tudor monarch, brought peace to England after a bitter civil war, the country still contained too many "over-mighty subjects," powerful local magnates who maintained armed retainers and who often paid little attention to royal authority. Henry possessed no standing army; his small navy intimidated no one. To be sure, the Tudors gave nominal allegiance to the pope in Rome, but unlike the rulers of Spain, they were not crusaders for Catholicism. Religion did not provide England's impetus for exploration.

A complex web of international diplomacy also worked against England's early entry into New World colonization. In 1509, to cement an alliance between Spain and England, the future Henry VIII married Catherine of Aragon. As a result of this marital arrangement, English merchants enjoyed limited rights to trade in Spain's

American colonies, but any attempt by England at independent colonization would have threatened those rights and would have jeopardized the alliance.

By the end of the sixteenth century, however, conditions within England had changed dramatically, in part as a result of the Protestant Reformation. As they did, the English began to consider their former ally, Spain, as the greatest threat to English aspirations. Tudor monarchs, especially Henry VIII (r. 1509–1547) and his daughter Elizabeth I (r. 1558–1603), developed a strong central administration, while England became more and more a Protestant society. This merger of English Protestantism and English nationalism affected all aspects of public life. It helped propel England into a central role in European affairs and was crucial in creating a powerful sense of an English identity among all classes of people.

Popular anticlericalism helped spark religious reformation in England. The English people had long resented paying monies to a distant pope. Early in the sixteenth century, opposition to and criticism of the clergy grew increasingly vocal. Cardinal Thomas Wolsey, the most powerful prelate in England, flaunted his immense wealth and unwittingly became a symbol of spiritual corruption. Parish priests were objects of ridicule. Poorly educated men for the most part, they seemed theologically ignorant and perpetually grasping. Anticlericalism did not run as deep in England as it had in Germany, but by the late 1520s, the Catholic church had lost the allegiance of the great mass of the population. The people's pent-up anger is central to an understanding of the English Reformation. Put simply, if common men and women throughout the kingdom had not supported separation from Rome, then Henry VIII could not have forced them to leave the church.

The catalyst for Reformation in England was the king's desire to rid himself of his wife, Catherine of Aragon, who happened to be the daughter of the former king of Spain. Their marriage had produced a daughter, Mary, but, as the years passed, no son. The need for a male heir obsessed Henry. He and his counselors assumed a female ruler could not maintain domestic peace and England would fall once again into civil war. The answer seemed to be remarriage. Henry petitioned Pope Clement VII for a divorce (technically, an annulment), but the Spanish had other ideas. Unwilling to tolerate the public humiliation of Catherine, they forced the pope to procrastinate. In 1527, time ran out. The passionate Henry fell in love with Anne Boleyn, who later bore him a daughter, Elizabeth. The king decided to divorce Catherine with or without papal consent.

The final break with Rome came swiftly. Between 1529 and 1536, the king, acting through Parliament, severed all ties with the pope, seized church lands, and dissolved many of the monasteries. In March 1534, the Act of Supremacy boldly announced, "The King's Majesty justly and rightfully is supreme head of the Church of England." The entire process, which one historian termed a "state reformation," was conducted with impressive unanimity. Land formerly owned by the Catholic church passed quickly into private hands, and within a short period, property holders throughout England had acquired a vested interest in Protestantism. Beyond breaking with the papacy, Henry showed little enthusiasm for theological change. Many Catholic ceremonies survived.

The split with Rome, however, could not be contained. The year 1539 saw the publication of an English Bible. Before then the Scripture had

The Tudor Monarchs

Henry VII
(d. 1509)
m.
Elizabeth of York

Arthur (d.1502) — Henry VIII (r. 1509–1547) — Margaret — Mary

m.

Catherine of Aragon — Anne Boleyn — Jane Seymour

Mary I (r. 1553–1558) — Elizabeth I (r. 1558–1603) — Edward VI (r. 1547–1553)

been available only in Latin, the language of an educated elite. For the first time in English history, ordinary people could read the word of God in the vernacular. It was a liberating experience that persuaded some men and women that Henry had not yet fully reformed the English church.

With Henry's death in 1547, England entered a period of acute political instability. Edward VI, Henry's young son by his third wife, Jane Seymour, came to the throne, but he was still a child and sickly besides. Militant Protestants took advantage of the political uncertainty, insisting the Church of England remove every trace of its Catholic origins. With the death of young Edward in 1553, these ambitious efforts came to a sudden halt. Henry's eldest daughter, Mary, next ascended the throne. Fiercely loyal to the Catholic faith of her mother, Catherine of Aragon, Mary I vowed to return England to the pope.

However misguided were the queen's plans, she possessed her father's iron will. Hundreds of Protestants were executed; others scurried off to the safety of Geneva and Frankfurt where they absorbed the most radical Calvinist doctrines of the day. When Mary died in 1558 and was succeeded by Elizabeth, these "Marian exiles" flocked back to England, more eager than ever to rid the Tudor church of Catholicism. Mary had inadvertently advanced the cause of Calvinism by creating so many Protestant martyrs, reformers burned for their faith and now celebrated in the woodcuts of the most popular book of the period, John Foxe's *Acts and Monuments,* commonly known as the *Book of Martyrs* (1563). The Marian exiles served as the leaders of the Elizabethan church, an institution that remained fundamentally Calvinist until the end of the sixteenth century.

Reformation in Europe

By the time Mary Tudor had come to the throne, the vast popular movement known as the Reformation swept across northern and central Europe, and as much as any of the later great political revolutions, it had begun to transform the character of the modern world. The Reformation started in Germany when, in 1517, a relatively obscure German monk, Martin Luther, publicly challenged the central tenets of Roman Catholicism. Within a few years, the religious unity of Europe was permanently shattered. The Reformation divided kingdoms, sparked bloody wars, and unleashed an extraordinary flood of religious publication.

Luther's message was straightforward, one ordinary people could easily comprehend. God spoke through the Bible, Luther maintained, not through the pope or priests. Scripture taught that women and men were saved by faith alone. Pilgrimages, fasts, alms, indulgences, none of these traditional ritual activities could assure salvation. Luther's radical ideas challenged the institutional structure of Catholicism, as they spread rapidly across northern Germany and Scandinavia.

Other Protestant theologians—religious thinkers who would determine the course of reform in England, Scotland, and the early American colonies—mounted an even more strident attack on Catholicism. The most influential of these was John Calvin, a lawyer turned theologian, who lived most of his adult life in the Swiss city of Geneva. Calvin stressed God's omnipotence over human affairs. The Lord, he maintained, chose some persons for "election," the gift of salvation, while condemning others to eternal damnation. There was nothing that a man or woman could do to alter this decision.

Common sense suggests that such a bleak doctrine might lead to fatalism or hedonism. After all, why not enjoy the world's pleasures to the fullest if such actions have no effect on God's judgment? But many sixteenth-century Europeans did not share modern notions of what constitutes common sense. Indeed, Calvinists were constantly up and doing, searching for signs that they had received God's gift of grace. The uncertainty of their eternal state proved a powerful psychological spur, for as long as people did not know whether they were scheduled for heaven or hell, they worked diligently to demonstrate that they possessed at least the seeds of grace. The doctrine of *predestination* became the distinguishing mark of this form of Protestantism.

John Calvin's *Institutes of the Christian Religion* (1536) contained a powerful statement of the new faith, and his teachings spawned religious movements in most northern European countries. In France, the Reformed Protestants were known as Huguenots. In Scotland, people of Calvinistic persuasion founded the Presbyterian church. And in

Foxe's Book of Martyrs (1563), *depicting the sufferings of those executed under Mary, provided powerful propaganda for the advance of the Protestant religion in England.*

seventeenth-century England and America, most of those who put Calvin's teachings into practice were called Puritans.

The Protestant Queen

Elizabeth demonstrated that Henry and his advisers had been mistaken about the capabilities of female rulers. She was a woman of such talent that modern biographers find little to criticize in her decisions. She governed the English people from 1558 to 1603, an intellectually exciting period during which some of her subjects took the first halting steps toward colonizing the New World.

Elizabeth recognized her most urgent duty as queen was to end the religious turmoil that had divided the country for a generation. She had no desire to restore Catholicism. After all, the pope openly referred to her as a woman of illegitimate birth. Nor did she want to recreate the church exactly as it had been in the final years of her father's reign. Rather, Elizabeth established a unique and heterogeneous institution, Catholic in much of its ceremony and government but clearly Protestant in doctrine. Under her so-called Elizabethan settlement, the queen assumed the title "Supreme Head of the Church." Some churchmen who had studied with Calvin in Geneva urged her to drop immediately all Catholic rituals, but she ignored these strident reformers. The young

queen understood she could not rule effectively without the full support of her people, and as the examples of Edward and Mary before her demonstrated, neither radical change nor widespread persecution gained a monarch lasting popularity.

The state of England's religion was not simply a domestic concern. One scholar aptly termed this period of European history "the Age of Religious Wars." Catholicism and Protestantism influenced the way ordinary men and women across the continent interpreted the experiences of everyday life. Religion shaped political and economic activities. Protestant leaders, for example, purged the English calendar of the many saints' days that had punctuated the agricultural year in Catholic countries. The Reformation certainly had a profound impact on the economic development of Calvinist countries. Max Weber, a brilliant German sociologist of the early twentieth century, argued in his *Protestant Ethic and Spirit of Capitalism* that a gnawing sense of self-doubt created by the doctrine of "predestination" drove Calvinists to extraordinary diligence. They generated large profits not because they wanted to become rich, but because they wanted to be doing the Lord's work, to show they might be among God's "elect."

Indeed, it is helpful to view Protestantism and Catholicism as warring ideologies, bundles of deeply held beliefs that divided countries and families much as communism and capitalism did during the late twentieth century. The confrontations between these two faiths affected Elizabeth's entire reign. Soon after she became queen, Pope Pius V excommunicated her, and in his papal bull *Regnans in Exelsis* (1570), he stripped Elizabeth of her "pretended title to the kingdom." Spain, the most fervently Catholic state in Europe, vowed to restore England to the "true" faith, and Catholic militants constantly plotted to overthrow the Tudor monarchy.

Religion, War, and Nationalism

Slowly, but steadily, English Protestantism and English nationalism merged. A loyal English subject in the late sixteenth century loved the queen, supported the Church of England, and hated Catholics, especially those who happened to live in Spain. Elizabeth herself came to symbolize this militant new chauvinism. Her subjects adored the Virgin Queen, and they applauded when her famed "Sea Dogs"—dashing figures such as Sir Francis Drake and Sir John Hawkins—seized Spanish treasure ships in American waters. The English sailors' raids were little more than piracy, but in this undeclared state of war, such instances of harassment passed for national victories. There seemed to be no reason that patriotic Elizabethans should not share in the wealth of the New World. With each engagement, each threat, each plot, English nationalism took deeper root. By the 1570s, it had become obvious the English people were driven by powerful ideological forces similar to those that had moved the subjects of Isabella and Ferdinand almost a century earlier.

In the mid-1580s, Philip II, who had united the empire of Spain and Portugal in 1580, decided that England's arrogantly Protestant queen could be tolerated no longer. He ordered the construction of a mighty fleet, hundreds of transport vessels designed to carry Spain's finest infantry across the English channel. When one of Philip's lieutenants viewed the Armada at Lisbon in May 1588, he described it as *la felicissima armada,* the invincible fleet. The king believed that with the support of England's oppressed Catholics, Spanish troops would sweep Elizabeth from power.

It was a grand scheme; it was an even grander failure. In 1588, a smaller, more maneuverable English navy dispersed Philip's Armada, and severe storms finished it off. Spanish hopes for Catholic England lay wrecked along the rocky coasts of Scotland and Ireland. English Protestants interpreted victory in providential terms: "God breathed and they were scattered."

REHEARSAL IN IRELAND FOR AMERICAN COLONIZATION

After the defeat of the Armada, it seemed as if England had fulfilled the prerequisites for American colonization. Before they crossed the Atlantic, however, English settlers moved to Ireland. Their experiences there powerfully shaped how later migrants would view the New World. It was on this island that enterprising Englishmen first learned to subdue a foreign population and to seize its lands. When Elizabeth assumed the throne, Ireland's one million inhabitants were scattered across the countryside. There were few villages, most of which were located along the coast. To the English eye, the Irish people seemed wild and barbaric. They were also fiercely independent and difficult to control. The English dominated a small region around Dublin by force of arms, but much of Ireland's territory remained in the hands of Gaelic-speaking Catholics who presumably lived beyond the reach of civilization.

English Colonization in Ireland

During the 1560s and 1570s, various enterprising English people decided that considerable fortunes could be made in Ireland. There were substantial risks, of course, not the least of which was the hostility of the Irish. Nevertheless, private "projectors" sponsored English settlements, and, in turn, these colonists forced the Irish either into tenancy or off the land altogether. It was during this period that semimilitary colonies were planted in Ulster and Munster.

As one might expect, colonization produced severe cultural strains. The English settlers, however humble their origins, felt superior to the Irish. After all, the English people had championed the Protestant religion. They had constructed a complex market economy and created a powerful nation-state. To the English settlers, the Irish appeared to be lazy, licentious, superstitious, even stupid. English settlers ridiculed unfamiliar local customs, and it is not surprising that even educated representatives of the two cultures found communication almost impossible. English colonists, for example, criticized the pastoral farming methods prevalent in sixteenth-century Ireland. It seemed perversely wasteful for the Irish to be forever moving about, since as any English person could see, such practices retarded the development of towns. Sir John Davies, a leading English colonizer, declared that if the Irish were left to themselves, they would "never (to the end of the world) build houses, make townships or villages or manure or improve the land *as it ought to be*." Such stubborn inefficiency—surely (the English reasoned) the Irish must have known better—became the standard English justification for the seizure of large tracts of land.

English Brutality

English ethnocentrism was relatively benign so long as the Irish accepted the subservient roles the colonizers assigned them. But when they rebelled against the invaders, something they did with great frequency, English condescension turned to violence. Resistance smacked of disrespect and, moreover, to ensure the safety of the English, it had to be crushed. The brutality of Sir Humphrey Gilbert in Ireland would have made even the most insensitive conquistadore uneasy. Gilbert was a talented man who wrote treatises on geography, explored the coast of North America, and entertained Queen Elizabeth with witty conversation. But as a colonizer in a strange land—in what some historians now call England's "permissive frontier"—he tolerated no opposition.

In 1569, he was appointed military governor of Munster, and when the Irish in his district rose up, he executed everyone he could catch, "mane, woman and childe." Gilbert's excesses would never have been permitted in England no matter how serious the rebellion. He cut off the heads of many enemy soldiers killed in battle, and in the words of one contemporary, Gilbert laid his macabre trophies "on the ground by each side of the way leading to his tent, so that none should come into his tent for any cause but commonly he must pass through a lane of heads." Such behavior was not only unprecedented, it was also calamitous. Instead of bringing peace and securi-

ty, it helped generate a hatred so deep that Ireland remains divided to this day.

The Irish experiments served as models for later English colonies in the New World. Indeed, one modern Irish scholar argues that "English colonization in Virginia was a logical continuation of the Elizabethan conquest of Ireland." English adventurers in the New World commonly compared Native Americans with the "wild" Irish, a kind of ethnocentric shorthand that equated all alien races. This mental process was a central element in the transfer of English culture to America. The English, like the Spanish and the French, did not perceive America in objective terms. Instead, they saw an America they had already constructed in their imaginations, and the people and objects that greeted them on the other side of the Atlantic were forced into Old World categories, one of which was "Irish."

ENGLAND TURNS TO AMERICA

By the 1570s, English interest in the New World had revived. An increasing number of gentlefolk were in an expansive mood, ready to challenge Spain and reap the profits of Asia and America. Yet the adventurers who directed Elizabethan expeditions were only dimly aware of Cabot's voyages, and their sole experience in settling distant outposts was in Ireland. Over the last three decades of the sixteenth century, English adventurers made almost every mistake one could possibly imagine. They did, however, acquire valuable information about winds and currents, supplies, and finance.

Roanoke Tragedy

In 1584, Sir Walter Ralegh dispatched two captains to the coast of present-day North Carolina to claim land granted to him by Elizabeth. The men returned with glowing reports, no doubt aimed in part at potential financial backers. "The soile," declared Captain Arthur Barlow, "is the most plentifull, sweete, fruitfull, and wholesome of all the world."

Ralegh diplomatically renamed this marvelous region Virginia, in honor of his patron, the Virgin Queen. Elizabeth encouraged her favorite in private conversation but rejected his persistent requests for money. With rumors of war in the air, she did not want to alienate Philip II unnecessarily by sponsoring a colony on land long ago claimed by Spain.

Ralegh finally raised the funds for his adventure, but his enterprise seemed ill fated from the start. Despite careful planning, everything went wrong. The settlement was poorly situated. Located inside the Outer Banks—perhaps to avoid detection by the Spanish—the Roanoke colony proved extremely difficult to reach. Even experienced navigators feared the treacherous currents and storms off Cape Hatteras. Sir Richard Grenville, the leader of the expedition, added to the colonists' troubles by destroying an entire Indian village in retaliation for the suspected theft of a silver cup.

Grenville hurried back to England in the autumn of 1585, leaving the colonists to fend for themselves. Although they coped quite well, a peculiar series of accidents transformed Ralegh's settlement into a ghost town. In the spring of 1586, Sir Francis Drake was returning from a Caribbean voyage and for reasons known only to himself, decided to visit Roanoke. Since an anticipated shipment of supplies was overdue, the colonists climbed aboard Drake's ships and went home.

In 1587, Ralegh launched a second colony. This time he placed in charge John White, a veteran administrator and talented artist, who a few years earlier had produced a magnificent sketchbook of the Algonquian Indians who lived near Roanoke. The new settlement contained women, children, and even two infants who were born within weeks after the colonists crossed the Atlantic. The settlers feasted on Roanoke's fish and game and bountiful harvests of corn and pumpkin.

Once again, Ralegh's luck turned sour. The Spanish Armada severed communication between England and America. Every available English vessel was pressed into military service, and between 1587 and 1590, no ship visited the Roanoke colonists. When rescuers eventually reached the island, they found the village deserted. The fate of the "lost" colonists remains a mystery. The best guess is that they were absorbed by neighboring groups of natives, some

The wife and daughter of an Algonquian chief, drawn by John White, a leader of the 1587 Roanoke settlement. The child is holding an English doll.

from as far as the southern shore of the James River.

Propaganda for Empire

Had it not been for Richard Hakluyt, the Younger, who publicized explorers' accounts of the New World, the dream of American colonization might have died in England. Hakluyt, a supremely industrious man, never saw America. Nevertheless, his vision of the New World powerfully shaped English public opinion. He interviewed captains and sailors upon their return from distant voyages and carefully collected their stories in a massive book entitled *The Principall Navigations, Voyages, and Discoveries of the English Nation* (1589). The work appeared to be

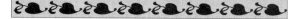

CHRONOLOGY

30,000–20,000 B.C. Indians cross the Bering Strait into North America

2000–1500 B.C. Agricultural revolution transforms Native American life

1001 A.D. Norsemen establish a small settlement in Vinland (Newfoundland)

1030 Death of War Jaabi (King of Takrur), first Muslim ruler in West Africa

1450 Gutenberg perfects movable type

1469 Marriage of Isabella and Ferdinand leads to the unification of Spain

1481 Portuguese build castle at Elmina on the Gold Coast of Africa

1492 Columbus lands at San Salvador

1497 Cabot leads first English exploration of North America

1498 Vasco da Gama of Portugal reaches India by sailing around Africa

1502 Montezuma becomes emperor of the Aztecs

1506 Columbus dies in Spain after four voyages to America

1517 Martin Luther's protest sparks Reformation in Germany

1521 Cortés defeats the Aztecs at Tenochtitlán

1529–1536 Henry VIII provokes English Reformation

1534 Cartier claims Canada for France

1536 Calvin's *Institutes* published

1540 Coronado explores the Southwest for Spain

1558 Elizabeth I becomes queen of England

1585 First Roanoke settlement established on coast of North Carolina

1588 Spanish Armada defeated by the English

1608 Champlain founds Quebec

a straightforward description of what these sailors had seen across the sea. That was its strength. In reality, Hakluyt edited each piece so it would drive home the book's central point: England needed American colonies. Indeed, they were essential to the nation's prosperity and independence. In Hakluyt's America, there were no losers. "The earth bringeth fourth all things in abundance, as in the first creations without toil or labour," he wrote of Virginia. His blend of piety, patriotism, and self-interest proved immensely popular, and his *Voyages* went through many editions.

As a salesperson for the New World, Hakluyt was as misleading as he was successful. He failed to appreciate, or purposely ignored, the rich cultural diversity of the Native Americans and the varied backgrounds of the Europeans. He said not a word about the sufferings of Africans in America. Instead, he and many other polemicists for colonization led the ordinary English men and women who traveled to America to expect nothing less than a paradise on earth.

Recommended Reading

The history of first contact has generated provocative, splendidly interdisciplinary scholarship, works that should be read not only to learn something about the conquest of America, but also about the current state of the discipline of history. Two excellent studies of encounters between Native Americans and Europeans—works that attempt to reconstruct the Indians' side of the story—are Inga Clendinnen, *Aztecs: An Interpretation* (1991) and James Axtell, *The Invasion Within: The Contest of Cultures in Colonial North America* (1986). Other innovative books explore how early European invaders imagined the New World, and how they translated what they saw into a familiar and unthreatening language: Stephen Greenblatt, *Marvelous Possessions: The Wonder of the New World* (1991) and Anthony Pagden, *European Encounters with the New World: From Renaissance to Romanticism* (1992). For a readable introduction to the heated controversy over Columbus, consider Kirkpatrick Sale, *The Conquest of Paradise: Christopher Columbus and the Columbian Legacy* (1990). For an excellent investigation of Indian culture in New Spain after the conquest see James Lockhart, *The Nahuas After the Conquest: A Social and Cultural History of the Indians of Central Mexico, Sixteenth Through Eighteenth Centuries* (1992).

Additional Bibliography

A. W. Crosby provides a fascinating study of the ecological impact of exploration on the New World as well as on the Old in *The Columbian Voyages, the Columbian Exchange, and Their Historians* (1987). William Cronon's provocative book, *Changes in the Land* (1983), investigates within early New England a cultural conflict over the meaning and use of land.

A list of the most original investigations of Native American cultures and the Indians' accommodation to radical social and environmental change would include James H. Merrell, *The Indians' New World: Catawbas and Their Neighbors from European Contact Through the Era of Removal* (1989); Neal Salisbury, *Manitou and Providence: Indians, Europeans, and the Making of New England* (1982); Bruce G. Trigger, *Natives and Newcomers: Canada's "Heroic Age" Reconsidered* (1987); Richard White, *The Roots of Dependency: Subsistence, Environment, and Social Change Among the Choctaws, Pawnees, and Navajos* (1983); and James Axtell, *The European and the Indian: Essays in the Ethnohistory of Colonial North America* (1981).

The literature of early West African history often focuses on the American slave trade. But as Philip Curtin and others remind us, the Africans had developed complex economies long before the arrival of the Europeans. An important study is Curtin's *Economic Change in Precolonial Africa: Senegambia in the Era of the Slave Trade* (1975). Other valuable works include Ray A. Kea, *Settlements, Trade, and Politics in the Seventeenth-Century Gold Coast* (1982); Joseph C. Miller, *Way of Death: Merchant Capitalism and the Angolan Slave Trade 1730–1830* (1988); Paul H. Lovejoy, *Transformations in Slavery: A History of Slavery in Africa* (1983).

The complicated and tragic story of the struggle to control Mexico is the subject of several strikingly original studies. See especially Tzvetan Todorov, *The Conquest of America: The Question of the Other* (1984) and Inga Clendinnen, *Ambivalent Conquests: Maya and Spaniard in the Yucatan, 1517–1570* (1987). Also helpful are James Lockhart and Stuart B. Schwartz, *Early Latin America: A History of Colonial Spanish America and Brazil* (1983); and Charles Gibson, *Spain in America* (1966).

The transformation of early modern Europe, especially economic shifts, is discussed in Ralph Davis's brilliant synthesis, *The Rise of Atlantic Economies* (1973). A valuable study that explores the European response to the discovery of the New World is J. H. Elliott, *The Old World and the New, 1492–1650* (1970). On the conquest of the Canary Islands, see Felipe Fernández-Armesto, *Before Columbus* (1987). Anyone curious about the religious background of early English settlement should look at William J. Bouwsma, *John Calvin: A Sixteenth-Century Portrait* (1988); Patrick Collinson, *The Religion of the Protestants: The Church in English Society 1559–1625* (1982); R. W. Scribner, *Popular Culture and Popular Movements in Reformation Germany* (1987).

One can easily obtain many excellent political and social histories of the major European powers on the eve of New World colonization. For Spain, the recommended start remains J. H. Elliott, *Imperial Spain 1469–1716* (1963). For England, G. R. Elton, *England Under the Tudors* (1974); Keith Wrightson, *English Society 1580–1641* (1979); and Lawrence Stone, *The Crisis of the Aristocracy 1558–1641* (1965) provide valuable insights. And for Ireland, the two most readable studies of this period are David B. Quinn, *The Elizabethans and the Irish* (1966) and Nicholas P. Canny, *Kingdom and Colony: Ireland in the Atlantic World, 1560–1800* (1988). Thorough accounts of the development of New France can be found in W. J. Eccles, *France in America* (rev. ed. 1990) and *The Canadian Frontier, 1534–1760* (rev. ed. 1983).

Competing Visions
English Colonization in the Seventeenth Century

*I*n the spring of 1644, John Winthrop, governor of Massachusetts Bay, learned that Indians had overrun the scattered tobacco plantations of Virginia, killing as many as five hundred colonists. Winthrop never thought much of the Chesapeake settlements. He regarded the people who had migrated to that part of America as grossly materialistic, and because Virginia had recently expelled several Puritan ministers, Winthrop decided the Indian hostilities were God's way of punishing the planters for their worldliness. "It was observable," he related, "that this massacre came upon them soon after they had driven out the godly ministers we had sent to them." When Virginians appealed to Massachusetts for military supplies, they received a cool reception. "We were weakly provided ourselves," Winthrop explained, "and so could not afford them any help of that kind."

In 1675, the tables turned. Indian forces declared all-out war against the New Englanders, and soon reports of the destruction of Puritan communities were circulating in Virginia. "The Indians in New England have burned Considerable Villages," wrote one leading tobacco planter, "and have made them [the New Englanders] desert more than one hundred and fifty miles of those places they had formerly seated."

Sir William Berkeley, Virginia's royal governor, was not displeased by news of New England's adversity. He and his friends held the Puritans in contempt. Indeed, the New Englanders reminded them of the religious fanatics who had provoked civil war in England and who in 1649 had executed Charles I. During this particular crisis, Berkeley noted that he might have shown more pity for the beleaguered New Englanders "had they deserved it of the King." The governor, sounding like a Puritan himself, described the warring Indians as the "Instruments" with which God intended "to destroy the King's Enemies." For good measure, Virginia outlawed the export of foodstuffs to their embattled northern neighbors.

Such extraordinary disunity—not to mention lack of compassion—comes as a surprise to anyone searching for the roots of American nationalism in this early period. But the world of Winthrop and Berkeley was most emphatically not that of Washington and Jefferson. English colonization in the seventeenth century did not spring from a desire to build a centralized empire in the New World similar to that of Spain or France. Instead, the English Crown awarded colonial charters to a wide variety of merchants, religious idealists, and aristocratic adventurers who established separate and profoundly different colonies. Not only did New Englanders have little in common with the earliest Virginians and Carolinians, but they were often divided among themselves.

Migration itself helps to explain this striking social diversity. At different times different colonies appealed to different sorts of people. Men and women moved to the New World for various reasons, and as economic, political, and religious conditions changed on both sides of the Atlantic during the course of the seventeenth century, so too did patterns of English migration.

DECISION TO EMIGRATE

English people in the early decades of the seventeenth century observed an accelerating pace of social change. What was most evident was the rapid growth of population. Between 1580 and 1650, a period during which many men and women elected to journey to the New World, the population of England expanded from about 3.5 million to over 5 million. Among other things, this expansion strained the nation's agrarian economy. Competition for food and land drove up prices, and people who needed work increasingly took to the roads. These migrants, many of them drawn into the orbit of London by tales of opportunity, frightened the propertied leaders of English society. To the propertied class, the wandering poor represented a threat to the traditional order, and, particularly during the early decades of the seventeenth century, they urged local magistrates throughout the kingdom to enforce the laws against vagrancy.

Even by modern standards, the English population of this period was quite mobile. To be sure, most men and women lived out their days rooted in the tiny country villages of their birth. A growing number of English people, however, were migrant laborers who took seasonal work. Many others relocated from the countryside to London, already a city of several hundred thousand inhabitants by the early seventeenth century. Because health conditions in London were poor, a large number of these new arrivals quickly died, and had their places not been taken by other migrants from the rural villages, the population of London would almost certainly have decreased.

Other, more exotic destinations also beckoned. A large number of English settlers migrated to Ireland, while lucrative employment and religious freedom attracted people to Holland. The Pilgrims, for example, initially hoped to make a new life in Leyden. These migrations within Europe serve as reminders that ordinary people had choices. A person who was upset about the state of the Church of England or who had lost a livelihood did not have to move to America. That some men and women consciously selected this much more dangerous and expensive journey clearly set them apart from their contemporaries.

English colonists crossed the Atlantic for many different reasons. Some wanted to institute a purer form of worship, more closely based on their reading of Scripture. Others dreamed of owning land and of bettering their social position. A few came to the New World to escape bad marriages, jail terms, and the dreary prospect of lifelong poverty. Since most seventeenth-century migrants, especially those who transferred to the Chesapeake colonies, left almost no records of their previous lives in England, it is futile to try to isolate a single cause or explanation for their decision to leave home.

In the absence of detailed personal information, historians have usually assumed that poverty, or the fear of soon falling into poverty, drove people across the Atlantic. No doubt such considerations figured heavily in the final decision. But so too did religion, and it was not uncommon for the poor of early modern England to be among those demanding the most radical ecclesiastical reform. As a recent historian of seventeenth-century migration concluded, "Individuals left for a variety of motives, some idealistic, others practical, some simple, others complex, many perhaps contradictory and imperfectly understood by the migrants themselves."

Whatever their reasons for crossing the ocean, English migrants to America in this period left a nation wracked by recurrent, often violent political and religious controversy. During the 1620s,

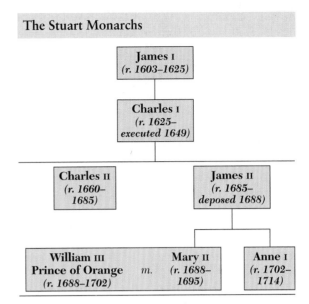

The Stuart Monarchs

James I (r. 1603–1625)

Charles I (r. 1625–executed 1649)

Charles II (r. 1660–1685)

James II (r. 1685–deposed 1688)

William III Prince of Orange (r. 1688–1702) m. Mary II (r. 1688–1695)

Anne I (r. 1702–1714)

the Stuart monarchs—James I (r. 1603–1625) and his son Charles I (r. 1625–1649)—who succeeded Queen Elizabeth on the English throne, fought constantly with the elected members of Parliament.

Many royal policies—the granting of lucrative commercial monopolies to court favorites, for example—fueled popular discontent, but the Crown's hostility to far-reaching religious reform sparked the most vocal protest. Throughout the kingdom, Puritans became adamant in their demand for radical change.

Tensions grew so severe that in 1629, Charles attempted to rule the country without Parliament's assistance. The strategy backfired. When Charles was finally forced to recall Parliament in 1640 because he was running out of money, Parliament demanded major constitutional reforms. Militant Puritans, supported by many members of Parliament, insisted on restructuring the church—abolishing the office of bishop was high on their list. In this angry political atmosphere, Charles took up arms against the supporters of Parliament. The confrontation between Royalists and Parliamentarians set off a long and bloody civil war. In 1649, the victorious Parliamentarians beheaded Charles, and for almost a decade Oliver Cromwell, a skilled general and committed Puritan, governed England.

In 1660, following Cromwell's death from natural causes, the Stuarts returned to the English throne. During a period known as the Restoration, neither Charles II (1660–1685) nor James II (1685–1688)—both sons of Charles I—were able to establish genuine political stability. When the authoritarian James openly patronized his fellow Catholics, the nation rose up in what the English people called the "Glorious Revolution" (1688) and sent James into permanent exile.

The Glorious Revolution altered the course of English political history and, therefore, that of the American colonies as well. The monarchs who followed James II surrendered some of the powers of government that had destabilized English politics for almost a century. The Crown was still a potent force in the political life of the nation, but never again would an English king or queen attempt to govern without an elected assembly.

Such political events, coupled with periodic economic recession and religious repression, determined, in large measure, the direction and flow of migration to America. During times of political turmoil, religious persecution, and economic insecurity, men and women thought more seriously about living in the New World than they did during periods of peace and prosperity. Obviously, people who moved to America at different times came from different social and political environments. A person who emigrated to Pennsylvania in the 1680s, for example, left a homeland unlike the one that a Virginian in 1607 or a Bay Colonist in 1630 might have known. Moreover, the young men and women who migrated to London in search of work and who then, in their frustration and poverty, decided to move to the Chesapeake, carried a very different set of memories than those people who moved directly to New England from the small rural villages of their homeland.

Regardless of the exact timing of departure, English settlers took with them a bundle of ideas and assumptions that helped them make sense of their everyday experiences in an unfamiliar environment. Their values were tested and sometimes transformed in the New World, but they were seldom destroyed. Settlement involved a complex process of adjustment. The colonists developed different subcultures in America, and in each of these, one can trace the interaction between the settlers' values and the physical elements, such as the climate, crops, and soil, of their new surroundings. The Chesapeake, the New England

colonies, the Middle Colonies, and the Southern Colonies formed distinct regional identities that persisted long after the first settlers had passed from the scene.

THE CHESAPEAKE: DREAMS OF WEALTH

After the Roanoke debacle in 1590 (see Chapter 1), interest in American settlement declined, and only a few aging visionaries such as Richard Hakluyt kept alive the dream of English colonies in the New World. These advocates argued that the North American mainland contained resources of incalculable value. An innovative group, they insisted, might reap great profits and at the same time supply the mother country with items that it would otherwise be forced to purchase from European rivals: Holland, France, and Spain.

Moreover, any enterprise that annoyed Catholic Spain or revealed its weakness in America seemed a desirable end in itself to patriotic English citizens. Anti-Catholicism and hatred of Spain became an integral part of English nationalism during this period, and unless one appreciates just how deeply these sentiments ran in the popular mind, one cannot fully understand why ordinary people who had no direct stake in the New World supported English efforts to colonize America. Soon after James I ascended to the throne, adventurers were given an opportunity to put their theories into practice in the colonies of Virginia and Maryland, an area known as the Chesapeake.

Jamestown Disaster

During Elizabeth's reign, the major obstacle to successful colonization of the New World had been money. No single person, no matter how rich or well connected, could underwrite the vast expenses a New World settlement required. The solution to this financial problem was the "joint-stock company," a business organization in which scores of people could invest without fear of bankruptcy. A merchant or landowner could purchase a share of stock at a stated price, and at the end of several years could anticipate recovering the initial investment plus a portion of whatever profits the company had made. Joint-stock

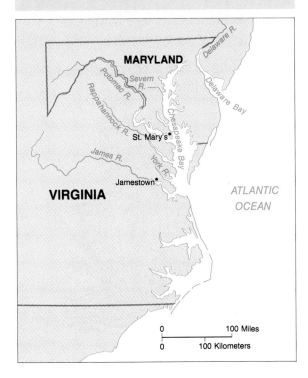

Chesapeake Colonies, 1640
The four regional maps in this chapter depict the full spectrum of English settlement on mainland North America.

some hundred miles up a large navigable river. The natural beauty and economic potential of the region was apparent to everyone. A voyager on this expedition reported seeing "faire meaddowes and goodly tall trees, with such fresh waters running through the woods, as almost ravished [us] at first sight."

The leaders of the colony selected—without consulting the local Native Americans—what the Europeans considered a promising location more than 30 miles from the mouth of the James River. A marshy peninsula jutting out into the river became the site for one of America's most ill-fated villages, Jamestown. Modern historians have criticized this choice, for the low-lying ground proved to be a disease-ridden death trap; even the drinking water was contaminated with salt. But the first Virginians were neither stupid nor suicidal. Jamestown seemed the ideal place to build a fort, since surprise attack rather than sickness appeared the more serious threat in the early months of settlement.

Almost immediately the colonists began quarreling. The adventurers were not prepared for the challenges that confronted them in America. Part of the problem was cultural. Most of these people had grown up in a depressed agricultural economy that could not provide full-time employment for all who wanted it. In England laborers shared what little work was available. One man, for example, might perform a certain chore while others simply watched. Later the men who had been idle were given an opportunity to work for an hour or two. This labor system may have been appropriate for England, but in Virginia it nearly destroyed the colony. Adventurers sat around Jamestown while other men performed crucial agricultural tasks. It made little sense, of course, to share work in an environment in which people were starving because too little labor was expended on the planting and harvesting of crops. Not surprisingly, some modern historians—those who assumed all workers should put in an eight-hour day—branded the early Virginians as lazy, irresponsible beings who preferred to play while others labored in the fields. In point of fact, however, these first settlers were merely attempting to replicate a traditional work experience.

Greed exacerbated these problems. The adventurers had traveled to the New World in search of the sort of instant wealth they imagined the

ventures sprang up like mushrooms. English citizens of means, and even some of more modest fortunes, rushed to invest in these companies, and as a result, some enterprises were able to amass large amounts of capital, enough certainly to finance a new colony in Virginia.

On April 10, 1606, James issued the first Virginia charter. This document authorized the London Company to establish plantations in Virginia. The London Company was a dynamic business venture. Its leader, Sir Thomas Smith, was reputedly London's wealthiest merchant. Smith and his partners gained possession of the territory lying between Cape Fear and the Hudson River. These were generous but vague boundaries, to be sure, but the Virginia Company—as the London Company soon called itself—set out immediately to find the treasure Hakluyt had promised.

In December 1606, the *Susan Constant,* the *Godspeed,* and the *Discovery* sailed for America. The ships carried 104 men and boys who had been instructed to establish a fortified outpost

Spaniards to have found in Mexico and Peru. Tales of rubies and diamonds lying on the beach may have inflamed their expectations. Even when it must have been apparent these expectations were unfounded, the first settlers often behaved in Virginia as if they fully expected to become rich. Instead of cooperating for the common good—guarding or farming, for example—each individual pursued personal interests. They searched for gold when they might have helped plant corn. No one was willing to take orders, and those who were supposed to govern the colony looked after their private welfare, while disease, war, and starvation ravaged the settlement.

The Indomitable Captain John Smith

Virginia might have gone the way of Roanoke had it not been for Captain John Smith. By any standard, he was a resourceful man. Before coming to Jamestown, he had traveled throughout Europe, fought with the Hungarian army against the Turks, and if Smith is to be believed, was saved from certain death by various beautiful women. Because of his reputation for boasting, historians have discounted Smith's account of life in early Virginia. Recent scholarship, however,

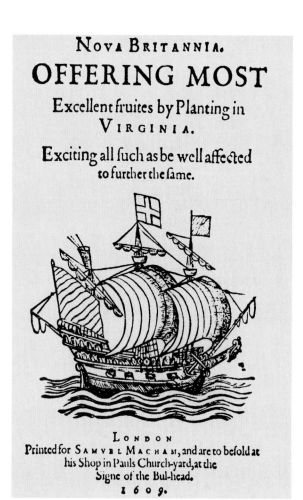

The title page of a 1609 brochure promoting the colony of Virginia. Pamphlets such as these promised the settlers instant wealth.

Much of our knowledge of early Virginia comes from the accounts and maps of Captain John Smith. Twentieth-century archaeological investigation has confirmed the map's overall accuracy. The vignette in the upper left corner of the map depicts the Indian Powhatan in a longhouse addressing his people.

has reaffirmed the truthfulness of his story. In Virginia, Smith brought order out of anarchy. While members of the council in Jamestown debated petty topics, he traded with the local Indians for food, mapped the Chesapeake Bay, and may even have been rescued from execution by a young Indian girl, Pocahontas. In the fall of 1608, he seized control of the ruling council and instituted a tough military discipline. Under Smith, no one enjoyed special privilege. Individuals whom he forced to work came to hate him. But he managed to keep them alive, no small achievement in such a deadly environment.

Leaders of the Virginia Company in London recognized the need to reform the entire enterprise. After all, they had spent considerable sums and had received nothing in return. In 1609, the company directors obtained a new charter from the king, which completely reorganized the Virginia government. Henceforth all commercial and political decisions affecting the colonists rested with the company, a fact that had not been made sufficiently clear in the 1606 charter. Moreover, in an effort to obtain scarce capital, the original partners opened the "joint-stock" to the general public. For a little more than £12—approximately one year's wages for an unskilled English laborer—a person or group of persons could purchase a stake in Virginia. It was anticipated that in 1616, the profits from the colony would be distributed among the shareholders. The company sponsored a publicity campaign; pamphlets and sermons extolled the colony's potential and exhorted patriotic English citizens to invest in the enterprise.

This burst of energy came to nothing. Bad luck and poor planning plagued the Virginia Company. A vessel carrying settlers and supplies went aground in Bermuda, and while this misadventure did little to help the people at Jamestown, it provided Shakespeare with the idea for *The Tempest*. The governor, Lord De La Warr, added to the confusion by postponing his departure for America. Even the indomitable Captain Smith suffered a gunpowder accident and was forced to return to England.

Between 1609 and 1611, the remaining Virginia settlers lacked capable leadership, and perhaps as a result, they lacked food. The terrible winter of 1609–1610 was termed the "starving time." A few desperate colonists were driven to cannibalism. In England, Smith heard that one colonist had killed his wife, powdered [salted] her, and "had eaten part of her before it was known; for which he was executed." The captain, who possessed a curious sense of humor, observed, "Now, whether she was better roasted, broiled, or carbonadoed, I know not, but such a dish as powdered wife I never heard of." Other people lost the will to live.

The presence of so many Indians complicated the situation. The first colonists found themselves living—or attempting to live—in territory controlled by what was probably the most powerful Native American confederation east of the Mississippi River. Under the leadership of their *werowance*, Powhatan, these Indians had by 1608 created a loose association of some thirty

tribes, and when Captain John Smith arrived to lead several hundred adventurers, the Powhatans (named for their king) numbered some 14,000 people, of whom 3,200 were warriors. These natives hoped initially to enlist the Europeans as allies against native enemies. When it became clear that the two peoples, holding such different notions about labor and property and about the exploitation of the natural environment, could not coexist in peace, the Powhatans tried to drive the invaders out of Virginia, once in 1622 and again in 1644. The failure of the second campaign ended in the complete destruction of the Powhatan empire.

In June 1610, the settlers who had survived despite starvation and conflicts with the natives actually abandoned Virginia. Through a stroke of

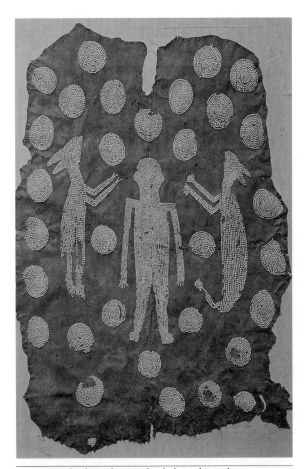

In 1608, Chief Powhatan, the father of Pocahontas, gave this shell-decorated ceremonial cloak to Captain Christopher Newport. Such gestures of friendship were short-lived, however, as coexistence became more and more difficult.

luck, however, they encountered De La Warr just as they commenced their voyage down the James River. The governor and the deputy governors who succeeded him, Sir Thomas Gates and Sir Thomas Dale, ruled by martial law. The new colonists, many of them male and female servants employed by the company, were marched to work by the beat of the drum. Such methods saved the colony but could not make it flourish. In 1616, company shareholders received no profits. Their only reward was the right to a piece of unsurveyed land located 3,000 miles from London.

A "Stinking Weed"

The solution to Virginia's problems grew in the vacant lots of Jamestown. Only Indians bothered to cultivate tobacco until John Rolfe, a settler who achieved notoriety by marrying Pocahontas, realized this local weed might be a valuable export. Rolfe experimented with the crop, eventually growing in Virginia a milder variety that had been developed in the West Indies and was more appealing to European smokers.

Virginians suddenly possessed a means to make money. Tobacco proved relatively easy to grow, and settlers who had avoided work now threw themselves into its production with single-minded diligence. In 1617, one observer found that Jamestown's "streets and all other spare places [are] planted with tobacco . . . the Colony dispersed all about planting tobacco." Although King James I originally considered smoking immoral and unhealthy, he changed his mind when the duties he collected on tobacco imports began to mount. He was neither the first nor the last ruler who decided a vice that generates revenue is not really a vice.

The company launched one last effort to transform Virginia into a profitable enterprise. In 1618, Sir Edwin Sandys (pronounced Sands) led a faction of stockholders that began to pump life into the dying organization by instituting a series of sweeping reforms and eventually ousting Sir Thomas Smith and his friends. Sandys wanted private investors to develop their own estates in Virginia. Before 1618, there had been little incentive to do so, but by relaxing Dale's martial law and promising a representative assembly called

Pocahontas married John Rolfe, a settler who pioneered the cultivation of tobacco as a cash crop. She converted to Christianity, taking the name Rebeka. This portrait, painted during a 1615 visit to London, shows her in court dress.

the House of Burgesses, Sandys thought the colony might be more attractive to wealthy speculators. Even more important was his method for distributing land. Colonists who covered their own transportation cost to America were guaranteed a "headright," a 50-acre lot for which they paid only a small annual rent. Adventurers were granted additional headrights for each servant they brought to the colony. This procedure allowed prosperous planters to build up huge estates at the same time they acquired dependent laborers. This land system persisted long after the company's collapse.

Sandys had only just begun. He also urged the settlers to diversify their economy. Tobacco alone, he argued, was not a sufficient base. He envisioned colonists busily producing iron and tar, silk and glass, sugar and cotton. There was no end to his suggestions. He scoured Europe for skilled artisans and exotic plant cuttings. To finance such a huge project, Sandys relied on a lottery, a game of chance that promised a contin-

The praises sung of tobacco and Virginia on this English tobacco label express the change in King James's attitude toward the "stinking weed" once he recognized the profit to be gained from it.

uous flow of capital into the company's treasury. The final element in the grand scheme was people. Sandys sent new settlers by the thousand to Jamestown, men and women swept up by the same hopes that had carried the colonists of 1607 to the New World.

Mortality in Virginia

Between 1619 and 1622, colonists arrived in Virginia in record number. Company records reveal that during this short period, 3,570 individuals were sent to the colony. These people seldom moved to Virginia in families. Although the first women arrived in Jamestown in 1608, most emigrants were single males in their teens or early twenties who came to the New World as indentured servants. In exchange for transportation across the Atlantic, they agreed to serve a master for a stated number of years. The length of service depended in part on the age of the servant. The younger the servant, the longer he or she served. In return, the master promised to give the laborers proper care and, at the conclusion of their contracts, to provide them with tools and clothes according to "the custom of the country."

Whenever possible, planters in Virginia purchased able-bodied workers, in other words, persons (preferably male) capable of performing hard agricultural labor. This preference dramatically skewed the colony's sex ratio. In the early decades, men outnumbered women by as much as six to one. As one historian, Edmund S. Morgan, explained, "Women were scarcer than corn or liquor in Virginia and fetched a higher price." Such gender imbalance meant that even if a male servant lived to the end of his indenture, he could not realistically expect to start a family of his own. Moreover, despite apparent legal safeguards, masters could treat dependent workers as they pleased; after all, these people were legally considered property. Servants were sold, traded, even gambled away in a hand of cards. It does not require much imagination to see that a society that tolerated such an exploitative labor system might later embrace slavery.

Most Virginians did not live long enough to worry about marriage. Death was omnipresent in this society. Indeed, extraordinarily high mortality was a major reason the Chesapeake colonies developed so differently from those of New England. On the eve of the 1618 reforms, Virginia's population stood at approximately 700. The company sent at least 3,000 more people, but by 1622 only 1,240 were still alive. "It Consequentilie followes," declared one angry shareholder, "that we had then lost 3,000 persons within those 3 yeares." The major killers were contagious diseases. Salt in the water supply also took a toll. And on Good Friday, March 22, 1622, the Powhatans slew 347 Europeans in a well-coordinated surprise attack.

No one knows for certain what effect such a horrendous mortality rate had on the men and women who survived. At the very least, it must have created a sense of impermanence, a desire to escape Virginia with a little money before sickness or Indians tragically ended the adventure. The settlers who drank to excess aboard the tavern ships anchored in the James River described the colony "not as a place of Habitacion but only of a short sojourninge."

Scandal and Reform

On both sides of the Atlantic people wondered who should be blamed. Why had so many colonists died in a land so rich in potential? The burden of responsibility lay in large measure with the Virginia Company. Sandys and his supporters were in too great a hurry to make a profit. Settlers were shipped to America, but neither housing nor food awaited them in Jamestown. Weakened by the long sea voyage, they quickly succumbed to contagious disease.

Company officials in Virginia also bore a share of guilt. They were so eager to line their own pockets that they consistently failed to provide for the common good. Various governors and their councillors grabbed up the indentured servants, sent them to their own private plantations to cultivate tobacco, and, as the 1622 tragedy demonstrated, ignored the colony's crumbling defenses. Jamestown took on the characteristics of a boomtown. There was no shared sense of purpose, no common ideology, except perhaps unrestrained self-advancement, to keep the society from splintering into highly individualistic, competitive fragments.

The company's scandalous mismanagement embarrassed the king, and in 1624 he dissolved the bankrupt enterprise and transformed Virginia into a royal colony. The Crown appointed a governor and a council. No provision was made, however, for continuing the local representative assembly, an institution the Stuarts heartily opposed. The House of Burgesses had first convened in 1619. While elections to the Burgesses were hardly democratic, the assembly did provide wealthy planters with a voice in government. Even without the king's authorization, the representatives gathered annually after 1629, and in 1639, Charles recognized the body's existence.

He had no choice. The colonists who served on the council or in the assembly were strong-willed, ambitious men. They had no intention of surrendering their control over local affairs. Since Charles was having political troubles of his own and lived 3,000 miles from Jamestown, he usually allowed the Virginians to have their own way. In 1634, the assembly divided the colony into eight counties. In each one, a group of appointed justices of the peace—the wealthy planters of the area—sat as a court of law as well as a governing body. The "county court" was the most important institution of local government in Virginia, and long after the American Revolution, it served as a center for social, political, and commercial activities.

Changes in government had little impact on the character of daily life in Virginia. The planters continued to grow tobacco, and as the Indians were killed, made into tributaries, or pushed north and south, Virginians took up large tracts of land along the colony's many navigable rivers. The focus of their lives was the isolated plantation, a small cluster of buildings housing the planter's family and dependent workers. These were modest wooden structures. Not until the eighteenth century did the Virginia gentry build the great Georgian mansions that still attract tourists. The dispersed pattern of settlement retarded the development of institutions such as schools and churches. Besides Jamestown there were no population centers, and as late as 1705, Robert Beverley, a leading planter, reported that Virginia did not have a single place "that may reasonably bear the Name of a Town."

Maryland: A Troubled Sanctuary

By the end of the seventeenth century, Maryland society looked remarkably like that of its Chesapeake neighbor, Virginia. At the time of first settlement in 1634, however, no one would have predicted that Maryland, a colony wholly owned by a Catholic nobleman, would have survived, much less become a flourishing tobacco colony.

The driving force behind the founding of Maryland was Sir George Calvert, later Lord Baltimore. Calvert, a talented and well-educated man, enjoyed the patronage of James I. He was awarded lucrative positions in the government, the most important being the king's secretary of state. In 1625, Calvert shocked almost everyone by publicly declaring his Catholicism; in this fiercely anti-Catholic society, persons who openly supported the Church of Rome were immediately stripped of civil office. Although forced to resign as secretary of state, Calvert retained the Crown's favor.

Before resigning, Calvert sponsored a settlement on the coast of Newfoundland, but after visiting the place, the proprietor concluded that no English person, whatever his or her religion, would transfer to a place where the "ayre [is] so intolerably cold." He turned his attention to the Chesapeake, and on June 30, 1632, Charles I

Cecilius Calvert, the second Lord Baltimore, is shown with his grandson.

granted George Calvert's son, Cecilius, a charter for a colony to be located north of Virginia. The boundaries of the settlement, named Maryland in honor of Charles's queen, were so vaguely defined that they generated legal controversies not fully resolved until the mid-eighteenth century when Charles Mason and Jeremiah Dixon surveyed their famous line between Pennsylvania and Maryland.

Cecilius, the second Lord Baltimore, wanted to create a sanctuary for England's persecuted Catholics. He also intended to make money. Without Protestant settlers, it seemed unlikely Maryland would prosper, and Cecilius instructed his brother Leonard, the colony's governor, to do nothing that might frighten off hypersensitive Protestants. The governor was ordered to "cause all Acts of the Roman Catholic Religion to be done as privately as may be and . . . [to] instruct all Roman Catholics to be silent upon all occa-

sions of discourse concerning matters of Religion." On March 25, 1634, the *Ark* and *Dove*, carrying about one hundred fifty settlers, landed safely, and within days, the governor purchased from the Yaocomico Indians a village that became St. Mary's City, the capital of Maryland.

The colony's charter was an odd document, a throwback to an earlier age. It transformed Baltimore into a "palatine lord," a proprietor with almost royal powers. Settlers swore an oath of allegiance not to the king of England but to Lord Baltimore. In the mother country, such practices had long ago passed into obsolescence, but for reasons not entirely clear, the Calverts obtained the right to create a vast feudal estate in America. As the proprietor, Lord Baltimore owned outright almost 6 million acres; he possessed absolute authority over anyone living in his domain.

On paper at least, everyone in Maryland was assigned a place in an elaborate social hierarchy. Members of a colonial ruling class, persons who purchased 6,000 acres from Baltimore, were called lords of the manor. These landed aristocrats were permitted to establish local courts of law. People holding less acreage enjoyed fewer privileges, particularly in government. Baltimore figured that land sales and rents would adequately finance the entire venture.

Baltimore's feudal system never took root in Chesapeake soil. People simply refused to play the social roles the lord proprietor had assigned. These tensions affected the operation of Maryland's government. Baltimore assumed his brother, acting as his deputy in America, and a small appointed council of local aristocrats would pass necessary laws and carry out routine administration. When an elected assembly first convened in 1635, Baltimore allowed the delegates to discuss only those acts he had prepared. The members of the assembly bridled at such restrictions, insisting on exercising traditional parliamentary privileges. Neither side gained a clear victory in the assembly, and for almost twenty-five years, legislative squabbling contributed to the widespread political instability that almost destroyed Maryland.

The colony drew both Protestants and Catholics, and the two groups might have lived in harmony had civil war not broken out in

England. When Cromwell and the Puritan faction came to power in the mother country, it seemed Baltimore might lose his colony. To head off such an event and to placate Maryland's restless Protestants, in 1649, the proprietor drafted the famous "Act concerning Religion," which extended toleration to all individuals who accepted the divinity of Christ. At a time when European rulers regularly persecuted people for their religious beliefs, Baltimore championed liberty of conscience.

However laudable the act may have been, it did not heal religious divisions in Maryland, and when local Puritans seized the colony's government, they promptly repealed the "Act." For almost two decades, vigilantes roamed the countryside, and during the "Plundering Time" (1644–1646), one armed group temporarily drove Leonard Calvert out of Maryland. In 1655, civil war flared again. No other mainland colony, with the possible exception of Rhode Island, experienced such extreme political disorder.

In this troubled sanctuary, ordinary planters and their workers cultivated tobacco on plantations dispersed along the riverfront. In 1678, Baltimore complained that he could not find fifty houses in a space of 30 miles. Tobacco affected almost every aspect of local culture. "In Virginia and Maryland," one Calvert explained, "Tobacco, as our Staple, is our all, and indeed leaves no room for anything Else." A steady stream of indentured servants supplied the plantations with dependent laborers, that is, until they were replaced by slaves at the end of the seventeenth century. The Europeans sacrificed much by coming to the Chesapeake. For most of the century, their standard of living was primitive when compared with that of people of the same social class who had remained in England. Two-thirds of the planters, for example, lived in houses of only two rooms and of a type associated with the poorest classes in contemporary English society.

CONQUEST OF NEW ENGLAND

The Pilgrims enjoy almost mythic status in American history. These brave refugees crossed the cold Atlantic in search of religious liberty, signed a democratic compact aboard the *Mayflower,* landed at Plymouth Rock, and gave us our Thanksgiving Day. As with most legends, this one contains only a core of truth.

The Pilgrims were not crusaders who set out to change the world. Rather, they were humble English farmers. Their story began in the early 1600s in Scrooby Manor, a small community located approximately 150 miles north of London. Many people living in this area believed the Church of England retained too many traces of its Catholic origin. To support such a corrupt institution was like winking at the devil. Its very rituals compromised God's true believers, and so, in the early years of the reign of James I, the Scrooby congregation formally left the state church. Like others who followed this logic, they were called "Separatists." Since English statute required citizens to attend Anglican services, the Scrooby Separatists moved to Holland in 1608–1609 rather than compromise their souls.

The Netherlands provided the Separatists with a good home—too good. The members of the little church feared they were losing their distinct identity; their children were becoming Dutch. In 1617, therefore, a portion of the original Scrooby congregation vowed to sail to America. Included in this group was William Bradford, a wonderfully literate man who wrote *Of Plymouth Plantation,* one of the first and certainly most moving accounts of an early American settlement. Poverty presented the major obstacle to their plans. They petitioned for a land patent from the Virginia Company of London. At the same time, they looked for someone willing to underwrite the staggering costs of colonization. These negotiations went well, or so it seemed. After stopping in England to take on supplies and laborers, the Pilgrims set off for America in 1620 aboard the *Mayflower,* armed with a patent to settle in Virginia and indebted to a group of English investors who were only marginally interested in separatism.

Because of an error in navigation, the Pilgrims landed not in Virginia, but in New England. The patent for which they had worked so diligently had no validity in this region. In fact, the Crown had granted New England to another company. Without a patent, the colonists possessed no authorization to form a civil government, a serious matter since some sailors who were not Pilgrims threatened mutiny. To preserve the struggling community from anarchy forty-one men agreed on November 11 to "covenant and combine our selves together into a civil body politick."

The Mayflower Compact could not ward off disease and hunger. During the first months in Plymouth, death claimed approximately half of the 102 people who had initially set out from England. Moreover, debts contracted in the mother country severely burdened the new colony. To their credit, the Pilgrims honored their financial obligations, but it took almost twenty years to satisfy the English investors. Without Bradford, whom they elected as governor, the settlers might have allowed adversity to overwhelm them. Through strength of will and self-sacrifice, however, Bradford persuaded frightened men and women that they could survive in America.

In time, the Pilgrims replicated the humble little farm communities they had once known in England. They formed Separatist congregations to their liking; the population slowly increased. The settlers experimented with commercial fishing and the fur trade, but these efforts never generated substantial income. Most families relied on mixed husbandry, grain, and livestock. Because Plymouth offered relatively few economic opportunities, it attracted only a trickle of new settlers. In 1691, the colony was absorbed into its larger and more prosperous neighbor, Massachusetts Bay.

Puritan Commonwealth

In the early decades of the seventeenth century, an extraordinary spirit of religious reform burst forth in England, and before it had burned itself out, Puritanism had transformed the face of England and America. Modern historians have difficulty comprehending this powerful force. Some consider the Puritans rather neurotic individuals who condemned liquor and sex, dressed in drab clothes, and minded their neighbors' business. This crude caricature is based on a fundamental misunderstanding of the actual nature of this broad popular movement. The seventeenth-century Puritans were more like today's radical political reformers, men and women committed to far-reaching institutional change, than like Victorian do-gooders. To their enemies, of course, the Puritans were a bother, always pointing out civil and ecclesiastical imperfections. A

The oldest timepiece in New England was this sundial, owned by John Endecott, first governor of the Massachusetts Bay Colony. The timepiece was made in 1630, the year the colony was established.

great many people, however, shared their vision, and not only did they found several American colonies, but they also sparked the English Civil War, an event that generated bold new thinking about republican government and popular sovereignty.

The Puritans were products of the Protestant Reformation. They accepted the notion that an omnipotent God predestined some people to salvation and damned others throughout eternity (see Chapter 1). But instead of waiting passively for Judgment Day, the Puritans examined themselves for signs of grace, for hints that God had in fact placed them among his "elect." A member of this select group, they argued, would try to live according to Scripture, to battle sin and eradicate corruption.

For the Puritans the logic of everyday life was clear. If the Church of England contained unscriptural elements—clerical vestments, for example—then they must be eliminated. If the pope in Rome was in league with the Antichrist, then Protestant kings had better not form alliances with Catholic states. If God condemned licentiousness and intoxication, then local officials should punish whores and drunks. There was nothing improper about an occasional beer or physical love within marriage, but when sex and drink became ends in themselves, the Puritans thought England's ministers and magistrates should speak out. Persons of this temperament were more combative than the Pilgrims had been. They wanted to purify the Church of England from within, and before the 1630s at least, separatism held little appeal for them.

From the Puritan perspective, the early Stuarts, James I and Charles I, seemed unconcerned about the spiritual state of the nation. James tolerated corruption within his own court; he condoned gross public extravagance. His foreign policy appeased European Catholic powers. At one time, he even tried to marry his son to a Catholic princess. Neither king showed interest in purifying the Anglican church. In fact, Charles assisted the rapid advance of William Laud, a cleric who represented everything the Puritans detested. Laud defended church ceremonies that they found obnoxious. He persecuted Puritan ministers, forcing them either to conform to his theology or lose their licenses to preach. As long as Parliament met, Puritan voters in the various boroughs and countries throughout the nation elected men sympathetic to their point of view. These outspoken representatives criticized royal policies and hounded Laud. Because of their defiance, Charles decided in 1629 to rule England without Parliament and four years later named Laud archbishop of Canterbury. The last doors of reform slammed shut. The corruption remained.

John Winthrop, the future governor of Massachusetts Bay, was caught up in these events. Little about his background suggested such an auspicious future. He owned a small manor in Suffolk, one that never produced sufficient income to support his growing family. He dabbled in law. But the core of Winthrop's life was his faith in God, a faith so intense his contemporaries immediately identified him as a Puritan. The Lord, he concluded, was displeased with England. Time for reform was running out. In May 1629 he wrote to his wife, "I am verily perswaded God will bringe some heavye Affliction upon this lande, and that speedylye." He was, however, confident that the Lord would "provide a shelter and a hidinge place for us."

John Winthrop served many terms as governor of Massachusetts and held the colony together during several major political crises.

Other Puritans, some of them wealthier and politically better connected than Winthrop, reached similar conclusions about England's future. They turned their attention to the possibility of establishing a colony in America, and on March 4, 1629, their Massachusetts Bay Company obtained a charter directly from the king. Charles and his advisers apparently thought the Massachusetts Bay Company was a commercial venture no different from the dozens of other joint-stock companies that had recently sprung into existence.

Winthrop and his associates knew better. On August 26, 1629, twelve of them met secretly and signed the Cambridge Agreement. They pledged to be "ready in our persons and with such of our severall familyes as are to go with us . . . to embark for the said plantation by the first of March next." There was one loophole. The charters of most joint-stock companies designated a specific place where business meetings were to be held. For reasons not entirely clear—a timely bribe is a good guess—the charter of the Massachusetts Bay Company did not contain this standard clause. It could hold meetings anywhere the stockholders, called "freemen," desired, even America, and if they were in America, the king could not easily interfere in their affairs.

"A City on a Hill"

The Winthrop fleet departed England in March 1630. By the end of the first year, almost 2,000 people had arrived in Massachusetts Bay, and before the "Great Migration" concluded in the early 1640s, over 16,000 men and women had arrived in the new Puritan colony.

A great deal is known about the background of these particular settlers. A large percentage of them originated in an area northeast of London called East Anglia, a region in which Puritan ideas had taken deep root. London, Kent, and the West Country also contributed to the stream of emigrants. In some instances, entire villages were reestablished across the Atlantic. Many Bay Colonists had worked as farmers in the mother country, but a surprisingly large number came from English industrial centers, like Norwich, where cloth was manufactured for the export trade.

Whatever their backgrounds, they moved to Massachusetts as nuclear families, fathers, mothers, and their dependent children, a form of migration strikingly different from the one that peopled Virginia and Maryland. Moreover, because the settlers had already formed families in England, the colony's sex ratio was more balanced than that found in the Chesapeake colonies. Finally, and perhaps more significantly, once they had arrived in Massachusetts, these men and women survived. Indeed, their life expectancy compares favorably to that of modern Americans. Many factors help explain this phenomenon—clean drinking water and a healthy climate, for example. While the Puritans could not have planned to live longer than did colonists in other parts of the New World, this remarkable accident reduced the emotional shock of long-distance migration.

The first settlers possessed another source of strength and stability. They were bound together by a common sense of purpose. God, they insisted, had formed a special covenant with the people of Massachusetts Bay. On his part, the Lord expected them to live according to Scripture, to reform the church, in other words, to create a

"city on a hill" that would stand as a beacon of righteousness for the rest of the Christian world. If they fulfilled their side of the bargain, the settlers could anticipate peace and prosperity. No one, not even the lowliest servant, was excused from this divine covenant, for as Winthrop stated, "Wee must be knitt together in this worke as one man." Even as the first ships were leaving England, John Cotton, a popular Puritan minister, urged the emigrants to go forth "with a publicke spirit, looking not on your owne things only, but also on the things of others." Many people throughout the ages have espoused such communal rhetoric, but these particular men and women went about the business of forming a new colony as if they truly intended to transform a religious vision into social reality.

In ecclesiastical affairs, the colonists proceeded by what one founder called "experimental footsteps." They arrived in Massachusetts Bay without a precise plan for their church. Although the rituals and ceremonies enforced by Laud had no place in Massachusetts, the American Puritans refused to separate formally from the Church of England. In this matter, they thought the Pilgrims had made a serious mistake. After all, what was the point of reforming an institution if the reformers were no longer part of it?

The Bay Colonists gradually came to accept a highly innovative form of church government known as Congregationalism. Under this system, each village church was independent of outside interference. The American Puritans, of course, wanted nothing of bishops. The people (the "saints") *were* the church, and as a body, they pledged to uphold God's law. In the Salem Church, for example, the members covenanted "with the Lord and with one another and do bind ourselves in the presence of God to walk together in all his ways."

Simply because a person happened to live in a certain community did not mean he or she automatically belonged to the local church. The churches of Massachusetts were voluntary institutions, and in order to join one a man or woman had to provide testimony—a confession of faith—before neighbors who had already been admitted as full members. It was a demanding process. Whatever the personal strains, however, most men and women in early Massachusetts aspired to full membership, which entitled them to the

Rituals of Public Execution: A Kind of Theater?

Public executions, however ghoulish they might appear to modern Americans, were not unusual events in colonial society. Indeed, they represented what one historian has described as a kind of theater or ritual performance.

Esther Rodgers, aged twenty-one, was hanged in Ipswich, Massachusetts, in July 1701. A local court had convicted her of murdering her own infant, a child fathered out of wedlock. According to a minister who witnessed the woman's last moments, "the manner of her Entertaining DEATH" astonished the crowd of four or five thousand spectators who crowded around the gallows. Rodgers's "Composure of Spirit, Cheerfulness of Countenance, pleasantness of Speech, and a sort of Complaisantness in Carriage towards the Ministers . . . melted the hearts of all that were within seeing or hearing, into Tears of affection."

Various members of a community, including the condemned criminals, played socially sanctioned roles in these public spectacles. It was important that the order of events be correct. Usually the felon—a person allegedly hardened by a life of sin—maintained his or her innocence during the trial. Following conviction, however, such persons often confessed. A

Mr. Richard Mather.

This primitive woodcut depicts Richard Mather, one of early New England's influential Puritan ministers.

minister recorded the full story, and on the day of the execution, he delivered a formal sermon attended by colonists who had sometimes traveled more than 50 miles just to see the hanging. Before they died, the criminals spoke to the spectators, and within a very short time, these last words along with the minister's execution sermon were published as pamphlets.

Clergymen played a central role in these public dramas. They engaged in what today we might call criminal sociology. Why, they asked, had the condemned man or woman come to such a tragic end? What lessons could be drawn from a close study of their lives? Not surprisingly the

answer to these questions involved sin. Long before the condemned person had contemplated murder or some equally heinous act, he or she had engaged in seemingly petty vices—disobedience to parents, pride, lying, profanity, irreligion, drunkenness—a range of ungodly behavior that inevitably led the unwary sinner to more serious transgressions. Seen from this perspective, of course, the average colonists became potential murderers or rapists, and only by resisting small temptations could they ever hope to avoid the fate of poor Esther Rodgers.

The ministers paid special attention to the young people in the audience; in other words, to those persons who seemed most likely to experiment with vice. Standing next to the condemned criminals, clergymen of New England thundered out their warnings. In 1674, for example, the famous Puritan divine Increase Mather observed that when "Children shall rebel against their Parents, their wickedness is excessively great. And such Children do usually die *before their Time.*" Lest the boys and girls missed his point, Mather added, "[it] is greatly to be observed that most of those that die upon the Gallows do confess that they have been guilty of disobedience to Parents."

In 1713, Cotton Mather, Increase's son, delivered an execution sermon specifically designed to strike terror in the hearts of the young. Look, he said pointing to a felon about to die, "[Here] is a poor Young man before you, that is just *going to the Dead*. God this day is holding up a *Young man* in Chains, that all the *Young People* of New England, may . . . be withheld from Sinning."

The execution ritual reaffirmed the traditional moral order; rebellion against elders was rebellion against God. The ministers knew the adolescents before them would probably not end their days as murderers or rapists. But by making a spectacle of an extreme case, by transforming the execution into a public drama, they hoped to discourage lesser vices.

Without the cooperation of the condemned, the execution lost much of its social meaning. Most men and women—people about to be hanged and without hope of clemency—not only voluntarily confessed to a host of moral failings, but also admonished the crowds to avoid a life of sin. Esther Rodgers ended her life with these words: "I beg of all to have Care. Be Obedient to your Parents and Masters; Run not at Nights, especially on Sabbath Nights, Refrain bad Company for the Lord's Sake. . . ." Her moving performance made for a "good" execution. James Morgan, a convicted murderer, also fulfilled everyone's expectations. "Have a care of that Sin of Drunkenness," he warned the citizens of Boston in 1686, "for that is a sin that leads to all manner of sins and wickedness." And

The Wages of Sin;
OR,
Robbery juſtly Rewarded;
A
P O E M;
Occaſioned by the untimely Death of
Richard Wilſon,
Who was Executed on *Boſton* Neck, for Burglary,
On *Thurſday* the 19th of *October*, 1732.

This Day from Goal muſt *Wilſon* be conveyed in a Cart, By Guards unto the Gallows-Tree, to die as his Deſert.

Here we may ſee what Men for Stealth and Robbing muſt endure; And what the Gain of ill got Wealth will in the End procure.

just before he died, Morgan cried out, "I am going out of this World; O take warning by me, and beg God to keep you from this Sin which hath been my ruine."

Though the ministers may have encouraged these public displays of penance—they may have even suggested the actual wording—there is no reason to doubt the criminals' sincerity. They too shared the religious values of the seventeenth-century, and however far from the accepted norms they may have strayed, they desired in some small way to win favor in the sight of the Lord. As the Reverend William Cooper observed in 1733, "It may be [that] there is no Place in the World, where such Pains are taken with condemned Criminals to prepare them for their Death; that *in the Destruction of the Flesh, the Spirit may be saved in the Day of the Lord Jesus*." Standing on the gallows, men and women rarely expressed even a hint of bitterness. In fact, they frequently praised their judges, noting that the magis-

trates had merely carried out God's will.

Soon after the execution colonial printers issued pamphlets containing the execution sermon, the criminal's dying confession, and in some cases, a lurid woodcut depicting an individual about to hang. These works sold quite well. The account of James Morgan's execution went through several editions. Others bore provocative titles such as *The Wicked Man's Portion* and *Death The Certain Wages of Sin*. The most ambitious production was Cotton Mather's *Pillars of Salt. An HISTORY OF SOME CRIMINALS Executed in this Land; for Capital Crimes. With some of their Dying Speeches; Collected and Published, For the WARNING of such as Live in Destructive Courses of Ungodliness (1699)*. What effect the execution rituals had upon colonial Americans—spectators as well as readers—is impossible to judge. Some may have reformed their evil ways; for others the theater of punishment may have involved no more than an "Entertaining DEATH."

sacraments, and gave some of them responsibility for choosing ministers, disciplining backsliders, and determining difficult questions of theology. Although women and blacks could not vote for ministers, they did become members of the Congregational churches. Over the course of the seventeenth century, women made up an increasingly large share of the membership.

There were limits on Congregational autonomy, to be sure, and colonial magistrates sometimes ferreted out heretical beliefs. Those who did not become church members were compelled to attend regular religious services. Perhaps because of the homogeneity of the colony's population, however, the loose polity of the Congregational churches held together for the entire colonial period.

In creating a civil government, the Bay Colonists faced a particularly difficult challenge. Their charter allowed the investors in a joint-stock company to set up a business organization. When the settlers arrived in America, however, company leaders—men like Winthrop—moved quickly to transform the commercial structure into a colonial government. An early step in this direction took place on May 18, 1631, when the category of "freeman" was extended to all adult males who had become members of a Congregational church. This decision greatly expanded the franchise of Massachusetts Bay, and historians estimate that during the 1630s at least 40 percent of the colony's adult males could vote in elections. While this percentage may seem low by modern or even Jacksonian standards, it was higher than anything the emigrants would have known in the mother country. The freemen voted annually for a governor, a group of magistrates called the Court of Assistants, and after 1634, deputies who represented the interests of the individual towns. Even military officers were elected in Massachusetts Bay.

Two popular misconceptions about this government should be dispelled. It was neither a democracy nor a theocracy. The magistrates elected in Massachusetts did not believe they represented the voters, much less the whole populace. They ruled in the name of the electorate; but their responsibility as rulers was to God. In 1638, Winthrop warned against overly democratic forms, since "the best part is always the least, and

of that best part the wiser is always the lesser." And second, the Congregational ministers possessed no formal political authority in Massachusetts Bay. They could not even hold civil office, and it was not unusual for the voters to ignore the recommendations of a respected minister such as John Cotton.

In this colony, the town, rather than the country, became the center of public life. Groups of men and women voluntarily covenanted together to live by certain rules. The community constructed a meetinghouse where church services and town meetings were held, formed a village government, passed bylaws regulating agricultural practices, and "warned out" those individuals who refused to accept local ordinances. Each townsman received land sufficient to build a house and to support a family. The house lots were clustered around the meetinghouse; the fields were located on the village perimeter. The land was given free. No one was expected to pay quitrents or other feudal dues. Villagers were obliged, however, to contribute to the minister's salary, pay local and colony taxes, and serve in the town militia.

Different Voices

The European settlers of Massachusetts Bay managed to live in peace—at least with each other. This was a remarkable achievement considering the chronic instability that plagued other colonies at this time. The Bay Colonists disagreed over many issues, sometimes vociferously; whole towns disputed with neighboring villages over common boundaries. But the people inevitably relied on the courts to mediate differences. They believed in a rule of law, and in 1648 the colonial legislature, called the General Court, drew up the *Lawes and Liberties*, the first alphabetized code of law printed in English. This is a document of fundamental importance in American constitutional history. In clear prose, it explained to the colonists their rights and responsibilities as citizens of the commonwealth. The code engendered public trust in government and discouraged magistrates from the arbitrary exercise of authority.

The most serious challenges to Puritan orthodoxy in Massachusetts Bay came from two remarkable individuals. The first, Roger

Williams, arrived in 1631 and immediately attracted a body of loyal followers. Indeed, everyone seems to have liked Williams as a person.

Williams's *ideas*, however, created controversy. He preached extreme separatism. The Bay Colonists, he exclaimed, were impure in the sight of the Lord so long as they remained even nominal members of the Church of England. Moreover, he questioned the validity of the colony's charter, since the king had not first purchased the land from the Indians, a view that threatened the integrity of the entire colonial experiment. Williams also insisted the civil rulers of Massachusetts had no business punishing settlers for their religious beliefs. It was God's responsibility, not men's, to monitor people's consciences. The Bay magistrates were prepared neither to tolerate heresy nor to accede to Williams's other demands, and in 1636, after attempts to reach a compromise had failed, they banished him from the colony. Williams worked out the logic of his ideas in Providence, a village he founded in what would become Rhode Island.

The magistrates of Massachusetts Bay believed Anne Hutchinson posed an even graver threat to the peace of the commonwealth. This extremely intelligent woman, her husband William, and her children followed John Cotton to the New World in 1634. Even contemporaries found her religious ideas, usually termed Antinomianism, somewhat confusing. Whatever her thoughts, Hutchinson shared them with other Bostonians, many of them women. Her outspoken views scandalized orthodox leaders of church and state. She suggested that all but two ministers in the colony had lost touch with the "Holy Spirit" and were preaching a doctrine in the Congregational churches that was little better than that of Archbishop Laud. When authorities demanded she explain her unusual opinions, she announced she experienced divine inspiration independently of either the Bible or the clergy. In other words, Hutchinson's teachings could not be tested by Scripture, a position that seemed dangerously subjective. Indeed, Hutchinson's theology called the very foundation of Massachusetts Bay into question. Without clear, external standards, one person's truth was as valid as that of anyone else, and from Winthrop's perspective, Hutchinson's teachings invited civil and religious anarchy.

When this woman described Congregational ministers—some of them the leading divines of Boston—as unconverted men, the General Court intervened. For two very tense days in 1637, the ministers and magistrates of Massachusetts Bay cross-examined Hutchinson; in this intense theological debate, she more than held her own. She knew as much about the Bible as did her inquisitors, and no doubt her brilliance at that moment provoked the Court's misogyny.

Hutchinson defied the ministers and magistrates to demonstrate exactly where she had gone wrong. Just when it appeared Hutchinson had outmaneuvered—indeed, thoroughly embarrassed—her opponents, she let down her guard, declaring forcefully that what she knew of God came "by an immediate revelation. . . . By the voice of his own spirit to my soul." Here was what her accusers had suspected all along but could not prove. She had confessed in open court that the Spirit can live without the Moral Law. This Antinomian statement challenged the authority of the Bay rulers, and they were relieved to exile Hutchinson and her followers to Rhode Island.

Breaking Away

Massachusetts Bay spawned four new colonies, three of which survived to the American Revolution. New Hampshire became a separate colony in 1677. Its population grew very slowly, and for much of the colonial period, New Hampshire remained economically dependent on Massachusetts, its neighbor to the south.

Far more people were drawn to the fertile lands of the Connecticut River Valley. In 1636, settlers founded the villages of Hartford, Windsor, and Wethersfield. No one forced these men and women to leave Massachusetts, and in their new surroundings, they created a society that looked much like the one they had known in the Bay Colony. Through his writings, Thomas Hooker, Connecticut's most prominent minister, helped all New Englanders define Congregational church polity. Puritans on both sides of the Atlantic read Hooker's beautifully crafted works. In 1639, representatives from the Connecticut towns passed the Fundamental Orders, a blueprint

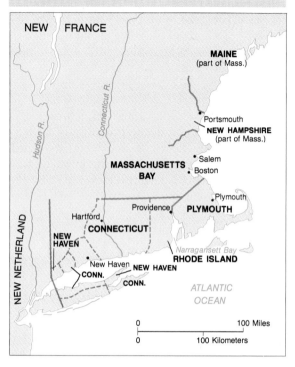

New England Colonies, 1650
The early settlers quickly carved up New England. New Haven briefly flourished as a separate colony before being absorbed into Connecticut in 1662. Long Island later became part of New York; Plymouth later joined Massachusetts.

for civil government, and in 1662, Charles II awarded the colony a charter of its own.

In 1638, another group, led by Theophilus Eaton and the Reverend John Davenport, settled New Haven and several adjoining towns along Long Island Sound. These emigrants, many of whom had come from London, lived briefly in Massachusetts Bay, but then insisted on forming a Puritan commonwealth of their own, one that established a closer relationship between church and state than the Bay colonists had allowed. The New Haven colony never prospered, and in 1662, it was absorbed into Connecticut.

Rhode Island experienced a wholly different history. From the beginning, it was populated by exiles and troublemakers, and according to one Dutch visitor, Rhode Island was "the receptacle of all sorts of riff-raff people. . . . All the cranks of New-England retire thither." This description, of course, was an exaggeration. Roger Williams founded Providence in 1636; two years later Anne

Hutchinson took her followers to Portsmouth. Other groups settled around Narragansett Bay. Not surprisingly, these men and women appreciated the need for toleration. No one was persecuted in Rhode Island for his or her religious beliefs.

One might have thought these separate Rhode Island communities would cooperate for the common good. They did not. Villagers fought over land and schemed with outside speculators to divide the tiny colony into even smaller pieces. In 1644, Parliament issued a patent for the "Providence Plantations," and in 1663, the Rhode Islanders obtained a royal charter. These successes did not calm political turmoil. For most of the seventeenth century, colonywide government existed in name only. Despite their constant bickering, however, the settlers of Rhode Island built up a profitable commerce in agricultural goods.

DIVERSITY IN THE MIDDLE COLONIES

New York, New Jersey, Pennsylvania, and Delaware were settled for quite different reasons. William Penn, for example, envisioned a Quaker sanctuary; the Duke of York worried chiefly about his own income. Despite the founders' intentions, however, some common characteristics emerged. Each colony developed a strikingly heterogeneous population, men and women of different ethnic and religious backgrounds. This cultural diversity became a major influence on the economic, political, and ecclesiastical institutions of the Middle Colonies. The raucous, partisan public life of the Middle Colonies foreshadowed later American society.

Anglo-Dutch Rivalry on the Hudson

By the early decades of the seventeenth century, the Dutch had established themselves as Europe's most aggressive traders. Holland—a small, loosely federated nation—possessed the world's largest merchant fleet. Its ships vied for the commerce of Asia, Africa, and America. Dutch rivalry with Spain, a fading though still formidable power,

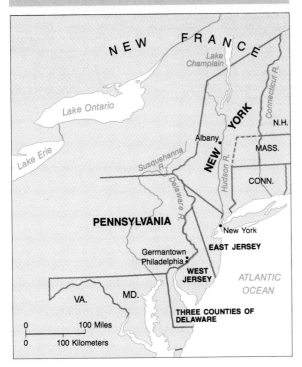

Middle Colonies, 1685

Until the Revolution, the Iroquois blocked white westward expansion in New York. The Jerseys initially attracted English and Irish Quakers, who were soon joined by thousands of Scotch-Irish and Germans.

was in large measure responsible for the settlement of New Netherland. While searching for the elusive Northwest Passage in 1609, Henry Hudson, an English explorer employed by a Dutch company, sailed up the river that now bears his name. Further voyages led to the establishment of trading posts in New Netherland, although permanent settlement did not occur until 1624. The area also seemed an excellent base from which to attack Spain's colonies in the New World.

The directors of the Dutch West India Company sponsored two small outposts, Fort Orange (Albany) located well up the Hudson River and New Amsterdam (New York City) on Manhattan Island. The first Dutch settlers were not actually colonists. Rather, they were salaried employees, and their superiors in Holland expected them to spend most of their time gathering animal furs. They did not receive land for their troubles. Needless to say, this arrangement attracted relatively few Dutch immigrants.

The colony's population may have been small, only 270 in 1628, but it contained an extraordinary ethnic mix. One visitor to New Amsterdam in 1644 maintained he had heard "eighteen different languages" spoken in the city. Even if this report was exaggerated, there is no doubt the Dutch colony drew English, Finns, Germans, and Swedes. By the 1640s, a sizable community of free blacks (probably former slaves who had gained their freedom through self-purchase) had developed in New Amsterdam, adding African tongues to the hodgepodge of languages. The colony's culture was further fragmented by New England Puritans who left Massachusetts and Connecticut to stake out farms on eastern Long Island.

New Netherland lacked capable leadership. The company sent a number of director-generals to oversee judicial and political affairs. Without exception, these men were temperamentally unsuited to govern an American colony. They adopted autocratic procedures, lined their own pockets, and in one case, blundered into a war that needlessly killed scores of Indians and settlers. The company made no provision for an elected assembly. As much as they were able, the scattered inhabitants living along the Hudson River ignored company directives. They felt no loyalty to the trading company that had treated them so shabbily. Long Island Puritans complained bitterly about the absence of representative institutions. The Dutch system has aptly been described as "unstable pluralism."

In August 1664, the Dutch lost their tenuous hold on New Netherland. The English Crown, eager to score an easy victory over a commercial rival, dispatched a fleet of warships to New Amsterdam. The commander of this force, Colonel Richard Nicolls, ordered the colonists to surrender. The last director-general, a colorful character named Peter Stuyvesant (1647–1664), rushed wildly about the city urging the settlers to resist the English. But no one obeyed. Even the Dutch remained deaf to Stuyvesant's appeals. They accepted the Articles of Capitulation, a generous agreement that allowed Dutch nationals to remain in the province and to retain their property.

Charles II had already granted his brother, James, the Duke of York, a charter for the newly captured territory and much else besides. The

Het Fort B. de Kerck C. de Wintmolen D. dese Vlagge wert op gehaelt als daer Schepen in de Haven komen. E. t'gevangen huys F. de H. Generaels huys G. t'Gerecht H. de Kaeck I. Compagnies Pachuys K. S.

New Amsterdam as it appeared about 1640. This city, which was founded as a trading out-post by the Dutch West Indies Company, was characterized by a diverse ethnic mix and a suc-cession of inept governors.

duke became absolute proprietor over Maine, Martha's Vineyard, Nantucket, Long Island, and the rest of New York all the way to Delaware Bay. The king perhaps wanted to encircle New England's potentially disloyal Puritan population, but whatever his aims may have been, he created a bureaucratic nightmare.

During the English Civil War, the duke acquired a thorough aversion to representative assemblies. After all, Parliament had executed the duke's father, Charles I, and raised up Oliver Cromwell. The new proprietor had no intention of letting participatory government take root in New York. "I cannot *but* suspect," the duke announced, that an assembly "would be of dangerous consequence." The Long Islanders felt betrayed. In part to appease these outspoken critics, Governor Nicolls—one of the few competent administrators to serve in the Middle Colonies—drew up in March 1665 a legal code known as the Duke's Laws. It guaranteed religious toleration and created local governments.

There was no provision, however, for an elected assembly, nor, for that matter, for democratic town meetings. The legal code disappointed the Puritan migrants on Long Island, and when the duke's officers attempted to collect taxes these people protested that "they are inslav'd under an Arbitrary Power."

The Dutch kept silent. For several decades they remained a large unassimilated ethnic group. They continued to speak their own language, worship in their own churches (Dutch Reformed Calvinist), and eye their English neighbors with suspicion. In fact, the colony seemed little different from what it had been under the Dutch West India Company, a loose collection of independent communities ruled by an ineffectual central government.

Confusion in New Jersey

Only three months after receiving a charter for New York, the Duke of York made a terrible blunder—something this stubborn, humorless man was prone to do. As a gift to two courtiers who had served Charles during the English Civil War, the duke awarded the land lying between the Hudson and Delaware rivers to John, Lord Berkeley, and Sir George Carteret. This colony was named New Jersey in honor of Carteret's birthplace, the Isle of Jersey in the English Channel. When Nicolls heard what the duke had done, he exploded. In his estimation this fertile region contained the "most improveable" land in all New York, and to give it away so casually seemed the height of folly.

The duke's impulsive act bred confusion. Soon it was not clear who owned what in New Jersey. Before Nicolls had learned of James's decision, the governor allowed migrants from New England to take up farms west of the Hudson River. He promised these settlers an opportunity to establish an elected assembly, a headright system, and liberty of conscience. In exchange for these privileges, Nicolls asked only that they pay a small annual quitrent to the duke. The proprietors, Berkeley and Carteret, recruited colonists on similar terms. They assumed, of course, that they would receive the rent money.

The result was chaos. Some colonists insisted Nicolls had authorized their assembly. Others, equally insistent, claimed Berkeley and Carteret had done so. Both sides were wrong. Neither the proprietors nor Nicolls possessed any legal right whatsoever to set up a colonial government. James could transfer land to favorite courtiers, but no matter how many times the land changed hands, the government remained his personal responsibility. Knowledge of the law failed to quiet the controversy. Through it all, the duke showed not the slightest interest in the peace and welfare of the people of New Jersey.

Berkeley grew tired of the venture. It generated headaches rather than quitrents, and in 1674, he sold his proprietary rights to a group of surprisingly quarrelsome Quakers. The sale necessitated the division of the colony into two separate governments known as East and West Jersey. Neither half prospered. Carteret and his heirs tried unsuccessfully to turn a profit in East Jersey. In 1677, the Quaker proprietors of West Jersey issued a remarkable democratic plan of government, the Laws, Concessions, and Agreements. But they fought among themselves with such intensity that not even William Penn could bring tranquillity to their affairs. Penn wisely turned his attention to the unclaimed territory across the Delaware River. The West Jersey proprietors went bankrupt, and in 1702, the Crown reunited the two Jerseys into a single royal colony.

In 1700, the population of New Jersey stood at approximately fourteen thousand. Largely because it lacked a good deep-water harbor, the colony never developed a commercial center to rival New York City or Philadelphia. Its residents lived on scattered, often isolated farms; villages of more than a few hundred people were rare. Visitors commented on the diversity of the settlers. There were colonists from almost every European nation. Congregationalists, Presbyterians, Quakers, Baptists, Anabaptists, and Anglicans somehow managed to live together peacefully in New Jersey.

QUAKERS IN AMERICA

The founding of Pennsylvania cannot be separated from the history of the Quaker movement. Believers in an extreme form of Antinomianism, the Quakers saw no need for a learned ministry, since one person's interpretation of Scripture was as valid as anyone else's. This radical religious sect, a product of the social upheaval in England

In this satirical drawing, The Quakers Unmasked (1691), the artist ridicules the mysterious nature of the sect and its leaders, including William Penn. Quakers, who believed that the "Inner Light" of Christ was present in everyone and thus all men and women were equal before the Lord, were harassed for their differences from the traditional social order. In their religious services, or meetings, members sat in silence until the spirit prompted an individual to speak.

during the Civil War, gained its name from the derogatory term that English authorities sometimes used to describe those who "tremble at the word of the Lord." The name persisted even though the Quakers preferred being called Professors of the Light or, more commonly, Friends.

By the time the Stuarts regained the throne in 1660, the Quakers had developed strong support throughout England. One person responsible for their remarkable success was George Fox (1624–1691), a poor shoemaker whose own spiritual anxieties sparked a powerful new religious message that pushed beyond traditional reformed Protestantism. According to Fox, he experienced despair "so that I had nothing outwardly to help me . . . [but] then, I heard a voice which said, 'There is one, even Christ Jesus, that can speak to thy condition.'" Throughout his life, Fox and his growing number of followers gave testimony to the working of the Holy Spirit. Indeed, they informed ordinary men and women that if only they would look, they too would discover they possessed an "Inner Light." This was a wonderfully liberating invitation, especially for persons of lower-class origin. With the Lord's personal assistance, they could attain greater spiritual perfection on earth. Gone was the stigma of original sin; discarded was the notion of eternal predestination. Everyone could be saved.

Quakers practiced humility in their daily lives. They wore simple clothes and employed old-fashioned forms of address that set them apart from their neighbors. Friends refused to honor worldly position and accomplishment or to swear oaths in courts of law. They were also pacifists. According to Fox, all persons were equal in the sight of the Lord, a belief that generally annoyed people of rank and achievement.

Moreover, the Quakers never kept their thoughts to themselves. They preached conversion constantly, spreading the "Truth" throughout England, Ireland, and America. The Friends played important roles in the early history of New Jersey, Rhode Island, and North Carolina, as well as Pennsylvania. In some places, the "publishers of Truth" wore out their welcome. English authorities harassed the Quakers. Thousands, including Fox himself, were jailed, and in Massachusetts Bay between 1659 and 1661, Puritan magistrates ordered several Friends put to death. Such measures proved counterproductive, for persecution only inspired the martyred Quakers to redouble their efforts.

Penn's "Holy Experiment"

William Penn lived according to the Inner Light, a commitment that led eventually to the founding of Pennsylvania. Penn possessed a curiously complex personality. He was an athletic person who threw himself into intellectual pursuits. He was a bold visionary capable of making pragmatic decisions. He came from an aristocratic family and yet spent his entire adult life involved with a religious movement associated with the lower class.

Penn's father had served with some distinction in the English navy. Through luck and skill, he acquired a considerable estate in Ireland, and as a wealthy landowner, he naturally hoped his son would be a favorite at the Stuart court. He befriended the king, the Duke of York, and several other powerful Restoration figures. But William disappointed his father. He was expelled from Oxford University for holding unorthodox religious views. Not even a grand tour through Europe could dissuade the young man from joining the Society of Friends. His political connections and driving intellect quickly propelled him to a position of prominence within the struggling sect. Penn wrote at least forty-two books testifying to his deep attachment to Quaker principles. Even two years in an English jail could not weaken his faith.

Precisely when Penn's thoughts turned to America is not known. He was briefly involved with the West Jersey proprietorship. This venture may have suggested the possibility of an even larger enterprise. In any case, Penn negotiated in 1681 one of the more impressive land deals in the history of American real estate. Charles II awarded Penn a charter making him the sole proprietor of a vast area called Pennsylvania (literally, Penn's woods). The name embarrassed the modest Penn, but he knew better than to look the royal gift horse in the mouth.

Why the king bestowed such generosity on a leading Quaker who had recently been released from prison remains a mystery. Perhaps Charles wanted to repay an old debt to Penn's father. The monarch may have regarded the colony as a means of ridding England of its troublesome Quaker population, or quite simply, he may have liked Penn. In 1682, the new proprietor purchased from the Duke of York the so-called Three Lower Counties that eventually became Delaware. This astute move guaranteed that Pennsylvania would have access to the Atlantic and determined even before Philadelphia had been established that it would become a commercial center.

Penn lost no time in launching his "Holy Experiment." In 1682, he set forth his ideas in an unusual document known as the Frame of Government. The charter gave Penn the right to create any form of government he desired, and his imagination ran wild. His plan blended traditional notions about the privileges of a landed aristocracy with quite daring concepts of personal liberty. Penn guaranteed that settlers would enjoy among other things liberty of conscience, freedom from persecution, no taxation without representation, and due process of law.

In designing his government, Penn drew heavily on the writings of James Harrington (1611–1677). This English political philosopher argued that no government could ever be stable unless it reflected the actual distribution of landed property within society. Both the rich and poor had to have a voice in political affairs; neither should be able to overrule the legitimate interests of the other class. The Frame of Government envisioned a governor appointed by the proprietor, a 72-member Provincial Council responsible for initiating legislation, and a 200-person Assembly that could accept or reject the bills presented to it. Penn apparently thought the Council would be filled by the colony's richest landholders, or in the words of the Frame, "persons of most note for their wisdom, virtue and ability." The governor and Council were charged with the routine administration of justice. Smaller landowners spoke through the Assembly. It was a clumsy structure, and in America the entire edifice crumbled under its own weight.

Penn promoted his colony aggressively throughout England, Ireland, and Germany. He had no choice. His only source of revenue was the sale of land and the collection of quitrents. Penn commissioned pamphlets in several languages extolling the quality of Pennsylvania's rich farmland. The response was overwhelming. People poured into Philadelphia and the surrounding area. In 1685 alone, eight thousand emigrants arrived. Most of these settlers were Irish, Welsh, and English Quakers, and they generally moved to America as families. But Penn opened the door to men and women of all nations. He asserted that the people of Pennsylvania "are a collection of divers nations in Europe, as French, Dutch, Germans, Swedes, Danes, Finns, Scotch, Irish, and English."

The settlers were by no means all Quakers. The founder of Germantown, Francis Daniel Pastorius, called the vessel that brought him to the New World a "Noah's Ark" of religions, and within his own household, there were servants who subscribed "to the Roman [Catholic], to the Lutheran, to the Calvinistic, to the Anabaptist, and to the Anglican church, and only one Quaker." Ethnic and religious diversity were crucial in the development of Pennsylvania's public institutions, and its politics took on a quarrelsome quality absent in more homogeneous colonies such as Virginia and Massachusetts.

Penn himself emigrated to America in 1682. His stay, however, was unexpectedly short and unhappy. The Council and Assembly—reduced now to more manageable size—fought over the right to initiate legislation. Wealthy Quaker merchants, most of them residents of Philadelphia, dominated the Council. By contrast, the Assembly included men from rural settlements and the Three Lower Counties who showed no concern for the "Holy Experiment."

Penn did not see his colony again until 1699. During his enforced absence much had changed. The settlement had prospered. Its agricultural products, especially its excellent wheat, were in demand throughout the Atlantic world. Despite this economic success, however, the population remained deeply divided. Even the Quakers had briefly split into hostile factions. Penn's hand-picked governors had failed to win general support for the proprietor's policies, and one of them exclaimed in anger that each Quaker "*prays* for his neighbor on First Days and then *preys* on him the other six." As the seventeenth century closed, few colonists still shared the founder's desire to create a godly, paternalistic society.

In 1701, legal challenges in England again forced Penn to depart for the mother country. Just before he sailed, Penn signed the Charter of Liberties, a new frame of government that established a unicameral or one-house legislature (the only one in colonial America) and gave the representatives the right to initiate bills. Penn also allowed the Assembly to conduct its business without proprietary interference. The charter provided for the political separation of the Three Lower Counties (Delaware) from Pennsylvania, something people living in this area had demanded for years. This hastily drafted document served as Pennsylvania's constitution until the American Revolution.

His experience in America must have depressed Penn, now both old and sick. In England, Penn was imprisoned for debts incurred by dishonest colonial agents, and in 1718, Pennsylvania's founder died a broken man.

PLANTING THE CAROLINAS

In some ways, Carolina society looked much like the one that had developed in Virginia and Maryland. In both areas, white planters forced African slaves to produce staple crops for a world market. But such superficial similarities masked substantial regional differences. In fact, "the South"—certainly the fabled solid South of the early nineteenth century—did not exist during the colonial period. The Carolinas, joined much later by Georgia, stood apart from their northern neighbors. As a historian of colonial Carolina explained, "the southern colonies were never a cohesive section in the same way that New England was. The great diversity of population groups . . . discouraged southern sectionalism."

Proprietors of the Carolinas

Carolina was a product of the Restoration of the Stuarts to the English throne. Court favorites who had followed the Stuarts into exile during the civil war demanded tangible rewards for their loyalty. New York and New Jersey were obvious plums. So too was Carolina. Sir John Colleton, a successful English planter returned from Barbados, organized a group of eight powerful courtiers who styled themselves the True and Absolute Lords Proprietors of Carolina. On March 24, 1663, the king granted these proprietors a charter to the vast territory between Virginia and Florida and running west as far as the "South Seas."

The failure of similar ventures in the New World taught the Carolina proprietors valuable lessons. Unlike the first Virginians, for example, this group did not expect instant wealth. Rather, the proprietors reasoned that they would obtain a steady source of income from rents. What they needed, of course, were settlers. Recruitment turned out to be no easy task. Economic and social conditions in the mother country improved considerably after the Civil War, and English

A Brief DESCRIPTION
OF
The Province
OF
CAROLINA
On the COASTS of FLOREDA.
AND
More perticularly of a New-Plantation begun by the *ENGLISH* at *Cape-Feare,* on that River now by them called *Charles-River,* the 29th. of *May.* 1664.

Wherein is set forth.
The *Healthfulness* of the *Air*; the *Fertility* of the *Earth*, and *Waters*; and the great *Pleasure* and *Profit* will accrue to those that shall go thither to enjoy the same.

Also,
Directions and advice to such as shall go thither whether on their own accompts, or to serve under another.

Together with
A most accurate MAP of the whole *PROVINCE.*

London, Printed for *Robert Horne* in the first Court of *Gresham-Colledge* neer *Bishopsgate street.* 1666.

This brochure attempted to lure settlers to the province of Carolina by promising pleasure and profit to all who would come to partake of the healthfulness of the air and the fertility of the land and waters.

people were no longer so willing to transfer to the New World. Even if they had shown interest, the cost of transporting settlers across the Atlantic seemed prohibitively expensive. The proprietors concluded, therefore, that with the proper incentives—a generous land policy, for example—they could attract men and women from established American colonies and thereby save themselves a great deal of money. Unfortunately for the men who owned Carolina, such people were not easily persuaded. They had begun to take for granted certain rights and privileges, and as the price of settlement, they demanded a representative assembly, liberty of conscience, and a liberal headright system.

The Carolina proprietors divided their grant into three distinct jurisdictions, anticipating no

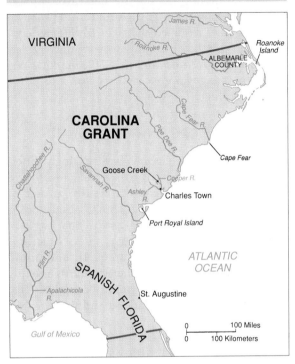

Carolina Proprietorship, 1685
Caribbean sugar planters migrated to the Goose Creek area where, with African American assistance, they eventually mastered rice cultivation. Poor harbors in North Carolina retarded European settlement in that region.

doubt that these areas would become the centers of settlement. The first region, called Albemarle, abutted Virginia. As the earlier ill-fated Roanoke colonists had discovered, the region lacked a good deep-water port. Nevertheless, it attracted a number of dissatisfied Virginians who drifted south in search of fresh land. Further south, the mouth of the Cape Fear River seemed a second likely site for development. And third, within the present state of South Carolina, the Port Royal region contained a maze of fertile islands and meandering tidal streams.

Colleton and his associates waited for the money to roll in, but to their dismay, no one seemed particularly interested in moving to the Carolina frontier. A tiny settlement at Port Royal failed. One group of New Englanders briefly considered taking up land in the Cape Fear area, but these people were so disappointed by what they saw that they departed, leaving behind only a sign that "tended not only to the disparagement of the Land . . . but also to the great discourage-

ment of all those that should hereafter come into these parts to settle." By this time, a majority of surviving proprietors had given up on Carolina.

The Barbadian Connection

Anthony Ashley Cooper, later Earl of Shaftesbury, was the exception. In 1669, he persuaded the remaining Carolinian proprietors to invest their own capital in the colony. Without such financial support, Ashley recognized, the project would surely fail. Once he received sufficient funds, this energetic organizer dispatched three hundred English colonists to Port Royal under the command of Joseph West. The fleet put in briefly at Barbados to pick up additional recruits, and in March 1670, after being punished by Atlantic gales that destroyed one ship, the expedition arrived at its destination. Only one hundred people were still alive. The unhappy settlers did not remain long at Port Royal, an unappealing, low-lying place badly exposed to Spanish attack. They moved northward, locating eventually along the more secure Ashley River. Later the colony's administrative center, Charles Town (it did not become Charleston until 1783) was established at the junction of the Ashley and Cooper rivers.

Ashley also wanted to bring order to the new society. With assistance from John Locke, the famous English philosopher (1632–1704), Ashley devised the Fundamental Constitutions of Carolina. Like Penn, Ashley had been influenced by the writings of Harrington. The constitutions created a local aristocracy consisting of proprietors and lesser nobles called *landgraves* and *cassiques,* terms as inappropriate to the realities of the New World as was the idea of creating an hereditary landed elite. Persons who purchased vast tracts of land automatically received a title and the right to sit in the Council of Nobles, a body designed to administer justice, oversee civil affairs, and initiate legislation. A parliament in which smaller landowners had a voice could accept or reject bills drafted by the council. The very poor were excluded from political life altogether. Ashley thought his scheme maintained the proper "Balance of Government" between aristocracy and democracy, a concept central to Harrington's philosophy. Not surprisingly, the constitutions had little impact on the actual structure of government. It reaffirmed religious toleration, but since so few men bought manors, the Council of Nobles remained a paper dream.

Before 1680, almost half the men and women who settled in the Port Royal area came from Barbados. This small Caribbean island, which produced an annual fortune in sugar, depended upon slave labor. By the third quarter of the seventeenth century, Barbados had become over-populated. Wealthy families could not provide their sons and daughters with sufficient land to maintain social status, and as the crisis intensi-fied, Barbadians looked to Carolina for relief.

These migrants, many of whom were quite rich, traveled to Carolina both as individuals and family groups. Some even brought gangs of slaves with them to the American mainland. The Barbadians carved out plantations on the tribu-taries of the Cooper River and established them-selves immediately as the colony's most powerful political faction. "So it was," writes historian Richard Dunn, "that these Caribbean pioneers helped to create on the North American coast a slave-based plantation society closer in temper to the islands they fled from than to any other mainland English settlement."

Much of the planters' time was taken up with the search for a profitable crop. The early settlers experimented with a number of plants: tobacco, cotton, silk, and grapes. The most successful items turned out to be beef, skins, and naval stores (especially tar used to maintain ocean ves-sels). By the 1680s, some Carolinians had built up great herds of cattle—seven or eight hundred head in some cases. Traders who dealt with Indians brought back thousands of deerskins from the interior, and they often returned with Indian slaves as well. These items together with tar and turpentine enjoyed a good market. It was not until the 1690s that the planters came to appreciate fully the value of rice, but once they had done so, it quickly became the colony's main staple.

Proprietary Carolina was in a constant politi-cal uproar. Factions vied for special privilege. The Barbadian settlers, known locally as the "Goose Creek Men," resisted the proprietors' policies at every turn. A large community of French Huguenots located in Craven County distrusted the Barbadians. The proprietors—an ineffectual group following the death of Shaftesbury—appointed a series of utterly incompetent gover-nors who only made things worse. One visitor observed that "the Inhabitants of Carolina should be as free from Oppression as any [people] in the Universe . . . if their own Differences amongst themselves do not occasion the contrary." By the end of the century, the Commons House of Assembly had assumed the right to initiate legis-lation. In 1719, the colonists overthrew the last proprietary governor, and in 1729, the king cre-ated separate royal governments for North and South Carolina.

THE FOUNDING OF GEORGIA

The early history of Georgia was strikingly differ-ent from that of Britain's other mainland colonies. Its settlement was really an act of aggression against Spain, a country that had as good a claim to this area as did the English. During the eighteenth century, the two nations were often at war (see Chapter 4), and South Carolinians worried that the Spaniards moving up from bases in Florida would occupy the dis-puted territory between Florida and the Carolina grant.

The colony owed its existence primarily to James Oglethorpe, a British general and member of Parliament who believed that he could thwart Spanish designs on the area south of Charleston while at the same time providing a fresh start for London's worthy poor, saving them from debtors' prison. Although Oglethorpe envisioned Georgia as an asylum as well as a garrison, the military aspects of his proposal were especially appealing to the leaders of the British govern-ment. In 1732, the king granted Oglethorpe and a board of trustees a charter for a new colony to be located between the Savannah and Altamaha rivers and from "sea to sea." The trustees living in the mother country were given complete con-trol over Georgia politics, a condition the settlers soon found intolerable.

During the first years of colonization, Georgia fared no better than had earlier utopian experi-ments. The poor people of England showed little desire to move to an inclement frontier, and the trustees, in their turn, provided little incentive for emigration. Each colonist received only 50 acres. Fifty additional acres could be added for each ser-vant transported to Georgia, but in no case could

England's Principal Mainland Colonies

Name	Original Purpose	Date of Founding	Principal Founder	Major Export	Estimated Population c. 1700
Virginia	Commercial venture	1607	Captain John Smith	Tobacco	64,560
New York (New Amsterdam)	Commercial venture	1613 (Made English colony, 1664)	Peter Stuyvesant, Duke of York	Furs, grain	19,107
Plymouth	Refuge for English Separatists	1620 (Absorbed by Massachusetts 1691)	William Bradford	Grain	Included with Massachusetts
New Hampshire	Commercial venture	1623	John Mason	Wood, naval stores	4,958
Massachusetts	Refuge for English Puritans	1628	John Winthrop	Grain, wood	55,941
Maryland	Refuge for English Catholics	1634	Lord Baltimore (George Calvert)	Tobacco	34,100
Connecticut	Expansion of Massachusetts	1635	Thomas Hooker	Grain	25,970
Rhode Island	Refuge for dissenters from Massachusetts	1636	Roger Williams	Grain	5,894
Delaware (New Sweden)	Commercial venture	1638 (Included in Penn grant, 1681; given separate assembly, 1703)	Peter Minuit William Penn	Grain	2,470
North Carolina	Commercial venture	1663	Anthony Ashley Cooper	Wood, naval stores, tobacco	10,720
South Carolina	Commercial venture	1663	Anthony Ashley Cooper	Naval stores, rice	5,720
New Jersey	Consolidation of new English territory, Quaker settlement	1664	Sir George Cartaret	Grain	14,010
Pennsylvania	Refuge for English Quakers	1681	William Penn	Grain	18,950
Georgia	Discourage Spanish expansion; charity	1733	James Oglethorpe	Silk, rice, wood, naval stores	5,200 (in 1750)

Sources: U.S. Bureau of Census, *Historical Statistics of the United States: Colonial Times to 1970*, Washington, D.C., 1975; John J. McCusker and Russell R. Menard, *The Economy of British America, 1607–1789*, Chapel Hill, 1985.

a settler amass more than 500 acres. Moreover, land could be passed only to an eldest son, and if a planter had no sons at the time of his death, the holding reverted to the trustees. Slavery was prohibited. So too was rum.

Almost as soon as they arrived in Georgia, the settlers complained. The colonists demanded slaves, pointing out to the trustees that unless the new planters possessed an unfree labor force, they could not compete economically with their South Carolina neighbors. The settlers also wanted a voice in local government. In 1738, 121 people living in Savannah petitioned for fundamental reforms in the colony's constitution. Oglethorpe responded angrily, "The idle ones are indeed for Negroes. If the petition is countenanced, the province is ruined." The settlers did not give up. In 1741, they again petitioned Oglethorpe, this time addressing him as "our Perpetual Dictator."

While the colonists grumbled about various restrictions, Oglethorpe tried and failed to capture the Spanish fortress at Saint Augustine (1740). This personal disappointment coupled with the growing popular unrest destroyed his interest in Georgia. The trustees were forced to compromise their principles. In 1738, they eliminated all restrictions on the amount of land a man could own; they allowed women to inherit land. In 1750, they permitted the settlers to import slaves. Soon Georgians could drink rum. In 1751, the trustees returned Georgia to the king, undoubtedly relieved to be free of what had become a hard-drinking, slave-owning plantation society much like that in South Carolina. The king authorized an assembly in 1751, but even with these social and political changes, Georgia attracted very few new settlers.

RUGGED AND LABORIOUS BEGINNINGS

Long after he had returned from his adventures in Virginia, Captain John Smith reflected on the difficulty of establishing colonies in the New World. It was a task for which most people were not temperamentally suited. "It requires," Smith counseled, "all the best parts of art, judgement, courage, honesty, constancy, diligence, and industry, [even] to do neere well." On another occasion, Charles I warned Lord Baltimore that new

CHRONOLOGY

1607	First English settlers arrive at Jamestown
1608–1609	Scrooby Congregation (Pilgrims) leaves England for Holland
1609–1611	"Starving time" in Virginia threatens survival of the colonists
1616–1618	Plague destroys Native American populations of coastal New England
1619	Virginia assembly, called House of Burgesses, meets for the first time • First slaves sold at Jamestown
1620	Pilgrims sign the Mayflower Compact
1622	Surprise Indian attack devastates Virginia
1624	Dutch investors create permanent settlements along Hudson River • James I, king of England, dissolves Virginia Company
1625	Charles I ascends English throne
1630	John Winthrop transfers Massachusetts Bay charter to New England
1634	Colony of Maryland is founded
1636	Harvard College established • Puritan settlers found Hartford and other Connecticut Valley towns
1638	Anne Hutchinson exiled to Rhode Island • Theophilus Eaton and John Davenport lead settlers to New Haven Colony
1639	Connecticut towns accept Fundamental Orders
1644	Second major Indian attack in Virginia
1649	Charles I executed during English Civil War
1660	Stuarts restored to the English throne
1663	Rhode Island obtains royal charter • Proprietors receive charter for Carolina
1664	English soldiers conquer New Netherland
1677	New Hampshire becomes a royal colony
1681	William Penn granted patent for his "Holy Experiment"
1702	East and West Jersey unite to form single colony
1732	James Oglethorpe receives charter for Georgia

settlements "commonly have rugged and laborious beginnings."

Over the course of the seventeenth century, women and men had followed leaders like Baltimore, Smith, Winthrop, Bradford, Penn, and Berkeley to the New World in anticipation of creating a successful new society. Some people were religious visionaries; others were hardheaded businessmen. The results of their efforts, their struggles to survive in an often hostile environment, and their interactions with various Native American groups, yielded a spectrum of settlements along the Atlantic coast, ranging from the quasi feudalism of South Carolina to the Puritan commonwealth of Massachusetts Bay.

The diversity of early English colonization must be emphasized precisely because it is so easy to overlook. Even though the colonists eventually banded together and fought for independence, persistent differences separated New Englanders from Virginians, Pennsylvanians from Carolinians. The interpretive challenge, of course, is to comprehend how European colonists managed over the course of the eighteenth century to overcome fragmentation and to develop the capacity to imagine themselves a nation.

Recommended Reading

The fullest discussion of the separate histories of England's thirteen mainland colonies can be found in Milton Klein and Jacob Cooke, eds., *A History of the American Colonies in Thirteen Volumes* (1973–1986). Each volume in this series has been written by a distinguished specialist. An older but still reliable account of the founding of the various settlements is Charles M. Andrews, *The Colonial Period of American History*, 4 vols. (1934–1938). A provocative guide to this rich historiography is Jack P. Greene and J. R. Pole, eds., *Colonial British America: Essays in the New History of the Early Modern Era* (1984).

Additional Bibliography

Some books that contribute to an understanding of the background of English colonization are Keith Wrightson, *English Society, 1580–1680* (1982); and Virginia D. Anderson, *New England's Generation: The Great Migration and the Formation of Society and Culture in the Seventeenth Century* (1991). T. H. Breen, *Puritans and Adventurers: Change and Persistence in Early America* (1980), specifically explores the problem of cultural transfer. Also helpful is David Grayson Allen, *In English Ways: The Movement of Societies and the Transferal of English Local Law and Custom* (1981).

On the execution ritual, see Lawrence W. Towner, "True Confessions and Dying Warnings in Colonial New England," in *Sibley's Heirs: A Volume in Memory of Clifford Kenyon Shipton*, Publications, Colonial Society of Massachusetts, Vol. 59: 523–539.

The best analysis of the early settlement of Virginia is Edmund S. Morgan, *American Slavery, American Freedom* (1975). For a masterful analysis of the current research on Chesapeake society, see Thad W. Tate and David L. Ammerman, eds., *The Chesapeake in the Seventeenth Century* (1979). New insights are offered in David B. Quinn, ed., *Early Maryland in a Wider World* (1982); Gloria L. Main, *Tobacco Colony: Life in Early Maryland, 1650–1720* (1982); and Lois G. Carr et al., *Robert Cole's World: Agriculture and Society in Early Maryland* (1991).

Two of Colonial New England's most capable historians were William Bradford and John Winthrop. See especially Bradford's *Of Plymouth Plantation*, edited by Samuel E. Morison (1952) and Winthrop's *History of New England*, edited by James K. Hosmer (2 vols., 1908). The most brilliant exploration of Puritan theology remains Perry Miller, *New England Mind: From Colony to Province* (1956). Also, see Stephen Foster, *The Long Argument: English Puritanism and the Shaping of New England Culture, 1570–1700* (1991); George D. Langdon, Jr., *Pilgrim Colony* (1966); T. H. Breen, *Character of the Good Ruler* (1970); David T. Konig, *Law and Society in Puritan Massachusetts* (1979); David D. Hall, *Worlds of Wonder, Days of Judgment: Popular Religious Belief in Early New England* (1989); and Charles E. Hambrick-Stowe, *The Practice of Piety* (1982). The better New England town studies—and there are many—are Kenneth A. Lockridge, *A New England Town: The First Hundred Years* (1970); Philip Greven, Jr., *Four Generations: Population, Land, and Family in Colonial Andover* (1970); and Stephen Innes, *Labor in a New Land* (1983).

Good accounts of early New York history are Oliver A. Rink, *Holland on the Hudson: An Economic and Social History of Dutch New York* (1986) and Robert C. Ritchie, *The Duke's Province* (1977). William Penn's life and political thought are the subject of Mary M. Dunn, *William Penn: Politics and Conscience* (1967). For newer interpretations see Richard and Mary Dunn, eds., *The World of William Penn* (1986).

Anyone curious about the founding of Carolina and Georgia should examine M. Eugene Sirmans, *Colonial South Carolina: A Political History, 1663–1763* (1966); and Harold E. Davis, *The Fledgling Province: Social and Cultural Life in Colonial Georgia, 1733–1776* (1976).

Putting Down Roots

Colonists in an Empire

he Witherspoon family moved from Great Britain to the South Carolina backcountry early in the eighteenth century. Though otherwise indistinguishable from the thousands of other ordinary families that put down roots in English America, the Witherspoons were made historical figures by the candid account of pioneer life produced by their son, Robert, who was only a small child at the time of their arrival. The Witherspoon's initial reaction to the New World—at least, that of the mother and children—was utter despondence. "My mother and us children were still in expectation that we were coming to an agreeable place," Robert confessed, "but when we arrived and saw nothing but a wilderness and instead of a fine timbered house, nothing but a very mean dirt house, our spirits quite sunk." For many years, the Witherspoons feared they would be killed by Indians, become lost in the woods, or be bitten by snakes.

The Witherspoons managed to survive these early difficult years on the Black River. To be sure, the Carolina backcountry did not look very much like the world they had left behind. The discrepancy, however, apparently did not greatly discourage Robert's father. He had a vision of what the Black River settlement might become. "My father," Robert recounted, "gave us all the comfort he [could] by telling us we would get all these trees cut down and in a short time [there] would be plenty of inhabitants, [and] that we could see from house to house."

Robert Witherspoon's story reminds us just how much the early history of colonial America was in fact a history created by families. Neither the peopling of the Atlantic frontier, the cutting down of the forests, nor the creation of new communities where one could see from "house to house" was a process that involved what we would today recognize as state policy. Men and women made significant decisions about the character of their lives within families. It was within this primary social unit that most colonists earned their livelihoods, educated their children, defined gender, sustained religious tradition, and nursed each other in sickness. In short, the family was the source of their societal and cultural identities.

Early colonial families did not exist in isolation but were part of larger societies. As we have already discovered, the characters of the first English settlements in the New World varied substantially (see Chapter 2). During much of the seventeenth century, these initial differences grew stronger as each region acquired its own history and developed its own traditions. The various local societies in which families like the Witherspoons put down roots reflected several critical elements: supply of labor, abundance of land, unusual demographic patterns, and commercial ties with European markets. In the Chesapeake, for example, an economy based almost entirely on a single commodity—tobacco—created an insatiable demand for indentured servants and black slaves. Moreover, in Massachusetts Bay, the extraordinary longevity of the founders generated a level of social and political stability that Virginians and Marylanders did not attain until the end of the seventeenth century.

By 1660, it seemed these regional differences had undermined the very idea of a unified English empire in America. During the reign of Charles II, however, a trend toward cultural convergence began. Although subcultures had evolved in strikingly different directions, countervailing forces such as common language and religion gradually pulled English American settlers together. Parliament took advantage of this trend and began to establish a uniform set of rules for the expanding American empire. The process was slow and uneven, often sparking violent colonial resistance, but by the end of the seventeenth century, England had made significant progress toward its goal.

TRADITIONAL SOCIETIES: THE NEW ENGLAND COLONIES OF THE SEVENTEENTH CENTURY

Seventeenth-century New Englanders successfully replicated in America a traditional social order they had known in England. The transfer of a familiar way of life to the New World seemed less difficult for these Puritan migrants than it did for the many English men and women who settled in the Chesapeake colonies. Their contrasting experiences, fundamental to an understanding of the development of both cultures, can be explained, at least in part, by the Puritan family tradition.

Immigrant Families and New Social Order

Early New Englanders believed God ordained the family for human benefit. It was essential to the maintenance of social order, since outside the family, men and women succumbed to carnal temptation. Such people had no one to sustain them or remind them of Scripture. "Without *Family care*," declared the Reverend Benjamin Wadsworth, "the labour of Magistrates and Ministers for Reformation and Propagating Religion, is likely to be in great measure unsuccessful."

The godly family, at least in theory, was ruled by a patriarch, father to his children, husband to his wife, the source of authority and object of unquestioned obedience. The wife shared responsibility for the raising of children, but in decisions of importance, especially those related to property, she was expected to defer to her spouse.

The New Englanders' concern about the character of the godly family is not surprising. This institution played a central role in shaping their society. In contrast to those who migrated to the colonies of Virginia and Maryland, New Englanders crossed the Atlantic within *nuclear* families. That is, they moved within established units consisting of a father, mother, and their dependent children, rather than as single youths and adults. People who migrated to America within families preserved local English customs more fully than did the youths who traveled to other parts of the continent as single men and women. The comforting presence of immediate family members reduced the shock of adjusting to a strange environment 3,000 miles from home. Even in the 1630s, the ratio of men to women in New England was fairly well balanced, about three males for every two females. Persons who had not already married in England before coming to the New World could expect to form nuclear families of their own.

The great migration of the 1630s and 1640s brought approximately twenty thousand persons to New England. After 1642, the English Civil War reduced the flood of people moving to Massachusetts Bay to a trickle. Nevertheless, by the end of the century, the population of New

Isaac Royal and Family (1741) by Robert Feke, known for his portraits of the leading citizens of his day. His portraits are distinguished primarily by an emphasis on elaborate dress.

England had reached almost 120,000, an amazing increase considering the small number of original immigrants. Historians have been hard pressed to explain this striking rate of growth. Some have suggested that New Englanders married very young, thus giving couples extra years in which to produce large families. Other scholars have maintained that New England women must have been more fertile than their Old World counterparts.

Neither theory adequately explains how so few migrants produced such a large population. Early New England marriage patterns, for example, did not differ substantially from those recorded in seventeenth-century England. The average age for men at first marriage was the mid-twenties. Wives were slightly younger than their husbands, the average age being about twenty-two. There is no evidence that New Englanders favored child brides. Nor, for that matter, were Puritan families unusually large by the standards of the period.

The explanation for the region's extraordinary growth turned out to be survival, rather than fertility. Put simply, people who, under normal conditions, would have died in contemporary Europe, lived in New England. Indeed, the life expectancy of seventeenth-century settlers was not very different from our own. Males who survived infancy might have expected to see their seventieth birthday. Twenty percent of the men of the first generation reached the age of eighty. The figures for women were only slightly lower. Why the early settlers lived so long is not entirely clear.

No doubt, pure drinking water, a cool climate that retarded the spread of fatal contagious disease, and a dispersed population promoted general good health.

Longer life altered family relations. New England males lived not only to see their own children reach adulthood, but also to witness the birth of grandchildren. One historian, John Murrin, has argued that New Englanders "invented" grandparents. In other words, this society produced *real* patriarchs. This may have been one of the first societies in recorded history in which a person could reasonably anticipate knowing his or her grandchildren, a demographic surprise that contributed to social stability. The traditions of particular families and communities literally remained alive in the memories of the colony's oldest citizens.

A Society of Families

The life cycle of the seventeenth-century New England family began with marriage. Young men and women generally initiated courtships. If parents exercised a voice in such matters, it was to discourage union with a person of unsound moral character. Puritan ministers advised single people to choose godly partners, warning:

The Wretch that is alone to Mammon Wed,
May chance to find a Satan in the bed.

In this highly religious society, there was not much chance that young people would stray far from traditional community values. The overwhelming majority of the region's population married, for in New England, the single life was not only morally suspect, but also physically difficult.

A couple without land could not support an independent and growing family in these agrarian communities. While men brought farmland, prospective brides were expected to possess a dowry worth approximately one-half what the bridegroom brought to the union. Women often contributed money or household goods.

The household was primarily a place of work—very demanding work. One historical geographer estimates that a Pennsylvania family of five needed 75 acres of cleared land just to feed itself. Additional cultivation allowed the farmer to pro-duce a surplus that could then be sold or bartered, and since agrarian families required items that could not be manufactured at home—metal tools, for example—they usually grew more than they consumed. Early American farmers were not economically self-sufficient; the belief that they were is a popular misconception.

During the seventeenth century, men and women generally lived in the communities of their parents and grandparents. New Englanders usually managed to fall in love with a neighbor, and most marriages took place between men and women living less than 13 miles apart. Moving to a more fertile region might have increased their earnings, but such thoughts seldom occurred to early New Englanders. Religious values, a sense of common purpose, and the importance of family reinforced traditional communal ties.

Towns, in fact, were collections of families, not individuals. Over time, these families intermarried, so the community became an elaborate kinship network. Social historians have discovered that in many New England towns the original founders dominated local politics and economic affairs for several generations. Not surprisingly, newcomers who were not absorbed into the family system tended to move away from the village with greater frequency than did the sons and daughters of the established lineage groups.

Congregational churches were also built on a family foundation. During the earliest years of settlement, the churches accepted persons who could demonstrate they were among God's "elect." Members were drawn from a broad social spectrum. Once the excitement of establishing a new society had passed, however, New Englanders began to focus more attention on the spiritual welfare of their own families. This quite normal parental concern precipitated a major ecclesiastical crisis. The problem was the status of the children within a gathered church. Sons and daughters of full church members regularly received baptism, usually as infants, but as these people grew to adulthood, they often failed to provide testimony of their own "election." Moreover, they wanted their own children to be baptized. A church synod—a gathering of Congregational ministers—responded to this generational crisis by adopting the so-called Half-Way Covenant (1662). This compromise allowed the grandchildren of persons in full communion

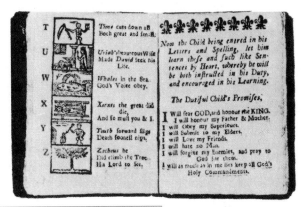

New England parents took seriously their responsibility for the spiritual welfare of their children. To seek the word of God, young people had to learn to read. The New England Primer, *shown here, was their primary vehicle.*

to be baptized even though *their* parents could not demonstrate conversion. Congregational ministers assumed "God cast the line of election in the loins of godly parents." Because of the New Englanders' growing obsession with family—termed *tribalism* by some historians—the Congregational churches by the end of the seventeenth century were increasingly turning inward, addressing the spiritual needs of particular lineage groups rather than reaching out to the larger Christian community.

Colonists regarded education as primarily a family responsibility. Parents were supposed to instruct children in the principles of Christianity; and so it was necessary to teach boys and girls how to read. In 1642, the Massachusetts General Court reminded the Bay Colonists of their obligation to catechize their families. Five years later, the legislature ordered towns containing at least fifteen families to open an elementary school supported by local taxes. Villages of a hundred or more families had to maintain more advanced grammar schools, which taught a basic Latin curriculum. At least eleven schools were operating in 1647, and despite their expense, new schools were established throughout the century.

This family-based education system worked. A large majority of the region's adult males could read and write, an accomplishment not achieved in the Chesapeake colonies for another century. The literacy rate for women was somewhat lower, but by the standards of the period, it was still impressive. A printing press operated in Cambridge as early as 1639. *The New-England Primer,* first published in 1690 in Boston by Benjamin Harris, taught children the alphabet as well as the Lord's Prayer. This primer announced:

> *He who ne'er learns his ABC,*
> *forever will a blockhead be.*
> *But he who to his book's inclined,*
> *will soon a golden treasure find.*

But the best-seller of seventeenth-century New England was Michael Wigglesworth's *The Day of Doom* (1662), a poem of 224 stanzas describing in terrifying detail the fate of sinners on Judgment Day. In words that even young readers could comprehend, Wigglesworth wrote of these unfortunate souls:

> *They cry, no, no: Alas! and wo!*
> *Our Courage all is gone:*
> *Our hardiness (fool hardiness)*
> *Hath us undone, undone.*

Many New Englanders memorized the entire poem.

After 1638, young men could attend Harvard College, the first institution of higher learning founded in England's mainland colonies. The school was originally intended to train ministers, and of the 465 students who graduated during the seventeenth century, over half became Congregational divines. Harvard had a demanding curriculum. The boys read logic, rhetoric, divinity, and several ancient languages, including Hebrew. Yale College followed Harvard's lead, admitting its first students in 1702.

Women in Puritan New England

The role of women in the agrarian societies north of the Chesapeake is a controversial subject among colonial historians. Some scholars point out that common law as well as English custom treated women as inferior to men. Other historians, however, depict the colonial period as a "golden age" for women. According to this interpretation, wives worked alongside their husbands. They were not divorced from meaningful, productive labor. They certainly were not transformed into the frail, dependent beings much admired by middle-class males of the nineteenth century. Both views provide insights into the lives of early American women, but neither fully recaptures their community experiences.

To be sure, women worked on family farms. They did not, however, necessarily do the same jobs that men performed. Women usually handled separate tasks, including cooking, washing, clothes making, dairying, and gardening. Their production of food was absolutely essential to the survival of most households. Sometimes wives—and the overwhelming majority of adult seventeenth-century women were married—raised poultry, and by selling surplus birds achieved some economic independence. When people in one New England community chided a man for allowing his wife to peddle her fowl, he responded, "I meddle not with the geese nor turkeys for they are hers." In fact, during this period women were often described as "deputy husbands," a label that drew attention to their dependence on

family patriarchs as well as to their roles as decision makers.

Women also joined churches in greater number than men. Within a few years of founding, many New England congregations contained two female members for every male, a process historians describe as the "feminization of colonial religion." Contemporaries offered different explanations for this gender shift. Cotton Mather, the leading Congregational minister of Massachusetts Bay, argued that God had created "far more *godly Women*" than men. Others thought the life-threatening experience of childbirth gave women a deeper appreciation of religion. The Quakers gave women an even larger role in religious affairs, which may help to explain the popularity of this sect among ordinary women.

In political and legal matters, society sharply curtailed the rights of colonial women. According to English common law, a wife exercised no control over property. She could not, for example, sell land, although if her husband decided to dispose of their holdings, he was free to do so without her permission. Divorce was extremely difficult to obtain in any colony before the American Revolution. Indeed, a person married to a cruel or irresponsible spouse had little recourse but to run away or accept the unhappy situation.

Yet most women were neither prosperous entrepreneurs nor abject slaves. Surviving letters indicate that men and women generally accommodated themselves to the gender roles they thought God had ordained. One of early America's most creative poets, Anne Bradstreet, wrote movingly of the fulfillment she had found with her husband. In a piece entitled "To my Dear and loving Husband," Bradstreet declared:

If ever two were one, then surely we.
   If ever man were lov'd by wife, then thee;
If ever wife was happy in a man,
   Compare with me the women if you can.

Although Puritan couples worried that the affection they felt for a husband or a wife might turn their thoughts away from God's perfect love, this was a danger they were willing to risk.

Rank and Status in New England Society

During the seventeenth century, the New England colonies attracted neither noblemen nor paupers. The absence of these social groups meant the American social structure seemed incomplete by contemporary European standards. The settlers were not displeased that the poor remained in the Old World. The lack of very rich persons—and in this period great wealth frequently accompanied noble title—was quite another matter. According to the prevailing hierarchical view of the structure of society, well-placed individuals were *natural rulers,* people intended by God to exercise political authority over the rank and file. Migration forced the colonists, however, to choose their rulers from men of more modest status. One minister told a Plymouth congregation that since its members were "not furnished with any persons of *special eminency above the rest,* to be chosen by you into office of government," they would have to make due with neighbors, "not beholding in them the *ordinariness of their persons.*"

The colonists gradually sorted themselves out into distinct social groupings. Persons who would never have been "natural rulers" in England became provincial gentry in the various northern colonies. It helped, of course, if an individual possessed wealth and education, but these attributes alone could not guarantee a newcomer would be accepted into the local ruling elite, at least not during the early decades of settlement. In Massachusetts and Connecticut, Puritan voters expected their leaders to join Congregational churches and defend orthodox religion.

The Winthrops, Dudleys, and Pynchons—just to cite a few of the more prominent families—fulfilled these expectations, and in public affairs they assumed dominant roles. They took their responsibilities quite seriously and certainly did not look kindly on anyone who spoke of their "ordinariness." A colonist who jokingly called a Puritan magistrate a "just ass" found himself in deep trouble with civil authorities.

The problem was that while most New Englanders accepted a hierarchical view of society, they disagreed over their assigned places. Both Massachusetts Bay and Connecticut passed sumptuary laws—statutes that limited the wearing of fine apparel to the wealthy and prominent—to curb the pretensions of those of lower status. Yet such restraints could not prevent some people from rising and others from falling within the social order.

Governor John Winthrop provided a marvelous description of the unplanned social mobility that occurred in early New England. During the 1640s, he recorded in his diary the story of a master who could not afford to pay a servant's wages. To meet this obligation, the master sold a pair of oxen, but the transaction barely covered the cost of keeping the servant. In desperation, the master asked the employee, a man of lower social status, "how shall I do . . . when all my cattle are gone?" The servant replied, "you shall then serve me, so you may have your cattle again." In the margin of his diary next to this account, Winthrop scribbled "insolent."

Most northern colonists were yeomen (independent farmers) who worked their own land. While few became rich in America, even fewer fell hopelessly into debt. Their daily lives, especially for those who settled New England, centered on scattered little communities where they participated in village meetings, church-related matters, and militia training. Possession of land gave agrarian families a sense of independence from external authority. As one man bragged to those who had stayed behind in England, "Here are no hard landlords to rack us with high rents or extorting fines. . . . Here every man may be master of his own labour and land . . . and if he have nothing but his hands he may set up his trade, and by industry grow rich."

During the seventeenth century, this independence was balanced by an equally strong feeling of local identity. Not until the late eighteenth century, when many New Englanders left their familial villages in search of new land, did many northern yeomen place personal material ambition above traditional community bonds.

It was not unusual for northern colonists to work as servants at some point in their lives. This system of labor differed greatly from the pattern of servitude that developed in seventeenth-century Virginia and Maryland. New Englanders seldom recruited servants from the Old World. The forms of agriculture practiced in this region, mixed cereal and dairy farming, made employment of large gangs of dependent workers uneconomic. Rather, New England families placed their adolescent children in nearby homes. These young persons contracted for four or five years and seemed more like apprentices than servants. Servitude was not simply a means by which one group exploited another. It was a form of vocational training program in which the children of the rich as well as the poor participated.

By the end of the seventeenth century, the New England Puritans had developed a compelling story about their own history in the New World. The founders had been extraordinarily godly men and women, and in an heroic effort to establish a purer form of religion, pious families had passed "over the vast ocean into this vast and howling wilderness." Although the children and grandchildren of the first generation sometimes questioned their ability to please the Lord, they recognized the mission to the New World had been a success: they were "as Prosperous as ever, there is Peace & Plenty, & the Country flourisheth."

THE PLANTERS' WORLD

An entirely different regional society developed in England's Chesapeake colonies. This contrast with New England seems puzzling. After all, the two areas were founded at roughly the same time by men and women from the same mother country. In both regions, settlers spoke English, accepted Protestantism, and gave allegiance to one crown. And yet, to cite an obvious example, seventeenth-century Virginia looked nothing like Massachusetts Bay. In an effort to explain the difference, colonial historians have studied environmental conditions, labor systems, and agrarian economies. The most important reason for the distinctiveness of these early southern plantation societies, however, turned out to be the Chesapeake's death rate, a frighteningly high mortality that tore at the very fabric of traditional family life.

Family Life in a Perilous Environment

Unlike New England's settlers, the men and women who emigrated to the Chesapeake region did not move in family units. They traveled to the New World as young unmarried servants, youths cut off from the security of traditional kin relations. Although these immigrants came from a cross section of English society, most had been poor to middling farmers in the mother country. It is now estimated that 70 to 85 percent of the white colonists who went to Virginia and Maryland during the seventeenth century were not free; that is, they owed four or five years' labor in exchange for the cost of passage to America. If the servant was under fifteen, he or she had to serve a full seven years. The overwhelming majority of these laborers were males between the ages of eighteen and twenty-two. In fact, before 1640, the ratio of males to females stood at 6 to 1. This figure dropped to about $2\frac{1}{2}$ to 1 by the end of the century, but the sexual balance in the Chesapeake was never as favorable as it had been in early Massachusetts.

Most immigrants to the Chesapeake region died soon after arriving. It is difficult to ascertain the exact cause of death in most cases, but malaria and other diseases took a frightful toll. Recent studies also indicate that drinking water contaminated with salt killed many colonists living in low-lying areas. Throughout the entire seventeenth century, high mortality rates had a profound effect on this society. Life expectancy for Chesapeake males was about forty-three, some ten to twenty years less than for men born in New England! For women, life was even shorter. A full 25 percent of all children died in infancy; another 25 percent did not see their twentieth birthdays. The survivors were often weak or ill, unable to perform hard physical labor.

These demographic conditions retarded normal population increase. Young women who might have become wives and mothers could not do so until they had completed their terms of servitude. They thus lost several reproductive years, and in a society in which so many children died in infancy, late marriage greatly restricted family size. Moreover, because of the unbalanced sex ratio, many adult males simply could not find wives. Migration not only cut them off from their English families, but also deprived them of an opportunity to form new ones. Without a constant flow of immigrants, the population of Virginia and Maryland would have actually declined.

High mortality compressed the family life cycle into a few short years. One partner in a marriage usually died within seven years. Only one in three

Seventeenth-century Puritan carvers transformed the production of gravestones into high art.

Chesapeake marriages survived as long as a decade. Not only did children not meet grandparents, they often did not even know their own parents. Widows and widowers quickly remarried, bringing children by former unions into their new homes, and it was not uncommon for a child to grow up with persons to whom he or she bore no blood relation. The psychological effects of such experiences on Chesapeake settlers cannot be measured. People probably learned to cope with a high degree of personal insecurity. However they adjusted, it is clear family life in this region was vastly more impermanent than it was in the New England colonies during the same period.

Women were obviously in great demand in the early southern colonies. Some historians have argued that scarcity heightened the woman's bargaining power in the marriage market. If she was an immigrant, she did not have to worry about obtaining parental consent. She was on her own in the New World and free to select whomever she pleased. If a woman lacked beauty or

strength, if she were a person of low moral standards, she could still be confident of finding an American husband. Such negotiations may have provided Chesapeake women with a means of improving their social status. Nevertheless, liberation from some traditional restraints on seventeenth-century women must not be exaggerated. As servants, women were vulnerable to sexual exploitation by their masters. Moreover, in this unhealthy environment, childbearing was extremely dangerous, and women in the Chesapeake usually died twenty years earlier than their New England counterparts.

Rank and Status in Plantation Society

Colonists who managed somehow to survive grew tobacco—as much tobacco as they possibly could. This crop became the Chesapeake staple, and since it was relatively easy to cultivate, anyone with a few acres of cleared land could produce leaves for export. Cultivation of tobacco did not, however, produce a society roughly equal in wealth and status. To the contrary, tobacco generated inequality. Some planters amassed large fortunes; others barely subsisted. Labor made the difference, for to succeed in this staple economy, one had to control the labor of other men and women. More workers in the fields meant larger harvests, and, of course, larger profits. Since free persons showed no interest in growing another man's tobacco, not even for wages, wealthy planters relied on white laborers who were not free, as well as on slaves. The social structure that developed in the seventeenth-century Chesapeake reflected a wild, often unscrupulous scramble to bring men and women of three races—black, white, and Indian—into various degrees of dependence.

Great planters dominated Chesapeake society. The group was small, only a trifling portion of the population of Virginia and Maryland. During the early decades of the seventeenth century, the composition of Chesapeake gentry was continually in flux. Some gentlemen died before they could establish a secure claim to high social status; others returned to England, thankful to have survived. Not until the 1650s did the family names of those who would become famous eighteenth-century gentry appear in the records. The first gentlemen were not—as genealogists sometimes discover to their dismay—dashing Cavaliers who had fought in the English civil war for King Charles I. Rather, such Chesapeake gentry as the Burwells, Byrds, Carters, and Masons consisted originally of the younger sons of English merchants and artisans.

These ambitious men arrived in America with capital. They invested immediately in laborers, and one way or another, they obtained huge tracts of the best tobacco-growing land. The members of this gentry were not technically aristocrats, for they did not possess titles that could be passed from generation to generation. They gave themselves military titles, sat as justices of the peace on the county courts, and directed local (Anglican) church affairs as members of the vestry. Over time, these gentry families intermarried so frequently that they created a vast network of cousins. During the eighteenth century, it was not uncommon to find a half dozen men with the same surname sitting simultaneously in the Virginia House of Burgesses.

Freemen formed the largest class in this society. Their origins were strikingly different from those of the gentry, or for that matter, from those of New England's yeomen farmers. Chesapeake freemen traveled to the New World as indentured servants and, by sheer good fortune, managed to remain alive to the end of their contracts. If they had dreamed of becoming great planters, they were gravely disappointed. Most seventeenth-century freemen lived on the edge of poverty. Some freemen, of course, did better in America than they would have in contemporary England, but in both Virginia and Maryland, historians have found a sharp economic division separating the gentry from the rest of white society.

Below the freemen came indentured servants. Membership in this group was not demeaning; after all, servitude was a temporary status. But servitude in the Chesapeake colonies was not the benign institution it was in New England. Great planters purchased servants to grow tobacco. No one worried whether these laborers received decent food and clothes, much less whether they acquired trade skills. These young people, thousands of them, cut off from family ties, sick often to the point of death, unable to obtain normal sexual release, regarded their servitude as a form of "slavery." Not surprisingly, the gentry worried

that unhappy servants and impoverished freemen, what the planters called the "giddy multitude," would rebel at the slightest provocation, a fear that turned out to be fully justified.

The character of social mobility—and this observation applies only to the whites—changed considerably during the seventeenth century. Until the 1680s, it was relatively easy for a newcomer who possessed capital to become a member of the planter elite. No one paid much attention to the reputation or social standing of one's English family.

Sometime after the 1680s, however—the precise date is impossible to establish—a dramatic demographic shift occurred. Although infant mortality remained high, life expectancy rates for those who survived childhood in the Chesapeake improved significantly, and for the first time in the history of Virginia and Maryland, important leadership positions went to men who had actually been born in America. This transition has been described by one political historian as the "emergence of a creole majority," in other words, as the rise of an indigenous ruling elite. Before this time, immigrant leaders had died without heirs or had returned as quickly as possible to England. The members of the new creole class took a greater interest in local government. Their activities helped give the Tobacco Colonies the kind of political and cultural stability that had eluded earlier generations of planter adventurers. Not surprisingly, it was during this period of demographic transition that creole leaders founded the College of William and Mary (1693) and authorized the construction of an impressive new capital called Williamsburg. These were changes that, in the words of one creole Virginian, provided the colony "with a sense of permanence and legitimacy . . . it had never before possessed."

The key to success in this creole society was ownership of slaves. Those planters who held more blacks could grow more tobacco, and thus could acquire fresh capital needed to purchase additional laborers. Over time, the rich not only became richer, they also formed a distinct ruling elite that newcomers found increasingly difficult to enter.

Opportunities for advancement also decreased for the region's freemen. Studies of mid-seventeenth-century Maryland reveal that some servants managed to become moderately prosperous farmers and small officeholders. But as the gentry consolidated its hold on political and economic institutions, ordinary people discovered it was much harder to rise in Chesapeake society. Those men and women with more ambitious dreams headed for Pennsylvania, North Carolina, or western Virginia.

Social institutions that figured importantly in the daily experience of New Englanders were either weak or nonexistent in the Chesapeake colonies. In part, this sluggish development resulted from the continuation of high infant mortality rates. There was little incentive to build elementary schools, for example, if half the children would die before reaching adulthood. The great planters sent their sons to England or Scotland for their education, and even after the founding of the College of William and Mary in Virginia in 1693, the gentry continued to patronize English schools. As a result of this practice, higher education in the South languished for much of the colonial period.

Tobacco influenced the spread of other institutions in this region. Planters were scattered along the rivers, often separated from their nearest neighbors by miles of poor roads. Since the major tobacco growers traded directly with English merchants, they had no need for towns. Whatever items they required were either made on the plantation or imported from Europe. Other than the centers of colonial government, Jamestown (and later Williamsburg) and St. Mary's (and later Annapolis), there were no villages capable of sustaining a rich community life before the late eighteenth century. Seventeenth-century Virginia did not even possess a printing press. In fact, Governor Sir William Berkeley bragged in 1671, "there are no free schools, nor printing in Virginia, for learning has brought disobedience, and heresy . . . into the world, and printing had divulged them . . . God keep us from both!"

THE AFRICAN AMERICAN EXPERIENCE

Many people who landed in the colonies had no desire to come to the New World. They were Africans taken as slaves to cultivate rice, sugar, and tobacco. As the Native Americans were exterminated and the supply of white indentured servants dried up, European planters demanded even more African laborers.

Roots of Slavery

A great deal is known about the transfer of African peoples across the Atlantic. During the entire history of this human commerce, between the sixteenth and nineteenth centuries, slave traders carried almost eleven million blacks to the Americas. Most of these men and women were sold in Brazil or in the Caribbean. Only a small number of Africans ever reached British North America, and of this group, the majority arrived after 1700. Because slaves performed hard physical labor, planters preferred purchasing young males. In many early slave communities, men outnumbered women by a ratio of two to one.

English colonists did not hesitate to enslave black people, or for that matter, Native Americans. While the institution of slavery had long before died out in the mother country, New World settlers quickly discovered how well this particular labor system operated in the Spanish and Portuguese colonies. The decision to bring African slaves to the colonies, therefore, was based primarily on economic considerations.

English masters, however, seldom justified the practice purely in terms of planter profits. Indeed, they adopted a quite different pattern of rhetoric. English writers associated blacks in Africa with heathen religion, barbarous behavior, sexual promiscuity—in fact, with evil itself. From such a racist perspective, the enslavement of Africans seemed unobjectionable. The planters maintained that if black slaves converted to Christianity, shedding their supposedly savage ways, they would benefit from their loss of freedom.

Africans first landed in Virginia in 1619. For the next fifty years, the status of the colony's black people remained unclear. English settlers classified some black laborers as slaves for life, as chattel to be bought and sold at the master's will. But other Africans became servants, presumably for stated periods of time, and it was even possible for a few blacks to purchase their freedom. Several seventeenth-century Africans became successful Virginia planters (see pp. 76–77).

One reason Virginia lawmakers tolerated such confusion was that the black population remained very small. By 1660, less than 1,500

The African Slave Trade

Between 1619 and 1760, about half a million African captives were brought to the thirteen mainland English colonies, far fewer than were taken to other parts of the Americas.

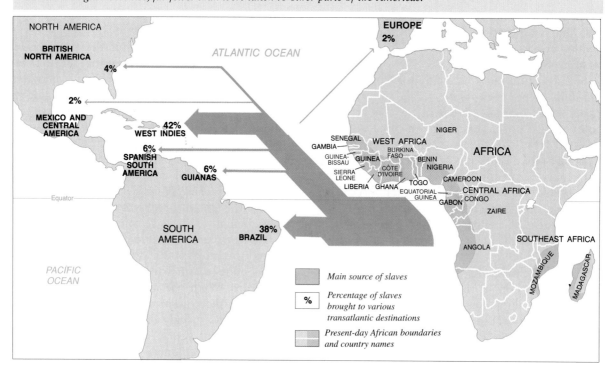

people of African origin lived in the entire colony (compared to a white population of approximately 26,000), and it hardly seemed necessary for the legislature to draw up an elaborate slave code to control so few men and women. If the planters could have obtained more black laborers, they certainly would have done so. There is no evidence that the great planters preferred white indentured servants to black slaves. The problem was supply. During this period, slave traders sold their cargoes on Barbados or the other sugar islands of the West Indies, where they fetched higher prices than Virginians could afford. In fact, before 1680, most blacks who reached England's colonies on the North American mainland came from Barbados or through New Netherland rather than directly from Africa.

By the end of the seventeenth century, the legal status of Virginia's black people was no longer in doubt. They were slaves for life, and so were their children after them. This transformation reflected changes in the supply of Africans to British North America. After 1672, the Royal African Company was chartered to meet the colonial

planters' demands for black laborers. Historian K.G. Davies terms this organization "the strongest and most effective of all European companies formed exclusively for the African trade." Between 1695 and 1709, over eleven thousand Africans were sold in Virginia alone; many others went to Maryland and the Carolinas. Although American merchants—most of them based in Rhode Island—entered the trade during the eighteenth century, the British continued to supply the bulk of the slaves to the mainland market for the entire colonial period.

The expanding black population apparently frightened white colonists, for as the number of Africans increased, lawmakers drew up ever stricter slave codes. It was during this period that racism, always a latent element in New World societies, was fully revealed. By 1700, slavery was unequivocally based on the color of a person's skin. Blacks fell into this status simply because they were black. A vicious pattern of discrimination had been set in motion. Even conversion to Christianity did not free the African from bondage. The white planter could deal with his

This watercolor, Slave Deck of the Albanoz (1846), *by naval officer Lieutenant Godfrey Meynell, shows slaves packed with cargo in the hold of a ship after being taken captive in West Africa. Because it was expected that many slaves would die en route, ship captains sometimes attempted to increase their profits by crowding even more slaves into the hold than regulations allowed.*

black property as he alone saw fit, and one revolting Virginia statute excused a master who had killed a slave, on the grounds that no rational person would purposely "destroy his own estate." Children born to a slave woman became slaves regardless of the father's race. Unlike the Spanish colonies, where persons of lighter color enjoyed greater privileges in society, the English colonies tolerated no mixing of the races. Mulattoes and pure Africans received the same treatment.

African American Cultures in English America

The slave experience varied substantially from colony to colony. The daily life of a black person in South Carolina, for example, was quite different from that of an African American who happened to live in Pennsylvania or Massachusetts Bay. The size and density of the slave population determined in large measure how successfully blacks could maintain a separate cultural identity.

In the lowlands of South Carolina during the eighteenth century, 60 percent of the population was black. These men and women were placed on large, isolated rice plantations, and their contact with whites was limited. In these areas blacks developed creole languages, which mixed the basic vocabulary of English with words borrowed from various African tongues. Until the end of the nineteenth century, one creole language, Gullah, was spoken on some of the Sea Islands along the Georgia–South Carolina coast. Slaves on these large rice plantations were also able to establish elaborate and enduring kinship networks that may have helped reduce the more dehumanizing aspects of bondage.

In the New England and Middle Colonies, and even in Virginia, African Americans made up a smaller percentage of the population: 40 percent in Virginia, 8 percent in Pennsylvania, and 3 percent in Massachusetts. In such environments, contact between blacks and whites was more frequent than in South Carolina and Georgia. These population patterns had a profound effect on

Anthony Johnson: Black Patriarch of Pungoteague Creek

During the first decades of settlement, a larger proportion of Virginia's black population achieved freedom than at any time until the Civil War ended slavery. Despite considerable obstacles, these free black men and women—their number in these early years was quite small—formed families, acquired property, earned community respect, and helped establish a distinctive African American culture. One member of this group was Anthony Johnson, an immigrant who rose from slavery to prominence on Virginia's Eastern Shore.

Johnson came to Virginia aboard the English vessel *James* in 1621, just two years after the first blacks had arrived in the colony. As a slave known simply as "Antonio a Negro," Johnson found life a constant struggle for survival. Working in the tobacco fields of the Bennett plantation located on the south side of the James River, he endured long hours, poor rations, fearful epidemics, and haunting loneliness, which, more often than not, brought an early death to slaves as well as indentured servants. Johnson, however, was a tough, intelligent, and lucky man.

Exactly how Johnson achieved freedom is not known. Early records reveal that while still living at the Bennett plantation, he took a wife "Mary a

Africans were sometimes given the opportunity to buy their freedom through labor. This arrangement, called self-purchase, may have been the means by which Anthony and Mary Johnson escaped bondage and became property owners.

Negro woman." Anthony was fortunate to find her. Because of an exceedingly unequal sex ratio in early Virginia, few males—regardless of color—had an opportunity to form families. Anthony and Mary reared at least four children. Even more remarkable, in a society in which most unions were broken by death within a decade, their marriage lasted over forty years.

Sometime during the 1630s, Anthony and Mary gained their freedom, perhaps with the help of someone named Johnson. Their bondage probably ended through self-purchase, an arrangement that allowed enterprising slaves to buy their liberty through labor. Later, again

under unknown circumstances, the Johnsons migrated to Northampton County on the Eastern Shore of Virginia. During the 1640s, they acquired an estate of 250 acres on Pungoteague Creek, where they raised cattle, horses, and hogs and cultivated tobacco. To work these holdings, Anthony Johnson apparently relied on the labor of indentured servants and at least one black slave named Casor.

As the "patriarch of Pungoteague Creek," Johnson participated as fully as most whites in Northampton society. He traded with wealthy white landowners and apparently shared their assumptions about the sanctity of property and the

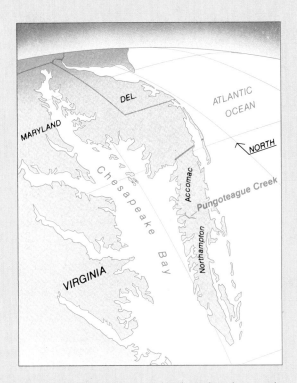

legitimacy of slavery. When two white neighbors attempted to steal Casor, Johnson hauled them into court and forced them to return his laborer. On another occasion, Johnson appealed to the court for tax relief after an "unfortunate fire" destroyed much of his plantation.

The Johnsons also maintained close ties with other free blacks, such as Anthony Payne and Emmanuel Driggus who had similarly attained freedom and prosperity through their own efforts. Johnson's strongest links were with his family. Although his children lived in separate homes after reaching adulthood, his two sons laid out holdings in the 1650s adjacent to their father's plantation, and in times of crisis, parents and children participated in family conferences. These close bonds persisted even after the Johnson clan moved to Somerset County, Maryland, in the 1660s, and Anthony Johnson's subsequent

death. When he purchased land in Somerset in 1677, Johnson's grandson, a third-generation free black colonist, named his plantation "Angola," perhaps in memory of his grandfather's African homeland.

Interpreting Johnson's remarkable life has proved surprisingly difficult. An earlier generation of historians considered Johnson a curiosity, a sort of black Englishman who did not fit neatly into familiar racial categories. Even some recent writers, concerned about tracing the roots of slavery and prejudice in the United States, have paid scant attention to Johnson and the other free blacks on the Eastern Shore.

Most historians would now agree that Johnson's life illustrated the complexity of race relations in early Virginia. His surprising progression from slave to slaveholder and his easy participation in the world of the white gentry and in a network of black

friendships and family ties demonstrated that relations among blacks and whites conformed to no single pattern in the fluid society of mid-seventeenth-century Virginia. Rather, they took a variety of forms—conflict, cooperation, exploitation, accommodation—depending on the goals, status, experience, and environment of the participants. Race was only one—and by no means the decisive—factor shaping relations among colonists.

The opportunities that had been available to Anthony Johnson and other Virginia blacks, however, disappeared during the last quarter of the seventeenth century. A growing reliance on slave labor rather than white indentured servitude brought about a rapid increase in the black population of Virginia and an accompanying curtailment of civil liberties on racial grounds. The rise of a group of great planters who dominated the colonial economy soon drove free black farmers into poverty. No longer did they enjoy the security, as had one black farmer in the 1640s, of having "myne owne ground and I will work when I please and play when I please." It is not surprising that after 1706, a time when Virginia's experiment in a genuinely multiracial free society was all but over, the Johnson family disappeared from colonial records. When modern Americans discuss the history of race relations in the United States, they might consider the factors that allowed some of the first blacks that settled in America to achieve economic and social success.

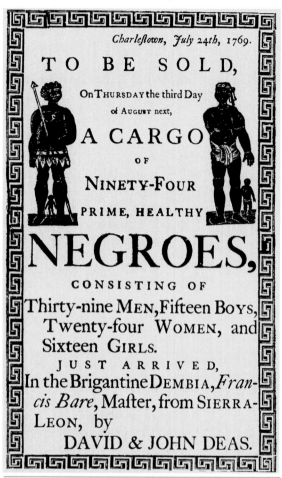

This notice publicizes a slave auction to be held at the Charles Town wharf (1769).

northern and Chesapeake blacks, for while they escaped the physical drudgery of rice cultivation, they found the preservation of an independent African identity difficult. In northern cities, slaves working as domestics and living in the houses of their masters saw other blacks, but had little opportunity to develop creole languages or reaffirm a common African past.

In eighteenth-century Virginia, native-born or creole blacks, people who had learned to cope with whites on a daily basis, looked with contempt on slaves who had just arrived from Africa. These "outlandish" Negroes, as they were called, were forced by blacks as well as whites to accept elements of English culture. It was especially important for newcomers to speak English. Consider, for example, the pain of young Olaudah Equiano, an African sold in Virginia in 1757. This twelve-year-old slave declared, "I was

now exceedingly miserable, and thought myself worse off than any . . . of my companions; for they could talk to each other [in English], but I had no person to speak to that I could understand. In this state I was constantly grieving and pining, and wishing for death."

Newly arrived men and women from Africa were far more likely to run away, assault their masters, and organize rebellion than were the creole slaves. The people described in colonial newspaper advertisements as "New Negroes" desperately tried to regain control over their lives. In 1770—just to cite one moving example—two young Africans, both recently sold in Virginia, "went off with several others, being persuaded that they could find their way back to their own Country."

Despite such wrenching experiences, black slaves creatively preserved elements of an African heritage. The process of establishing African American traditions involved an imaginative reshaping of African and European customs into something that was neither African nor European. It was African American. The slaves accepted Christianity, but they did so on their own terms—terms their masters seldom fully understood. Blacks transformed Christianity into an expression of religious feeling in which an African element remained vibrant. In music and folk art, they gave voice to a cultural identity that even the most degrading conditions could not eradicate.

A major turning point in the history of African American people occurred during the early decades of the eighteenth century. At this time, blacks living in England's mainland colonies began to reproduce successfully. The number of live births exceeded deaths, and from that date, the expansion of the African American population owed more to natural increase than to the importation of new slaves. Even though thousands of new Africans arrived each year, the creole population was always much larger than that of the immigrant blacks. This demographic shift did not take place in the Caribbean or South American colonies until a much later date. Historians believe North American blacks enjoyed a healthier climate and better diet than other New World slaves.

Although mainland blacks lived longer than the blacks of Jamaica or Barbados, they were,

Old Plantation, *a watercolor by an unknown artist (about 1800), shows that some African identity and customs survived plantation life. The man and women in the center dance (possibly to celebrate a wedding) to the music of drum and banjo. Instruments, turbans, and scarves have African elements.*

after all, still slaves. They protested their debasement in many ways, some in individual acts of violence, others in organized revolt. The most serious slave rebellion of the colonial period was the Stono Uprising, which took place in September 1739. One hundred and fifty South Carolina blacks rose up, and seizing guns and ammunition, murdered several white planters. "With Colours displayed, and two Drums beating," they marched toward Spanish Florida where they had been promised freedom. The local militia soon overtook the rebellious slaves and killed most of them. Although the uprising was short-lived, such incidents helped persuade whites everywhere that their own blacks might secretly be planning bloody revolt. Fear bred paranoia. When an unstable white servant woman in New York City announced in 1741 that blacks intended to burn the town, frightened authorities executed 32 suspected arsonists and dispatched 175 others to the West Indies. While the level of inter-racial violence in colonial society was quite low, everyone recognized that the blacks—in the words of one Virginia governor—longed "to Shake off the fetters of Slavery."

BLUEPRINT FOR EMPIRE

In 1661, John Norton, a respected Congregational minister, delivered a remarkable sermon before the assembled legislators of Massachusetts Bay. "It is not a Gospel-spirit to be against Kings," Norton lectured, "'tis neither Gospel nor English Spirit for any of us to be against the Government by Kings, Lords and Commons." It was as if after some thirty years of virtual freedom, the American Puritans had to be reminded of the political ties that bound them to England. As Norton sensed, however, the times were changing. The newly restored Stuart monarchy was beginning to establish rules for the entire empire, and the planters of the Chesapeake as well as the Puritans of New England would soon discover they were not as independent as they had imagined.

Until the middle of the seventeenth century, English political leaders largely ignored the American colonists. Private companies and aristocratic proprietors had created these societies, some for profit, others for religious sanctuary, but in no case did the Crown provide financial or military assistance. After the Restoration of Charles II in 1660, intervention replaced indifference. Englishmen of various sorts—courtiers, merchants, parliamentarians—concluded that the colonists should be brought more tightly under the control of the mother country. The regulatory policies that evolved during this period formed a framework for an empire that survived with only minor adjustment until 1765.

A New Commercial System

The famous eighteenth-century Scottish economist, Adam Smith, coined the term *mercantilist system* to describe Great Britain's commercial regulations, and ever since, his phrase has appeared in history books. Smith's term, however, is misleading. It suggests that English policymakers during the reign of Charles II had developed a well-integrated set of ideas about the nature of international commerce and a carefully planned set of mercantilist government policies to implement them.

They did nothing of the sort. Administrators responded to particular problems, usually on an individual basis. In 1668, Charles informed his sister, "The thing which is nearest the heart of the nation is trade and all that belongs to it." National interest alone, however, did not shape public policy. Instead, the needs of several powerful interest groups led to the rise of English commercial regulation.

Each group looked to colonial commerce to solve a different problem. For his part, the king wanted money. For their part, English merchants were eager to exclude Dutch rivals from lucrative American markets and needed government assistance to compete successfully with the Dutch, even in Virginia or Massachusetts Bay. From the perspective of the landed gentry who sat in

Parliament, England needed a stronger navy and that in turn meant expansion of the domestic shipbuilding industry. And almost everyone agreed England should establish a more favorable balance of trade; that is, increase exports, decrease imports, and grow richer at the expense of other European states. None of these ideas was particularly innovative, but taken together they provided a blueprint for England's first empire.

Navigation Acts Transform Colonial Society

After some legislation in that direction during the Commonwealth, Parliament passed a Navigation Act in 1660. This statute was the most important piece of imperial legislation drafted before the American Revolution. Colonists from New

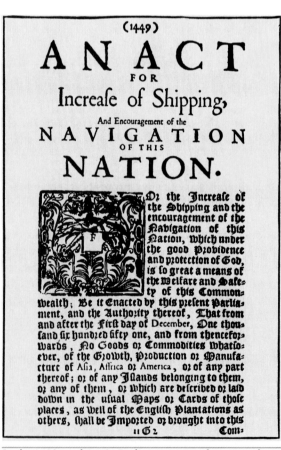

In the 1650s and 1660s Parliament enacted a series of measures known collectively as the Navigation Acts, which were designed to protect English shipping, enrich the treasury, and exploit colonial economies. Shown here is the title page of the Navigation Act of 1651.

Hampshire to Georgia paid close attention to the details of this statute, which stated (1) that no ship could trade in the colonies unless it had been constructed in either England or America and carried a crew that was at least 75 percent English (for these purposes colonists counted as Englishmen), and (2) that certain *enumerated* goods of great value that were not produced in England—tobacco, sugar, cotton, indigo, dye-woods, ginger—could be transported from the colonies *only* to an English or another colonial port. In 1704, Parliament added rice and molasses to the enumerated list; in 1705, rosins, tars, and turpentines needed for shipbuilding were included.

The act of 1660 was masterfully conceived. It encouraged the development of domestic shipbuilding and prohibited European rivals from obtaining enumerated goods anywhere except in England. Since the Americans had to pay import duties in England (for this purpose colonists did *not* count as Englishmen) on such items as sugar and tobacco, the legislation also provided the Crown with another source of income.

In 1663, Parliament supplemented this legislation with a second Navigation Act known as the *Staple Act,* which stated that, with a few noted exceptions, nothing could be imported into America unless it had first been transshipped through the mother country, a process that greatly added to the price ultimately paid by colonial consumers.

The Navigation Acts attempted to eliminate the Dutch, against whom the English fought three wars in this period (1652–1654, 1664–1667, and 1672–1674), as the middlemen of American commerce. Just as English merchants were celebrating their victory, however, an unanticipated rival appeared on the scene. New England merchantmen sailed out of Boston, Salem, and Newport to become formidable world competitors in maritime commerce.

During the 1660s, the colonists showed little enthusiasm for the new imperial system. Reaction to these regulations varied from region to region. Virginians bitterly protested the Navigation Acts. The collection of English customs on tobacco greatly reduced the colonial planters' profits. Moreover, the exclusion of the Dutch from the trade meant that growers often had to sell their crops at artificially low prices. The Navigation Acts hit the small planters especially hard, for they were least able to absorb increased production costs. Even though the governor of Virginia lobbied on the planters' behalf, the Crown turned a deaf ear. By 1670, import duties on tobacco accounted for almost £100,000, a sum the king could scarcely do without.

At first, New Englanders simply ignored the commercial regulations. Indeed, one Massachusetts merchant reported in 1664 that Boston entertained "near one hundred sail of ships, this year, of ours and strangers." The strangers, of course, were the Dutch, who had no intention of obeying the Navigation Acts so long as they could reach colonial ports. Some New England merchants found clever ways to circumvent the Navigation Acts. These crafty traders picked up cargoes of enumerated goods such as sugar or tobacco, sailed to another colonial port (thereby technically fulfilling the letter of the law), and then made directly for Holland or France. Along the way they paid no customs.

To plug this loophole, Parliament passed the Navigation Act of 1673. This statute established a *plantation duty,* a sum of money equal to normal English customs duties to be collected on enumerated products at the various colonial ports. New Englanders could now sail wherever they pleased within the empire, but they could not escape paying customs. Parliament also extended the jurisdiction of the London Customs Commissioners to America. And in 1675, as part of this new imperial firmness, the Privy Council formed a powerful subcommittee, the Lords of Trade, whose members monitored colonial affairs.

Despite these legal reforms, serious obstacles impeded the execution of imperial policy. The customs service did not have enough effective agents in American ports to enforce the Navigation Acts fully, and some men sent from the mother country did more harm than good. Edward Randolph, head of the imperial customs service in New England, was such a person. He was dispatched to Boston in 1676 to gather information about the conduct of colonial trade. New England Puritans did not look kindly on intervention in their affairs, but even considering their irritability, Randolph seems to have been extraordinarily inept. His behavior was so obnoxious, his reports about New Englanders so condescending, that he became the most hated man in late seventeenth-century Massachusetts.

Parliament passed the last major piece of imperial legislation in 1696. Among other things, the statute tightened enforcement procedures, putting pressure specifically on the colonial governors to keep England's competitors out of American ports. The act of 1696 also expanded the American customs service, and for the first time set up vice-admiralty courts in the colonies. This decision eventually rankled the colonists. Established to settle disputes that occured at sea, vice-admiralty courts required neither juries nor oral cross-examination, both traditional elements of the common law. But they were effective and sometimes even popular for resolving maritime questions quickly enough to send the ships to sea again with little delay. The year 1696 witnessed one other significant change in the imperial system. William III replaced the ineffective Lords of Trade with a body of policy advisers that came to be known as the Board of Trade. This group was expected to monitor colonial affairs closely and to provide government officials with the best available advice on commercial and other problems. For several decades at least, it energetically carried out its responsibilities.

The members of Parliament believed these reforms would belatedly compel the colonists to accept the Navigation Acts, and in large measure they were correct. By 1700, American goods transshipped through the mother country accounted for a quarter of *all* English exports, an indication the colonists found it profitable to obey the commercial regulations. In fact, during the eighteenth century, smuggling from Europe to America dried up almost completely.

The Navigation Acts of the seventeenth century also shaped the colonists' material culture. Over time, Americans grew increasingly accustomed to purchasing English goods; they established close ties with specific merchant houses in London, Bristol, or Glasgow. It is not surprising, therefore, that by the mid-eighteenth century the colonists preferred the manufactures of the mother country over those of England's commercial rivals. In other words, the Navigation Acts influenced the development of consumer habits throughout the empire, and it is not an exaggeration to suggest that this regulatory system was in large part responsible for the anglicization of eighteenth-century American culture (see Chapter 4).

POLITICAL UNREST, 1676–1691: COLONIAL GENTRY IN REVOLT

The Navigation Acts created an illusion of unity. English administrators superimposed a system of commercial regulation on a number of different, often unstable American colonies and called it an empire. But these statutes did not remove long-standing differences. Within each society, men and women struggled to bring order out of disorder, to establish stable ruling elites, to diffuse ethnic and racial tensions, and to cope with population pressures that imperial planners only dimly understood. During the final decades of the seventeenth century, these efforts sometimes sparked revolt.

First, the Virginians rebelled, and then a few years later, political violence swept through Maryland, New York, and Massachusetts Bay, England's most populous mainland colonies. Historians once interpreted these events as rehearsals for the American Revolution, or even for Jacksonian Democracy. They perceived these rebels as frontier democrats, rising in protest against an entrenched aristocracy.

Recent research suggests, however, that this view seriously misconstrued the character of these late seventeenth-century rebellions. These uprisings certainly did not involve confrontations between ordinary people and their rulers. Indeed, these events were not in any modern sense of the word ideological. In each colony, the local gentry split into factions, usually the "outs" versus the "ins," and each side proclaimed its political legitimacy.

Civil War in Virginia: Bacon's Rebellion

After 1660, the Virginia economy steadily declined. Returns from tobacco had not been good for some time, and the Navigation Acts reduced profits even further. Into this unhappy environment came thousands of indentured servants, people drawn to Virginia, as the governor explained, "in hope of bettering their condition in a Growing Country."

The reality bore little relation to their dreams. A hurricane destroyed one entire tobacco crop, and in 1667, Dutch warships captured the tobacco fleet just as it was about to sail for England. Indentured servants complained about lack of food and clothing. No wonder that Virginia's governor, Sir William Berkeley, despaired of ever ruling "a People where six parts of seven at least are Poor, Endebted, Discontented and Armed." In 1670, he and the House of Burgesses disfranchised all landless freemen, persons they regarded as troublemakers, but the threat of social violence remained.

Enter Nathaniel Bacon. This ambitious young man arrived in Virginia in 1674. He came from a respectable English family and set himself up immediately as a substantial planter. But he wanted more. Bacon envied the government patronage monopolized by Berkeley's cronies, a group known locally as the "Green Spring" faction. When Bacon attempted to obtain a license to engage in the fur trade, he was rebuffed. This lucrative commerce was reserved for the governor's friends. If Bacon had been willing to wait, he probably would have been accepted into the ruling clique, but as subsequent events would demonstrate, Bacon was not a man of patience.

Events beyond Bacon's control thrust him suddenly into the center of Virginia politics. In 1675, Indians reacting to white encroachment attacked several outlying plantations, killing a few colonists, and Virginians expected the governor to send an army to retaliate. Instead, early in 1676 Berkeley called for the construction of a line of defensive forts, a plan that seemed to the settlers both expensive and ineffective. Indeed, this strategy raised embarrassing questions. Was Berkeley protecting his own fur monopoly? Was he planning to reward his friends with contracts to build useless forts?

While people speculated about such matters, Bacon stepped forward. He boldly offered to lead a volunteer army against the Indians at no cost to the hard-pressed Virginia taxpayers. All he demanded was an official commission from Berkeley giving him military command, and the right to attack other Indians, not just the hostile Susquehannocks. The governor steadfastly refused. With some justification, Berkeley regarded his upstart rival as a fanatic on the subject of Indians. The governor saw no reason to exterminate peaceful tribes simply to avenge the death of a few white settlers.

What followed would have been comic had not so many people died. Bacon thundered against the governor's treachery; Berkeley labeled Bacon a traitor. Both men appealed to the populace for support. On several occasions, Bacon marched his followers to the frontier, but they either failed to find the enemy, or worse, massacred friendly Indians. At one point, Bacon burned Jamestown to the ground, forcing the governor to flee to the colony's Eastern Shore. Bacon's bumbling lieutenants chased Berkeley across Chesapeake Bay only to be captured themselves. Thereupon, the governor mounted a new campaign.

As the civil war dragged on, it became increasingly apparent that Bacon and his gentry supporters had only the vaguest notion of what they were trying to achieve. The members of the planter elite never seemed fully to appreciate that the rank-and-file soldiers, often black slaves and poor white servants, had serious, legitimate grievances against Berkeley's corrupt government, and they were demanding substantial reforms, not just a share in the governor's fur monopoly.

Although women had not been allowed to vote in colony elections, they made their political views clear enough during the rebellion. Some were apparently more violent than others. Sarah Glendon, for example, agitated so aggressively in support of Bacon that Berkeley later refused to grant her a pardon. Another outspoken rebel, Lydia Chiesman, defended her husband before Governor Berkeley, noting that the man would not have joined Bacon's forces had she not persuaded him to do so. "Therefore," Lydia Chiesman concluded, ". . . since what her husband had done, was by her meanes, and so, by consequence, she most guilty, that she might be hanged and he pardoned."

When Charles II learned of the fighting in Virginia, he dispatched a thousand regular soldiers to Jamestown. By the time they arrived, Berkeley had regained full control over the colony's government. In October 1676, Bacon died after a brief illness, and within a few months, his band of rebel followers had dispersed.

Berkeley, now an old and embittered man, was recalled to England in 1677. His successors, especially Lord Culpeper (1680–1683) and Lord Howard of Effingham (1683–1689), seemed interested primarily in enriching themselves at the expense of the Virginia planters. Their self-serving policies, coupled with the memory of near anarchy, helped heal divisions within the Virginia ruling class. For almost a century, in fact, the local gentry formed a united front against greedy royal appointees.

The Glorious Revolution in the Bay Colony

During John Winthrop's lifetime, Massachusetts settlers developed an inflated sense of their independence from the mother country. After 1660, however, it became difficult even to pretend that the Puritan colony was a separate state. Royal officials like Edward Randolph demanded full compliance with the Navigation Acts. Moreover, the growth of commerce attracted new merchants to the Bay Colony, men who were Anglicans rather than Congregationalists and who maintained close business contacts in London. These persons complained loudly of Puritan intolerance. The Anglican faction was never large, but its presence, coupled with Randolph's unceasing demands, divided Bay leaders. A few Puritan ministers and magistrates regarded compromise with England as treason, a breaking of the Lord's covenant. Other spokesmen, recognizing the changing political realities within the empire, urged a more moderate course.

In 1675, in the midst of this ongoing political crisis, the Indians dealt the New Englanders a terrible setback. Metacomet, a Wampanoag chief the whites called King Philip, declared war against the colonists. The powerful Narragansetts, whose lands the settlers had long coveted, joined Metacomet, and in little more than a year of fighting, the Indians destroyed scores of frontier villages, killed hundreds of colonists, and disrupted the entire regional economy. More than one thousand Indians and New Englanders died in the conflict. The war left the people of Massachusetts deeply in debt and more than ever uncertain of their future. As in other parts of colonial America, the defeated Indians were forced off their lands, compelled by events to become either refugees or economically marginal figures in white society.

In 1684, the debate over the Bay Colony's relation to the mother country ended abruptly. The Court of Chancery, sitting in London and acting on a petition from the king, annulled the charter of the Massachusetts Bay Company. In one stroke of a pen, the patent that Winthrop had so lovingly carried to America in 1630, the founda-

Metacomet, the Wampanoag chief, also known as King Philip, led Native Americans in a major war designed to remove the Europeans from New England.

tion for a "city on a hill," was gone. The decision forced the most stubborn Puritans to recognize they were part of an empire run by people who did not share their particular religious vision.

James II, a monarch who disliked representative institutions—after all, Parliament, a representative assembly, had executed his father, Charles I—decided to restructure the government of the entire region in the Dominion of New England. In various stages from 1686 to 1689, the Dominion incorporated Massachusetts, Connecticut, Rhode Island, Plymouth, New York, New Jersey, and New Hampshire under a single appointed royal governor. For this demanding position, James selected Sir Edmund Andros (pronounced Andrews), a military veteran of tyrannical temperament. Andros arrived in Boston in 1686, and within a matter of months he had alienated every-

William II and Mary II, joint monarchs of England after the Glorious Revolution of 1688. Mary ascended the throne when her father, James II, was deposed. Her husband William ruled Holland before ascending the English throne.

one: Puritans, moderates, and even Anglican merchants. Not only did Andros abolish elective assemblies, but he also enforced the Navigation Acts with such rigor that he brought about commercial depression. Andros declared normal town meetings illegal, collected taxes the people never approved, and packed the courts with strangers who detested the local population. Eighteenth-century historian and governor Thomas Hutchinson compared Andros unfavorably with the Roman tyrant Nero.

Early in 1689, news of the Glorious Revolution reached Boston. The previous fall, the ruling class of England had deposed James II, an admitted Catholic, and placed his daughter Mary and her husband, William of Orange, on the throne as joint monarchs (see the chart of the Stuart monarchs on p. 33). As part of the settlement, William and Mary accepted a Bill of Rights, a document stipulating the constitutional rights of all Englishmen. Almost immediately the Bay Colonists overthrew the hated Andros regime. The New England version of the Glorious Revolution

(April 18, 1689) was so popular that no one came to the governor's defense. Andros was jailed without a single shot having been fired. According to Cotton Mather, a leading Congregational minister, the colonists were united by the "most *Unanimous Resolution* perhaps that was ever known to have Inspir'd any people."

However united as they may have been, the Bay Colonists could not take the Crown's support for granted. William III could have declared the New Englanders rebels and summarily reinstated Andros. But thanks largely to the tireless efforts of Increase Mather, Cotton's father, who pleaded the colonists' case in London, William abandoned the Dominion of New England, and in 1691, Massachusetts received a new royal charter. This document differed substantially from the company patent of 1629. The freemen no longer selected their governor. The choice now belonged to the king. Membership in the General Court was determined by annual election, and these representatives in turn chose the men who sat in the council or upper house, subject always to the governor's veto. Moreover, the franchise, restricted here as in other colonies to adult males, was determined on the basis of personal property rather than church membership, a change that brought Massachusetts into conformity with general English practice. On the local level, town government remained much as it had been in Winthrop's time.

Contagion of Witchcraft

The instability of the Massachusetts government following Andros's arrest—what Reverend Samuel Willard described as "the short *Anarchy* accompanying our late Revolution"—allowed what under normal political conditions would have been an isolated, though ugly, local incident to expand into a major colonial crisis. Hysterical men and women living in Salem Village, a small unprosperous farming community, nearly overwhelmed the new rulers of Massachusetts Bay. Accusations of witchcraft were not uncommon in seventeenth-century New England. Puritans believed an individual might make a compact with the devil, but during the first decades of settlement, authorities executed only about fifteen alleged witches. Sometimes villagers simply left suspected witches alone. Never before had fears of witchcraft plunged an entire community into panic.

The terror in Salem Village began in late 1691, when several adolescent girls began to behave in strange ways. They cried out for no apparent reason; they twitched on the ground. When concerned neighbors asked what caused their suffering, the girls announced they were victims of witches, seemingly innocent persons who lived in the community. The arrest of several alleged witches did not relieve the girls' "fits," nor did prayer solve the problem. Additional accusations were made, and at least one person confessed, providing a frightening description of the devil as "a thing all over hairy, all the face hairy, and a long nose." In June 1692, a special court convened and began to send men and women to the gallows. By the end of the summer, the court had hanged nineteen people; another was pressed to death. Many more suspects awaited trial.

Then suddenly, the storm was over. Led by Increase Mather, a group of prominent Congregational ministers belatedly urged leniency and restraint. Especially troubling to the clergymen was the court's decision to accept "spectral evidence," that is, reports of dreams and visions in which the accused appeared as the devil's agent. Worried about convicting people on such dubious testimony, Mather declared, "It were better that ten suspected witches should escape, than that one innocent person should be condemned." The colonial government accepted the ministers' advice and convened a new court, which promptly acquitted, pardoned, or released the remaining suspects. After the Salem nightmare, witchcraft ceased to be a capital offense.

No one knows exactly what sparked the terror in Salem Village. The community had a history of religious discord, and during the 1680s, the people split into angry factions over the choice of a minister. Economic tensions played a part as well. Poorer, more traditional farmers accused members of prosperous, commercially oriented families of being witches. The underlying misogyny of the entire culture meant the victims were more often women than men. Whatever the ultimate social and psychological sources of this event may have been, jealousy and bitterness apparently festered to the point that adolescent girls who normally would have been disciplined were allowed to incite judicial murder. As so often happens in incidents like this one—the McCarthy hearings of the 1950s, for example—the accusers later came to their senses and apologized to the survivors for the needless suffering they had inflicted on the community. (For further discussion of the Salem witchcraft trials, see the essay "Witches and the Law," pp. 90–95.)

The Glorious Revolution in New York and Maryland

The Glorious Revolution in New York was more violent than it had been in Massachusetts Bay. Divisions within New York's ruling class ran deep and involved ethnic as well as religious differences. English newcomers and powerful Anglo-Dutch families who had recently risen to commercial prominence in New York City opposed the older Dutch elite.

Much like Nathaniel Bacon, Jacob Leisler was a man entangled in events beyond his control. Leisler, the son of a German minister, emigrated to New York in 1660, and through marriage

The publication of Cotton Mather's Memorable Providences, Relating to Witchcrafts and Possessions *(1689) contributed to the hysteria that resulted in the Salem witchcraft trials of the 1690s, but he did not take part in the trials. He is shown here surrounded by some of the forms a demon assumed in the "documented" case of an English family besieged by witches.*

aligned himself with the Dutch elite. While he achieved moderate prosperity as a merchant, Leisler resented the success of the Anglo-Dutch.

When news of the Glorious Revolution reached New York City in May 1689, Leisler raised a group of militiamen and seized the local fort in the name of William and Mary. He apparently expected an outpouring of popular support, but it was not forthcoming. His rivals waited, watching while Leisler desperately attempted to legitimize his actions. Through bluff and badgering, Leisler managed to hold the colony together, especially after French forces burned Schenectady (February 1690), but he never established a secure political base.

In March 1691, a new royal governor, Henry Sloughter, reached New York. He ordered Leisler to surrender his authority, but when Sloughter refused to prove he had been sent by William rather than by the deposed James, Leisler hesitated. The pause cost Leisler his life. Sloughter declared Leisler a rebel, and in a hasty trial, a court sentenced him and his chief lieutenant, Jacob Milbourne, to be hanged "by the Neck and being Alive their bodyes be Cutt downe to Earth and Their Bowells to be taken out and they being Alive, burnt before their faces. . . ." In 1695, Parliament officially pardoned Leisler, but he not being "Alive," the decision arrived a bit late. Long after his death, political factions calling themselves Leislerians and Anti-Leislerians struggled to dominate New York government. Indeed, in no other eighteenth-century colony was the level of bitter political rivalry so high.

During the last third of the seventeenth century, the colony of Maryland stumbled from one political crisis to another. Protestants in the colony's lower house resisted Lord Baltimore's Catholic friends in the upper house or council. When news of James's overthrow reached Maryland early in 1689, pent-up antiproprietary and anti-Catholic sentiment exploded. John

Coode, a member of the assembly and an outspoken Protestant, formed a group called the Protestant Association, which in August forced Baltimore's governor, William Joseph, to resign.

Coode avoided Leisler's fatal mistakes. The Protestant Association, citing many wrongs suffered at the hands of local Catholics, petitioned the Crown to transform Maryland into a royal colony. After reviewing the case, William accepted Coode's explanation, and in 1691, the king dispatched a royal governor to Maryland. A new assembly dominated by Protestants declared Anglicanism the established religion. Catholics

were excluded from public office on the grounds they might be in league with French Catholics in Canada. Lord Baltimore lost control of the colony's government, but he and his family did retain title to Maryland's undistributed lands. In 1715, the Crown restored to full proprietorship the fourth Lord Baltimore, who had been raised a member of the Church of England, and Maryland remained in the hands of the Calvert family until 1776.

COMMON EXPERIENCES, SEPARATE CULTURES

"It is no little Blessing of God," Cotton Mather announced proudly in 1700, "that we are part of the *English* nation." A half century earlier, John Winthrop would not have spoken these words, at least not with such enthusiasm. The two men were, of course, products of different political cultures. It was not so much that the character of Massachusetts society had changed. In fact, the Puritan families of 1700 were much like those of the founding generation. Rather, the difference was in England's attitude toward the colonies. Rulers living more than 3,000 miles away now made political and economic demands that Mather's contemporaries could not ignore.

The creation of a new imperial system did not, however, erase profound sectional differences. By 1700, for example, the Chesapeake colonies were more, not less, committed to the cultivation of tobacco and slave labor. Although the separate regions were being pulled slowly into England's commercial orbit, they did not have much to do with each other. The elements that sparked a powerful sense of nationalism among colonists dispersed over a huge territory would not be evident for a very long time. It would be a mistake, therefore, to anticipate the coming of the American Revolution.

Recommended Reading

The best account of the way seventeenth-century New Englanders thought about the family remains Edmund S. Morgan, *The Puritan Family* (1956). One should complement this book with one of the fine demography studies of a New England town. Philip J. Greven's *Four Generations* (1970) provides an excellent introduction to the field. Morgan has also produced a masterful analysis of development of early Chesapeake society.

His *American Slavery, American Freedom: The Ordeal of Colonial Virginia* (1975) examines the impact of an extraordinarily high death rate upon an evolving triracial plantation society. Anyone interested in the history of slavery in early America would do well to start with Winthrop D. Jordan, *White over Black: American Attitudes Toward the Negro, 1550–1812* (1968) and David B. Davis, *The Problem of Slavery in Western Culture* (1966). A complete discussion of the drafting of the Navigation Acts and England's efforts to enforce them can be found in C. M. Andrews, *The Colonial Period of American History*, vol. 4 (1938). David S. Lovejoy provides a comprehensive survey of the various late seventeenth-century colonial rebellions in *The Glorious Revolution in America* (1972). Perhaps the most readable biography of a leading figure from this period is Kenneth Silverman, *The Life and Times of Cotton Mather* (1984).

Additional Bibliography

The historical literature dealing with early New England is vast. The religious culture is explored in C. Hambrick-Stowe, *Practice of Piety* (1982), D. D. Hall, *Worlds of Wonder; Days of Judgment* (1989); and Patricia U. Bonomi, *Under the Cope of Heaven: Religion, Society, and Politics in Colonial America* (1986). There is no completely satisfactory examination of daily life in the other northern colonies, but James T. Lemon's *Best Poor Man's Country* (1972) is a valuable investigation of the rural economy of early Pennsylvania. Also see Barry Levy, *Quakers and the American Family: British Settlement in the Delaware Valley* (1988) and Joan Jensen, *Loosening the Bonds: Mid-Atlantic Farm Women, 1750–1850* (1986).

The dynamics of gender definition in colonial society is imaginatively explored in Laurel T. Ulrich, *Good Wives: Image and Reality in the Lives of Women in Northern New England 1650–1750* (1982). The best single discussion of colonial women in the Chesapeake is Lois G. Carr and Lorena S. Walsh, "The Planter's Wife: The Experience of White Women in Seventeenth-Century Maryland," *William and Mary Quarterly*, 3rd ser., 34 (1977): 542–571. Julia C. Spruill's *Women's Life and Work in the Southern Colonies* (1938) remains a valuable study.

Education and literacy are examined from different perspectives in James Axtell, *The School upon A Hill* (1974); and Kenneth Lockridge, *Literacy in Colonial New England* (1974).

Various aspects of the development of colonial society in the South are explored in three splendid essay collections: T. Tate and D. L. Ammerman, eds., *The Chesapeake in the Seventeenth Century* (1979); A. C. Land et al., eds., *Law, Society, and Politics in Early Maryland* (1977); and Lois Carr et al., eds., *Colonial Chesapeake Society* (1988). Anyone interested in the sociopolitical history of Virginia should read Bernard Bailyn, "Politics and Social Structure in Virginia," in J. M. Smith, ed., *Seventeenth-Century America* (1959). In *Colonists in Bondage* (1947), A. E. Smith discusses indentured servitude; one should also see David W. Galenson, *White Servitude in Colonial America: An Economic Analysis* (1981). In *Puritans and Adventurers* (1980), T. H. Breen speculates on the cultural values of early Virginians and compares them with those of the New Englanders. A quite different treatment of the same general theme can be found in Jack P. Greene, *Pursuits of Happiness* (1988). A pioneering study of a Virginia community is Darrett B. Rutman and Anita H. Rutman, *A Place in Time: Middlesex County, Virginia, 1650–1750* (1984).

The African American experience has been the topic of several recent interdisciplinary studies of very high quality: Philip D. Curtin, *The Atlantic Slave Trade: A Census* (1969); Patrick Manning, *Slavery and African Life* (1990); Peter Wood, *Black Majority* (1974); Allan Kulikoff, *Tobacco and Slaves: The Development of Southern Cultures in the Chesapeake, 1680–1800* (1986); Mechal Sobel, *The World They Made Together: Black and White Values in Eighteenth-Century Virginia* (1987). The creation of a free black community in early Virginia is the focus of T. H. Breen and Stephen Innes, *"Myne Owne Ground," Race and Freedom on Virginia's Eastern Shore* (1980).

Several good studies of the rebellions in specific colonies are available: W. Washburn, *The Governor and the Rebel* (1957) on Bacon's Rebellion; Thomas J. Archdeacon, *New York City, 1664–1710* (1976) on Leisler's Rebellion; and Lois Carr and D. W. Jordan, *Maryland's Revolution of Government* (1974) on Coode's Uprising. On King Philip's War, the fullest account is Douglas Leach, *Flintlock and Tomahawk* (1958). Of the many studies of witchcraft in seventeenth-century New England, some of the more imaginative are Paul Boyer and Stephen Nissenbaum, *Salem Possessed* (1974); John Demos, *Entertaining Satan: Witchcraft and the Culture of Early New England* (1982); Carol F. Karlsen, *The Devil in the Shape of a Woman: Witchcraft in Colonial New England* (1987); Richard Godbeer, *The Devil's Dominion* (1992); and Richard P. Gildrie, *The Profane, the Civil, and the Godly* (1994).

LAW & SOCIETY I

Witches and the Law

A Problem of Evidence in 1692

The events that occurred at Salem Village in 1692 still haunt modern memory. In popular American culture the incident has come to represent our worst nightmare—a community-sanctioned witch hunt that ferrets out deviants in the name of law. What seems most unsettling about the incident is the failure of allegedly good men and women to bear witness against judicial terror. The ordeal of Salem Village links a distant colonial past with the infamous McCarthy hearings of the 1950s as well as other, more recent witch hunts. The story of this deeply troubled town challenges us to confront the possibility that we, too, might allow law and authority to become instruments of injustice.

Our challenge is how best to interpret the Salem trials. It would be easy to insist that Puritan magistrates were gross hypocrites, figures who consciously manipulated the law for their own hateful purposes. But such conclusions are simplistic; they fail to place the Salem nightmare in proper historical context. The participants in this intense social drama acted on a complex set of seventeenth-century assumptions—legal, religious, and scientific—and if judges and jurors wronged innocent people, they did so by the standards of a society very different from our own.

Few New Englanders doubted the existence of witches. For centuries European communities had identified certain persons as agents of the Devil, and when the Puritans migrated to America, they carried these beliefs with them. They recognized no conflict between rational religion and the possible existence of a satanic world populated by witches. Ordinary farmers regarded unusual events—the strange death of a farm animal, for example—as evidence of witchcraft. New England's intellectual leaders sustained popular superstition in impressive scientific publications. In his *Memorable Providences, Relating to*

Witchcrafts and Possessions (1689), the Reverend Cotton Mather declared, "I am resolv'd . . . never to use . . . one grain of patience with any man that shall . . . impose upon me a Denial of Devils, or of Witches. I shall . . . count him down-right Impudent if he Assert the Non-Existence of things which we have had such palpable Convictions of."

Colonial New Englanders did more than talk and write about witches; as early as 1647 they executed several. Before the Salem outbreak, ninety-one people had been tried for witchcraft in Massachusetts and Connecticut, and eighteen of them were hanged (not burned as some historians have claimed). In addition, hundreds of people had accused neighbors of witchcraft but for many reasons—usually lack of convincing evidence—they stopped short of taking such disputes before the court. These were isolated incidents. Before 1692 fear of witches had not sparked mass hysteria.

Salem Village was different. In this instance charges of witchcraft shattered a community already deeply divided against itself. The predominantly agricultural Salem Village lay a few miles up the Ipswich Road from the bustling commercial port of Salem Town. The farmers of the Village envied their neighbors' prosperity. Even more, they resented the control that Town authorities exerted over the Village church and government. This tension found expression in numerous personal and family rivalries. In 1689, the congregation at Salem Village ordained the Reverend Samuel Parris, a troubled figure who provoked "disquietness" and "restlessness" and who fanned the factionalism that had long plagued the community.

The witchcraft crisis began suddenly in mid-January of 1692 when two girls in the Parris household experienced violent convulsions and frightening visions. A local physician examined the afflicted children but found no "natural" cause for their condition. Soon anxious families raised the possibility of witchcraft, a move which set off a storm of accusations that did not abate until October. By that time, 19 people had died and over 150 prisoners still awaited trial.

Although the witch hysteria affected everyone—men and women, rich and poor, farmers and merchants—the accusers and their targets were not evenly distributed among the population of Salem Village. Twenty of the thirty-four persons who claimed to have been bewitched were girls between the ages of eleven and twenty. Women a full generation older than the accusers were most likely to be identified as witches; over 40 percent of the accused fell into this category. Although men and women from many different backgrounds were accused, one widely shared characteristic was a history of socially unacceptable behavior. Sarah Good, for example, smoked a pipe and was known for cursing her enemies. John Aldin's accusers described him as "a bold fellow . . . who lies with Indian squaws . . . [and stands] with his hat on before the judges." Bridget Bishop ran a scandalous tavern and dressed in a particularly flashy, immodest manner. Those who testified against the supposed witches came from all classes, both genders, and every age group. Indeed, virtually the entire community was drawn into the ugly business of charge and countercharge, fear and betrayal.

No contemporary illustrations of the Salem witchcraft trials exist, but this recreation depicts the wife of Giles Corey standing in the dock as her accuser brings the charge of witchcraft against her.

New England's intellectual leaders—most of them Harvard-educated clergymen—tried to make sense out of reports coming out of Salem. Since the colonies did not yet have a newspaper, the reflections of these prominent figures significantly shaped how the entire society interpreted the frightening events of 1692. During the spring of that year, accusations of witchcraft mounted while magistrates interrogated everyone touched by the contagion.

Arriving from England in mid-May at the height of the witch hunt, the new royal governor of Massachusetts Bay, William Phips, appointed a special court of law (a court of "oyer and terminer") to try the cases at Salem Village. The seven judges he appointed all had previous experience in the colony's law courts. Phips wanted the trials to be as fair as possible and procedurally correct. A proper jury was impaneled. Despite precautions, however, the court itself soon succumbed to the frenzy. Chief judge and deputy governor William Stoughton, for example, staunchly believed the girls had been bewitched, and he had little doubt that "real" witches were responsible for the trouble at Salem Village. By contrast, Nathaniel Saltonstall was highly skeptical of the witchcraft charges. After witnessing the first round of executions, Saltonstall resigned from the court and turned to alcohol to persuade himself the court had not made a terrible mistake. Although the judges and jury may have felt ambivalent about what was happening, the law stated that persons convicted as witches must die.

Everything turned on evidence. Confession offered the most reliable proof of witchcraft, and it occurred surprisingly often. We will never know what compelled people to confess. Some may have actually believed they had cast spells on their neighbors or had foretold the future. Many women, though believing themselves innocent, may have confessed because of guilt for impure thoughts that they had privately entertained. Perhaps the psychological strain of imprisonment, coupled with intense social scrutiny, convinced them they might have unwittingly entered into a contract with the Devil. Regardless, the stories they told undoubtedly mortified those who heard them and fueled the growing frenzy. Imagine the reaction to Ann Foster's July 18 confession:

> *Ann Foster . . . confessed that the devil in the shape of a black man appeared to*

Increase Mather.

ly had a "witch's teat," usually a flap of skin located anywhere on the body, from which they gave suck to the Devil. The judges subjected almost every defendant to a humiliating physical examination in order to find such biological abnormalities. Witches could also be discovered by having them touch a girl in the midst of her torments. If the girl's fits ceased, then the person who touched her was assumed responsible for her agony. Since this form of evidence was immediately observable, judges relied on it heavily, oftentimes parading accused witches before the possessed girls waiting to see whose touch would calm them.

Had the terrible ordeal turned solely on unsightly warts, the trials might have ended without further note. But that did not happen. The judges allowed the jury to entertain a different sort of evidence, *spectral evidence*, and it was this material that hanged people at Salem Village. New Englanders believed that witches worked by dispatching a specter, a phantom spirit, to torment their victims. This meant that witches had power over great distances; they were invisible. They entered people's dreams, and dozens of good New Englanders complained of having been bitten, pinched, or even choked by specters that looked a lot like their neighbors. The judges regularly accepted spectral testimony of the sort offered by the eighteen-year-old John Cook.

her with [Martha] Carrier about six yeare since when they made her a witch and that she promised to serve the devill two years: upon which the Devill promised her prosperity and many things but never performed it, that she and Martha Carrier did both ride on a stick or pole when they went to the witch meeting at Salem Village and that the stick broak: as they were carried in the air above the tops of the trees and they fell but she did hang fast about the neck of [Martha] Carrier and were presently at the village, . . . she further saith that she heard some of the witches say that there was three hundred and five in the whole Country and that they would ruin that place the Village . . .

Most of the accused did not confess, however, forcing the judges to produce tangible evidence of witchcraft. The charge was difficult because the crime of bewitchment was, by nature, an invisible act. Earthly laws and magistrates had difficulty dealing with crimes that occurred in the spiritual world. In this situation, the beleaguered judges used a few customary tests. All witches supposed-

. . . one morning about sun rising as I was in bed . . . I saw [Bridget] Bishop . . . Standing in the chamber by the window and she looked on me & . . . presently struck me on the Side of the head w'ch did very much hurt me & then I Saw her goe Out under the End window at a little Creviss about So bigg as I Could thrust my hand into. I Saw her again the Same day . . . walke & Cross the roome & having at the time an apple in my hand it flew Out of my hand into my mothers lapp who stood Six or Eight foot distance from me & then She disappeared & though my mother & Severall others were in the Same room yet they affirmed they Saw her not.

As far as the witch hunters were concerned, Bridget Bishop had been caught in the act. To the

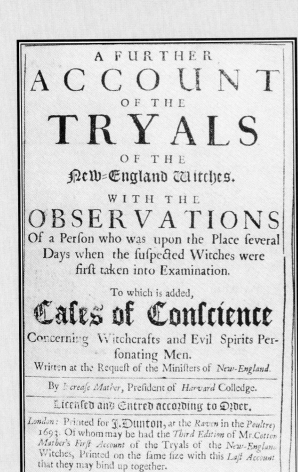

A FURTHER
ACCOUNT
OF THE
TRYALS
OF THE
New-England Witches.

WITH THE
OBSERVATIONS
Of a Person who was upon the Place several
Days when the suspected Witches were
first taken into Examination.

To which is added,
Cases of Conscience
Concerning Witchcrafts and Evil Spirits Per-
sonating Men.
Written at the Request of the Ministers of New-England.

By Increase Mather, President of Harvard Colledge.

Licensed and Entred according to Order.

London: Printed for J. Dunton, at the Raven in the Poultrey
1693. Of whom may be had the Third Edition of Mr.Cotton
Mather's First Account of the Tryals of the New-England
Witches, Printed on the same size with this Last Account
that they may bind up together.

Title page of A Further Account of the Tryals of the New England Witches (1693), *Increase Mather's reflection on the incidents at Salem Village. Mather's* Cases of Conscience Concerning Witchcrafts and Evil Spirits *is credited with helping end the witchcraft executions in Salem.*

modern observer, however, the problems with this kind of evidence seem obvious. First, how could one tell if Cook was lying? The power of his story lay in its inability to be corroborated, for one could never check the authenticity of an intensely private dream or vision. The second problem was that persons accused of being witches had no defense against spectral testimony. When Captain John Aldin stood before his accusers, for example, they immediately fell to the ground, writhing in pain. When asked why he tormented the girls Aldin firmly denied any wrongdoing, inquiring why the judges "suppose[d he had] no better things to do than to come to Salem to afflict these persons that I never knew or saw before?" Aldin's defense did not

carry much weight when set against the testimony of the suffering girls, and rather than conclude the accusers manifested a "lying spirit," the judges admitted all spectral evidence as incontestable proof of witchcraft.

Very early in the trials, a few people expressed doubts about the reliability of this particular form of evidence. Cotton Mather and other ministers, for example, issued a statement urging the judges to use spectral evidence with "a very critical and exquisite caution." Some feared the Devil could assume the shape of innocent people. If this was the case, then the visions of the afflicted proved nothing but the Devil's ability to deceive humans. In the absence of spectral evidence, the cases against most of the witches boiled down to little more than long-standing complaints against obnoxious neighbors. The fury of prosecution silenced these skeptical voices, however, and when the trials resumed in late June, chief judge William Stoughton continued to accept dreams and visions as proof of witchcraft.

Fantastic testimony about flying witches and pinching specters lent an almost circuslike air to the proceedings at Salem. Before the judges and the members of the jury, the afflicted girls would fall to the ground, convulsing and screaming, claiming to see witches that remained invisible to the court. Hundreds of spectators sat horrified as Satan caused suffering before their own eyes. For seventeenth-century New Englanders who felt the presence of the spiritual world in their everyday lives, the courtroom at Salem offered the opportunity to witness the struggle between the forces of darkness and light. Because of the gravity of the situation, no one expected the judges to deal lightly with those who had sworn allegiance to the Devil. Indeed, in the interest of obtaining a confession, the judges conducted harsh interrogations, usually assuming the guilt of the defendant. The intense psychological pressure inflicted on the defendants is revealed in the questioning of Sarah Good, a woman subsequently hanged as a witch.

JUDGE. *Sarah Good, what evil spirit have you familiarity with?*

GOOD. *None.*

JUDGE. *Why do you hurt these children?*

GOOD. *I do not hurt them. I scorn it.*

JUDGE. *Who do you employ then to do it?*

GOOD. *I employ nobody.*

JUDGE. *Have you made a contract with the devil?*

GOOD. *No.*

JUDGE. *Sarah Good . . . why do you not tell us the truth? Why do you thus torment these poor children?*

GOOD. *I do not torment them.*

Even the ministers who advised caution applauded the judges' "assiduous endeavors" and encouraged the "vigorous prosecution" of the witches. As the witch hysteria gained momentum, few people dared to defend the witches for fear of being accused themselves. The humble pleas of those who genuinely thought themselves innocent fell on the deaf ears of a community convinced of its own righteousness.

By late September, with nineteen people already executed, the emotional intensity that had sustained the witch hunt in its early stages began to ebb. For one thing, the accusations spun wildly out of control as the afflicted girls began naming unlikely candidates as witches: prominent ministers, a judge's mother-in-law, and even the governor's wife! Such accusations discredited the entire procedure by which the witches had been discovered. Also, although the jails could barely hold the 150 people still awaiting trial, the accusations kept coming. The terror was feeding on itself.

In mid-October, Governor Phips dismissed the original court and appointed a new one, this time barring spectral evidence. All remaining defendants were quickly acquitted although, curiously enough, three women still confessed to having practiced witchcraft. Phips explained his decision to end the trials in a letter to the king, claiming "the people" had become "dissatisfied and disturbed." Men and women who had been so eager to purify the community of evil, to murder neighbors in the name of a higher good, now spoke of their fear of divine retribution. Perhaps the dying words of Sarah Good, uttered in response to the assistant minister of Salem Town, echoed in their ears: "I am no more a witch than you are a wizard, and if you take away my life, God will give you blood to drink."

Soon after the trials ended, the witch hunters quickly turned confessors. In 1706, Ann Putnam, one of the most prolific accusers, publicly asked for forgiveness: "I desire to be humbled before

God. . . . It was a great delusion of Satan that deceived me in that time." Nine years earlier, the Salem jurors had issued a similar statement, asking the community to understand the particular pressures that compelled them to convict so many people:

> We confess that we . . . were not capable to understand, nor able to withstand the mysterious delusions of the Powers of Darkness. . . ; but were for want of Knowledge in our selves, and better Information from others, prevailed with to take up with such Evidence against the Accused, as on further consideration, and better Information, we justly fear was insufficient for the touching the Lives of any . . . whereby we fear we have been instrumental with others, tho Ignorantly and unwittingly, to bring upon our selves, and this People of the Lord, the Guilt of Innocent Blood.

The state never again executed citizens for witchcraft. The experience at Salem had taught New Englanders that, although witches may have existed, no human court could identify a witch beyond a reasonable doubt. The Reverend Increase Mather summed up the attitude of a post-Salem New England: "It were better that ten suspected witches should escape than that one innocent person should be condemned."

What triggered the tragic events of 1692 remains a mystery. Some historians view the witch hunt as a manifestation of Salem Village's socioeconomic troubles. This interpretation helps explain why the primary accusers came from the agrarian village while the alleged witches either resided in or were somehow connected to the market-oriented town. Perhaps the charge of witchcraft masked a deep resentment for their neighbors' monetary success and the new set of values that accompanied the market economy. Other historians believe the witch hunt reflected a deep ambivalence about gender roles in New England society. Young girls lashed out at older nonconforming women because they symbolized a freedom that was achievable within New England society, yet vehemently criticized. Facing the choice between becoming their husbands' servants or being free, the accusers may have expressed this cultural frustration in lethal ways. These and many other factors contributed to the witch phenomenon.

Regardless of which interpretation one favors, however, one must acknowledge that Salem Village had indeed been possessed. The blame rests on the community as a whole, not just on a few vindictive judges. In 1697, another repentant witch hunter, the Reverend John Hale, tried to explain how well-meaning people had caused such harm:

> I am abundantly satisfyed that those who were most concerned to act and judge in those matters, did not willingly depart from the rules of righteousness. But such was the darkness of that day, . . . that we walked in the clouds, and could not see our way.

Hale's words ring hollow. They came a little too late to do much good. As other communities have learned, it is easier to apologize after the fact than to stand up courageously against the first injustice.

Frontiers of Empire
Eighteenth-Century America

illiam Byrd II (1674–1744) was a type of English-American that one would not have encountered during the earliest years of settlement. This successful Tidewater planter was a product of a new, more cosmopolitan environment, and as an adult, Byrd seemed as much at home in London as in his native Virginia. In 1728, at the height of his political influence in Williamsburg, the capital of colonial Virginia, Byrd accepted a commission to help survey a disputed boundary between North Carolina and Virginia. During his long journey into the distant backcountry, Byrd kept a detailed journal, a satiric, often bawdy chronicle of daily events that is now regarded as a classic of early American literature.

On his trip into the wilderness, Byrd met many different people. No sooner had he departed a familiar world of tobacco plantations than he came across a self-styled "Hermit," an Englishman who apparently preferred the freedom of the woods to the constraints of society. "He has no other Habitation but a green Bower or Harbour," Byrd reported, "with a Female Domestick as wild & as dirty as himself."

As the boundary commissioners pushed further into the backcountry, they encountered highly independent men and women of European descent, small frontier families that Byrd regarded as living no better than savages. He attributed their uncivilized behavior to a diet of too much pork. "The Truth of it is, these People live so much upon Swine's flesh . . . [that it] makes them . . . extremely hoggish in their Temper, & many of them seem to Grunt rather than Speak in their ordinary conversation." The wilderness journey also brought Byrd's party of surveyors into regular contact with Native Americans, whom he properly distinguished as Catawabas, Tuscaroras, Usherees, and Sapponis.

Byrd's journal invites us to view the eighteenth-century backcountry from a fresh perspective. It was not a vast empty territory awaiting the arrival of European settlers. Maps often sustain this erroneous impression. They depict cities and towns, farms and plantations clustered along the Atlantic Coast; they suggest a "line of settlement" steadily pushing outward into a huge blank area with no mark of civilization. The people Byrd met on his journey into the backcountry

would not have understood such maps. After all, the empty space on the maps was their home. They experienced the frontier as a populous multicultural zone stretching from the English and French settlements in the north all the way to the Spanish borderlands in the far southwest.

The point is not to discount the significance of the older Atlantic settlements. During the eighteenth century, Britain's thirteen colonies underwent a profound transformation. The population in the colonies grew at unprecedented rates. German and Scotch-Irish immigrants arrived in huge numbers. So too did African slaves.

Wherever they lived, colonial Americans of this period found they were not as isolated from each other as they had been during most of the seventeenth century. Indeed, after 1690, men and women expanded their cultural horizons, becoming part of a larger Anglo-American world. The change was striking. Colonists whose parents or grandparents had come to the New World to confront a "howling wilderness" now purchased imported European manufactures, read English

William Byrd II. Byrd's History of the Dividing Line Run in the Year 1728 *contains a marvelously satirical account of a survey of the Virginia–North Carolina boundary.*

journals, participated in imperial wars, and sought favors from a growing number of resident royal officials. No one—not even the inhabitants of the distant frontiers—could escape the influence of Britain. The cultural, economic, and political links connecting the colonists to the imperial center in London grew stronger with time.

This surprising development raises a difficult question for the modern historian. If the eighteenth-century colonists were so powerfully attracted to Great Britain, then why did they ever declare independence? The answer may well be that as the colonists became more British, they inevitably became more American as well. This was a development of major significance, for it helps to explain the appearance after mid-century of genuine nationalist sentiment. Political, commercial, and military links that brought the colonists into more frequent contact with Great Britain also made them more aware of other colonists. It was within an expanding, prosperous empire that they first began seriously to consider what it meant to be American.

EXPANDING EMPIRE

The phenomenal growth of British America during the eighteenth century amazed Benjamin Franklin, one of the first persons to bring scientific rigor to the study of demography. The population of the English colonies doubled approximately every twenty-five years, and according to calculations Franklin made in 1751, if the expansion continued at such an extraordinary rate for another century or so, "the greatest Number of Englishmen will be on this Side [of] the water." Not only was the total population increasing at a very rapid rate, it also was becoming more dispersed and heterogeneous. Each year witnessed the arrival of thousands of non-English Europeans, most of whom soon moved to the backcountry of Pennsylvania and the Southern Colonies.

Accurate population data from the colonial period are extremely difficult to find. The first national census did not occur until 1790. Still, various sources surviving from prerevolutionary times indicate quite clearly that the total white population of Britain's thirteen mainland colonies

Estimated Population, 1720–1760				
		New England Colonies	Middle Colonies	Southern Colonies
1720	White	166,937	92,259	138,110
	Black	3,956	10,825	54,098
1730	White	211,233	135,298	191,893
	Black	6,118	11,683	73,220
1740	White	281,163	204,093	270,283
	Black	8,541	16,452	125,031
1750	White	349,029	275,723	309,588
	Black	10,982	20,736	204,702
1760	White	436,917	398,855	432,047
	Black	12,717	29,049	284,040

New England Colonies New Hampshire, Massachusetts, Rhode Island, and Connecticut

Middle Colonies New York, New Jersey, Pennsylvania, and Delaware

Southern Colonies Maryland, Virginia, North Carolina, South Carolina, and (after 1740) Georgia

Source: From *The American Colonies* by R. C. Simmons. Copyright © 1976 by R. C. Simmons. Reprinted by permission of Harold Matson Company, Inc.

rose from about 250,000 in 1700 to 2,150,000 in 1770, an annual growth rate of 3 percent.

Few societies in recorded history have expanded so rapidly, and if the growth rate had not dropped substantially during the nineteenth and twentieth centuries, the current population of the United States would stand at well over one billion people. Natural reproduction was responsible for most of the growth. More families bore children who in turn lived long enough to have children of their own. Because of this sudden expansion, the population of the late colonial period was strikingly young; approximately one-half of the populace at any given time was under the age of sixteen.

Convicts for America

The African slaves were not the only large group of people coerced into moving to the New World. In 1718, Parliament passed the Transportation Act, allowing judges in England, Scotland, and Ireland to send convicted felons to the American

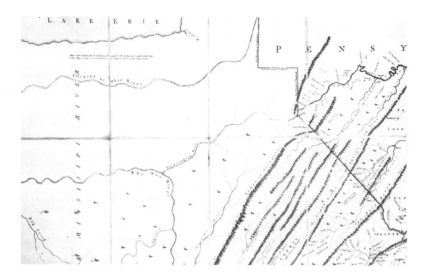

Detail from the 1751 "Map of the Inhabited Part of Virginia" by Joshua Fry and Peter Jefferson showing the northwest quadrant. The map depicts plentiful rivers and mountains but little settlement.

colonies. Between 1718 and 1775, the courts shipped approximately fifty thousand convicts across the Atlantic. Some of these men and women may actually have been dangerous criminals, but the majority seem to have committed minor crimes against property. Although transported convicts—almost 75 percent of whom were young males—escaped the hangman, they found life difficult in the colonies. Eighty percent of them were sold in the Chesapeake colonies as indentured servants. At best they faced an uncertain future, and it is probably not surprising that few former convicts prospered in America.

British authorities lavished praise on this system. According to one writer, transportation drained "the Nation of its offensive Rubbish, without taking away their Lives." Although Americans purchased the convict servants, they expressed fear that these men and women would create a dangerous criminal class. In one irate essay, Benjamin Franklin asked his readers to consider just how the colonists might repay the leaders of Great Britain for shipping so many felons to America. He suggested that rattlesnakes might be the appropriate gift. "I would propose to have them carefully distributed. . . ," Franklin wrote, "in the Gardens of all the Nobility and Gentry throughout the Nation; but particularly in the Gardens of the *Prime Ministers,* the *Lords of Trade* and *Members of Parliament.*" The Revolution forced the British courts to redirect the flow of convicts to another part of the world; an indirect result of American independence was the founding of Australia by transported felons.

CULTURES OF THE BACKCOUNTRY

The eighteenth century also witnessed fresh waves of voluntary European migration. Unlike those seventeenth-century English settlers who had moved to the New World in search of religious sanctuary (see Chapter 2), the newcomers generally transferred in hope of obtaining their own land and setting up as independent farmers. These people often traveled to the backcountry, a region stretching approximately 800 miles from western Pennsylvania to Georgia. Although they planned to follow customs they had known in Europe, they found the challenge of surviving on the British frontier far more demanding than they anticipated. They plunged into a complex, fluid, often violent society that included large numbers of Native Americans and African Americans as well as other Europeans.

Scotch-Irish and Germans

Non-English colonists poured into American ports throughout the eighteenth century, creating rich ethnic diversity in areas originally settled by Anglo-Saxons. The largest group of newcomers consisted of Scotch-Irish. The experiences of these people in Great Britain influenced not only their decision to move to the New World but also their behavior once they arrived.

During the seventeenth century, English rulers thought they could thoroughly dominate Catholic Ireland by transporting thousands of lowland Scottish Presbyterians to the northern region of that war-torn country. The plan failed. English officials who were members of the Anglican church discriminated against the Presbyterians. They passed laws that placed the Scotch-Irish at a severe disadvantage when they traded in England; they taxed them at exorbitant rates. After several poor harvests, many of the Scotch-Irish elected to emigrate to America where they hoped to find the freedom and prosperity that had been denied in Ireland. "I have seen some of their letters to their friends here [Ireland]," one British agent reported in 1729, ". . . in which after they set forth and recommend the fruitfulness and commodities of the country [America], they tell them, that if they will but carry over a little money with them, they may for a small sum purchase considerable tracts of land." It is estimated that about 150,000 Scotch-Irish migrated to the colonies before the Revolution.

Most Scotch-Irish immigrants landed initially in Philadelphia, but instead of remaining in that city, they carved out farms on Pennsylvania's western frontier. The colony's proprietors welcomed the influx of new settlers, for it seemed they would form an ideal barrier between the Indians and the older, coastal communities. The Penn family soon had second thoughts, however. The Scotch-Irish squatted on whatever land looked best, and when colony officials pointed out that large tracts had already been reserved, the immigrants retorted "it was against the laws of God and nature that so much land should be idle when so many Christians wanted it to labour on and to raise their bread." Wherever they located, the Scotch-Irish challenged established authority.

A second large body of non-English settlers, more than 100,000 people, came from the upper Rhine Valley, the German Palatinate. Some of the migrants, especially those who relocated to America around the turn of the century, belonged to small pietistic Protestant sects whose religious views were somewhat similar to those of the Quakers. These Germans moved to the New World primarily in hope of finding religious toleration. Under the guidance of Francis Daniel Pastorius (1651–1720), a group of Mennonites established a prosperous community in Pennsylvania known as Germantown.

By mid-century, however, the characteristics of the German migration had begun to change.

Large numbers of Lutherans transferred to the Middle Colonies. Unlike members of the pietistic sects, these men and women were not in search of religious freedom. Rather, they traveled to the New World looking to better their material lives. The Lutheran church in Germany initially tried to maintain control over the distant congregations, but even though the migrants themselves fiercely preserved many aspects of traditional German culture, they were eventually forced to accommodate to new social conditions. Henry Melchior Muhlenberg (1711–1787), a tireless leader, helped German Lutherans through a difficult cultural adjustment, and in 1748, Muhlenberg organized a meeting of local pastors and lay delegates that ordained ministers of their own choosing, an act of spiritual independence that has been called "the most important single event in American Lutheran history."

The German migrants—mistakenly called Pennsylvania Dutch because the English confused *deutsch* (meaning German) with *Dutch* (a person from Holland)—began reaching Philadelphia in large numbers after 1717, and by 1766, persons of German stock accounted for more than one-third of Pennsylvania's total population. Even their most vocal detractors admitted the Germans were the best farmers in the colony.

Ethnic differences in Pennsylvania bred disputes. The Scotch-Irish as well as the Germans preferred to live with people of their own background, and they sometimes fought to keep members of the other nationality out of their neighborhoods. The English were suspicious of both groups. They could not comprehend why the Germans insisted on speaking German in America. In 1753, for example, Franklin described these settlers as "the most stupid of their nation." He warned that "unless the stream of [German] importation could be turned from this to other colonies . . . they will soon outnumber us, . . . [and] all the advantages we have, will in my opinion, be not able to preserve our language, and even our government will become precarious."

Such prejudice may have persuaded members of both groups to search for new homes. After 1730, Germans and Scotch-Irish pushed south from western Pennsylvania into the Shenandoah Valley, thousands of them settling in the backcountry of Virginia and the Carolinas. The

Elizabeth Canning, convicted of perjury, stands at the bar to receive her sentence from the London court. For her crime, she was sentenced to one month's imprisonment and transport for seven years to the American colonies.

Germans usually remained wherever they found unclaimed fertile land. By contrast, the Scotch-Irish often moved two or three times, acquiring a reputation as a rootless people.

Wherever the newcomers settled, they often found themselves living beyond the effective authority of the various colonial governments. To be sure, backcountry residents petitioned for assistance during wars against the Indians, but most of the time they preferred to be left alone. These conditions heightened the importance of religious institutions within the small ethnic communities. Although the original stimulus for coming to America may have been a desire for economic independence and prosperity, backcountry families—especially the Scotch-Irish—flocked to evangelical Protestant preachers, to Presbyterian, Baptist, and later, Methodist ministers who not only fulfilled the settlers' spiritual needs, but also gave these scattered backcountry communities a pronounced moral character that survived long after the colonial period.

"Middle Ground"

In some histories of the colonial period, Native Americans make only a brief appearance, usually during the earliest years of conquest and settlement. After initial contact with the first European invaders, the Indians seem mysteriously to disappear from the central narrative of colonization, and it is not until the nineteenth century that they turn up again, this time to wage a last desperate battle against the encroachment of white society.

This obviously inadequate account slights one of the richer chapters of Native American history. To be sure, during much of the seventeenth century various Indian groups who contested the English settlers for control of coastal lands suffered terribly, sometimes from war, but more often from the spread of contagious diseases such as smallpox. The two races found it very difficult to live in close proximity. As one Indian informed the members of the Maryland assembly in 1666, "Your hogs & Cattle injure Us, You come too near Us to live & drive Us from place to place.

This folk art painting, from the cover of a clothes box, shows a typical eighteenth-century German farmer.

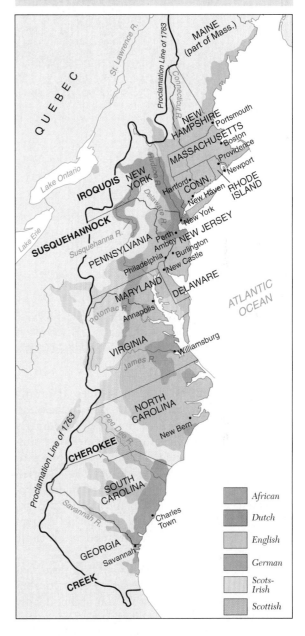

We can fly no farther; let us know where to live & how to be secured for the future from the Hogs & Cattle."

Against such odds the Indians managed to survive. By the eighteenth century, the site of the most intense and creative contact between the races had shifted to the Cis-Mississippian west; that is, to the huge territory between the Appalachian Mountains and the Mississippi River, where several hundred thousand Native Americans made their homes.

Many Indians had only recently migrated to this area. The Delawares, for example, retreated to far western Pennsylvania and the Ohio Valley to escape almost continuous confrontation with advancing European invaders. Other Indians drifted west in less happy circumstances. They were refugees, the remnants of Native American groups who had lost so many people they could no longer sustain an independent cultural identity. These survivors joined with other Indians to establish new multiethnic communities. In this respect the Native American villages may not have seemed all that different from the mixed European settlements of the backcountry.

Stronger groups of Indians such as the Creeks, Choctaws, Chickasaws, Cherokees, and Shawnees generally welcomed the refugees. Strangers were

This certificate of William Johnson, superintendent of Indian affairs, signifies an alliance between the English settlers and the Native Americans in the "middle ground." Calumets (ceremonial pipes), wampum belts, and medals were other tokens used to mark alliances.

formally adopted to take the places of family members killed in battle or overcome by sickness, and we should appreciate that many seemingly traditional Indian villages of the eighteenth century actually represented innovative responses to rapidly shifting external conditions. As historian Peter Wood explains, "Physically and linguistically diverse groups moved to form loosely organized confederacies, unions of mutual convenience, that effectively restrained interethnic hostilities."

The concept of a *middle ground*—a term that has only recently entered the interpretive vocabulary—helps us more fully to comprehend how eighteenth-century Indians held their own in the backcountry beyond the Appalachian Mountains. The Native Americans never intended to isolate themselves completely from European contact. They relied on white traders, French as well as English, to provide essential metal goods and weapons. The goal of the Indian confederacies was rather to maintain a strong independent voice in these commercial exchanges, and so long as they had sufficient military strength—that is, large numbers of healthy armed warriors—they compelled everyone who came to negotiate in the "middle ground" to give them proper respect. It would be incorrect, therefore, to characterize their relations with the Europeans as a stark choice between resistance or accommodation, between total war or abject surrender. Native Americans took advantage of rivals when possible; they compromised when necessary. It is best to imagine the Indians' middle ground as an open, dynamic process of creative interaction.

The Susquehannas understood the rules of the middle ground. Indeed, they mastered the eighteenth-century language of commercial negotiation. When backcountry traders charged the Indians seemingly exorbitant prices for European goods, the angry Susquehannas took their complaint to James Hamilton, the lieutenant governor of Pennsylvania. In fact, they forced Hamilton to give them a short lecture on international economics, an event that shows the Indians were fully capable of grasping the essential elements of modern capitalism. "You know we dont make the Goods ourselves," Hamilton whined, "they are made in England, and the Transporting them over the Seas is dangerous in time of War and very expensive, so that . . . their prices change, as the risque and demand for them is greater or less."

The survival of the middle ground depended ultimately on factors over which the Native Americans had little control. Imperial competition between France and Great Britain enhanced the Indians' bargaining position, but after the British defeated the French in 1763, the Indians no longer received the same solicitous attention as they had in earlier times. Keeping old allies happy seemed to the British a needless expense. Moreover, contagious disease continued to take a fearful toll. In the southern backcountry between 1685 and 1790 the Indian population dropped an astounding 72 percent. In the Ohio Valley the numbers suggest similar rates of decline. By the time the United States took control of this region, the middle ground itself had become a casualty of history.

SPANISH BORDERLANDS OF THE EIGHTEENTH CENTURY

Until 1821 when Mexico declared independence from Madrid, Spanish authorities struggled to control a vast northern frontier. During the eighteenth century the Spanish Empire in North America included widely dispersed settlements such as San Francisco, San Diego, Santa Fe, San Antonio, and St. Augustine. In these borderland communities European colonists mixed with peoples of other races and backgrounds, forming multicultural societies. According to historian Ramón A. Gutiérrez, the Spanish provinces present a story of "the complex web of interactions between men and women, young and old, rich and poor, slave and free, Spaniard and Indian, all of whom fundamentally depended on the other for their own self-definition."

Conquering the Northern Frontier

Tales of gold and silver attracted the attention of the earliest Spaniards. Eager to duplicate Cortés's feat (see Chapter 1), several lesser known con-

quistadores explored the lands to the north of Mexico. Between 1539 and 1541, Hernando de Soto trekked across the Southeast in search of treasure. At roughly the same time, Francisco Vázquez de Coronado departed New Spain looking for the fabled "Seven Cities of Cibola," centers of wealth that on closer inspection turned out to be Zuni pueblos. Coronado's quixotic journey took him to the present states of Texas, Kansas, New Mexico, and Arizona.

Not until late in the sixteenth century did Spanish settlers, led by Juan de Oñate, establish European communities north of the Rio Grande. The Pueblos resisted the invasion of colonists, soldiers, and missionaries, and in a major rebellion in 1680 led by El Popé, the native peoples drove the whites completely out of New Mexico. "The heathen have conceived a mortal hatred for our holy faith and enmity for the Spanish nation," concluded one imperial bureaucrat. Not until 1692 were the Spanish able to reconquer this fiercely contested area. By then, Native American hostility coupled with the settlers' failure to find precious metal had cooled Spain's enthusiasm for the northern frontier.

Concern over French encroachment in the Southeast led Spain to colonize St. Augustine (Florida) in 1565. Although this enterprise never flourished, it claims attention as the first permanent European settlement established in what would become the United States, predating the founding of Jamestown and Plymouth by several decades. Pedro Menéndez de Avilés brought some fifteen hundred soldiers and settlers to St. Augustine, where they constructed an impressive fort, but the colony failed to attract additional Spanish migrants. "It is hard to get anyone to go to St. Augustine because of the horror with which Florida is painted," the governor of Cuba complained in 1673. "Only hoodlums and the mischievous go there from Cuba."

California never figured prominently in Spain's plans for the New World. Early explorers reported finding only impoverished Indians living along the Pacific Coast. Adventurers saw no natural resources worth mentioning, and since the area proved extremely difficult to reach from Mexico City—the overland trip could take months—California received little attention. Fear that the Russians might seize the entire region belatedly sparked Spanish activity, however, and after

1769 two indomitable servants of empire, Fra Junípero Serra and Don Gaspar de Portolá, organized permanent missions and *presidios* (forts) at San Diego, Monterey, San Francisco, and Santa Barbara.

Peoples of the Spanish Borderlands

In sharp contrast to the English frontier settlements of the eighteenth century, the Spanish outposts in North America grew very slowly. A few Catholic priests and imperial administrators traveled to the northern provinces, but the danger of Indian attack as well as a harsh physical environment discouraged ordinary colonists. The European migrants were overwhelmingly male, most of them soldiers in the pay of the empire. Although some colonists came directly from Spain, most had been born in other Spanish colonies such as Minorca, the Canaries, or New

Spain, and because European women rarely appeared on the frontier, Spanish males formed relationships with Indian women, fathering large numbers of *mestizos,* children of mixed race.

As in other European frontiers of the eighteenth century, encounters with Spanish soldiers, priests, and traders altered Native American cultures. The experience here was quite different from that of the whites and Indians in the British backcountry. The Spanish exploited Native American labor, reducing entire Indian villages to servitude. Many Indians moved to the Spanish towns, and although they lived in close proximity to the Europeans—something rare in British America—they were consigned to the lowest social class, objects of European contempt. However much their material conditions changed, the Indians of the Southwest resisted strenuous efforts to convert them to Catholicism. The Pueblos maintained their own religious forms—often at great personal risk—and they sometimes murdered priests who became too intrusive. Angry Pueblos at Taos reportedly fed the hated Spanish friars corn tortillas containing urine and mice meat.

The Spanish empire never had the resources necessary to secure the northern frontier fully. The small military posts were intended primarily to discourage other European powers such as France, Great Britain, and Russia from taking possession of territory claimed by Spain. It would be misleading, however, to stress the fragility of Spanish colonization. The urban design and public architecture of many southwestern cities still reflect the vision of the early Spanish settlers, and to a large extent, the old borderlands remain Spanish speaking to this day.

BRITISH COLONIES IN AN ATLANTIC WORLD

The character of the older, more established Atlantic colonies changed almost as rapidly as that of the backcountry. The rapid growth of an urban cosmopolitan culture impressed eighteenth-century commentators, and even though most Americans still lived on scattered farms, they had begun to participate aggressively in a exciting consumer marketplace that expanded their imaginative horizons.

Acoma Pueblo near present-day Albuquerque, New Mexico. In 1540, a party sent by the explorer Coronado reached the site, which is situated atop a rock mesa more than 300 feet high with steep sides and approached along a difficult trail. Captured in 1599 by Juan de Oñate, Acoma joined in the revolt against the Spanish led by El Popé in 1680.

Provincial Cities

Considering the rate of population growth, it is surprising to discover how few eighteenth-century Americans lived in cities. Boston, Newport, New York, Philadelphia, and Charleston—the five largest cities—contained only about 5 percent of the colonial population. In 1775, none had more than forty thousand persons. The explanation for the relatively slow development of colonial American cities lies in their highly specialized commercial character. Colonial port towns served as entrepôts, intermediary trade and shipping centers where bulk cargoes were broken up for inland distribution and where agricultural products were gathered for export. They did not support large-scale manufacturing. Indeed, the pool of free urban laborers was quite small, since the type of person who was forced to work for wages in Europe usually became a farmer in America.

Yet despite the limited urban population, cities profoundly influenced colonial culture. It was in the cities that Americans were exposed to and welcomed the latest English ideas. Wealthy colonists—merchants and lawyers—tried to emulate the culture of the mother country. They sponsored concerts and plays; they learned to dance. Women as well as men picked up the new fashions quickly, and even though most of them had never been outside the colony of their birth, they sometimes appeared to be the products of London's best families.

It was in the cities, also, that wealthy merchants transformed commercial profits into architectural splendor, for in their desire to outdo one another, they built grand homes of enduring beauty. Most of these buildings are described as Georgian because they were constructed during the reign of Britain's early Hanoverian kings, who all happened to be named George. Actually these homes were provincial copies of grand country houses of Great Britain. They drew their inspiration from the great Italian Renaissance architect Andrea Palladio (1508–1580), who had incorporated classical themes into a rigidly symmetrical form. Palladio's ideas were popularized in the colonies by James Gibbs, an Englishman whose *Book of Architecture* (1728) provided blueprints for the most spectacular homes of mid-eighteenth-century America.

Their owners filled these houses with fine furniture. Each city patronized certain skilled craftsmen, but the artisans of Philadelphia were known for producing magnificent copies of the works of Thomas Chippendale, Great Britain's most famous furniture designer. These developments gave American cities an elegance they had not possessed in the previous century. One foreign visitor noted of Philadelphia in 1748, ". . . its natural advantages, trade, riches and power, are by no means inferior to any, even of the most ancient towns of Europe." As this traveler understood, the cultural impact of the cities went far beyond the number of people who actually lived there.

	Boston	%	Newport	%	New York	%	Philadelphia	%	Charleston	%
1720	12,000	—	3,800	—	7,000	—	10,000	—	3,500	—
1730	13,000	8	4,640	22	8,622	23	11,500	15	4,500	29
1740	15,601	20	5,840	26	10,451	21	12,654	10	6,269	39
1750	—	—	6,670	14	14,225	36	18,202	44	7,134	14
1760	15,631	—	7,500	12	18,000	27	23,750	30	8,000	12
1770	15,877	2	9,833	31	22,667	26	34,583	46	10,667	33

Estimated Population of Colonial Cities, 1720–1770, showing decennial percentage increases

Source: From *The American Colonies* by R. C. Simmons. Copyright © 1976 by R. C. Simmons. Reprinted by permission of Harold Matson Company, Inc.

Westover, the huge Virginia estate of William Byrd II (see p. 98) shows the influence of the architectural style of Andrea Palladio on eighteenth-century Georgian buildings.

Benjamin Franklin

Benjamin Franklin (1706–1790) absorbed the new cosmopolitan culture. European thinkers regarded him as a genuine *philosophe,* a person of reason and science, a role that he self-consciously cultivated when he visited England and France in later life. Franklin had little formal education, but as a young man working in his brother's print shop, he managed to keep up with the latest intellectual currents. In his *Autobiography,* Franklin described the excitement of discovering a new British journal. It was like a breath of fresh air to a boy growing up in Puritan New England. "I met with an odd volume of *The Spectator,*" Franklin recounted, ". . . I had never before seen any of them. I bought it, read it over and over, and was much delighted with it. I thought the writing excellent, and wished if possible to imitate it."

Franklin's opportunity came in August 1721 when he and his brother founded *The New England Courant,* a weekly newspaper that satirized Boston's political and religious leaders in the manner of the contemporary British press. Writing under the name "Silence Dogood," young Franklin asked his readers "Whether a Commonwealth suffers more by hypocritical Pretenders to Religion, or by the openly Profane?" Proper Bostonians were not prepared for a journal that one minister described as "full freighted with Nonesense, Unmannerliness, Railery, Prophaneness, Immorality, Arrogance,

Benjamin Franklin (left) exemplified the scientific curiosity and search for practical knowledge characteristic of thinkers of the eighteenth century. Franklin's experiments on electricity became world famous and inspired many others to study the effects of this strange force. The ordinary citizens shown above (right), eager to try out a new phenomenon, are rubbing metal rods together to produce static electricity.

Calumnies, Lyes, Contradictions, and what not, all tending to Quarrels and Divisions and to Debauch and Corrupt the Minds and Manners of New England." Franklin got the point; he left Massachusetts in 1723 in search of a less hostile intellectual environment.

After he had moved to Philadelphia, leaving behind an irritable brother as well as New England Puritanism, Franklin devoted himself to the pursuit of useful knowledge, ideas that would increase the happiness of his fellow Americans. Franklin never denied the existence of God. Rather, he pushed the Lord aside, making room for the free exercise of human reason. Franklin tinkered, experimented, and reformed. Almost everything he encountered in his daily life aroused his curiosity. His investigation of electricity brought him world fame, but Franklin was never satisfied with his work in this field until it yielded practical application. In 1756, he invented the lightning rod. He also designed a marvelously efficient stove that is still used today. In modern America, Franklin has become exactly what he would have wanted to be, a symbol of material progress through human ingenuity.

Franklin energetically promoted the spread of reason. In Philadelphia, he organized groups that discussed the latest European literature, philosophy, and science. In 1727, for example, he "form'd most of my ingenious Acquaintances into a Club for mutual Improvement, which we call'd the Junto." Four years later Franklin took a leading part in the formation of the Library Company, a voluntary association that for the first time allowed people like himself to pursue "useful knowledge." The members of these societies communicated with Americans living in other colonies, providing them not only with new information but also with models for their own clubs and associations. Such efforts broadened the intellectual horizons of many colonists, especially those who lived in cities.

Economic Transformation

The colonial economy kept pace with the stunning growth in population. During the first three-quarters of the eighteenth century, the population increased at least tenfold, and yet even with so many additional people to feed and clothe, the per capita income did not decline. Indeed, with the exception of poor urban dwellers, such as sailors whose employment varied with the season, white Americans did quite well. An abundance of land and the extensive growth of agriculture accounted for their economic success. New farmers were not only able to provide for their families' well-being but also to sell their crops in European and West Indian markets as well. Each year, more Americans produced more tobacco, wheat, or rice—just to cite the major export crops—and by this means, they maintained a high level of individual prosperity without developing an industrial base.

At mid-century, colonial exports flowed along well-established routes. Over half of American goods produced for export went to Great Britain. The Navigation Acts (see Chapter 3) were still in effect and "enumerated" items such as tobacco had to be landed first at a British port. Furs were added to the restricted list in 1722. The White Pines Acts passed in 1711, 1722, and 1729 forbade Americans from cutting white pine trees without a license. The purpose of this legislation was to reserve the best trees for the use of the Royal Navy. The Sugar Act of 1733—also called the Molasses Act—placed a heavy duty on molasses imported from foreign ports; the Hat and Felt Act of 1732 and the Iron Act of 1750 attempted to limit the production of colonial goods that competed with British exports.

These statutes might have created tensions between the colonists and the mother country had they been rigorously enforced. Crown officials, however, generally ignored the new laws. New England merchants imported molasses from French Caribbean islands without paying the full customs; ironmasters in the Middle Colonies continued to produce iron. Even without the Navigation Acts, however, a majority of colonial exports would have been sold on the English market. The emerging consumer society in Great Britain was beginning to create a new generation of buyers who possessed enough income to purchase American goods, especially sugar and

tobacco. This rising demand was the major market force shaping the colonial economy.

Colonial merchants operating out of Boston, Newport, and Philadelphia also carried substantial tonnage to the West Indies. In 1768, this market accounted for 27 percent of all American exports. If there was a triangular trade that included the west coast of Africa, it does not seem to have been economically significant. Colonial ships carrying food sailed for the Caribbean and returned immediately to the Middle Colonies or New England with cargoes of molasses, sugar, and rum. In fact, recent research indicates that during the eighteenth century, trade with Africa involved less than 1 percent of all American exports. Slaves were transported directly to colonial ports where they were sold for cash or credit.

The West Indies played a vital role in preserving American credit in Europe. Without this source of income, colonists would not have been able to pay for the manufactured items they purchased in the mother country. To be sure, they exported American products in great quantity to Great Britain, but the value of these exports seldom equaled the cost of British goods shipped back to the colonists. To cover this small but recurrent deficit, colonial merchants relied on profits made in the West Indies.

Birth of a Consumer Society

After mid-century, however, the balance of trade turned dramatically against the colonists. The reasons for this change were complex, but in simplest terms, Americans began buying more English goods than their parents or grandparents had done. Between 1740 and 1770, English exports to the American colonies increased by an astounding 360 percent.

In part, this shift reflected a fundamental transformation in the British economy. Although the Industrial Revolution was still far in the future, the pace of the British economy picked up dramatically after 1690. Small factories produced certain goods more efficiently and more cheaply than the colonists could. The availability of these products altered the lives of most Americans, even those with modest incomes. Staffordshire china replaced crude earthenware; imported cloth replaced homespun. Franklin noted in his *Autobiography* how changing consumer habits affected his life. For years, he had eaten his breakfast in an earthenware bowl with a pewter spoon, but on one morning it was served "in a china bowl, with a spoon of silver." Franklin observed that "this was the first appearance of plate and china in our house which afterwards in the course of years, as our wealth increased, augmented gradually to several hundred pounds in value." In this manner, British industrialization undercut American handicraft and folk art.

To help Americans purchase manufactured goods, British merchants offered generous credit. Colonists deferred settlement by agreeing to pay interest on their debts. The temptation to acquire English finery blinded many people to hard economic realities. They gambled on the future, hoping bumper farm crops would reduce their dependence on the large merchant houses of London and Glasgow. Obviously, some persons lived within their means, but the aggregate American debt continued to grow. By 1760, total indebtedness had reached £2 million. Colonial leaders tried various expedients to remain solvent—issuing paper money, for example—and while these efforts delayed a crisis, the balance of payments problem was clearly very serious.

The eighteenth century also saw a substantial increase in intercoastal trade. Southern planters sent tobacco and rice to New England and the Middle Colonies where these staples were exchanged for meat and wheat as well as goods imported from Great Britain. By 1760, approximately 30 percent of the colonists' total tonnage capacity was involved in this extensive "coastwise" commerce. In addition, backcountry farmers in western Pennsylvania and the Shenandoah Valley carried their grain to market along an old Iroquois trail that became known as the "Great Wagon Road," a rough, hilly highway that by the time of the Revolution stretched 735 miles along the Blue Ridge Mountains to Camden, South Carolina. Most of their produce was carried in long, gracefully designed Conestoga wagons. These vehicles—sometimes called the "wagons of empire"—had been invented by German immigrants living in the Conestoga River Valley in Lancaster County, Pennsylvania.

The shifting patterns of trade had immense effects on the development of an American culture. First, the flood of British imports eroded local and regional identities. Commerce helped to "anglicize" American culture by exposing colo-

The Great Wagon Road
By the mid-eighteenth century, this road had become the major avenue for the settlers in the Virginia and Carolina backcountry.

nial consumers to a common range of British manufactured goods. Deep sectional differences remained, of course, but Americans from New Hampshire to Georgia were increasingly drawn into a sophisticated economic network centered in London. Second, the expanding coastal and overland trade brought colonists of different backgrounds into more frequent contact. Ships that sailed between New England and South Carolina, and between Virginia and Pennsylvania, provided dispersed Americans with a means to exchange ideas and experiences on a more regular basis. Mid-eighteenth-century printers, for example, established several dozen new journals; these were weekly newspapers that carried information not only about the mother country and world commerce but also about events in other colonies.

RELIGIOUS REVIVALS IN PROVINCIAL SOCIETIES

The Great Awakening had a profound impact on the lives of ordinary people. This unprecedented evangelical outpouring altered the course of

*G*ood Manners and the Creation of an American Middle Class
The Eighteenth Century

Manners generate anxiety. A wrong dessert spoon, an ill-chosen wine glass, an inappropriate outfit—such errors of judgment can expose a man or woman to the ridicule of polite society. George Washington dreaded the possibility of appearing an "awkward country fellow," and as a young ambitious Virginian, he did what socially insecure persons have done for centuries: he obtained a reliable book of etiquette, the functional equivalent of "Miss Manners" for eighteenth-century Americans.

A teenage Washington busily copied over a hundred points of good manners in a little volume entitled *Rules of Civility & Decent Behaviour in Company*

and Conversation. Some entries strike modern readers as uncontroversial: "Associate yourself with Men of good Quality if you Esteem your own Reputation; for 'tis better to be alone than in bad Company" or "When another speaks be attentive yourself and disturb not the audience . . . interrupt him not."

Some of Washington's rules, however, seem bizarre. They suggest that relaxed modern standards of etiquette in this country are still a great deal more demanding than those of the eighteenth century. One wonders, for example, why Washington had to remind himself "When in company, put not your hands to any part of the

body, not usually discovered." Another rule counseled polite colonial Americans to "Kill no vermin as fleas, lice, ticks, &c. in the sight of others; if you see any filth or thick spittle, put your foot dexteriously [sic] upon it; if it be upon the clothes of your companions, put it off privately; and if it be upon your own clothes, return thanks to him who puts it off." Even stranger, Washington copied in his little book, "Do not Puff up the Cheeks, Loll not out the tongue . . . thrust out the lips, or bite them or keep the Lips too open or too Close."

The image of Washington puffing up his cheeks or lolling his tongue during a polite conversation is amusing. For the

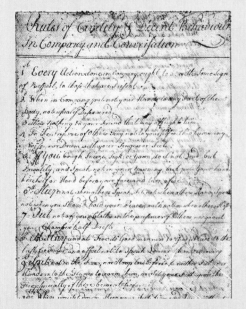

Among Washington's Rules of Civility and Decent Behaviour in Company and Conversation *were admonitions to* "Let your recreations be manful not sinful" *and* "Labour to keep alive in your breast that little celestial fire called conscience."

ambitious young planter, however, the fear of exposure was very real. Obsession with gentility swept through the Anglo-American world of the mid-eighteenth century. Everyone thought it important to be polite—or, if not polite in fact, then at least to appear polite. And in their quest for advice, people like Washington turned to surprising sources. The rules he reproduced had a long history stretching back to the Italian Renaissance. Much of this literature had been intended originally for courtiers, for the creatures who flattered Europe's kings and queens, and whatever else he may have been, Washington was no courtier. In eighteenth-century society, manners—the nervous concern over polite behavior—had spread to a fast-growing Anglo-American middle class.

Few Americans of Washington's background questioned the need to maintain visible class distinctions. Indeed, colonists agreed a gentleman should stand apart from ordinary farmers and small merchants. The problem in a largely rural and agrarian society, one that claimed no genuine aristocrats, was discovering who was the authentic gentleman. Any literate person could read the etiquette books and learn the rules of gentility. Moreover, in a relatively open commercial society, almost everyone had opportunities to purchase manufactured goods, such as bright cloth for

garments and pretty buckles and buttons. Such widespread access to imported finery and print culture meant a stranger might be a proper gentleman or someone who had managed to dress like a gentleman, in other words, a counterfeit.

A curious exchange between two travelers highlights the difficulty of establishing one's social rank at mid-century. A Scottish physician, Dr. Alexander Hamilton (no relation to the secretary of the treasury), never doubted his own gentility. He refused, however, to accept a Pennsylvania land speculator as his social peer. According to Hamilton, the other man appeared a "very rough spun, forward, clownish blade, much addicted to swearing, [and] at the same time desirous to pass for a gentleman." The Pennsylvanian felt insulted. Although he wore only "a greasy jacket and breeches and a dirty worsted cap," he believed himself as good a gentleman as the physician. In his own defense, the land speculator protested that "though he seemed to be but a plain, homely fellow, yet . . . he was able to afford better [clothes] than many that went finer." In fact, his "little woman at home drank tea twice a day."

The land speculator and his tea-drinking "little woman" were not about to be bullied by the likes of a Hamilton. Such middle-class Americans—white freeholders and artisans—strove

to master the trappings of the new gentility. The tea service presented the most demanding test, for during such complex social rituals the chance of making a major faux pas was very great. At such tense moments a young man like Washington may have had to remind himself: "Clense not your teeth with the Table Cloth, Napkin, Fork, or Knife, but if Others do it, let it be done with a Pick Tooth."

The spread of print and the sudden availability of so many consumer goods at mid-century fueled the obsession with "civility and decent behaviour." As middle-class Americans soon discovered, however, there was a heavy price to be paid. The rush to gentility generated new social anxieties. Americans—even those who purchased fancy imports and devoured the etiquette books—worried that manners might represent no more than a polite shell, an external set of appearances that indicated perhaps the absence of sincere principle. The acquisition of a tea set could signal an addiction, leading not to the attainment of true gentility, but rather to the emulation of the moral standards of sniveling European courtiers. The deep tension between private manners and public morality, raised so forcefully for the first time during the mid-eighteenth century, perplexes Americans to this day.

Rigid rules of etiquette prescribed the social ritual of the tea service. In this eighteenth-century overmantle (oil on wood), the family slave attends John Potter and his family of Matunuck, Rhode Island, as they take their tea.

American history. In our own time, of course, we have witnessed the force of religious revival in different regions throughout the world. It is no exaggeration to claim that a similar populist movement took place in mid-eighteenth-century America, for it caused men and women of all backgrounds to rethink basic assumptions about church and state, institutions and society.

Only with hindsight does the Great Awakening seem a unified religious movement. Revivals occurred in different places at different times; the intensity of the events varied from region to region. The first signs of a spiritual awakening appeared in New England during the 1730s, but within a decade the revivals in this area had burned themselves out. It was not until the 1750s and 1760s that the Awakening made more than a superficial impact on the people of Virginia. The revivals were most important in Massachusetts, Connecticut, Rhode Island, Pennsylvania, New Jersey, and Virginia. Their effect on religion in New York, Delaware, and the Carolinas was marginal. No single religious denomination or sect monopolized the Awakening. In New England, revivals shattered Congregational churches, and in the South, especially in Virginia, they had an impact on Presbyterians, Methodists, and Baptists. Moreover, there was nothing peculiarly American about the Great Awakening. Mid-eighteenth-century Europe experienced a similar burst of religious emotionalism.

Whatever their origins, the seeds of revival were generally sown on fertile ground. In the early decades of the century, many Americans—but especially New Englanders—complained that organized religion had lost vitality. They looked back at Winthrop's generation with nostalgia, assuming that common people at that time must have possessed greater piety than did later, more worldly colonists. Congregational ministers seemed obsessed with dull, scholastic matters; they no longer touched the heart. And in the southern colonies, there were simply not enough ordained ministers to tend to the religious needs of the population.

The Great Awakening arrived unexpectedly in Northampton, a small farm community in western Massachusetts, sparked by Jonathan Edwards, the local Congregational minister. Edwards accepted the traditional teachings of Calvinism (see Chapter 1), reminding his parish-

ioners that their eternal fate had been determined by an omnipotent God, there was nothing they could do to save themselves, and they were totally dependent on the Lord's will. He thought his fellow ministers had grown soft. They left men and women with the mistaken impression that sinners might somehow avoid eternal damnation simply by performing good works. "How dismal will it be," Edwards told his complacent congregation, "when you are under these racking torments, to know assuredly that you never, never shall be delivered from them." Edwards was not exaggerating his message in an attempt to be dramatic. He spoke of God's omnipotence with such calm self-assurance that even people who had not thought deeply about religious matters were shaken by his words.

Why this uncompromising message set off several religious revivals during the mid-1730s is not known. Whatever the explanation for the popular response to Edwards's preaching, young people began flocking to the church. They experienced a searing conversion, a sense of "new birth" and utter dependence on God. "Surely," Edwards pronounced, "this is the Lord's doing, and it is marvelous in our eyes." The excitement spread, and evangelical ministers concluded that God must be preparing Americans, his chosen people, for the millennium. "What is now seen in America and especially in New England," Edwards explained, "may prove the dawn of that glorious day."

Religion of the People

Edwards was a brilliant theologian, but he did not possess the dynamic personality required to sustain the revival. That responsibility fell to George Whitefield, a young, inspiring preacher from England who toured the colonies from New Hampshire to Georgia. While Whitefield was not an original thinker, he was an extraordinarily effective public speaker. According to Edwards's wife, Sarah, it was wonderful to witness what a spell Whitefield ". . . casts over an audience . . . I have seen upwards of a thousand people hang on his words with breathless silence, broken only by an occasional half-suppressed sob."

Whitefield's audiences came from all groups of American society: rich and poor, young and old, rural and urban. One obscure Connecticut farmer,

The fervor of the Great Awakening was intensified by the eloquence of itinerant preachers such as George Whitefield, the most popular evangelical of the mid-eighteenth century.

volumes, the itinerant minister possessed an almost intuitive sense of how this burgeoning consumer society could be turned to his own advantage, and he embraced the latest merchandising techniques. He appreciated, for example, the power of the press in selling the revival, and he regularly promoted his own work in advertisements placed in British and American newspapers. The crowds flocked to hear Whitefield, while his critics grumbled about the commercialization of religion. One anonymous writer in Massachusetts noted there is "a very wholesome law of the province to discourage Pedlars in Trade" and it seems high time "to enact something for the discouragement of Pedlars in Divinity also."

Other, American-born itinerant preachers followed Whitefield's example. The most famous was Gilbert Tennent, a Presbyterian of Scotch-Irish background who had been educated in the Middle Colonies. His sermon, "On the Danger of an Unconverted Ministry," printed in 1741 set off a storm of protest from established ministers who were understandably insulted. Lesser known revivalists traveled from town to town, colony to colony, challenging local clergymen who seemed hostile to evangelical religion. Men and women who thronged to hear the itinerants were called "New Lights," and during the 1740s and 1750s, many congregations split between defenders of the new emotional preaching and those who regarded the entire movement as dangerous nonsense.

Despite Whitefield's successes, many ministers remained suspicious of the itinerants and their methods. Some complaints may have amounted to little more than sour grapes. One "Old Light" spokesman labeled Tennent "a monster! impudent and noisy." He claimed Tennent told anxious Christians that "they were *damned! damned! damned!* This charmed them; and, in the most dreadful winter I ever saw, people wallowed in snow, night and day, for the benefit of his beastly brayings; and many ended their days under these fatigues." Charles Chauncy, minister of the prestigious First Church of Boston, raised much more troubling issues. How could the revivalists be certain God had sparked the Great Awakening? Perhaps the itinerants had relied too much on emotion? "Let us esteem those as friends of religion," Chauncy warned, ". . . who warn us of the

Nathan Cole, left a moving account of a sermon Whitefield delivered in Middletown in 1741. Rushing with his wife Anne along the dirt roads, Cole encountered "a stedy streem of horses & their riders scarcely a horse more than his length behind another all of a lather and fome with swet ther breath rooling out of their noistrels in the cloud of dust every jump every hors seemed to go with all his might to carry his rider to hear the news from heaven for the saving of their Souls." When Cole heard the great preacher, the farmer experienced what he called "a heart wound." While Whitefield described himself as a Calvinist, he welcomed all Protestants. He spoke from any pulpit that was available. "Don't tell me you are a Baptist, an Independent, a Presbyterian, a dissenter," he thundered, "tell me you are a Christian, that is all I want."

Whitefield was a brilliant entrepreneur. Like Franklin, with whom he published many popular

danger of enthusiasm, and would put us on our guard, that we may not be led aside by it."

While Tennent did not condone the excesses of the Great Awakening, his attacks on formal learning invited the crude anti-intellectualism of such fanatics as James Davenport. This deranged revivalist traveled along the Connecticut coast in 1742 playing upon popular emotion. At night, under the light of smoky torches, he danced and stripped, shrieked and laughed. He also urged people to burn books written by authors who had not experienced the new light as defined by Davenport. Like so many fanatics throughout history who have claimed a special knowledge of the "truth," Davenport later recanted and begged pardon for his disruptive behavior.

To concentrate on the bizarre activities of Davenport—as many critics of the Great Awakening have done—is to obscure the positive ways in which this vast revival changed American society. First, despite occasional anti-intellectual outbursts, the New Lights founded several important centers of higher learning. They wanted to train young men who would carry on the good works of Edwards, Whitefield, and Tennent. In 1746, New Light Presbyterians established the College of New Jersey, which later became Princeton University. Just before his death, Edwards was appointed its president. The evangelical minister, Eleazar Wheelock, launched Dartmouth (1769); other revivalists founded Brown (1764) and Rutgers (1766).

The Great Awakening also encouraged men and women who had been taught to remain silent before traditional figures of authority to speak up, to take an active role in their salvation. They could no longer rely on ministers or institutions. The individual alone stood before God. Knowing this, New Lights made religious choices that shattered the old harmony among Protestant sects, and in its place, they introduced a noisy, often bitterly fought competition. As one New Jersey Presbyterian explained, "There are so many particular *sects* and *Parties* among professed Christians . . . that we know not . . . in which of these different *paths,* to steer our course for *Heaven.*"

Expressive evangelicalism struck a particularly responsive chord among African Americans. Itinerant ministers frequently preached to large sympathetic audiences of slaves. Richard Allen (1760–1831), the founder of the African Methodist

Episcopal Church (AME), reported he owed his freedom in part to a traveling Methodist minister who persuaded Allen's master of the sinfulness of slavery. Allen himself was converted, as were thousands of other black colonists. According to one historian, evangelical preaching "shared enough with traditional African styles and beliefs such as spirit possession and ecstatic expression . . . to allow for an interpenetration of African and Christian religious beliefs."

With religious contention came an awareness of a larger community, a union of fellow believers that extended beyond the boundaries of town and colony. In fact, evangelical religion was one of several forces at work during the mid-eighteenth century that brought scattered colonists into contact with one another for the first time. In this sense, the Great Awakening was a "national" event long before a nation actually existed.

People who had been touched by the Great Awakening shared an optimism about the future of America. With God's help, social and political progress was possible, and from this perspective, of course, the New Lights did not sound much different than the mildly rationalist American spokesmen of the Enlightenment. Both groups prepared the way for the development of a revolutionary mentality in colonial America.

CLASH OF POLITICAL CULTURES

The political history of this period illuminates a growing tension within the empire. Americans of all regions repeatedly stated their desire to replicate British political institutions. Parliament, they claimed, provided a model for the American assemblies. They revered the English constitution. However, the more the colonists studied British political theory and practice—in other words, the more they attempted to become British—the more aware they became of major differences. By trying to copy Great Britain, they unwittingly discovered something about being American.

The English Constitution

During the eighteenth century, political discussion began with the British constitution. It was the object of universal admiration. Unlike the

U.S. Constitution, the British constitution was not a formal written document. It was something much more elusive. The English constitution was a growing body of law, court decisions, and statutes, a sense of traditional political arrangements that people of all classes believed had evolved out of the distant past, preserving life, liberty, and property. Eighteenth-century political commentators admitted with great reluctance that the constitution had in fact changed. Historic confrontations between king and parliament had generated new understandings about what the constitution did or did not allow. Nevertheless, almost everyone regarded change as dangerous and destabilizing, a threat to the political tradition that seemed to explain Britain's greatness.

In theory, the English constitution contained three distinct parts. The monarch was at the top, advised by handpicked court favorites. Next came the House of Lords, a body of 180 aristocrats who served with 26 Anglican bishops as the upper house of Parliament. And third was the House of Commons, composed of 558 members elected by various constituencies scattered throughout the realm.

Political theorists waxed eloquent on workings of the British constitution. Each of the three parts of government, it seemed, represented a separate socioeconomic interest: king, nobility, and common people. Acting alone each body would run to excess, even tyranny, but operating within a mixed system, they automatically checked each other's ambitions for the common good. "Herein consists the excellence of the English government," explained the famed eighteenth-century jurist Sir William Blackstone, "that all parts of it form a mutual check upon each other." Unlike the delegates who wrote the Constitution of the United States, eighteenth-century Englishmen did not perceive the constitution as a balance of executive, legislative, and judicial branches.

The Reality of British Politics

The reality of daily political life in Great Britain, however, bore little relation to theory. The three elements of the constitution did not, in fact, represent distinct socioeconomic groups. Men elected to the House of Commons often came from the same social background as those who served in the House of Lords. All represented the inter-

ests of Britain's landed elite. Moreover, there was no attempt to maintain strict constitutional separation. The king, for example, organized parliamentary associations, loose groups of political followers who sat in the House of Commons and who openly supported the monarch's policies in exchange for patronage or pension.

The claim that the members of the House of Commons represented all the people of England also seemed farfetched. As of 1715, roughly no more than 20 percent of Britain's adult males had the right to vote. Property qualifications or other restrictions often greatly reduced the number of eligible voters. In addition, the size of the electoral districts varied throughout the kingdom. In some boroughs, representatives to Parliament were chosen by several thousand voters. In many districts, however, a handful of electors controlled the result. These tiny, or "rotten" boroughs were an embarrassment. The Methodist leader, John Wesley, complained that Old Sarum, an almost uninhabited borough, "in spite of common sense, without house or inhabitant, still sends two members to the parliament." Since these districts were so small, a wealthy lord or ambitious politician could easily bribe or otherwise "influence" the entire constituency, something they did regularly throughout the century.

Before 1760, few people spoke out against these constitutional abuses. The main exception was a group of radical publicists whom historians have labeled the "Commonwealthmen." These writers decried the corruption of political life, noting that a nation that compromised civic virtue, that failed to stand vigilant against fawning courtiers and would-be despots, deserved to lose its liberty and property. The most famous Commonwealthmen were John Trenchard and Thomas Gordon, who penned a series of essays entitled *Cato's Letters* between 1720 and 1723. If England's rulers were corrupt, they warned, then the people could not expect the balanced constitution to save them from tyranny. In one typical article, Trenchard and Gordon observed "The Appitites . . . of Men, especially of Great Men, are carefully to be observed and stayed, or else they will never stay themselves. The Experience of every Age convinces us, that we must not judge of Men by what they ought to do, but by what they will do."

But however shrilly these writers protested, they won little support for political reforms.

The Election *by William Hogarth illustrates just one aspect of electoral corruption in England—voters were openly willing to sell their votes to either (or both) sides in an election.*

Most eighteenth-century Englishmen admitted there was more than a grain of truth in the commonwealth critique, but they were not willing to tamper with a system of government that had so recently survived a civil war and a Glorious Revolution. Americans, however, took Trenchard and Gordon to heart.

Governing the Colonies: The American Experience

The colonists assumed—perhaps naively—that their own governments were modeled on the balanced constitution of Great Britain. They argued that within their political systems, the governor corresponded to the king, and the governor's council to the House of Lords. The colonial assemblies were perceived as American reproductions of the House of Commons and were expected to preserve the interests of the people against those of the monarch and aristocracy. As the colonists discovered, however, general theories about a mixed constitution were even less relevant in America than they were in Britain.

By mid-century a majority of the mainland colonies had royal governors appointed by the Crown. Many were career army officers who through luck, charm, or family connection had gained the ear of someone close to the king. These patronage posts did not generate income sufficient to interest the most powerful or talented personalities of the period, but they did draw middle-level bureaucrats who were ambitious, desperate, or both. It is perhaps not surprising that most governors decided simply not to "consider any Thing further than how to sit easy."

George Clinton, who served as New York's governor from 1743 to 1753, was probably typical of the men who hoped to "sit easy." Before coming to the colonies, Clinton had compiled an extraordinary record of ineptitude as a naval officer. He gained the governorship more as a means to get him out of England than as a sign of respect. When he arrived in New York City, Clinton ignored the colonists. "In a province given to hospitality," wrote one critic, "he [Clinton] erred by immuring himself in the fort, or retiring to a grotto in the country, where his time was spent with his bottle and a little trifling circle."

Whatever their demerits, royal governors in America possessed enormous powers. In fact, royal governors could do certain things in America that a king could not do in eighteenth-century Britain. Among these were the right to veto legislation and dismiss judges. The governors also served as military commanders in each province.

Political practice in America differed from the British model in another crucial respect. Royal governors were advised by a council, usually a body of about twelve wealthy colonists selected by the Board of Trade in London upon the recommendation of the governor. During the seventeenth century, the council had played an important role in colonial government, but its ability to exercise independent authority declined steadily over the course of the eighteenth century. Its members certainly did not represent a distinct aristocracy within American society.

If royal governors did not look like kings, nor American councils like the House of Lords, colonial assemblies bore but a faint resemblance to the eighteenth-century House of Commons. The major difference was the size of the American franchise. In most colonies, adult white males who owned a small amount of land could vote in colonywide elections. One historian estimates that 95 percent of this group in Massachusetts were eligible to participate in elections. The number in Virginia was about 85 percent. These high figures—much larger than those of contemporary England—have led some scholars to view the colonies as "middle-class democracies," societies run by moderately prosperous yeomen farmers who—in politics at least—exercised independent judgment. There were too many of them to bribe, no "rotten" boroughs, and when these people moved west, colonial assemblies usually created new electoral districts.

Colonial governments were not democracies in the modern sense of that term. Possessing the right to vote was one thing, exercising it quite another. Americans participated in elections when major issues were at stake—the formation of banks in mid-eighteenth-century Massachusetts, for example—but most of the time they were content to let members of the rural and urban gentry represent them in the assemblies. To be sure, unlike modern democracies, these colonial politics excluded women and nonwhites from voting. The point to remember, however, is that the power to expel legislative rascals was always present in

America, and it was this political reality that kept autocratic gentlemen from straying too far from the will of the people.

Colonial Assemblies

Elected members of the colonial assemblies believed that they had a special obligation to preserve colonial liberties. They perceived any attack on the legislature as an assault on the rights of Americans. The elected representatives brooked no criticism, and several colonial printers landed in jail because they criticized actions taken by a lower house.

So aggressive were these bodies in seizing privileges, determining procedures, and controlling money bills that some historians have described the political development of eighteenth-century America as "the rise of the assemblies." No doubt this is exaggerated, but the long series of imperial wars against the French, demanding large public expenditures, transformed the small, amateurish assemblies of the seventeenth century into the more professional, vigilant legislatures of the eighteenth.

This political system seemed designed to generate hostility. There was simply no reason for the colonial legislators to cooperate with appointed royal governors. Alexander Spotswood, Virginia's governor from 1710 to 1722, for example, attempted to institute a bold new land program backed by the Crown. He tried persuasion and gifts, and when these failed, chicanery. But the members of the House of Burgesses refused to support a plan that did not suit their own interests. Before leaving office, Spotswood gave up trying to carry out royal policy in America. Instead, he allied himself with the local Virginia gentry who controlled the House as well as the Council, and because they awarded their new friend with large tracts of land, he became a wealthy man.

A few governors managed briefly to recreate in America the political culture of patronage, the system that eighteenth-century Englishmen took for granted. Most successful in this endeavor was William Shirley, who held office in Massachusetts from 1741 to 1757. The secret to his political successes in America was connection to people who held high office in Great Britain. But Shirley's practices—and those of men like him—clashed with the colonists' perception of politics. They *really* believed in the purity of the balanced constitution. They insisted on complete separation of executive and legislative authority. Therefore, when Americans suspected a governor, or even some of their own representatives, of employing patronage to influence government decisions, their protests seem to have been lifted directly from the pages of *Cato's Letters*.

A major source of shared political information was the weekly journal, a new and vigorous institution in American life. In New York and Massachusetts especially, weekly newspapers urged readers to preserve civic virtue, to exercise extreme vigilance against the spread of privileged power. In the first issue of the *Independent Reflector* published in New York (November 30, 1752), the editor announced defiantly that no discouragement shall ". . . deter me from vindicating the *civil* and *religious RIGHTS* of my Fellow-Creatures: From exposing the peculiar Deformity of publick *Vice*, and *Corruption*; and displaying the amiable Charms of *Liberty*, with the detestable Nature of *Slavery* and *Oppression*." Through such journals, a pattern of political rhetoric that in Britain had gained only marginal respectability, became after 1765 America's normal form of political discourse.

The rise of the assemblies shaped American culture in other, subtler ways. Over the course of the century, the language of the law became increasingly anglicized. The Board of Trade, the Privy Council, and Parliament scrutinized court decisions and legislative actions from all thirteen mainland colonies. As a result, varying local legal practices that had been widespread during the seventeenth century became standardized. Indeed, according to one historian, the colonial legal system by 1750 "was substantially that of the mother country." Not surprisingly, many men who served in colonial assemblies were either lawyers or persons who had received legal training. When Americans from different regions met—as they frequently did in the years before the Revolution—they discovered they shared a commitment to the preservation of the English common law.

As eighteenth-century political developments drew the colonists closer to the mother country, they also brought Americans a greater awareness of each other. As their horizons widened, they learned they operated within the same general

North America, 1750
By 1750, the French had established a chain of settlements southward through the heart of the continent from Quebec to New Orleans. The English saw this as a menace to their seaboard colonies, which were expanding westward.

imperial system, and the problems confronting the Massachusetts House of Representatives were not too different from those facing Virginia's House of Burgesses or South Carolina's Commons House. Like the revivalists and merchants—people who crossed old boundaries—colonial legislators laid the foundation for a larger cultural identity.

CENTURY OF IMPERIAL WAR

The scope and character of warfare in the colonies changed radically during the eighteenth century. The founders of England's mainland colonies had engaged in intense local conflicts with the Indians, such as King Philip's War (1675–1676) in New England. But after 1690, the colonists were increasingly involved in hostilities that originated on the other side of the Atlantic, in rivalries between Great Britain and France over political and commercial ambitions. The external threat to security forced people in different colonies to devise unprecedented measures of military and political cooperation.

On paper at least, the British settlements enjoyed military superiority over the settlements of New France. Louis XIV (1643–1715) possessed an impressive army of 100,000 well-armed troops, but he dispatched few of them to the New World. He left the defense of Canada and the Mississippi Valley to the companies engaged in the fur trade. Meeting this challenge seemed almost impossible for the French outposts strung out along the Saint Lawrence River and the Great Lakes. In 1754, New France contained only 75,000 inhabitants as compared to 1.2 million people living in Britain's mainland colonies.

For most of the century, the theoretical advantages enjoyed by the English colonists did them little good. While the British settlements possessed a larger and more prosperous population, they were divided into separate governments that sometimes seemed more suspicious of each other than of the French. When war came, French officers and Indian allies exploited these jealousies with considerable skill. Moreover, although the population of New France was comparatively small, it was concentrated along the Saint Lawrence, so that while the French found it difficult to mount effective offensive operations against the English, they could easily mass the forces needed to defend Montreal and Quebec.

King William's and Queen Anne's Wars

Colonial involvement in imperial war began in 1689, when England's new king, William III, declared war on Louis XIV. Europeans called this struggle the War of the League of Augsburg, but to the Americans, it was simply King William's War. Canadians commanded by the Comte de Frontenac raided the northern frontiers of New York and New England, and while they made no territorial gains, they caused considerable suffering among the civilian populations of Massachusetts and New York.

Native Americans often depended on trade goods supplied by the British and sometimes adopted British dress as shown in this engraving of a Mohawk chief, "Old Hendrick," published in London in 1740.

The war ended with the Treaty of Ryswick (1697), but the colonists were drawn almost immediately into a new conflict. Queen Anne's War, known in Europe as the War of Spanish Succession (1702–1713), was fought across a large geographic area. The bloody combat along the American frontier ended in 1713 when Great Britain and France signed the Treaty of Utrecht. European negotiators showed little interest in the military situation in the New World. Their major concern was preserving a balance of power among the European states. More than two decades of intense fighting had taken a heavy toll in North America, but neither French nor English colonists had much to show for their sacrifice.

After George I replaced Anne on the throne in 1714, parliamentary leaders were determined to preserve peace—mainly because of the rising cost of war. Yet on the American frontier, the hostilities continued with raids and reprisals. As people on both sides of this conflict now realized, the

A Century of Conflict: Major Wars, 1689–1763

Dates	European Name	American Name	Major Allies	Issues
1689–1697	War of the League of Augsburg	King William's War	Britain, Holland, Spain, their colonies, and Native American allies against France, its colonies, and Native American allies	Opposition to French bid for control of Europe
1702–1713	War of the Spanish Succession	Queen Anne's War	Britain, Holland, their colonies, and Native American allies against France, Spain, their colonies, and Native American allies	Austria and France hold rival claims to Spanish throne
1739–1748	War of the Austrian Succession (War of Jenkin's Ear)	King George's War	Britain, its colonies and Native American allies, and Austria against France, Spain, their Native American allies, and Prussia	Struggle among Britain, Spain, and France for control of New World territory; among France, Prussia, and Austria for control of central Europe.
1756–1763	Seven Years' War	French and Indian War	Britain, its colonies, and Native American allies against France, its colonies, and Native American allies.	Struggle among Britain, Spain, and France for worldwide control of colonial markets and raw materials

stakes of war were very high; they were fighting for control over the entire West, including the Mississippi Valley.

Both sides viewed this great contest in conspiratorial terms. From South Carolina to Massachusetts Bay, colonists believed the French planned to "encircle" the English settlements, to confine the English to a narrow strip of land along the Atlantic Coast. The English noted that in 1682, La Salle had claimed for the king of France, a territory—Louisiana—that included all the people and resources located on "streams and Rivers" flowing into the Mississippi River. To make good on their claim, the French constructed forts on the Chicago and Illinois rivers. In 1717, they established a military post 200 miles up the Alabama River, well within striking distance of the Carolina frontier, and in 1718, they settled New Orleans. One New Yorker declared in 1715 that ". . . it is impossible that we and the French can

both inhabit this Continent in peace but that one nation must at last give way to the other."

On their part, the French suspected their rivals intended to seize all of North America. Land speculators and frontier traders pushed aggressively into territory claimed by the French and owned by the Native Americans. In 1716, one Frenchman urged his government to hasten the development of Louisiana, since "it is not difficult to guess that their [the British] purpose is to drive us entirely out . . . of North America."

To their great sorrow and eventual destruction, the original inhabitants of the frontier, the Native Americans, were swept up in this undeclared war. The Indians maneuvered to hold their own in the "middle ground." The Iroquois favored the British; the Algonquian peoples generally supported the French. But regardless of the groups to which they belonged, Indian warriors—acting independently and for their own strategic

Major American Battle	Treaty
New England troops assault Quebec under Sir William Phips (1690)	Treaty of Ryswick (1697)
Deerfield Massacre (1704)	Treaty of Utrecht (1713)
New England forces capture Louisbourg under William Pepperrell (1745)	Treaty of Aix-la-Chappelle (1748)
British and Continental forces capture Quebec under Major General James Wolfe (1759)	Peace of Paris (1763)

reasons—found themselves enmeshed in imperial policies set by distant European kings.

King George's War and Its Aftermath

In 1743, the Americans were dragged once again into the imperial conflict. During King George's War (1743–1748), known in Europe as the War of Austrian Succession, the colonists scored a magnificent victory over the French. Louisbourg, a gigantic fortress on Cape Breton Island, the easternmost promontory of Canada, guarded the approaches to the Gulf of Saint Lawrence and Quebec. It was described as the "Gibraltar of the New World." An army of New England troops under the command of William Pepperrell captured Louisbourg in June 1745, a feat that demonstrated the British colonists were able to fight and to mount effective joint operations.

The Americans, however, were in for a shock. When the war ended with the signing of the Treaty of Aix-la-Chapelle in 1748, the British

government handed Louisbourg back to the French in exchange for concessions elsewhere. Such decisions exposed the deep and continuing ambivalence the colonists felt about participation in imperial wars. They were proud to support Great Britain, of course, but the Americans seldom fully understood why the wars were being fought, why certain tactics had been adopted, and why the British accepted treaty terms that so blatantly ignored colonial interests.

The French were not prepared to surrender an inch. But as they recognized, time was running against them. Not only were the English colonies growing more populous, they also possessed a seemingly inexhaustible supply of manufactured goods to trade with the Indians. The French decided in the early 1750s, therefore, to seize the Ohio Valley before the Virginians could do so. They established forts throughout the region, the most formidable being Fort Duquesne, located at the strategic fork in the Ohio River, later renamed Pittsburgh.

Although France and England had not officially declared war, British officials advised the governor of Virginia to "repell force by force." The Virginians needed little encouragement. They were eager to make good their claim to the Ohio Valley, and in 1754, militia companies under the command of a promising young officer, George Washington, constructed Fort Necessity not far from Fort Duquesne. The plan failed. French and Indian troops overran the badly exposed outpost (July 3, 1754). Among other things, this humiliating setback revealed that a single colony could not defeat the French.

Albany Congress and Braddock's Defeat

Benjamin Franklin, for one, appreciated the need for intercolonial cooperation. When British officials invited representatives from the northern colonies to Albany (June 1754) to discuss relations with the Iroquois, Franklin used the occasion to present a bold blueprint for colonial union. His so-called Albany Plan envisioned the formation of a Grand Council, made up of elected delegates from the various colonies, to oversee matters of common defense, western expansion, and Indian affairs. A President General appointed by the king would preside. Franklin's most daring suggestion involved taxation. He insisted the

This mid-eighteenth-century lithograph portrays colonial assault troops, under the command of William Pepperrell, establishing a beachhead at Freshwater Cove near Louisbourg. Pepperrell's troops went on to capture Louisbourg.

council be authorized to collect taxes to cover military expenditures.

First reaction to the Albany Plan was enthusiastic. To take effect, however, it required the support of the separate colonial assemblies as well as Parliament. It received neither. The assemblies were jealous of their fiscal authority, and the English thought the scheme undermined the Crown's power over American affairs.

In 1755, the Ohio Valley again became the scene of fierce fighting. Even though there was still no formal declaration of war, the British resolved to destroy Fort Duquesne, and to that end, they dispatched units of the regular army to America. In command was Major General Edward Braddock, an obese, humorless veteran who inspired neither fear nor respect. One colonist described Braddock as ". . . very indolent, Slave to his passions, women & wine, as great an Epicure as could be in his eating, tho a brave man."

On July 9, Braddock led a joint force of twenty-five hundred British redcoats and colonists to humiliating defeat. The French and Indians opened fire as Braddock's army waded across the Monongahela River, about 8 miles from Fort Duquesne. Along a narrow road already congested with heavy wagons and confused men, Braddock ordered a counterattack, described by one of his officers as "without any form or order but that of a parcell of school boys coming out of s[c]hool." Nearly 70 percent of Braddock's troops were killed or wounded in western Pennsylvania. The general himself died in battle. The French, who suffered only light casualties, remained in firm control of the Ohio Valley.

The entire affair profoundly angered Washington, who fumed, "We have been most scandalously beaten by a trifling body of men." The British thought their allies the Iroquois might desert them after this embarrassing defeat. The Indians, however, took the news in stride, observing that "they were not at all surprised to hear it, as they [Braddock's redcoats] were men who had crossed the Great Water and were unacquainted with the arts of war among the Americans."

Seven Years' War

Britain's imperial war effort had hit bottom. No one in England or America seemed to possess the leadership necessary to drive the French from the Mississippi Valley. The cabinet of George II (1727–1760) lacked the will to organize and finance a sustained military campaign in the New World, and colonial assemblies balked every time Britain asked them to raise men and money. On May 18, 1756, the British officially declared war on the French, a conflict called the French and Indian War in America and the Seven Years' War in Europe.

Had it not been for William Pitt, the most powerful minister in George's cabinet, the military stalemate might have continued. This supremely self-confident Englishman believed he was the only person capable of saving the British empire, an opinion he publicly expressed. When he became effective head of the Ministry in December 1756, Pitt had an opportunity to demonstrate his talents.

In the past, warfare on the European continent had worked mainly to France's advantage. Pitt saw no point in continuing to concentrate on Europe, and in 1757 he advanced a bold new imperial policy, one based on commercial assumptions. In Pitt's judgment, the critical confrontation would take place in North America, where Britain and France were struggling to control colonial markets and raw materials. Indeed, according to Pitt, America was "where England and Europe are to be fought for." He was determined, therefore, to expel the French from the continent, however great the cost.

To effect this ambitious scheme, Pitt took personal command of the army and navy. He mapped strategy. He even promoted young promising officers over the heads of their superiors. He also recognized that the success of the war effort could not depend on the generosity of the colonial assemblies. Great Britain would have to foot most of the bill. Pitt's military expenditures, of course, created an enormous national debt that would soon haunt both Britain and its colonies, but at the time, no one foresaw the fiscal consequences of victory in America.

To direct the grand campaign, Pitt selected two relatively obscure officers, Jeffrey Amherst and James Wolfe. It was a masterful choice, one that

The first political cartoon to appear in an American newspaper was created by Benjamin Franklin in 1754 to emphasize the importance of the Albany Plan.

a less self-assured man than Pitt would never have risked. Both officers were young, talented, and ambitious, and on July 26, 1758, forces under their direction captured Louisbourg, the same fortress the colonists had taken a decade earlier!

This victory cut the Canadians' main supply line with France. The small population of New France could no longer meet the military demands placed on it. As the situation became increasingly desperate, the French forts of the Ohio Valley and the Great Lakes began to fall. Duquesne was simply abandoned late in 1758 as French and Indian troops under the Marquis de Montcalm retreated toward Quebec and Montreal. During the summer of 1759, the French surrendered key forts at Ticonderoga, Crown Point, and Niagara.

The climax to a century of war came dramatically in September 1759. Wolfe, now a major general, assaulted Quebec with nine thousand men. But it was not simply force of arms that brought victory. Wolfe proceeded as if he were preparing to attack the city directly, but under cover of darkness, his troops scaled a cliff to dominate a less well-defended position. At dawn on September 13, 1759, they took the French from the rear by surprise. The decisive action occurred on the Plains of Abraham, a bluff high above the Saint Lawrence River. Both Wolfe and Montcalm were mortally wounded. When an aide informed Wolfe the French had been routed, he

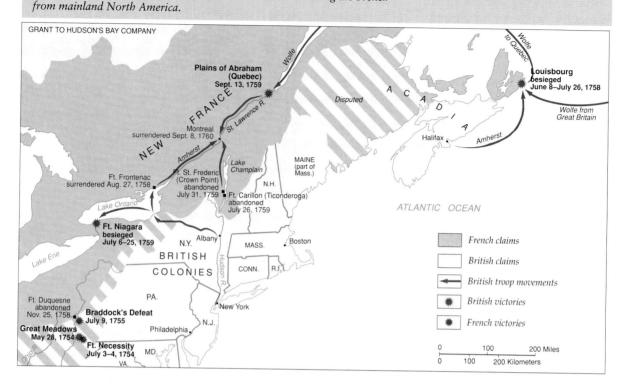

The Seven Years' War, 1756–1763
Major battle sites. The conflict ended with Great Britain driving the French from mainland North America.

GRANT TO HUDSON'S BAY COMPANY

Plains of Abraham
(Quebec)
Sept. 13, 1759

Wolfe
to Quebec

Louisbourg
besieged
June 8–July 26, 1758

Wolfe from
Great Britain

Montreal
surrendered Sept. 8, 1760

St. Lawrence R.

A C A D I A

NEW FRANCE

Disputed

Amherst

Halifax

Amherst

Ft. Frontenac
surrendered Aug. 27, 1758

Ft. St. Frederic
(Crown Point)
abandoned
July 31, 1759

Lake
Champlain

MAINE
(part of
Mass.)

N.H.

Ft. Carillon (Ticonderoga)
abandoned
July 26, 1759

ATLANTIC OCEAN

Lake Ontario

Ft. Niagara
besieged
July 6–25, 1759

N.Y.

Albany

MASS.

Boston

Lake Erie

BRITISH

COLONIES

Hudson R.

CONN.

R.I.

PA.

Ft. Duquesne
abandoned
Nov. 25, 1758

Braddock's Defeat
July 9, 1755

New York

N.J.

Great Meadows
May 28, 1754

Philadelphia

Ft. Necessity
July 3–4, 1754

MD.

Ohio R.

VA.

	French claims
	British claims
←	British troop movements
✳	British victories
✳	French victories

0   100   200 Miles
0   100   200 Kilometers

sighed, "Now, God be praised, I will die in peace." On September 8, 1760, Amherst accepted the final surrender of the French army at Montreal.

The Peace of Paris signed on February 10, 1763, almost fulfilled Pitt's grandiose dreams. Great Britain took possession of an empire that stretched around the globe. Only Guadeloupe and Martinique, the Caribbean sugar islands, were given back to the French. After a century-long struggle, the French had been driven from the mainland of North America. Even Louisiana passed out of France's control into Spanish hands. The treaty gave Britain title to Canada, Florida, and all the land east of the Mississippi River. Moreover, with the stroke of a diplomat's pen, eighty thousand French-speaking Canadians, most of them Catholics, became the subjects of George III.

The Americans were overjoyed. It was a time of good feelings and national pride. Together, the English and their colonial allies had thwarted the "Gallic peril." Samuel Davies, a Presbyterian who had brought the Great Awakening to Virginia, announced confidently that the long-awaited victory would inaugurate "*a new heaven and a new earth.*"

Perceptions of War

The Seven Years' War made a deep impression on American society. Even though Franklin's Albany Plan had failed, the military struggle had forced the colonists to cooperate on an unprecedented scale. It also drew them into closer contact with Britain. They became aware of being part of a great empire, but in the very process of waging war, they acquired a more intimate sense of an America that lay beyond the plantation and the village. Conflict had carried thousands of young men across colonial boundaries, exposing them to a vast territory full of opportunities for a booming population. Moreover, the war trained a corps of American officers, people like George Washington, who learned from firsthand experience that the British were not invincible.

British officials later accused the Americans of ingratitude. England, they claimed, had sent troops and provided funds to liberate the colonists from the threat of French attack. The Americans, appreciative of the aid from England, cheered on the British but dragged their feet at every stage, refusing to pay the bills. These charges were later incorporated into a general argument justifying parliamentary taxation in America.

The British had a point. The colonists were, in fact, slow in providing the men and materials needed to fight the French. Nevertheless, they did make a significant contribution to the war effort, and it was perfectly reasonable for Americans to regard themselves at the very least as junior partners in the empire. After all, they had supplied almost twenty thousand soldiers and spent well over £2 million. In a single year, in fact, Massachusetts enlisted five thousand men out of an adult male population of about fifty thousand, a commitment that, in the words of one military historian, meant "the war was being waged on a scale comparable to the great wars of modern times." After making such a sacrifice—indeed, after demonstrating their loyalty to the mother country—the colonists would surely have been disturbed to learn that General James Wolfe, the hero of Quebec, had stated, "The Americans are in general the dirtiest, the most contemptible, cowardly dogs that you can conceive. There is no depending upon them in action. They fall down in their own dirt and desert in battalions, officers and all."

North America After 1763
The Peace of Paris (1763) redrew the map of North America. Great Britain received all the French holdings except a few islands in the Caribbean.

RULE BRITANNIA?

James Thomson, an Englishman, understood the hold of empire on the popular imagination of the eighteenth century. In 1740, he composed words that British patriots have proudly sung for more than two centuries:

Rule Britannia, rule the waves
Britons never will be slaves

Colonial Americans—at least, those of British background—joined the chorus. By mid-century they took their political and cultural cues from Great Britain. They fought its wars, purchased its consumer goods, flocked to hear its evangelical preachers, and read its many publications. Without question, the empire provided the colonists with a compelling source of identity.

An editor justified the establishment of New Hampshire's first newspaper in precisely these terms. "By this Means," the publisher observed, "the spirited *Englishman*, the mountainous *Welshman*, the brave *Scotchman*, and *Irishman*, and the loyal *American*, may be firmly united and mutually RESOLVED to guard the glorious Throne of BRITANNIA. . . . as *British Brothers*, in defending the Common Cause." Even new immigrants, the Germans, Scotch-Irish, and

CHRONOLOGY

1680	Popé leads Pueblo revolt against the Spanish in New Mexico
1689	William and Mary accede to the English throne
1706	Birth of Benjamin Franklin
1714	George I of Hanover becomes monarch of Great Britain
1732	Colony of Georgia is established • Birth of George Washington
1734–1736	First expression of the Great Awakening at Northampton, Massachusetts
1740	George Whitefield electrifies listeners at Boston
1745	Colonial troops capture Louisbourg • First American Lutheran ministers ordained in Philadelphia
1754	Albany Congress meets
1755	Braddock is defeated by the French and Indians in western Pennsylvania
1756	Seven Years' War is formally declared
1759	British are victorious at Quebec. Wolfe and Montcalm are killed in battle
1760	George III becomes king of Great Britain
1763	Peace of Paris ending French and Indian War is signed
1769	Junípero Serra begins to build missions in California
1821	Mexico declares independence from Spain

Recommended Reading

A comprehensive examination of Anglo-American relations in the late colonial period is Lawrence H. Gipson, *British Empire Before the American Revolution*, 8 vols. (1936-1949). A much shorter, and in many ways more useful, introduction to eighteenth-century colonial society is Richard Hofstadter, *America at 1750: A Social Portrait* (1971). A stimulating survey of English culture and politics can be found in Roy Porter, *English Society in the Eighteenth Century* (1982). For the wars of empire, see Howard H. Peckham, *The Colonial Wars, 1689–1762* (1964), and Fred Anderson's splendid social history of colonial soldiering, *A People's Army: Massachusetts Soldiers and Society in the Seven Years' War* (1984). Sydney E. Ahlstrom provides an encyclopedic review of eighteenth-century religion in *Religious History of the American People* (1972). Also valuable is Patricia Bonomi, *Under the Cope of Heaven: Religion, Society, and Politics in Colonial America* (1986). The most imaginative analysis of colonial politics remains Bernard Bailyn, *The Origin of American Politics* (1968). And recently, Bailyn has produced a masterful study of European migration entitled *Voyagers to the West* (1986).

Additional Bibliography

The significance of American population growth in this period is thoughtfully examined in John J. McCusker and Russell R. Menard, *The Economy of British America, 1607–1789* (1985). The transfer of various British subcultures is the topic of David H. Fischer's provocative *Albion's Seed: Four British Folkways in America* (1989). A useful review of the recent literature can be found in Bernard Bailyn and Philip D. Morgan, eds., *Strangers Within the Realm: Cultural Margins of the First British Empire* (1991). A. G. Roeber provides an impressively original interpretation of the transfer of German culture in *Palatines, Liberty, and Property: German Lutherans in Colonial British America* (1993). For the Scots, see Ned Landsman, *Scotland and Its First American Colony* (1985). Roger A. Ekirch offers a thorough analysis of the convict servant trade in *Bound for America* (1987).

The most exciting recent historical literature deals with the formation of a multicultural backcountry. These studies are especially good on the development of Native American societies: Daniel H. Unser, Jr., *Indians, Settlers, and Slaves in a Frontier Exchange Economy* (1992); Michael N. McConnell, *A Country Between: The Upper Ohio Valley and Its Peoples,*

Africans, who felt no political loyalty to Great Britain and no affinity to English culture, had to assimilate to some degree to the dominant English culture of the colonies.

Americans hailed Britannia. In 1763, they were the victors, the conquerors of the backcountry. In their moment of glory the colonists assumed that Britain's rulers saw the Americans as "Brothers," as equal partners in the business of empire. Only slowly would they learn the British had a differ-

1724–1774 (1992); Richard White, *The Middle Ground: Indians, Empires, and Republics in the Great Lakes Region* (1991); Daniel K. Richter, *The Ordeal of the Longhouse: The Peoples of the Iroquois League in the Era of European Colonization* (1992); Peter H. Wood et al., eds., *Powhatan's Mantle: Indians in the Colonial Southeast* (1989); and Peter C. Mancall, *Valley of Opportunity: Economic Culture Along the Upper Susquehanna* (1991).

The complex story of Spanish colonization is told masterfully in David J. Weber, *The Spanish Frontier in North America* (1992). Weber also edited a book of valuable essays entitled *New Spain's Far Northern Frontier* (1979). One of the most original works in this field, one that explores the meaning of gender, is Ramón A. Gutiérrez, *When Jesus Came, the Corn Mothers Went Away: Marriage, Sexuality, and Power in New Mexico, 1500–1846* (1991).

Eighteenth-century English politics, theory and practice, is the subject of an increasingly sophisticated literature. Read Linda Colley, *Britons: Forging the Nation, 1707–1837* (1992); Gerald Newman, *The Rise of English Nationalism: A Cultural History* (1987); and Lawrence Stones, ed., *An Imperial State at War* (1994).

The way Americans living in different colonies interpreted contemporary British political culture is discussed in Bernard Bailyn, *The Origins of American Politics* (1968); Jack P. Greene, *Peripheries and Center* (1986); Richard Bushman, *King and People in Provincial Massachusetts* (1985); and T. H. Breen, *Tobacco Culture: The Great Tidewater Planters on the Eve of Revolution* (1986). Also see J. Greene, *Quest for Power* (1983); Patricia Bonomi, *A Factious People: Politics and Society in Colonial New York* (1977); Robert Weir, *"The Last American Freemen," Studies in the Political Culture of the Colonial and Revolutionary South* (1986).

On the Great Awakening, see George Whitefield's *Journals* (1969) as well as *The Great Awakening* (1967), edited by Alan Heimert and Perry Miller. Also useful are Alan Heimert, *Religion and the American Mind* (1966); Harry S. Stout, *The New England Soul* (1988); John Butler, *Awash in a Sea of Faith* (1990); and Frank Lambert, *"Pedlar in Divinity": George Whitefield and the Transatlantic Revivals* (1994). For an explanation of the eighteenth-century concern for good manners, see Richard L. Bushman, *The Refinement of America: Persons, Houses, Cities* (1992).

The American Revolution

From Gentry Protest to Popular Revolt, 1763–1783

During the revolutionary war, a captured British officer spent some time at the plantation of Colonel Thomas Mann Randolph, a leader of Virginia's gentry. The Englishman described the arrival of three farmers who were members of the local militia. He characterized the militiamen as "peasants," for without asking their host's permission, the Americans drew chairs up to the fire, pulled off their muddy boots, and began spitting. The British officer was appalled; after the farmers departed, he observed they had not shown Randolph proper deference. The colonel responded that such behavior had come to be expected, for "the spirit of independency" had been transformed into "equality." Indeed, every American who "bore arms" during the Revolution considered himself as good as his neighbors. "No doubt," Randolph remarked to the officer, "each of these men conceives himself, in every respect, my equal."

This chance encounter illuminates the character of the American Revolution. The initial stimulus for rebellion came from the gentry, from the rich and wellborn, who resented Parliament's efforts to curtail their rights within the British empire. They voiced their unhappiness in carefully reasoned statements and in speeches before elected assemblies. Passionate rhetoric made them uneasy.

But as these influential planters, wealthy merchants, and prominent clergymen discovered, the revolutionary movement generated a momentum that they could not control. As relations with Britain deteriorated, particularly after 1765, the traditional leaders of colonial society invited the ordinary folk to join the protest—as rioters, as petitioners, and finally, as soldiers. Newspapers, sermons, and pamphlets helped transform what had begun as a squabble among the gentry into a mass movement, and as Randolph learned, once the people had become involved in shaping the nation's destiny, they could never again be excluded.

A second, often overlooked, aspect of the American Revolution involved a massive military commitment. If common American soldiers had not been willing to stand up to seasoned British troops, to face the terror of the bayonet charge, independence would have remained a dream of intellectuals. Proportionate to the population, a greater percentage of Americans died in military service during the Revolution than in any war in American history, with the exception of the Civil War. The concept of liberty so magnificently expressed in revolutionary pamphlets was not, therefore, simply an abstraction, an exclusive concern of political theorists like Thomas Jefferson and John Adams. It also motivated ordinary folk—mud-covered Virginia militiamen, for example—to take up weapons and risk death. Those who survived the ordeal were never quite the same, for the very experience of fighting, of assuming responsibility in battle and perhaps even of taking the lives of British officers, gave dramatic new meaning to social equality.

AN EXPECTANT SOCIETY

Colonists who were alive during the 1760s did not anticipate the coming of independence. It is only from our modern perspective that we see how the events of this period would lead to the formation of a new nation. The colonists, of course, did not know what the future would bring. They would probably have characterized these years as "postwar," as a time of heightened economic and political expectation following the successful conclusion of the Seven Years' War (see Chapter 4).

For many Americans, it was a period of optimism. The population continued to grow. Indeed, in 1776, approximately 2.5 million people, black and white, were living in Great Britain's thirteen mainland colonies. The population was extremely young. Nearly 60 percent of the American people were under twenty-one. This is a fact of considerable significance. At any given time, most people in this society were small children, and many of the young men who fought the British during the Revolution either had not been alive during the Stamp Act crisis or, if they were alive, had been infants. Any explanation for the coming of independence, therefore, must take into account the continuing political mobilization of so many young people.

Postwar Americans also experienced a high level of prosperity. To be sure, some major port cities went through a difficult period as colonists who had been employed during the fighting were thrown out of work. Sailors and ship workers, for example, were especially vulnerable to layoffs of this sort. In general, however, white Americans did very well. In fact, the quality of their material lives was not substantially lower than that of the English. In 1774, the per capita wealth of the Americans—this figure includes blacks as well as whites—was £37.4. This sum exceeds the per capita wealth of most developing countries today. On the eve of revolution, £37.4 would have purchased about 310 bushels of wheat, 1,600 pounds of rice, 11 cows, or 6 horses. A typical white family of five—a father, mother, and three dependent children—would have been able to afford not only decent food, clothing, and housing, but would also have had money left over with which to purchase consumer goods. Even the poorest colonists seem to have benefited from a rising standard of living, and although they may not have done as well as their wealthier neighbors, they too wanted to preserve gains they had made.

Wealth, however, was not evenly distributed in this society. Regional variations were striking. The southern colonies enjoyed the highest levels of personal wealth in America, which can be explained in part by the ownership of slaves. Over 90 percent of America's unfree workers lived in the South, and they represented a huge capital investment. Even without including the slaves in these wealth estimates, the South did quite well. In terms of aggregate wealth, the Middle Colonies also scored impressively. In fact, only New England lagged noticeably behind, a reflection of its relative inability to produce large amounts of exports for a growing world market.

Roots of Imperial Crisis

Ultimate responsibility for preserving the empire fell to George III. When he became king of England in 1760, he was a young man, only twenty-two years of age. In public, contemporaries praised the new monarch. In private, however, they expressed grave reservations. The youth had led a sheltered, loveless life; his father, an irresponsible playboy, died in 1751 before ascending the throne. Young George had not received a good education, and even though he

Despite his insecurity over an inadequate education, George III was determined to take an active role in reigning over Parliament and the colonies.

demonstrated considerable mechanical ability, his grandfather, George II, thought his grandson dull-witted, an opinion widely shared. As one might expect, George grew up hating not only his grandfather, but almost everyone associated with the reign of George II.

To hide his intellectual inadequacies, the new king adopted a pedantic habit of correcting people for small faults, a characteristic made all the more annoying by his obvious inability to grasp the larger implications of government policy. During a difficult period that demanded imagination, generosity, and wisdom, George muddled along as best he could.

The new monarch was determined to play an aggressive role in government. This decision caused considerable dismay among England's political leaders. For decades a powerful, though loosely associated, group of men who called themselves "Whigs" had set policy and controlled patronage. George II had accepted this situation, and so long as the Whigs in Parliament did not meddle with his beloved army, the king had let them rule the nation.

In one stroke, George III destroyed this cozy relationship. He selected as his chief minister the Earl of Bute, a Scot whose only qualification for office appeared to be his friendship with the young king. The Whigs who dominated Parliament were outraged. Bute had no ties with the members of the House of Commons; he owed them no favors. It seemed to the Whigs that with the appointment of Bute, George was trying to turn back the clock, to reestablish a personal Stuart monarchy free from traditional constitutional restraints. The Whigs blamed Bute for every wrong, real or imagined. George did not, in fact, harbor such arbitrary ambitions, but his actions threw customary political practices into doubt.

By 1763, Bute had despaired of public life and left office. His departure, however, neither restored the Whigs to preeminence nor dampened the king's enthusiasm for domestic politics. Everyone agreed George had the right to select whomever he desired for cabinet posts, but until 1770, no one seemed able to please the monarch. Ministers came and went, often for no other reason than George's personal distaste. Because of this chronic instability, subministers (minor bureaucrats who directed routine colonial affairs) did not know what was expected of them. In the absence of long-range policy, some ministers made narrowly based decisions; others did nothing. Most devoted their energies to finding a political patron capable of satisfying the fickle king. Talent played little part in the scramble for office, and incompetent hacks were advanced as frequently as were men of vision. With such turbulence surrounding him, the king showed little interest in the American colonies.

The king, however, does not bear the sole blame for England's loss of empire. The members of Parliament who actually drafted the statutes that gradually drove a wedge between the colonists and Britain must share the blame, for they failed to provide innovative answers to the explosive constitutional issues of the day. The

problem was not stupidity, or even obstinancy, qualities that are found in equal measure among all peoples.

In part, the impasse resulted from sheer ignorance. Few Englishmen active in government had ever visited America. For those who attempted to follow colonial affairs, accurate information proved extremely difficult to obtain. Packet boats carrying passengers and mail sailed regularly between London and the various colonial ports, but the voyage across the Atlantic required at least four weeks. Furthermore, all correspondence was laboriously copied in longhand by overworked clerks serving in understaffed offices. One could not expect to receive from America an answer to a specific question in less than three months. As a result of the lag in communication between England and America, rumors sometimes passed for true accounts, and misunderstanding influenced the formulation of colonial policy.

But failure of communication alone was not to blame for the widening gap between the colonists and England. Even when complete information was available, the two sides were often unable to understand each other's positions. The central element in this Anglo-American debate was a concept known as *parliamentary sovereignty*. The English ruling classes viewed the role of Parliament from a historical perspective that most colonists never shared. They insisted that Parliament was the dominant element within the constitution. Indeed, this elective body protected rights and property from an arbitrary monarch. During the reign of the Stuarts, especially under Charles I (1625–1649), the authority of Parliament had been challenged, and it was not until the Glorious Revolution of 1688 that the English Crown formally recognized Parliament's supreme authority in matters such as taxation. Almost no one, including George III, would have dissented from a speech made in 1766 before the House of Commons in which a representative declared, "The parliament hath, and must have, from the nature and essence of the constitution, has had, and ever will have a sovereign supreme power and jurisdiction over every part of the dominions of the state, *to make laws in all cases whatsoever*."

Such a constitutional position did not leave much room for compromise. Most members of

Parliament took a hard line on this issue. The notion of dividing or sharing sovereignty simply made no sense to the English ruling class. As Thomas Hutchinson, royal governor of Massachusetts, explained, no middle ground existed "between the supreme authority of Parliament and the total dependence of the colonies: it is impossible there should be two independent legislatures in one and the same state."

The logic of this argument seemed self-evident to the British. In fact, Parliamentary leaders could never quite understand why the colonists were so difficult to persuade. In frustration, Lord Hillsborough, the British Secretary of State, admonished the colonial agent for Connecticut, "It is essential to the constitution to preserve the supremacy of Parliament inviolate; and tell your friends in America . . . that it is as much their interest to support the constitution and preserve the supremacy of Parliament as it is ours."

No Taxation Without Representation: The American Perspective

Americans most emphatically did not see it in their "interest" to maintain the "supremacy of Parliament." The crisis in imperial relations forced the colonists first to define and then to defend principles deeply rooted in their own political culture. For more than a century, their ideas about the colonies' role within the British empire had remained a vague, untested bundle of assumptions about personal liberties, property rights, and representative institutions.

By 1763, however, certain fundamental American beliefs had become clear. From Massachusetts to Georgia, colonists aggressively defended the powers of the provincial assemblies. They drew on a rich legislative history of their own. Over the course of the century, the American assemblies had steadily expanded their authority over taxation and expenditure. Since no one in Britain bothered to clip their legislative wings, these provincial bodies assumed a major role in policy making and routine administration. In other words, by mid-century the assemblies looked like American copies of Parliament. It seemed unreasonable, therefore, for the British suddenly to insist on the supremacy of Parliament, for as the legislators of Massachusetts observed in 1770, "This house has the same inherent rights in this province as the house of commons in Great Britain."

The constitutional debate turned ultimately on the meaning of representation itself. In 1764, a British official informed the colonists that even though they had not elected members to Parliament—indeed, even though they had had no direct contact with the current members—they were nevertheless "virtually" represented by that august body. The members of parliament, he declared, represented the political interests of everyone who lived in the British empire. It did not really matter whether they had cast a vote.

The colonists ridiculed this argument. The only representatives the Americans recognized as legitimate were those actually chosen by the people for whom they spoke. On this crucial point they would not compromise. As John Adams insisted, a representative assembly should actually mirror its constituents: "It should think, feel, reason, and act like them." Since the members of Parliament could not possibly "think" like Americans, it followed logically they could not represent them. And if they were not genuine representatives, the members of Parliament—pretensions to sovereignty not withstanding—had no business taxing the American people. Thus, in 1764 the Connecticut Assembly declared in bold letters, "NO LAW CAN BE MADE OR ABROGATED WITHOUT THE CONSENT OF THE PEOPLE BY THEIR REPRESENTATIVES."

Politics of Virtue

The political ideology that had the greatest popular appeal among the colonists contained a strong moral component, one that British rulers and American loyalists (people who sided with the king and Parliament during the Revolution) never fully understood. The origins of this highly religious perspective on civil government are difficult to locate with precision, but certainly, the Great Awakening created a general awareness of an obligation to conduct public as well as private affairs according to Scripture (see Chapter 4).

Americans expressed their political beliefs in a language they had borrowed from English writers. The person most frequently cited was John Locke, the great seventeenth-century philosopher whose *Two Treatises of Government* (first published in 1690) seemed to colonial readers at least a brilliant description of what was in fact American political practice. Locke claimed that all people possessed natural and inalienable rights. In order to preserve these God-given rights—the rights of life, liberty, and property, for example—free men (the status of women in Locke's work was less clear) formed contracts. These agreements were the foundation of human society as well as civil government, and they required the consent of the people who were actually governed. There could be no coercion. Locke justified rebellion against arbitrary forms of government that were by their very nature unreasonable. Americans delighted in Locke's ability to unite traditional religious values with a spirited defense of popular government, and even when they did not fully understand his technical writings, they seldom missed a chance to quote from the works of "the Great Mr. Locke."

Colonial Americans also enthusiastically subscribed to the so-called Commonwealthman tradition, a body of political assumptions generally identified with two eighteenth-century English publicists, John Trenchard and Thomas Gordon (see Chapter 4). The writings of such figures—most of whom spent their lives in political opposition—helped persuade the colonists that *power* was extremely dangerous, a force that would surely destroy liberty unless it was countered by *virtue*. Persons who shared this highly charged moral outlook regarded bad policy as not simply the result of human error. Rather, it was an indication of sin and corruption.

Insistence on public virtue—sacrifice of self-interest to the public good—became the dominant theme of revolutionary political writing. American pamphleteers seldom took a dispassionate, legalistic approach to their analysis of power and liberty. More commonly, they exposed plots hatched by corrupt courtiers, such as the Earl of Bute. None of them—nor their readers—had any doubt that Americans were more virtuous than were the people of England.

During the 1760s, however, popular writers were not certain how long the colonists could hold out against arbitrary taxation, standing armies, Anglican bishops—in other words, against a host of external threats designed to crush American liberty. In 1774, for example, the people of Farmington, Connecticut, declared that "the present ministry, being instigated by the devil and led by their wicked and corrupt hearts, have a design to take away our liberties and properties, and to enslave us forever." Indeed, these Connecticut farmers described Britain's leaders as "pimps and parasites." This highly emotional, conspiratorial rhetoric sometimes shocks modern readers who assume America's revolutionary leaders were products of the Enlightenment, persons who relied solely on reason to solve social and political problems. Whatever the origins of their ideas may have been, the colonial pamphleteers successfully roused ordinary men and women to resist Britain with force of arms.

Colonial newspapers spread these ideas through a large dispersed population. A majority of adult white males—especially in the Northern Colonies—were literate, and it is not surprising that the number of journals published in this country increased dramatically during the revolutionary period. For the first time in American his-

Samuel Adams, seen here in a portrait by John Singleton Copley, was a fervid republican ideologue who urged the American colonists to defend their political virtue against British corruption.

tory, persons living in various parts of the continent could closely follow events that occurred in distant American cities. Because of the availability of newspapers, the details of Bostonians' confrontations with British authorities were known throughout the colonies, and these shared political experiences drew Americans more closely together, making it possible—in the words of John Adams—for "Thirteen clocks . . . to strike together—a perfection of mechanism which no artist had ever before effected."

ERODING THE BONDS OF EMPIRE: CHALLENGE AND RESISTANCE

The Seven Years' War saddled Great Britain with a national debt so huge that over half of the annual national budget went to pay the interest on it. Almost everyone in government assumed that with the cessation of hostilities, the troops would be disbanded, thus saving a lot of money. George III had other plans. He insisted on keeping the largest peacetime army in British history on active duty, supposedly to protect Indians from predatory frontiersmen and to preserve order in the newly conquered territories of Florida and Quebec.

Maintaining such a force so far distant from the mother country fueled the budgetary crisis. The growing financial burden weighed heavily on restive English taxpayers and sent government leaders scurrying in search of new sources of revenue.

For their part, colonists doubted the value of this very expensive army. First, Britain did not leave enough troops in America to maintain peace effectively. The weakness of the army was dramatically demonstrated during the spring of 1763. The native peoples of the backcountry—the Senecas, Ottawas, Miamis, Creeks, and Cherokees—had begun discussing how they might turn back the tide of white settlement. The powerful spiritual leader Neolin, known as the Delaware Prophet, helped these Indians articulate their fear and anger. He urged them to restore their cultures to the "original state that they were in before the white people found out their country." If moral regeneration required violence, so be it. Neolin converted Pontiac, an Ottawa warrior, to the cause, and he, in turn, coordinated an uprising among the western Indians who had formerly been French allies and who hated all British people—even those sent to protect them from land-grabbing colonists. In May, Pontiac attacked Detroit; other Indians harassed the Pennsylvania and Virginia frontiers. At the end of the year, after his followers began deserting, Pontiac sued for peace. During even this brief outbreak, the British army proved unable to defend exposed colonial settlements, and several thousand Americans lost their lives.

Second, the colonists fully intended to settle the fertile region west of the Appalachian Mountains. After the British government issued the Proclamation of 1763, which prohibited governors from granting land beyond the headwaters of rivers flowing into the Atlantic, disappointed Americans viewed the army as an obstruction to legitimate economic development, a domestic police force that cost too much money.

The task of reducing England's debt fell to George Grenville, the rigid, somewhat unimaginative chancellor of the exchequer who replaced Bute in 1763 as the king's first minister. After carefully reviewing the state of Britain's finances, Grenville concluded that the colonists would have to contribute to the maintenance of the army. The first bill he steered through Parliament was the Revenue Act of 1764, known as the Sugar Act.

This legislation placed a new burden on the Navigation Acts that had governed the flow of colonial commerce for almost a century (see Chapter 3). Those acts had forced Americans to trade almost exclusively with Britain. The statutes were not, however, primarily intended as a means to raise money for the British government. The Sugar Act—and the acts that soon followed—redefined the relationship between America and Great Britain. Parliament now expected the colonies to generate revenue. The preamble of the Sugar Act proclaimed explicitly: "It is just and necessary that a revenue be raised . . . in America for defraying the expenses of defending, protecting, and securing the same." The purpose of the Sugar Act was to discourage smuggling, bribery, and other illegalities that prevented the Navigation Acts from being profitable. Parliament reduced the duty on molasses (set originally by the Molasses Act of 1733) from six to three pence per gallon. At so low a rate, Grenville reasoned, colonial mer-

Colonial Products and Trade

The American colonies produced many goods that were valuable to Britain,
but they were also dependent on British manufactures such as cloth, metal goods, and ceramics.

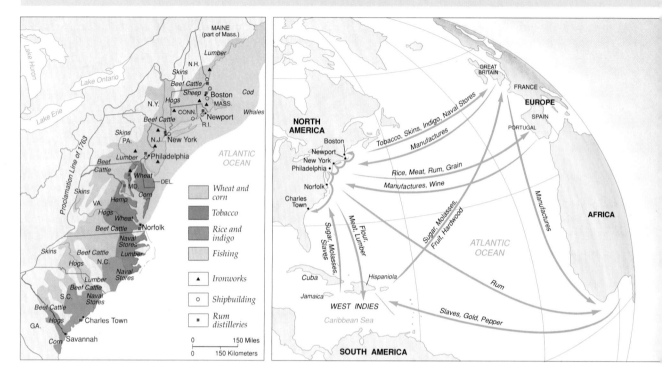

chants would have little incentive to bribe customs collectors. Much needed revenue would be diverted from the pockets of corrupt officials into the Treasury so that it might be used to maintain the army.

Grenville had been too clever by half. The Americans immediately saw through his unconstitutional scheme. According to the members of the Rhode Island Assembly, the Sugar Act taxed the colonists in a manner "inconsistent with their rights and privileges as British subjects." James Otis, a fiery orator from Massachusetts, exclaimed the legislation deprived Americans of "the right of assessing their own taxes."

The Act generated no violence. In fact, ordinary men and women were only marginally involved in the drafting of formal petitions. The protest was still confined to the members of the colonial assemblies, to the merchants, and to the well-to-do Americans who had personal interests in commerce.

Birth of Popular Politics

Passage of the Stamp Act in 1765 transformed conversation among gentlemen into a mass political movement. The crisis might have been avoided. Colonial agents had presented Grenville with alternative schemes for raising money in America. But Grenville was a stubborn man, and he had little fear of parliamentary opposition. The majority of the House of Commons assumed that Parliament possessed the right to tax the colonists, and when the chancellor of the exchequer announced a plan to squeeze £60,000 annually out of the Americans by requiring them to purchase special seals or stamps to validate legal documents, the members responded with enthusiasm. The Stamp Act was scheduled to go into effect on November 1, 1765, and in anticipation of brisk sales, Grenville appointed stamp distributors for every colony.

During discussion of the act in Parliament, several members warned the act would raise a storm of protest in the colonies. Colonel Isaac Barré, a veteran of the Seven Years' War, reminded his colleagues that the Americans were "sons of liberty" and would not surrender their rights without a fight. But Barré's appeal fell on deaf ears.

Word of the Stamp Act reached America in May, and it was soon clear that Barré had gauged the colonists' response correctly. The most dramatic incident occurred in Virginia's House of Burgesses. Patrick Henry, young and eloquent, whom contemporaries compared in fervor to evangelical preachers, introduced five resolutions protesting the Stamp Act on the floor of the assembly. He timed his move carefully. It was late in the session; many of the more conservative burgesses had already departed for their plantations. Even then, Henry's resolves declaring that Virginians had the right to tax themselves as they alone saw fit passed by narrow margins. The fifth resolution, stricken almost immediately from the legislative records, announced that any attempt to collect stamp revenues in America was "illegal, unconstitutional, and unjust, and has a manifest tendency to destroy British as well as American liberty." Henry was carried away by the force of his own rhetoric. He reminded his fellow Virginians that Caesar had had his Brutus, Charles I his Cromwell, and he hoped that "some good American would stand up for his country. . ." An astonished speaker of the house cut Henry off in mid-sentence, accusing him of treason.

The Virginia Resolves might have remained a local matter had it not been for the colonial press. Newspapers throughout America printed Henry's resolutions, but perhaps because editors did not really know what had happened in Williamsburg, they reported that all five resolutions had received the burgesses' full support. Several journals even carried two resolves that Henry had not dared to introduce. The result of this misunderstanding, of course, was that the Virginians appeared to have taken an extremely radical position on the issue of the supremacy of Parliament, one that other Americans now trumpeted before their own assemblies. No wonder Francis Bernard, royal governor of Massachusetts, called the Virginia Resolves an "alarm bell."

Not to be outdone by Virginia, Massachusetts called a general meeting to protest Grenville's policy. Nine colonies sent representatives to the Stamp Act Congress that convened in New York City in October 1765. It was the first intercolonial gathering held since the abortive Albany Congress of 1754; if nothing else, the new congress provided leaders from different regions with an opportunity to discuss common problems. The delegates drafted petitions to the king and Parliament that restated the colonists' belief "that no taxes should be imposed on them, but with their own consent, given personally, or by their representatives." The tone of the meeting was restrained, even conciliatory. The congress studiously avoided any mention of independence or disloyalty to the Crown.

Resistance to the Stamp Act soon spread from the assemblies to the streets. By taxing deeds, marriage licenses, and playing cards, the Stamp Act touched the lives of ordinary women and men. Anonymous artisans and seamen, angered by Parliament's apparent insensitivity and fearful the statute would increase unemployment and poverty, organized mass protests in the major colonial ports.

In Boston, the "Sons of Liberty" burned in effigy the local stamp distributor, Andrew Oliver, and when that action failed to bring about his resignation, they tore down one of his office buildings. Even after he resigned, the mob nearly demolished the elegant home of Oliver's close associate, Lieutenant Governor Thomas Hutchinson. The violence frightened colonial leaders, yet evidence suggests they encouraged the lower classes to intimidate royal officials. Popular participation in these protests was an exciting experience for people who had traditionally deferred to their social betters. After 1765, it was impossible for either royal governors or patriot leaders to take the ordinary folk for granted.

By November 1, 1765, stamp distributors in almost every American port had publicly resigned, and without distributors, the hated revenue stamps could not be sold. The courts soon reopened; most newspapers were published. Daily life in the colonies was undisturbed with one exception: the Sons of Liberty persuaded—some said coerced—colonial merchants to boycott British goods until Parliament repealed the Stamp Act. The merchants showed little enthusiasm for such tactics, but the threat of tar and feathers stimulated cooperation.

Because the Stamp Act touched the lives of ordinary men and women, they were vocal and demonstrative in their protests against the measure. Here a crowd in New Hampshire displays the hanged effigy of the stamp master.

The boycott movement was in itself a masterful political innovation. The colonists depended on British imports—cloth, metal goods, and ceramics—and each year they imported more consumer goods than they could possibly afford. In this highly charged moral atmosphere, one in which ordinary people talked constantly of conspiracy and corruption, it is not surprising that Americans of different classes and backgrounds advocated a radical change in buying habits. Private acts suddenly became part of the public sphere. Personal excess threatened to contaminate the entire political community. This logic explains the power of an appeal made in a Boston newspaper: "Save your money and you can save your country."

The boycotts mobilized colonial women. They were excluded from voting and civil office, but such legal discrimination did not mean women were not part of the broader political culture. Since wives and mothers spent their days involved with household chores, they assumed special responsibility to reform consumption, to root out luxury, and to promote frugality. Indeed, in this realm they possessed real power; they monitored the ideological commitment of the entire family. Throughout the colonies women altered styles of dress, made homespun cloth, and shunned imported items on which Parliament had placed a tax.

British Reaction

What most Americans did not yet know—after all, communication with Britain required months—was that in July, Grenville had fallen from power. This unexpected shift came about not because the king thought Grenville's policies inept, but rather because George did not like the man. His replacement as first lord of the treasury, Lord Rockingham, was young, inexperienced, and terrified of public speaking, a serious handicap to launching a brilliant parliamentary career. The Rockinghamites—as his followers were called—envisioned a prosperous empire founded on an expanding commerce and local government under the gentle guidance of Parliament. In this unified structure, it seemed improbable that Parliament would ever be obliged to exercise control in a manner likely to offend the Americans. Rockingham wanted to repeal the Stamp Act, but because of the shakiness of his own political coalition, he could not announce such a decision until it enjoyed broad national support. He, therefore, urged merchants and manufacturers throughout England to petition Parliament for repeal of the act, claiming the American boycott would soon drive them into bankruptcy.

Grenville, now simply a member of Parliament, would tolerate no retreat on the issue of supremacy. He urged his colleagues in the House of

Commons to be tough, to condemn "the outrageous tumults and insurrections which have been excited and carried on in North America." But William Pitt, the architect of victory in the Seven Years' War and a hero throughout America, eloquently defended the colonists' position, and after the Rockingham ministry gathered additional support from prominent figures such as Benjamin Franklin, who happened to be visiting England, Parliament felt strong enough to recommend repeal. On March 18, 1766, the House of Commons voted 275 to 167 to rescind the Stamp Act.

Lest its retreat on the Stamp Act be interpreted as weakness, the House of Commons passed the Declaratory Act (March 1766), a shrill defense of parliamentary supremacy over the Americans "in all cases whatsoever." The colonists' insistence on no taxation without representation failed to impress British rulers. England's merchants, supposedly America's allies, claimed sole responsibility for the Stamp Act repeal. The colonists had only complicated the task, the merchants lectured, and if the Americans knew what was good for them, they would keep quiet. To George Mason, a leading political figure in Virginia, such advice sounded patronizing. The British merchants seemed to be saying, "We have with infinite difficulty and fatigue got you excused this one time; pray be a good boy for the future, do what your papa and mama bid you, and hasten to return them your most grateful acknowledgements for condescending to let you keep what is your own." To this, Mason snapped "ridiculous!"

The Stamp Act crisis also eroded the colonists' respect for imperial officeholders in America. Suddenly, these men—royal governors, customs collectors, military personnel—appeared alien, as if their interests were not those of the people over whom they exercised authority. One person who had been forced to resign the post of stamp distributor for South Carolina noted several years later that "The Stamp Act had introduc'd so much Party Rage, Faction, and Debate that the ancient Harmony, Generosity, and Urbanity for which these People were celebrated is destroyed, and at an End." Similar reports came from other colonies, and it is testimony to the Americans' lingering loyalty to the British Crown and constitution that rebellion did not occur in 1765.

Townshend's Boast: Tea and Sovereignty

Rockingham's ministry soon gave way to a government headed once again by William Pitt, who was now the Earl of Chatham. The aging Pitt suffered horribly from gout, and during his long absences from London, Charles Townshend, his chancellor of the exchequer, made important policy decisions. Townshend was an impetuous man whose mouth often outran his mind. During a parliamentary debate in January 1767, he surprised everyone by blithely announcing he knew a way to obtain revenue from the Americans. The members of the House of Commons were so pleased with the news, they promptly voted to lower English land taxes, an action that threatened fiscal chaos.

A budgetary crisis forced Townshend to make good on his extraordinary boast. His scheme turned out to be a grab bag of duties on American imports of paper, glass, paint, lead, and tea, which collectively were known as the Townshend Revenue Acts (June–July 1767). He hoped to generate sufficient funds to pay the salaries of royal governors and other imperial officers, thus freeing them from dependence on the colonial assemblies.

The chancellor recognized that without tough instruments of enforcement, his duties would not produce the promised revenues. Therefore, he created an American Board of Customs Commissioners, a body based in Boston and supported by reorganized vice-admiralty courts located in Boston, Philadelphia, and Charles Town. And for good measure, Townshend induced Parliament to order the governor of New York to veto all bills passed by that colony's assembly until it supplied resident British troops in accordance with the Quartering Act (May 1765) that required the colonies to house soldiers in barracks, taverns, and vacant buildings, and to provide the army with firewood, candles, and beer, among other items. Many Americans regarded this as more taxation without representation, and in New York at least, colonists refused to pay.

Colonists showed no more willingness to pay Townshend's duties than they had to buy Grenville's stamps. No congress was called; none was necessary. Recent events had taught people how to coordinate protest, and they moved to resist the unconstitutional revenue acts. In major ports, the Sons of Liberty organized boycotts of British goods. Protest often involved what one historian has termed "rituals of nonconsumption." In some large towns, these were moments of public moral reaffirmation. Men and women took oaths before neighbors promising not to purchase certain goods until Parliament repealed unconstitutional taxation. In Boston, ordinary people were encouraged to sign "Subscription Rolls." "The Selectmen strongly recommend this Measure to Persons of *all ranks*," announced the *Boston Gazette*," as the most honorable and effectual way of giving *public* Testimony of their Love to their Country, and of endeavouring to save it from ruin."

On February 11, 1768, the Massachusetts House of Representatives drafted a circular letter, which it then sent to other colonial assemblies. The letter requested suggestions on how best to thwart the Townshend Acts; not surprisingly, legislators in other parts of America, busy with local matters, simply ignored this general appeal. But not Lord Hillsborough, England's secretary for American affairs. This rather mild action struck him as gross treason, and he ordered the Massachusetts representatives to rescind their "seditious paper." After considering Hillsborough's demand, the legislators voted 92 to 17 to defy him.

Suddenly, the circular letter became a cause célèbre. The royal governor of Massachusetts hastily dissolved the House of Representatives. That decision compelled the other colonies to demonstrate their support for Massachusetts. Assembly after assembly now felt obligated to take up the circular letter, an action Hillsborough had specifically forbidden. Assemblies in other colonies were dissolved, creating a much broader crisis of representative government. Throughout America, the number 92 (the number of legislators who voted against Hillsborough) immediately became a symbol of patriotism. In fact, Parliament's challenge had brought about the very results it most wanted to avoid: a foundation for intercolonial communication and a strengthening of conviction among the colonists of the righteousness of their position.

The Boston Massacre Heightens Tensions

In October 1768, British rulers made another mistake, one that raised tensions almost to the pitch they had reached during the Stamp Act riots. The issue at the heart of the trouble was the army. In part to save money and in part to intimidate colonial troublemakers, the ministry transferred four thousand regular troops from Nova Scotia and Ireland to Boston. Most of the army had already been withdrawn from the frontier to the seacoast to save revenue, thereby raising more acutely than ever the issue of why troops were in America at all. The armed strangers camped on Boston Commons, and when citizens passed the site, redcoats shouted obscenities. Sometimes in accordance with martial law, an errant soldier was whipped within an inch of his life, a bloody sight that sickened Boston civilians. To make relations worse, redcoats—men who were ill treated and underpaid—competed in their spare time for jobs with local dockworkers and artisans. Work was already in short supply, and the streets crackled with tension.

When colonists questioned why the army had been sent to a peaceful city, pamphleteers responded that it was there to further a conspiracy originally conceived by Bute to oppress Americans, to take away their liberties, to collect illegal revenues. Grenville, Hillsborough, Townshend: they were all, supposedly, part of the plot. Such rhetoric sounds excessive, but to Americans who had absorbed the political theories of the Commonwealthmen, a pattern of tyranny seemed obvious.

Colonists had no difficulty interpreting the violence that erupted in Boston on March 5, 1770. In the gathering dusk of that afternoon, young boys and street toughs bombarded a small isolated patrol outside the offices of the hated customs commissioners in King Street with rocks and snowballs. The details of this incident are obscure, but it appears that as the mob grew and became more threatening, the soldiers panicked. In the confusion, the troops fired, leaving five Americans dead.

Pamphleteers promptly labeled the incident a "massacre." The victims were seen as martyrs and were memorialized in extravagant terms. In one eulogy, Joseph Warren addressed the dead men's widows and children, dramatically recreating the gruesome scene in King Street. "Behold thy murdered husband gasping on the ground," Warren cried, ". . . take heed, ye orphan babes, lest, whilst your streaming eyes are fixed upon the ghastly corpse, your feet slide on the stones

The BLOODY MASSACRE perpetrated in King street Boston on March 5th 1770 by a party of the 29th Regt.

Unhappy Boston! see thy Sons deplore,
Thy hallow'd Walks besmear'd with guiltless Gore:
While faithless P——n and his savage Bands,
With murd'rous Rancour stretch their bloody Hands;
Like fierce Barbarians grinning o'er their Prey,
Approve the Carnage, and enjoy the Day.

If scalding drops from Rage from Anguish Wrung,
If speechless Sorrows lab'ring for a Tongue,
Or if a weeping World can ought appease
The plaintive Ghosts of Victims such as these;
The Patriot's copious Tears for each are shed,
A glorious Tribute which embalms the Dead.

But know, Fate summons to that awful Goal,
Where Justice strips the Murd'rer of his Soul:
Should venal C——ts the scandal of the Land,
Snatch the relentless Villain from her Hand,
Keen Execrations on this Plate inscrib'd,
Shall reach a Judge who never can be brib'd.

Outrage over the Boston Massacre was fanned by propaganda, such as this etching by Paul Revere, which showed British redcoats firing on well-dressed men and women. In subsequent editions, the blood spurting from the dying Americans became more conspicuous.

bespattered with your father's brains." Apparently to propagandists like Warren, it mattered little that the five civilians had been bachelors! Paul Revere's engraving of the massacre, appropriately splattered with blood, became an instant bestseller. Confronted with such intense reaction and with the possibility of massive armed resistance, crown officials wisely moved the army to an island in Boston harbor.

At this critical moment, the king's new first minister restored a measure of tranquillity. Lord North, congenial, well meaning, but not very talented, became chancellor of the exchequer following Townshend's death in 1767. North became the first minister in 1770, and for the next twelve years—indeed, throughout most of the American crisis—he managed to retain his office. His secret formula seems to have been an ability to get along with George III and to build an effective majority in Parliament.

One of North's first recommendations to Parliament was the repeal of the Townshend duties. Not only had these ill-conceived duties unnecessarily angered the colonists, they also hurt English manufacturers, a cardinal sin in the mer-

cantilist system. By taxing British exports such as glass and paint, Parliament had only encouraged the Americans to develop their own industries; thus without much prodding, the House of Commons dropped all the Townshend duties—with the notable exception of tea. The tax on tea was retained not for revenue purposes, North insisted, but as a reminder that England's rulers still subscribed to the principles of the Declaratory Act. They would not compromise the supremacy of Parliament. In mid-1770, however, the matter of tea seemed trivial to most Americans. The colonists had drawn back from the precipice, a little frightened by the events of the past two years, and desperately hoped to head off future confrontation with the British.

An Interlude of Order, 1770–1773

For a short while, American colonists and British officials put aside their recent animosities. Like England's rulers, some colonial gentry were beginning to pull back from protest, especially violent confrontation with estab-

Popular Culture and Revolutionary Ferment

No one knows exactly why men and women rebel against governments. Economic deprivation and political frustration contribute to unrest, but the spark that ignites popular passions, that causes common people to risk their lives in battle, often arises from a society's most basic traditions and beliefs.

The American Revolution illustrates this complex process of revolt. The educated elite in the colonies may have found their inspiration in reading classical history or political pamphlets, but the common people, those who protested British taxation in the streets, seem to have gained resolution from a deep Protestant tradition, a set of religious values recently reinforced during the Great Awakening (see Chapter 4). For ordinary men and women, the American Revolution may have seemed a kind of morality play, a drama that transformed complicated issues of representation and sovereignty into a stark conflict between American good and British evil.

Even before colonial protests against British taxation led to bloodshed, religious passions helped draw thousands of people into the streets of Boston on Pope's Day, a traditional anti-Catholic holiday celebrated on November 5. (In England, the holiday was known as Guy Fawkes Day and commemorated exposure of the Gunpowder Plot of 1605, a con-spiracy organized by English Catholics to blow up Parliament that was thwarted at the last minute.) For the holiday, Bostonians arranged elaborate processions, complete with effigies of the pope and the devil, which they burned at the climax of the festivities. Sometimes the annual celebration turned ugly, as rival gangs from the north and south ends of the city tried to disrupt each other's parade. During the Seven Years' War, the crowds grew increasingly unruly, as the pageantry triggered an outpouring of emotions that sprang from the New Englanders' fervent commitment to the Reformation and their desire to rid Canada of Catholic domination.

The Pope's Day celebrations provided a model for demonstrations against the Stamp Act. The first public protest against the British law in Boston, on August 14, 1765, began with a rally under a large elm, the original colonial "Liberty Tree." Hanging from its branches were effigies of Andrew Oliver, Boston's first stamp collector, and the devil, whose pitchforks men-

Pope's Day celebrations—complete with burning effigies and more than a touch of rowdyism—provided colonists with a model that they could use for later anti-British political demonstrations.

Defcription of the POPE, 1769.

Toafts on the Front of the large Lanthorn.
Love and Unity.---The American Whig.---Confufion to the
Torries, and a total Bar ifhment to Bribery and Corruption.
On the Right Side of the fame.—An Acroftick.

J nfulting Wretch, we'll him expofe,
O 'er the whole World his Deeds difclofe,
H ell now gaups wid : to take him in,
N ow he is ripe, Oh Lump of Sin.
M ean is the Man, M --N is his Name,
E nough he's fpread his hellifh Fame,
I nfernal Furies hurl his Soul,
N ine Million Times from Pole to Pole.

aced Oliver. A label attached to the effigy of Oliver read:

Fair Freedom's glorious cause I've meanly quitted For the sake of self; But ah! the Devil had me outwitted, And instead of stamping others, I've hang'd myself

As night fell, a diverse crowd of gentlemen, workers, and even a few women carried the effigies through the streets of Boston. After destroying a building owned by Oliver, they marched to Fort Hill where "they made a burnt offering of the effigies for these sins of the people which had caused such heavy judgments as the Stamp Act, etc. to be laid upon them." This symbolic protest ended with a sort of conversion; in much the same way that anxious sinners renounced evil at evangelical meetings, Oliver announced publicly that he would resign as stamp collector.

The devil was a familiar feature in American political cartoons. In one famous illustration, published in 1774, the devil held a list of crimes committed by Governor Thomas Hutchinson of Massachusetts, as the viper of death prepared to punish the royal official for his sins. This gruesome imagery revealed that patriots thought of Hutchinson not only as a political opponent but also as a moral traitor. No one who saw these macabre figures could fail to appreciate the accompanying warning: "Let the destroyers of mankind behold and tremble!"

A similar message was at the heart of the patriot practice of tarring and feathering. Crowds in Boston usually reserved this humiliating punishment for informers who reported violations to the hated customs officers. The victim

became the main actor in a public morality play, in which he was wheeled in a cart before jeering crowds and forced to repent. This spectacle recalled a verse often repeated on Pope's Day:

See the informer how he stands If anyone now takes his part An enemy to all the Land He'll go to Hell without a cart.

Patriots regarded military traitors as the worst of sinners. When General Benedict Arnold, who had been a hero during the early stages of the war, went over to the British in 1780, Americans accused him of selling out to the devil. A huge parade held in Philadelphia included a two-faced Arnold riding in front of Satan. The devil held a bag of gold—presumably the source of Arnold's fall—and a pitchfork that he used to prod the traitor along the path to Hell.

Revolutionary leaders also tapped long-standing Puritan hostility to the theater. Puritans and other strict Protestants indicted the theater for encouraging idleness, hypocrisy, deceit, and even effeminacy, since men usually played women's roles. But their greatest objection was that the stage appealed to those emotions and lusts that God-fearing men and women tried to restrain through knowledge of Scripture. Theaters, they believed, were nothing less than enemies of the church. "Those therefore who serve the Devill in Playes and Playhouses; it's impossible for them to serve the Lord in prayers and Churches," asserted one Puritan thinker.

Patriot leaders also considered the stage a rival for popular loyalties. In 1766, the Sons of Liberty in New York City demolished a theater. And in 1774, the First Continental Congress resolved to

"discontenance and discourage every species of extravagance and dissipation especially . . . shews, plays and other expensive diversions and entertainments." Such proclamations helped to channel Protestant moral fervor into a commitment to the patriot cause.

During the war itself—when soldiers were actually fighting and dying—religion helped sustain patriotism. In 1775, for example, a company of Massachusetts soldiers on their way to Quebec camped briefly at Newburyport, where George Whitefield had been buried. Before the troops resumed their long march to Canada, some of them opened the minister's tomb and cut off small pieces of Whitefield's collar and wristband, an act that seems ghoulish only to those who do not fully comprehend the importance of religion in the lives of the common soldiers.

Religious symbol and ritual thus galvanized common men and women by expressing in moral terms the issues that divided the colonies from England. The Great Awakening had prepared the colonists to view the contest in terms of American virtue and English vice, of God and the devil. By appealing to the strong Protestant tradition in the colonies, patriots mobilized the American people for revolution.

lished authority, in fear that the lower orders were becoming too assertive. It was probably in this period that Loyalist Americans emerged as an identifiable group. Colonial merchants returned to familiar patterns of trade, pleased no doubt to end the local boycotts that had depressed the American economy. British goods flooded into colonial ports; the level of American indebtedness soared to new highs. In this period of apparent reconciliation, the people of Massachusetts—even of Boston—decided they could accept their new governor, Thomas Hutchinson. After all, he was one of their own, an American.

But appearances were deceiving. The bonds of imperial loyalty remained fragile, and even as Lord North attempted to win the colonists' trust, crown officials in America created new strains. Customs commissioners whom Townshend had appointed to collect his duties remained in the colonies long after his Revenue Acts had been repealed. If they had been honest, unobtrusive administrators, perhaps no one would have taken notice of their behavior. But the customs commissioners regularly abused their powers of search and seizure and in the process lined their own pockets. In Massachusetts, Rhode Island, and South Carolina—to cite the most notorious cases—these officials drove local citizens to distraction by enforcing the Navigation Acts with such rigor that a skiff could not cross Narragansett Bay with a load of firewood without first obtaining a sheaf of legal documents. One slip, no matter how minor, could bring confiscation of ship and cargo.

The commissioners were not only corrupt, they were also short-sighted. If they had restricted their extortion to the common folk, they might have avoided becoming a major American grievance. But they could not control their greed. Some customs officers harassed the wealthiest, most powerful men around, men like John Hancock of Boston and Henry Laurens of Charles Town. The commissioners' actions drove some members of the colonial ruling class into opposition to the king's government. When in the summer of 1772 a group of disguised Rhode Islanders burned a customs vessel, the *Gaspee*, Americans cheered. A special royal commission sent to arrest the culprits discovered that not a single Rhode Islander had the slightest idea how the ship could have come to such an end.

Samuel Adams (1722–1803) refused to accept the notion that the repeal of the Townshend duties had secured American liberty. During the early 1770s, while colonial leaders turned to other matters, Adams kept the cause alive with a drumfire of publicity. He reminded the people of Boston that the tax on tea remained in force. He organized public anniversaries commemorating the repeal of the Stamp Act and the Boston Massacre. Adams was a genuine revolutionary, an ideologue filled with a burning sense of indignation at the real and alleged wrongs suffered by his countrymen. To his contemporaries, this man resembled a figure out of New England's Puritan past. He seemed obsessed with the preservation of public virtue. The American goal, he declared, was the creation of a "Christian Sparta," an ideal commonwealth in which vigilant citizens would constantly guard against the spread of corruption, degeneracy, and luxury.

With each new attempt by Parliament to assert its supremacy over the colonists, more and more Bostonians listened to what Adams had to say. He observed ominously that the British intended to use the tea revenue to pay judicial salaries, thus freeing the judges from dependence on the assembly. When in November 1772 Adams suggested the formation of a committee of correspondence to communicate grievances to villagers throughout Massachusetts, he received broad support. Americans living in other colonies soon copied his idea. It was a brilliant stroke. Adams developed a structure of political cooperation completely independent of royal government.

The Final Provocation: The Boston Tea Party

In May 1773, Parliament passed the Tea Act, legislation the Americans might have welcomed. After all, it lowered the price for their favorite beverage. Parliament wanted to save one of Britain's largest businesses, the East India Company, from possible bankruptcy. This commercial giant imported Asian tea into England, where it was resold to wholesalers. The tea was also subject to heavy duties. The Company tried to pass these charges on to the consumers, but American tea drinkers preferred the cheaper leaves that were smuggled in from Holland.

The Tea Act changed the rules. Parliament not only allowed the Company to sell directly to American retailers, thus cutting out middlemen, but also eliminated the duties paid in England. If all had gone according to plan, the agents of the East India Company in America would have undersold their competitors, including the Dutch smugglers, and with the new profits would have saved the business.

But Parliament's logic was flawed. First, since the tax on tea, collected in American ports, remained in effect, this new act seemed a devious scheme to win popular support for Parliament's right to tax the colonists without representation. Second, the act threatened to undercut powerful colonial merchants who did a good business trading in smuggled Dutch tea. Considering the American reaction, the British government might have been well advised to devise another plan to rescue the ailing company. In Philadelphia, and then at New York City, colonists turned back the tea ships before they could unload.

In Boston, however, the issue was not so easily resolved. Governor Hutchinson, a strong-willed man, would not permit the vessels to return to England. Local patriots would not let them unload. And so, crammed with the East India Company's tea, the ships sat in Boston Harbor waiting for the colonists to make up their minds. On the night of December 16, 1773, they did so in dramatic style. A group of men disguised as Mohawks boarded the ships and pitched 340 chests of tea worth £10,000 over the side. Whether Samuel Adams organized the famed "Tea Party" is not known. No doubt he and his allies were not taken by surprise. Even at the time, John Adams, Samuel's distant cousin, sensed the event would have far-reaching significance. "This Destruction of the Tea," he scribbled in his diary, "is so bold, so daring, so firm, intrepid, and inflexible, and it must have so important consequences, and so lasting, that I can't but consider it as an epocha in history."

When news of the Tea Party reached London in January 1774, the North ministry was stunned. The people of Boston had treated parliamentary supremacy with utter contempt, and British rulers saw no humor whatsoever in the destruction of private property by subjects of the Crown dressed in costume. To quell such rebelliousness, Parliament passed a series of laws called the Coercive Acts. (In America, they were referred to as the Intolerable Acts.) This legislation (1) closed the port of Boston until the city fully compensated the East India Company for the lost tea, (2) restructured the Massachusetts government by transforming the upper house from an elective to an appointed body and restricting the number of legal town meetings to one a year, (3) allowed the royal governor to transfer British officials arrested for offenses committed in the line of duty to England where there was little likelihood they would be convicted, and (4) authorized the army to quarter troops wherever they were needed, even if this required the compulsory requisition of uninhabited private buildings. George III enthusiastically supported this tough policy; he appointed General Thomas Gage to serve as the colony's new royal governor. Gage apparently won the king's favor by announcing that in America "Nothing can be done but by forcible means."

This sweeping denial of constitutional liberties confirmed the colonists' worst fears. To men like Samuel Adams, it seemed as if Britain really intended to enslave the American people. Colonial moderates found their position shaken by the vindictiveness of the Coercive Acts. Edmund Burke, one of America's last friends in Parliament, noted sadly on the floor of Commons, "this is the day, then, that you wish to go to war with all America, in order to conciliate that country to this . . . "

In the midst of this constitutional crisis, Parliament announced plans to establish a new civil government for the Canadian province of Quebec (Quebec Act, June 22, 1774). This territory had been ruled by military authority following the Seven Years' War. The Quebec Act not only failed to create an elective assembly—an institution the Americans regarded as essential for the protection of liberty—but also awarded French Roman Catholics a large voice in local political affairs. Moreover, since Quebec extended all the way south to the Ohio River and west to the Mississippi River, Americans concluded that Parliament wanted to deny the American settlers and traders in this fast-developing region their constitutional rights, a threat that affected all colonists, not just those of Massachusetts Bay.

If in 1774 the House of Commons thought it could isolate Boston from the rest of America, it was in for a rude surprise. Colonists living in

This drawing of the Boston Tea Party appeared in W. D. Cooper's History of North America, *published in London in 1789. The British lion on the prow of the ship seems to look on disapprovingly as the colonists, disguised as Indians, dump the tea in the harbor.*

other parts of the continent recognized immediately that the principles at stake in Boston affected all Americans. As one Virginian explained, ". . . there were no Heats and Troubles in Virginia till the Blockade of Boston." Few persons advocated independence, but they could not remain passive while Boston was destroyed. They sent food and money and, during the fall of 1774, reflected more deeply than ever on what it meant to be a colonist in the British empire.

The sticking point remained—as it had been in 1765—the sovereignty of Parliament. No one in Britain could think of a way around this constitutional impasse. In 1773, Benjamin Franklin had offered a suggestion. "The Parliament," he observed, "has no right to make any law whatever, binding on the colonies . . . the king, and not the king, lords, and commons collectively, is their sovereign." But so long as it still seemed possible to coerce the Americans into obedience, to punish these errant children, Britain's rulers had little incentive to accept such a humiliating compromise.

DECISION FOR INDEPENDENCE

During the summer of 1774, committees of correspondence analyzed the perilous situation in which the colonists found themselves. Something, of course, had to be done. But what? Would the Southern Colonies support resistance in New England? Would Pennsylvanians stand up to Parliament? Not surprisingly, the committees endorsed a call for a

Continental Congress, a gathering of fifty-five elected delegates from twelve colonies (Georgia sent none but agreed to support the action taken). This momentous gathering convened in Philadelphia on September 5. It included some of America's most articulate, respected leaders; among them were John and Samuel Adams, Patrick Henry, Richard Henry Lee, Christopher Gadsden, and George Washington.

The delegates were strangers to one another. They knew little about the customs and values, the geography and economy of Britain's other provinces. As John Adams explained on September 18, "It has taken Us much Time to get acquainted with the Tempers, Views, Characters, and Designs of Persons and to let them into the Circumstances of our Province." During the early sessions of the Congress, the delegates eyed each other closely, trying to gain a sense of the strength and integrity of the men with whom they might commit treason.

Differences of opinion soon surfaced. Delegates from the Middle Colonies—Joseph Galloway of Pennsylvania, for example—wanted to proceed with caution, but Samuel Adams and other more radical members pushed the moderates toward confrontation. Boston's master politician engineered congressional commendation of the Suffolk Resolves, a bold statement drawn up in Suffolk County, Massachusetts, that encouraged forcible resistance of the Coercive Acts.

After this decision, the tone of the meeting was established. Moderate spokesmen introduced conciliatory measures, which received polite discussion but failed to win a majority vote. Just

Legislation	Date	Provisions	Colonial Reaction
Sugar Act	April 5, 1764	Revised duties on sugar, coffee, tea, wine, other imports; expanded jurisdiction of vice-admiralty-courts	Several assemblies protest taxation for revenue
Stamp Act	March 22, 1765; repealed March 18, 1766	Printed documents (deeds, newspapers, marriage licenses, etc.) issued only on special stamped paper purchased from stamp distributors	Riots in cities; collectors forced to resign; Stamp Act Congress (October 1765)
Quartering Act	May 1765	Colonists must supply British troops with housing other items (candles, firewood, etc.)	Protest in assemblies; New York Assembly punished for failure to comply 1767
Declaratory Act	March 18, 1766	Parliament declares its sovereignty over the colonies "in all cases whatsoever"	Ignored in celebration over repeal of the Stamp Act
Townshend Revenue Acts	June 26, 29, July 2, 1767; all repealed—except duty on tea, March 1770	New duties on glass, lead, paper, paints, tea; customs collections tightened in America	Nonimportation of British goods; assemblies protest; newspapers attack British policy
Tea Act	May 10, 1773	Parliament gives East India Company right to sell tea directly to Americans; some duties on tea reduced	Protests against favoritism shown to monopolistic company; tea destroyed in Boston (December 16, 1773)
Coercive Acts (Intolerable Acts)	March–June 1774	Closes port of Boston; restructures, Massachusetts government; restricts town meetings; troops quartered in Boston; British officials accused of crimes sent to England or Canada for trial	Boycott of British goods; First Continental Congress convenes (September 1774)
Prohibitory Act	December 22, 1775	Declares British intention to coerce Americans into submission; embargo on American goods; American ships seized	Drives Continental Congress closer to decision for independence

before returning to their homes (September 1774), the delegates created the "Association," an intercolonial agreement to halt all commerce with Britain until Parliament repealed the Intolerable Acts. This was a totally revolutionary decision. The Association authorized a vast network of local committees to enforce nonimportation. In many of the communities, they *were* the government, distinguishing in the words of James Madison, "Friends from Foes." George III sneered at these activities. "I am not sorry," he confided, "that the line of conduct seems now chalked out ... the New England Governments are in a state of Rebellion, blows must decide whether they are to be subject to this country or independent."

Shots Heard Around the World

The king was correct. Before Congress reconvened, "blows" fell at Lexington and Concord, two small farm villages in eastern Massachusetts. On the evening of April 18, 1775, General Gage dispatched troops from Boston to seize rebel supplies. Paul Revere, a renowned silversmith and active patriot, warned the colonists the redcoats were coming. The militia of Lexington, a collection of ill-trained farmers, boys as well as old men, decided to stand on the village green on the following morning, April 19, as the British soldiers passed on the road to Concord. No one planned to fight, but in a moment of confusion someone (probably a colonist) fired; the redcoats discharged a volley, and eight Americans lay dead.

Word of the incident spread rapidly, and by the time the British force reached its destination, the countryside swarmed with "minutemen," special companies of Massachusetts militia prepared to respond instantly to military emergencies. The redcoats found nothing of significance in Concord, and so returned. The long march back to Boston turned into a rout. Lord Percy, a British officer who brought up reinforcements, remarked more in surprise than bitterness, "whoever looks upon them [the American soldiers] as an irregular mob, will find himself much mistaken." On June 17, colonial militiamen again held their own against seasoned troops at the battle of Bunker Hill (actually Breed's Hill). The British finally took the hill, but after this costly "victory" in which he suffered 40 percent casualties, Gage complained that the Americans had displayed "a conduct and spirit against us, they never showed against the French."

The Second Continental Congress Directs the War Effort

Members of the Second Continental Congress gathered in Philadelphia in May 1775. They faced an awesome responsibility. British government in the mainland colonies had almost ceased to function, and with Americans fighting redcoats, the country desperately needed strong central leadership. Slowly, often reluctantly, Congress took control of the war. The delegates formed a Continental army and appointed George Washington its commander, in part because he seemed to have greater military experience than anyone else available and in part because he looked like he should be commander in chief. The delegates were also eager to select someone who did not come from Massachusetts, a colony that seemed already to possess too much power in national councils. The members of Congress purchased military supplies and, to pay for them, issued paper money. But while they were assuming the powers of a sovereign government, the congressmen refused to declare independence. They debated and fretted, listened to the appeals of moderates who played on the colonists' remaining loyalty to Britain, and then did nothing.

Indecision drove men like John Adams nearly mad. In one tirade against his timid colleagues, he exclaimed that they possessed "the vanity of the ape, the tameness of the ox, or the stupid servility of the ass." Haste, however, would have been a terrible mistake. While Adams and Richard Henry Lee of Virginia were willing to sever ties with Britain, many Americans were not convinced that such a step was either desireable or necessary. If Congress had moved too quickly, it might have become vulnerable to charges of extremism, in which case the rebellion would have seemed—and indeed, might have been—more like an overthrow by a faction or clique than an expression of popular will.

The British government appeared intent on transforming colonial moderates into angry rebels. In December 1775, Parliament passed the Prohibitory Act, declaring war on American commerce. Until the colonists begged for pardon, they could not trade with the rest of the world. The

This 1775 engraving by Amos Doolittle, an eyewitness, shows the attack on the British regulars as they marched from Concord back to Boston. The minutemen fired from cover. It is not certain who fired the first shot at Lexington.

British navy blockaded their ports and seized American ships on the high seas. Lord North also hired German mercenaries (the Russians drove too hard a bargain) to put down the rebellion. And in America, royal governors like Lord Dunmore further undermined the possibility of reconciliation by urging Virginia's slaves to take up arms against their masters. Few did so, but the effort to stir up black rebellion infuriated the Virginia gentry.

Thomas Paine (1737–1809) pushed the colonists even closer to independence. Nothing in this man's background suggested he would write the most important pamphlet in American history. In England, Paine had tried and failed in a number of jobs, and exactly why he elected to move to America in 1774 is not clear. While still in England, Paine had the good fortune to meet Benjamin Franklin, who presented him with letters of introduction to the leading patriots of Pennsylvania. At the urging of his new American

friends, Paine produced *Common Sense,* an essay that became an instant best-seller. In only three months it sold over 120,000 copies. Paine confirmed in forceful prose what the colonists had been thinking but had been unable to state in coherent form. "My motive and object in all my political works," he declared, ". . . have been to rescue man from tyranny and false systems of government, and enable him to be free."

Common Sense systematically stripped kingship of historical and theological justification. For centuries, the English had maintained the fiction that the monarch could do no wrong. When the government oppressed the people, the royal counselors received the blame. The Crown was above suspicion. To this, Paine cried nonsense. Monarchs ruled by force. George III was simply a "royal brute," who by his arbitrary behavior had surrendered his claim to the colonists' obedience. The pamphlet also attacked the whole idea of a mixed and balanced constitution. Indeed,

Common Sense was a powerful democratic manifesto.

Paine's greatest contribution to the revolutionary cause was persuading common folk to sever their ties with Great Britain. It was not reasonable, he argued, to regard England as the mother country. "Europe, and not England," he explained, "is the parent country of America. This new world hath been the asylum for the persecuted lovers of civil and religious liberty from *every part* of Europe." No doubt that message made a deep impression on Pennsylvania's German population. The time had come for the colonists to form an independent republic. "We have it in our power," Paine wrote in one of his most moving statements, "to begin the world over again . . . the birthday of a new world is at hand."

On July 2, 1776, after a long and tedious debate, Congress finally voted for independence. The motion passed; twelve states for, none against. Thomas Jefferson, a young Virginia lawyer and planter who enjoyed a reputation as a graceful writer, drafted a formal declaration that was accepted with alterations two days later. Much of the Declaration of Independence consisted of a list of specific grievances against George III and his government. Like the skilled lawyer he was, Jefferson presented the evidence for independence. But the document did not become famous for those passages. Long after the establishment of the new Republic, the declaration challenged Americans to make good on the principle that "all men are created equal." John Adams nicely expressed the patriots' fervor when he wrote on July 3: "Yesterday the greatest question was decided, which ever was debated in America, and a greater perhaps, never was or will be decided among men."

WAR FOR INDEPENDENCE

Only fools and visionaries were optimistic about America's prospects of winning independence in 1776. The Americans had taken on a formidable military power. The population of Britain was perhaps four times that of its former colonies. England also possessed a strong manufacturing base, a well-trained regular army supplemented

The message of Thomas Paine's pamphlet Common Sense *(title page shown) was clear and direct. Paine's stark phrases calling for "The Free and Independent States of America" reverberated throughout America.*

by thousands of hired German troops (Hessians), and a navy that dominated the world's oceans. Many British officers had battlefield experience. They already knew what the Americans would slowly learn: waging war requires great discipline, money, and sacrifice.

The British government entered the conflict fully confident it could beat the Americans. In 1776, Lord North and his colleagues regarded the war as a police action. They anticipated a mere show of armed force would intimidate the upstart colonists. As soon as the rebels in Boston had been humbled, the British argued, people living in other colonies would desert the cause for independence. General Gage, for example, told the king that the colonists "will be Lions, whilst we are Lambs, . . . if we take a resolute part they will undoubtedly prove very weak." Since this advice confirmed George's views, he called Gage "an honest determined man."

As later events demonstrated, of course, Britain had become involved in an impossible military situation, in some ways analogous to that in which the United States found itself in Vietnam. Three separate elements neutralized advantages held by the larger power over its adversary. First, the British had to transport men and supplies across the Atlantic, a logistic chal-

Congress Voting Independence, *oil painting by Robert Edge Pine and Edward Savage, 1785. The committee appointed by Congress to draft a declaration of independence included (center, standing) John Adams, Roger Sherman, Robert Livingston, Thomas Jefferson, and (center foreground, seated) Benjamin Franklin. The committee members are shown submitting Jefferson's draft to the Speaker.*

lenge of unprecedented complexity. Unreliable lines of communication broke down under the strain of war.

Second, America was too vast to be conquered by conventional military methods. Redcoats might gain control over the major port cities, but as long as the Continental army remained intact, the rebellion continued. As Washington explained, ". . . the possession of our Towns, while we have an Army in the field, will avail them little. . . . It is our Arms, not defenceless Towns, they have to subdue." Even if England had recruited enough soldiers to occupy the entire country, it would still have lost the war. As one Loyalist instructed the king, "if all America becomes a garrison, she is not worth your attention." Britain could only win by crushing the American will to resist.

And third, British strategists never appreciated the depth of the Americans' commitment to a political ideology. In the wars of eighteenth-century Europe, such beliefs had seldom mattered. European troops before the French Revolution served because they were paid or because the military was a vocation, but most certainly not because they hoped to advance a set of constitutional principles. Americans were different. To be sure, some young men were drawn to the military by bounty money or by the desire to escape unhappy families. A few were drafted. But taking such people into account, one still encounters among the American troops a remarkable commitment to republican ideals. As one French officer reported from the United States, "It is incredible that soldiers composed of men of every age, even of children of fifteen, of whites and blacks, almost naked, unpaid, and rather poorly fed, can march so well and withstand fire so steadfastly."

During the earliest months of rebellion, American soldiers—especially those of New England—suffered no lack of confidence. Indeed, they interpreted their courageous stands at Concord and Bunker Hill as evidence that brave yeomen farmers could lick British regulars on any battlefield. George Washington spent the first years of the war disabusing the colonists of this foolishness, for as he had learned during the French and Indian War, military success depended on endless drill, careful planning, and tough discipline—rigorous preparation that did not characterize the minutemen's methods.

Washington insisted on organizing a regular well-trained field army. Some advisers urged the commander in chief to wage a guerrilla war, one in which small partisan bands would sap Britain's will to rule Americans. But Washington rejected that course. He recognized the Continental army served not only as a fighting force but also as a symbol of the republican cause. Its very existence would sustain American hopes, and so long as the

Overview of the Revolutionary War

Maps that follow on pages 156, 157 and 160 are enlargements of the insets on this map.

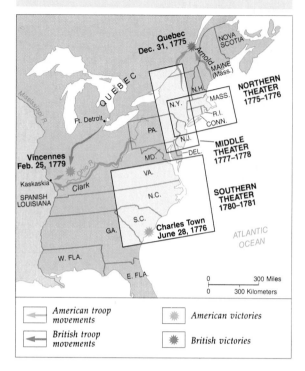

American troop movements

British troop movements

American victories

British victories

Britain . . . [but] They appeared to be penitent of their former conduct, [and] professed themselves convinced . . . that there was no such thing as remaining neuters." Without local political coercion, Washington's task would have been considerably more difficult.

For the half million African American colonists, most of them slaves, the fight for independence took on special poignance. After all, they wanted to achieve personal as well as political freedom, and many African Americans supported those who seemed most likely to deliver them from bondage. As one historian explained, "the black soldier was likely to join the side that made him the quickest and best offer in terms of those 'unalienable rights' of which Mr. Jefferson had spoken." It is estimated that some five thousand African Americans took up arms to fight against the British. The Continental army included two all-black units, one from Massachusetts and the other from Rhode Island. In 1778, the legislature of Rhode Island voted to free any slave who volunteered to serve, since according to the lawmakers, history taught that "the wisest, the

In this 1774 woodcut, a Daughter of Liberty stands ready to take up arms in support of colonial militia.

army survived, American agents could plausibly solicit foreign aid. This thinking shaped Washington's wartime strategy; he studiously avoided "general actions" in which the Continental army might be destroyed. Critics complained about Washington's caution, but as they soon discovered, he understood better than they what independence required.

If the commander in chief was correct about the army, however, he failed to comprehend the importance of the militia. These scattered, almost amateur, military units seldom altered the outcome of battle, but they did maintain control over large areas of the country not directly affected by the British army. Throughout the war, they compelled men and women who would rather have remained neutral to support actively the American effort. In 1777, for example, the militia of Farmington, Connecticut, visited a group of suspected Tories, as Loyalists were called, and after "educating" these people in the fundamentals of republican ideology, a militia spokesman announced, "They were indeed grossly ignorant of the true grounds of the present war with Great

freest, and bravest nations . . . liberated their slaves, and enlisted them as soldiers to fight in defence of their country." In the South, especially in Georgia and South Carolina, more than ten thousand African Americans supported the British, and after the patriots had won the war, these men and women left the United States, relocating to Nova Scotia, Florida, and Jamaica, with some eventually resettling in Africa.

Early Disasters Test the American Will

After the embarrassing defeats in Massachusetts, the king appointed General Sir William Howe to replace the ill-fated Gage. British rulers now understood that a simple police action would not be sufficient to crush the American rebellion. Parliament authorized sending over fifty thousand troops to the mainland colonies, and after evacuating Boston—an untenable strategic position—the British forces stormed ashore at Staten Island in New York harbor on July 3, 1776. From this more central location, Howe believed he could cut the New Englanders off from the rest of America. He enjoyed the powerful support of the British navy under the command of his brother, Admiral Lord Richard Howe.

When Washington learned the British were planning to occupy New York City, he transferred many of his inexperienced soldiers to Long Island, where they suffered a major defeat (August 27, 1776). In a series of disastrous engagements for the Americans, Howe drove the Continental army across the Hudson River into New Jersey. Because of his failure to take full advantage of the situation, however, General Howe lost what seemed in retrospect an excellent opportunity to annihilate Washington's entire army. Nevertheless, the Americans were on the run, and in the fall of 1776, contemporaries predicted the rebels would soon capitulate.

"Times That Try Men's Souls"

Swift victories in New York and New Jersey persuaded General Howe that few Americans enthusiastically supported independence. He issued a general pardon, therefore, to anyone who would swear allegiance to George III. The results were encouraging. Over three thousand men and women who lived in areas occupied by the British

army took the oath. This group included one signer of the Declaration of Independence. Howe perceived that a lasting peace in America would require his troops to treat "our enemies as if they might one day become our friends." A member of Lord North's cabinet grumbled that this was "a sentimental manner of making war," a shortsighted view considering England's experience in attempting to pacify the Irish. The pardon plan eventually failed not because Howe lacked toughness but because his soldiers and officers regarded loyal Americans as inferior provincials, an attitude that did little to promote good relations. In any case, as soon as the redcoats left a pardoned region, the rebel militia retaliated against those who had deserted the patriot cause.

In December 1776, Washington's bedraggled army retreated across the Delaware River into Pennsylvania. American prospects appeared bleaker than at any other time during the war. The Continental army lacked basic supplies, and many men who had signed up for short-term enlistments prepared to go home. "These are the times that try men's souls," Paine wrote in a pamphlet entitled *American Crisis*. "The summer soldier and the sunshine patriot will, in this crisis, shrink from the service of their country, but he that stands it *now* deserves . . . love and thanks. . . " Before winter, Washington determined to attempt one last desperate stroke.

Howe played into Washington's hands. The British forces were dispersed in small garrisons across the state of New Jersey, and while the Americans could not possibly have defeated the combined British army, they did possess the capacity—with luck—to capture an exposed post. On the night of December 25, Continental soldiers slipped over the ice-filled Delaware River and at Trenton took nine hundred sleeping Hessian mercenaries by complete surprise.

Cheered by success, Washington returned a second time to Trenton, but on this occasion the Continental army was not so fortunate. A large British force under Lord Cornwallis trapped the Americans. Instead of standing and fighting—really an impossible challenge—Washington secretly, by night, marched his little army around Cornwallis's left flank. On January 3, 1777, the Americans surprised a British garrison at Princeton. Washington then went into winter quarters. The British, fearful of losing more out-

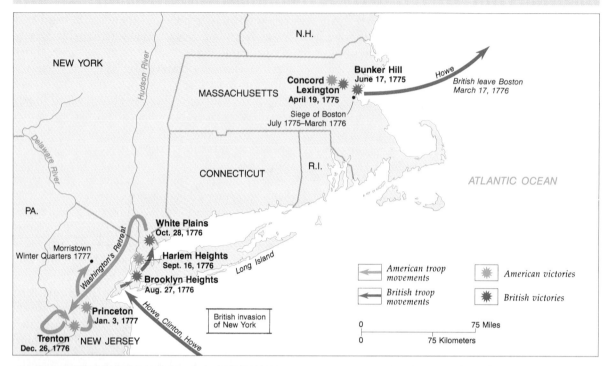

Northern Theater of War, 1775–1776
The major battles of the first years of the war, from the spontaneous rising at Concord in 1775 to Washington's well-coordinated attack on Trenton in December 1776, occurred in the northern colonies.

N.H.

NEW YORK

Hudson River

MASSACHUSETTS

Bunker Hill
June 17, 1775

Howe

Concord
Lexington
April 19, 1775

British leave Boston
March 17, 1776

Siege of Boston
July 1775–March 1776

Delaware River

CONNECTICUT

R.I.

ATLANTIC OCEAN

PA.

White Plains
Oct. 28, 1776

Morristown
Winter Quarters 1777

Washington's Retreat

Harlem Heights
Sept. 16, 1776

Long Island

Brooklyn Heights
Aug. 27, 1776

Princeton
Jan. 3, 1777

Howe, Clinton, Howe

Trenton
Dec. 26, 1776

NEW JERSEY

British invasion
of New York

← *American troop movements*

← *British troop movements*

✦ *American victories*

✶ *British victories*

0   75 Miles

0   75 Kilometers

Defeat of the British at the Battle of Princeton, oil painting by William Mercer, ca. 1786–1790. The painting shows George Washington (left, on horseback) directing cannon fire with his sword. Shouting "It's a fine fox chase, my boys!" he led the rout of the British rear guard. The artist's father was mortally wounded in the battle.

posts, consolidated their troops, thus leaving much of the state in the hands of the patriot militia.

Victory in a Year of Defeat

In 1777, England's chief military strategist, Lord George Germain, still perceived the war in conventional European terms. A large field army would somehow maneuver Washington's Continental troops into a decisive battle in which the British would enjoy a clear advantage. Complete victory over the Americans certainly seemed within England's grasp. Unfortunately for the men who advocated this plan, the Continental forces proved extremely elusive, and while one British army vainly tried to corner Washington in Pennsylvania, another was forced to surrender in the forests of upstate New York.

In the summer of 1777, General John Burgoyne, a dashing though overbearing officer, descended from Canada with a force of over seven thousand troops. They intended to clear the Hudson Valley of rebel resistance, join Howe's army, which was to come up to Albany, and thereby cut New England off from the other states. Burgoyne fought in a grand style. Accompanied by a German band, thirty carts filled with the general's liquor and belongings, and two thousand dependents and camp followers, the British set out to thrash the Americans. The campaign was a disaster. Military units, mostly from New England, cut the enemy force apart in the deep woods north of Albany. At the battle of Bennington (August 16), the New Hampshire militia under Brigadier General John Stark overwhelmed a thousand German mercenaries. After this setback, Burgoyne's forces struggled forward, desperately hoping Howe would rush to their rescue, but when it became clear their situation at Saratoga was hopeless, the haughty Burgoyne was forced to surrender fifty-eight hundred men to the American General Horatio Gates (October 17).

Soon after Burgoyne left Canada, General Howe quite unexpectedly decided to move his main army from New York City to Philadelphia. Exactly what he hoped to achieve was not clear, even to Britain's rulers, and of course, when Burgoyne called for assistance, Howe was sitting in the new nation's capital still trying to devise a way to destroy the Continental army. Howe's campaign began in late July. The British forces sailed to the head of the Chesapeake Bay and

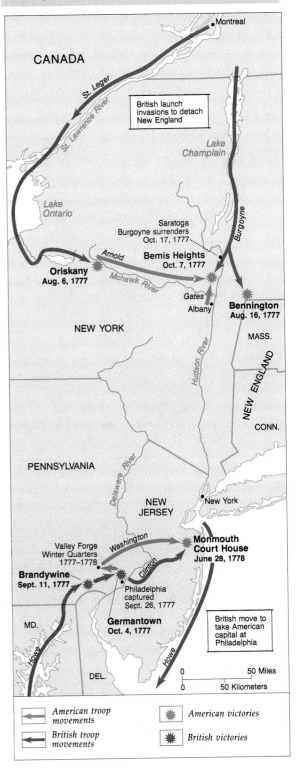

The Middle Years of the War
Burgoyne's attempt to cut New England off from the rest of the states failed when his army was defeated at Saratoga.

then marched north to Philadelphia. Washington's troops obstructed the enemy's progress, first at Brandywine Creek (September 11) and then at Paoli (September 20), but the outnumbered Americans could not stop the British from entering Philadelphia.

Anxious lest these defeats discourage Congress and the American people, Washington attempted one last battle before the onset of winter. In an engagement at Germantown (October 4), the Americans launched a major counterattack on a fog-covered battlefield, but just at the moment when success seemed assured, the Americans broke off the fight. "When every thing gave the most flattering hopes of victory," Washington complained, "the troops began suddenly to retreat." Bad luck, confusion, and incompetence contributed to the failure. A discouraged Continental army dug in at Valley Forge, 20 miles outside of Philadelphia, where camp diseases took twenty-five hundred American lives. In their misery, few American soldiers realized their situation was not nearly as desperate as it had been in 1776.

The French Alliance

Even before the Americans declared their independence, agents of the government of Louis XVI began to explore ways to aid the colonists, not so much because the French monarchy favored the republican cause, but because it hoped to embarrass the English. The French deeply resented the defeat they had sustained during the Seven Years' War. During the early months of the Revolution, the French covertly sent tons of essential military supplies to the Americans. The negotiations for these arms involved secret agents and fictitious trading companies, the type of clandestine operation more typical of modern times than of the eighteenth century. But when American representatives, Benjamin Franklin for one, pleaded for official recognition of American independence or for outright military alliance, the French advised patience. The international stakes were too great for the king openly to back a cause that had little chance of success.

The American victory at Saratoga convinced the French that the rebels had formidable forces and were serious in their resolve. Indeed, Lord North drew the same conclusion. When news of Saratoga reached London, North muttered, "this

damned war." In private conversation he expressed doubts about England's ability to win the contest, knowing the French would soon enter the fray.

In April 1778, North tried to avert a greatly expanded war by sending a peace commission to America. He instructed this group, headed by the Earl of Carlisle, to bargain with the Continental Congress "as if it were a legal body." If the colonists would agree to drop their demand for independence, they could turn the imperial calendar back to 1763. Parliament belatedly conceded the right of Americans to tax themselves, even to elect their own governors. It also promised to remove all British troops in times of peace. The proposal might have gained substantial support back in 1776. The war, however, had hardened American resolve; the Congress refused to deal with Carlisle.

In Paris, Franklin performed brilliantly. In meetings with French officials, he hinted that the Americans might accept a British peace initiative. If the French wanted the war to continue, if they really wanted to embarrass their old rival, then they had to do what the English refused: formally recognize the independence of the United States.

The stratagem paid off handsomely. On February 6, 1778, the French presented American representatives with two separate treaties. The first, called the Treaty of Amity and Commerce, established commercial relations between France and the United States. It tacitly accepted the existence of a new, independent republic. The Treaty of Alliance was even more generous, considering America's obvious military and economic weaknesses. In the event that France and England went to war (they did so on June 14 as everyone expected), the French agreed to reject "either Truce or Peace with Great Britain . . . until the independence of the United States shall have been formally or tacitly assured by the Treaty or Treaties that shall terminate the War." Even more amazing, France surrendered its claim to all territories formerly owned by Great Britain east of the Mississippi River. The Americans pledged they would not sign a separate peace with Britain without first informing their new ally. And in return, France made no claim to Canada, asking only for the right to take possession of certain British islands in the Caribbean. Never had

Franklin worked his magic to greater effect.

French intervention instantly transformed British military strategy. What had been a colonial rebellion suddenly became a world conflict, a continuation of the great wars for empire of the late seventeenth century (see Chapter 4). Scarce military resources, especially newer fighting ships, had to be diverted from the American theater to guard the English Channel. In fact, there was talk in London of a possible French invasion. While the threat of such an assault was not very great until 1779, the British did not have cause for concern. The French navy posed a serious challenge to the overextended British fleet. By concentrating their warships in a specific area, the French could hold off or even defeat British squadrons, an advantage that would figure significantly in the American victory at Yorktown.

The Final Campaign

British General Henry Clinton replaced Howe, who resigned after the battle of Saratoga. Clinton was a strangely complex individual. As a subordinate officer, he had impressed his superiors as imaginative but easily provoked to anger. When he took command of the British army, his resolute self-confidence suddenly dissolved. Perhaps he feared failure. Whatever the explanation for his vacillation, Clinton's record in America was little better than Howe's or Gage's.

Military strategists calculated that Britain's last chance of winning the war lay in the Southern Colonies, a region largely untouched in the early years of fighting. Intelligence reports reaching London indicated that Georgia and South Carolina contained a sizable body of Loyalists, men who would take up arms for the Crown if only they received support and encouragement from the regular army. The southern strategy devised by Germain and Clinton in 1779 turned the war into a bitter guerrilla conflict, and during the last months of battle, British officers worried that their search for an easy victory had inadvertently opened a Pandora's box of uncontrollable partisan furies.

The southern campaign opened in the spring of 1780. Savannah had already fallen, and Clinton reckoned that if the British could take Charles Town, they would be able to control the entire South. A large fleet carrying nearly eight thousand redcoats reached South Carolina in February. Complacent Americans had allowed the city's fortifications to decay, and in a desperate, last-minute effort to preserve Charles Town, General Benjamin Lincoln's forces dug trenches and reinforced walls, but to no avail. Clinton and his second in command, General Cornwallis, gradually encircled the city, and on May 12, Lincoln surrendered an American army of almost six thousand men.

The defeat took Congress by surprise, and without making proper preparations, it dispatched a second army to South Carolina under Horatio Gates, the hero of Saratoga. He too failed. At Camden, Cornwallis outmaneuvered the raw American recruits, capturing or killing 750 during the course of battle (August 16). Poor Gates galloped from the scene and did not stop until he reached Hillsboro, North Carolina, 200 miles away.

Even at this early stage of the southern campaign, the dangers of partisan warfare had become evident. Tory raiders showed little interest in serving as regular soldiers in Cornwallis's army. They preferred night riding, indiscriminate plundering or murdering of neighbors against whom they harbored ancient grudges. The British had unleashed a horde of banditti across South Carolina. Men who genuinely supported independence or who had merely fallen victim to the Loyalist guerrillas bided their time. They retreated westward waiting for their enemies to make a mistake. Their chance came on October 7 at King's Mountain, North Carolina. The backwoodsmen decimated a force of British regulars and Tory raiders who had strayed too far from base. This was the most vicious fighting of the Revolution. One witness reported that when a British officer tried to surrender, he was summarily shot down by at least seven American soldiers.

Cornwallis, badly confused and poorly supplied, proceeded to squander his strength chasing American forces across the Carolinas. Whatever military strategy had compelled him to leave Charles Town had long since been abandoned, and in early 1781, Cornwallis informed Clinton that "Events alone can decide the future Steps." Events, however, did not run in the British favor. Congress sent General Nathanael Greene to the South with a new army. This young Rhode Islander was the most capable general on Washington's staff. Greene joined Daniel

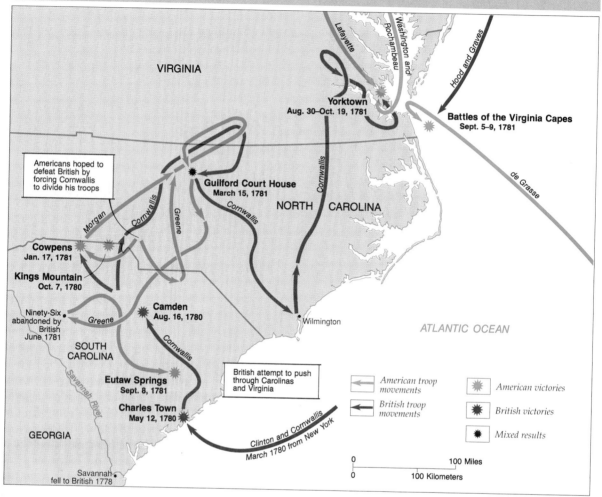

Southern Theater of War, 1780–1781
Major battles from the fall of Savannah to the final victory at Yorktown.

VIRGINIA

Lafayette

Washington and Rochambeau

Hood and Graves

Yorktown
Aug. 30–Oct. 19, 1781

Battles of the Virginia Capes
Sept. 5–9, 1781

de Grasse

Americans hoped to defeat British by forcing Cornwallis to divide his troops

Cornwallis

Guilford Court House
March 15, 1781

NORTH CAROLINA

Cornwallis

Morgan

Greene

Cowpens
Jan. 17, 1781

Kings Mountain
Oct. 7, 1780

Ninety-Six abandoned by British June 1781

Greene

Camden
Aug. 16, 1780

Wilmington

ATLANTIC OCEAN

SOUTH CAROLINA

Cornwallis

Savannah River

Eutaw Springs
Sept. 8, 1781

British attempt to push through Carolinas and Virginia

Charles Town
May 12, 1780

GEORGIA

Clinton and Cornwallis
March 1780 from New York

Savannah
fell to British 1778

American troop movements

British troop movements

American victories

British victories

Mixed results

| 0 | 100 Miles |
| 0 | 100 Kilometers |

Morgan, leader of the famed Virginia Riflemen, and in a series of tactically brilliant engagements, they sapped the strength of Cornwallis's army, first at Cowpens, South Carolina (January 17, 1781), and later at Guilford Courthouse, North Carolina (March 15). Clinton fumed in New York City. In his estimation, the inept Cornwallis had left "two valuable colonies behind him to be overrun and conquered by the very army which he boasts to have completely routed but a week or two before."

Cornwallis pushed north into Virginia, planning apparently to establish a base of operations on the coast. He selected Yorktown, a sleepy tobacco market town located on a peninsula bounded by the York and James rivers. Washington watched these maneuvers closely.

The canny Virginia planter knew this territory intimately, and he sensed that Cornwallis had made a serious blunder. When Washington learned the French fleet could gain temporary dominance in the Chesapeake Bay, he rushed south from New Jersey. With him marched thousands of well-trained French troops under Comte de Rochambeau. All the pieces fell into place. The French admiral, Comte de Grasse, cut Cornwallis off from the sea, while Washington and his lieutenants encircled the British on land. On October 19, 1781, Cornwallis surrendered his entire army of six thousand men. When Lord North heard of the defeat at Yorktown, he moaned, "Oh God! It is all over." The British still controlled New York City and Charles Town, but except for a few skirmishes, the fighting ended. The task of securing the independence of the United States was now in the hands of the diplomats.

THE LOYALIST DILEMMA

The war lasted longer than anyone had predicted in 1776. While the nation won its independence, many Americans paid a terrible price. Indeed, a large number of men and women decided that however much they loved living in America, they could not accept the new government.

No one knows for certain how many Americans actually supported the Crown during the Revolution. Some Loyalists undoubtedly kept silent and avoided making a public commitment that might have led to banishment or loss of property. But for many persons, neutrality proved impossible. Almost one hundred thousand men and women permanently left America. While a number of these exiles had served as imperial officeholders—Thomas Hutchinson, for example—in the main, they came from all ranks and backgrounds. A large number of humble farmers, more than thirty thousand, resettled in Canada. Others relocated to England, the West Indies, or Africa.

The political ideology of the Loyalists was not substantially different from that of their opponents. Like other Americans, they believed men and women were entitled to life, liberty, and the pursuit of happiness. The Loyalists were also convinced that independence would destroy those values by promoting disorder. By turning their backs on Britain, a source of tradition and stability, the rebels seemed to have encouraged licentiousness, even anarchy in the streets. The Loyalists suspected that Patriot demands for freedom were self-serving, even hypocritical, for as Perserved Smith, a Loyalist from Ashfield, Massachusetts, observed, "Sons of liberty . . . did not deserve the name, for it was evident all they wanted was liberty from oppression that they might have liberty to oppress!"

The Loyalists were caught in a difficult squeeze. The British never quite trusted them. After all, they were Americans. During the early stages of the war, Loyalists organized militia companies and hoped to pacify large areas of the countryside with the support of the regular army.

The British generals were unreliable partners, however, for no sooner had they called on loyal Americans to come forward, than the redcoats marched away, leaving the Tories exposed to rebel retaliation. And in England, the exiles found themselves treated as second-class citizens. While many of them received monetary compensation for their sacrifice, they were never regarded as the equals of native-born English citizens. Not surprisingly, the Loyalist community in London was gradually transformed into a collection of bitter men and women who felt unwelcome on both sides of the Atlantic.

Americans who actively supported independence saw these people as traitors who deserved their fate of constant, often violent, harassment. In many states—but especially in New York—revolutionary governments confiscated Loyalist property. Other friends of the king received beatings, or as the rebels called them, "grand Toory [sic] rides." A few were even executed. According to one patriot, "A Tory is a thing whose head is in England, and its body in America, and its neck ought to be stretched."

Long after the victorious Americans turned their attentions to the business of building a new republic, Loyalists remembered a receding colonial past, a comfortable, ordered world that had been lost forever at Yorktown. Although many Loyalists eventually returned to their homes, a sizable number could not do so. For them, the sense of loss remained a heavy emotional burden. Perhaps the most poignant testimony came from a young mother living in exile in Nova Scotia. "I climbed to the top of Chipman's Hill and watched the sails disappear in the distance," she recounted, "and such a feeling of loneliness came over me that though I had not shed a tear through all the war I sat down on the damp moss with my baby on my lap and cried bitterly."

WINNING THE PEACE

Congress appointed a splendid delegation to negotiate a peace treaty: Benjamin Franklin, John Adams, and John Jay. According to their official instructions, they were to insist only on the recognition of the independence of the United States. On other issues, Congress ordered

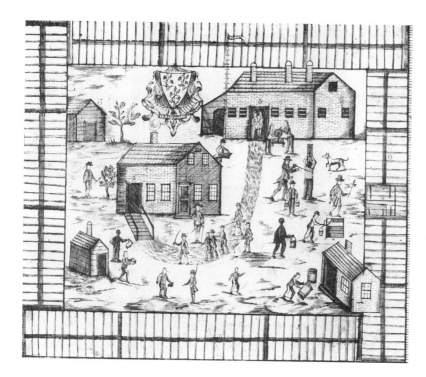

Between 1776 and 1783, the revolutionary state governments passed "Test Acts" requiring repudiation of the British Crown and setting various punishments for those who remained loyal to Britain. The Connecticut assembly, for example, passed a law threatening imprisonment for anyone who criticized the state assembly or the Continental Congress. This engraving, "A Prospective View of Old Newgate Connecticut's State Prison" is attributed to Richard Brunton and was probably done ca. 1800–1801 while Brunton was imprisoned for counterfeiting.

its delegates to defer to the counsel of the French government.

But the political environment in Paris was much different than the diplomats had been led to expect. The French had formed a military alliance with Spain, and French officials announced that they could not consider the details of an American settlement until after the Spanish had recaptured Gibraltar from the British. The prospects for a Spanish victory were not good, and in any case, it was well known that Spain coveted the lands lying between the Appalachian Mountains and the Mississippi River. Indeed, there were even rumors afloat in Paris that the great European powers might intrigue to deny the United States its independence.

While the three American delegates publicly paid their respects to French officials, they secretly entered into negotiations with an English agent. The peacemakers drove a remarkable bargain, a much better one than Congress could have expected. The prelimi-

nary agreement signed on September 3, 1783, not only guaranteed the independence of the United States, it also transferred all the territory east of the Mississippi River, except Spanish Florida, to the new Republic. The treaty established generous boundaries on the north and south and gave the Americans important fishing rights in the North Atlantic. In exchange, Congress promised to help British merchants collect debts contracted before the Revolution and compensate Loyalists whose lands had been confiscated by the various state governments. Even though the Americans negotiated separately with the British, they did not sign a separate peace. The preliminary treaty did not become effective until France reached its own agreement with Great Britain. Thus did the Americans honor the French alliance. It is difficult to imagine how Franklin, Adams, and Jay could have negotiated a more favorable conclusion to the war. In the fall of 1783, the last redcoats sailed from New York City, ending 176 years of colonial rule.

CHRONOLOGY

1763	Peace of Paris ends the Seven Years' War
1764	Parliament passes Sugar Act to collect American revenue
1765	Stamp Act receives support of House of Commons (March) • Stamp Act Congress meets in New York City (October)
1766	Stamp Act repealed the same day that Declaratory Act becomes law (March 18)
1767	Townshend Revenue Acts stir American anger (June–July)
1768	Massachusetts assembly refuses to rescind circular letter (February)
1770	Parliament repeals all Townshend duties except one on tea (March) • British troops "massacre" Boston civilians (March)
1772	Samuel Adams forms committee of correspondence
1773	Lord North's government passes Tea Act (May) • Bostonians hold Tea Party (December)
1774	Parliament punishes Boston with Coercive Acts (March–June) • First Continental Congress convenes (September)
1775	Patriots take stand at Lexington and Concord (April) • Second Continental Congress gathers (May) • Americans hold their own at Bunker Hill (June)
1776	Congress votes for independence; Declaration of Independence is signed • British defeat Washington at Long Island (August) • Americans score victory at Trenton (December)
1777	General Burgoyne surrenders at Saratoga (October)
1778	French treaties recognize independence of the United States (February)
1780	British take Charles Town (May)
1781	Washington forces Cornwallis to surrender at Yorktown (October)
1783	Peace treaty signed (September) • British evacuate New York City (November)

REPUBLICAN CHALLENGE

The American people had waged war against the most powerful nation in Europe and emerged victorious. The treaty marked the conclusion of a colonial rebellion, but it remained for the men and women who had resisted taxation without representation to work out the full implications of republicanism. What would be the shape of the new government? What powers would be delegated to the people, the states, the federal authorities? How far would the wealthy, well-born leaders of the rebellion be willing to extend political, social, and economic rights? No wonder that Dr. Benjamin Rush explained, "There is nothing more common than to confound the terms of American Revolution with those of the late American war. The American war is over, but this is far from being the case with the American Revolution. On the contrary, nothing but the first act of the great drama is closed."

Recommended Reading

The Revolution has generated a rich historiography. No sooner had the fighting ceased than the participants, Loyalists as well as Patriots, began to interpret the events leading to the creation of an independent republic. The most enjoyable book is David Ramsay's *The History of the American Revolution,* originally published in 1789, but recently reprinted in volumes edited by Lester H. Cohen (1990). A general guide to the period is provided by Jack Greene and J. R. Pole, eds., *Blackwell Encyclopedia of the American Revolution* (1991). Two reliable surveys are Merrill Jensen, *The Founding of a Nation* (1968), and Edmund S. Morgan, *Birth of the Republic* (rev. ed. 1992). Two books that transformed how an entire generation interpreted the revolution are Edmund S. Morgan and Helen M. Morgan, *The Stamp Act Crisis* (1953), and Bernard Bailyn, *The Ideological Origins of the American Revolution* (1967).

Additional Bibliography

The literature dealing with British politics on the eve of the American Revolution is impressive. One important study is John Brooke, *King George III* (1974). The most useful recent investigation of parliamentary politics is John Brewer, *Party Ideology and Popular Politics at the Accession of George III* (1976). Also helpful are J. C. D. Clark, *The Language of Liberty 1660–1832: Political Discourse and Social Dynamics in the Anglo-American World* (1994) and P. D. G.

Thomas's *The Townshend Duties Crisis* (1987) and *Tea Party to Independence* (1991).

The American interpretation of changing British politics can be explored in Pauline Maier, *From Resistance to Revolution: Colonial Radicals and the Development of American Opposition to Britain* (1972), and John Phillip Reid, *Constitutional History of the American Revolution* (1986). Other more specialized studies include John Shy, *Toward Lexington* (1965); Richard D. Brown, *Revolutionary Politics in Massachusetts: The Boston Committee of Correspondence and the Towns* (1970); and David Hackett Fischer, *Paul Revere's Ride* (1994). For an innovative interpretation of the cultural tensions in revolutionary society, see Jay Fliegelman's *Declaring Independence: Jefferson, Natural Language, and the Culture of Performance* (1993) as well as his *Prodigals and Pilgrims: The American Revolution Against Patriarchal Authority* (1982).

Several studies show how local communities tried to make sense out of political and social change: Rhys Isaac, *Transformation of Virginia, 1740–1790* (1983); Robert A. Gross, *The Minutemen and Their World* (1976); Edward Countryman, *A People in Revolution: The American Revolution and Political Society in New York* (1982); and T. H. Breen, *Tobacco Culture: The Mentality of the Great Tidewater Planters on the Eve of Revolution* (1985). For a balanced biography of the author of *Common Sense,* see Eric Foner, *Tom Paine and Revolutionary America* (1976). An excellent essay collection remains Alfred F. Young, ed., *The American Revolution: Explorations in American Radicalism* (1976).

Alice H. Jones provides a full analysis of the economic structure of colonial America in *Wealth of a Nation to Be* (1980). The experiences of the merchants are discussed in Thomas Doerflinger, *A Vigorous Spirit of Enterprise* (1986) and John W. Tyler, *Smugglers and Patriots* (1986). A splendid reconstruction of city life, especially the growth of class tensions, can be found in Gary Nash, *Urban Crucible: Social Change, Political Consequences, and the Origins of the American Revolution* (1979). Also see Billy G. Smith, *The "Lower Sort": Philadelphia's Laboring People, 1750–1800* (1990).

Anyone interested in the experiences of American women during this period should start with Linda Kerber, *Women of the Republic* (1980). Also helpful are Mary Beth Norton, *Liberty's Daughters: The Revolutionary Experience of American Women, 1750–1800* (1980) and Marylynn Salmon, *Women and the Law of Property in Early America* (1986). The rituals of rebellion are interpreted in T. H. Breen, "Narrative of Commercial Life: Consumption, Ideology, and Community on the Eve of the American Revolution," *William & Mary Quarterly,* 3rd ser., 50 (1993), 471–501. A good account of the Iroquois remains Barbara Graymont, *The Iroquois in the American Revolution* (1972).

Two valuable studies of the war are Don Higginbotham, *The War of Independence: Military Attitudes, Policies, and Practices* (1983), and Howard H. Peckham, *The War for Independence: A Military History* (1958). The British side of the story is well told in Piers Mackesy, *The War for America, 1775–1783* (1964). For an innovative interpretation of the political role of the militia see John Shy, *A People Numerous and Armed* (rev. ed. 1990). The Americans' changing attitudes toward the Continental army are traced in Charles Royster, *A Revolutionary People at War* (1979). Also see a classic study of African American soldiers, Benjamin Quarles, *The Negro in the American Revolution* (1961) as well as Sidney Kaplan, *The Black Presence in the Era of the American Revolution 1770–1800* (1973).

The Loyalists are examined in Wallace Brown, *The King's Friends: The Composition and Motives of the American Loyalist Claimants* (1965); Robert M. Calhoon, *The Loyalists in Revolutionary America, 1760–1781* (1973); and Janice Potter, *Liberty We Seek: Loyalist Ideology in Colonial New York and Massachusetts* (1983). A good study of American relations with foreign powers is Jonathan Dull, *The Diplomatic History of the American Revolution* (1985).

The Republican Experiment

A curious controversy shattered the harmony of Boston in 1785. The dispute broke out soon after a group of young adults, sons and daughters of the city's wealthiest families, announced the formation of a tea assembly or "Sans Souci Club." The members of this select group gathered once a week for the pleasure of good conversation, a game of cards, some dancing, and perhaps a glass of Madeira wine.

These meetings outraged other Bostonians, many of them old patriots. Samuel Adams, who dreamed of creating a "Christian Sparta," a virtuous society committed to republican purity, sounded the alarm. "Say, my country," he thundered, "why do you suffer all the intemperances of Great Britain to be fostered in our bosom, in all their vile luxuriance?" The club's very existence threatened the "republican principles" for which Americans had so recently fought a revolution.

FROM MONARCHY TO REPUBLIC

Today, the term *republican* no longer possesses the evocative powers it did for Americans of the late eighteenth century. Adams and his contemporaries—some of whom probably visited the Sans Souci Club—believed creating a new nation-state involved more than simply winning independence from Great Britain. The American people had taken on a responsibility to establish an elective system of government. It was a bold experiment, and the precedents were not very encouraging. Indeed, the history books of that period offered disturbing examples of failure, of young republics that after a promising beginning had succumbed to political instability and military impotence.

More than did any other form of government, a republic demanded an exceptionally high degree of public morality. If American citizens substituted "luxury, prodigality, and profligacy" for "prudence, virtue, and economy," then their revolution surely would have been in vain. Maintaining popular virtue was crucial to success. An innocent tea party, therefore, set off alarm bells. Such "foolish gratifications" in Boston seemed to compromise republican goals. It is not surprising that

in this situation Adams thundered, "Rome, Athens, and all the cities of renown, whence came your fall?"

White Americans were optimistic about their country's chances. They came out of the Revolution with an almost euphoric sense of America's special destiny. This expansive outlook, encountered among so many ordinary men and women, owed much to the spread of Protestant evangelicalism. However skeptical Jefferson and Franklin may have been about revealed religion, the great mass of American people subscribed to a millennial vision of the country's future. To this republic, God had promised progress and prosperity. The signs were there for everyone to see. "There is not upon the face of the earth a body of people more happy or rising into consequence with more rapid stride," one man announced in 1786, "than the Inhabitants of the United States of America. Population is increasing, new houses building, new lands clearing, new settlements forming, and new manufactures establishing with a rapidity beyond conception."

Such optimism did not translate easily or smoothly into the creation of a strong central government. Modern Americans tend to take for granted the acceptance of the Constitution. Its merits seem self-evident largely because it has survived for two centuries. But in the early 1780s, no one could have predicted the Constitution as we know it would have been written, much less ratified. It was equally possible the Americans would have supported a weak confederation, or perhaps, allowed the various states and regions to go their separate ways.

In this uncertain political atmosphere, Americans divided sharply over the relative importance of *liberty* and *order*. The revolutionary experience had called into question the legitimacy of any form of special privilege. As one republican informed an aristocratic colleague in the South Carolina assembly, "the day is Arrived when *goodness*, and not *Wealth*, are the only *Criterions of greatness*." A legislative leader in Pennsylvania put the point even more bluntly: "no man has a greater claim of special privilege for his $100,000 than I have for my $5." The man who passionately defended social equality for those of varying economic status, however, may still have resisted the extension of civil rights to women or blacks. Nevertheless, liberty was contagious, and Americans of all backgrounds began to make new demands on society and government. For them, the Revolution had suggested radical alternatives, and in many forums throughout the nation—especially in the elected state assemblies—they insisted on being heard.

In certain quarters, the celebration of liberty met with mixed response. Some Americans—often the very men who had resisted British tyranny—worried the citizens of the new nation were caught up in a wild, destructive scramble for material wealth. Democratic excesses seemed to threaten order, to endanger the rights of property. Surely a republic could not long survive unless its citizens showed greater self-control. For people concerned about the loss of order, the state assemblies appeared the greatest source of instability. Popularly elected representatives lacked what men of property defined as real civic virtue.

Working out the tensions between order and liberty, between property and equality, generated an outpouring of political genius. At other times in American history, persons of extraordinary talent have been drawn to theology, commerce, or science, but during the 1780s, the country's intellectual leaders—Thomas Jefferson, James Madison, Alexander Hamilton, and John Adams among others—focused their creative energies on the problem of how republicans ought to govern themselves.

REPUBLICAN SOCIETY

Revolution changed American society, often in ways no one had planned. This phenomenon is not surprising. The great revolutions of modern times produced radical transformations in French, Russian, and Chinese societies. By comparison, the immediate results of the American Revolution appear much tamer, less wrenching. Nevertheless, national independence compelled people to reevaluate hierarchical social relations that they had taken for granted during the colonial period. The faltering first steps of independence raised fundamental questions about the meaning of equality in American society, many that still have not been answered satisfactorily.

Social and Political Reform

Following the war, Americans aggressively ferreted out and, with republican fervor, denounced any traces of aristocratic presence. As colonists, they had long resented the claims that certain Englishmen made to special privilege simply because of noble birth. Even so committed a republican as George Washington had to be reminded that artificial status was contrary to republican principles. In 1783, he and the officers who had served during the Revolution formed the Society of the Cincinnati, a hereditary organization in which membership passed from father to eldest son. The soldiers meant no harm; they simply wanted to maintain old friendships. But anxious republicans throughout America let out a howl of protest and one South Carolina legislator, Aedanus Burke, warned that the Society intended to create "an hereditary peerage . . . [which would] undermine the Constitution and destroy civil liberty." After an embarrassed Washington called for appropriate reforms of the Society's bylaws, the Cincinnati crisis receded. The fear of privilege remained, however, and wealthy Americans dropped honorific titles such as "esquire." Lawyers of republican persuasion chided judges who had adopted the English custom of wearing great flowing wigs to court.

The appearance of equality was as important as its actual achievement. In fact, the distribution of wealth in postwar America was more uneven than it had been in the mid-eighteenth century. The sudden accumulation of large fortunes by new families made other Americans particularly sensitive to aristocratic display, for it seemed intolerable that a revolution waged against a monarchy should produce a class of persons legally, or even visibly, distinguished from their fellow citizens.

In an effort to root out the notion of a privileged class, states abolished laws of primogeniture and entail. In colonial times, these laws allowed a landholder either to pass his entire estate to his eldest son or to declare that his property could never be divided, sold, or given away. Jefferson claimed that the repeal of these practices would eradicate "antient [sic] and future aristocracy; a foundation [has been] laid for a government truly republican." Jefferson exaggerated the social impact of this reform. In neither Virginia nor North Carolina did the abolition of

Questions of equality in the new Republic extended to the rights of women. In this illustration, which appeared as the frontispiece in the 1792 issue of The Lady's Magazine and Repository of Entertaining Knowledge, *the "Genius of the Ladies Magazine" and the "Genius of Emulation" (holding in her hand a laurel crown) present to Liberty a petition for the rights of woman.*

no man can be "free & independent" unless he possesses "a voice . . . in the choice of the most important Officers in the Legislature." Pennsylvania and Georgia allowed all white male taxpayers to participate in elections. Other states were less democratic, but with the exception of Massachusetts, they reduced property qualifications. These reforms, however, did not significantly expand the American electorate. Long before the Revolution, an overwhelming percentage of free white males had owned enough land to vote. In any case, during the 1780s republican lawmakers were not prepared to experiment with universal manhood suffrage, for as John Adams observed, if the states pushed these reforms too far, "New claims will arise, women will demand a vote . . . and every man who has not a farthing, will demand an equal vote with any other."

The most important changes in voting patterns were the result of western migration. As Americans moved to the frontier, they received full political representation in their state legislatures, and because new districts tended to be poorer than established coastal settlements, their representatives seemed less cultured, less well trained than those sent by eastern voters. Moreover, western delegates resented traveling so far to attend legislative meetings, and they lobbied successfully to transfer state capitals to more convenient locations. During this period, Georgia moved the seat of its government from Savannah to Augusta, South Carolina from Charles Town to Columbia, North Carolina from New Bern to Raleigh, Virginia from Williamsburg to Richmond, New York from New York City to Albany, and New Hampshire from Portsmouth to Concord.

After gaining independence, Americans also reexamined the relation between church and state. Republican spokespersons like Thomas Jefferson insisted that rulers had no right to interfere with the free expression of an individual's religious beliefs. As governor of Virginia, he strenuously advocated the disestablishment of the Anglican church, an institution that had received tax monies and other benefits during the colonial period. Jefferson and his allies regarded such special privilege not only as a denial of religious freedom—after all, rival denominations did not receive tax money—but also as a vestige of aristocratic society.

primogeniture greatly affect local custom. The great tobacco planters had seldom encumbered their estates with entail, and they generally provided all their children—daughters as well as sons—with land. Nonetheless, republican legislators wanted to cleanse traces of the former feudal order from the statute books.

Republican ferment also encouraged many states to lower property requirements for voting. After the break with Great Britain, such a step seemed logical. As one group of farmers declared,

In 1786, Virginia cut the last ties between church and state. Other southern states disestablished the Anglican church, but in Massachusetts and New Hampshire, Congregational churches continued to enjoy special status. Moreover, while Americans championed toleration, they seldom favored philosophies that radically challenged Christian values.

African Americans in the New Republic

Revolutionary fervor forced Americans to confront the most appalling contradiction to republican principles—slavery. The Quaker leader, John Woolman (1720–1772), probably did more than any other white person of the era to remind people of the evils of this institution. A trip he took through the Southern Colonies as a young man forever impressed upon Woolman "the dark gloominess" of slavery. In a sermon, this outspoken humanitarian declared "that Men having Power too often misapplied it; that though we made Slaves of the Negroes, and the Turks made Slaves of the Christians, I believed that Liberty was the natural Right of all Men equally."

During the revolutionary period, abolitionist sentiment spread. Both in private and in public, people began to criticize slavery in other than religious language. No doubt, the double standard of their own political rhetoric embarrassed many white Americans. They hotly demanded liberation from parliamentary enslavement at the same time that they held several hundred thousand blacks in permanent bondage.

By keeping the issue of slavery before the public by writing and petitioning, African Americans powerfully undermined arguments advanced in favor of human bondage. They demanded freedom, reminding white lawmakers that African American men and women had the same right to liberty as did other Americans. In 1779, for example, a group of African Americans living in Connecticut pointedly asked the members of the state assembly "whether it is consistent with the present Claims, of the United States, to hold so many Thousands, of the Race of Adam, our Common Father, in perpetual Slavery." In New Hampshire, nineteen persons who called themselves "natives of Africa" reminded local legislators that "private or public tyranny and slavery are alike detestable to minds conscious of the equal dignity of human nature."

The scientific accomplishments of Benjamin Banneker (1731–1806), Maryland's African American astronomer and mathematician, and the international fame of Phillis Wheatley (1753–1784), Boston's celebrated "African muse," made it increasingly difficult for white Americans to maintain credibly that African Americans could not hold their own in a free society. Wheatley's poems went through many editions, and after reading her work, the great French philosopher, Voltaire, rebuked a friend who had claimed "there never would be Negro poets." As Voltaire discovered, Wheatley "writes excellent verse in English." Banneker, like Wheatley, enjoyed a well-deserved reputation for his contributions as a scientist. After receiving a copy of an almanac that Banneker had published in Philadelphia, Thomas Jefferson concluded "that nature has given to our black brethren, talents equal to those of the other colors of men."

In the northern states, there was no real economic justification for slavery, and white laborers, often recent European immigrants, resented having to compete in the workplace against slaves. This economic situation, combined with the acknowledgment of the double standard represented by slavery, contributed to the establishment of antislavery societies. In 1775, Franklin helped organize a group in Philadelphia called The Society for the Relief of Free Negroes, Unlawfully Held. John Jay, Alexander Hamilton, and other prominent New Yorkers founded a Manumission Society in 1785. By 1792, antislavery societies were meeting from Virginia to Massachusetts, and in the northern states at least, these groups working for the same ends as various Christian evangelicals put slaveholders on the intellectual defensive for the first time in American history.

In several states north of Virginia, the abolition of slavery took a number of different forms. Even before achieving statehood, Vermont drafted a constitution (1777) that specifically prohibited slavery. In 1780, the Pennsylvania legislature passed a law effecting the gradual emancipation of slaves. Although the Massachusetts assembly refused to address the issue directly, the state courts took up the challenge and liberated the African Americans. A judge ruled slavery unconstitutional in Massachusetts because it conflicted with a clause in the state bill of rights declaring "all men . . . free and equal." According to one enthusiast, this decision freed "a Grate [sic] number of Blacks . . . who . . . are held in a state of slavery within the bowels of a free and christian Country." By 1800, slavery was well on the road to extinction in the northern states.

These positive developments did not mean white people accepted blacks as equals. In fact, in the very states that outlawed slavery, African Americans faced systematic discrimination. Free blacks were generally excluded from voting, juries, and militia duty—they were denied rights and responsibilities usually associated with full citizenship. They rarely enjoyed access to education, and in cities like Philadelphia and New York, where African Americans went to look for work, they wound up living in segregated wards or neighborhoods. Even in the churches—institutions that had often spoken out against slavery—

Born to slaves, Richard Allen became a zealous minister and converted his master, who allowed him to buy his freedom. Allen was ordained a bishop in 1799.

This engraving of Phillis Wheatley appeared in her volume of verse, Poems on Various Subjects, Religious and Moral *(1773), the first book published by an African American.*

free African Americans were denied equal standing with white worshippers. Humiliations of this sort persuaded African Americans to form their own churches. In Philadelphia, Richard Allen, a former slave, founded the Bethel Church for Negro Methodists (1793). This man later organized the African Methodist Episcopal Church (1814), an institution of great cultural as well as religious significance for nineteenth-century American blacks.

Even in the South, where African Americans made up a large percentage of the population, slavery disturbed thoughtful white republicans. Some planters simply freed their slaves, and by 1790, the number of free blacks living in Virginia numbered 12,766. By 1800, the figure had reached 30,750. There is no question that this trend reflected the uneasiness among white masters. Richard Randolph, one of Virginia's wealthier planters, explained that he freed his slaves "to make retribution, as far as I am able, to an unfortunate race of bond-men, over whom my ancestors have usurped and exercised the most lawless and monstrous tyranny." George Washington also manumitted his slaves. To be sure, most southern slaveholders, especially those living in South Carolina and Georgia, rejected this course of action. Their economic well-being depended on slave labor. Perhaps more significant, however, is the fact that no southern leader during the era of republican experimentation defended slavery as a positive good. Such overtly racist rhetoric did not become part of the public discourse until the nineteenth century.

Despite promising starts in that direction, the southern states did not abolish slavery. The economic incentives to maintain a servile labor force, especially after the invention of the cotton gin in 1793, and the opening up of the Alabama and Mississippi frontier, overwhelmed the initial abolitionist impulse. An opportunity to translate the principles of the American Revolution into social practice had been lost, at least temporarily. Jefferson reported sadly in 1805, "I have long since given up the expectation of any early provision for the extinction of slavery among us." Unlike some contemporary Virginians, the man who wrote the Declaration of Independence could not bring himself to free his own slaves.

Rethinking Gender

The revolutionary experience accelerated changes in the way ordinary people viewed the family. At the beginning of the eighteenth century, fathers claimed authority over other members of their families simply on the grounds that they were fathers. As patriarchs, they merited obedience. If they behaved like brutal despots, so be it; fathers could treat wives and children however they pleased. The English philosopher John Locke (1632–1704) helped to expose the fallacy of this view, and at the time of the American Revolution few seriously accepted the notion that fathers—be they tyrannical kings or heads of ordinary families—enjoyed unlimited powers over women and children. Indeed, people in England as well as America increasingly described the family in terms of love and companionship. Instead of duties, they spoke of affection. This transformation in the way men and women viewed relations of power within the family was most evident in the popular novels of the period. Americans devoured *Pamela* and *Clarissa*, stories by the English writer Samuel Richardson about women

who were the innocent victims of unreformed males, usually deceitful lovers and unforgiving fathers.

It was in this changing intellectual environment that American women began making new demands not only on their husbands, but also on republican institutions. Abigail Adams, one of the generation's most articulate women, instructed her husband, John, as he set off for the opening of the Continental Congress: "I desire you would Remember the Ladies, and be more generous and favourable to them than your ancestors. Do not put such unlimited power into the hands of the Husbands." John responded in a condescending manner. The "Ladies" would have to wait until the country achieved independence. In 1777, Lucy Knox took an even stronger line with her husband, General Henry Knox. When he was about to return home from the army, she warned him, "I hope you will not consider yourself as commander in chief in your own house—but be convinced . . . that there is such a thing as equal command."

If Knox accepted Lucy's argument, he did so because she was a good republican wife and mother. In fact, women justified their assertiveness largely on the basis of political ideology. If survival of republics really depended on the virtue of its citizens, they argued, then it was the special responsibility of women as mothers to nurture the right values in their children and as wives to instruct their husbands in proper behavior. Contemporaries claimed that the woman who possessed "virtue and prudence" could easily "mold the taste, the manners, and the conduct of her admirers, according to her pleasure." In fact, "nothing short of a general reformation of manners would take place, were the ladies to use their power in discouraging our licentious manners."

Ill-educated women could not possibly fulfill these high expectations. Women required education that was at least comparable to what men received. Scores of female academies were established during this period to meet what many Americans, men as well as women, now regarded as a pressing social need. These schools may have received widespread encouragement precisely because they did not radically alter traditional gender roles. After all, the educated republican woman of the late eighteenth century did not pursue a career; she returned to the home where she

Abigail Adams, wife of patriot John Adams, was a brilliant woman whose plea to limit the power of husbands gained little sympathetic attention.

followed a familiar routine as wife and mother. The frustration of not being allowed to develop her talents may explain the bitterness of a graduation oration delivered by an otherwise obscure woman in 1793: "Our high and mighty Lords . . . have denied us the means of knowledge, and then reproached us for want of it. . . . They doom'd the sex to servile or frivolous employments, on purpose to degrade their minds, that they themselves might hold unrivall'd, the power and preeminence they had usurped."

During this period, women began to petition for divorce on new grounds. One case is particularly instructive concerning changing attitudes toward women and the family. In 1784, John Backus, an undistinguished Massachusetts silversmith, was hauled before a local court and asked why he beat his wife. He responded that "it was Partly owing to his Education for his father treated his mother in the same manner." The difference between Backus's case and his father's was that Backus's wife refused to tolerate such abuse,

and she sued successfully for divorce. Studies of divorce patterns in Connecticut and Pennsylvania show that after 1773, women divorced on about the same terms as men.

The war itself presented some women with fresh opportunities. In 1780, Ester DeBerdt Reed founded a large volunteer women's organization in Philadelphia—the first of its kind in the United States—that raised over $300,000 for Washington's army. Other women ran family farms and businesses while their husbands fought the British. And in 1790, the New Jersey legislature explicitly allowed women who owned property to vote.

Despite these scattered gains, republican society still defined women's roles exclusively in terms of mother, wife, and homemaker. Other pursuits seemed unnatural, even threatening, and it is perhaps not surprising, therefore, that in 1807, New Jersey lawmakers—apparently angry over a close election in which women voters apparently determined the result—repealed female suffrage in the interests of "safety, quiet, and good order and dignity of the state."

The Promise of Liberty

The Revolution did not bring about a massive restructuring of American society, at least not in the short term. Nevertheless, republicans like Samuel Adams and Thomas Jefferson raised issues of immense significance for the later history of the United States. They insisted that equality, however narrowly defined, was an essential element of republican government. Even though they failed to abolish slavery, institute universal manhood suffrage, or apply equality to women, they vigorously articulated a set of assumptions about people's rights and liberties that challenged future generations of Americans to make good on the promise of the Revolution.

THE STATES: THE LESSONS OF REPUBLICANISM

In May 1776, the Second Continental Congress invited the states to adopt constitutions. The old colonial charters filled with references to king and Parliament were clearly no longer adequate, and within a few years, most states had taken action. Rhode Island and Connecticut already enjoyed republican government by virtue of their

Westtown Boarding School in Pennsylvania was established by the Society of Friends to expand educational opportunities for women in the mid-Atlantic states. Instituted in 1794, the school opened in 1799.

unique seventeenth-century charters that allowed the voters to select both governors and legislators. Eleven other states plus Vermont created new political structures, and their deliberations reveal how Americans living in different regions and reacting to different social pressures defined fundamental republican principles.

Several constitutions were boldly experimental, and some states later rewrote documents that had been drafted in the first flush of independence. These early constitutions were provisional, but they nevertheless provided the framers of the federal Constitution of 1787 with invaluable insights into the strengths and weaknesses of government based on the will of the people.

Blueprints for State Government

Despite disagreements over details, Americans who wrote the various state constitutions shared certain political assumptions. First, they insisted on preparing *written* documents. For many of them, of course, this seemed a natural step. As colonists, they had lived under royal charters, documents that described the workings of local government in detail. The Massachusetts Bay Charter of 1629, for example (see Chapter 2), guaranteed that the Puritans would enjoy the rights of Englishmen even after they had moved to the New World. And in New England, Congregationalists drew up church covenants stating in clear contractual language the rights and responsibilities of the entire congregation.

However logical the decision to produce written documents may have seemed to the Americans, it represented a major break with English practice. Political philosophers in the mother country had long boasted of Britain's unwritten constitution, a collection of judicial reports and parliamentary statutes. But this highly vaunted system had not protected the colonists from oppression; hence, after declaring independence, Americans demanded that their state constitutions explicitly define the rights of the people as well as the power of their rulers.

Natural Rights and the State Constitutions

The authors of the state constitutions believed men and women possessed certain natural rights over which government exercised no control whatsoever. So that future rulers—potential tyrants—would know the exact limits of authority, these fundamental rights were carefully spelled out. Indeed, the people of Massachusetts rejected the proposed state constitution of 1778 largely because it lacked a full statement of their basic rights. They demanded a guarantee of "rights of conscience, and . . . security of persons and property, which every member in the State hath a right to expect from the supreme power."

Eight state constitutions contained specific "Declarations of Rights." The length and character of these lists varied, but in general, they affirmed three fundamental freedoms: religion, speech, and press. They protected citizens from unlawful searches and seizures; they upheld trial by jury. George Mason, a shrewd political thinker who had written important revolutionary pamphlets, penned the most influential Declaration of Rights. It was appended to the Virginia Constitution of 1776, and the words were incorporated into other state constitutions as well as the famed Bill of Rights of the federal Constitution.

In almost every state, delegates to constitutional conventions drastically reduced the power of the governor. The constitutions of Pennsylvania and Georgia abolished the governor's office. In four other states, terms like *president* were substituted for *governor*. Even when those who designed the new state governments provided for a governor, they severely circumscribed his authority. He was allowed to make almost no political appointments, and while the state legislators closely monitored his activities, he possessed no veto over their decisions (Massachusetts being the lone exception). Most early constitutions lodged nearly all effective power in the legislature. This decision made good sense to men who had actually served under powerful royal governors during the late colonial period. These ambitious crown appointees had used executive patronage to influence members of the colonial assemblies, and as the Americans drafted their new republican constitutions, they were determined to bring their governors under tight control. In fact, the writers of the state constitutions were so fearful of the concentration of power in the hands of a single person, they failed to appreciate that elected governors—like the representatives themselves—were now the servants of a free people.

The legislature dominated early state government. The constitutions of Pennsylvania and Georgia provided for a unicameral, or one-house system, and since any male taxpayer could cast a ballot in these states, their legislatures became the nation's most democratic. Other states authorized the creation of two houses, but even as they did so, some of the more demanding republicans wondered why America needed a senate or upper house at all. What social and economic interests, they asked, did that body represent that could not be more fully and directly voiced in the lower house? After all, America had just freed itself of an aristocracy. The two-house form survived the

Revolution largely because it was familiar and because some persons had already begun to suspect that certain checks on the popular will, however arbitrary they might appear, were necessary to preserve minority rights.

Power to the People

Massachusetts did not adopt a constitution until 1780, several years after the other states had done so. The experience of the people of Massachusetts is particularly significant because in their efforts to establish a workable system of republican government they hit on a remarkable political innovation. After the rejection of two constitutions drafted by the state legislature, the responsibility fell to a specially elected convention of delegates whose sole purpose was the "formation of a new Constitution."

John Adams took a position of leadership at this convention and served as the chief architect of the governmental framework of Massachusetts. This framework included a house and senate, a popularly elected governor—who, unlike the chief executives of other states, possessed a veto over legislative bills—and property qualifications for officeholders as well as voters. The most striking aspect of the 1780 constitution, however, was its opening sentence: "We . . . the people of Massachusetts . . . agree upon, ordain, and establish." This powerful vocabulary would be echoed in the federal Constitution. The Massachusetts experiment reminded Americans that ordinary officeholders could not be trusted to define fundamental rights. That important task required a convention of delegates who could legitimately claim to speak for the people.

In 1780, no one knew whether the state experiments would succeed. There was no question a different type of person had begun to appear in public office, one that seemed, to the local gentry at least, a little poorer and less polished than they would have liked. When one Virginian surveyed the newly elected House of Burgesses in 1776, he discovered it was "composed of men not quite so well dressed, nor so politely educated, nor so highly born as some Assemblies I have formerly seen." This particular Virginian approved of such change, for he believed that "the People's men," however plain they might appear, possessed honesty and sincerity. They were, in fact, representative republicans, people who insisted they were anyone's equal in this burgeoning society.

Other Americans were less optimistic about the nation's immediate prospects. The health of a small republic depended entirely on the virtue of its people. If they or their elected officials succumbed to material temptation, if they failed to comprehend the moral dimensions of political power, or if personal liberty threatened the rights of property, then the state constitutions were no more than worthless pieces of paper. The risk of excess seemed great. In 1778, a group of New Englanders, fearful unbridled freedom would create political anarchy, observed, "The idea of liberty has been held up in so dazzling colours that some of us may not be willing to submit to that subordination necessary in the freest states."

CREATING A NEW NATIONAL GOVERNMENT

When the Second Continental Congress convened in 1775, the delegates found themselves waging war in the name of a country that did not yet exist. As the military crisis deepened, Congress gradually—often reluctantly—assumed greater authority over national affairs, but everyone agreed such narrowly conceived measures were a poor substitute for a legally constituted government. The separate states could not possibly deal with the range of issues that now confronted the American people. Indeed, if independence meant anything in a world of sovereign nations, it implied the creation of a central authority capable of conducting war, borrowing money, regulating trade, and negotiating treaties.

Articles of Confederacy

The challenge of creating a viable central government proved more difficult than anyone anticipated. Congress appointed a committee to draw up a plan for confederation. John Dickinson, the lawyer who had written an important revolutionary pamphlet entitled *Letters from a Farmer in Pennsylvania,* headed the committee. Dickinson envisioned the creation of a strong central government, and the report his committee presented on July 12, 1776, shocked delegates who assumed the constitution would authorize a loose confederation of states. Dickinson's plan placed the western territories, land claimed by the separate states, under congressional control. In addition,

John Dickinson, a highly respected lawyer, conceived a bold plan in 1776 for a strong central government, but the members of Congress saw it as a dangerous threat to the sovereignty of the states.

Dickinson's committee called for equal state representation in Congress.

Since some states, such as Virginia and Massachusetts, were more populous than others, the plan fueled tensions between large and small states. Also unsettling was Dickinson's recommendation that taxes be paid to Congress on the basis of a state's total population, black as well as white, a formula that angered Southerners who did not think slaves should be counted. Indeed, even before the British evacuated Boston, Dickinson's committee raised many difficult political questions that would divide Americans for several decades.

Not surprisingly, the draft of the plan—the Articles of Confederation—that Congress finally approved in November 1777 bore little resemblance to Dickinson's original plan. The Articles jealously guarded the sovereignty of the states. The delegates who drafted this framework shared a general republican conviction that power—especially power so far removed from the people—was inherently dangerous and that the only way to preserve liberty was to place as many constraints as possible on federal authority.

The result was a government that many people regarded as powerless. The Articles provided for a single legislative body consisting of representatives selected annually by the state legislatures. Each state possessed a single vote in Congress. It could send as many as seven delegates, as few as two, but if they divided evenly on a certain issue, the state lost its vote. There was no independent executive and no veto over legislative decisions. The Articles also denied Congress the power of taxation, a serious oversight in time of war. The national government could obtain funds only by asking the states for contributions, called requisitions, but if a state failed to cooperate—and many did—Congress limped along without financial support. Amendments to this constitution required assent by *all* thirteen states. The authors of the new system expected the weak national government to handle foreign relations, military matters, Indian affairs, and interstate disputes. They most emphatically did not award Congress ownership of the lands west of the Appalachian Mountains.

The new constitution sent to the states for ratification encountered apathy and hostility. Most Americans were far more interested in local affairs than in the actions of Congress. When a British army marched through a state, creating a need for immediate military aid, people spoke positively about central government, but as soon as the threat had passed, they sang a different tune. During this period, even the slightest encroachment on state sovereignty rankled the republicans who feared centralization would inevitably promote corruption.

Meeting a Crisis

The major bone of contention with the Articles, however, was the disposition of the vast, unsurveyed territory west of the Appalachians that everyone hoped the British would soon surrender. Some states, such as Virginia and Georgia, claimed land all the way from the Atlantic Ocean to the elusive "South Sea," in effect extending their boundaries to the Pacific Coast by virtue of royal charters. State legislators—their appetites whetted by aggressive land speculators—anticipated generating large revenues through land sales. Connecticut, New York, Pennsylvania, and North Carolina also announced intentions to seize blocks of western land.

Other states were not blessed with vague or ambiguous royal charters. The boundaries of Maryland, Delaware, and New Jersey had been established many years earlier, and it seemed as if people living in these states would be permanently cut off from the anticipated bounty. In protest, these "landless" states stubbornly refused to ratify the Articles of Confederation. Marylanders were particularly vociferous. All the states had made sacrifices for the common good during the Revolution, they complained, and it appeared only fair that all states should profit from the fruits of victory, in this case, from the sale of western lands. Maryland's spokesmen feared that if Congress did not void Virginia's excessive claims to all of the Northwest Territory (the land west of Pennsylvania and north of the Ohio River) as well as to a large area south of the Ohio, beyond the Cumberland Gap, known as Kentucky, then Marylanders would desert their home state in search of cheap Virginia farms, leaving Maryland an underpopulated wasteland.

Virginians scoffed at these pleas for equity. They knew that behind the Marylanders' statements of high purpose lay the greed of speculators. Private land companies had sprung up before the Revolution and purchased large tracts from the Indians in areas claimed by Virginia. Their agents petitioned Parliament to legitimize these questionable transactions. Their efforts failed. After the Declaration of Independence, however, the companies shifted the focus of their lobbying to Congress, particularly to the representatives of landless states like Maryland. By liberally distributing shares of stock, officials of the Indiana, Illinois, and Wabash companies gained powerful supporters such as Benjamin Franklin, Robert Morris, and Thomas Johnson, governor of Maryland. These activities encouraged Delaware and New Jersey to modify their demands and join the Confederation, while Maryland held out for five years. The leaders of Virginia, though, remained firm. Why, they asked, should Virginia surrender its historic claims to western lands to enrich a handful of selfish speculators?

The states resolved this bitter controversy in 1781 as much by accident as by design. Virginia agreed to cede its holdings north of the Ohio River to the Confederation on condition that Congress nullify the land companies' earlier purchases from the Indians. A practical consideration had softened Virginia's resolve. Republicans such as Jefferson worried about expanding their state beyond the mountains; with poor transportation links, it seemed impossible to govern such a large territory effectively from Richmond. The western settlers might even come to regard Virginia as a colonial power insensitive to their needs. Marylanders who dreamed of making fortunes on the land market grumbled, but when a British army appeared on their border, they prudently accepted the Articles (March 1, 1781). Congress required another three years to work out the details of the Virginia cession. Other landed states followed Virginia's example. These transfers established an important principle, for after 1781, it was agreed the West belonged not to the separate states, but to the United States. In this matter at least, the national government now exercised full sovereignty.

No one greeted ratification of the Articles with much enthusiasm. When they thought about national politics at all, Americans concerned themselves primarily with winning independence. The new government gradually developed an administrative bureaucracy, and in 1781, it formally created the Departments of War, Foreign Affairs, and Finance. By far the most influential figure in the Confederation was Robert Morris (1734–1806), a freewheeling Philadelphia merchant who was appointed the first superintendent of finance. Although he was a brilliant manager, Morris's decisions as superintendent provoked controversy, indeed, deep suspicion. He hardly seemed a model republican. Morris mixed public funds under his control with personal accounts, and he never lost an opportunity to make a profit. While such practices were not illegal, his apparent improprieties undermined his own political agenda. He desperately wanted to strengthen the central government, but highly vocal critics resisted, labeling Morris a "pecuniary dictator."

The Confederation's Major Achievement

Whatever the weaknesses of Congress may have been, it did score one impressive triumph. Congressional action brought order to western settlement, especially in the Northwest Territory, and incorporated frontier Americans into an expanding federal system. In 1781, the prospects for success did not seem promising. For years, colonial authorities had ignored people who migrated far inland, sending neither money nor soldiers to protect them from Indian attack. Tensions between the seaboard colonies and the frontier regions had sometimes flared into violence. In 1763, a group of Scotch-Irish frontiersmen calling themselves the "Paxton Boys" had protested Pennsylvania's inadequate defenses by killing innocent Indians and marching on the colonial capital. Similar disorders occurred in South Carolina in 1767, in North Carolina in 1769, and in Vermont in 1777. With thousands of men and women, most of them squatters, pouring across the Appalachian Mountains, Congress had to act quickly to avoid the past errors of royal and colonial authorities.

The initial attempt to deal with this explosive problem came in 1784. Jefferson, then serving as a member of Congress, drafted an ordinance that became the basis for later, more enduring legislation. Jefferson recommended carving ten new states out of the western lands located north of the Ohio River and recently ceded to the United States by Virginia. He specified that each new state establish a republican form of government. When the population of a territory equaled that of the smallest state already in the Confederation, the region could apply for full statehood. In the meantime, free white males could participate in local government, a democratic guarantee that frightened some of Jefferson's more conservative colleagues.

The impoverished Congress was eager to sell off the western territory as quickly as possible. After all, the frontier represented a source of income that did not depend on the unreliable generosity of the states. A second ordinance, passed in 1785 and called the Land Ordinance, established an orderly process for laying out new townships and marketing public lands.

The 1785 scheme possessed geometric elegance. Surveyors marked off townships, each running directly from east to west. These units, 6

Western Land Claims Ceded by the States

After winning the war, the major issue facing the Continental Congress under the Articles of Confederation was mediating conflicting states' claims to rich western land. By 1802, the states had ceded all rights to the federal government.

miles square, were subdivided into 36 separate sections of 640 acres (1 square mile) each. (Roads and property boundaries established according to this grid pattern survived long after the Confederation had passed into history.) The government planned to auction off its holdings at prices of not less than $1 an acre. Congress set the minimum purchase at 640 acres, and near-worthless paper money was not accepted as payment. Section 16 was set aside for public education; the federal government reserved four other sections for its own use.

Public response disappointed Congress. Surveying the lands took far longer than antici-

Land Ordinance of 1785

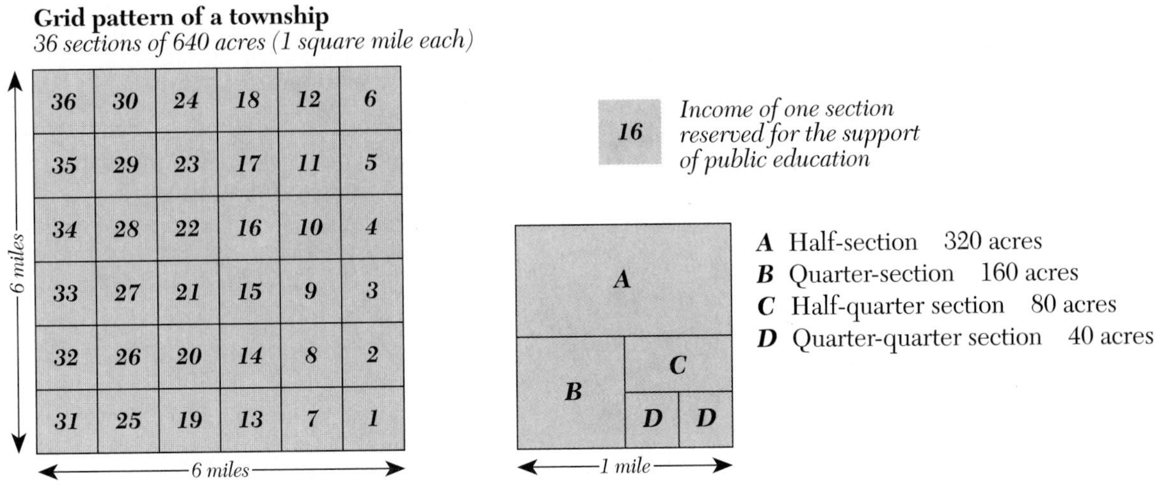

Grid pattern of a township
36 sections of 640 acres (1 square mile each)
36 30 24 18 12 6
35 29 23 17 11 5
34 28 22 16 10 4
33 27 21 15 9 3
32 26 20 14 8 2
31 25 19 13 7 1
6 miles
6 miles
16
Income of one section reserved for the support of public education
A
B
C
D D
1 mile
A Half-section 320 acres
B Quarter-section 160 acres
C Half-quarter section 80 acres
D Quarter-quarter section 40 acres

pated, and few persons possessed enough hard currency to make even the minimum purchase. Finally, a solution to the problem came from Manasseh Cutler, a New England minister turned land speculator and congressional lobbyist, and his associates, who included several former officers of the Continental army.

Cutler and his associates, representing the Ohio and Scioto companies, offered to purchase more than 6 million unsurveyed acres of land located in present-day southeastern Ohio by persuading Congress to accept, at full face value, government loan certificates that had been issued to soldiers during the Revolution. On the open market, the Ohio company could pick up these certificates for as little as 10 percent of their face value; thus, the company stood to make a fortune. Like so many other get-rich-quick schemes, however, this one failed to produce the anticipated millions. Unfortunately for Cutler and his friends, small homesteaders settled wherever they pleased, refusing to pay either government or speculators for the land.

Congress worried about the excess liberty on the frontier. In the 1780s, the West seemed to be filling up with people who by eastern standards were uncultured. Timothy Pickering, a New Englander, declared that "the emigrants to the frontier lands are the least worthy subjects in the United States. They are little less savage than the Indians; and when possessed of the most fertile spots, for want of industry, live miserably." The charge was as old as the frontier itself. Indeed, seventeenth-century Englishmen had said the same things of the earliest Virginians. The lawless image stuck, however, and even a sober observer like Washington insisted the West crawled with "banditti." The Ordinance of 1784 placed the government of the territories in the hands of people about whom congressmen and speculators had second thoughts.

These various currents shaped the Ordinance of 1787, one of the final acts passed under the Confederation. This bill, also called the Northwest Ordinance, provided a new structure for government of the Northwest Territory. The plan authorized the creation of between three and five territories, each to be ruled by a governor, a secretary, and three judges appointed by Congress. When the population reached five thousand, voters who owned property could elect an assembly, but its decisions were subject to the governor's absolute veto. Once sixty thousand persons resided in a territory, they could write a constitution and petition for full statehood. While these procedures represented a retreat from Jefferson's original proposal, the Ordinance of 1787 contained several significant features. A bill of rights guaranteed the settlers the right to trial by jury, freedom of religion, and due process of law. In addition, this act outlawed slavery, a prohibition that freed the future states of Ohio, Indiana, Illinois, Michigan, and Wisconsin from the curse of human bondage.

By contrast, settlement south of the Ohio River received far less attention from Congress. Long before the end of the war, thousands of Americans streamed through the Cumberland Gap into a part of Virginia known as Kentucky. The most famous of these settlers was Daniel Boone. In 1775, the population of Kentucky was approximately one hundred; by 1784, it had jumped to thirty thousand. Speculators purchased large tracts from the Indians, planning to resell this acreage to settlers at handsome profits. In 1776, one land company asked Congress to reorganize the company's holdings into a new state called Transylvania. While nothing came of this self-serving request, another, even more aggressive group of speculators in 1784 carved the state of Franklin out of a section of present-day Tennessee, then claimed by North Carolina. Rival speculators prevented formal recognition of Franklin's government. By 1790, the entire region south of the Ohio River had been transformed into a crazy quilt of claims and counterclaims that generated lawsuits for many years to come.

SEARCH FOR ORDER

Despite its success in bringing order to the Northwest Territory, the Confederation increasingly came under heavy fire from critics who wanted a stronger central government. Complaints varied from region to region, from person to person, but most disappointment reflected economic frustration. Americans had assumed that peace would restore economic growth, but recovery following the Revolution was slow.

The Nationalist Critique

Even before England signed a treaty with America, its merchants flooded American ports with consumer items and offered easy credit. Families that had postponed purchases of imported goods—either because of British blockade or personal hardship—now rushed to buy European finery.

This sudden renewal of trade with Great Britain on such a large scale strained the American economy. Gold and silver flowed back across the Atlantic, leaving the United States desperately short of hard currency, and when large merchant houses called in their debts, ordinary American consumers often found themselves on the brink of bankruptcy. "The disagreeable state of our commerce," observed James Wilson, an advocate of strong national government, has been the result "of extravagant and injudicious importation. . . . [w]e seemed to have forgot that to pay was as necessary in trade as to purchase."

To blame the Confederation alone for the economic depression would be unfair. Nevertheless, during the 1780s, many people agreed a stronger central government could somehow have brought greater stability to the struggling economy. In their rush to acquire imported luxuries, Americans seemed to have deserted republican

The widespread land speculation in the territory south of the Ohio River did not go unnoticed by European political cartoonists of the day. The French caption to the original cartoon explained that "Citizen Mignard signs today for some English companions who are selling imaginary lands in the United States. The better to ensnare dupes, they draw geological maps, converting rocky deserts into fertile plains, show roads cutting through impassable cliffs, and offer shares in lands that do not belong to them."

principles, and a weak Congress was helpless to restore national virtue.

Critics pointed to the government's inability to regulate trade. Whenever a northern congressman suggested restricting British access to American markets, southern representatives, who feared any controls on the export of tobacco or rice, bellowed in protest. Southerners anticipated that navigation acts written by the Confederation would put planters under the yoke of northern shipping interests.

The country's chronic fiscal instability increased public anxiety. While the war was still in progress, Congress printed well over $200 million in paper money, but because of extraordinarily high inflation, the rate of exchange for Continental bills soon declined to a fraction of their face value. In 1781, Congress, facing insolvency, turned to the states for help. They were asked to retire the depreciated currency. The situation was spinning out of control. Several states—pressed to pay their own war-related debts—not only recirculated the Continental bills, but also issued nearly worthless money of their own.

A heavy burden of state and national debt compounded the general sense of economic crisis. Revolutionary soldiers had yet to be paid. Women and men who had loaned money and goods to the government clamored for reimbursement. Foreign creditors demanded interest on funds advanced during the Revolution. These pressures grew, but Congress was unable to respond. The Articles specifically prohibited Congress from taxing the American people. It required little imagination to see the Confederation would soon default on its legal obligations unless something was done quickly.

In response, an aggressive group of men announced they knew how to save the Confederation. The "nationalists"—persons like Alexander Hamilton, James Madison, and Robert Morris—called for major constitutional reforms, the chief of which was an amendment allowing Congress to collect a 5 percent tax on imported goods sold in the states. Revenues generated by the proposed Impost of 1781 would be used by the Confederation to reduce the national debt. On this point they were adamant. The nationalists recognized that whoever paid the public debt would gain the public trust. If the states assumed

"Not worth a Continental!" became a common oath when inflation eroded the value of Continental currency. Most currency issued by the states was equally valueless.

the responsibility, then the country could easily fragment into separate republics. "A national debt," Hamilton explained in 1781, "if it is not excessive, will be to us a national blessing. It will be a powerful cement to our union." Twelve states accepted the Impost amendment, but Rhode Island—where local interests argued the tax would make Congress "independent of their constituents"—resolutely refused to cooperate. One negative vote on this proposed constitutional change and the taxing scheme was dead. Subsequent attempts to put the country's finances on a firm footing were also narrowly defeated on the state level.

State leaders frankly thought the nationalists were up to no good. The "localists" were especially apprehensive of fiscal plans advanced by Robert Morris. His profiteering as superintendent of finance appeared a threat to the moral fiber of the young republic. Richard Henry Lee and Samuel Adams, men of impeccable patriotic credentials, decried Morris's efforts to create a national bank. Such an institution would bring forth a flock of social parasites, the kind of persons that Americans associated with corrupt monarchical government. One person declared that if an impost ever passed, Morris "will have all [the money] in his Pocket."

The nationalists regarded their opponents as economically naive. A country with the potential of the United States required a complex, centralized fiscal system. But for all their pretensions to realism, the nationalists of the early 1780s were politically inept. They underestimated the depth of republican fears, and in their rush to strengthen the Articles, they overplayed their hand.

A group of extreme nationalists even appealed to the army for support. To this day, no one knows the full story of the Newburgh Conspiracy of 1783. Officers of the Continental army stationed at Newburgh, New York, worried Congress would disband them without funding their pensions, began to lobby intensively for relief. In March, they scheduled general meetings to protest the weakness and duplicity of Congress. The officers' initial efforts were harmless enough, but frustrated nationalists such as Morris and Hamilton hoped that if the army exerted sufficient pressure on the government, perhaps even threatened a military takeover, then stubborn Americans might be compelled to amend the Articles.

The conspirators failed to take George Washington's integrity into account. No matter how much he wanted a strong central government, he would not tolerate insubordination by the military. Washington confronted the officers directly at Newburgh, intending to read a prepared statement. Fumbling with his glasses before his men, he commented, "Gentlemen, you must pardon me. I have grown gray in your service and now find myself growing blind." The unexpected vulnerability of this great soldier reduced the troops to tears, and in an instant, the rebellion was broken. Washington deserves credit for preserving civilian rule in this country.

In April 1783, Congress proposed a second impost, but it too failed to win unanimous ratification. Even a personal appeal by Washington could not save the amendment. As one opponent explained, if "permanent Funds are given to Congress, the aristocratic Influence, which predominates in more than a major part of the United States, will fully establish an arbitrary Government." With this defeat, nationalists gave up on the Confederation. Morris retired from government, and Madison returned to Virginia utterly depressed by what he had witnessed.

Diplomatic Humiliation

In foreign affairs, Congress endured further embarrassment. It could not even enforce the provisions of its own peace treaty. American negotiators had promised Great Britain that its citizens could collect debts contracted before the Revolution. The states, however, dragged their heels, and several even passed laws obstructing the settlement of legitimate prewar claims. Congress was powerless to force compliance. The British responded to this apparent provocation by refusing to evacuate troops from posts located in the Northwest Territory. A strong national government would have driven the redcoats out, but without adequate funds, the weak Congress could not provide soldiers for such a mission.

Congress's postrevolutionary dealings with Spain were equally humiliating. That nation refused to accept the southern boundary of the United States established by the Treaty of Paris. Spain claimed sovereignty over much of the land located between Georgia and the Mississippi River, and its agents schemed with Indian tribes in this region to resist American expansion. On July 21, 1784, Spain fueled the controversy by closing the lower Mississippi River to citizens of the United States.

This unexpected decision devastated western farmers. Free use of the Mississippi was essential to the economic development of the entire Ohio Valley. Because of the prohibitively high cost of transporting freight for long distances over land, western settlers—and southern planters eyeing future opportunities in this area—demanded a secure water link with the world's markets. Their spokesmen in Congress denounced anyone who claimed that navigation of the Mississippi was a negotiable issue.

In 1786, a Spanish official, Don Diego de Gardoqui, opened talks with John Jay, a New Yorker appointed by Congress to obtain rights to navigation of the Mississippi. Jay soon discovered that Gardoqui would not compromise. After making little progress, Jay seized the initiative. If

Gardoqui would allow American merchants to trade directly with Spain, thus opening up an important new market to ships from New England and the middle states, then the United States might forgo navigation of the Mississippi for twenty-five years. When southern delegates heard of Jay's concessions, they were outraged. It appeared to them as if representatives of northern commerce were ready to abandon the southern frontier. Angry congressmen accused New Englanders of attempting to divide the United States into separate confederations, for as one Virginian exclaimed, the proposed Spanish treaty "would weaken if not destroy the union by disaffecting the Southern States . . . to obtain a trivial commercial advantage." Congress wisely terminated the negotiations with Spain.

By the mid-1780s, the Confederation could claim several notable achievements. It designed an administrative system that lasted far longer than did the Articles. It also brought order out of the chaos of conflicting western land claims. Still, as anyone could see, the government was struggling. Congress met irregularly. Some states did not even bother to send delegates, and pressing issues often had to be postponed for lack of a quorum. The nation even lacked a permanent capital, and Congress drifted from Philadelphia to Princeton, to Annapolis to New York City, prompting one humorist to suggest the government purchase an air balloon. This newly invented device, he explained, would allow the members of Congress to "float along from one end of the continent to the other" and "suddenly pop down into any of the states they please."

RESTRUCTURING THE REPUBLIC

Many Americans, especially those who had provided leadership during the Revolution, agreed something had to be done. By 1785, the country seemed to have lost direction. The buoyant optimism that sustained revolutionary patriots had dissolved into pessimism and doubt. In 1786, Washington bitterly observed, "What astonishing changes a few years are capable of producing. Have we fought for this? Was it with these expectations that we launched into a sea of trouble, and have bravely struggled through the most threatening dangers?"

A Crisis Mentality

The conviction of people such as Washington that the nation was indeed in a state of crisis reflected tensions within republican thought. To be sure, they supported open elections and the right of individuals to advance their own economic well-being, but when these elements seemed to undermine social and political order, they expressed the fear that perhaps liberty had been carried too far. The situation had changed quite rapidly. As recently as the 1770s, men of republican persuasion had insisted the greatest threat to the American people was concentration of power in the hands of unscrupulous rulers. With this principle in mind, they transformed state governors into mere figureheads and emasculated the Confederation in the name of popular liberties.

By the mid-1780s, persons of property and standing saw the problem in a different light. Recent experience suggested to them that ordinary citizens did not in fact possess sufficient virtue to sustain a republic. The states had been plagued not by executive tyranny but by an excess of democracy, by a failure of the majority to preserve the property rights of the minority, by an unrestrained individualism that promoted anarchy rather than good order.

Many state leaders did not seem particularly concerned about the fiscal health of the national government. Local presses churned out worthless currency, and in some states, assemblies passed laws impeding the collection of debt. In Rhode Island, the situation became absurd. State legislators made it illegal for merchants to reject Rhode Island money even though everyone knew it had no value. No wonder Governor William Livingston of New Jersey declared in 1787, "We do not exhibit the virtue that is necessary to support a republican government."

As Americans tried to interpret these experiences within a republican framework, they were checked by the most widely accepted political wisdom of the age. Baron de Montesquieu (1689–1755), a French political philosopher of immense international reputation, declared flatly that a republican government could not flourish in a large territory. The reasons were clear. If the people lost direct control over their representatives, they would fall prey to tyrants. Large distances allowed rulers to hide their corruption; physical separation presented aristocrats with opportunities to seize power.

In the United States, most learned men treated Montesquieu's theories as self-evident truths. His writings seemed to demonstrate the importance of preserving the sovereignty of the states, for however much these small republics abused the rights of property and ignored minority interests, it was plainly unscientific to maintain that a republic consisting of thirteen states, several million people, and thousands of acres of territory could long survive.

James Madison rejected Montesquieu's argument, and in so doing, helped Americans to think of republican government in radical new ways. This soft-spoken, rather unprepossessing Virginian was the most brilliant American political thinker of his generation. One French official described Madison as "a man one must study a long time in order to make a fair appraisal." Those who listened carefully to what Madison had to say, however, soon recognized his genius for translating theory into practice.

Madison delved into the writings of a group of Scottish philosophers, the most prominent being David Hume (1711–1776), and from their works he concluded that Americans need not fear a greatly expanded republic. Madison perceived that "inconveniences of popular States contrary to prevailing Theory, are in proportion not to the extent, but to the narrowness of their limits." Indeed, it was in small states like Rhode Island that legislative majorities tyrannized the propertied minority. In a large territory, Madison explained, "the Society becomes broken into a greater variety of interest, of pursuits, of passions, which check each other, whilst those who may feel a common sentiment have less opportunity of communication and contact."

Madison did not, however, advocate a modern "interest-group" model of political behavior. The contending parties were incapable of working for the common good. They were too mired in their own local, selfish concerns. Rather, Madison thought competing factions would neutralize each other, leaving the business of running the central government to the ablest, most virtuous persons the nation could produce. In other words, Madison's federal system was not a small state writ large; it was something entirely different, a government based on the will of the people and yet detached from their narrowly based demands. This thinking formed the foundation of Madison's most famous political essay, *The Federalist* No. 10.

Movement Toward Constitutional Reform

A concerted movement to overhaul the Articles of Confederation began in 1786 when Madison and his friends persuaded the Virginia assembly to recommend a convention to explore the creation of a unified system of "commercial regulations." Congress supported the idea. In September, delegates from five states arrived in Annapolis, Maryland, to discuss issues that extended far beyond commerce. The small turnout was disappointing, but the occasion provided strong nationalists with an opportunity to hatch an even bolder plan. The Annapolis delegates advised Congress to hold a second meeting in Philadelphia "to take into consideration the situation of the United States, to devise such further provisions as shall appear to them necessary to render the constitution of the Federal Government adequate to the exigencies of the Union." Whether staunch states' rights advocates in Congress knew what was afoot is not clear. In any case, Congress authorized a grand convention to gather in May 1787.

Events played into Madison's hands. Soon after the Annapolis meeting, an uprising known as Shays's Rebellion, involving several thousand impoverished farmers, shattered the peace of western Massachusetts. No matter how hard these men worked the soil, they always found themselves in debt to eastern creditors. They complained of high taxes, of high interest rates, and, most of all, of a state government insensitive to their problems. In 1786, Daniel Shays, a veteran of the battle of Bunker Hill, and his armed neighbors closed a county courthouse where creditors were suing to foreclose farm mortgages. At one point, the rural insurgents threatened to seize the federal arsenal located at Springfield. Congress did not have funds sufficient to support an army, and the arsenal might have fallen had not a group of wealthy Bostonians raised an army of four thousand troops to put down the insurrection. The victors were in for a surprise. At the next general election, the voters of Massachusetts

This 1787 woodcut portrays Daniel Shays with one of his chief officers, Jacob Shattucks. Shays led a band of fellow farmers in revolt against a state government that was insensitive to rural needs. Their rebellion strengthened the demand for a strong new federal government.

selected representatives sympathetic to Shays's demands, and a new liberal assembly reformed debtor law.

Nationalists throughout the United States were not so forgiving. From their perspective, Shays' Rebellion symbolized the breakdown of law and order that they had long predicted. "Great commotions are prevailing in Massachusetts," Madison wrote. "An appeal to the sword is exceedingly dreaded." The time had come for sensible people to speak up for a strong national government. The unrest in Massachusetts persuaded persons who might otherwise have ignored the Philadelphia meeting to participate in drafting a new constitution.

The Philadelphia Convention

In the spring of 1787, fifty-five men representing twelve states traveled to Philadelphia. Rhode Island refused to take part in the proceedings, a decision that Madison attributed to its "wickedness and folly." Thomas Jefferson described the convention as an "assembly of demi-Gods," but this flattering depiction is misleading. However much modern Americans revere the Constitution, they should remember that the individuals who wrote it did not possess divine insight into the nature of government. They were practical people—lawyers, merchants, and planters—many of

whom had fought in the Revolution and served in the Congress of the Confederation. The majority were in their thirties or forties. The gathering included George Washington, James Madison, George Mason, Robert Morris, James Wilson, John Dickinson, Benjamin Franklin, and Alexander Hamilton, just to name some of the more prominent participants. Absent were John Adams and Thomas Jefferson, who were conducting diplomacy in Europe; Patrick Henry, a localist suspicious of strong central government, remained in Virginia, announcing he "smelled a rat."

As soon as the convention opened on May 25, the delegates made several procedural decisions of the utmost importance. First, they voted "that nothing spoken in the House be printed, or communicated without leave." The rule was stringently enforced. Sentries guarded the doorways to keep out uninvited visitors, windows stayed shut in the sweltering heat to prevent sound from either entering or leaving the chamber, and members were forbidden to copy the daily journal without official permission. As Madison explained, the secrecy rule saved "both the convention and the community from a thousand erroneous and perhaps mischievous reports." It also has made it extremely difficult for modern lawyers and judges to determine exactly what the delegates had in mind when they wrote the

Constitution (see pages 188–189, "The Elusive Constitution: Search for Original Intent").

In a second procedural move, the delegates decided to vote by state, but to avoid the kinds of problems that had plagued the Confederation, they ruled that key proposals needed the support of only a majority instead of the nine states required under the Articles.

Inventing a Federal Republic

Madison understood that whoever sets the agenda, controls the meeting. Even before all the delegates had arrived, he drew up a framework for a new federal system known as the "Virginia Plan." Madison wisely persuaded Edmund Randolph, Virginia's popular governor, to present this scheme to the convention on May 29. Randolph claimed the Virginia Plan merely revised sections of the Articles, but everyone, including Madison, knew better. "My ideas," Madison confessed, "strike . . . deeply at the old Confederation." He was determined to restrain the state assemblies, and in the original Virginia Plan, Madison gave the federal government power to veto state laws.

The Virginia Plan envisioned a national legislature consisting of two houses, one elected *directly* by the people, the other chosen by the first house from nominations made by the state assemblies. Representation in both houses was proportional to the state's population. The Virginia Plan also provided for an executive elected by Congress. Since most delegates at the Philadelphia convention sympathized with the nationalist position, Madison's blueprint for a strong federal government initially received broad support, and the Virginia Plan was referred to further study and debate. A group of men who allegedly had come together to reform the Confederation found themselves discussing the details of "a *national* Government . . . consisting of a *supreme* Legislature, Executive, and Judiciary."

The Virginia Plan had been pushed through the convention so fast that opponents hardly had an opportunity to present their objections. On June 15, they spoke up. William Paterson, a New Jersey lawyer, advanced the so-called New Jersey Plan, a scheme that retained the unicameral legislature in which each state possessed one vote, and at the same time gave Congress extensive new powers to tax and regulate trade. Paterson argued that these revisions, while more modest than Madison's plan, would have greater appeal for the American people. "I believe," he said, "that a little practical virtue is to be preferred to the finest theoretical principles, which cannot be carried into effect." The delegates listened politely and then soundly rejected the New Jersey Plan on June 19. Indeed, only New Jersey, New York, and Delaware voted in favor of Paterson's scheme.

Rejection of this framework did not resolve the most controversial issue before the convention. Paterson and others feared that under the Virginia Plan, small states would lose their separate identities. These delegates maintained that unless each state possessed an equal vote in Congress, the small states would find themselves at the mercy of their larger neighbors.

This argument outraged the delegates who favored a strong federal government. It awarded too much power to the states. "For whom [are we] forming a Government?" Wilson cried. "Is it for men, or for the imaginary beings called States?" It seemed absurd to claim that Rhode Island with only 68,000 people should have the same voice in Congress as Virginia's 747,000 inhabitants.

Compromise Saves the Convention

The mood of the convention was tense. Hard work and frustration, coupled with Philadelphia's sweltering summer heat, frayed nerves, prompted some members to predict that this meeting would accomplish nothing of significance. But despite the growing pessimism, the gathering did not break up. The delegates desperately wanted to produce a constitution, and they refused to give up until they had explored every avenue of reconciliation. Perhaps cooler heads agreed with Washington: "To please all is impossible, and to attempt it would be vain. The only way, therefore, is . . . to form such a government as will bear the scrutinizing eye of criticism, and trust it to the good sense and patriotism of the people."

Mediation clearly offered the only way to overcome what Roger Sherman, a Connecticut delegate, called "a full stop." On July 2, a "grand committee" of one person from each state was elected by the convention to resolve persistent differences between the large and small states. Franklin, at eighty-one the oldest delegate, served as chair. The two fiercest supporters of proportional representation based on population, Madison and Wilson, were left off the "grand committee," a sure sign the small states would salvage something from the compromise.

The committee recommended the states be equally represented in the upper house of Congress, while representation was to be proportionate in the lower house. Only the lower house could initiate money bills. Franklin's committee also decided one member of the lower house should be selected for every forty thousand inhabitants of a state. Southern delegates insisted this number include slaves. In the so-called three-fifths rule, the committee agreed that for the purpose of determining representation in the lower house slaves would be counted, but not as much as free persons. For every five slaves, a congressional district received credit for three free voters, a deal that gave the South much greater power in the new government than it would have otherwise received. As with most compromise solutions, the one negotiated by Franklin's committee fully satisfied no one. It did, however, overcome a major impasse, and after the small states gained an assured voice in the upper house, the Senate, they cooperated enthusiastically in creating a strong central government.

A Republic with Slaves

During the final days of August, a deeply disturbing issue came before the convention. It was a harbinger of the great sectional crisis of the nineteenth century. Many northern representatives detested the slave trade and wanted it to end immediately. They despised the three-fifths ruling that seemed to award slaveholders extra power in government simply because they owned slaves. "It seemed now to be pretty well understood," Madison jotted in his private notes, "that the real difference of interest lay, not between the large and small but between the N. and Southn. States. The institution of slavery and its consequences formed a line of discrimination."

Whenever northern delegates—and on this point they were by no means united—pushed too aggressively, Southerners threatened to bolt the convention, thereby destroying any hope of establishing a strong national government. Curiously, even recalcitrant Southerners avoided using the word *slavery*. They seemed embarrassed to call an institution by its true name, and in the Constitution itself, slaves were described as "other persons," "such persons," "persons held to Service or Labour," in other words, as everything but slaves.

A few northern delegates such as Roger Sherman of Connecticut sought at every turn to mollify the Southerners, especially the South Carolinians who spoke so passionately about preserving slavery. Gouverneur Morris, a Pennsylvania representative, would have none of it. He regularly reminded the Convention that, "the inhabitant of Georgia and S.C. who goes to the Coast of Africa, and in defiance of the most sacred laws of humanity tears away his fellow creatures from their dearest connections and damns them to the most cruel bondage, shall have more votes in a Government instituted for the protection of the rights of mankind, than the Citizen of Pa. or N. Jersey."

Largely ignoring Morris's stinging attacks, the delegates reached an uneasy understanding on the continuation of the slave trade. Southerners feared the new Congress would pass commercial regulations adversely affecting the planters—taxes on the export of rice and tobacco, for example. They demanded, therefore, that no trade laws be passed without a two-thirds majority of the federal legislature. They backed down on this point, however, in exchange for guarantees that Congress would not interfere with the slave trade until 1808 (see Chapter 8). The South even came away with a clause assuring the return of fugitive slaves. "We have obtained," Charles Cotesworth Pinckney told the planters of South Carolina, "a right to recover our slaves in whatever part of America they may take refuge, which is a right we had not before."

Although these deals revolted many Northerners, they conceded that establishing a strong national government was of greater immediate importance than ending the slave trade. "Great as the evil is," Madison wrote, "a dismemberment of the union would be worse."

The Elusive Constitution
Search for Original Intent

Many prominent national leaders, alarmed at a perceived "judicial imperialism" in recent activist courts, have urged that judges interpret the Constitution strictly according to the "intent of the Framers." Arguing that a "jurisprudence of original intent" is the "only legitimate basis for constitutional decision making," *intentionalists* demand that judges measure decisions against a "demonstrable consensus among the Framers and ratifiers as to principles stated or implied in the Constitution."

Yet when one considers circumstances surrounding the Constitution's framing, demonstration of the Founders' intent proves elusive indeed. Delegates to Philadelphia in 1787 deliberately veiled the purpose of the Convention in secrecy to avoid pressure by local constituencies who harbored deep suspicions concerning strong central government. Newspapers, barred from access to the Convention, printed only occasional rumors. Delegates refused to speak or correspond with outsiders concerning the proceedings.

The strictness with which delegates observed the rule of secrecy not only restricted contemporary knowledge of what transpired, but has also limited the number of sources in which subsequent generations may search for original intent. Only three members preserved complete accounts of Convention debates. These records remained unpublished for more than thirty years, forcing the first generation of lawyers and federal judges to rely on the words of the Constitution alone for clues to the Framers' intent.

The publication of the three accounts did not necessarily make the delegates' intent more accessible. The *Journal, Acts and Proceedings of the Convention Assemblies in Philadelphia*, recorded by the Convention Secretary, William Jackson, provided only a chronological listing of motions, resolutions, and vote tallies. His unpublished manuscript of convention debates, which could have fleshed out the published *Journal's* "mere skeleton" of the proceedings, was lost.

The notes of New York delegate Robert Yates appeared in 1821 as *Secret Proceedings and Debates of the Convention Assembled at Philadelphia*, but the circumstances of their publication rendered them thoroughly unreliable. Their editor, the for-

---

Though complete sets of notes were penned by both the convention secretary, William Jackson (center, left) and James Madison (opposite page), neither set provides indisputable evidence to support a particular theory of original intent. Jackson's published notes provide only listings to parliamentary procedures; Madison's notes, though accurate, must be considered incomplete.

mer French minister Citizen Edmond Genêt, attained notoriety in the 1790s when he violated American neutrality in the Anglo-French war by commissioning American privateers against British shipping. Genêt supported states' rights and popular government and manipulated Yates's notes to support his views. A comparison of *Secret Proceedings* with the two surviving pages of Yates's manuscript reveals that Genêt altered or deleted more than half the original text.

If the intent of the delegates survives anywhere, Madison's *Notes of Debates in the Federal Convention of 1787* provides its likeliest repository. The "father of the Constitution" as contemporaries called him, carefully preserved notes on Convention proceedings and took every measure to ensure their accuracy. Recognizing his own limitations as a stenographer, Madison did not try to record everything said, but sought manuscript copies of delegates' speeches that he incorporated into his notes at the end of each day. Madison also waited until the end of each day to record his own speeches, every one of which was extemporaneous, from memory. At the convention's end, he obtained a manuscript copy of Secretary Jackson's notes, which he used to supplement and correct his own. Though Madison tinkered at times with his notes over the next thirty years, recent analysis has demonstrated that none of these minor corrections impaired the faithfulness of the text.

Yet in spite of the meticulous care that Madison lavished on his notes, they remain, at best, incomplete repositories of the

Framers' original intent. Each day's notes contain only a few minutes of oral discourse, whereas actual delivery occupied between five and seven hours. Furthermore, written manuscripts of speeches may have approximated only roughly what the debaters actually said. Madison's speech on the benefits of a large republic, for example, occupies two closely reasoned pages in his notes. Yet others who took notes seem to have recorded a much shorter and far less impressive oral version. Such discrepancies raise important questions. How did Framers understand the actual speeches on the Convention floor? How did understanding shape their intentions? How much of their intent is lost in the vast omissions?

These questions take on even greater significance when one considers that the Constitution was forged through a series of compromises among representatives whose interests and intentions differed widely. No delegate was completely satisfied, and the finished document permitted some functions none had intended. Madison himself complained, for example, that the principle of judicial review "was never intended and can never be proper."

Moreover, he thought it would be a mistake to search for the original intent of Convention delegates. The delegates' intent could never possibly determine Constitutional interpretation, he argued, for "the only authoritative intentions were those of the people of the States, as expressed thro' the Conventions which ratified the Constitution."

Yet the works most common-

James Madison

ly cited from the time of state ratification raise problems with the application of this principle as well. Stenographers who recorded the *Debates of the Several State Conventions on the Adoption of the Federal Constitution* did not possess skills adequate to their task, and Federalist partisans edited the speeches with abandon in order to promote their own views. Evidence also suggests that Jonathan Eliot, the journalist who published the debates in 1836, altered them further.

Given the limitations of sources most often cited by modern judges and lawyers, the original intent of most Framers remains as elusive today as it was for the first generation who had no access to those documents. The Constitution's often ambiguous wording, which furnished the sole guide to the Framers' intent in their day, remains the best recourse in our own.

The Last Details

On July 26, the convention formed a Committee of Detail, a group that prepared a rough draft of the Constitution. After it completed its work—writing a document that still, after so many hours of debate, preserved the fundamental points of the Virginia Plan—the delegates reconsidered each article. The task required the better part of a month.

During these sessions, the members of the convention concluded that the president, as they now called the executive, should be selected by an electoral college, a body of prominent men in each state chosen by local voters. The number of "electoral" votes held by each state equaled its number of representatives and senators. This awkward device guaranteed the president would not be indebted to the Congress for his office. Whoever received the second largest number of votes in the electoral college automatically became vice president. In the event that no person received a majority of the votes, the election would be decided by the lower house—the House of Representatives—with each state casting a single vote. Delegates also armed the chief executive with veto power over legislation as well as the right to nominate judges. Both privileges, of course, would have been unthinkable a decade earlier, but the state experiments revealed the importance of having an independent executive to maintain a balanced system of republican government.

As the meeting was concluding, some delegates expressed concern about the absence in the Constitution of a bill of rights. Such declarations had been included in most state constitutions, and Virginians like George Mason insisted that the states and their citizens needed explicit protection from possible excesses by the federal government. While many delegates sympathized with Mason's appeal, they noted that the hour was late and, in any case, that the proposed Constitution provided sufficient security for individual rights. During the hard battles over ratification, the delegates to the convention may have regretted passing over the issue so lightly.

We, the People

The delegates adopted an ingenious procedure for ratification. Instead of submitting the Constitution to the various state legislatures, all of which had a vested interest in maintaining the status quo and most of which had two houses, either of which could block approval, they called for the election of thirteen state conventions especially chosen to review the new federal government. The delegates may have picked up this idea from the Massachusetts experiment of 1780. Moreover, the Constitution would take effect after the assent of only nine states. There was no danger, therefore, that the proposed system would fail simply because a single state like Rhode Island withheld approval.

The convention asked Gouverneur Morris, a delegate from Pennsylvania noted for his urbanity, to make final stylistic changes in the wording of the Constitution. When Morris examined the working draft, he discovered it spoke of the collection of states forming a new government. This wording presented problems. Ratification required only nine states. No one knew whether all the states would accept the Constitution, and if not, which nine would. A strong possibility existed that several New England states would reject the document. Morris's brilliant phrase, "We, the People of the United States," eliminated this difficulty. The new nation was a republic of the people, not of the states.

On September 17, thirty-nine men signed the Constitution. A few members of the convention, like Mason, could not support the document. Others had already gone home. For over three months, Madison had served as the convention's driving intellectual force. He now generously summarized the experience: "There never was an assembly of men, charged with a great and arduous trust, who were more pure in their motives, or more exclusively or anxiously devoted to the object committed to them."

WHOSE CONSTITUTION? THE STRUGGLE FOR RATIFICATION

Supporters of the Constitution recognized ratification would not be easy. After all, the convention had been authorized only to revise the Articles, but instead it produced a new plan that fundamentally altered relations between the states and the central government. The delegates dutifully dispatched copies of the Constitution to the Congress of Confederation, then meeting in New

	Articles of Confederation	Constitution
Mode of ratification or amendment	Require confirmation by every state legislature	Requires confirmation by $3/4$ of state conventions or legislatures
Number of houses in legislature	One	Two
Mode of representation	1–7 Delegates represent each state, each state holding only one vote in Congress	Two senators represent each state in upper house; each senator holds one vote. One representative to lower house represents every 30,000 people (in 1788) in a state; each representative holds one vote
Mode of election and term of office	Delegates appointed annually by state legislatures	Senators chosen by state legislatures for six-year term (direct election after 1913); representatives chosen by vote of citizens for two-year term
Executive	No separate executive: delegates annually elect one of their number as president, who possesses no veto, no power to appoint officers or to conduct policy. Administrative functions of government theoretically carried out by Committee of States; practically by various single-headed departments	Separate executive branch: president elected by electoral college to four-year term, granted veto, power to conduct policy, to appoint ambassadors, judges, and officers of executive departments established by legislation
Judiciary	Most adjudication left to state and local courts, Congress final court of appeal in disputes between states	Separate branch consisting of Supreme Court and inferior courts established by Congress to enforce federal law
Taxation	States alone can levy taxes, Congress funds the Common Treasury by making requisitions for state contributions	Federal government granted powers of taxation
Regulation of commerce	Congress regulates foreign commerce by treaty, but holds no check on conflicting state regulations	Congress regulates foreign commerce by treaty; all state regulations must obtain congressional consent

York City, and that powerless body referred the document to the separate states without any specific recommendation. The fight for ratification had begun.

Federalists and Antifederalists

Proponents of the Constitution enjoyed great advantages over the unorganized opposition. In the contest for ratification, they took no chances.

Their most astute move was the adoption of the label *Federalist*. This term cleverly suggested that they stood for a confederation of states rather than for the creation of a supreme national authority. Critics of the Constitution, who tended to be somewhat poorer, less urban, and less well educated than their opponents, cried foul, but there was little they could do. They were stuck with the name *Antifederalist*, a misleading term that made their cause seem far more obstructionist than it actually was.

The Federalists recruited the most prominent public figures of the day. In every state convention, speakers favoring the Constitution were more polished and more fully prepared than were their opponents. In New York, the campaign to win ratification sparked publication of *The Federalist,* a brilliant series of essays written by Madison, Hamilton, and Jay during the fall and winter of 1787 and 1788. The nation's newspapers threw themselves overwhelmingly behind the new government. In fact, few journals even bothered to carry Antifederalist writings. In some states, the Federalists adopted tactics of questionable propriety in order to gain ratification. In Pennsylvania, for example, they achieved a legal quorum for a crucial vote by dragging several opposition delegates into the meeting from the streets. In New York, Hamilton intimidated upstate Antifederalists with threats that New York City would secede from the state unless the state ratified the Constitution.

In these battles, the Antifederalists articulated a political philosophy that had broad popular appeal. They spoke the language of the Commonwealthmen (see Chapter 4). Like the extreme republicans who drafted the first state constitutions, the Antifederalists were deeply suspicious of political power. During the debates over ratification, they warned that public officials, however selected, would be constantly scheming to expand their authority.

The preservation of individual liberty required constant vigilance. It seemed obvious that the larger the republic, the greater the opportunity for political corruption. Local voters could not possibly know what their representatives in a distant national capital were doing. The government outlined in the Constitution invited precisely the kinds of problems that Montesquieu had described in his famous essay. "In so extensive a republic," one Antifederalist declared, "the great officers of government would soon become above the control of the people, and abuse their power."

Antifederalists demanded direct, personal contact with their representatives. They argued that elected officials should reflect the character of their constituents as closely as possible. It seemed unlikely that in large congressional districts, the people would be able to preserve such close ties with their representatives. According to the Antifederalists, the Constitution favored persons wealthy enough to have forged a reputation that extended beyond a single community. Samuel Chase told the members of the Maryland ratifying convention that under the new system "the distance between the people and their representatives will be so great that there is no probability of a farmer or planter being chosen . . . only the *gentry*, the *rich*, and the well-born will be elected."

Federalist speakers mocked their opponents' localist perspective. The Constitution deserved general support precisely because it ensured future Americans would be represented by "natural aristocrats," individuals possessing greater insights, skills, and training than did the ordinary citizen. These talented leaders, the Federalists insisted, could discern the interests of the entire population. They were not tied to the selfish needs of local communities. "The little demagogue of a petty parish or country will find his importance annihilated [under the Constitution] and his intrigues useless," predicted Charles Cotesworth Pinckney, a South Carolina Federalist.

Historians have generally accepted the Federalist critique. It would be a mistake, however, to see the Antifederalists as "losers" or as persons who could not comprehend social and economic change. Although their rhetoric echoed an older moral view of political culture, they accepted more easily than did many Federalists a liberal marketplace in which ordinary citizens competed as equals with the rich and well-born. They believed the public good was best served by allowing individuals like themselves to pursue their own private interests. That is what they had been doing on the local level during the 1780s, and they resented the imposition of elite controls over their affairs. Although the Antifederalists lost the battle over ratification, their ideas about political economy later found many champions in the "Age of Andrew Jackson."

The Constitution drew support from many different types of people. In fact, historians have been unable to discover sharp correlations between wealth and occupation on the one hand

and attitudes toward the proposed system of central government on the other. In general, Federalists lived in more commercialized areas than did their opponents. In the cities, artisans as well as merchants called for ratification, while those farmers who were only marginally involved in commercial agriculture frequently voted Antifederalist.

Despite passionate pleas from Patrick Henry and other Antifederalists, most state conventions quickly adopted the Constitution. Delaware acted first (December 7, 1787), and a number of other states soon followed. Within eight months of the Philadelphia meeting, eight of the nine states required to launch the government had ratified

the document. The contests in New York and Virginia (June 1788) generated bitter debate, but they too joined the union, leaving only North Carolina and Rhode Island outside the United States. Eventually (November 21, 1789 and May 29, 1790), even these states ratified the Constitution. Still, the vote had been very close. The Constitution was ratified in New York by a tally of 30 to 27, in Massachusetts by 187 to 168, and in Virginia by 89 to 79. A swing of a few votes in several key states could have defeated the new government.

While the state conventions sparked angry rhetoric, Americans soon closed ranks behind the Constitution. An Antifederalist who represented

Ratification of the Constitution
Advocates of the new Constitution called themselves Federalists and those who opposed its ratification were known as Antifederalists.

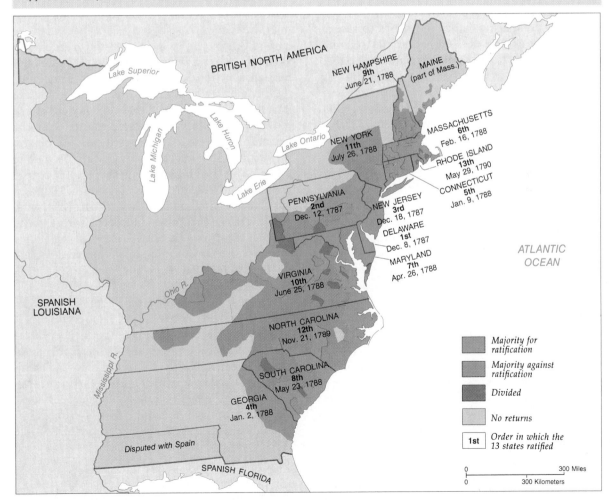

one Massachusetts village explained that "he had opposed the adoption of this Constitution; but that he had been overruled . . . by a majority of wise and understanding men [and that now] he should endeavor to sow the seeds of union and peace among the people he represented."

Adding the Bill of Rights

The first ten amendments to the Constitution are the major legacy of the Antifederalist argument. In almost every state convention, opponents of the Constitution pointed to the need for greater protection of individual liberties, rights that people presumably had possessed in a state of nature. "It is necessary," wrote one Antifederalist, "that the sober and industrious part of the community should be defended from the rapacity and violence of the vicious and idle. A bill of rights, therefore, ought to set forth the purposes for which the compact is made, and serves to secure the minority against the usurpation and tyranny of the majority." The list of fundamental rights varied from state to state, but most Antifederalists demanded specific guarantees for jury trial and freedom of religion. They wanted prohibitions against cruel and unusual punishments. There was also considerable, though not universal, support for freedom of speech and freedom of the press.

Madison and others regarded these proposals with little enthusiasm. In *The Federalist* No. 84, Hamilton bluntly reminded the American people that "the constitution is itself . . . a BILL OF RIGHTS." But after the adoption of the Constitution had been assured, Madison moderated his stand. If nothing else, passage of a bill of rights would appease able men such as George Mason and Edmund Randolph, who might otherwise remain alienated from the new federal system. "We have in this way something to gain," Madison concluded, "and if we proceed with caution, nothing to lose."

The crucial consideration was caution. A number of people throughout the nation advocated calling a second constitutional convention, one that would take Antifederalist criticism into account. Madison wanted to avoid such a meet-

ing, and he feared some members of the first Congress might use a bill of rights as an excuse to revise the entire Constitution or to promote a second convention.

Madison carefully reviewed these recommendations as well as the various declarations of rights that had appeared in the early state constitutions, and on June 8, 1789, he placed before the House of Representatives a set of amendments designed to protect individual rights from government interference. Madison told the members of Congress that the greatest dangers to popular liberties came from "the majority [operating] against the minority." A committee compressed and revised his original ideas into ten amendments that were ratified and became known collectively as the Bill of Rights. For many modern Americans these amendments are the most important section of the Constitution. Madison had hoped that additions would be inserted into the text of the Constitution at the appropriate places, not tacked onto the end, but he was overruled.

The Bill of Rights protected the freedoms of assembly, speech, religion, and the press; guaranteed speedy trial by an impartial jury; preserved the people's right to bear arms; and prohibited unreasonable searches. Other amendments dealt with legal procedure. Some opponents of the Constitution urged Congress to provide greater safeguards for states' rights, but Madison had no intention of backing away from a strong central government. Only the Tenth Amendment addressed the states' relation to the federal system. This crucial article, designed to calm Antifederalist fears, specified that those "powers not delegated to the United States by the Constitution, nor prohibited by it to the States, are reserved to the States respectively, or to the people."

On September 25, 1789, the Bill of Rights passed both houses of Congress, and by December 15, 1791, these amendments had been ratified by three-fourths of the states. Madison was justly proud of his achievement. He had effectively secured individual rights without undermining the Constitution. When he asked his friend Jefferson for his opinion of the Bill of Rights, Jefferson responded with typical republican candor: "I like [it] . . . as far as it goes; but I should have been for going further."

The Signing of the Constitution (1875) by Thomas Rossiter. Paintings like this, in which Washington appears enthroned in a radiant aura, contributed to the mythic reputations of the men who framed the Constitution at the 1787 convention in Independence Hall, Philadelphia.

A NEW BEGINNING

By 1789, one phase of American political experimentation had come to an end. During these years, the people gradually, often haltingly, learned that in a republican society they themselves were sovereign. They could no longer blame the failure of government on inept monarchs or greedy aristocrats. They bore a great responsibility. Americans had demanded a government of the people only to discover during the 1780s that in some situations the people could not be trusted with power, majorities could tyrannize minorities, and the best of governments could abuse individual rights.

Contemporaries had difficulty deciding just what had been accomplished. A writer in the *Pennsylvania Packet* thought the American people had preserved *order.* "The year 1776 is cele-brated," the newspaper observed, "for a revolution in favor of liberty. The year 1787 . . . will be celebrated with equal joy, for a revolution in favor of Government." But some aging patriots grumbled that perhaps order had been achieved at too high a price. In 1788, Richard Henry Lee remarked, "Tis really astonishing that the same people, who have just emerged from a long and cruel war in defense of liberty, should now agree to fix an elective despotism upon themselves and their posterity."

But most Americans probably would have accepted Franklin's optimistic assessment. As he watched the delegates to the Philadelphia convention come forward to sign the Constitution, he noted that there was a sun carved on the back of George Washington's chair. "I have," the aged philosopher noted, ". . . often in the course of the session . . . looked at [the sun] behind the

CHRONOLOGY

1776   Second Continental Congress authorizes colonies to create republican government (May) • Eight states draft new constitutions; two others already enjoy republican government by virtue of former colonial charters

1777   Congress accepts Articles of Confederation after long debate (November)

1780   Massachusetts finally ratifies state constitution

1781   States ratify Articles of Confederation following settlement of Virginia's western land claims • British army surrenders at Yorktown (October)

1782   States fail to ratify proposed Impost tax

1783   Newburgh Conspiracy thwarted (March) • Society of the Cincinnati raises a storm of criticism • Treaty of peace signed with Great Britain (September)

1785   Land Ordinance for Northwest Territory passed by Congress

1786   Jay-Gardoqui negotiations over Mississippi navigation anger southern states • Annapolis Convention suggests second meeting to revise the Articles of Confederation (September) • Shays's Rebellion frightens American leaders

1787–1788   The federal Constitution is ratified by all states except North Carolina and Rhode Island

1791   Bill of Rights (first ten amendments of the Constitution) ratified by states

---

enduring value are Jensen's *Articles of Confederation* (1959) and *The New Nation: A History of the United States During the Confederation, 1781–1789* (1950) as well as Main's *The Sovereign States, 1775–1783* (1973) and *The Antifederalists, Critics of the Constitution, 1781–1788* (1961). Gordon S. Wood brilliantly reinterpreted this entire period in *The Creation of the American Republic, 1776–1787* (1969), a work now supplemented by his provocative *Radicalism of the American Revolution* (1992). The failure of Congress during the 1780s is the subject of Jack N. Rakove's *The Beginning of National Politics: An Interpretive History of the Continental Congress* (1979). Peter S. Onuf provides a penetrating analysis of one major piece of legislation in *Statehood and Union: A History of the Northwest Ordinance* (1987). A splendid collection of contempory writings can be found in Bernard Bailyn, ed., *The Debate on the Constitution* (1993).

Additional Bibliography

In a masterful essay, *The American Revolution Considered as a Social Movement* (1926), Franklin Jameson challenged American historians not only to explore social effects of the Revolution, but also to compare the patriots' achievement with the actions of other revolutionaries throughout the world. Although no one responded fully to this ambitious challenge, some scholars provide a provocative comparative framework. See, for example, Patrice Higonnet, *Sister Republics: The Origins of French and American Republicanism* (1988). Good general discussions of some of these issues can be found in Joyce Appleby, *Liberalism and Republicanism in the Historic Imagination* (1992) and Peter Onuf, ed., *Jeffersonian Legacies* (1993).

Many able studies focus on specific reforms. The extension of political participation is discussed in J. R. Pole, *Political Representation in England and the Origins of the American Republic* (1966). On African Americans, see Winthrop Jordan, *White Over Black: American Attitudes Toward the Negro, 1550–1812* (1968); Benjamin Quarles, *The Negro in the American Revolution* (1961); Arthur Zilversmit, *The First Emancipation* (1961); Gary Nash, *Race and Revolution* (1990); Ira Berlin and Ronald Hoffman, eds., *Slavery and Freedom in the Age of the American Revolution* (1983); and Sylvia R. Frey, *Water from the Rock: Black Resistance in a Revolutionary Age* (1991).

Recent historians have transformed our understanding of women in postrevolutionary society. One might start an investigation of this field with Linda Kerber, *Women of the Republic* (1980); Mary Beth Norton, *Liberty's Daughters* (1980); and Ronald Hoffman and Peter J. Albert, eds., *Women in the Age of the*

President without being able to tell whether it was rising or setting; but now at length I have the happiness to know that it is a rising and not a setting sun."

Recommended Reading

The best general accounts of this period have been written by Merrill Jensen and Jackson Turner Main. Of

American Revolution (1990). Important articles are Jan Lewis, "The Republican Wife," *William and Mary Quarterly*, 3rd ser., 44(1987): 689–721; and Ruth H. Bloch, "The Gendered Meaning of Virtue in Revolutionary America," *Signs: Journal of Women in Culture and Society*, 8(1987): 37–58. Bernard Bailyn writes about immigrants and speculators in his *Voyagers to the West: A Passage in the Peopling of America on the Eve of the Revolution* (1986).

The early state constitutions are discussed in Wood's *Creation of the American Republic* (1969); and Willi Paul Adams, *The First American Constitutions: Republican Ideology and the Making of the State Constitutions* (1980). A classic exploration of political and economic history at the state level is Oscar and Mary Handlin, *Commonwealth: A Study of the Role of Government in the American Economy, Massachusetts, 1774–1861*, rev. ed. (1969). The Newburgh Conspiracy is covered in Richard H. Kohn, *Eagle and Sword: The Federalists and the Creation of the Military Establishment in America, 1783–1802* (1975). On Shays's Rebellion, see Robert A. Gross, ed., *In Debt to Shays: The Bicentennial of an Agrarian Rebellion* (1993).

The best source on the Constitution remains Max Farrand, ed., *Records of the Federal Convention of 1787*, 4 vols. (1911–1937). Charles A. Beard's *Economic Interpretation of the Constitution of the United States* (1913) caused a generation of historians to examine the financial accounts of convention delegates, but as Forrest McDonald demonstrates in *We The People* (1958), Beard's thesis simply does not hold up. The intellectual background of the Founders is examined in Forrest McDonald, *Novus Ordo Seclorum: The Intellectual Origins of the Constitution* (1985); Douglass Adair, *Fame and the Founding Fathers*, edited by Trevor Colbourn (1974); Garrett W. Sheldon, *Political Philosophy of Thomas Jefferson* (1991); and J. G. A. Pocock, *The Machiavellian Moment: Florentine Political Thought and the Atlantic Republican Tradition* (1975). The practical implications of republican ideas on state government are explored in Rosemarie Zagarri, *The Politics of Size: Representation in the United States, 1776–1850* (1987).

In *Visionary Republic: Millennial Themes in American Thought, 1756–1800* (1985), Ruth H. Bloch argues persuasively that historians of this period have not fully appreciated evangelical Protestantism in shaping political ideas. For a thoughtful investigation of the many different meanings of republicanism, see Richard Beeman, et al., eds., *Beyond Confederation: Origins of the Constitution and American National Identity* (1987). The best introduction to Antifederalist thought is Herbert J. Storing, ed., *The Complete Antifederalist*, 7 vols. (1981).

Setting the Agenda
Federalists and Republicans, 1788–1800

*W*hile presiding over the first meeting of the U.S. Senate in 1789, Vice President John Adams called the senators' attention to a pressing procedural question.

How would they address George Washington, the newly elected president? Adams insisted that Washington deserved an impressive title, a designation lending dignity and weight to his office. The vice president warned the senators that if they called Washington simply "president of the United States," the "common people of foreign countries [as well as] the sailors and soldiers [would] despise him to all eternity." Adams recommended "His Highness, the President of the United States, and Protector of their Liberties," but some senators favored "His Elective Majesty" or "His Excellency."

Adams's initiative caught many persons, including Washington, completely by surprise. They regarded the entire debate as ridiculous. James Madison, a member of the House of Representatives, announced that pretentious European titles were ill suited to the "genius of the people" and "the nature of our Government." Thomas Jefferson, who was then residing in Paris, could not comprehend what motivated the vice president, and in private correspondence, he repeated Benjamin Franklin's judgment that Adams "means well for his Country, is always an honest Man, often a wise one, but sometimes, and in some things, absolutely out of his senses." When the senators learned their efforts embarrassed Washington, they dropped the topic. The leader of the new republic would be called president of the United States. One wag, however, dubbed the portly Adams, "His Rotundity."

FORCE OF PUBLIC OPINION

The comic-opera quality of this debate should not obscure the participants' serious concern about setting government policy. The members of the first Congress could not take the survival of republican government for granted. All of them, of course, wanted to secure the Revolution. The recently ratified Constitution transferred sovereignty from the states to the people, a bold and unprecedented decision that many Americans feared would generate chronic instability.

Translating constitutional abstractions into practical legislation would under the most favorable conditions have been difficult. But these were especially trying times. Great Britain and France, rivals in a century of war, put nearly unbearable pressures on the leaders of the new republic and, in the process, made foreign policy a bitterly divisive issue.

Although no one welcomed them, political parties gradually took shape during this period. Neither the Jeffersonians nor the Federalists—as the two major groups were called—doubted that the United States would one day become a great commercial power. They differed, however, on how best to manage the transition from an agrarian household economy to an international system of trade and industry. The Federalists encouraged rapid integration of the United States into a world economy, but however enthusiastic they were about capitalism, they did not trust the people or local government to do the job effectively. A modern economy, they insisted, required strong national institutions that would be directed by a social elite who understood the financial challenge and who would work in the best interests of the people.

Such claims frightened persons who called themselves Jeffersonians. Strong financial institutions, they thought, had corrupted the government of Great Britain from which they had just dissociated themselves. They searched for alternative ways to accommodate to the needs of commerce and industry. Unlike the Federalists, the Jeffersonians put their political faith in the people. The Jeffersonians felt that if ordinary entrepreneurs could be freed from too many government regulations, they could be trusted to resist greed and crass materialism and to sustain the virtue of the republic.

During the 1790s, former friends were surprised to discover themselves at odds over such basic political issues. One person—Hamilton, for example—would stake out a position. Another, such as Jefferson or Madison, would respond, perhaps speaking a little more extravagantly than a specific issue demanded, goaded by the rhetorical nature of public debate. The first in turn would rebut passionately the new position. By the middle of the decade, this dialectic had almost spun out of control, taking the young republic to the brink of political violence.

Leaders of every persuasion had to learn to live with "public opinion." The revolutionary gentry had invited the people to participate in government, but the gentlemen assumed ordinary voters would automatically defer to their social betters. Instead, the founders discovered they had created a rough-and-tumble political culture. The "public" followed the great debates of the period through articles they read in hundreds of highly partisan newspapers and magazines. Just as television has done in our own century, print journalism opened politics to a large audience that previously might have been indifferent to the activities of elected officials. By the time John Adams left the presidency in 1800, he had learned this lesson well. The ordinary workers and farmers of the United States, feisty individuals who thought they were as good as anyone else and who were not afraid to let their political opinions be known, were not likely to let their president become an "Elective Majesty."

ESTABLISHING GOVERNMENT

In 1788, George Washington enjoyed great popularity throughout the nation. The people remembered him as the selfless leader of the Continental army, and even before the states had ratified the Constitution, everyone assumed he would be chosen president of the United States. He received the unanimous support of the electoral college, an achievement that no subsequent president has duplicated. Adams, a quick-tempered New Englander who championed national independence in 1776, was selected vice president. As Washington left his beloved Virginia plantation, Mount Vernon, for New York City, he recognized that the people—now so vocal in their support—could be fickle. "I fear," he explained with mature insight, "if the issue of public measures should not correspond with their sanguine expectations, they will turn the extravagant . . . praise . . . into equally extravagant . . . censures."

Washington bore great responsibility. The political stability of the young republic depended in large measure on how he handled himself in office. In the eyes of his compatriots, he had been transformed into a living symbol of the new government (see "The Man Who Could Not Tell a Lie," pp. 202–203), and during his presidency

(1789–1797), he carried himself with studied dignity and reserve—never ostentatious, the embodiment of classical republican values. Contemporaries sensed that although Washington put himself forward for elective office, he somehow stood above the hurly-burly of routine politics. A French diplomat who witnessed Washington's first inauguration in New York City reported in awe: "He has the soul, look and figure of a hero united in him." But the adulation of Washington—however well meant—seriously affected the conduct of public affairs, for criticism of his administration was regarded as an attack on the president and by extension, on the republic itself. During the early years of Washington's presidency, therefore, American public opinion discouraged partisan politics.

Washington created a strong, independent presidency. While he discussed pressing issues with the members of his cabinet—indeed, solicited their opinions—he left no doubt that he alone made policy. Moreover, the first president resisted congressional efforts to restrict executive authority, especially in foreign affairs.

The first Congress quickly established executive departments. Some congressmen wanted to prohibit presidents from dismissing cabinet-level appointees without Senate approval, but James Madison—still a voice for a strong, independent executive—led a successful fight against this restriction on presidential authority. Madison recognized that the chief executive could not function unless he had personal confidence in the people with whom he worked. In 1789, Congress created the Departments of War, State, and the Treasury, and as secretaries, Washington nominated Henry Knox, Thomas Jefferson, and Alexander Hamilton, respectively. Edmund Randolph served as part-time attorney general, a position that ranked slightly lower in prestige than the head of a department. Since the secretary of the treasury oversaw the collection of customs and other future federal taxes, Hamilton could anticipate having several thousand jobs to dispense, an obvious source of political patronage.

To modern Americans accustomed to a large federal bureaucracy, the size of Washington's government seems amazingly small. When Jefferson arrived in New York to take over the State Department, for example, he found two chief clerks, two assistants, and a part-time trans-

The Man Who Could Not Tell a Lie

The American Star, *painted by Frederick Kemmelmeyer, commemorates Washington's first inauguration.*

Every schoolchild can recite the more memorable incidents of George Washington's life: how as a small boy, the future father of his country chopped down a cherry tree or how he threw a stone across the broad Rappahannock River, a feat no contemporary had the strength to duplicate. Yet these stories are false, wholly without historical foundation. That such tall tales came to provide the most enduring images of Washington is attributable to the scribblings of one man, Mason Locke Weems, better known as "Parson" Weems.

Credited with inventing many Washington myths, Weems grew up in colonial Maryland, the youngest of nineteen children. He studied abroad during the Revolutionary War, first for the medical profession and then for the ministry. Ordained in England in 1784, he returned to become the rector of a Maryland parish. Apparently, he soon tired of being a parson and took up a more lucrative calling—selling books, mainly Bibles. Weems traveled widely with his literary offerings, dabbling at times in writing and publishing. Although he wrote several advice pamphlets, like *Hymen's Recruiting Sergeant,* a tract recommending premarital chastity, and the *Bad Wife's Looking Glass,* Weems's greatest success as an author came with his first biography, *The Life of Washington,* a book that went through eighty editions.

Several months before Washington's death in December 1799, Weems began to gather anecdotes about the first president. Always on the lookout for a quick profit, Weems wrote to his publisher friend Matthew Carey that a pamphlet on Washington "could make [Carey] a world of pence and popularity." Shortly after Washington's fatal illness plunged the nation into mourning, Weems wrote again to Carey, "Millions are gaping to read something about him. I am very nearly primed and cocked for 'em." Weems wanted to print a morally uplifting history that would "show that [Washington's] unparalleled rise & elevation were due to his Great Virtues."

When Carey ignored Weems's scheme, the persistent parson turned to another publisher, this time with more satisfactory results. At least three editions of his eighty-page pamphlet appeared in 1800. *The Life of Washington* proved extremely popular, outselling everything else in Weems's mobile bookstore. In the sixth edition and in all future editions, Weems described himself as the former rector of Mount Vernon parish, although no such parish existed. By 1808, he had lengthened the pamphlet to two hundred pages filled with exciting new anecdotes "Equally Honourable to [Washington] and Exemplary To His Young Countrymen."

Among the stories Weems invented to pad the original pamphlet was the unforgettable fable of the cherry tree. Supposedly, a distant relative who frequently visited Washington's family during her girlhood recounted the inci-

The image of the first president, captured in tapestry.

dent for Weems. Calling the anecdote "too valuable to be lost, and too true to be doubted," Weems explained how the six-year-old George had received a hatchet as a gift. He chopped down everything in sight, including his father's favorite cherry tree. When the elder Washington discovered the mischief, he questioned his son, who in Weems's rich imagination at least, admitted to the crime, crying "I can't tell a lie, Pa." This extraordinary show of honesty earned young George his father's praise rather than his punishment. "Run to my arms, you dearest boy," exclaimed his father. "Such an act of heroism in my son is worth more than a thousand trees."

Also new to the 1808 *Life* was a prophetic dream that Washington's mother, Mary Ball Washington, had allegedly had

long before the Revolution. She dreamed that the family home was on fire and no adult seemed capable of extinguishing the blaze. Five-year-old George, playing with a plow in the fields, rushed to the scene and inspired the confused servants to attack the flames just as he would later inspire American soldiers to fight the British. With this dream, Weems symbolically linked Washington to Cincinnatus, the patriot who set aside his plow to defend Rome. As Weems explained, Cincinnatus "unyoked his oxen [and] . . . hastened to the army—who at his appearance, felt as did our troubled fathers in 1774 [sic] when the godlike figure of Washington stood before them on the plains of Boston to fight the battles of liberty."

Portraying Washington as a

Cincinnatus seemed plausible to nineteenth-century Americans, since much of Washington's behavior had in fact corresponded to that of the mythic hero. After crushing the enemy, Cincinnatus had returned without hesitation to his farm, unmoved by the civic honors that others attempted to thrust on him. Like that virtuous Roman, Washington had neglected his plantation while in the service of his countrymen. At the conclusion of the Revolution, he enthusiastically threw himself into farming. And after two terms as a reluctant though popular president, America's agrarian warrior retired to his beloved Mount Vernon, content to exchange political authority for the joys of country life.

However outlandish Weems's images of Washington as Cincinnatus or as a child hero now appear, they reveal something important about the way Americans perceive national character. Washington embodied humility, quiet dignity, and a selfless devotion to country. A comparison with his famed contemporary Napoleon is instructive. The French celebrated Napoleon's martial triumphs; he was depicted in extravagant splendor as the god of war or as Zeus, the king of the gods. Washington remained, even in Weems's account, a somewhat plain figure, a republican soldier, a reluctant politician, a farmer rather than a warrior. Yet if Washington seems somewhat dull to modern Americans, his reserve in office and virtue in private life may have set a tone that discouraged later would-be presidents from attempting to become military adventurers.

The First Cabinet, *engraving from a painting by Alonzo Chappell (1866). The first meeting of the cabinet took place at Washington's Mount Vernon home.*

lator. With this tiny staff, he not only maintained contacts with the representatives of foreign governments, collected information about world affairs, and communicated with U.S. officials living overseas, but also organized the entire federal census! Jefferson immediately recognized that his new job would allow him little leisure for personal interests. The situation in other departments was similar. Overworked clerks scribbled madly just to keep up with the press of correspondence. John Adams, reviewing a bundle of letters and memos, grumbled "often the handwriting is almost illegible." Considering these working conditions, it is not surprising that the president had difficulty persuading able people to accept positions in the new government. It is even more astonishing that Hamilton and Jefferson were able to accomplish as much as they did with so little assistance.

Congress also provided for a federal court system. The Judiciary Act of 1789, the work primarily of Connecticut Congressman Oliver Ellsworth,

created a Supreme Court staffed by a chief justice and five associate justices. In addition, the statute set up thirteen district courts authorized to review the decisions of the state courts. John Jay, a leading figure in New York politics, agreed to serve as chief justice, but since federal judges in the 1790s were expected to travel hundreds of miles over terrible roads to attend sessions of the inferior courts, few persons of outstanding talent and training joined Jay on the federal bench. One who did, Judge James Iredell, complained that service on the Supreme Court had transformed him into a "travelling postboy."

Remembering the financial insecurity of the old Confederation government, the newly elected congressmen passed the tariff of 1789, a tax of approximately 5 percent on imports. Even before it went into effect, however, the act sparked controversy. Southern planters, who relied heavily on European imports and the northern shippers who could control the flow of imports into the South, claimed the tariff discriminated against southern interests in favor of those of northern merchants. The new levy generated considerable revenue for the young republic.

JEFFERSON AND HAMILTON

Washington's first cabinet included two extraordinary personalities, Alexander Hamilton and Thomas Jefferson. Both had served the country with distinction during the Revolution, were recognized by contemporaries as men of special genius as well as high ambition, and brought to public office a powerful vision of how the American people could achieve greatness. The story of their opposing views during the decade of the 1790s provides insight into the birth and development of political parties. It also reveals how a common political ideology, republicanism, could be interpreted in such vastly different ways that decisions about government policy turned friends into adversaries. Indeed, the falling out of Hamilton and Jefferson reflected deep, potentially explosive political divisions within American society.

Hamilton was a brilliant, dynamic young lawyer who had distinguished himself as Washington's aide-de-camp during the Revolution. Born in the West Indies, the child of an adulterous relationship, Hamilton employed charm, courage, and intellect to fulfill his inexhaustible ambition. He strove not for wealth but reputation. Men and women who fell under his spell found him almost irresistible, but to enemies, Hamilton appeared a dark, calculating, even evil, genius. He advocated a strong central government and refused to be bound by the strict wording of the Constitution, a document Hamilton once called "a shilly shally thing." While he had fought for American independence, he admired British culture, and during the 1790s, he advocated closer commercial and diplomatic ties with the former mother country with whom "we have a similarity of tastes, language, and general manners."

Jefferson possessed a profoundly different temperament. This tall Virginian was more reflective and shone less brightly in society than Hamilton. Contemporaries sometimes interpreted his retiring manner as lack of ambition. They misread Jefferson. He thirsted not for power or wealth but for an opportunity to advance the democratic principles that he had stated so eloquently in the Declaration of Independence. When Jefferson became secretary of state in January 1790, he had just returned from Paris where he witnessed the first exhilarating moments of the French Revolution. These earthshaking events, he believed, marked the beginning of a worldwide republican assault on absolute monarchy and aristocratic privilege. His European experiences biased Jefferson in favor of France over Great Britain when the two nations clashed.

The contrast between these two powerful figures during the early years of Washington's administration should not be exaggerated. They shared many fundamental beliefs. Indeed, both Hamilton and Jefferson insisted they were working for the creation of a strong, prosperous republic, one in which commerce would play an important role. Hamilton was publicly accused of being a secret monarchist, but he never repudiated the ideals of the American Revolution. Rather than being spokespersons for competing ideologies, Hamilton and Jefferson were different kinds of republicans who, during the 1790s, attempted as best they could to cope with unprecedented political challenges.

However much these two men had in common, serious differences emerged. Washington's secretaries disagreed on precisely how the United States should fulfill its destiny. As head of the treasury department, Hamilton urged his fellow citizens to think in terms of bold commercial development, of farms and factories embedded within a complex financial network that would reduce the nation's reliance on foreign trade. Because Great Britain had already established an elaborate system of banking and credit, the secretary looked to that country for economic models that might be reproduced on this side of the Atlantic.

Hamilton also voiced concerns about the role of the people in shaping public policy. His view of human nature caused him to fear total democracy. He assumed that in a republican society, the gravest threat to political stability was anarchy rather than monarchy. "The truth," he claimed, "unquestionably is, that the only path to a subversion of the republican system of the Country is, by flattering the prejudices of the people, and exciting their jealousies and apprehensions, to throw affairs into confusion and bring on civil commotion." The best hope for the survival of the republic, Hamilton believed, lay with the country's monied classes. If the wealthiest people could be persuaded their economic self-interest could be advanced—or at least made less insecure—by the central government, then they would work to strengthen it, and by so doing, bring a greater measure of prosperity to the common people. From Hamilton's perspective, there was no conflict between private greed and public good; one was the source of the other.

On almost every detail, Jefferson challenged Hamilton's analysis. The secretary of state assumed the strength of the American economy lay not in its industrial potential, but in its agricultural productivity. The "immensity of land" represented the country's major economic resource. Contrary to the claims of some critics, Jefferson did not advocate agrarian self-sufficiency or look back nostalgically to a golden age dominated by simple yeomen. He recognized the necessity of change, and while he thought that persons who worked the soil were more responsible citizens than were those who labored in factories for wages, he encouraged the nation's farmers to participate in an expanding international market. Americans could exchange raw materials "for finer manufactures than they are able to execute themselves."

During the first years of Washington's administration, neither Hamilton (left) nor Jefferson (right) recognized the full extent of their differences. But as events forced the federal government to make decisions on economic and foreign affairs, the two secretaries increasingly came into open conflict.

Unlike Hamilton, Jefferson expressed faith in the ability of the American people to shape policy. Throughout this troubled decade, even when the very survival of constitutional government seemed in doubt, Jefferson maintained a boundless optimism in the judgment of the common folk. He instinctively trusted the people, feared that uncontrolled government power might destroy their liberties, and insisted public officials follow the letter of the Constitution, a frame of government he described as "the wisest ever presented to men." The greatest threat to the young republic, he argued, came from the corrupt activities of pseudo aristocrats, persons who placed the protection of "property" and "civil order" above the preservation of "liberty." To tie the nation's future to the selfish interests of a privileged class—bankers, manufacturers, speculators—seemed cynical as well as dangerous. He despised speculators who encouraged "the rage of getting rich in a day," since such "gaming" activities inevitably promoted the kinds of public vice that threatened republican government. To mortgage the future of the common people by creating a large national debt struck Jefferson as particularly insane. But the responsibility for shaping the economy of the new nation fell mainly to Alexander Hamilton as the first secretary of the treasury.

HAMILTON'S GRAND DESIGN

The unsettled state of the nation's finances presented the new government with a staggering challenge. In August 1789, the House of Representatives announced that "adequate provision for the support of public credit [is] a matter of high importance to the national honor and prosperity." However pressing the problem appeared, no one was prepared to advance a solution, and the House asked the secretary of the treasury to make suggestions.

Congress may have received more than it bargained for. Hamilton threw himself into the task. He read deeply in abstruse economic literature. He even developed a questionnaire designed to find out how the U.S. economy really worked and sent it to scores of commercial and political leaders throughout the country. But when Hamilton's three major reports—on public credit, on banking, and on manufacturers—were complete, they bore the unmistakable stamp of his own creative genius. The secretary synthesized a vast amount of information into an economic blueprint so complex, so innovative that even his allies were slightly baffled. Theodore Sedgwick, a congressman who supported Hamilton's program, explained weakly that the secretary's ideas were "difficult to understand . . . while we are in our infancy in the knowledge of Finance." Certainly, Washington never fully grasped the subtleties of Hamilton's plan.

The secretary presented his *Report on the Public Credit* to Congress on January 14, 1790. His research revealed that the nation's outstanding debt stood at approximately $54 million. This sum represented various obligations that the U.S. government had incurred during the Revolutionary War. In addition to foreign loans, the figure included loan certificates the government had issued to its own citizens and soldiers. But that was not all. The states still owed creditors approximately $25 million. During the 1780s, Americans desperate for cash had been forced to sell government certificates to speculators at greatly discounted prices, and it was estimated that approximately $40 million of the nation's debt was owed to twenty thousand people, only 20 percent of whom were the original creditors.

Funding and Assumption

Hamilton's *Report on the Public Credit* contained two major recommendations covering the areas of funding and assumption. First, under his plan the United States promised to fund its foreign and domestic obligations at full face value. Current holders of loan certificates, whoever they were and no matter how they obtained them, could exchange the old certificates for new government bonds bearing a moderate rate of interest. Second, the secretary urged the federal government to assume responsibility for paying the remaining state debts.

Hamilton reasoned that his credit system would accomplish several desirable goals. It would significantly reduce the power of the individual states in shaping national economic policy, something Hamilton regarded as essential in maintaining a strong federal government. Moreover, the creation of a fully funded national debt signaled to investors throughout the world that the United States was now solvent, that its bonds represented a good risk. Hamilton argued that investment capital, which might otherwise flow to Europe, would remain in this country, providing a source of money for commercial and industrial investment. In short, Hamilton invited the country's wealthiest citizens to invest in the future of the United States. Critics claimed that

the only people who stood to profit from the scheme were Hamilton's friends—some of whom sat in Congress and who had purchased great numbers of public securities at very low prices.

To Hamilton's great surprise, Madison—his friend and collaborator in writing *The Federalist*—attacked the funding scheme in the House of Representatives. The Virginia congressman agreed that the United States should honor its debts. He worried, however, about the citizens and soldiers who, because of personal financial hardship, had been compelled to sell their certificates at prices far below face value. Why should wealthy speculators now profit from their hardship? If the government treated the current holders of certificates less generously, Madison declared, then there might be sufficient funds to provide equitable treatment for the distressed patriots. Whatever the moral justification for Madison's plan may have been, it proved unworkable on the national level. Far too many records had been lost since the Revolution for the Treasury Department to be able to identify all the original holders. In February 1790, Congress soundly defeated Madison's proposal.

Assumption unleashed even greater criticism. Some states had already paid their revolutionary debts, and Hamilton's program seemed designed to reward certain states—Massachusetts and South Carolina, for example—simply because they had failed to put their finances in order. In addition, the secretary's opponents in Congress became suspicious that assumption was merely a ploy to increase the power and wealth of Hamilton's immediate friends. "The Secretary's people scarce disguise their design," observed William Maclay, a crusty Scotch-Irish senator from Pennsylvania, "which is to create a mass of debts which will justify them in seizing all the sources of government."

No doubt, Maclay and others expressed genuine fears. Some of those who protested, however, were simply looking after their own speculative schemes. These men had contracted to purchase huge tracts of vacant western lands from the state and federal governments. They anticipated that when settlers finally arrived in these areas, the price of land would skyrocket. In the meantime, the speculators had paid for the land with revolutionary certificates, often purchased on the open market at fifteen cents on the dollar. This meant that one could obtain 1,000 acres for only $150. Hamilton's assumption proposal threatened to destroy these lucrative transactions by cutting off the supply of cut-rate securities. On April 12, a rebellious House led by Madison defeated assumption.

The victory was short-lived. Hamilton and congressional supporters resorted to legislative horse trading to revive his foundering program. In exchange for locating the new federal capital on the Potomac River, a move that would stimulate the depressed economy of northern Virginia, several key congressmen who shared Madison's political philosophy changed their votes on assumption. Hamilton may also have offered to give the state of Virginia more federal money than it actually deserved. Whatever the details of these negotiations may have been, in August, Washington signed assumption and funding into law. The first element of Hamilton's design was now securely in place.

The Controversial Bank of the United States

The persistent Hamilton submitted his second report to Congress in January 1791. He proposed that the U.S. government charter a national bank, much like the Bank of England. This privately owned institution would be funded in part by the federal government. Indeed, since the bank would own millions of dollars of new U.S. bonds, its financial stability was tied directly to the strength of the federal government and, of course, to the success of the Hamiltonian program. The secretary of the treasury argued that a growing financial community required a central bank to facilitate increasingly complex commercial transactions. The institution not only would serve as the main depository of the U.S. government but also would issue currency acceptable in payment of federal taxes. Because of that guarantee, the money would maintain its value while in circulation.

Madison and others in Congress immediately raised a howl of protest. While they were not oblivious to the many important services a national bank might provide for a growing country, they suspected that banks—especially those modeled on British institutions—might "perpetuate a larged monied interest" in this country. And what about the Constitution? That document said nothing specifically about chartering financial corporations, and they warned that if Hamilton and his supporters were allowed to stretch fundamental law on this occasion, they could not be held back in the future. Popular liberties would be at the mercy of whoever happened to be in office. "To take a single step," Jefferson warned, "beyond the boundaries thus specifically drawn around the powers of Congress is to take possession of a boundless field of power, no longer susceptible to definition." On this issue, Hamilton stubbornly refused to compromise, announcing angrily, "This is the first symptom of a spirit which must either be killed or will kill the constitution of the United States."

This intense controversy involving his closest advisers worried the president. Even though the bank bill passed Congress (February 8), Washington seriously considered vetoing the legislation on constitutional grounds. Before doing so, however, he requested written opinions from the members of his cabinet. Jefferson's rambling, wholly predictable attack on the bank was not one of his more persuasive performances. By contrast, in only a few days, Hamilton prepared a masterful essay entitled "Defense of the Constitutionality of the Bank." He assured the president that Article I, Section 8 of the Constitution—"The Congress shall have Power. . . . To make all Laws which shall be necessary and proper for carrying into Execution the foregoing Powers"—justified issuing charters to national banks. The "foregoing Powers" on which Hamilton placed so much weight were taxation, regulation of commerce, and making war. He boldly articulated a doctrine of *implied powers,* an interpretation of the Constitution that neither Madison nor Jefferson had anticipated. Hamilton's "loose construction" carried the day, and on February 25, 1791, Washington signed the bank act into law.

Hamilton triumphed in Congress, but the general public looked on his actions with growing fear and hostility. Many persons associated huge national debts and privileged banks with the decay of public virtue. Men of Jefferson's temperament believed Great Britain—a country Hamilton held in high regard—had compromised the purity of its ancient constitution by allowing speculators to worm their way into positions of political power.

Hamilton seemed intent on reproducing this corrupt system in the United States. When news of his proposal to fund the national debt at full face value leaked out, for example, urban speculators rushed to rural areas, where they purchased loan certificates from unsuspecting citizens at bargain prices. To backcountry farmers, making money without actually engaging in physical labor appeared immoral, unrepublican, and certainly, un-American. When the greed of a former treasury department official led to several serious bankruptcies in 1792, ordinary citizens began to listen more closely to what Madison, Jefferson, and their associates were saying about growing corruption in high places.

Setback for Hamilton

In his third major report, *Report on Manufactures,* submitted to Congress in December 1791, Hamilton revealed the final details of his grand design for the economic future of the United States. This lengthy document suggested ways by which the federal government might stimulate manufacturing. If the country wanted to free itself from dependence on European imports, Hamilton observed, then it had to develop its own industry, textile mills for example. Without direct government intervention, however, the process would take decades. Americans would continue to invest in agriculture. But, according to the secretary of the treasury, protective tariffs and special industrial bounties would greatly accelerate the growth of a balanced economy, and with proper planning, the United States would soon hold its own with England and France.

In Congress, the battle lines were clearly drawn. Hamilton's opponents—not yet a disciplined party but a loose coalition of men who shared Madison's and Jefferson's misgivings about the secretary's program—ignored his economic arguments. Instead, they engaged him on moral and political grounds. Madison railed against the dangers of "consolidation," a process that threatened to concentrate all power in the federal government, leaving the states defenseless. Under the Confederation, of course, Madison had stood with the nationalists against the advocates of extreme states' rights (see Chapter 6). His disagreements with Hamilton over economic policy, coupled with the necessity of pleasing the voters of his Virginia congressional district every two years, transformed Madison into a spokesman for the states.

Jefferson attacked the *Report on Manufactures* from a different angle. He assumed—largely because he had been horrified by Europe's urban poverty—that cities breed vice. The government, Jefferson argued, should do nothing to promote their development. He believed Hamilton's proposal guaranteed that American workers would leave the countryside and crowd into urban centers. "I think our government will remain virtuous for many centuries," Jefferson explained, "as long as they [the people] are chiefly agricultural. . . . When they get piled upon one another in large cities, as in Europe, they will become corrupt as in Europe." And southern congressmen saw tariffs and bounties as vehicles for enriching Hamilton's northern friends at the planters' expense. The recommendations in the *Report on Manufactures* were soundly defeated in the House of Representatives.

Washington detested political squabbling. The president, of course, could see the members of his cabinet disagreed on many issues, but in 1792, he still believed that Hamilton and Jefferson—and the people who looked to them for advice—could be reconciled. In August, he begged them personally to rise above the "internal dissensions [which are] . . . harrowing and tearing at our vitals." The appeal came too late. By the conclusion of Washington's first term, neither secretary trusted the other's judgment. Their sparring had produced congressional factions, but as yet no real political parties with permanent organizations that engaged in campaigning had come into existence. At this point, Hamilton and Jefferson only dimly appreciated the force of public opinion in shaping federal policy.

FOREIGN AFFAIRS: A CATALYST TO THE BIRTH OF POLITICAL PARTIES

During Washington's second term (1793–1797), war in Europe dramatically thrust foreign affairs into the forefront of American life. The impact of this development on the conduct of domestic politics was devastating. Officials who had formerly disagreed on economic policy now began to identify their interests with either Britain or France, the world's most powerful nations. Differences of political opinion, however trivial, were suddenly cited as evidence that one group or the other had entered into treasonous correspondence with external enemies eager to compromise the independence and prosperity of the United States. As Jefferson observed in the troubled summer of 1793, European conflict "kindled and brought forward the two parties with an ardour which our own interests merely, could never excite."

Formal political organizations—the Federalists and Republicans—were born in this poisonous atmosphere. The clash between these groups developed over how best to preserve the new republic. The Republicans (Jeffersonians) advocated states' rights, strict interpretation of the Constitution, friendship with France, and vigilance against "the avaricious, monopolizing Spirit of Commerce and Commercial Men." The Federalists urged a strong national government, central economic planning, closer ties with Great Britain, and maintenance of public order, even if that meant calling out federal troops.

Threats to U.S. Neutrality

Great Britain treated the United States with arrogance. The colonists had defeated the redcoats on land, but on the high seas, the Americans were no match for the British navy, the strongest in the world. Indeed, the young republic could not even compel its old adversary to comply with the Treaty of 1783, in which the British had agreed to vacate military posts in the Northwest Territory. In 1794, approximately a thousand British soldiers still occupied American land, an obstruction that Governor George Clinton of New York claimed had excluded U.S. citizens "from a very valuable trade to which their situation would naturally have invited them." Moreover, even though 75 percent of American imports came from Great Britain, that country refused to grant the United States full commercial reciprocity. Among other provocations, it barred American shipping from the lucrative West Indian trade.

France presented a very different challenge. In May 1789, Louis XVI, desperate for revenue, authorized a meeting of a representative assembly known as the Estates General. By so doing, the king unleashed explosive revolutionary forces that toppled the monarchy and cost him his life (January 1793). The men who seized power—and they came and went rapidly—were militant

republicans, ideologues eager to liberate all Europe from feudal institutions. In the early years of the Revolution, France drew on the American experience, and Thomas Paine and the Marquis de Lafayette enjoyed great popularity. But the French found they could not stop the Revolution. Constitutional reform turned into bloody purges, and one radical group, the Jacobins, guillotined thousands of people—many wrongfully—who were suspected of monarchist sympathies during the so-called Reign of Terror (October 1793–July 1794). These events left Americans confused. While those who shared Jefferson's views cheered the spread of republicanism, those others who sided with Hamilton condemned French expansionism and political violence.

In the face of growing international tension, neutrality seemed the most prudent course for the United States. But that policy was easier for a weak country to proclaim than to defend. In February 1793, France declared war on Great Britain—what the leaders of revolutionary France called the "war of all peoples against all kings"— and these powerful European rivals immediately challenged the official American position on shipping: "free ships make free goods," meaning that belligerents should not interfere with the shipping of neutral carriers. To make matters worse, no one was certain whether the Franco-American Treaties of 1778 (see Chapter 5) legally bound the United States to support its old ally against Great Britain.

Both Hamilton and Jefferson wanted to avoid war. The secretary of state believed nations desiring American goods should be forced to honor American neutrality. If Britain treated the United States as a colonial possession, if the Royal Navy stopped American ships on the high seas and forced seamen to serve the king—in other words, if it impressed American sailors—then the United States should award France special commercial advantages. Hamilton thought Jefferson's scheme insane. He pointed out that Britain possessed the largest navy in the world and was not likely to be coerced by American threats. The United States, he counseled, should appease the former mother country even if that meant swallowing national pride.

A newly appointed French minister to the United States, Edmond Genêt, precipitated the first major diplomatic crisis. This unstable young

The execution of Louis XVI by French revolutionaries served to deepen the growing political division in America. Republicans, although they deplored the excesses of the Reign of Terror, continued to support the French people. Federalists feared that the violence and lawlessness would spread to the United States.

man arrived in Charleston, South Carolina, in April 1793. He found considerable popular enthusiasm for the French Revolution and, buoyed by this reception, he authorized privately owned American vessels to seize British ships in the name of France. Such actions clearly violated U.S. neutrality and invited British retaliation. When government officials warned Genêt to desist, he threatened to take his appeal directly to the American people, who presumably loved France more than members of the Washington administration.

This confrontation particularly embarrassed Jefferson, the most outspoken pro-French member of the cabinet. He described Genêt as "hot headed, all imagination, no judgment, passionate, disrespectful and even indecent towards the President." Washington did not wait to discover if the treaties of 1778 were still in force. Before he had formally received the impudent French minister, the president issued a Proclamation of Neutrality (April 22). Ironically, when Genêt

learned the Jacobins intended to cut off his head if he returned to France, he requested asylum, married into an extremely wealthy family, and spent the remainder of his life residing in New York.

Jay's Treaty Divides the Nation

Great Britain failed to take advantage of Genêt's insolence. Instead, it pushed the United States to the brink of war. British forts in the Northwest Territory remained a constant source of tension. In June 1793, a new element was added. The London government blockaded French ports to neutral shipping, and in November, its navy captured several hundred American vessels trading in the French West Indies. The British had not even bothered to give the United States advance warning of a change in policy. Outraged members of Congress, especially those who identified with Jefferson and Madison, demanded retaliation, an embargo, a stoppage of debt payment, even war.

Before this rhetoric produced armed struggle, Washington made one final effort to preserve peace. In May 1794, he sent Chief Justice John Jay to London to negotiate a formidable list of grievances. Jay's main objectives were removal of the British forts, payment for ships taken in the West Indies, improved commercial relations, and acceptance of the American definition of neutral rights.

Jefferson's supporters—by now openly called the "Republican interest"—anticipated a treaty favorable to the United States. After all, they explained, the war with France had not gone well for Great Britain, and the British people were surely desperate for American foodstuffs. Even before Jay departed, however, his mission stood little chance of success. Hamilton, anxious as ever to placate the British, had already secretly informed British officials that the United States would compromise on most issues.

Not surprisingly, when Jay reached London, he encountered polite but firm resistance. The chief justice did persuade the British to abandon their frontier posts and to allow small American ships to trade in the British West Indies, but they rejected out of hand the U.S. position on neutral rights. The Royal Navy would continue to search American vessels on the high seas for contraband and to impress sailors suspected of being British citizens. Moreover, there would be no compensation for the ships seized in 1793 until the Americans paid British merchants for debts contracted before the Revolution. And to the particular annoyance of Southerners, not a word was said about the slaves the British army had carried off at the conclusion of the war. While Jay salvaged the peace, he appeared to have betrayed the national interest.

News of Jay's Treaty—perhaps more correctly called Hamilton's Treaty—produced an angry outcry in the nation's capital. Even Washington was apprehensive. He submitted the document to the Senate without recommending ratification, a sign the president was not entirely happy with the results of Jay's mission. After an extremely bitter debate, the upper house, controlled by Federalists, accepted a revised version of the treaty (June 1795). The vote was 20 to 10, a bare two-thirds majority.

The details of the Jay agreement soon leaked to the press. This was an important moment in American political history. The popular journals

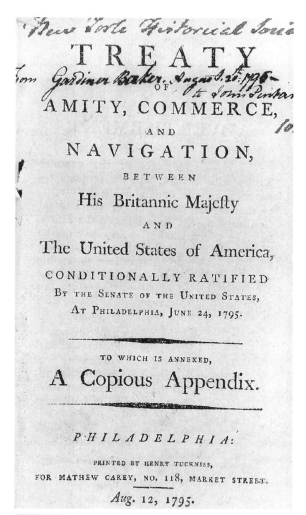

Printer Matthew Carey helped fire the protest over Jay's Treaty by printing the terms of the agreement and adding a series of comments to the appendix.

sparked a firestorm of protest. Throughout the country, people who had generally been apathetic about national politics were swept up in a wave of protest. Urban mobs condemned Jay's alleged sellout; rural settlers burned him in effigy. Jay jokingly told friends he could find his way across the country simply by following the light of these fires. Southerners announced they would not pay prerevolutionary debts to British merchants. The Virginia legislature proposed a constitutional amendment reducing the Senate's role in the treaty-making process. As Fisher Ames, a Federalist congressman, noted darkly, "These little whirlwinds of dry leaves and dirt portend a hurricane."

His prediction proved accurate. The storm broke in the House of Representatives. Republican congressmen, led by Madison, thought they could stop Jay's Treaty by refusing to appropriate funds for its implementation. As part of their plan, they demanded that Washington show the House state papers relating to Jay's mission. The challenge raised complex issues of constitutional law. The House, for example, was claiming a voice in treaty ratification, a power explicitly reserved to the Senate. Second, there was the question of executive secrecy in the interest of national security. Could the president withhold information from the public? According to Washington—as well as all subsequent presidents—the answer was yes. He took the occasion to lecture the rebellious representatives that "the nature of foreign negotiations requires caution; and their success must often depend on secrecy."

The president still had a trump card to play. He raised the possibility that the House was really contemplating his impeachment. Such an action was, of course, unthinkable. Even criticizing Washington in public was politically dangerous, and as soon as he redefined the issue before Congress, petitions supporting the president flooded into the nation's capital. The Maryland legislature, for example, declared its "unabated reliance on the integrity, judgment, and patriotism of the President of the United States," a statement that clearly called into question the patriotism of certain Republican congressmen. The Federalists won a stunning tactical victory over the opposition. Had a less popular man than Washington occupied the presidency, however, they would not have fared so well. The division between the two parties was beyond repair. The Republicans labeled the Federalists "the British party"; the Federalists believed the Republicans were in league with the French.

By the time Jay's Treaty became law (June 14, 1795), the two giants of Washington's first cabinet had retired. Late in 1793, Jefferson returned to his Virginia plantation, Monticello, where despite his separation from day-to-day political affairs, he remained the chief spokesman for the Republican party. His rival, Hamilton, left the Treasury in January 1795 to practice law in New York City. He maintained close ties with important Federalist officials, and even more

than Jefferson, Hamilton concerned himself with the details of party organization.

Diplomacy in the West

Before Great Britain finally withdrew its troops from the Great Lakes and Northwest Territory, its military officers encouraged local Indian groups—the Shawnee, Chippewa, and Miami—to attack settlers and traders from the United States. The Indians, who even without British encouragement fully appreciated the newcomers intended to seize their land, won several impressive victories over federal troops in the area that would become western Ohio and Indiana. In 1790, General Josiah Harmar led his soldiers into an ambush. The following year, an army under General Arthur St. Clair suffered more than nine hundred casualties near the Wabash River. But the Indians were militarily more vulnerable than they realized, for when confronted with a major U.S. army under the command of General Anthony Wayne, they received no support from their former British allies. At the battle of Fallen Timbers (August 20, 1794), Wayne's forces crushed Indian resistance in the Northwest Territory, and the native peoples were compelled to sign the Treaty of Greenville, formally ceding to the U.S. government the land that became Ohio. In 1796, the last British soldiers departed for Canada.

Shrewd negotiations mixed with pure luck helped secure the nation's southwestern frontier. For complex reasons having to do with the state of European diplomacy, Spanish officials in 1795 encouraged the U.S. representative in Madrid to discuss the navigation of the Mississippi River. Before this initiative, the Spanish government not only had closed the river to American commerce but also had incited the Indians of the region to harass settlers from the United States (see Chapter 6). Relations between the two countries would probably have deteriorated further had the United States not signed Jay's Treaty. The Spanish assumed—quite erroneously—that Great Britain and the United States had formed an alliance to strip Spain of its North American possessions.

To avoid this imagined disaster, officials in Madrid offered the American envoy, Thomas Pinckney, extraordinary concessions: the opening

Conquest of the West

Withdrawal of the British, defeat of Native Americans, and negotiations with Spain secured the nation's frontiers.

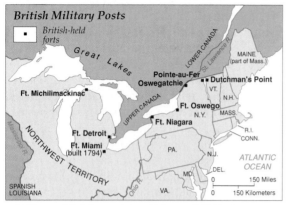

British Military Posts

- ■ British-held forts

Great Lakes
LOWER CANADA
St. Lawrence R.
MAINE (part of Mass.)
Pointe-au-Fer
Oswegatchie
■ Dutchman's Point
VT.
Ft. Michilimackinac
UPPER CANADA
Ft. Oswego
N.H.
MASS.
Ft. Niagara
N.Y.
Ft. Detroit
R.I.
CONN.
Ft. Miami (built 1794)
PA.
N.J.
DEL.
NORTHWEST TERRITORY
MD.
VA.
ATLANTIC OCEAN
Mississippi R.
Ohio R.
SPANISH LOUISIANA
0   150 Miles
0   150 Kilometers

Major Indian Battles

- ✳ Major Indian battles

UPPER CANADA
Ft. Detroit
N.Y.
Lake Erie
Fallen Timbers Aug. 20, 1794
Ft. Miami (Br.)
Harmer's Defeat Oct. 22, 1790
Maumee R.
PA.
Treaty of Greenville Line, 1795
Pittsburgh
St. Clair's Defeat Nov. 4, 1791
Ohio R.
NORTHWEST TERRITORY
Cincinnati
VA.
Wabash R.
KY.
0   100 Miles
0   100 Kilometers

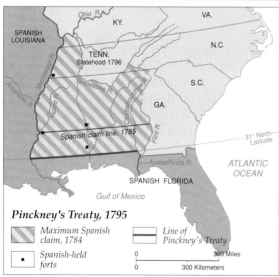

Ohio R.
SPANISH LOUISIANA
KY.
VA.
Mississippi R.
TENN. Statehood 1796
N.C.
Arkansas R.
Yazoo R.
Tennessee R.
S.C.
Chattahoochee R.
GA.
Spanish claim line, 1785
Flint R.
31° North Latitude
Apalachicola R.
ATLANTIC OCEAN
SPANISH FLORIDA
Gulf of Mexico

Pinckney's Treaty, 1795

- ▨ Maximum Spanish claim, 1784
- ■ Spanish-held forts
- ▭ Line of Pinckney's Treaty

0   300 Miles
0   300 Kilometers

GEORGE WASHINGTON PRESIDENT. 1792.

This engraved medallion is typical of the commemorative medals the United States presented to the chief of the Native American groups with whom it signed treaties.

of the Mississippi, the right to deposit goods in New Orleans without paying duties, a secure southern boundary on the thirty-first parallel (a line roughly parallel to the northern boundary of Florida and running west to the Mississippi), and a promise to stay out of Indian affairs. An amazed Pinckney signed the Treaty of San Lorenzo (also called Pinckney's Treaty) on October 27, 1795, and in March the Senate ratified the document without a single dissenting vote. Pinckney, who came from a prominent South Carolina family, instantly became the hero of the Federalist party.

POPULAR POLITICAL CULTURE

More than any other event during Washington's administration, ratification of Jay's Treaty generated intense political strife. Even as members of Congress voted as Republicans or Federalists, they condemned the rising partisan spirit as a grave threat to the stability of the United States. Popular writers equated "party" with "faction," and "faction" with "conspiracy to overthrow legitimate authority." Party conflict also suggested that Americans had lost the sense of common purpose that had united them during the Revolution. Contemporaries did not appreciate the beneficial role that parties could play by presenting alternative solutions to foreign and domestic problems. Organized opposition smacked of disloyalty and therefore had to be eliminated by any means—fair or foul. These intellectual currents coupled with the existence of two parties created an atmosphere that bred suspicion. In the name of national unity, Federalists as well as Republicans advocated the destruction of political adversaries.

The Partisan Role of Newspapers and Political Clubs

More than any other single element, newspapers transformed the political culture of the United States. Americans were voracious readers. In 1789, a foreign visitor observed, "The common people [here] are on a footing, in point of literature, with the middle ranks of Europe. They all read and write, and understand arithmetic; almost every little town now furnishes a circulating library."

A rapidly expanding number of newspapers appealed to this large literate audience. John Fenno established the *Gazette of the United States* (1789), a journal that supported Hamilton's political philosophy. The Republicans responded in October 1790 with Philip Freneau's influential *National Gazette*. While the format of these publications was similar to that of the colonial papers, their tone was quite different. These fiercely partisan journals presented rumor and opinion as fact. Public officials were regularly dragged through the rhetorical mud. Jefferson, for example, was accused of cowardice; Hamilton, vilified as an adulterer. As party competition became more bitter, editors showed less restraint. One Republican paper even suggested George Washington had been a British agent during the Revolution. No wonder Fisher Ames announced in 1801, "The newspapers are an overmatch for any government."

Even poets and essayists were caught up in the political fray. The better writers—and this was not a period of outstanding artistic achievement in the United States—often produced party propaganda. However much Freneau aspired to fame as a poet, he is remembered today chiefly as a champion of the Republican cause. Noah Webster, who later published *An American Dictionary of the English Language* (1828), spent the 1790s editing a strident Federalist journal, *American Minerva*, in New York City. And Joel Barlow, a Connecticut poet of modest talent, celebrated the French Revolution in verse, thus clearly identifying himself with the party of Jefferson. American writers sometimes complained that the culture of the young republic was too materialistic, too unappreciative of the subtler forms of art then popular in Europe. But it was clear that poets who ignored patriotism and politics simply did not sell well in the United States.

This decade also witnessed the birth of political clubs. These "Democratic" or "Republican" associations, as they were called, first appeared in 1793 and were modeled on the political debating societies that sprang up in France during the early years of the French Revolution. Perhaps because of the French connection, Federalists assumed the American clubs represented the interests of the Republican party. Their purpose was clearly political indoctrination. The Philadelphia Society announced it would "cultivate a just knowledge of rational liberty." A "Democratic" club in New York City asked each member to declare himself a "firm and steadfast friend of the EQUAL RIGHTS OF MAN."

By 1794, at least twenty-four clubs were holding regular meetings. How many Americans actually attended their debates is not known, but regardless of the number, the clubs obviously complemented the newspapers in providing the common people with highly partisan political information.

Whiskey Rebellion Linked to Republican Incendiaries

Political tensions became explosive in 1794. The Federalists convinced themselves the Republicans were actually prepared to employ violence against the U.S. government. Though the charge was without foundation, it took on plausibility in the context of growing party strife.

The crisis developed when a group of farmers living in western Pennsylvania protested a federal excise tax on distilled whiskey that Congress had originally passed in 1791. These men did not relish paying any taxes, but this tax struck them as particularly unfair. They made a good deal of money distilling their grain into whiskey, and the excise threatened to put them out of business.

Largely because the Republican governor of Pennsylvania refused to suppress the angry farmers, Washington and other leading Federalists assumed the insurrection represented a direct political challenge. The president called out fifteen thousand militiamen, and accompanied by Hamilton, he marched against the rebels. The expedition was an embarrassing fiasco. The distillers disappeared, and predictably enough, no one living in the Pittsburgh region seemed to know where the troublemakers had gone. Two supposed rebels were convicted of high crimes against the United States, one reportedly a "simpleton" and the other insane. Washington eventually pardoned both men. As peace returned to the frontier, Republicans gained much electoral support from voters the Federalists had alienated.

In the national political forum, however, the Whiskey Rebellion had just begun. Spokesmen for both parties offered sinister explanations for this seemingly innocuous affair. Washington blamed the "Republican" clubs for promoting civil unrest. He apparently believed the opposition party had dispatched French agents to western Pennsylvania to undermine the authority of the federal government. In November 1794, Washington informed Congress that these "self-created societies"—in other words, the Republican political clubs—had inspired "a spirit inimical to all order." Indeed, the Whiskey Rebellion had been "fomented by combinations of men who . . . have disseminated, from an ignorance or perversion of facts, suspicions, jealousies, and accusations of the whole Government."

The president's interpretation of this rural tax revolt was no less charitable than the conspiratorial explanation offered by the Republicans. Jefferson labeled the entire episode a Hamiltonian device to create an army for the purpose of intimidating Republicans. How else could one explain the administration's gross overreaction to a few disgruntled farmers? "An insurrection was announced and proclaimed and armed against," Jefferson noted, "but could never be found." The response of both parties reveals a pervasive fear of some secret evil design to destroy the republic. The clubs and newspapers—as yet unfamiliar tools for mobilizing public opinion—fanned these anxieties, convincing many government officials

Tarring and feathering federal officials was one way in which western Pennsylvanians protested the tax on whiskey in 1794. Washington's call for troops to put down the insurrection drew more volunteers than he had been able to raise during most of the Revolution.

that the First Amendment should not be interpreted as protecting political dissent.

Washington's Farewell

In September 1796, Washington published his famed "Farewell Address," formally declaring his intention to retire from the presidency. In the address, which was printed in newspapers throughout the country, Washington warned against all political factions. Written in large part by Hamilton, who drew on a draft prepared several years earlier by Madison, the address served narrowly partisan ends. The product of growing political strife, it sought to advance the Federalist cause in the forthcoming election. By waiting until September to announce his retirement, Washington denied the Republicans valuable time to organize an effective campaign. There was an element of irony in this initiative. Washington had always maintained he stood above party. While he may have done so in the early years of his presidency, events such as the signing of Jay's Treaty and the suppression of the Whiskey Rebellion transformed him in the eyes of many Americans into a spokesman solely for Hamilton's Federalist party.

Washington also spoke to foreign policy matters in the address. He counseled the United States to avoid making any permanent alliances with distant nations that had no real interest in promoting American security. This statement guided foreign relations for many years and became the credo of later American isolationists, who argued the United States should steer clear of foreign entanglements.

THE ADAMS PRESIDENCY

The election of 1796 took place in an atmosphere of mutual distrust. Jefferson, soon to be the vice president, informed a friend that "an Anglican and aristocratic party has sprung up, whose avowed object is to draw over us the substance, as they have already done the forms, of British government." On their part, the Federalists were convinced their Republican opponents wanted to hand the government over to French radicals. By modern standards, the structures of both political parties were still primitive. Leaders of national stature such as Madison and Hamilton wrote let-

The Election of 1796

Candidate	Party	Electoral Vote
J. Adams	Federalist	71
Jefferson	Republican	68
T. Pinckney	Federalist	59
Burr	Republican	30

ters encouraging local gentlemen around the country to support a certain candidate, but no one attempted to canvass the voters in advance of the election.

During the campaign the Federalists sowed the seeds of their eventual destruction. Party stalwarts agreed John Adams should stand against the Republican candidate, Thomas Jefferson. Hamilton, however, could not leave well enough alone. From his law office in New York City, he schemed to deprive Adams of the presidency. His motives were obscure. He apparently feared an independent-minded Adams would be difficult to manipulate. He was correct.

Hamilton exploited an awkward feature of the electoral college. In accordance with the Constitution, each elector cast two ballots, and the person who gained the most votes became president. The runner-up, regardless of party affiliation, served as vice president. Ordinarily the Federalist electors would have cast one vote for Adams and one for Thomas Pinckney, the hero of the negotiations with Spain and the party's choice for vice president. Everyone hoped, of course, there would be no tie. Hamilton secretly urged southern Federalists to support only Pinckney even if that meant throwing away an elector's second vote. If everything had gone according to plan, Pinckney would have received more votes than Adams, but when New Englanders loyal to Adams heard of Hamilton's maneuvering, they dropped Pinckney. When the votes were counted, Adams had 71, Jefferson 68, and Pinckney 59. Hamilton's treachery not only angered the new president but also heightened tensions within the Federalist party.

Adams assumed the presidency under intolerable conditions. He found himself saddled with the members of Washington's old cabinet, a group of second-raters who regularly consulted with

Hamilton behind Adams's back. The two most offensive were Timothy Pickering, secretary of state, and James McHenry, secretary of war. But to have dismissed them summarily would have called Washington's judgment into question, and Adams was not prepared to take that risk publicly.

Adams also had to work with a Republican vice president. Adams hoped he and Jefferson could cooperate as they had during the Revolution—they had served together on the committee that prepared the Declaration of Independence—but partisan pressures soon overwhelmed the president's good intentions. Jefferson recorded their final attempt at reconciliation. Strolling home one night after dinner, Jefferson and Adams reached a place "where our road separated, his being down Market Street, mine along Fifth, and we took leave; and he [Adams] never after that . . . consulted me as to any measure of the government."

The XYZ Affair and Domestic Politics

Foreign affairs immediately occupied Adams's full attention. The French government regarded Jay's Treaty as an affront. By allowing Great Britain to define the conditions for neutrality, the United States had in effect sided with that nation against the interests of France.

Relations between the two countries had steadily deteriorated. The French refused to receive Charles Cotesworth Pinckney, the U.S. representative in Paris. Pierre Adet, the French minister in Philadelphia, openly tried to influence the 1796 election in favor of the Republicans. His meddling in domestic politics not only embarrassed Jefferson, it also offended the American people. The situation then took a violent turn. In 1797, French privateers began seizing American ships. Since neither the United States nor France officially declared war, the hostilities came to be known as the Quasi-War.

Hamilton and his friends welcomed a popular outpouring of anti-French sentiment. The "High Federalists"—as Hamilton's wing of the party was called—counseled the president to prepare for all-out war, hoping war would purge the United States of French influence. Adams was not persuaded to escalate the conflict. He dispatched a special commission in a final attempt to remove the sources of antagonism. This famous negotiat-

ing team consisted of Charles Pinckney, John Marshall, and Elbridge Gerry. They were instructed to obtain compensation for the ships seized by French privateers as well as release from the treaties of 1778. Federalists still worried that this old agreement might oblige the United States to defend French colonies in the Caribbean against British attack, which they were extremely reluctant to do. In exchange, the commission offered France the same commercial privileges granted to Great Britain in Jay's Treaty. While the diplomats negotiated for peace, Adams talked of strengthening American defenses, rhetoric that pleased the militant members of his own party.

The commission was shocked by the outrageous treatment it received in France. Instead of dealing directly with Talleyrand, the minister of foreign relations, they met with obscure intermediaries who demanded a huge bribe. The commission reported that Talleyrand would not open negotiations unless he was given $250,000. In addition, the French government expected a "loan" of millions of dollars. The Americans refused to play this insulting game. Pinckney angrily sputtered, "No, no, not a sixpence," and with Marshall he returned to the United States. When they arrived home, Marshall offered his much-quoted toast: "Millions for defense, but not one cent for tribute."

Diplomatic humiliation set off a domestic political explosion. When Adams presented the commission's official correspondence before Congress—the names of Talleyrand's lackeys were labeled X, Y, and Z—the Federalists burst out with a war cry. At last, they would be able to even old scores with the Republicans. In April 1798, a Federalist newspaper in New York City announced ominously that any American who refused to censure France" . . . must have a soul black enough to be *fit* for *treasons, strategems, and spoils."* Rumors of conspiracy spread throughout the country. Personal friendships between Republicans and Federalists were shattered. Jefferson described the tense political atmosphere in a letter to an old colleague: "You and I have formerly seen warm debates and high political passions. But gentlemen of different politics would then speak to each other, and separate the business of the Senate from that of society. It is not so now. Men who have been intimate all their lives, cross the streets to avoid meeting, and

This cartoon, Property Protected, a la Francoise *(1798), captures the anti-French sentiment many Americans felt after President Adams disclosed the papers of the XYZ affair. America—depicted as a young maiden—is being plundered by five Frenchmen, who represent the five directors of the French government.*

turn their heads another way, lest they should be obliged to touch their hats."

Crushing Political Dissent

In the spring of 1798, High Federalists assumed that it was just a matter of time until Adams asked Congress for a formal declaration of war. In the meantime, they pushed for a general rearmament, new fighting ships, additional harbor fortifications, and most important, a greatly expanded U.S. Army. About the need for land forces, Adams remained understandably skeptical. He saw no likelihood of French invasion.

The president missed the political point. The army the Federalists wanted was intended not to thwart French aggression but to stifle internal opposition. Indeed, militant Federalists used the XYZ affair as the occasion to institute what Jefferson termed the "reign of witches." The threat to the Republicans was not simply a figment of the vice president's overwrought imagination. When Theodore Sedgwick, now a Federalist senator from Massachusetts, first learned of the commission's failure, he observed in words that capture the High Federalists' vindictiveness, "It will afford a glorious opportunity to destroy faction. Improve it."

During the summer of 1798, a provisional army gradually came into existence. George Washington agreed to lead the troops, but he would do so only on condition that Adams appoint Hamilton as second-in-command. This demand placed the president in a terrible dilemma. Several revolutionary veterans—Henry Knox, for example—outranked Hamilton. Moreover, the former secretary of the treasury had consistently undermined Adams's authority, and to give Hamilton a position of real power in the government seemed awkward at best. When Washington insisted, however, Adams was forced to support Hamilton.

The chief of the High Federalists threw himself into the task of recruiting and supplying the troops. No detail escaped his attention. He and Secretary of War McHenry made certain that in this political army only loyal Federalists received commissions. They even denied Adams's son-in-law a post. The entire enterprise took on an air of unreality. Hamilton longed for military glory, and he may have contemplated attacking Spain's Latin American colonies. His driving obsession, however, was the restoration of political order. No doubt, he agreed with a Federalist senator from Connecticut who predicted the Republicans "never will yield till violence is introduced; we must have a partial civil war . . . and the bayonet must convince some, who are beyond the reach of other arguments."

Hamilton should not have treated Adams with such open contempt. After all, the Massachusetts statesman was still the president, and without presidential cooperation, Hamilton could not fulfill his grand military ambitions. Yet whenever pressing questions concerning the army arose, Adams was nowhere to be found. He let commissions lie on his desk unsigned; he took overlong vacations to New England. He made it quite clear his first love was the navy. In May 1798, the president persuaded Congress to establish the Navy Department. For this new cabinet position, he selected Benjamin Stoddert, a person who did not take orders from Hamilton. Moreover, Adams further infuriated the High Federalists by refusing to ask Congress for a formal declaration of war. When they pressed him, Adams threatened to resign, making Jefferson president. As the weeks passed, the American people increasingly regarded the idle army as an expensive extravagance.

Silencing Political Opposition: The Alien and Sedition Acts

The Federalists did not rely solely on the army to crush political dissent. During the summer of 1798, the party's majority in Congress passed a group of bills known collectively as the Alien and Sedition Acts. This legislation authorized the use of federal courts and the powers of the presidency to silence the Republicans. The acts were born of fear and vindictiveness, and in their efforts to punish the followers of Jefferson, the Federalists created the nation's first major crisis over civil liberties.

Congress drew up three separate Alien Acts. The first, the Alien Enemies Law, vested the president with extraordinary wartime powers. On his own authority, he could detain or deport citizens of nations with which the United States was at war and who behaved in a manner he thought suspicious. Since Adams refused to ask for a declaration of war, this legislation never went into effect. A second act, the Alien Law, empowered the president to expel any foreigner from the United States simply by executive decree. Congress limited the acts to two years, and while Adams did not attempt to enforce them, the mere threat of arrest caused some Frenchmen to flee the country. The

third act, the Naturalization Law, was the most flagrantly political of the group. The act established a fourteen-year probationary period before foreigners could apply for full U.S. citizenship. Federalists recognized that recent immigrants, especially the Irish, tended to vote Republican. The Naturalization Law, therefore, was designed to keep "hordes of wild Irishmen" away from the polls for as long as possible.

The Sedition Law struck at the heart of free political exchange. It defined criticism of the U.S. government as criminal libel; citizens found guilty by a jury were subject to fines and imprisonment. Congress entrusted enforcement of the act to the federal courts. Republicans were justly worried that the Sedition Law undermined rights guaranteed by the First Amendment. When they protested, however, the High Federalists dismissed their complaints. The Constitution, they declared, did not condone "the most groundless and malignant lies, striking at the safety and existence of the nation." They were determined to shut down the opposition press and were willing to give the government what seemed almost dictatorial powers to achieve that end. The Jeffersonians also expressed concern over the federal judiciary's expanded role in punishing sedition. They believed such matters were best left to state officials.

Americans living in widely scattered regions of the country soon witnessed political repression firsthand. District courts staffed by Federalist appointees indicted seventeen people for criticizing the government. Several cases were absurd. In Newark, New Jersey, for example, a drunkard staggered out of a tavern to watch a sixteen-gun salute fired in honor of President Adams. When the man expressed the hope a cannonball might lodge in Adams's ample posterior, he was arrested. No wonder a New York City journal declared, "joking may be very dangerous even to a free country."

The most celebrated trial occurred in Vermont. A Republican congressman, Matthew Lyon, who was running for reelection, publicly accused the Adams administration of mishandling the Quasi-War. This was not the first time this Irish immigrant had angered the Federalists. On the floor of the House of Representatives, Lyon once spit in the eye of a Federalist congressman from Connecticut. Lyon was immediately labeled the "Spitting Lyon," and one Bostonian declared, "I

feel grieved that the saliva of an Irishman should be felt upon the face of an American & he, a New Englandman." A Federalist court was pleased to have the opportunity to convict him of libel. But Lyon enjoyed the last laugh. While he sat in jail, his constituents reelected him to Congress.

As this and other cases demonstrated, the federal courts had become political tools. While the fumbling efforts at enforcement of the Sedition Law did not silence opposition—indeed, they sparked even greater criticism and created martyrs—the actions of the administration persuaded Republicans the survival of free government was at stake. Time was running out. "There is no event," Jefferson warned, " ... however atrocious, which may not be expected."

The Republicans Appeal to the States

By the fall of 1798, Jefferson and Madison were convinced the Federalists envisioned the creation of a police state. According to Madison, the Sedition Law "ought to produce universal alarm." It threatened the free communication of ideas which he "deemed the only effectual guardian of every other right." Some extreme Republicans such as John Taylor of Virginia recommended secession from the Union; others advocated armed resistance. But Jefferson wisely counseled against such extreme strategies. "This is not the kind of opposition the American people

will permit," he reminded his desperate supporters. The last best hope for American freedom lay in the state legislatures.

As the crisis deepened, Jefferson and Madison drafted separate protests known as the Virginia and Kentucky Resolutions. Both statements vigorously defended the right of individual state assemblies to interpret the constitutionality of federal law. Jefferson wrote the Kentucky Resolutions in November 1798, and in an outburst of partisan anger, he flirted with a doctrine of nullification as dangerous to the survival of the United States as anything advanced by Hamilton and his High Federalist friends.

In the Kentucky Resolutions, Jefferson described the federal union as a compact. The states transferred certain explicit powers to the national government, but in his opinion, they retained full authority over all matters not specifically mentioned in the Constitution. Jefferson rejected Hamilton's broad interpretation of the "general welfare" clause. "Every state," Jefferson argued, "has a natural right in cases not within the compact . . . to *nullify* of their own authority all assumptions of power by others within their limits." Carried to an extreme, this logic could have led to the breakup of the federal government, and in 1798, Kentucky legislators were not prepared to take such a radical stance. While they diluted Jefferson's prose, they fully accepted his belief that the Alien and Sedition Acts were unconstitutional and ought to be repealed.

When Madison drafted the Virginia Resolutions in December, he took a stand more temperate than Jefferson's. Madison urged the states to defend the rights of the American people, but he resisted the notion that a single state legislature could or should have the authority to overthrow federal law.

The Virginia and Kentucky Resolutions must be viewed in proper historical context. They were not intended as statements of abstract principles and most certainly not as a justification for southern secession. They were pure political party propaganda. Jefferson and Madison dramatically reminded American voters during a period of severe domestic tension that the Republicans offered a clear alternative to Federalist rule. No other state legislatures passed the Resolutions, and even in Virginia where the Republicans enjoyed broad support, several important figures such as John Marshall and George Washington censured the states' rights argument.

Adams's Finest Hour

In February 1799, President Adams belatedly declared his independence from the Hamiltonian wing of the Federalist party. Throughout the confrontation with France, Adams had shown little enthusiasm for war. Following the XYZ debacle, he began to receive informal reports that Talleyrand had changed his tune. The French foreign minister told Elbridge Gerry and other Americans that the bribery episode had been an unfortunate misunderstanding and that if the United States sent new representatives, he was prepared to negotiate in good faith. The High Federalists ridiculed this report. But Adams, still brooding over Hamilton's appointment to the army, decided to throw his own waning prestige behind peace. In February, he suddenly asked the Senate to confirm William Vans Murray as U. S. representative to France.

The move caught the High Federalists totally by surprise. They sputtered with outrage. "It is solely the President's act," Pickering cried, "and we were all thunderstruck when we heard of it." Adams was just warming to the task. In May, he fired Pickering and McHenry, an action he should have taken months earlier. With peace in the offing, American taxpayers complained more and more about the cost of maintaining an unnecessary army. The president was only too happy to dismantle Hamilton's dream.

When the new negotiators—Oliver Ellsworth and William Davie joined Murray—finally arrived in France in November 1799, they discovered that yet another group had come to power there. This government, headed by Napoleon Bonaparte, cooperated in drawing up an agreement known as the Convention of Mortefontaine. The French refused to compensate the Americans for vessels taken during the Quasi-War, but they did declare the treaties of 1778 null and void. Moreover, the convention removed annoying French restrictions on U.S. commerce. Not only had Adams avoided war, he had also created an atmosphere of mutual trust that paved the way for the purchase of the Louisiana Territory. The president declared with considerable justification that the second French mission was "the most disinterested, the most determined and the most

John Adams in the suit and sword he wore for his 1797 inauguration. The portrait is by English artist William Winstanley, 1798. Throughout his presidency, Adams was plagued by political extremists, Federalist as well as Republican.

successful [act] of my whole life." It also cost him reelection.

THE PEACEFUL REVOLUTION: THE ELECTION OF 1800

On the eve of the election of 1800, the Federalists were fatally divided. Adams enjoyed wide popularity among the Federalist rank and file, especially in New England, but articulate party spokesleaders such as Hamilton vowed to punish the president for his betrayal of their militant policies. Hamilton even composed a scathing pamphlet entitled *Letter Concerning the Public Conduct and Character of John Adams,* an essay that questioned Adams's ability to hold high office.

Once again the former secretary of the treasury attempted to rig the voting in the electoral college so that the party's vice presidential candidate, Charles Cotesworth Pinckney, would receive more ballots than Adams, and America would be saved from "the fangs of Jefferson." As in 1796, the conspiracy backfired. The Republicans gained 73 votes, while the Federalists trailed with 65.

But to everyone's surprise, the election was not resolved in the electoral college. When the ballots were counted, Jefferson and his running mate, Aaron Burr, had tied. This accident—a Republican elector should have thrown away his second vote—sent the selection of the next president to the House of Representatives, a "lame duck" body still controlled by members of the Federalist party.

As the House began its work on February 27, 1801, excitement ran high. Each state delegation cast a single vote, with nine votes needed for election. On the first ballot, Jefferson received the support of eight states, Burr six, and two states divided evenly. People predicted a quick victory for Jefferson, but after dozens of ballots, the House had still not selected a president. "The scene was now ludicrous," observed one witness. "Many had sent home for night-caps and pillows, and wrapped in shawls and great-coats, lay about the floor of the committee-rooms, or sat sleeping in their seats." The drama dragged on for days. To add to the confusion, Burr unaccountably refused to withdraw. Contemporaries thought his ambition had overcome his good sense.

The Election of 1800		
Candidate	Party	Electoral Vote
Jefferson	Republican	73
Burr	Republican	73
J. Adams	Federalist	65
C. Pinckney	Federalist	64

The logjam finally broke when leading Federalists decided that Jefferson, whatever his faults, would make a more responsible president than would the shifty Burr. Even Hamilton labeled Burr "the most dangerous man of the community." On the thirty-sixth ballot, Representative James A. Bayard of Delaware announced he no longer supported Burr. This decision, coupled with Burr's inaction, gave Jefferson the presidency, ten states to four.

The Twelfth Amendment, ratified in 1804, saved the American people from repeating this potentially dangerous turn of events. Henceforth, the electoral college cast separate ballots for president and vice president.

During the final days of his presidency, Adams appointed as many Federalists as possible to the federal bench. Jefferson protested the hasty manner in which these "midnight judges" were selected. One of them, John Marshall, became chief justice of the United States, a post he held with distinction for thirty-four years. But behind the last-minute flurry of activity lay bitterness and disappointment. Adams never forgave Hamilton. "No party," the Federalist president wrote, "that ever existed knew itself so little or so vainly overrated its own influence and popularity as ours. None ever understood so ill the causes of its own power, or so wantonly destroyed them." On the morning of Jefferson's inauguration, Adams slipped away from the capital—now located in Washington, D.C.—unnoticed and unappreciated.

Peaceful Transition

In the address that Adams missed, Jefferson attempted to quiet partisan fears. "We are all republicans; we are all federalists," the new president declared. By this statement he did not mean to suggest party differences were no longer important. Jefferson reminded his audience that whatever the politicians might say, the people shared a deep commitment to a federal Union based on republican ideals set forth during the American Revolution. Indeed, the president interpreted the election of 1800 as a revolutionary episode, a fulfillment of the principles of 1776.

Recent battles, of course, colored Jefferson's judgment. The contests of the 1790s had been hard fought; the outcome often in doubt. Jefferson looked back at this period as a confrontation between the "advocates of republican and those of kingly government," and he believed only the vigilance of his own party had saved the country from Federalist "liberticide."

The Federalists were thoroughly dispirited by the entire experience. In the end, it had not been Hamilton's foolish electoral schemes that destroyed the party's chances in 1800. Rather, the Federalists had lost touch with a majority of the American people. In office, Adams and Hamilton—whatever their own differences may have been—betrayed their doubts about popular sovereignty too often, and when it came time to marshal broad support, to mobilize public opinion in favor of the party of wealth and privilege, few responded. As Secretary of War Oliver Wolcott observed on hearing of Jefferson's victory, "Have our party shown that they possess the necessary skill and courage to deserve . . . to govern? What have they done? . . . They write *private* letters. To whom? To each other, but they do nothing to give a proper direction to the public mind."

From a broader historical perspective, the election of 1800 seems noteworthy for what did not occur. There were no riots in the streets, no attempted coup by military officers, no secession from the Union, nothing except the peaceful transfer of government from the leaders of one political party to those of the opposition. Americans had weathered the Alien and Sedition Acts, the meddling by predatory foreign powers in domestic affairs, the shrilly partisan rhetoric of hack journalists, and now at the start of a new century, they were impressed with their own achievement. As one woman who attended Jefferson's inauguration noted, "The changes of administration which in every government and in every age have most generally been epochs of

CHRONOLOGY

1787 Constitution of the United States signed (September)

1789 George Washington inaugurated (April) • Louis XVI of France calls meeting of the Estates General (May)

1790 Congress approves Hamilton's plan for funding and assumption (July)

1791 Bank of the United States is chartered (February) • Hamilton's *Report on Manufactures* rejected by Congress (December)

1793 France's revolutionary government announces a "war of all people against all kings" (February) • Genêt affair strains relations with France (April) • Washington issues Proclamation of Neutrality (April) • Spread of "Democratic" Clubs alarms Federalists • Jefferson resigns as secretary of state (December)

1794 Whiskey Rebellion put down by U.S. Army (July–November) • General Anthony Wayne defeats Indians at Battle of Fallen Timbers (August)

1795 Hamilton resigns as secretary of the treasury (January) • Jay's Treaty divides the nation (June) • Pinckney's Treaty with Spain is a welcome surprise (October)

1796 Washington publishes "Farewell Address" (September) • John Adams elected president (December)

1797 XYZ Affair poisons U.S. relations with France (October)

1798–1800 Quasi-War with France

1798 Congress passes the Alien and Sedition Acts (June and July) • Provisional army is formed • Virginia and Kentucky Resolutions protest the Alien and Sedition Acts (November and December)

1799 George Washington dies (December)

1800 Convention of Mortefontaine is signed with France, ending Quasi-War (September)

1801 House of Representatives elects Thomas Jefferson president (February)

confusion, villainy and bloodshed, in this our happy country take place without any species of distraction, or disorder."

Recommended Reading

The best general survey of political events is Stanley Elkins and Eric McKitrick, *The Age of Federalism: The Early American Republic* (1993). Forrest McDonald has produced two highly original portraits of major figures of this period: *The Presidency of George Washington* (1974) and *Alexander Hamilton* (1979). Merrill D. Peterson provides an encyclopedic account of Jefferson's political career in *Thomas Jefferson and the New Nation: A Biography* (1970). For a thoughtful reinterpretation of the ideological issues separating Hamilton from Jefferson, see Drew McCoy, *The Elusive Republic: The Political Economy in Jeffersonian America* (1980). Richard Hofstadter offers a valuable discussion of the development of political parties in this period in *The Idea of a Party System, 1780–1840* (1969).

Additional Bibliography

Some of the better biographies of Hamilton, Madison, and Jefferson include Dumas Malone's classic *Jefferson and the Rights of Man* (1951) and *Jefferson and the Ordeal of Liberty* (1962); Gerald Stourzh, *Alexander Hamilton and the Idea of Republican Government* (1970); Jacob Ernest Cooke, *Alexander Hamilton* (1982); and Jack N. Rakove, *James Madison and the Creation of the American Republic* (1990). For students doing research in this period or for people just curious about the powerful personalities that shaped the politics of the new nation, the published papers of George Washington, John Adams, Thomas Jefferson, Alexander Hamilton, John Jay, and James Madison provide invaluable insights.

Political ideologies of the 1790s are discussed in Lance Banning, *The Jeffersonian Persuasion: Evolution of Party Ideology* (1978); Richard Buel, Jr., *Securing the Revolution: Ideology in American Politics, 1789–1815* (1972); Joyce Appleby, *Capitalism and a New Social Order* (1984); and Robert E. Shalhope, *The Roots of Democracy: American Thought and Culture* (1990). Two good regional studies are Andrew Cayton, *Frontier Republic: Ideology and Politics in the Ohio Country, 1780–1825* (1986) and Alan Taylor, *Liberty Men and Great Proprietors* (1990).

Several books take a more cultural perspective on the period: Steven Watts, *The Republic Reborn: War and the Making of Liberal America, 1790–1820* (1987); and David Shi, *The Simple Life: Plain Living and High Thinking in American Culture* (1985).

For a discussion of Parson Weems as well as the changing public image of Washington throughout American history, see Mason Locke Weems, *The Life of Washington,* edited by Marcus Cunliffe (1962); Gary Wills, *Cincinnatus: George Washington and the Enlightenment* (1984); and Paul K. Longmore, *Invention of George Washington* (1989).

The problems associated with the development of political parties are examined in William N. Chambers, *Political Parties in a New Nation: The American Experience, 1776–1809* (1963); Noble E. Cunningham, Jr., *The Jeffersonian Republicans: The Formation of Party Organization, 1789–1801* (1957); and Alfred F. Young, *The Democratic Republicans of New York: The Origins 1763–1797* (1963). The relation between literature and society is the topic of three challenging books: Michael Warner, *Letters of the Republic: Publication and the Public Sphere* (1990); Emory Elliott, *Revolutionary Writers: Literature and Authority in the New Republic, 1725–1810* (1982); and Cathy N. Davidson, *Revolution and the Word: The Rise of the Novel in America* (1986).

Detailed treatments of the complex negotiations and treaty fights include Alexander De Conde, *Entangling Alliance: Politics and Diplomacy Under George Washington* (1958) and *The Quasi-War: Politics and Diplomacy of the Undeclared War with France 1797–1801* (1966); Gerald A. Combs, *The Jay Treaty: Political Battleground of the Founding Fathers* (1970); Albert H. Bowman, *The Struggle for Neutrality: Franco-American Diplomacy During the Federalist Era* (1974); and William Stinchcombe, *The XYZ Affair* (1960).

The attempts by the Federalists to restrict constitutional rights is masterfully explored in James Morton Smith, *Freedom's Fetters: The Alien and Sedition Laws and American Civil Liberties* (1956). Richard H. Kohn's *Eagle and Sword: The Federalists and the Creation of the Military Establishments in America, 1783–1803* (1975) describes the plans to form a Federalist army. The implications of using armed force against citizens are analyzed in Thomas P. Slaughter, *The Whiskey Rebellion: Frontier Epilogue to the American Revolution* (1986).

Jeffersonian Ascendancy

Theory and Practice of Government

*B*ritish visitors often expressed contempt for Jeffersonian society. Wherever they traveled in the young republic, they met ill-mannered people inspired with a ruling passion for liberty and equality. Charles William Janson, an Englishman who lived in the United States for thirteen years, recounted an exchange he found particularly unsettling that had occurred at the home of an American acquaintance. "On knocking at the door," he reported, "it was opened by a servant maid, whom I had never before seen." The woman's behavior astonished Janson. "The following is the dialogue, word for word, which took place on this occasion:—'Is your master at home?'—'I have no master.'—'Don't you live here?'—'I *stay* here.'—'And who are you then?'—'Why, I am Mr. ———————'s *help*. I'd have you know, *man,* that I am no *sarvant* [sic]; none but *negers* [sic] are *sarvants.*'"

Standing on his friend's doorstep, Janson encountered the authentic voice of Jeffersonian republicanism—self-confident, assertive, blatantly racist, and having no intention of being relegated to low social status. The maid who answered the door believed she was her employer's equal, perhaps not in wealth but surely in character. She may have even dreamed of someday owning a house staffed with "*help.*" American society fostered such ambition. In the early nineteenth century, thousands of settlers poured across the Appalachian Mountains or moved to cities in search of opportunity. Thomas Jefferson and individuals who stood for public office under the banner of the Republican party spoke for these people.

The limits of the Jeffersonian vision were obvious even to contemporaries. The people who spoke most eloquently about equal opportunity often owned slaves. As early as the 1770s, the famed English essayist Samuel Johnson had chided Americans for their hypocrisy. "How is it," he asked the indignant rebels, "that we hear the loudest yelps for liberty from the drivers of Negroes?" Little had changed since the Revolution. African Americans, who represented one-fifth of the population of the United States, were totally excluded from the new opportunities opening up in the cities and the West. Indeed, the maid in the incident just described insisted—with no apparent sense of inconsistency—that her position was superior to that of blacks, who were brought to lifelong servitude involuntarily.

It is not surprising that leaders of the Federalist party accused the Republicans, especially those who lived in the South, of disingenuousness, and in 1804, one Massachusetts Federalist sarcastically defined "Jeffersonian" as "an Indian word, signifying '*a great tobacco planter, who had herds of black slaves.*'" The race issue simply would not go away. Beneath the political maneuvering over the acquisition of the Louisiana Territory and the War of 1812 lay fundamental disagreement about the spread of slavery to the western territories.

In other areas, the Jeffersonians did not fulfill even their own high expectations. As members of an opposition party during the presidency of John Adams, they insisted on a strict interpretation of the Constitution, peaceful foreign relations, and a reduction of the role of the federal government in the lives of the average citizens. But following the election of 1800, Jefferson and his supporters discovered that unanticipated pressures, foreign and domestic, forced them to moderate these goals. Before he retired from public office, Jefferson interpreted the Constitution in a way that permitted the government to purchase the Louisiana Territory when the opportunity arose; he regulated the national economy with a rigor that would have made Alexander Hamilton blush, and he led the country to the brink of war. Some Americans praised the president's pragmatism; others felt betrayed. For a man who had played a leading role in the revolt against George III, it must have been shocking in 1807 to find himself labeled a "despot" in a popular New England newspaper. "Give ear no longer to the siren voice of democracy and Jeffersonian liberty," the editor shrieked. "It is a cursed delusion, adopted by traitors, and recommended by sycophants."

DEVELOPING REGIONAL IDENTITIES

During the early decades of the nineteenth century, the population of the United States experienced substantial growth. The 1810 census counted 7,240,000 Americans, a jump of almost two million in just ten years. Of this total, approximately 20 percent were blacks, the majority of whom lived in the South. The large population increase in the nation was the result primarily of natural reproduction, since during Jefferson's presidency few immigrants moved to the New World. The largest single group in this society was children, boys and girls who were born after Washington's administration and who came of age at a time when the nation's boundaries were rapidly expanding.

Even as Americans defended the rights of individual states, they were forming strong regional identifications. In commerce and politics, they perceived themselves as representatives of distinct subcultures—as Southerners, New Englanders, or Westerners. No doubt, the broadening geographic horizons reflected improved transportation links that enabled people to travel more easily within the various sections. But the growing regional mentality was also the product of defensiveness. While local writers celebrated New England's cultural distinctiveness, for example, they were clearly uneasy about the region's rejection of the democratic values that were sweeping the rest of the nation. Moreover, during this period people living south of the Potomac River began describing themselves as Southerners, not as citizens of the Chesapeake or the Carolinas as they had done in colonial times.

This shifting focus of attention resulted not only from an awareness of shared economic interests but also from a sensitivity to outside attacks on slavery. Several times during the first fifteen years of the nineteenth century, conspirators actually advocated secession, and while these harebrained schemes failed, they revealed the powerful sectional loyalties that undermined national unity.

Western Conquest

The most striking changes occurred in the West. Before the end of the American Revolution, only Indian traders and a few hardy settlers had ventured across the Appalachians. After 1790, however, a flood of people rushed west to stake out farms on the rich soil. Many settlers followed the so-called northern route across Pennsylvania or New York into the old Northwest Territory. Pittsburgh and Cincinnati, both strategically located on the Ohio River, became important commercial ports. In 1803, Ohio joined the Union, and territorial governments were formed

in Indiana (1800), Louisiana (1805), Michigan (1805), Illinois (1809), and Missouri (1812). Southerners poured into the new states of Kentucky (1792) and Tennessee (1796). Wherever they located, Westerners depended on water transportation. Because of the extraordinarily high cost of hauling goods over land, riverboats represented the only economical means of carrying agricultural products to distant markets. The Mississippi River was the crucial commercial link for the entire region, and Westerners did not feel secure so long as New Orleans, the southern gate to the Mississippi, remained under Spanish control.

Families who moved west attempted to transplant familiar eastern customs to the frontier. In some areas such as the Western Reserve, a narrow strip of land along Lake Erie in northern Ohio, the influence of New England remained strong. In general, however, a creative mixing of peoples of different backgrounds in a strange environment generated distinctive folkways. Westerners developed their own heroes like Mike Fink, the legendary keelboatman of the Mississippi River; Daniel Boone, the famed trapper and Indian fighter; and the eye-gouging "alligator-men" of Kentucky and Tennessee. Americans who crossed the mountains were ambitious and self-confident, excited by the challenge of almost unlimited geographic mobility. A French traveler observed in 1802 that throughout the region he visited there was not a single farm "where one cannot with confidence ask the owner from whence he had emigrated, or, according to the light manners of the Americans, 'What part of the world do you come from?'" These rootless people, he explained, "incline perpetually toward the most distant fringes of American settlement."

At the beginning of the nineteenth century, a substantial number of Native Americans lived in the region; the land belonged to them. The tragedy was that the Indians, many dependent on trade with the white people and ravaged by disease, lacked unity. Small groups of Native Americans, allegedly representing the interests of an entire tribe, sold off huge pieces of land, often for whiskey and trinkets.

Such fraudulent transactions disgusted the two Shawnee leaders, Tecumseh and his brother Tenskwatawa (known as the Prophet). Tecumseh rejected classification as a Shawnee and may have been the first native leader to identify himself self-

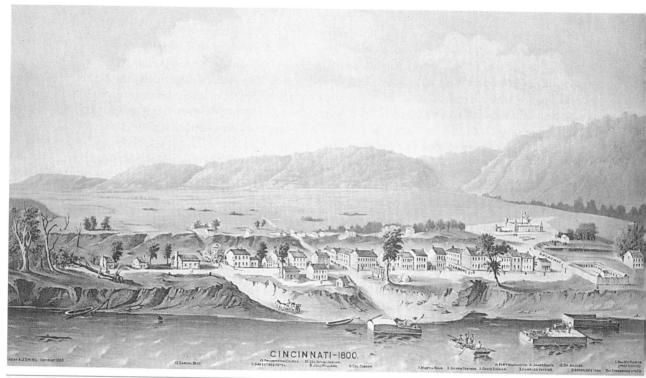

By 1800, Cincinnati—one of the new western cities—had become a busy trading center on the Ohio River with a post office, a Presbyterian church, and the Green Tree Hotel.

consciously as "Indian." These men desperately attempted to revitalize native cultures, and against overwhelming odds, they briefly persuaded Native Americans living in the Indiana Territory to avoid contact with whites, to resist alcohol, and most important, to hold on to their land. White intruders saw Tecumseh as a threat to progress, and during the War of 1812, they shattered the Indians' dream of cultural renaissance (see discussion on p. 252). The populous Creek nation, located in the modern states of Alabama and Mississippi, also resisted the settlers' advance, but its warriors were crushed by Andrew Jackson's Tennessee militia at the battle of Horseshoe Bend (March 1814).

Well-meaning Jeffersonians disclaimed any intention to destroy the Indians. The president talked of creating a vast reservation beyond the Mississippi River, just as the British had talked before the Revolution of a sanctuary beyond the Appalachian Mountains. He sent federal agents to "civilize" the Indians, to transform them into yeoman farmers. But even the most enlightened white thinkers of the day did not believe the Indians possessed cultures worth preserving. In

fact, in 1835 the Democratic national convention selected a vice presidential candidate whose major qualification for high office seemed to be that he killed Tecumseh.

Commercial Capitalism

Before 1820, the prosperity of the United States depended primarily on its agriculture and trade. Jeffersonian America was by no stretch of the imagination an industrial economy. The overwhelming majority of the population—84 percent in 1810—was directly involved in agriculture. Southerners concentrated on staple crops, tobacco, rice, and cotton, which they sold on the European market. In the North, people generally produced livestock and cereal crops. Regardless of location, however, the nation's farmers followed a back-breaking work routine that did not differ substantially from that of their parents and grandparents. Except for the cotton gin, important chemical and mechanical inventions did not appear in the fields for another generation. Probably the major innovation of this period was the agricultural fair, an idea first advanced in

1809 by a Massachusetts farmer, Elkanah Watson. In hopes of improving animal breeding, he offered prizes for the best livestock in the country. The experiment was a great success, for as Watson reported, "Many farmers, and even women, were excited by curiosity to attend this first novel, and humble exhibition."

The merchant marine represented an equally important element in America's preindustrial economy. At the turn of the century, ships flying the Stars and Stripes transported a large share of the world's trade. Merchants in Boston, New York, and Philadelphia received handsome profits from this commerce. Their ships provided essential links between European countries and their Caribbean colonies. France, for example, relied heavily on American vessels for its sugar. These lucrative transactions, coupled with the export of domestic staples, especially cotton, generated great fortunes. Between 1793 and 1807, the year that Jefferson imposed the embargo against Britain and France, American commerce enjoyed a more than 300 percent increase in the value of exports and in net earnings. Unfortunately, the boom did not last. The success of the "carrying trade" depended in large measure on friendly relations between the United States and the major European powers. When England and France began seizing American ships—as they both did after 1805—national prosperity suffered.

The cities of Jeffersonian America functioned chiefly as depots for international trade. Only about 7 percent of the nation's population lived in urban centers, and most of these people owed their livelihoods either directly or indirectly to the "carrying trade." Artisans maintained the fleet; skilled workers produced new ships; laborers loaded cargoes. And as some merchant families became wealthy, they demanded luxury items such as fine furniture. This specialized market drew a small, but highly visible, group of master craftspeople, and their extraordinarily beautiful and intricate pieces—New England tall clocks, for example—were perhaps the highest artistic achievement of the period.

Despite these accomplishments, American cities exercised only a marginal influence on the nation's vast hinterland. Because of the high cost of land transportation, urban merchants seldom purchased goods for export—flour, for example—from a distance of more than 150 miles. The

Tenskwatawa, known as the Prophet, provided spiritual leadership for the union of the native peoples he and his brother Tecumseh organized to resist white encroachment on Native American lands.

separation between rural and urban Americans was far more pronounced during Jefferson's presidency than it was after the development of canals and railroads a few decades later.

The booming carrying trade may actually have retarded the industrialization of the United States. The lure of large profits drew investment capital—a scarce resource in a developing society—into commerce. By contrast, manufacturing seemed too risky. One contemporary complained, "The brilliant prospects held out by commerce, caused our citizens to neglect the mechanical and manufacturing branches of industry."

He may have exaggerated slightly to make his point. Samuel Slater, an English-born designer of textile machinery, did establish several cotton spinning mills in New England, but before the 1820s these plants employed only a small number of workers. In fact, during this period far more cloth was produced in individual households than in factories. Another farsighted inventor, Robert Fulton, sailed the first American steamship up the Hudson River in 1807. In time, this marvelous innovation opened new markets for domestic

Although cotton was an important trade item in the early nineteenth century, technological advances in textile production were slow in taking hold. Some spinning mills such as the one pictured here were built in New England.

manufacturers, especially in the West. At the conclusion of the War of 1812, however, few people anticipated how greatly power generated by fossil fuel would eventually transform the character of the American economy.

Ordinary workers often felt threatened by the new machines. Skilled artisans who had spent years mastering trade and who took pride in producing an object that expressed their own personalities found the industrial workplace alienating (see "Machines Ingeniously Constructed," pp. 234–235). Moreover, they rightly feared that innovative technology designed to achieve greater efficiency might throw traditional craftspeople out of work or, if not that, transform independent entrepreneurs into dependent wage laborers. One New Yorker, for example, writing in the *Gazette and General Advertiser* in 1801 warned the tradespeople to be on guard against those who "will screw down the wages to the last thread . . . [and destroy] the independent spirit, so distinguished at present in our mechanics, and so useful in republics."

REPUBLICAN ASCENDANCY

The District of Columbia seemed an appropriate capital for a Republican president. At the time of Jefferson's first inauguration, Washington was still an isolated rural village, a far cry from the cosmopolitan centers of Philadelphia and New York. Jefferson fit comfortably into Washington society. He despised formal ceremony and sometimes shocked foreign dignitaries by meeting them in his slippers or a threadbare jacket. He spent as much time as his official duties allowed in reading and reflection. Isaac, one of Jefferson's slaves, recounted, "Old master had abundance of books: sometimes would have twenty of 'em down on the floor at once; read fust one then tother."

The president was a poor public speaker. He wisely refused to deliver annual addresses before Congress. In personal conversation, however, Jefferson exuded considerable charm. His dinner parties were major intellectual as well as social events, and in this forum, the president regaled politicians with his knowledge of literature, philosophy, and science. According to Margaret Bayard Smith, the wife of a congressman, the president "has more ease than grace—all the winning softness of politeness, without the artificial polish of courts."

Notwithstanding his commitment to the life of the mind, Jefferson was a politician to the core. He ran for the presidency in order to achieve specific goals: the reduction of the size and cost of federal government, the repeal of obnoxious Federalist legislation such as the Alien Acts, and the maintenance of international peace. To

The busy carrying trade conducted in the harbor surrounding lower Manhattan in New York is pictured in Cannon House and Wharf *(1792) by Jonathan Budington.*

accomplish his program, Jefferson realized he needed the full cooperation of congressional Republicans, some of whom were fiercely independent men. Over such figures Jefferson exercised political mastery. He established close ties with the leaders of both houses of Congress, and while he seldom announced his plans in public, he made certain his legislative lieutenants knew exactly what he desired. Contemporaries who described Jefferson as a weak president—and some Federalists did just that—did not read the scores of memoranda he sent to political friends or witness the informal meetings he held at the executive mansion with important Republicans. In two terms as president, Jefferson never had to veto a single act of Congress.

Jefferson carefully selected the members of his cabinet. During Washington's administration, he had witnessed—even provoked—severe infighting; as president, he nominated only those who enthusiastically supported his programs. James Madison, the leading figure at the Constitutional Convention, became secretary of state. For the Treasury, Jefferson chose Albert Gallatin, a Swiss-born financier who understood the complexities of the federal budget. "If I had the universe to choose from," the president announced,

"I could not change one of my associates to my better satisfaction."

Jeffersonian Reforms

A top priority of the new government was cutting the national debt. Throughout American history, presidents have advocated such reductions, but in the twentieth century, few have achieved them. Jefferson succeeded. He and Gallatin regarded a large federal deficit as dangerous to the health of republican institutions. In fact, both men associated debt with Alexander Hamilton's Federalist financial programs (see Chapter 7), measures they considered harmful to republicanism. Jefferson claimed that legislators elected by the current generation did not have the right to mortgage the future of unborn Americans.

Jefferson also wanted to diminish the activities of the federal government. He urged Congress to repeal all direct taxes, including the hated Whiskey Tax that had sparked an insurrection in 1794. Secretary Gallatin linked federal income to the carrying trade. He calculated that the entire cost of national government could be borne by customs receipts. As long as commerce flourished, revenues provided sufficient sums. When

"Machines Ingeniously Constructed"
Tensions of Technology in the Early Republic

On July 4, 1788, a parade sponsored by the Pennsylvania Society for the Encouragement of Manufactures and the Useful Arts sparked a mild workers' protest as its members marched in Philadelphia's Federal Procession. A 30-foot carriage at the head of the parade carried several operators who demonstrated the latest devices for making cloth: a carding machine that prepared cotton for spinning, a spinning jenny that produced eighty spindles of yarn at once, a large handloom, and a cloth-printing machine. Independent weavers and Society wage earners marched proudly behind the carriage. Handspinners, however, refused to parade with the jenny that threatened their livelihoods by replacing their wheels.

Eli Whitney's inventions (such as the cotton gin shown here in a cutaway) had a tremendous impact on the growth of manufacturing at the turn of the nineteenth century.

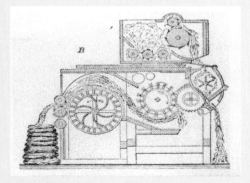

From the earliest days of independence, a tension between mechanization and craftsmanship marked the American quest for technological advance. Manufacturing enthusiasts such as Alexander Hamilton joined Enlightenment figures like Benjamin Rush to celebrate the advent of "machines ingeniously constructed." George Washington urged the First Congress to pass a patent law for the "effectual encouragement" of new inventions that could improve American productivity, reduce reliance on foreign manufactures, and thereby promote genuine independence.

Yet other Americans expressed grave misgivings about the new technology. Thomas Jefferson urged citizens of the new republic to preserve individual independence by letting "our work-shops remain in Europe." While few craftspeople followed his advice, most resisted mechanization and clung to the methods their fathers had taught them.

To be sure, the U. S. Patent Office recognized several important technological achievements among the 1,179 patents it issued between 1790 and 1810. Eli Whitney secured fame by modifying the design of earlier cotton gins so that his model could separate fibers from seeds and husks of the short staple cotton grown in the South. Samuel Slater made great strides in importing and improving English textile technology for northeastern merchant investors. The New York patrician Robert Livingston's financing enabled Robert Fulton's *Claremont* to succeed in 1807 where steamboats of the 1790s had failed, and the Hudson River provided the enterprising inventor a profitable route.

Despite such achievements, traditional methods of transportation and production comprised the bulk of the early republic's economic activity. Even textile manufacturers, the first to mechanize extensively, were still relying as late as the mid-nineteenth century on weavers using hand looms to make the finer grades of cloth. Managers sought to increase productivity by moving weaving from the household to the factory where they could impose stricter work discipline, hoping thus to gain as much from "the labor of thirty men" as they could from "one hundred loom weavers in families."

Such attempts met with resistance from weavers who, like other craftspeople, had traditionally enjoyed the freedom to set their own hours, work at their own pace, and interrupt their professional duties to tend to small farms or simply to socialize. Most master weavers refused to make cloth on factory-owned looms, and many less skilled journeymen worked in textile factories only long enough to acquire the means and experience needed to set up independent shops.

Despite the risk of antagonizing craftspeople, other fledgling American industries increased productivity by combining small technological advances with an imposition of industrial discipline and a reorganization of the manufacturing process through the division of labor. Connecticut clockmakers, for example, increased output by applying water power to conventional drills and lathes and by introducing templates, gauges, and pattern pieces for measuring parts. Craftspeople lacking such tools had built the entire works of every clock, custom shaping each piece to ensure proper operation. Now each worker could use the pattern piece to shape a single interchangeable part for later assembly. By 1820, the new division of labor was enabling the workers of a small factory to turn out more clocks in a month than a traditional clockmaker could produce in a lifetime.

Where imposition of labor discipline had undermined the craftsperson's traditional independence, specialization threatened to reduce his or her competence to a small portion of a manufacturing process that the worker had earlier performed in its entirety. The decrease in requisite skills often undermined wages by enabling employers to hire unskilled workers for simple tasks formerly carried out by craftspeople.

Gunsmiths at the federal armory in Harpers Ferry, Virginia, were keenly aware of this and carried on a running battle with the federal Ordinance Department to prevent mechanization of their trade. The secretary of war and his chief of ordinance, however, were anxious on their part to increase efficiency and to develop guns with interchangeable parts that could be repaired quickly on the field. True interchangeability eluded arms manufacturers until 1830, but the drive for uniformity and efficiency fostered technological advances that enabled Harpers Ferry manager James Stubblefield to employ extensive specialization. Where the armory had begun operations in the 1790s with a threefold division of labor, by 1816 Stubblefield

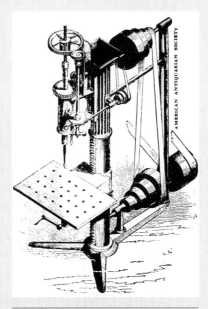

Drill presses like the one shown here were used in musket factories to make identical, interchangeable parts.

doubled the productivity of his work force by increasing to fifty-five the number of specialized tasks involved in manufacturing each gun.

While Stubblefield's gunsmiths acquiesced in the division of labor, they clung to many of their traditional craft prerogatives. Armorers resisted changes in labor discipline, retaining control of their own hours, working at their own pace, taking frequent holidays and drinking on the job. They welcomed machines such as a new barrel lathe, which improved work conditions by replacing a dangerous method. Yet older craftspeople, refusing to become "slaves of machines," continued practicing much that they had learned in Pennsylvania workshops. Metalworkers still hand-welded barrels long after other arms manufacturers were welding by machine. Woodworkers, scorning stock-turning lathes, meticulously hand-carved and custom-fitted each stock to its barrel until the 1830s. Yankee technicians sent to introduce machine-assisted processes at Harpers Ferry complained of poor treatment and sabotaged equipment.

Such behavior slowed but did not halt mechanization and the division of labor. By 1825, even Thomas Jefferson was boasting of "manufactures . . . now very nearly on a footing with those of England." Yet his early admonition—that Americans not sacrifice personal independence merely to achieve independence from foreign manufactured goods—voiced a deep-rooted ambivalence toward the new methods of production that has persisted into the modern age.

Georgetown and Federal City (which would later be renamed Washington, D.C.) are visible in this 1801 view of the Potomac. The Capitol moved here from Philadelphia in 1800, during John Adams's presidency.

international war closed foreign markets, however, the flow of funds dried up.

To help pay the debt inherited from the Adams administration, Jefferson ordered substantial cuts in the national budget. The president closed several American embassies in Europe. He also slashed military spending. In his first term, Jefferson reduced the size of the U.S. Army by 50 percent. This decision left only three thousand soldiers to guard the entire frontier. In addition, he retired a majority of the navy's warships. When New Englanders claimed these cuts left the country defenseless, Jefferson countered with a disarming argument. As ships of the U.S. Navy sailed the world's oceans, he claimed, they were liable to provoke hostilities, perhaps even war; hence by reducing the size of the fleet, he promoted peace.

More than budgetary considerations prompted Jefferson's military reductions. He was deeply suspicious of standing armies. In the event of foreign attack, he reasoned, the militia would rise in defense of the republic. No doubt, his experiences during the Revolution influenced his thinking on military affairs, for in 1776, an aroused populace had taken up arms against the British. To ensure that the citizen soldiers would receive professional leadership in battle, Jefferson created the Army Corps of Engineers and the military academy at West Point in 1802.

Political patronage was a great burden to the new president. Loyal Republicans throughout the United States had worked hard for Jefferson's victory, and as soon as he took office, they stormed the executive mansion seeking federal employment. While the president controlled several hundred jobs, he refused to dismiss all the Federalists. To be sure, he acted quickly to remove the so-called midnight appointees, highly partisan selections that Adams had made after learning of Jefferson's election. But to transform federal hiring into an undisciplined spoils system, especially at the highest levels of the federal bureaucracy, seemed to Jefferson to be shortsighted. Moderate Federalists might be converted to the Republican party, and in any case, there was a good chance they possessed the expertise needed to run the government. At the end of his first term, one-half of the people holding office were appointees of Washington and Adams.

Jefferson's political moderation helped hasten the demise of the Federalist party. This loose organization had nearly destroyed itself during the election of 1800 (see Chapter 7), and following Adams's defeat, prominent Federalist spokesmen such as Fisher Ames and John Jay withdrew from national affairs. They refused to adopt the popular forms of campaigning that the Republicans had developed so successfully during the late 1790s. The mere prospect of flattering the common people was odious enough to drive some Federalists into political retirement.

Many of them also sensed that national expansion worked against their interests. The creation of new states and congressional reapportionment inevitably seemed to increase the number of Republican representatives in Washington. By 1805, the Federalists retained only a few seats in New England and Delaware. "The power of the [Jefferson] Administration," confessed John Quincy Adams in 1802, "rests upon the support of a much stronger majority of the people throughout the Union than the former administrations ever possessed since the first establishment of the Constitution."

After 1804, a group of younger Federalists belatedly attempted to pump life into the dying party. They experimented with popular election techniques. In some states they tightened party organization, held nominating conventions, and campaigned energetically for office. These were essential reforms, but with the exception of a brief Federalist revival in the Northeast between 1807 and 1814, the results of these activities were disappointing. Even the younger Federalists felt it was demeaning to appeal for votes. The diehards like Timothy Pickering promoted wild secessionist schemes in New England, while the most promising moderates—John Quincy Adams, for example—joined the Republicans.

The Louisiana Purchase

When Jefferson first took office, he was confident that Louisiana as well as Florida would eventually become part of the United States. After all, Spain owned the territory, and Jefferson assumed he could persuade the rulers of that notoriously weak nation to sell their colonies. If that peaceful strategy failed, the president was prepared to threaten forceable occupation.

In May 1801, however, prospects for the easy or inevitable acquisition of Louisiana suddenly darkened. Jefferson learned that Spain had secretly transferred title to the entire region to France, its powerful northern neighbor. To make matters worse, the French leader Napoleon seemed intent on reestablishing an empire in North America. Even as Jefferson sought additional information concerning the details of the transfer, Napoleon was dispatching a large army to put down a rebellion in France's sugar-rich Caribbean colony, Haiti. From that island stronghold in the West Indies, French troops could occupy New Orleans and close the Mississippi River to American trade.

A sense of crisis enveloped Washington. Some congressmen urged Jefferson to prepare for war

President Jefferson recognized the strategic location of New Orleans and determined to buy it from the French. By 1803, when this view was painted, New Orleans was already a thriving port and an important outlet for products from the growing frontier.

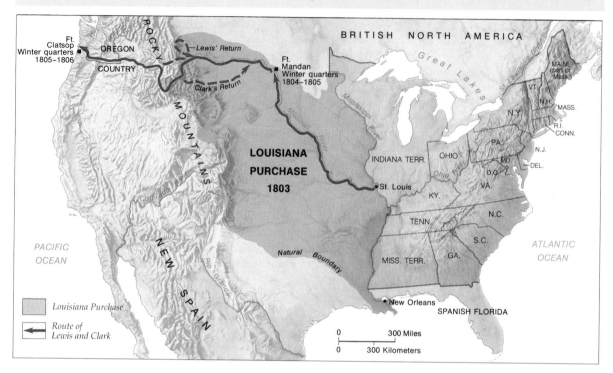

The Louisiana Purchase and the Route of Lewis and Clark

Not until Lewis and Clark had explored the far West did citizens of the United States realize just how much territory Jefferson had acquired through the Louisiana Purchase.

against France. Tensions increased when the Spanish officials who still governed New Orleans announced the closing of that port to American commerce (October 1802). Jefferson and his advisers assumed the Spanish had acted on orders from France, but despite this serious provocation, the president preferred negotiations to war. In January 1803, he asked James Monroe, a loyal Republican from Virginia, to join the American minister, Robert Livingston, in Paris. The president instructed the two men to explore the possibility of purchasing the city of New Orleans. Lest they underestimate the importance of their diplomatic mission, Jefferson reminded them, "There is on the globe one single spot, the possessor of which is our natural and habitual enemy. It is New Orleans." If Livingston and Monroe failed, Jefferson realized he would be forced to turn to Great Britain for military assistance. Dependence on that country seemed repellent, but he recognized that as soon as French troops moved into Louisiana, "we must marry ourselves to the British fleet and nation."

By the time Monroe joined Livingston in France, Napoleon had lost interest in establishing an American empire. The army he sent to Haiti succumbed to tropical diseases. By the end of 1802, over thirty thousand veteran troops had died. In a fit of disgust, Napoleon announced, "Damn sugar, damn coffee, damn colonies . . . I renounce Louisiana." The diplomats from the United States knew nothing of these developments. They were taken by complete surprise, therefore, when they learned that Talleyrand, the French minister for foreign relations, had offered to sell the entire Louisiana Territory in April 1803. For only $15 million, the Americans doubled the size of the United States. In fact, Livingston and Monroe were not certain how much land they had actually purchased. When they asked Talleyrand whether the deal included Florida, he responded ambiguously, "You have made a noble bargain for yourselves, and I suppose you will make the most of it." Even at that moment, Livingston realized the transaction would alter the course of American history.

"From this day," he wrote, "the United States take their place among the powers of first rank."

The American people responded enthusiastically to news of the Louisiana Purchase. The only criticism came from a few disgruntled Federalists in New England who thought the United States was already too large. Jefferson, of course, was immensely relieved. The nation had avoided war with France. Nevertheless, he worried that the treaty might be unconstitutional. The president pointed out that the Constitution did not specifically authorize the acquisition of vast new territories and the incorporation of thousands of foreign citizens. To escape this apparent legal dilemma, Jefferson proposed an amendment to the Constitution. Few persons, even his closest advisers, shared the president's scruples. Events in France soon forced Jefferson to adopt a more pragmatic course. When he heard that Napoleon had become impatient for his money, Jefferson rushed the treaty to a Senate eager to ratify the agreement, and nothing more was said about amending the Constitution.

Jefferson's fears about the incorporation of this new territory were not unwarranted. The area that eventually became the state of Louisiana (1812) contained many people of French and Spanish background who possessed no familiarity with representative institutions. Their laws had been autocratic; their local government corrupt. To allow such persons to elect a representative assembly struck the president as dangerous. He did not even know whether the population of Louisiana would remain loyal to the United States. Jefferson, therefore, recommended to Congress a transitional government consisting entirely of appointed officials. In March 1804, the Louisiana Government Bill narrowly passed the House of Representatives. Members of the president's own party attacked the plan. After all, it imposed taxes on the citizens of Louisiana without their consent. According to one outspoken Tennessee congressman, the bill "establishes a complete despotism." Most troubling perhaps was the fact that the legislation ran counter to Jefferson's well-known republican principles.

The Lewis and Clark Expedition

In the midst of the Louisiana controversy, Jefferson dispatched a secret message to Congress requesting $2,500 for the exploration of the Far West (January 1803). How closely this decision was connected to the Paris negotiations is not clear. Whatever the case may have been, the president asked his talented private secretary, Meriwether Lewis, to discover whether the Missouri River "may offer the most direct & practicable water communication across this continent for the purposes of commerce." The president also regarded the expedition as a wonderful opportunity to collect precise data about flora and fauna. He personally instructed Lewis in the latest techniques of scientific observation. While preparing for this great adventure, Lewis's second-in-command, William Clark, assumed such a prominent role that the effort became known as the Lewis and Clark Expedition. The exploring party set out from St. Louis in May 1804, and after barely surviving crossing the snow-covered Rocky Mountains, with their food supply running dangerously low, the Americans reached the Pacific Ocean in November 1805. The group returned safely the following September. The results of this expedition not only fulfilled Jefferson's scientific expectations, but also reaffirmed his faith in the future economic prosperity of the United States.

Conflict with the Barbary States

During this period, Jefferson dealt with another problem. For several decades, Morocco, Algiers, Tripoli, and Tunis—the Barbary States—had preyed on commercial shipping. Most European nations paid these pirates tribute, hoping thereby to protect merchants trading in the Mediterranean. In 1801, Jefferson, responding to Tripoli's increased demand for tribute, decided this extortion had become intolerable, and dispatched a small fleet to the Barbary Coast, where according to one commander, the Americans intended to negotiate "through the mouth of a cannon." Tripoli put up stiff resistance, however, and in one mismanaged engagement it captured the U. S. frigate *Philadelphia*. Ransoming the crew cost Jefferson's government another $60,000. An American land assault across the Libyan desert provided inspiration for the words of the Marine hymn—"to the shores of Tripoli"—but no smashing victory.

Despite a generally unimpressive American military record, a vigorous naval blockade

The large drawing at right is from the 1812 edition of Patrick Gass's Journal, *one of the first authentic accounts of Lewis and Clark's expedition. Samples of the drawings Clark made in his field diary include one of a salmon trout and a diagram showing how the Chinook flattened their infants' heads by binding them between two boards.*

brought hostilities to a conclusion. In 1805, the president signed a treaty formally ending the Barbary War. One diplomat crowed, "It must be mortifying to some of the neighboring European powers to see that the Barbary States have been taught their first lessons of humiliation from the Western World."

Jefferson concluded his first term on a wave of popularity. He had maintained the peace, reduced taxes, and expanded the boundaries of the United States. Not surprisingly, he overwhelmed his Federalist opponent in the presidential election of 1804. In the electoral college, Jefferson received 162 votes to Charles Cotesworth Pinckney's 14. Republicans controlled Congress. John Randolph, the most articulate member of the House of Representatives, exclaimed, "Never was there an administration more brilliant than that of Mr.

Jefferson up to this period. We were indeed in 'the full tide of successful experiment!'"

SOURCES OF POLITICAL DISSENSION

At the moment of Jefferson's greatest electoral victory, a perceptive person might have seen signs of serious division within the Republican party and within the country. The president's heavy-handed attempts to reform the federal courts stirred deep animosities. Republicans had begun sniping at other Republicans, and one leading member of the party, Aaron Burr, became involved in a bizarre plot to separate the West from the rest of the nation. Congressional debates over the future of the slave trade revealed the

The Barbary States

In 1801, President Jefferson refused to continue paying the tribute that pirates of the Barbary States had received for decades.

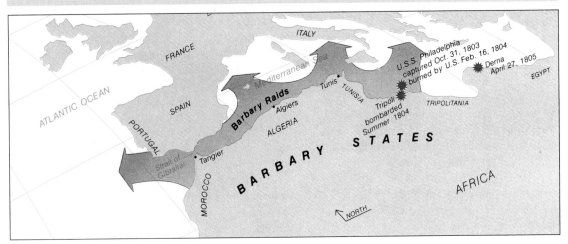

Attack on the Judges

Jefferson's controversy with the federal bench commenced the moment he first became president. The Federalists, realizing they would soon lose control over the executive branch, had passed the Judiciary Act of 1801. This bill created several circuit courts and sixteen new judgeships. Through his "midnight" appointments, Adams had quickly filled these positions with stalwarts of the Federalist party. Such blatantly partisan behavior angered Jefferson. In the courts, he explained, the Federalists hoped to preserve their political influence, and "from that battery all the works of Republicanism are to be beaten down and erased." Even more infuriating was Adams's appointment of John Marshall as the new chief justice. This shrewd, largely self-educated Virginian of Federalist background, whose training in the law consisted of a series of lectures he attended at William and Mary College in 1780, was clearly a man who could hold his own against the new president.

In January 1802, Jefferson's congressional allies called for repeal of the Judiciary Act. In public debate they studiously avoided the obvious political issue. The new circuit courts should be closed not only because they were staffed by Federalists but also, as they argued, because they were needlessly expensive. The judges did not hear enough cases to warrant continuance. The Federalists mounted an able defense. The Constitution, they observed, provided for the removal of federal judges only when they were found guilty of high crimes and misdemeanors. By repealing the Judiciary Act, the legislative branch would in effect be dismissing judges without a trial, a clear violation of their constitutional rights. This argument made little impression on the Republican party. In March, the House, following the Senate, voted for repeal.

While Congress debated the Judiciary Act, another battle erupted. One of Adams's "midnight" appointees, William Marbury, complained that the new administration would not give him his commission for the office of justice of the peace for the District of Columbia. He sought redress before the Supreme Court, demanding that the federal justices compel James Madison, the secretary of state, to deliver the necessary papers. When they learned that Marshall had agreed to hear this case, the Republicans were furious. Apparently the chief justice wanted to provoke a confrontation with the executive branch.

Marshall was too clever to jeopardize the independence of the Supreme Court over this relatively minor issue. In his celebrated *Marbury* v. *Madison* decision (February 1803), Marshall

The Election of 1804

Candidate	Party	Electoral Vote
Jefferson	Republican	162
Pinckney	Federalist	14

berated the secretary of state for withholding Marbury's commission. Nevertheless, he concluded that the Supreme Court did not possess jurisdiction over such matters. Poor Marbury was out of luck. The Republicans proclaimed victory. In fact, they were so pleased with the outcome, they failed to examine the logic of Marshall's decision. He had ruled that part of the earlier act of Congress, the one on which Marbury based his appeal, was unconstitutional. This was the first time the Supreme Court asserted its right to judge the constitutionality of congressional acts, and while contemporaries did not fully appreciate the significance of Marshall's doctrine, *Marbury* v. *Madison* later served as an important precedent for judicial review of federal statutes.

Neither Marbury's defeat nor repeal of the Judiciary Act placated extreme Republicans. They insisted that federal judges should be made more responsive to the will of the people. One solution, short of electing federal judges, was impeachment. This clumsy device provided the legislature with a way of removing particularly offensive individuals. Early in 1803, John Pickering, an incompetent judge from New Hampshire, presented the Republicans with a curious test case. This Federalist appointee suffered from alcoholism as well as insanity. While his outrageous behavior on the bench embarrassed everyone, Pickering had not committed any high crimes against the U. S. government. Ignoring such legal niceties, Jefferson's congressional allies pushed for impeachment. Although the Senate convicted Pickering (March 1804), many senators refused to compromise the letter of the Constitution and were conspicuously absent on the day of the final vote.

Jefferson was apparently so eager to purge the courts of Federalists that he failed to heed these warnings. By the spring of 1803, he had set his sights on a target far more important than John Pickering. In a Baltimore newspaper, the presi-

dent stumbled on the transcript of a speech allegedly delivered before a federal grand jury. The words seemed almost treasonous. The person responsible was Samuel Chase, a justice of the Supreme Court, who had frequently attacked Republican policies. Jefferson leapt at the chance to remove Chase from office. Indeed, the moment he learned of Chase's actions, the president wrote to a leading Republican congressman, asking, "Ought the seditious and official attack on the principles of our Constitution . . . go unpunished?" The congressman took the hint. In a matter of weeks, the Republican-controlled House of Representatives indicted Chase.

Even at this early stage of the impeachment, some members of Congress expressed uneasiness. The charges drawn up against the judge were purely political. There was no doubt the judge's speech had been indiscreet. He had told the Baltimore jurors that "our late reformers"—in other words, the Republicans—threatened "peace and order, freedom and property." But while Chase lacked good judgment, his attack on the Jefferson administration hardly seemed criminal. Nathaniel Macon, a powerful Republican congressman from North Carolina, wondered aloud, "Is error of opinion to be dreaded where enquiry is free?" This was the sort of question that Jefferson himself had asked the Federalists following passage of the Alien and Sedition Acts, but in 1804, Macon went unanswered. It was clear that if the Senate convicted Chase, every member of the Supreme Court, including Marshall, might also be dismissed.

Chase's trial before the U. S. Senate was one of the most dramatic events in American legal history. Aaron Burr, the vice president, organized the proceedings. For reasons known only to himself, Burr redecorated the Senate chamber so that it looked more like the British House of Lords than the meeting place of a republican legislature. In this luxurious setting, Chase and his lawyers conducted a masterful defense. By contrast, John Randolph, the congressman who served as chief prosecutor, behaved in an erratic manner, betraying repeatedly his ignorance of relevant points of law. While most Republican senators personally disliked the arrogant Chase, they refused to expand the constitutional definition of impeachable offenses to suit Randolph's argument, and on March 1, 1805, the Senate acquitted the jus-

REPORT
OF THE
T R I A L
OF THE
HON. SAMUEL CHASE,
ONE OF THE ASSOCIATE JUSTICES
OF THE
SUPREME COURT OF THE UNITED STATES,
BEFORE THE
HIGH COURT OF IMPEACHMENT,
COMPOSED OF THE
Senate of the United States,
FOR CHARGES EXHIBITED AGAINST HIM BY THE
HOUSE OF REPRESENTATIVES,
In the name of themselves, and of all the People of the United States,
FOR
HIGH CRIMES & MISDEMEANORS,
SUPPOSED TO HAVE BEEN BY HIM COMMITTED;
WITH THE NECESSARY
DOCUMENTS AND OFFICIAL PAPERS,
From his Impeachment to final Acquital.

TAKEN IN SHORT HAND,
BY CHARLES EVANS,
AND THE ARGUMENTS OF COUNSEL REVISED BY THEM
FROM HIS MANUSCRIPT.

BALTIMORE:
PRINTED FOR SAMUEL BUTLER AND GEORGE KEATINGE.
1805.

Presiding officer Aaron Burr ordered extra seating installed in the Senate chamber to accommodate the spectators who attended Justice Chase's impeachment trial.

tice of all charges. The experience apparently convinced Chase of the need for greater moderation. After returning to the federal bench, he refrained from attacking Republican policies. His Jeffersonian opponents also learned something important. American politicians did not like tampering with the Constitution in order to get rid of specific judges, even an imprudent one like Chase.

Politics of Desperation

The collapse of the Federalists on the national level encouraged dissension within the Republican party. Extremists in Congress insisted on monopolizing the president's ear, and when he listened to political moderates, they rebelled. The members of the most vociferous faction called themselves "the *good old* republicans"; the newspapers labeled them the "Tertium Quids," loosely translated as "nothings" or "No Accounts." During Jefferson's second term, the Quids argued that the president's policies, foreign and domestic, sacrificed virtue for pragmatism. Their chief spokesmen were two members from Virginia, John Randolph and John Taylor of Caroline (the name of his plantation), both of whom were convinced that Jefferson had betrayed the republican purity of the Founding Fathers. They both despised commercial capitalism. Taylor urged Americans to return to a simple agrarian way of life. Randolph's attacks were particularly shrill. He saved his sharpest barbs for Gallatin and Madison, Republican moderates who failed to appreciate the congressman's self-righteous posturing.

The Yazoo controversy raised the Quids from political obscurity. This complex legal battle began in 1795 when a thoroughly corrupt Georgia assembly sold 35 million acres of western land, known as the Yazoo claims, to private companies at bargain prices. It soon became apparent that every member of the legislature had been bribed, and in 1796, state lawmakers rescinded the entire agreement. Unfortunately, some land had already changed hands. When Jefferson became president, a specially appointed federal commission attempted to clean up the mess. It recommended that Congress set aside 5 million acres for buyers who had unwittingly purchased land from the discredited companies.

Randolph immediately cried foul. Such a compromise, however well meaning, condoned fraud. Republican virtue hung in the balance. For months the Quids harangued Congress about the Yazoo business, but in the end their impassioned oratory accomplished nothing. The Marshall Supreme Court upheld the rights of the original purchasers in *Fletcher* v. *Peck* (1810). The justices unanimously declared that legislative fraud did not impair private contracts and that the Georgia assembly of 1796 did not have authority to take away lands already sold to innocent buyers. This important case upheld the Supreme Court's authority to rule on the constitutionality of state laws.

The Burr Conspiracy

Vice President Aaron Burr created far more serious difficulties for the president. The two men had never been close. Burr's strange behavior during the election of 1800 (see Chapter 7) raised suspicions that he had conspired to deprive Jefferson of the presidency. Whatever the truth may have been, the vice president entered the new administration under a cloud. He played only a marginal role in shaping policy, a situation extremely frustrating for a person as ambitious as Burr.

In the spring of 1804, Burr decided to run for the governorship of New York. Although he was a Republican, he entered into political negotiations with High Federalists who were plotting the secession of New England and New York from the Union. In a particularly scurrilous contest—and New York politics were always abusive—Alexander Hamilton described Burr as ". . . a dangerous man . . . who ought not to be trusted with the reins of government" and urged Federalists in the state to vote for another candidate.

Whether Hamilton's appeals influenced the voters is not clear. Burr, however, blamed Hamilton for his subsequent defeat and challenged his tormentor to a duel. Even though Hamilton condemned this form of violence—his own son had recently been killed in a duel—he accepted Burr's "invitation." On July 11, 1804, at Weehawken, New Jersey, the vice president shot and killed the former secretary of the treasury. Both New York and New Jersey indicted Burr for murder. If he returned to either state, he would immediately be arrested. His political career lay in shambles.

In his final weeks as vice president, Burr hatched a scheme so audacious that the people with whom he dealt could not decide whether he was a genius or a madman. On a trip down the Ohio River in April 1805 after his term as vice president was over, he hinted broadly that he was planning a private military adventure against a Spanish colony, perhaps Mexico. Burr also suggested that he envisioned separating the western states and territories from the Union. The region certainly seemed ripe for secession. The citizens of New Orleans acted as if they wanted no part of the United States. Burr covered his tracks well.

Frustrated in his attempt to win national political power, Aaron Burr initiated a series of maneuvers that led eventually to his downfall.

No two contacts ever heard the same story. Wherever Burr traveled, he recruited adventurers; he mingled with the leading politicians of Kentucky, Ohio, and Tennessee. James Wilkinson, commander of the U. S. Army in the Mississippi Valley, accepted an important role in this vaguely defined conspiracy. The general was a thoroughly corrupt opportunist. Randolph described him as "the only man that I ever saw who was from bark to the very core a villain."

In the late summer of 1806, Burr put his ill-defined plan into action. A small group of volunteers constructed riverboats on a small island in the Ohio River owned by Harman Blennerhassett, an Irish immigrant who found Burr's charm irresistible. By the time this armed band set out to join Wilkinson's forces, however, the general had experienced a change of heart. He frantically dispatched letters to Jefferson denouncing Burr.

Wilkinson's betrayal destroyed any chance of success, and conspirators throughout the West rushed pell-mell to save their own skins. Facing certain defeat, Burr tried to escape to Spanish Florida. It was already too late. Federal authorities arrested Burr in February 1807 and took him to Richmond to stand trial for treason. The prospect of humiliating his old rival was hardly displeasing to the president. Even before a jury had been called, Jefferson announced publicly that Burr's guilt "is placed beyond all question."

Jefferson spoke prematurely. John Adams wisely observed, if Burr's "guilt is as clear as the Noon day Sun, the first Magistrate ought not to have pronounced it so before a Jury had tryed him." The trial judge was John Marshall, a strong Federalist not likely to do the Republican administration any favors. During the entire proceedings, Marshall insisted on a narrow constitutional definition of treason. He refused to hear testimony regarding Burr's supposed intentions. "Troops must be embodied," Marshall thundered, "men must be actually assembled." He demanded two witnesses to each overt act of treason.

Burr, of course, had been too clever to leave this sort of evidence. While Jefferson complained bitterly about the miscarriage of justice, the jurors declared on September 1, 1807, that the defendant was "not proved guilty by any evidence submitted to us." The public was outraged, and Burr prudently went into exile in Europe. The president threatened to introduce an amendment to the Constitution calling for the election of federal judges. Nothing came of his proposal. And Marshall, who behaved in an undeniably partisan manner, inadvertently helped protect the civil rights of all Americans. If the chief justice had allowed circumstantial evidence into the Richmond courtroom, if he had listened to rumor and hearsay, he would have made it much easier for later presidents to use trumped-up conspiracy charges to silence legitimate political opposition.

The Slave Trade

Slavery sparked angry debate at the Constitutional Convention of 1787 (see Chapter 6). If delegates from the northern states had refused to compromise on this issue, Southerners would not have supported the new government. The slave states demanded a great deal in return for cooperation. According to an agreement that determined the size of a state's congressional delegation, a slave counted as three-fifths of a free white male. This political formula meant that while blacks did not vote, they helped increase the number of southern representatives. The South in turn gave up very little, agreeing only that after 1808 Congress *might consider* banning the importation of slaves into the United States. Slaves even influenced the outcome of national elections. Had the three-fifths rule not been in effect in 1800, for example, Adams would surely have had the votes to defeat Jefferson in the electoral college.

In an annual message sent to Congress in December 1806, Jefferson urged the representatives to prepare legislation outlawing the slave trade. During the early months of 1807, congressmen debated various ways of ending this embarrassing commerce. It was clear that the issue cut across party lines. Northern representatives generally favored a strong bill; some even wanted to make smuggling slaves into the country a capital offense. But there was a serious problem. The northern congressmen could not figure out what to do with black people captured by the customs agents who would enforce the legislation. To sell these Africans would involve the federal government in slavery, which many Northerners found morally repugnant. Nor was there much sympathy for freeing them. Ignorant of the English language and lacking personal possessions, it seemed unlikely that these blacks could long survive free in the American South.

Southern congressmen responded with threats and ridicule. They explained to their northern colleagues that no one in the South regarded slavery as evil. It appeared naive, therefore, to expect local planters to enforce a ban on the slave trade or to inform federal agents when they spotted a smuggler. The notion that these culprits deserved capital punishment seemed viciously inappropriate. At one point in the debate, Peter Early, a congressman from Georgia, announced that the South wanted "no civil wars, no rebellions, no insurrections, no resistance to the authority of government." All he demanded, in fact, was to let the *states* regulate slavery. To this, a Republican congressman from western Pennsylvania retorted that Americans who hated slavery would not be "terrified by the threat of civil war."

The bill that Jefferson finally signed in March 1807 probably pleased no one. The law prohibited the importation of slaves into the United States after the new year. Whenever customs officials captured a smuggler, the slaves were turned over to state authorities and disposed of according to local custom. Southerners did not cooperate, and for many years African slaves continued to pour into southern ports. Even more blacks would have been imported had Great Britain not outlawed the slave trade in 1807. As part of their ban of the slave trade, ships of the Royal Navy captured American slave smugglers off the coast of Africa, and when anyone complained, the British explained that they were merely enforcing the laws of the United States.

FAILURE OF FOREIGN POLICY

During Jefferson's second term (1805–1809), the United States found itself in the midst of a world at war. A brief peace in Europe ended abruptly in 1803, and the two military giants of the age, France and Great Britain, fought for supremacy on land and sea. This was a kind of total war unknown in the eighteenth century. Napoleon's armies carried the ideology of the French Revolution across the Continent. The emperor—as Napoleon Bonaparte called himself after December 1804—transformed conquered nations into French satellites. Only Britain offered effective resistance. On October 21, 1805, Admiral Horatio Nelson destroyed the main French fleet at the battle of Trafalgar, demonstrating decisively the absolute supremacy of the Royal Navy. But only a few weeks later (December 2, 1805), Napoleon crushed Britain's allies, Austria and Russia, at the battle of Austerlitz and confirmed his clear superiority on land.

During the early stages of the war, the United States profited from European adversity. As "neutral carriers," American ships transported goods to any port in the world where they could find a buyer, and American merchants grew wealthy serving Britain and France. Since the Royal Navy did not allow direct trade between France and its colonies, American captains conducted "broken voyages." American vessels sailing out of French ports in the Caribbean would put in briefly in the United States, pay nominal customs, and then leave for France. For several years, the British did little to halt this obvious subterfuge.

Napoleon's successes on the battlefield, however, quickly strained Britain's economic resources. In July 1805, a British admiralty court announced in the *Essex* decision that henceforth "broken voyages" were illegal. The Royal Navy began seizing American ships in record number. Moreover, as the war continued, the British stepped up the impressment of sailors on ships flying the U. S. flag. Estimates of the number of men impressed ranged as high as nine thousand.

Beginning in 1806, the British government issued a series of trade regulations known as "Orders in Council." These proclamations forbade neutral commerce with the Continent and threatened any ship that violated these orders with seizure. The declarations created what were in effect "paper blockades," for even the powerful British navy could not monitor the activities of every Continental port.

Napoleon responded to Britain's commercial regulations with his own "paper blockade," called the Continental System. In the Berlin Decree of November 1806 and the Milan Decree of December 1807, he announced the closing of all Continental ports to British trade. Since French armies occupied most of the territory between Spain and Germany, the decrees obviously cut the British out of a large market. The French emperor also declared that neutral vessels carrying British goods were liable to seizure. For the Americans there was no escape. They were caught between two conflicting systems. The British ordered American ships to stop off to pay duties and secure clearances in England on the way to the Continent; Napoleon was determined to seize any vessel that obeyed the British.

This unhappy turn of international events baffled Jefferson. He had assumed that civilized countries would respect neutral rights; justice obliged them to do so. Appeals to reason, however, made little impression on states at war. "As for France and England," the president growled, ". . . the one is a den of robbers, the other of pirates." In a desperate attempt to avoid hostilities for which the United States was ill prepared, Jefferson ordered James Monroe and William Pinckney to negotiate a commercial treaty with Great Britain. The document they signed on

December 31, 1806, said nothing about impressment, and an angry president refused to submit the treaty to the Senate for ratification.

The United States soon suffered an even greater humiliation. A ship of the Royal Navy, the *Leopard,* sailing off the coast of Virginia, commanded an American warship to submit to a search for deserters (June 22, 1807). When the captain of the *Chesapeake* refused to cooperate, the *Leopard* opened fire, killing three men and wounding eighteen. The attack clearly violated the sovereignty of the United States. Official protests received only a perfunctory apology from the British government, and the American people demanded revenge.

Despite the pressure of public opinion, however, Jefferson played for time. He recognized that the United States was unprepared for war against a powerful nation like Great Britain. The president worried that an expensive conflict with Great Britain would quickly undo the fiscal reforms of his first term. As Gallatin explained, in the event of war the United States "will be poorer, both as a nation and as a government, our debt and taxes will increase, and our progress in every respect be interrupted."

Embargo Divides the Nation

Jefferson found what he regarded as a satisfactory way to deal with European predators with a policy he called "peaceable coercion." If Britain and France refused to respect the rights of neutral carriers, then the United States would keep its ships at home. Not only would this action protect them from seizure, it would also deprive the European powers of much needed American goods, especially food. The president predicted that a total embargo of American commerce would soon force Britain and France to negotiate with the United States in good faith. "Our commerce is so valuable to them," he declared, "that they will be glad to purchase it when the only price we ask is to do us justice." Congress passed the Embargo Act by large majorities, and it became law on December 22, 1807.

"Peaceable coercion" turned into a Jeffersonian nightmare. The president apparently believed the American people would enthusiastically support the embargo. That was a naive assumption. Compliance required a series of enforcement acts that over fourteen months became increasingly harsh.

By the middle of 1808, Jefferson and Gallatin were involved in the regulation of the smallest details of American economic life. Indeed, in the words of one of Jefferson's biographers, the president assumed the role of "commissar of the nation's economy." The federal government supervised the coastal trade, lest a ship sailing between two states slip away to Europe or the West Indies. Overland trade with Canada was proscribed. When violations still occurred, Congress gave customs collectors the right to seize a vessel merely on suspicion of wrongdoing. A final desperate act, passed in January 1809, prohibited the loading of any U. S. vessel, regardless of size, without authorization from a customs officer who was supported by the army, navy, and local militia. Jefferson's eagerness to pursue a reasonable foreign policy blinded him to the fact that he and a Republican Congress would have had to establish a police state to make it work.

Northerners hated the embargo. Persons living near Lake Champlain in upper New York state simply ignored the regulations, and they roughed up collectors who interfered with the Canadian trade. The administration was determined to stop the smugglers. Jefferson urged the governor of

The Ograb me (embargo spelled backwards) snapping turtle, created by cartoonist Alexander Anderson, is shown here grabbing at an American tobacco smuggler who is breaking the embargo.

New York to call out the militia. "I think it so important," the president explained in August 1808, ". . . to crush these audacious proceedings, and to make the offenders feel the consequences of individuals daring to oppose a law by force, that no effort should be spared to compass the object." In a decision that Hamilton might have applauded, Jefferson dispatched federal troops—led by the conspiratorial General Wilkinson—to overawe the citizens of New York.

New Englanders regarded the embargo as lunacy. Merchants of the region were willing to take their chances on the high seas, but for reasons that few people understood, the president insisted that it was better to preserve ships from possible seizure than to make profits. Sailors and artisans were thrown out of work. The popular press maintained a constant howl of protest. One writer observed that embargo in reverse spelled "O grab me!" A poem published in July 1808 captured the growing frustration:

> Our ships, all in motion,
> Once whitened the ocean,
>   They sail'd and returned with a cargo;
> Now doom'd to decay
> They have fallen a prey
>   To Jefferson, worms, and Embargo.

Dolly Madison, in a portrait by Gilbert Stuart, 1804, host-ed popular informal entertainments at the White House.

Not surprisingly, the Federalist party experienced a brief revival in New England, and a few extremists suggested the possibility of state assemblies nullifying federal law.

By 1809, the bankruptcy of Jefferson's foreign policy was obvious. The embargo never seriously damaged the British economy. In fact, British merchants rushed to take over the lucrative markets that the Americans had been forced to abandon. Napoleon liked the embargo, since it seemed to harm Great Britain more than it did France. Faced with growing popular opposition, the Republicans in Congress panicked. One newly elected representative declared that "peaceful coercion" was a "miserable and mischievous failure" and joined his colleagues in repealing the embargo a few days before James Madison's inauguration. Relations between the United States and the great European powers were much worse in 1809 than they had been in 1805. During his

second term, the pressures of office weighed heavily on Jefferson, and after so many years of public service, he welcomed retirement to Monticello.

A New Administration Goes to War

As president, James Madison suffered from several personal and political handicaps. Although his intellectual abilities were great, he lacked the qualities necessary for effective leadership. In public gatherings, he impressed people as being "exceedingly modest," and one foreign visitor claimed that the new president ". . . always seems to grant that the one with whom he talks is his superior in mind and training." Critics argued that Madison's humility revealed a weak, vacillating character.

During the election of 1808, Randolph and the Quids tried unsuccessfully to persuade James

The Election of 1808		
Candidate	Party	Electoral Vote
Madison	Republican	122
Pinckney	Federalist	47

Monroe to challenge Madison's candidacy. Jefferson favored his old friend Madison. In the end, a caucus of Republican congressmen gave the official nod to Madison, the first time in American history that such a congressional group controlled a presidential nomination. The former secretary of state defeated his Federalist rival, Charles Cotesworth Pinckney, in the electoral college by a vote of 122 to 47, with New Yorker George Clinton receiving six ballots. The margin of victory was substantially lower than Jefferson's had been in 1804, a warning of political troubles ahead. The Federalists also made impressive gains in the House of Representatives, raising their delegation from 24 to 48.

The new president confronted the same foreign policy problems that had occupied his predecessor. Neither Britain nor France showed the slightest interest in respecting American neutral rights. Threats against either nation rang hollow so long as the United States failed to develop its military strength. Out of weakness, therefore, Madison was compelled to put the Non-Intercourse Act into effect. Congress passed this clumsy piece of legislation at the same time it repealed the embargo (March 1, 1809). The new bill authorized the resumption of trade between the United States and all nations of the world *except* Britain and France. Either of these countries could restore full commercial relations simply by promising to observe the rights of neutral carriers.

The British immediately took advantage of this offer. Their minister to the United States, David M. Erskine, informed Madison that the British government had modified its position on a number of sensitive commercial issues. The president was so encouraged by these talks that he publicly announced that trade with Great Britain could resume in June 1809. Unfortunately, Erskine had not conferred with his superiors on the details of these negotiations. George Canning, the British foreign secretary, rejected the agreement out of

hand, and while an embarrassed Madison fumed in Washington, the Royal Navy seized the American ships that had already put to sea.

Canning's apparent betrayal led the artless Madison straight into a French trap. In May 1810, Congress passed Macon's Bill Number Two, an act sponsored by Nathanial Macon of North Carolina. In a complete reversal of strategy, this poorly drafted legislation reestablished trade with *both* England and France. It also contained a curious carrot-and-stick provision. As soon as either of these European states repealed restrictions upon neutral shipping, the U. S. government promised to halt all commerce with the other.

Napoleon spotted a rare opportunity. He informed the U. S. minister in Paris that France would no longer enforce the hated Berlin and Milan decrees. Again, Madison acted impulsively. Without waiting for further information from Paris, he announced that unless Britain repealed the Orders in Council by November, the United States would cut off commercial relations. Only later did the president learn that Napoleon had no intention of living up to his side of the bargain; his agents continued to seize American ships. Madison, who had been humiliated by the Erskine experience, decided to ignore the French provocations, to pretend the emperor was behaving in an honest manner. The British could not explain why the United States tolerated such obvious deception. No one in London would have suspected that the president really had no other options left.

Events unrelated to international commerce fueled anti-British sentiment in the newly conquered parts of the United States. Westerners believed—incorrectly as it turned out—that British agents operating out of Canada had persuaded Tecumseh's warriors to resist the spread of American settlement. According to the rumors that ran through the region, the British dreamed of monopolizing the fur trade. In any case, General William Henry Harrison, governor of the Indiana Territory, marched an army to the edge of a large Shawnee Village at the mouth of Tippecanoe Creek near the banks of the Wabash River. On the morning of November 7, 1811, the American troops routed the Indians at the battle of Tippecanoe. Harrison immediately became a

This colored lithograph from 1889 commemorates the Battle of Tippecanoe. While Tecumseh was away, Shawnee warriors engaged U. S. troops led by General William Henry Harrison. Although his troops lost more men than did the Shawnee, Harrison claimed the victory.

national hero, and several decades later the American people rewarded "Tippecanoe" by electing him president. This incident forced Tecumseh—a brilliant leader who was trying to restore the confidence and revitalize tribal cultures of the Indians of the Indiana Territory—to seek British military assistance in battling the Americans, something he probably would not have done had Harrison left him alone.

Fumbling Toward Conflict

In 1811, the anti-British mood of Congress intensified. A group of militant representatives, some of them elected to Congress for the first time in the election of 1810, announced they would no longer tolerate national humiliation. They called for action, for resistance to Great Britain, for any course that promised to achieve respect for the United States and security for its republican institutions. These aggressive nationalists, many of them elected in the South and West, have sometimes been labeled the "War Hawks." The group included Henry Clay, an earthy Kentucky congressman who served as Speaker of the House, and John C. Calhoun, a brilliant South Carolinian. These fiery orators spoke of honor and pride, as if foreign relations were a sort of duel between gentlemen. While the War Hawks were Republicans, they repudiated Jefferson's policy of peaceful coercion.

Madison surrendered to the "War Hawks." On June 1, 1812, he sent Congress a declaration of war against Great Britain. The timing of his action was peculiar. Over the preceding months, tensions between the two nations had relaxed. No new attacks had occurred. Indeed, at the very moment Madison called for war, the British government was suspending the Orders in Council, a conciliatory gesture that in all likelihood would have preserved the peace.

However inadequately Madison communicated his goals, he did seem to have had a plan. His major aim was to force the British to respect American maritime rights, especially in Caribbean waters. The president's problem was to figure out how a small, militarily weak nation like the United States could bring effective pressure on Great Britain. Madison's answer seemed to be Canada. This colony supplied Britain's Caribbean possessions with much needed foodstuffs. The president reasoned, therefore, that by threatening to seize Canada, the Americans might compel the British to make concessions on maritime issues. It was this logic that Secretary of State James Monroe had in mind when he explained in June 1812 that "it might be necessary to invade Canada, not as an object of the war but as a means to bring it to a satisfactory conclusion."

Congressional War Hawks, of course, may have had other goals in mind. Some expansionists were probably more concerned about conquering Canada than they were about the impressment of American seamen. For others, the whole affair may have truly been a matter of national pride. Andrew Jackson wrote, *"For what are we going to fight? . . . we are going to fight for the reestablishment of our national character, misunderstood and vilified at home and abroad."* New

Englanders in whose commercial interests the war would supposedly be waged ridiculed such chauvinism. The vote in Congress was close, 79 to 49 in the House, 19 to 13 in the Senate. With this doubtful mandate, the country marched to war against the most powerful maritime nation in Europe. Division over the war question was reflected in the election of 1812. A faction of antiwar Republicans nominated De Witt Clinton of New York, who was endorsed by the Federalists. Nevertheless Madison, the Republican, won narrowly, gaining 128 electoral votes to Clinton's 89.

THE STRANGE WAR
OF 1812

Optimism ran high. The War Hawks apparently believed that even though the United States possessed only a small army and navy, it could easily sweep the British out of Canada. Such predictions flew in the face of political and military realities. Not only did the Republicans fail to appreciate how unprepared the country was for war, they also refused to mobilize needed resources. The House rejected proposals for direct taxes and authorized naval appropriations only with the greatest reluctance. Indeed, even as they planned for battle, the Republican members of Congress were haunted by the consequences of their political and economic convictions. They did not seem to understand that a weak, highly decentralized government—the one that Jeffersonians championed—was incapable of waging an expensive war against the world's greatest sea power.

New Englanders refused to cooperate with the war effort. In July 1812, one clergyman in Massachusetts urged the people of the region to "proclaim an honourable neutrality." Many persons did just that. New Englanders carried on a lucrative, though illegal, commerce with the enemy. When the U. S. Treasury appealed for loans to finance the war, wealthy northern merchants failed to respond. The British government apparently believed the New England states might negotiate a separate peace, and during the first year of war, the Royal Navy did not bother to blockade the major northern ports.

American military operations focused initially on the western forts. The results were discourag-

The Election of 1812

Candidate	Party	Electoral Vote
Madison	Republican	128
Clinton	Republican* (antiwar faction)	89

*Clinton was nominated by a convention of antiwar Republicans and endorsed by the Federalists.

The War of 1812

Major battles of the War of 1812 brought few lasting gains to either the British or the Americans.

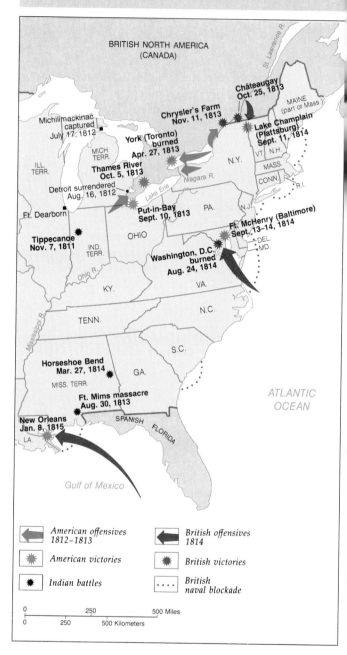

ing. On August 16, 1812, Major General William Hull surrendered an entire army to a smaller British force at Detroit. Michilimackinac was lost. Poorly coordinated marches against the enemy at Niagara and Montreal achieved nothing. These experiences demonstrated that the militia, led by aging officers with little military aptitude, no matter how enthusiastic, was no match for well-trained European veterans. On the sea, the United States did much better. In August, Captain Isaac Hull's *Constitution* defeated the H. M. S. *Guerriere* in a fierce battle, and American privateers destroyed or captured a number of British merchantmen. These successes were somewhat deceptive, however. So long as Napoleon threatened the Continent, Great Britain could spare few warships for service in America. As soon as peace returned to Europe in the spring of 1814, Britain redeployed its fleet and easily blockaded the tiny U. S. Navy.

The campaigns of 1813 revealed that conquering Canada would be more difficult than the War Hawks ever imagined. Both sides in this war recognized that whoever controlled the Great Lakes controlled the West. On Lake Erie, the Americans won the race for naval superiority. On September 10, 1813, Oliver Hazard Perry destroyed a British fleet at Put-in-Bay, and in a much quoted letter written immediately after the battle, Perry exclaimed, "We have met the enemy; and they are ours." On October 5, General Harrison overran an army of British troops and Indian warriors at the battle of Thames River. During this engagement Tecumseh was killed. On the other fronts, however, the war went badly for the Americans. General Wilkinson suffered an embarrassing defeat near Montreal (battle of Chrysler's Farm,

November 11), and the British Navy held its own on Lake Ontario.

In 1814, the British took the offensive. Following their victory over Napoleon, British strategists planned to increase pressure on three separate American fronts: the Canadian frontier,

This scene of the battle of New Orleans, painted from sketches drawn during the engagement, shows the Americans standing their ground against the British frontal assault. The Americans suffered only light casualties in the battle, but more than two thousand British soldiers were killed or wounded.

Chesapeake coastal settlements, and New Orleans. Sir George Prevost, commander of the British forces in Canada, marched his army south into upper New York State. A hastily assembled American fleet led by Captain Thomas Macdonough turned back a British flotilla off Plattsburg on Lake Champlain (September 11, 1814). When Prevost learned of this setback, he retreated quickly into Canada. Although the Americans did not realize the full significance of this battle, the triumph accelerated peace negotiations, for after news of Plattsburg reached London, the British government concluded that major land operations along the Canadian border were futile.

Throughout the year, British warships harassed the Chesapeake coast. To their surprise, the British found the region almost totally undefended, and on August 24, 1814, in retaliation for the Americans' destruction of the capital of Upper Canada (York, Ontario), a small force of British marines burned the American capital, a victory more symbolic than strategic. Encouraged by their easy success and contemptuous of America's ragtag soldiers, the

British launched a full-scale attack on Baltimore (September 14). To everyone's surprise, the fort guarding the harbor held out against a heavy naval bombardment, and the British gave up the operation. The survival of Fort McHenry inspired Francis Scott Key to write "The Star-Spangled Banner."

The battle of New Orleans should never have occurred. The British landed a large assault force under General Edward Pakenham at precisely the same time that diplomats in Europe were preparing the final drafts of a peace treaty. The combatants, of course, knew nothing of these distant developments, and on January 8, 1815, Pakenham foolishly ordered a frontal attack against General Andrew Jackson's well-defended positions. In a short time, the entire British force had been destroyed. The Americans suffered only light casualties. The victory not only transformed Jackson into a national folk hero, it also provided the people of the United States with a much needed source of pride. Even in military terms, the battle was significant, for if the British had managed to occupy New Orleans, they would have been difficult to dislodge regardless of the specific provisions of the peace treaty.

Hartford Convention: The Demise of the Federalists

In the fall of 1814, a group of leading New England politicians, most of them moderate Federalists, gathered in Hartford to discuss relations between the people of their region and the federal government. The delegates were angry and hurt by the Madison administration's seeming insensitivity to the economic interests of the New England states. The embargo had soured New Englanders on Republican foreign policy, but the events of the War of 1812 added insult to injury. When British troops occupied the coastal villages of Maine, then part of Massachusetts, the president did nothing to drive out the enemy. Of course, the self-righteous complaints of convention organizers overlooked New England's tepid support for the war effort.

The men who met at Hartford on December 15 did not advocate secession from the Union. Although people living in other sections of the country cried treason, the convention delegates only recommended changes in the Constitution. They drafted a number of amendments that reflected the New Englanders' growing frustration. One proposal suggested that congressional representation be calculated on the basis of the number of white males living in a state. New England congressmen were tired of the three-fifths rule that gave southern slaveholders a disproportionally large voice in the House. The convention also wanted to limit each president to a single term in office, a reform that New Englanders hoped might end Virginia's monopoly of the executive mansion. And finally, the delegates insisted that a two-thirds majority was necessary before Congress could declare war, pass commercial regulations, or admit new states to the Union. The moderate Federalists of New England were confident these changes would protect their region from the tyranny of southern Republicans.

The convention dispatched its resolutions to Washington, but soon after an official delegation reached the federal capital, the situation became extremely awkward. Everyone was celebrating the victory of New Orleans and the announcement of peace. Republican leaders in Congress accused the hapless New Englanders of disloyalty, and people throughout the country were persuaded that a group of wild secessionists had attempted to destroy the Union. The Hartford Convention accelerated the final demise of the Federalist party.

Treaty of Ghent Ends the War

In August 1814, the United States dispatched a distinguished negotiating team to Ghent, a Belgian city where the Americans opened talks with their British counterparts. During the early weeks of discussion, the British made impossible demands. They insisted on territorial concessions from the United States, the right to navigate the Mississippi River, and the creation of a large Indian buffer state in the Northwest Territory. The Americans listened to this presentation, more or less politely, and then rejected the entire package. In turn, they lectured their British counterparts about maritime rights and impressment.

Fatigue finally broke the diplomatic deadlock. The British government realized no amount of military force could significantly alter the outcome of hostilities in the United States. When one important minister asked the Duke of Wellington, the hero of the Napoleonic Wars, for his assessment of British prospects following the battle of Plattsburg, the general replied, "I do not know where you could carry on . . . an operation which would be so injurious to the Americans as to force them to sue for peace."

Weary negotiators signed the Treaty of Ghent on Christmas Eve 1814. The document dealt with virtually none of the topics contained in Madison's original war message. Neither side surrendered territory; Great Britain refused even to discuss the topic of impressment. In fact, after more than two years of hostilities, the adversaries merely agreed to end the fighting, postponing the vexing issues of neutral rights until a later date. The Senate apparently concluded that stalemate was preferable to continued conflict and ratified the treaty 35 to 0.

Most Americans—except perhaps the diehard Federalists of New England—viewed the War of 1812 as an important success. Even though the country's military accomplishments had been unimpressive, the people of the United States had been swept up in a contagion of nationalism. The Hartford debacle served to discredit secessionist fantasies for several decades. Americans had waged a "second war of independence" and in the process transformed the Union into a symbol of national destiny. "The war," reflected Gallatin, had made Americans "feel and act more as a nation; and I hope that the permanency of the Union is thereby better secured." That nationalism had flourished in times of war was an irony that Gallatin's contemporaries did not fully appreciate. After the Treaty of Ghent, however, Americans came gradually to realize they had nothing further to fear from Europe, and in an era of peace, the process of sectional divergence began to quicken, threatening to destroy the republic that Jefferson and Madison had worked so hard to preserve.

REPUBLICAN LEGACY

During the 1820s, it became fashionable to visit retired presidents. These were not, of course, ordinary leaders. Jefferson, Adams, and Madison linked a generation of younger men and women to the heroic moments of the early republic. When they spoke about the Declaration of Independence or the Constitution of the United States, their opinions carried symbolic weight for a burgeoning society anxious about its political future.

A remarkable coincidence occurred on July 4, 1826, the fiftieth anniversary of the Declaration of Independence. On that day, Thomas Jefferson died at Monticello. His last words were "Is it the Fourth?" On the same day several hundred miles to the north, John Adams also passed his last day on earth. His mind was on his old friend and sometimes adversary, and during his final moments, Adams found comfort in the assurance that "Thomas Jefferson still survives."

James Madison lived on at his Virginia plantation, the last of the "founding fathers." Throughout a long and productive career, he had fought for republican values. He championed a Jeffersonian vision of a prosperous nation in which virtuous, independent citizens pursued their own economic interests. He tolerated no aristocratic pretensions. Leaders of a Jeffersonian persuasion—and during his last years that probably included John Adams—brought forth a democratic, egalitarian society. Although they sometimes worried that the obsessive grubbing for wealth might destroy public virtue, they were justly proud of the republic they had helped to create.

But many visitors who journeyed to Madison's home at Montpelier before he died in 1836 were worried about another legacy of the founding generation. Why, they asked the aging president, had the early leaders of this nation allowed slavery to endure? How did African Americans fit into the republican scheme? Try as they would, neither Madison nor the politicians who claimed the Jeffersonian mantle could provide satisfactory answers. In an open, egalitarian society, there seemed no place for slaves, and a few months before Madison died, a visitor reported sadly, "With regard to slavery, he owned himself almost to be in despair."

Recommended Reading

The best written and in many ways the fullest account of the first two decades of the nineteenth century remains Henry Adams's classic *History of the United States During the Administration of Jefferson and Madison*, 9 vols. (1889–1891). A solid account of the period is Marshall Smelser, *The Democratic Republic, 1801–1815* (1968). Anyone interested in the problems that Jefferson faced as president should start with Merrill D. Peterson, *Thomas Jefferson and the New Nation: A Biography* (1970) and Forrest McDonald, *The Presidency of Thomas Jefferson* (1976). A brilliant exploration of the evolution of republican ideas after the retirement of Madison is Drew R. McCoy, *The Last of the Founding Fathers: James Madison and the Republican Legacy* (1989). Nathan O. Hatch provides an excellent account of popular religion in his *The Democratization of American Christianity* (1989). Laurel Ulrich has written a splendid study of a remarkable woman in the age of Jefferson: *A Midwife's Tale* (1990).

Additional Bibliography

The economic developments of this period are the subject of several valuable studies. The most provocative is Thomas C. Cochran, *Frontiers of Change: Early Industrialization of America* (1981). Also see Stuart Bruchey, *The Roots of American Economic Growth, 1607–1861* (1965); Douglass C. North, *The Economic Growth of the United States, 1790–1860* (1961); Winifred B. Rothenberg, *From Market-Places to a*

CHRONOLOGY

1800 Thomas Jefferson elected president

1801 Adams makes "midnight" appointments of federal judges

1802 Judiciary Act is repealed (March)

1803 Chief Justice John Marshall rules on *Marbury* v. *Madison* (February); sets precedent for judicial review • Louisiana Purchase concluded with France (May)

1803–1806 Lewis and Clark explore the Northwest

1804 Aaron Burr kills Alexander Hamilton in a duel (July) •Jefferson elected to second term

1805 Justice Samuel Chase acquitted by Senate (March)

1807 Burr is tried for conspiracy (August-September) • Embargo Act passed (December)

1808 Slave trade is ended (January) • Madison elected president

1809 Embargo is repealed; Non-Intercourse Act passed (March)

1811 Harrison defeats Indians at Tippecanoe (November)

1812 Declaration of war against Great Britain (June) • Madison elected to second term, defeating De Witt Clinton of New York

1813 Perry destroys British fleet at battle of Put-in-Bay (September)

1814 Jackson crushes Creek Indians at Horseshoe Bend (March) • British marines burn Washington, D.C. (August) • Hartford Convention meets to recommend constitutional changes (December) • Treaty of Ghent ends War of 1812 (December)

1815 Jackson routs British at battle of New Orleans (January)

Market Economy: The Transformation of Rural Massachusetts, 1750–1850 (1992).The problems of adjusting to new industrial technologies is addressed in Merritt Roe Smith, *Harper's Ferry Armory and the New Technology: The Challenge of Change* (1977) and Brooke Hindle and Steven Lubar, *Engines of Change: The American Industrial Revolution, 1790–1860* (1986).

A thoughtful study of working class culture is Howard B. Rock, *Artisans of the New Republic: The Tradesmen of New York City in the Age of Jefferson* (1979). Charles W. Jansen's account of American society along with other contemporary documents can be found in Gordon S. Wood, ed., *The Rising Glory of America, 1760–1820* (1971).

A good introduction to the history of the western settlements is Reginald Horsman, *The Frontier in the Formative Years, 1783–1815* (1970). Also see John M. Faragher, *Daniel Boone, the Life and Legend of an American Pioneer* (1992); Andrew R. L. Cayton, *The Midwest and the Nation* (1990); Anthony F. C. Wallace, *Death and Rebirth of the Seneca* (1970); William McLoughlin, *Cherokees and Missionaries, 1789–1839* (1984); and B. Gilbert, *God Gave Us This Country: Takamthi and the First American Civil War* (1989).

The challenges confronting Jefferson as president are discussed in Dumas Malone, *Jefferson and His Time*, vols. 4 and 5 (1970, 1974). Several works focus more narrowly on political problems: Noble E. Cunningham, Jr., *The Process of Government Under Jefferson* (1978); and James Sterling Young, *The Washington Community, 1800–1828* (1966). See also Richard E. Ellis's masterful *The Jeffersonian Crisis: Courts and Politics in the Young Republic* (1971); Leonard W. Levy, *Emergence of a Free Press* (1985); and Morton J. Horowitz, *The Transformation of American Law, 1780–1860* (1977).

The Louisiana Purchase is the subject of Alexander DeConde, *The Affair of Louisiana* (1976). On the Lewis and Clark expedition, see James P. Ronda, *Lewis and Clark Among the Indians* (1984); and Donald Jackson, *Thomas Jefferson and the Stony Mountains: Exploring the West from Monticello* (1981).

Two Republicans who gave Jefferson so much trouble are discussed in Robert E. Shalhope, *John Taylor of Caroline: Pastoral Republican* (1980); and Robert Dawidoff, *The Education of John Randolph* (1979). For Burr's strange career, see Milton Lomask, *Aaron Burr*, vols. 1 and 2 (1979, 1982). Thoughtful explorations of the relation of slavery to politics are Donald L. Robinson, *Slavery in the Structure of American Politics, 1765–1820* (1971); and John C. Miller, *Wolf by the Ears: Thomas Jefferson and Slavery* (1991).

The country's foreign policy is analyzed in Bradford Perkins, *Prologue to War: England and the United States, 1805–1812* (1961); and Burton Spivak, *Jefferson's English Crisis: Commerce, Embargo, and* the Republican Revolution (1974). For Madison's presidency, see Irving Brant, *James Madison*, vols. 4–6 (1953–1961) as well as Ralph Ketcham, *James Madison: A Biography* (1971). A good account of the War of 1812 can be found in J. C. A. Stagg, *Mr. Madison's War: Politics, Diplomacy, and Warfare in the Early American Republic* (1983).

The problems facing the Federalist party are the subject of David Hackett Fischer, *The Revolution of American Conservatism* (1965); Linda Kerber, *Federalists in Dissent: Imagery and Ideology in Jeffersonian America* (1970); and James M. Banner, Jr., *To the Hartford Convention* (1970).

Nationalism and Nation-Building

Mr. Barnhard. A vender give to little Lewis Miller, the first Barlo-Knife as A present. 1799.

When the Marquis de Lafayette revisited the United States in 1824, he marveled at how the country had changed in the more than forty years since he had served with George Washington. During his thirteen-month grand tour, the great French hero of the American Revolution traveled to all parts of the country. He was greeted by adoring crowds in places that had been unsettled or beyond the nation's borders four decades earlier. Besides covering the eastern seaboard, Lafayette went west to New Orleans, then up the Mississippi and the Ohio by steamboat. He thus sampled a new mode of transportation that was helping to bring the far-flung outposts and settlements of a much enlarged nation into regular contact with each other. Such travel was still hazardous. Lafayette had to be rescued from a sinking steamboat on the Ohio before he could complete his journey to Cincinnati, hub city of the newly settled trans-Appalachian West.

Everywhere Lafayette was greeted with patriotic oratory celebrating the liberty, prosperity, and progress of the new nation. Speaking before a joint session of both houses of Congress, the old hero responded in kind, telling his hosts exactly what they wanted to hear. He hailed "the immense improvements" and "admirable communications" that he had witnessed and declared himself deeply moved by "all the grandeur and prosperity of these happy United States, which . . . reflect on every part of the world the light of a far superior political civilization."

Americans had good reasons to make Lafayette's return the occasion for patriotic celebration and reaffirmation. Since the War of 1812, the nation had been free from serious foreign threats to its independence and way of life. It was growing rapidly in population, size, and wealth. Its republican form of government, which many had considered a risky experiment at the time of its origin, was apparently working well. James Monroe, the current president, had proclaimed in his first inaugural address that "the United States have flourished beyond example. Their citizens individually have been happy and the nation prosperous." Expansion "to the Great Lakes and beyond the sources of the great rivers which communicate through our whole interior," meant that "no country was ever happier with respect to

its domain." As for the government, it was so near to perfection that "in respect to it we have no essential improvement to make."

Beneath the optimism and self-confidence, however, lay undercurrents of doubt and anxiety about the future. The visit of the aged Lafayette signified the passing of the Founding Fathers. Less than a year after his departure, Jefferson and Adams, the last of the great Founders, would die within hours of each other on the fiftieth anniversary of the Declaration of Independence. Could their example of republican virtue and self-sacrifice be maintained in an increasingly prosperous and materialistic society? Many in fact believed public virtue had declined since the heroic age of the Revolution. And what about the place of black slavery in a "perfect" democratic republic? Lafayette himself noted with disappointment that the United States had not yet extended freedom to southern slaves.

But the peace following the War of 1812 did open the way for a great surge of nation-building. As new lands were acquired or opened up for settlement, hordes of pioneers often rushed in. Improvements in transportation soon gave many of them access to distant markets, and advances in the processing of raw materials led to the first stirrings of industrialization. Politicians looked for ways to encourage this process of growth and expansion, and an active judiciary handed down decisions that served to promote economic development and assert the priority of national over state and local interests. To guarantee the peace and security essential for internal progress, statesmen proclaimed a foreign policy designed to insulate America from external involvements. A new nation of great potential wealth and power was emerging.

EXPANSION AND MIGRATION

The peace concluded with Great Britain in 1815 allowed Americans to shift their attention from Europe and the Atlantic to the vast lands of North America. Although the British had withdrawn from the region north of the Ohio, they continued to lay claim to the Pacific Northwest. Spain still possessed Florida and much of the present-day American West. Between the Appalachians and the Mississippi, settlement had already begun in earnest, especially in the new states of Ohio, Kentucky, and Tennessee. In the lower Mississippi Valley, the former French colony of Louisiana had been admitted as a state in 1812, and a thriving settlement existed around Natchez in the Mississippi Territory. Elsewhere, however, the trans-Appalachian West was only sparsely settled by whites, and much good land remained in Indian hands. Diplomacy, military action (or at least the threat of it), and the westward movement of vast numbers of settlers were all needed before the continent would yield up its wealth.

Extending the Boundaries

The first goal of postwar expansionists was to obtain Florida from Spain. In the eyes of the Spanish, their possession extended along the Gulf Coast to the Mississippi. Between 1810 and 1812, however, the United States had annexed the area between the Mississippi and the Perdido rivers in what became Alabama, claiming it was part of the Louisiana Purchase. The remainder, known as East Florida, became a prime object of territorial ambition for President James Monroe and his energetic secretary of state, John Quincy Adams. Adams had a grand design for continental expansion that required nullifying or reducing Spanish claims west of the Mississippi as well as east of it; he eagerly awaited an opportunity to apply pressure for that purpose.

General Andrew Jackson provided such an opportunity. In 1816, U. S. troops first crossed into East Florida in pursuit of hostile Seminole Indians. This raid touched off a wider conflict, and after taking command in late 1817, Jackson went beyond his official orders and occupied East Florida in April and May of 1818. Except for Adams, all the members of Monroe's cabinet privately condemned this aggressive action; so did a report of the House of Representatives. But no disciplinary action was taken, mainly because public opinion rallied behind the hero of New Orleans.

In November 1818, Secretary Adams informed the Spanish government the United States had acted in self-defense and that further conflict would be avoided only if East Florida was ceded to the United States. The Madrid government, weakened by Latin American revolutions and the

North America, 1819

Historian Henry Adams described the North American continent as "an uncovered ore bed." But it would take diplomacy, military action, and massive settlement before its riches could be mined.

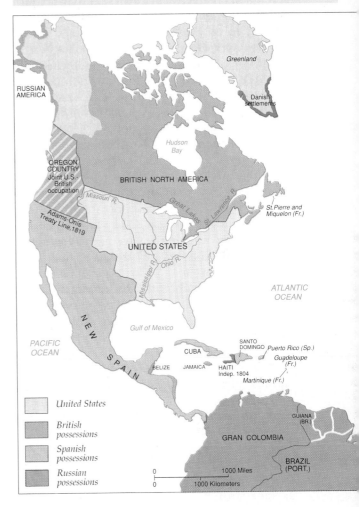

breaking up of its empire, was in no position to resist American bullying. As part of the Adams-Onís Treaty, signed on February 22, 1819, Spain relinquished Florida to the United States. In return, the United States assumed $5 million of the financial claims of American citizens against Spain.

A strong believer that the United States had a continental destiny, Adams also used the confrontation over Florida to make Spain give up its claim to the Pacific Coast north of California, thus opening a path for future American expansion. Taking advantage of Spain's desire to keep its title to Texas—a portion of which the United States had previously claimed as part of the Louisiana Purchase—Adams induced the Spanish minister Luis de Onís to agree to the creation of a new boundary between American and Spanish territory that ran north of Texas but extended all the way to the Pacific. Great Britain and Russia still had competing claims to the Pacific Northwest, but the United States was now in a better position to acquire some frontage on a second ocean.

Interest in exploitation of the Far West continued to grow during the second and third decades of the nineteenth century. In 1811, a New York merchant, John Jacob Astor, founded the fur trading post of Astoria at the mouth of the Columbia River in the Oregon country. Astor's American Fur Company, which later sold its interests to a British firm, operated out of St. Louis in the 1820s and 1830s, with fur traders working their way up the Missouri to the northern Rockies and beyond. First they limited themselves to trading for furs with the Indians, but later, businesses such as the Rocky Mountain Fur Company, founded in 1822, relied on trappers or "mountain men" who went after game on their own and sold the furs to agents of the company at an annual "rendezvous."

These colorful characters, who included such legendary figures as Jedediah Smith, Jim Bridger, Kit Carson, and Jim Beckwourth (one of the many African Americans who contributed to the opening of the West as fur traders, scouts, or settlers), accomplished prodigious feats of survival under harsh natural conditions. Following Indian trails, they explored many parts of the Rockies and the Great Basin. They often married Indian women and assimilated much of the culture and technology of the Native Americans. Although they actually depleted the animal resources on which the Indians depended, these mountain men were portrayed in American literature and popular mythology as exemplars of a romantic ideal of lonely self-reliance in harmony with unspoiled nature.

Reports of military expeditions provided better documented information about the Far West than the tales of illiterate mountain men. The most notable of the postwar expeditions was mounted by Major Stephen S. Long in 1819–1820. Long surveyed parts of the Great Plains and Rocky Mountains, but his reports encouraged the mis-

leading view that the plains beyond the Missouri were a "great American desert" unfit for cultivation or settlement. For the time being, the Far West remained beyond American dreams of agrarian expansion. The real focus of attention between 1815 and the 1840s was the nearer West, the rich agricultural lands between the Appalachians and the Mississippi that were being opened up for settlement.

Settlement to the Mississippi

To completely occupy and exploit the trans-Appalachian interior, white Americans generally believed they had to displace the Indian communities still inhabiting that region in 1815. In the Ohio Valley and the Northwest Territory, military defeat had already made Native Americans only a minor obstacle to the ambitions of white settlers and land speculators. When the British withdrew from the Old Northwest in 1815, they left their former Indian allies virtually defenseless before the tide of whites who rushed into the region. Consigned by treaty to reservations outside the main lines of white advance, most of the tribes were eventually forced west of the Mississippi. The last stand of the Indians in this region occurred in 1831–1832, when a faction of the confederated Sac and Fox Indians under Chief Black Hawk refused to abandon their lands east of the Mississippi. Federal troops and Illinois state militia pursued Black Hawk's band and drove it back to the river, where it was almost exterminated while attempting to cross to the western bank.

Uprooting once populous Indian communities of the Old Northwest was part of a national program for removing Indians of the eastern part of the country to an area beyond the Mississippi. Whites of the time viewed Indian society and culture as radically inferior to their own and doomed by the march of "progress." Furthermore, the fact that Indians based property rights to land on use rather than absolute ownership was regarded as an insuperable obstacle to economic development. As originally conceived by Thomas Jefferson, removal would have allowed those Indians who became "civilized" to remain behind on individually owned farms and qualify for American citizenship. This policy

Mountain men like Jim Beckwourth (far left) and Native Americans met at a rendezvous to trade their furs to company agents in exchange for food, ammunition, and other goods. Feasting, drinking, gambling, and sharing exploits were also part of the annual event. Moccasins (left) trimmed with trade beads and worn by both Native Americans and trappers, show how trade influenced both cultures. The painting Rendezvous *(ca. 1837) is by Alfred Jacob Miller.*

would reduce Indian holdings without appearing to violate American standards of justice. But during the Monroe era it became clear that white settlers wanted nothing less than the removal of all Indians, civilized or not. The issue was particularly pressing in the South. Greed combined with racism as land-grabbing state governments pressed for the total extinction of Indian land titles within their borders.

In the South, as in the Old Northwest, a series of treaties negotiated between 1815 and 1830 reduced tribal holdings and provided for the eventual removal of most Indians to the trans-Mississippi West. But some southern tribes held on tenaciously to their homelands. Many members of the five so-called civilized tribes—the Cherokees, Creeks, Seminoles, Choctaws, and Chickasaws—had become settled agriculturalists. It was no easy task to induce the civilized tribes to give up the substantial and relatively prosperous enclaves in Georgia, Florida, Alabama, and Mississippi that they still held in the 1820s. But the pressure continued to mount. The federal government used a combination of deception, bribery, and threats to induce land cessions. When federal action did not yield results fast enough to suit southern whites who coveted Indian land for mining, speculation, and cotton production, state governments began to act on their own, proclaiming state jurisdiction over lands still allotted by federal treaty to Indians within the state's borders. The stage was thus set for the forced removal of the five civilized tribes to Oklahoma during the administration of

View of the Great Treaty Held at Prairie du Chien *(1825). Representatives of eight Native American tribes met with government agents at Prairie du Chien, Wisconsin, in 1825 to define the boundaries of their respective land claims. The United States claimed the right to make "an amicable and final adjustment" of the claims. Within twenty-five years most of the tribes present at Prairie du Chien had ceded their land to the government.*

Andrew Jackson. (See Chapter 10 for a more complete discussion.)

While Indians were being hustled or driven beyond the Mississippi, settlers poured across the Appalachians and filled the agricultural heartland of the United States. In 1810, only about one-seventh of the American population lived beyond the Appalachians; by 1840, more than one-third did. During that period, Illinois grew from a territory with 12,282 inhabitants to a state with 476,183; Mississippi's population of about 40,000 increased tenfold; and Michigan grew from a remote frontier area with less than 5,000 people into a state with more than 200,000. Eight new western states were added to the Union during this period. Because of the government's removal policies, few settlers actually had to fight Indians. But they did have to obtain possession of land and derive a livelihood from it. For many, this was no easy task.

Much of the vast acreage opened up by the westward movement passed through the hands of land speculators before it reached farmers and planters. Government lands in the western territories were first surveyed and then sold at auction. After a financial panic in 1819 brought ruin to many who had purchased tracts on credit, the minimum price was lowered from $2.00 to $1.25 an acre, but full payment was required in cash.

Since few settlers could afford the necessary outlays, wealthy speculators continued to acquire most good land. In the prosperous period following the War of 1812, and again during the boom of the early to mid-1830s, speculation in public lands proceeded at a massive and feverish rate.

Eventually most of the land did find its way into the hands of actual cultivators. In some areas, squatters arrived before the official survey and formed claims associations that policed land auctions to prevent "outsiders" from bidding up the price and buying their farms out from under them. Squatters also agitated for formal "preemption" rights from the government. Between 1799 and 1830, Congress passed a number of special acts that granted squatters in specific areas the right to buy the land that they had already improved at the minimum price. In 1841, the right to farm on public lands with the assurance of a *future* preemption right was formally acknowledged by Congress.

Settlers who arrived after speculators had secured title had to deal with land barons. Fortunately for the settlers, most speculators operated on credit and needed a quick return on their investment. They did this by selling land at a profit to settlers who had some capital, renting out farms until tenants had earned enough to buy them, or loaning money to squatters until they

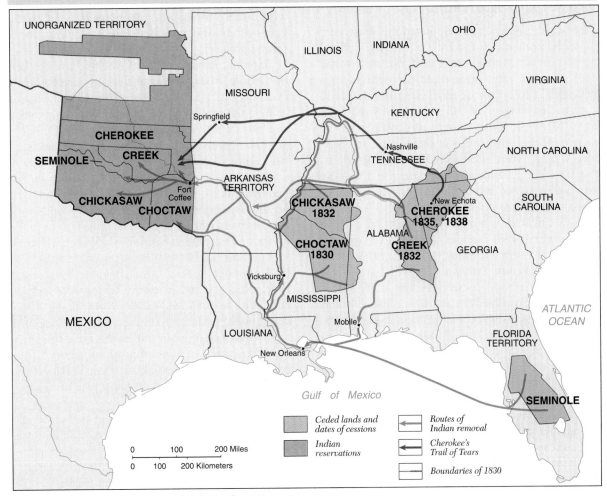

Indian Removal

Because so many Native Americans, uprooted from their lands in the East, died on the forced march to Oklahoma, the route they followed became known as the "Trail of Tears."

UNORGANIZED TERRITORY

OHIO

ILLINOIS   INDIANA

VIRGINIA

MISSOURI

Springfield

KENTUCKY

CHEROKEE

CREEK

NORTH CAROLINA

SEMINOLE

Nashville

TENNESSEE

ARKANSAS
TERRITORY

New Echota

SOUTH
CAROLINA

CHICKASAW   Fort
Coffee

CHICKASAW
1832

CHEROKEE
1835, *1838

CHOCTAW

ALABAMA

CREEK
1832

GEORGIA

CHOCTAW
1830

Vicksburg

MEXICO

MISSISSIPPI

ATLANTIC
OCEAN

Mobile

LOUISIANA

FLORIDA
TERRITORY

New Orleans

Gulf of Mexico

SEMINOLE

Ceded lands and dates of cessions		Routes of Indian removal
Indian reservations		Cherokee's Trail of Tears
		Boundaries of 1830

0   100   200 Miles

0   100   200 Kilometers

* Treaty signed in 1835 by minority factions forced removal in 1838.

were in a position to pay for the land in install-ments. As a result, the family farm or owner-operated plantation became the characteristic unit of western agriculture.

Since the pioneer family was likely to be sad-dled with debt of one kind or another, it was often forced from the beginning to do more than simply raise enough food to subsist. Farmers also had to produce something for market. Not sur-prisingly, most of the earliest settlement was along rivers that provided a natural means of transportation for flatboats loaded with corn, wheat, cotton, or cured meat. From more remote areas, farmers drove livestock over primitive trails and roads to eastern markets. To turn bulky

grain, especially corn, into a more easily trans-portable commodity, farmers in these remote regions often distilled it into whiskey. To meet the needs of farmers, local marketing centers quickly sprung up, usually at river junctions. Some of these grew into small cities virtually overnight. In the Midwest especially, the rapid rise of towns and cities serving surrounding farm-ing areas greatly accelerated regional develop-ment.

Most frontier people welcomed the opportuni-ty to sell some of their crops in order to acquire the consumer goods they could not produce for themselves, but many of them also valued self-sufficiency and tried to produce enough of the necessities of life to survive when cash crops failed or prices were low.

The People and Culture of the Frontier

Most of the settlers who populated the West were farmers from the seaboard states. Rising land prices and declining fertility of the soil in the older regions often motivated their migration. Few sought to escape or repudiate the "civilized" and settled way of life they had known in the East. Most moved in family units and tried to recreate their former ways of life as soon as possible. Women were often reluctant to migrate in the first place, and when they arrived in new areas, they strove valiantly to recapture the comfort and stability they had left behind.

New Englanders moving to western New York or northern Ohio, Indiana, and Illinois brought with them their churches, schools, notions of community uplift, Puritan ideals of hard work and self-denial, and respect for law and government. The Southerners who emigrated from Virginia, the Carolinas, and Georgia to Kentucky, Tennessee, Alabama, and Mississippi, as well as the lower part of the Midwest, were more devoted to the defense of personal or family honor and independence. They therefore tended to be less committed to the development of public authority and institutions.

In general, pioneers sought out the kind of terrain and soil with which they were already familiar. People from eastern uplands favored western hill country. Piedmont and tidewater farmers or planters usually made for the lower and flatter areas. The fertile prairies of the Midwest were avoided by early settlers, who preferred river bottoms or wooded sections because they were more like home and could be farmed by tried-and-true methods. Rather than being the bold and deliberate innovators pictured in American mythology, typical agricultural pioneers were deeply averse to changing their habits.

Yet adjustments were necessary simply to survive under frontier conditions. Initially, at least, a high degree of self-sufficiency was required on isolated homesteads. Men usually cut down trees, built cabins, broke the soil, and put in crops; besides cooking, keeping house, and caring for children, women made clothes, manufactured soap and other household necessities, churned butter, preserved food for the winter, and worked in the fields at busy times; at one time or another, women performed virtually all the tasks required by frontier farming. Crops had to be planted, harvested, and readied for home consumption with simple tools brought in wagons from the East—often little more than an axe, a plow, and a spinning wheel.

But this picture of frontier self-reliance is not the whole story. Most settlers in fact found it extremely difficult to accomplish all these tasks using only family labor. A more common practice was the sharing of work by a number of pioneer families. Except in parts of the South, where frontier planters had taken slaves with them, the normal way to get heavy labor done in newly settled regions was through mutual aid. Assembling the neighbors to raise a house, burn the woods, roll logs, harvest wheat, husk corn, pull flax, or make quilts helped turn collective work into a festive social occasion. Passing the jug was a normal feature of these "bees," and an uproarious good time often resulted from the various contests or competitions that speeded the work along. These communal events represented a creative response to the shortage of labor and at the same time provided a source for community solidarity. They probably tell us more about the "spirit of the frontier" than the conventional image of the pioneer as a lonely individualist.

While some settlers remained in one place and "grew up with the country," many others moved on after a relatively short time. The wandering of young Abraham Lincoln's family from Kentucky to Indiana and finally to Illinois between 1816 and 1830 was fairly typical. The physical mobility characteristic of nineteenth-century Americans in general was particularly pronounced in frontier regions. Improved land could be sold at a profit and the proceeds used to buy new acreage beyond the horizon where the soil was reportedly richer. The temptations of small-scale land speculation and the lure of new land further west induced a large proportion of new settlers to pull up stakes and move on after only a few years. Few early nineteenth-century American farmers developed the kind of attachment to the land that often characterized rural populations in other parts of the world.

Americans who remained in the East often ignored the frontier farmers and imagined the West as an untamed American wilderness inhabited by Indians and solitary white "pathfinders"

American Log House (1822), a watercolor by John Hackett. The log cabin and split rail fence of the typical frontier farmstead were cut from trees on the land. Other trees were burnt to clear the land for farming.

who turned their backs on civilization and learned to live in harmony with nature. James Fenimore Cooper, the first great American novelist, fostered this mythic view of the West in his stories of the frontier. He began in 1823 to publish a series of novels featuring Natty Bumppo, or "Leatherstocking"—a character who became the prototype for the western hero of popular fiction. Natty Bumppo was a hunter and scout who preferred the freedom of living in the forest to the constraints of civilization. Through Natty Bumppo, Cooper engendered a main theme of American romanticism—the superiority of a solitary life in the wilderness to the kind of settled existence among families, schools, and churches to which most real pioneers aspired.

After the War of 1812, political leaders realized that national security, economic progress, and political unity were all more or less dependent on a greatly improved transportation network. Accordingly, President Madison called for a federally supported program of "internal improvements" in 1815. Recommending such a program in Congress, Congressman John C. Calhoun described it as a great nationalizing enterprise: "Let us, then, bind the nation together with a perfect system of roads and canals. Let us conquer space." In ensuing decades, Calhoun's vision of a transportation revolution was realized to a considerable extent, although the direct role of the federal government proved to be less important than anticipated.

TRANSPORTATION AND THE MARKET ECONOMY

It took more than the spread of settlements to bring prosperity to new areas and ensure that they would identify with older regions or with the country as a whole. Along the eastern seaboard, land transportation was so primitive that in 1813 it took seventy-five days for one wagon of goods drawn by four horses to make a trip of about 1,000 miles from Worcester, Massachusetts, to Charleston, South Carolina. Coastal shipping eased the problem to some extent in the East and stimulated the growth of port cities. Traveling west over the mountains, however, meant months on the trail.

A Revolution in Transportation: Roads and Steamboats

Americans who wished to get from place to place rapidly and cheaply needed, as a bare minimum, new and improved roads. The first great federal transportation project was the building of the National Road between Cumberland, Maryland, on the Potomac, and Wheeling, Virginia, on the Ohio (1811–1818). This impressive toll road had a crushed stone surface and immense stone bridges. It was subsequently extended to reach Vandalia, Illinois, in 1838. Another thoroughfare to the west completed during this period was the Lancaster Turnpike connecting Philadelphia and Pittsburgh. Other major cities were also linked by

On the frontier, women were responsible for preparing all the food, even for sometimes butchering the animals (top). The sketch, by artist Lewis Miller, is from the early 1800s. Quilting bees (bottom), depicted in Quilting Bee, a ca. 1855 work by an anonymous artist, offered men and women a rare opportunity to socialize.

"turnpikes"—privately owned toll roads chartered by the states. By about 1825, southern New England, upstate New York, much of Pennsylvania, and northern New Jersey were crisscrossed by thousands of miles of turnpikes.

By themselves, however, the toll roads failed to meet the demand for low-cost transportation over long distances. For the most part, travelers benefited more than transporters of bulky freight. The latter usually found that total expenses—toll plus the cost and maintenance of heavy wagons and great teams of horses—were too high to guarantee a satisfactory profit from haulage. Hence traffic was less than anticipated, and the tolls collect-

ed were often insufficient to provide an adequate return to investors.

Even the National Road itself had severe limitations. Although it was able to carry a substantial east-west traffic of settler parties and wagonloads of manufactured goods, as well as a reverse flow of livestock being driven to market, it could not offer the low freight costs required for the long-distance hauling of wheat, flour, and the other bulky agricultural products of the Ohio valley. For these commodities, water transportation of some sort was required.

The United States's natural system of river transportation was one of the most significant reasons for its rapid economic development. The Ohio-Mississippi system in particular provided ready access to the rich agricultural areas of the interior and a natural outlet for their products. By 1815, large numbers of flatboats loaded with wheat, flour, and salt pork were making the 2,000-mile trip from Pittsburgh to New Orleans. On the lower Mississippi and its main tributaries, cotton could be loaded from plantation or town wharfs onto river craft or small seagoing vessels and carried to the same destination. Even after the coming of the steamboat, flatboats continued to carry a major share of the downriver trade.

The flatboat trade, however, was necessarily one way. A farmer from Ohio or Illinois, or someone hired to do the job, could float down to New Orleans easily enough, but there was generally no way to get back except by walking overland through rough country. Until the problem of upriver navigation was solved, the Ohio-Mississippi could not carry the manufactured goods that farmers desired in exchange for their crops.

Fortunately, a solution was readily at hand— the use of steam power. Late in the eighteenth century, a number of American inventors had experimented with steam-driven riverboats. John Fitch even exhibited an early model to delegates at the Constitutional Convention. But making a commercially successful craft required further refinement. In 1807, inventor Robert Fulton, backed by Robert R. Livingston—a New Yorker of great wealth and political prominence— demonstrated the full potential of the steamboat by successfully propelling the Clermont 150 miles up the Hudson River. The first steamboat launched in the West was the New Orleans, which made the long trip from Pittsburgh to New

Fairview Inn or Three Mile House, Frederick Road, Baltimore *(1889), a watercolor by Thomas Ruckle. On their way west to the Alleghenies, a party of settlers leads their Conestoga wagons, loaded with freight, past the Fairview Inn on the National Road near Baltimore. Heading east is a herd of cattle being driven to market.*

Orleans in 1811–1812. Besides becoming a principal means of passenger travel on the inland waterways of the East, the river steamboat revolutionized western commerce. In 1815, the *Enterprise* made the first return trip from New Orleans to Pittsburgh. Within five years, sixty-nine steamboats with a total capacity of 13,890 tons were plying western waters.

Steam transport was a great boon for farmers and merchants. It reduced costs, increased the speed of moving goods and people, and allowed a two-way commerce on the Mississippi and Ohio. Eastern manufacturers and merchants now had a better way to reach interior markets than the old method of hauling everything over the Appalachians by road.

The steamboat quickly captured the American imagination. Great paddle wheelers became luxurious floating hotels, the natural habitats of gamblers, confidence men, and mysterious women. For the pleasure of passengers and onlookers, steamboats sometimes raced against each other, and their more skillful pilots became folk heroes. But the boats also had a lamentable safety record, frequently running aground, colliding, or blowing up. The most publicized disasters of antebellum

America were spectacular boiler explosions that claimed the lives of hundreds of passengers. As a result of such accidents, the federal government began in 1838 to attempt to regulate steamboats and monitor their construction and operation. This legislation, which failed to create an agency capable of enforcing minimum safety standards, stands as virtually the only federal effort in the pre–Civil War period to regulate domestic transportation.

The Canal Boom

A transportation system based solely on rivers and roads had one enormous gap—it did not provide an economical way to ship western farm produce directly east to ports engaged in transatlantic trade or to the growing urban market of the seaboard states. The solution offered by the politicians and merchants of the Middle Atlantic and midwestern states was to build a system of canals that linked seaboard cities directly to the Great Lakes, the Ohio, and ultimately the Mississippi.

The best natural location for a canal connect-

The Clermont on the Hudson *(probably 1830–1835) by Charles Pensee. Although some called his Clermont "Fulton's Folly," Robert Fulton immediately turned a profit from his fleet of steamboats, which reduced the cost and increased the speed of river transport.*

ing a river flowing into the Atlantic with one of the Great Lakes was between Albany and Buffalo, a relatively flat stretch of 364 miles. The potential value of such a project had long been recognized, but when it was actually approved by the New York legislature in 1817, it was justly hailed as an enterprise of breathtaking boldness. At that time, no more than about 100 miles of canal existed in the entire United States, and the longest single canal extended only 26 miles. Credit for the project belongs mainly to New York's vigorous and farsighted governor, De Witt Clinton. He persuaded the New York state legislature to underwrite the project by issuing bonds, and construction began in 1818. In less than two years, 75 miles were already finished, and the first tolls were being collected. In 1825, the entire canal was opened with great public acclaim and celebration.

At 364 miles long, 40 feet wide, 4 feet deep, and containing 84 locks, the Erie Canal was the most spectacular engineering achievement of the young republic. Furthermore, it was a great economic success. It reduced the cost of moving goods from Buffalo to Albany to one-twelfth the previous rate. It not only lowered the cost of western products in the East but caused an even sharper decline in the price of goods imported

from the East by Westerners. It also helped to make New York City the commercial capital of the nation.

The great success of the Erie Canal inspired other states to extend public credit for canal building. Between 1826 and 1834, Pennsylvania constructed an even longer and more elaborate canal, covering the 395 miles from Philadelphia to Pittsburgh and requiring twice as many locks as its New York competitor. But the Pennsylvania Main Line Canal did not do as well as the Erie, partly because of a bottleneck at the crest of the Alleghenies where an inclined-plane railroad had to haul canal boats over a high ridge. Ohio also embarked on an ambitious program of canal construction, completing an artificial waterway from the Ohio River to Cleveland on Lake Erie in 1833. Shorter canals were built in many other states connecting navigable rivers with sea or lake ports. The last of these was the Illinois and Michigan Canal, completed in 1848. It linked Chicago and the Great Lakes with the Illinois River and the Mississippi.

The canal boom ended when it became apparent in the 1830s and 1840s that most of these waterways were unprofitable. State credit had been overextended, and the panic and depression of the late 1830s and early 1840s forced retrenchment. Moreover, by this time railroads were beginning to compete successfully for the same traffic, and a new phase in the transportation revolution was beginning.

But canals should not be written off as economic failures that contributed little to the improvement of transportation. Some of them continued to be important arteries up to the time of the Civil War and well beyond. Furthermore, the "failure" of many of the canals was due solely to their inability to yield an adequate return on the money invested in them. Concerning one failing canal, a contemporary argued it "has been more useful to the public, than to the owners." Had the canals been thought of as providing a service rather than yielding a profit—in the manner, for example, of modern interstate highways—their vital contribution to the nation's economic development would have been better appreciated.

Emergence of a Market Economy

The desire to reduce the costs and increase the speed of shipping heavy freight over great distances laid the groundwork for a new economic system. Canals made it less expensive and more profitable for western farmers to ship wheat and flour to New York and Philadelphia and also gave manufacturers in the East ready access to an interior market. Steamboats reduced shipping costs on the Ohio and Mississippi, and put farm-

ers in the enviable position of receiving more for their crops and paying less for the goods they needed to import. Hence improved transport increased farm income and stimulated commercial agriculture.

At the beginning of the nineteenth century, the typical farming household consumed most of what it produced and sold only a small surplus in nearby markets. Most manufactured articles were produced at home. Easier and cheaper access to distant markets caused a decisive change in this pattern. Between 1800 and 1840, agricultural output increased at an annual rate of approximately 3 percent a year, and a rapidly growing portion of this production consisted of commodities grown for sale rather than consumed at home. This rise in productivity was partly due to technological advances. Iron or steel plows proved better than wooden ones, the grain cradle displaced the scythe for harvesting, and better varieties or strains of crops, grasses, and livestock were introduced. But the availability of good land and the revolution in marketing were the most important spurs to profitable commercial farming. Good land made for high yields, at least for a time; and when excessive planting wore out the soil, a farmer could migrate to more fertile lands farther west. The existence or extension of transportation facilities made distant markets available and plugged farmers into a commercial network that provided credit and relieved them of the need to do their own selling.

Erie Canal Scene (1884) by William R. Miller. Shallow-draft canal barges were used to transport goods on the four-foot deep Erie Canal. These barges were often towed by horses or mules from footpaths on the shore.

Agriculture, Transportation, and Trade

Connecting the new crop-producing regions of the frontier with eastern markets depended on improved transportation networks. Although the new toll roads helped in some of the inland areas, most trade was still carried out along the major waterways—the Mississippi River, the Great Lakes, and the Atlantic seaboard.

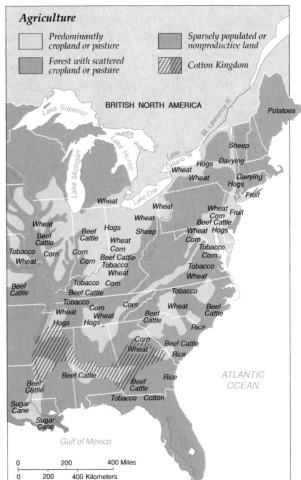

Agriculture

- Predominantly cropland or pasture
- Forest with scattered cropland or pasture
- Sparsely populated or nonproductive land
- Cotton Kingdom

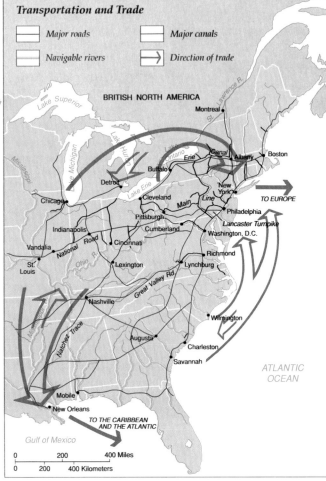

Transportation and Trade

- Major roads
- Navigable rivers
- Major canals
- Direction of trade

This emerging exchange network encouraged movement away from diversified farming and toward regional concentration on staple crops. Wheat was the main cash crop of the North, and the center of its cultivation moved westward as soil depletion, pests, and plant diseases lowered yields in older regions. In 1815, the heart of the wheat belt was New York and Pennsylvania. By 1839, Ohio was the leading producer and Indiana and Illinois were beginning to come into their own. On the rocky hillsides of New England, sheep raising was displacing the mixed farming of an earlier era. But the prime examples of successful staple production in this era were in the South. Tobacco continued to be a major cash crop of the upper South (despite declining fertility and a shift to wheat in some areas), rice was important in coastal South Carolina, and sugar was a staple of southern Louisiana. Cotton, however, was the "king" crop in the lower South as a whole. In the course of becoming the nation's principal export commodity, it brought wealth and prosperity to a belt of states running from South Carolina to Louisiana.

A number of factors made the Deep South the world's greatest producer of cotton. First was the great demand generated by the rise of textile manufacturing in England and, to a lesser extent, in New England. Second was the effect of the cotton gin on processing. Invented by Eli Whitney in

1793, this simple device cut the labor costs involved in cleaning short-staple cotton, thus making it an easily marketable commodity.

A third reason for the rise of cotton was the availability of good land in the Southwest. As yields fell in original areas of cultivation—mainly South Carolina and Georgia—the opening of the rich and fertile plantation areas or "black belts" of Alabama, Mississippi, and Louisiana shifted the Cotton Kingdom westward and resulted in a vast increase in total production. In 1816, New Orleans, the great marketing center for western crops, received 37,000 bales; in 1830, 428,000 arrived; and in 1840, the annual number had reached 923,000. Between 1817 and 1840, the amount of cotton produced in the South tripled from 461,000 bales to 1,350,000.

A fourth factor—the existence of slavery, which provided a flexible system of forced labor—permitted operations on a scale impossible for the family labor system of the agricultural North. Finally, the cotton economy benefited from the South's splendid natural transportation system—its great network of navigable rivers extending deep into the interior from the cotton ports of Charleston, Savannah, Mobile, and, of course, New Orleans. The South had less need than other agricultural regions for artificial internal improvements such as canals and good roads. Planters could simply establish themselves on or near a river and ship their crops to market via natural waterways.

Commerce and Banking

As regions specialized in growing commercial crops, a new system of marketing emerged. During the early stages in many areas, farmers did their marketing personally, even when it required long journeys overland or by flatboat. With the growth of country towns, local merchants took charge of the crops near their sources, bartering clothing and other manufactured goods for produce. These intermediaries shipped the farmers' crops to larger local markets like Pittsburgh, Cincinnati, and St. Louis. From there the commodities could be sent on to Philadelphia, New York, or New Orleans. Cotton growers in the South were more likely to deal directly with factors or agents in the port cities from which their crop was exported. But even in the South, commission merchants in such inland

towns as Macon, Atlanta, Montgomery, Shreveport, and Nashville became increasingly important as intermediaries.

Credit was a crucial element in the whole system. Farmers borrowed from local merchants, who received an advance of their own when they consigned crops to a commission house or factor. The commission agents relied on credit from merchants or manufacturers at the ultimate destination, which might be Liverpool or New York City. The intermediaries all charged fees and interest, but the net cost to the farmers was less than when they had handled their own marketing. The need for credit encouraged the growth of money and banking.

Before the revolutions in transportation and marketing, small-scale local economies could survive to a considerable extent on barter. Farmers could give grain to blacksmiths who could in turn exchange grain for iron from a local forge. But long-distance transactions involving credit and deferred payment required money and lots of it. Under the Constitution, the U. S. government is the only agency authorized to coin money and regulate its value. But in the early to mid-nineteenth century, the government printed no paper money and produced gold and silver coins in such small quantities that it utterly failed to meet the expanding economy's need for a circulating currency.

Private or state banking institutions filled the void by issuing bank notes, promises to redeem their paper in *specie*—gold or silver—on the bearer's demand. After Congress failed to recharter the Bank of the United States in 1811, existing state-chartered banks took up the slack. Many of them, however, lacked adequate reserves and were forced to suspend specie payments during the War of 1812. The demand for money and credit during the immediate postwar boom led to a vast increase in the number of state banks—from 88 to 208 within two years. The resulting flood of state bank notes caused this form of currency to depreciate well below its face value and threatened a runaway inflation. In an effort to stabilize the currency, Congress established a second Bank of the United States in 1816. The Bank was expected to serve as a check on the state banks by forcing them to resume specie payments.

But it did not perform this task well in its early years. In fact, its own free lending policies contributed to the overextension of credit that led to financial panic and depression in 1819. When the economy collapsed, as it would do again in 1837, many Americans questioned whether the new system of banking and credit was as desirable as it had seemed to be in times of prosperity. As a result, hostility to banks became a prominent feature of American politics.

Early Industrialism

The growth of a market economy also created new opportunities for industrialists. In 1815, most manufacturing in the United States was carried on in households, in the workshops of skilled artisans, or in small mills, which used waterpower to turn wheat into flour or timber into boards. The factory form of production, in which supervised workers tended or operated machines under one roof, was rare. It was found mainly in southern New England where a number of small spinning mills, relying heavily on the labor of women and children, accomplished one step in the manufacture of cotton textiles. But most spinning of thread, as well as the weaving, cutting, and sewing of cloth, was still done by women working at home.

As late as 1820, about two-thirds of the clothing worn by Americans was made entirely in households by female family members—wives and daughters. A growing proportion, however, was produced for market rather than direct home consumption. Under the "putting-out system" of manufacturing, merchant capitalists provided raw material to people in their own homes, picked up finished or semifinished products, paid the workers, and took charge of distribution. Items such as simple shoes and hats were also made under the putting-out system. Home manufacturing of this type was centered in the Northeast and often involved farm families making profitable use of their slack seasons. It did not usually present a direct challenge to the economic preeminence of agriculture, nor did it seriously disrupt the rural pattern of life.

The making of articles that required greater skill—such as high-quality shoes and boots, carriages or wagons, mill wheels, and barrels or kegs—was mostly carried on by artisans working in small shops in towns. But in the decades after 1815, shops expanded in size, masters tended to become entrepreneurs rather than working artisans, and journeymen often became wage earners

rather than aspiring masters. At the same time, the growing market for low-priced goods led to a stress on speed, quantity, and standardization in the methods of production. Even where no substantial mechanization was involved, shops dealing in handmade goods for a local clientele tended to become small factories turning out cheaper items for a wider public.

A fully developed factory system emerged first in textile manufacturing. The establishment of the first cotton mills utilizing the power loom as well as spinning machinery—thus making it possible to turn fiber into cloth in a single factory—resulted from the efforts of a trio of Boston merchants: Francis Cabot Lowell, Nathan Appleton, and Patrick Tracy Jackson. On a visit to England in 1810 and 1811, Lowell succeeded in memorizing the closely guarded industrial secret of how a power loom was constructed. Returning to Boston, he joined with Appleton and Jackson to acquire a water site at Waltham and to obtain a corporate charter for textile manufacturing on a new and expanded scale.

Under the name of the Boston Manufacturing Company, the associates began their Waltham operation in 1813. Its phenomenal success led to the erection of a larger and even more profitable mill at Lowell in 1822 and another at Chicopee in 1823. Lowell became the great showplace for early American industrialization. Its large and seemingly contented work force of unmarried young women residing in supervised dormitories, its unprecedented scale of operation, its successful mechanization of almost every stage of the production process—all captured the American middle-class imagination in the 1820s and 1830s. (See "The Evolution of a 'Mill Girl,'" pp. 276–277.) Other mills using similar methods sprang up throughout New England, and the region became the first important manufacturing area in the United States.

The shift in textile manufacture from domestic to factory production shifted the locus of female economic activity. As the New England textile industry grew, the putting-out system rapidly declined. Between 1824 and 1832, household production of textiles dropped from 90 to 50 percent in most parts of New England. The shift to factory production changed the course of capitalistic activity in the region. Before the 1820s, New England merchants concentrated mainly on international trade, and Boston mercantile houses made great profits. A major source of capital was the lucrative China trade carried on by fast, well-built New England vessels. When the success of Waltham and Lowell became clear, many merchants shifted their capital away from oceanic trade and into manufacturing. This change had important political consequences, as leading politicians such as Daniel Webster no longer advocated a low tariff that favored importers over exporters. They now became leading proponents of a high duty rate designed to protect manufacturers from foreign competition.

The development of other "infant industries" of the postwar period was less dramatic and would not come to fruition until the 1840s and 1850s. Technology to improve the rolling and refining of iron was imported from England; it gradually encouraged a domestic iron industry centered in Pennsylvania. The use of interchangeable parts in the manufacture of small arms, pioneered by Eli Whitney and Simeon North, not only helped to modernize the weapons industry but also contributed more generally to the growth of new forms of mass production.

Although most manufacturing was centered in the Northeast, the West also experienced modest industrial progress. Increasing rapidly in number and size were facilities for processing farm products, such as grist mills, slaughterhouses, and tanneries. Distilleries in Kentucky and Ohio began during the 1820s to produce vast quantities of corn whiskey for a seemingly insatiable public.

One should not assume, however, that America had already experienced an industrial revolution by 1840. In that year, 63.4 percent of the nation's labor force was still employed in agriculture. Only 8.8 percent were directly involved in factory production (others were employed in trade, transportation, and the professions). Although this represented a significant shift since 1810 when the figures were 83.7 and 3.2 percent, the numbers would have to change a good deal more before it could be said that industrialization had really arrived. The revolution that did occur during these years was essentially one of distribution rather than production. The growth of a market economy of national scope—still based mainly on agriculture but involving a rapid flow of capital, commodities, and services from region to region—was the major economic development of this period. And it was one that had vast repercussions for all aspects of American life.

For those who benefited from it most directly, the market economy provided firm evidence of progress and improvement. But many of those who suffered from its periodic panics and depressions regretted the loss of the individual independence and security that had existed in a localized economy of small producers. These victims of boom and bust were receptive to politicians and reformers who attacked corporations and "the money power."

THE POLITICS OF NATION-BUILDING AFTER THE WAR OF 1812

Geographic expansion, economic growth, and the changes in American life that accompanied them were bound in the long run to generate political controversy. Farmers, merchants, manufacturers, and laborers were affected by the changes in different ways. So were Northerners, Southerners, and Westerners. Federal and state policies meant to encourage or control growth and expansion did not benefit all these groups or sections equally, and unavoidable conflicts of interest and ideology occurred.

But for a time these conflicts were not prominently reflected in the national political arena. During the period following the War of 1812, a single party dominated politics. Without a party system in place, politicians did not have to band together to offer the voters a choice of programs and ideologies. A myth of national harmony prevailed, culminating in the "Era of Good Feeling" during James Monroe's two terms as president. Behind this facade, individuals and groups fought for advantage, as always, but without the public accountability and need for broad popular approval that a party system would have required. As a result, popular interest in national politics fell.

The absence of party discipline and programs did not completely immobilize the federal government. Congress did manage to legislate on some matters of national concern. Although the president had little control over congressional action, he could still take important initiatives in foreign policy. The third branch of government—the Supreme Court—was in a position to make far-reaching decisions affecting the relationship between the federal government and the states. The common theme of the public policies that

The Evolution of a "Mill Girl"

Sarah Bagley became a "mill girl" when she left home in 1837 to work in a textile factory in Lowell, Massachusetts. In their own quiet way, Bagley and her fellow workers at the cotton mills, nearly all of them young women from rural families, initiated a struggle for women's rights that still continues.

The struggle was not planned. The mills of the 1820s and 1830s utilized amazing new machines for transforming raw cotton into textiles, but initially lacked people to run them. Cheap land and entrepreneurial opportunities had drained away the pool of potential male laborers; the early part of the nineteenth century was still a time when men would work under no boss unless absolutely necessary.

Women, with few other opportunities for earning a living, were perceived as a willing and docile labor alternative. As the *Lowell Offering* (a magazine published by the mills and written by the women operatives) said, women were to be "submissive, cheerful and contented" and to "remain entirely neutral in political and economic matters." Operating within that dominant ideology, the owners of the mills, understandably, considered women the perfect solution to the labor shortage.

Initially the mill owners were

right. Visitors and new operatives alike marvelled at the early mills' corporate paternalism. The assigned boardinghouses where most women operatives lived were clean and "morally pure," which is to say the supervisors prohibited any behavior that deviated from a church-defined norm. At night, until their 10 P.M. curfew, operatives read books, magazines, and newspapers made available by the mills and attended lyceum lectures and evening classes. Sunday church attendance was required.

Such paternalism inspired Sarah Bagley in her early mill-working days to write about

such topics as "The Pleasures of Factory Life," in which she spoke of her male bosses as kindly patriarchs: "We are placed in the care of overseers who feel under moral obligation to look after our interests."

Soon, however, she began with other operatives to write about an increasingly oppressive working environment: conditions had begun to contradict the image of benign paternalism. Her new ideas carried her into labor organization. In 1844, she helped found the Lowell Female Labor Reform Association (FLRA), making the New England Workingmen's Association the first labor organization in America to include both men and women. Quasi-spontaneous strikes in 1834 and 1836, called "turn-outs," had generally failed because they lacked an organizational backing, a clearly focused complaint, and the sympathetic intervention of outsiders. Women strikers had stressed their hereditary ties to the American Revolution and its yeomanry by calling themselves "daughters of freemen," but in most cases mill owners ("Tories in disguise") had simply fired all strikers. In the 1840s, owners slashed wages and instituted harsher work rules to maintain factory profits in the face of increased competition and a depressed economy.

Lowell, Massachusetts, ca. 1849.

The economic burden fell largely on the operatives. "It is *very* hard indeed," a two-year veteran of the mills wrote about her work, "and sometimes I think I shall not be able to endure it." Her pay, "about two dollars a week," must have been enough to keep her on the job, but it was less than one-third of the average weekly pay for a farmhand. "Perhaps you would like [to know] something about our regulations about going in and coming out of the mill," wrote a seventeen-year-old operative to her widowed father in 1845. "At half past 4 in the morning the bell rings for us to get up and at five for us to go into the mill. At seven we are called out to breakfast, are allowed half an hour between bells and the same at noon. . . . We have dinner at half past 12 and supper at seven."

Operatives worked a daily average of thirteen and a half hours: monotonous, noisy, and stifling labor. The mills were poorly ventilated, with fumes from whale-oil lamps permeating stale, lint-filled air that could not circulate because, in order to maintain the high humidity nec-essary to keep threads from breaking, overseers nailed all windows shut. Operatives often became ill, reportedly "going home to die" after working at the mills for a few years.

The FLRA responded by orga-nizing the Ten-Hour-Day move-ment—gathering petitions and lobbying for legislation limiting factory workers to ten-hour days. The FLRA objected not only to the length of working days but also to the absolute power of employers to set inhu-man work assignments for the operatives. In particular, the FLRA attempted to introduce legislation to regulate three employer innovations: the speedup, the stretch-out, and the bonus system. Speeding up referred simply to making each machine turn faster; stretching-out was the practice of gradually forcing operatives to control more machines at once; and the bonus system rewarded some overseers for getting more pro-duction from their operatives than other overseers could. Efforts at regulating those prac-tices through political channels failed. (Not until 1874 did Massa-chusetts pass a ten-hour-day law.)

Under its "Try again!" motto the FLRA then turned to a strat-egy of direct agitation against such innovations. In May 1846, when one mill tried to get its mill girls to operate four instead of three looms simultaneously, the *Voices of Industry* threatened to print the name of any woman who refused to sign a pledge against "stretching-out" to four looms. All the women in the plant signed the pledge, and management yielded.

Such victories on behalf of the women operatives were rare. By the end of the 1840s, immi-grants, many coming from con-ditions worse than those at the mills, replaced most native-born mill girls. Sarah Bagley dropped out of the labor movement in 1847 to live in a utopian com-munity, but would soon reap-pear as the nation's first female telegraph operator. (See discus-sion of utopian societies in Chapter 10.) Her refusal to stay "submissive, cheerful and con-tented" typified the reactions of many nineteenth-century women whose reality differed from the contemporary ideal of "true womanhood."

emerged between the War of 1812 and the Age of Jackson, which began in the late 1820s, was an awakening nationalism—a sense of American pride and purpose that reflected the expansionism and material progress of the period.

The Republicans in Power

By the end of the War of 1812, the Federalist party was no longer capable of winning a national election. The party of Jefferson, now known simply as the Republicans, was so completely dominant that it no longer had to distinguish itself from its opponents. Retreating from their original philosophy of states' rights and limited government, party leaders now openly embraced some of the programs of their former Federalist rivals—policies that seemed dictated by postwar conditions. In December 1815, President Madison proposed to Congress that it consider such measures as the reestablishment of a national bank, a mildly protective tariff for industry, and a program of federally financed internal improvements to bind "more closely together the various parts of our extended confederacy." Thus did Jefferson's successor endorse parts of a program enunciated by Alexander Hamilton.

In Congress, Henry Clay of Kentucky took the lead in advocating that the government take action to promote economic development. The keystone of what Clay called the "American system" was a high protective tariff to stimulate industrial growth and provide a "home market" for the farmers of the West, making the nation economically self-sufficient and free from a dangerous dependence on Europe.

In 1816, Congress took the first step toward establishing a neo-Federalist "American System." It enacted a tariff raising import duties an average of 25 percent. This legislation was deemed necessary because a flood of British manufactured goods was beginning to threaten the infant industries that had sprung up during the period when imports had been shut off by the embargo and the war. The tariff had substantial support in all parts of the country, both from a large majority of congressmen from New England and the Middle Atlantic states, and from a respectable minority of the southern delegation. In 1816, manufacturing was not so much a powerful interest as a patriotic concern. Many Americans believed the preservation of political independence and victory in future wars required industrial independence for the nation. Furthermore, important sectors of the agricultural economy also felt the need of protection—especially hemp growers of Kentucky, sugar planters of Louisiana, and wool producers of New England.

Later the same year, Congress voted to establish the second Bank of the United States. The new national Bank had a twenty-year charter, an authorized capital of $35 million, and the right to establish branches throughout the country as needed. Organized much like the first bank, it was a mixed public-private institution, with the federal government owning one-fifth of its stock and appointing five of its twenty-five directors. The Bank served the government by providing a depository for its funds, an outlet for marketing its securities, and a source of redeemable bank notes that could be used to pay taxes or purchase public lands. The bank bill was opposed by state banking interests and strict constructionists, but the majority of Congress found it a necessary and proper means for promoting financial stability and meeting the constitutional responsibility of the federal government to raise money from taxation and loans.

Legislation dealing with internal improvements made less headway in Congress because it aroused stronger constitutional objections and invited disagreements among sectional groups over who would benefit from specific projects. Except for the National Road, the federal government undertook no major transportation projects during the Madison and Monroe administrations. Both presidents believed that internal improvements were desirable but that a constitutional amendment was required before federal monies could legally be used for the building of roads and canals within individual states. In 1817, just before leaving office, Madison vetoed a bill that would have distributed $1.5 million among the states for local transportation projects.

The following year, the House of Representatives held a lengthy debate on the question of whether Congress had the authority to make appropriations for internal improvements. Although a preliminary vote approved the principle, further discussion led to its rejection. In 1822, Monroe vetoed legislation for the repair and administration of the National Road, arguing

The Election of 1816

Candidate	Party	Electoral Vote
Monroe	Republican	183
King	Federalist	34

that even this modest activity was beyond the constitutional powers of Congress. Consequently, public aid for the building of roads and canals continued to come mainly from state and local governments.

Monroe as President

As did Jefferson before him, President Madison chose his own successor in 1816. James Monroe thus became the third successive Virginian to occupy the White House. He served two full terms and was virtually uncontested in his election to each. Monroe was well qualified in terms of experience, having been an officer in the Revolution, governor of Virginia, a special emissary to France, and secretary of state. He was reliable, dignified, and high principled, as well as stolid and unimaginative, lacking the intellectual depth and agility of his predecessors. He projected an image of a disinterested statesman in the tradition of the Founders. (He even dressed in the outmoded fashions of the revolutionary era.) Nominated, as was the custom of the time, by a caucus of Republicans in the House of Representatives, Monroe faced only nominal Federalist opposition in the general election.

Monroe avoided controversy in his effort to maintain the national harmony that was the keynote of his presidency. His first inaugural address expressed the complacency and optimism of the time, and he followed it up with a goodwill tour of the country, the first made by a president since Washington. A local newspaper was so impressed with Monroe's warm reception in Federalist Boston that it announced that party strife was a thing of the past and that an "era of good feelings" had begun.

A principal aim of Monroe's administrations was to encourage these good feelings. He hoped to accommodate or conciliate all the sectional or economic interests of the country and devote his main attention to the task of asserting American power and influence on the world stage.

The first challenge to Monroe's hopes for domestic peace and prosperity was the panic of 1819, which brought an abrupt end to the postwar boom. After a period of rampant inflation, easy credit, and massive land speculation, the Bank of the United States pricked the bubble by calling in loans and demanding the immediate redemption in specie of the state bank notes in its possession. This retrenchment brought a drastic downturn in the economy, as prices fell sharply, businesses failed, and land bought on credit was foreclosed upon.

In 1821, Congress responded weakly to the resulting depression by passing a relief act that eased the terms for paying debts owed on public land. Monroe himself had no program to relieve the economic crisis because he did not feel called on to exert this kind of leadership, and the voters did not seem to have expected it of him. The one-party system then prevailing left the president without the ability to work through an organized majority party in Congress; one-party rule had in fact degenerated into a chaotic "no-party" system. More easily than later presidents, Monroe could retain his popularity during a depression.

Monroe prized national harmony even more than economic prosperity. But during his first administration, a bitter controversy developed between the North and the South over the admission of Missouri to the Union. Once again Monroe remained above the battle and suffered little damage to his own prestige. It was left entirely to the legislative branch of the government to deal with the nation's most serious domestic political crisis between the War of 1812 and the late 1840s.

The Election of 1820

Candidate	Party	Electoral Vote
Monroe	Republican	231
J. Q. Adams -	No party designation	1

The Missouri Compromise

In 1817, the Missouri territorial assembly applied for statehood. Since there were two to three thousand slaves already in the territory and the petition made no provision for their emancipation or for curbing further introduction of slaves, it was clear that Missouri would enter the Union as a slave state unless Congress took special action. Missouri was slated to be the first state, other than Louisiana, to be carved out of the Louisiana Purchase, and resolution of the status of slavery there would have implications for the rest of the trans-Mississippi West.

When the question came before Congress in early 1819, sectional fears and anxieties bubbled to the surface. Many Northerners resented southern control of the presidency and the fact that the three-fifths clause of the Constitution, by which every five slaves were counted as three persons in figuring the state's population, gave the South's free population added weight in the House of Representatives and the electoral college. The South, on the other hand, feared for the future of what it regarded as a necessary balance of power between the sections. Up until 1819, a strict equality had been maintained by alternately admitting slave and free states; in that year, there were eleven of each. But northern population was growing more rapidly than southern, and the North had built up a decisive majority in the House of Representatives. Hence the South saw its equal vote in the Senate as essential for preservation of the balance.

In February 1819, Congressman James Tallmadge of New York introduced an amendment to the statehood bill banning further introduction of slaves into Missouri and requiring steps toward the gradual elimination of slavery within the state. After a heated debate, the House approved the Tallmadge amendment by a narrow margin. The Senate, however, voted it down. The issue remained unresolved until a new Congress convened in December 1819. In the great debate that ensued in the Senate, the Federalist leader Rufus King of New York argued that Congress was within its rights to require restriction of slavery before Missouri could become a state. Southern senators protested that denying Missouri's freedom in this matter was an attack on the principle of equality among the states and showed that Northerners were conspiring to upset the balance of power between the sections.

A separate statehood petition from the people of Maine, who were seeking to be separated from Massachusetts, suggested a way out of the impasse. In February 1820, the Senate voted to couple the admission of Missouri as a slave state with the admission of Maine as a free state. A further amendment was also passed prohibiting slavery in the rest of the Louisiana Purchase north of the southern border of Missouri, or above the latitude of 36°30', and allowing it below that line. The Senate's compromise then went to the House, where it was initially rejected. Through the adroit maneuvering of Henry Clay—who broke the proposal into three separate bills—it eventually won House approval. The measure authorizing Missouri to frame a constitution and apply for admission as a slave state passed by a razor-thin margin of 90 to 87 with most northern representatives remaining opposed.

A major sectional crisis had been resolved. But the Missouri affair had ominous overtones for the future of North-South relations. Thomas Jefferson described the controversy as "a fire bell in the night," threatening the peace of the Union. In 1821, he wrote prophetically of future dangers: "All, I fear, do not see the speck on our horizon which is to burst on us as a tornado, sooner or later. The line of division lately marked out between the different portions of our confederacy is such as will never, I fear, be obliterated." The congressional furor had shown that when the issue of slavery or its extension came directly before the people's representatives, regional loyalties took precedence over party or other considerations. An emotional rhetoric of morality and fundamental rights issued from both sides, and votes followed sectional lines much more closely than on any other issue. If the United States were to acquire any new territories in which the status of slavery had to be determined by Congress, renewed sectional strife would be unavoidable.

Postwar Nationalism and the Supreme Court

While the Monroe administration was proclaiming national harmony and congressional leaders were struggling to reconcile sectional differences, the third branch of government—the Supreme Court—was making a more substantial and enduring contribution to the growth of national-

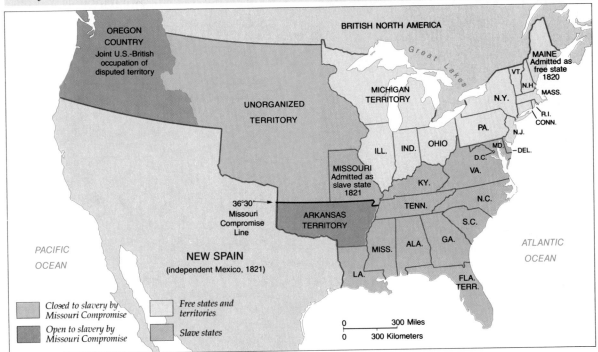

The Missouri Compromise, 1820–1821

The Missouri Compromise kept the balance of power in the Senate by admitting Missouri as a slave state and Maine as a free state. The agreement temporarily settled the argument over slavery in the territories.

OREGON COUNTRY
Joint U.S.-British occupation of disputed territory

BRITISH NORTH AMERICA

Great Lakes

MAINE
Admitted as free state 1820

UNORGANIZED TERRITORY

MICHIGAN TERRITORY

VT.
N.H.
N.Y.
MASS.
R.I.
CONN.
PA.
N.J.

ILL.   IND.   OHIO
MD.
D.C.   DEL.
VA.

MISSOURI
Admitted as slave state 1821

KY.

36°30'
Missouri Compromise Line

ARKANSAS TERRITORY

TENN.

N.C.

S.C.

PACIFIC OCEAN

NEW SPAIN
(independent Mexico, 1821)

MISS.   ALA.   GA.

LA.

FLA. TERR.

ATLANTIC OCEAN

Closed to slavery by Missouri Compromise

Open to slavery by Missouri Compromise

Free states and territories

Slave states

0   300 Miles
0   300 Kilometers

ism and a strong federal government. Much of this achievement was due to the firm leadership and fine legal mind of the chief justice of the United States, John Marshall.

A Virginian, a Federalist, and the devoted disciple and biographer of George Washington, Marshall served as chief justice from 1801 to 1835, and during that entire period dominated the Court as no other chief justice has ever done. Discouraging dissent and seeking to hammer out a single opinion on almost every case that came before the Court, he played a role that has been compared to that of a symphony conductor who is also composer of the music and principal soloist.

As the author of most of the major opinions issued by the Supreme Court during its formative period, Marshall gave shape to the Constitution and clarified the crucial role of the Court in the American system of government. He placed the protection of individual liberty, especially the right to acquire property, above the attainment of political, social, or economic equality. Ultimately he was a nationalist, believing the strength, secu-

rity, and happiness of the American people depended mainly on economic growth and the creation of new wealth.

The role of the Supreme Court, in Marshall's view, was to interpret and enforce the Constitution in a way that encouraged economic development, especially against efforts of state legislatures to interfere with the constitutionally protected rights of individuals or combinations of individuals to acquire property through productive activity. To limit state action, he cited the contract clause of the Constitution that prohibited a state from passing a law "impairing the obligation of contracts." As the legal watchdog of an enterprising, capitalistic society, the Court could also approve a liberal grant of power for the federal government so the latter could fulfill its constitutional responsibility to promote the general welfare by encouraging economic growth and prosperity.

In a series of major decisions between 1819 and 1824, the Marshall Court enhanced judicial power and used the contract clause of the Constitution to limit the power of state legislatures.

Chief Justice John Marshall affirmed the Supreme Court's authority to overrule state laws and congressional legislation that it held to be in conflict with the Constitution. The portrait is by Chester Harding, ca. 1829.

It also strengthened the federal government by sanctioning a broad or loose construction of its constitutional powers and by clearly affirming its supremacy over the states.

In *Dartmouth College* v. *Woodward* (1819), the Court was asked to rule on whether the legislature of New Hampshire had the right to convert Dartmouth from a private college into a state university. Daniel Webster, arguing for the college and against the state, contended Dartmouth's original charter of 1769 was a valid and irrevocable contract. The Court accepted his argument. Speaking for all the justices, Marshall made the far-reaching determination that any charter granted by a state to a private corporation was fully protected by the contract clause.

In practical terms, the Court's ruling in the Dartmouth case meant that the kind of business enterprises then being incorporated by state governments—such as turnpike or canal companies and textile manufacturing firms—could hold on indefinitely to any privileges or favors that had been granted in their original charters. The deci-

sion therefore increased the power and independence of business corporations by weakening the ability of the states to regulate them or withdraw their privileges. This ruling helped foster the growth of the modern corporation as a profit-making enterprise with only limited public responsibilities.

About a month after the Dartmouth ruling, in March 1819, the Marshall Court handed down its most important decision. The case of *McCulloch* v. *Maryland* arose because the state of Maryland had levied a tax on the Baltimore branch of the Bank of the United States. The unanimous opinion of the Court, delivered by Marshall, was that the Maryland tax was unconstitutional. The two main issues were whether Congress had the right to establish a national bank and whether a state had the power to tax or regulate an agency or institution created by Congress.

In response to the first question, Marshall set forth his doctrine of "implied powers." Conceding that no specific authorization to charter a bank could be found in the Constitution, the chief justice argued that such a right could be deduced from more general powers and from an understanding of the "great objects" for which the federal government had been founded. Marshall thus struck a blow for "loose construction" of the Constitution and a broad grant of power to the federal government to encourage economic growth and stability.

In answer to the second question—the right of a state to tax or regulate a federal agency—Marshall held that the Bank was indeed such an agency and that giving a state the power to tax it would also give the state the power to destroy it. In an important assertion of the supremacy of the national government, Marshall argued that the American people "did not design to make their government dependent on the states." This opinion ran counter to the view of many Americans, particularly in the South, that the Constitution did not take away sovereignty from the states. This debate over federal-state relations was not finally resolved until the northern victory in the Civil War decisively affirmed the dominance of federal authority. But Marshall's decision gave great new weight to a nationalist constitutional philosophy.

The case of *Gibbons* v. *Ogden* in 1824 led to a decision that bolstered the power of Congress to regulate interstate commerce. A steamboat monopoly granted by the state of New York was challenged by a competing ferry service operating between New York and New Jersey. The Court declared the New York grant unconstitutional because it amounted to state interference with Congress's exclusive right to regulate interstate commerce. Until this time, it had not been clearly established that "commerce" included navigation, and the Court's ruling went a long way toward freeing private interests engaged in furthering the transportation revolution from state interference.

This case clearly showed the dual effect of Marshall's decision making. It broadened the power of the federal government at the expense of the states while at the same time encouraging the growth of a national market economy. The actions of the Supreme Court provide the clearest and most consistent example of the main nationalistic trends of the postwar period—the acknowledgment of the federal government's major role in promoting the growth of a powerful and prosperous America and the rise of a nationwide capitalist economy.

Nationalism in Foreign Policy: The Monroe Doctrine

The new spirit of nationalism was also reflected in foreign affairs. The main diplomatic challenge facing Monroe after his reelection in 1820 was how to respond to the successful revolt of most of Spain's Latin American colonies after the Napoleonic wars. In Congress, Henry Clay called for immediate recognition of the new republics. In doing so, he expressed the belief of many Americans that their neighbors to the south were simply following the example of the United States in its own struggle for independence.

Before 1822, the administration stuck to a policy of neutrality. Monroe and Secretary of State Adams feared that recognizing the revolutionary governments would antagonize Spain and impede negotiations to acquire Florida. But pressure for recognition grew in Congress; in 1821, the House of Representatives, responding to Clay's impassioned oratory, passed a resolution of sympathy for Latin American revolutionaries and made it clear to the president that he would have the support of Congress if and when he decided to accord recognition. After the Florida treaty had

been formally ratified in 1821, Monroe agreed to recognition and the establishment of diplomatic ties with the Latin American republics. Mexico and Colombia were recognized in 1822, Chile and Argentina in 1823, Brazil (which had separated from Portugal) and the Federation of Central American States in 1824, and Peru in 1826.

Recognizing the republics put the United States on a possible collision course with the major European powers. Austria, Russia, and Prussia were committed to rolling back the tides of liberalism, self-government, and national self-determination that had arisen during the French Revolution and its Napoleonic aftermath. After Napoleon's first defeat in 1814, the monarchs of Europe had joined in a "Grand Alliance" to protect "legitimate" authoritarian governments from democratic challenges. Originally Great Britain was a member of this concert of nations but withdrew when it found its own interests conflicted with those of the other members. In 1822, the remaining alliance members, joined now by the restored French monarchy, gave France the green light to invade Spain and restore a Bourbon regime that might be disposed to reconquer the empire. Both Great Britain and the United States were alarmed by this prospect.

Particularly troubling to American policymakers was the role of Tsar Alexander I of Russia in these maneuverings. Not only was the tsar an outspoken and active opponent of Latin American independence, but he was attempting to extend Russian claims on the Pacific Coast of North America south to the fifty-first parallel—into the Oregon country the United States wanted for itself.

The threat from the Grand Alliance pointed to a need for American cooperation with Great Britain, which had its own reasons for wanting to prevent a restoration of Spanish or French power in the New World. Independent nations offered better and more open markets for British manufactured goods than the colonies of other nations, and the spokesmen for burgeoning British industrial capitalism anticipated a profitable economic dominance over Latin America. In early 1823, the British foreign secretary, George Canning, tried to exact from the French a pledge that they would make no attempt to acquire territories in Spanish America. When that venture failed, he sought to involve the United States in a joint policy to prevent the Grand Alliance from intervening in Latin America.

In August 1823, Canning broached the possibility of joint Anglo-American action against the designs of the Alliance to Richard Rush, U. S. minister to Great Britain, and Rush referred the suggestion to the president. Monroe welcomed the British initiative because he believed the United States should take an active role in trans-Atlantic affairs by playing one European power against another. When Monroe presented the question to his cabinet, however, he encountered the opposition of Secretary of State Adams, who favored a different approach. Adams distrusted the British and differed from the president in his general view of proper relations between the United States and Europe. Adams believed the national interest would best be served by avoiding all entanglements in European politics while at the same time discouraging European intervention in the Americas.

Political ambition also predisposed Adams against joint action with Great Britain; he hoped to be the next president and did not wish to give his rivals the chance to label him as pro-British. He therefore advocated unilateral action by the United States rather than some kind of joint declaration with the British. As he told the cabinet in November, "It would be more candid, as well as more dignified, to avow our principles explicitly to Russia and France, than to come in as a cockboat of the British man-of-war."

In the end, Adams managed to swing Monroe and the cabinet around to his viewpoint. In his annual message to Congress on December 2, 1823, Monroe included a far-reaching statement on foreign policy that was actually written mainly by Adams. What came to be known as the Monroe Doctrine solemnly declared the United States opposed any further colonization in the Americas or any effort by European nations to extend their political systems outside of their own hemisphere. In return, the United States pledged not to involve itself in the internal affairs of Europe or to take part in European wars. The statement envisioned a North and South America composed entirely of independent republics— with the United States preeminent among them.

Although the Monroe Doctrine made little impression on the great powers of Europe at the time it was proclaimed, it signified the rise of a new sense of independence and self-confidence in American attitudes toward the Old World. The United States would now go its own way free of involvement in European conflicts and would energetically protect its own sphere from European interference.

Adams and the End of the Era of Good Feelings

Monroe endorsed John Quincy Adams to succeed him as president. An intelligent and high-minded New Englander and the son of the second president, Adams seemed remarkably well qualified for the highest office in the land. More than anyone, except perhaps Monroe himself, he seemed to stand for a nonpartisan nationalism that put the public good above special interests. Early in

John Quincy Adams, in an 1828 portrait by Gilbert Stuart, the outstanding American portrait painter. As secretary of state under James Monroe, Adams advocated a policy of national self-interest and freedom from entanglement in European affairs.

his career, he had lost a seat in the Senate for supporting the foreign policies of Thomas Jefferson in defiance of the Federalist majority of his home state of Massachusetts. After becoming a National Republican, he served mainly in diplomatic posts, culminating in his tenure as secretary of state. In this office, he did more than negotiate treaties. Believing the rising greatness of America should be reflected not only in economic development and territorial expansion but also in scientific and intellectual achievement, he single-handedly produced a monumental report prescribing a uniform system of weights and measures for the United States. For three years, he rose early every morning in order to put in several hours of research on this project before doing a full day's work conducting the nation's foreign policy. Uniformity of weights and measures, he argued, was essential to scientific and technological progress. Showing that his nationalism was not of a narrow and selfish kind, he called for an agreement with Great Britain and France to promote a single universal system.

Adams represented a type of leadership that could not survive the growth of the sectional and economic divisions foreshadowed by the Missouri controversy and the fallout from the panic of 1819. Adams did become president, but only after a hotly contested election that led to the revival of partisan political conflict (see Chapter 10). As the nation's chief executive, he tried to gain support for government-sponsored scientific research and higher education, only to find the nation was in no mood for public expenditures that offered nothing immediate and tangible to most voters. As a highly educated "gentleman," he projected an image that was out of harmony with a rising spirit of democracy and veneration of "the common man."

The consensus on national goals and leadership that Monroe had represented could not sustain itself. The "era of good feelings" turned out to be a passing phase and something of an illusion. Although the pursuit of national greatness would continue, there would be sharp divisions over how it should be achieved. A general commitment to settlement of the West and the development of agriculture, commerce, and industry would endure despite serious differences over what role government should play in the process; but the idea that an elite of nonpartisan statesmen could define common purposes and harmonize competing elements—the concept of leadership that Monroe and Adams had advanced—would no longer be viable in the more contentious and democratic America of the Jacksonian era.

CHRONOLOGY

1813	Boston Manufacturing Company founds cotton mill at Waltham, Massachusetts
1815	War of 1812 ends
1816	James Monroe elected president
1818	Andrew Jackson invades Florida
1819	Supreme Court hands down far-reaching decision in Dartmouth College case and in *McCulloch* v. *Maryland* • Adams-Onís treaty cedes Spanish territory to the United States • Financial panic is followed by a depression lasting until 1823
1820	Missouri Compromise resolves nation's first sectional crisis • Monroe reelected president unanimously
1823	Monroe Doctrine proclaimed
1824	Lafayette revisits the United States • Supreme Court decides *Gibbons* v. *Ogden*
1825	Erie Canal completed; Canal Era begins

Recommended Reading

The standard surveys of the period between the War of 1812 and the Age of Jackson are two works by George Dangerfield: *The Era of Good Feelings* (1952) and *Awakening of American Nationalism, 1815–1828* (1965); but see also the early chapters of Charles Sellers, *The Market Revolution: Jacksonian America, 1815–1846* (1991). A lively narrative of westward expansion is Dale Van Every, *The Final Challenge: The American Frontier, 1804–1845* (1964); but Malcolm J. Rohrbough, *The Trans-Appalachian Frontier* (1978), is more comprehensive and authoritative. Outstanding studies of economic transformation and the rise of a market economy are George R. Taylor, *The Transportation Revolution, 1815–1860* (1951); Paul

W. Gates, *The Farmer's Age: Agriculture, 1815–1860* (1960); Stuart Bruchey, *Growth of the Modern American Economy* (1975); and Douglas C. North, *The Economic Growth of the United States, 1790–1860* (1961). An incisive study of the Marshall Court's decisions is Robert K. Faulkner, *The Jurisprudence of John Marshall* (1968). Samuel F. Bemis, *John Quincy Adams and the Foundations of American Policy* (1949), provides the classic account of the statesmanship that led to the Monroe Doctrine. But see also Ernest May, *The Making of the Monroe Doctrine* (1976), for a persuasive newer interpretation of how the doctrine originated.

Additional Bibliography

Good accounts of Lafayette's visit and what Americans made of it can be found in Fred Somkin, *Unquiet Eagle: Memory and Desire in the Idea of American Freedom, 1815–1860* (1967) and Anne C. Loveland, *Emblem of Liberty: The Image of Lafayette in the American Mind* (1971). For general accounts of the westward movement, see Frederick Jackson Turner, *The Frontier in American History* (1920), Ray A. Billington, *Westward Expansion* (1974), and Richard White, *It's Your Misfortune and None of My Own* (1992). On the removal of Native Americans, see A. H. DeRosier, *The Removal of the Choctaw Indians* (1970); Francis P. Prucha, *American Indian Policy in the Formative Years* (1962); Dale Van Every, *Disinherited: The Lost Birthright of the American Indian* (1966); and William G. McLoughlin, *Cherokee Renascence in the New Republic* (1986). Insights into life in the frontier areas can be derived from Frank Owsley, *Plain Folk of the Old South* (1948); Allen G. Bogue, *From Prairie to Corn Belt* (1963); Richard L. Power, *Planting Corn Belt Culture* (1953); and R. C. Buley, *The Old Northwest: Pioneer Period,* 2 vols. (1950). On exploration and fur trading in the trans-Mississippi West, see William H. Goetzmann, *Exploration and Empire* (1966) and David J. Wishart, *The Fur Trade of the American West, 1817–1840* (1979). On popular and literary images of the West and the frontier, see Henry Nash Smith, *Virgin Land: The American West as Symbol and Myth* (1950), and Richard Slotkin, *The Fatal Environment: The Myth of the Frontier in the Age of Industrialization* (1985).

Major works on the development of internal waterways are Carter Goodrich, *Government Promotion of American Canals and Railroads* (1960); Harry N. Schieber, *Ohio Canal Era* (1969); Ronald E. Shaw, *Erie Water West* (1966); and Erik E. Haites et al., *Western River Transportation* (1975). On agricultural development, see Percy W. Bidwell and John I. Falconer, *History of Agriculture in the Northern United States* (1925) and Lewis C. Gary, *History of Agriculture in the Southern United States to 1860,* 2 vols. (1933). The early growth of manufacturing is treated in Caroline F. Ware *The Early New England Cotton Manufacture* (1931); Arthur H. Cole, *The American Wool Manufacture,* 2 vols. (1926); Peter Temin, *Iron and Steel in Nineteenth Century America* (1964); H. J. Habakkuk, *American and British Technology in the Nineteenth Century* (1962); David J. Jeremy, *Transatlantic Industrial Revolution* (1981); and Robert F. Dalzell, *The Boston Associates and the World They Made* (1987). On early mill workers, see Bernice Selden, *The Mill Girls* (1983), and Thomas Dublin, *Women at Work: The Transformation of Work and Community in Lowell, Massachusetts, 1826–1860* (1979).

The politics of postwar nationalism are examined in Shaw Livermore, Jr., *The Twilight of Federalism* (1962); Harry Ammon, *James Monroe* (1971); James S. Young, *The Washington Community, 1800–1828* (1966); and Robert V. Remini, *Henry Clay: Statesman for the Union* (1991). The Marshall Court is covered in Leonard Baker, *John Marshall* (1974); Albert J. Beveridge, *John Marshall,* 4 vols. (1916–1919); and R. Kent Newmyer, *The Supreme Court Under Marshall and Taney* (1968). Morton J. Horwitz, *The Transformation of American Law, 1780–1860* (1977), deals with broader aspects of legal change.

On diplomacy and the Monroe Doctrine, see Philip C. Brooks, *Diplomacy and the Borderlands* (1939); Walter LaFeber, ed., *John Quincy Adams and American Continental Empire* (1965); and Dexter Perkins, *The Monroe Doctrine, 1823–1826* (1927) and *Hands Off: A History of the Monroe Doctrine* (1941).

The Triumph of
White Men's Democracy

So many Americans were moving about in the 1820s and 1830s that new industries sprung up just to meet their needs. To service the rising tide of travelers, transients, and new arrivals, entrepreneurs erected large hotels in the center of major cities. There they provided lodging, food, and drink on an unprecedented scale. These establishments were as different from the inns of the eighteenth century as the steamboat was from the flatboat. A prototype of the new hotel was the Boston Exchange Hotel with its 8 stories and 300 rooms. Opened in 1809, the Exchange burned down nine years later; and the depression that followed the financial panic of 1819 put a damper on hotel building. After the return of prosperity in 1825, the "first-class hotel" soon became a prominent feature of the American scene. The splendor and comforts of the Baltimore City Hotel, Gadsby's National Hotel in Washington, and the Tremont House of Boston—all of which opened in the late 1820s—dazzled travelers and local residents alike. By the 1830s, imposing hotels were springing up in commercial centers all over the country. The grandest of these was New York's Astor House, completed in 1836.

According to the historian Doris Elizabeth King, "the new hotels were so obviously 'public' and 'democratic' in their character that foreigners were often to describe them as a true reflection of American society." Their very existence showed that many people, white males in particular, were on the move geographically and socially. Among the hotels' patrons were traveling salesmen, ambitious young men seeking to establish themselves in a new city, and restless pursuers of "the main chance"(unexpected economic opportunities) not yet ready to put down roots.

Hotel managers shocked European visitors by failing to enforce traditional social distinctions among their clientele. Under the "American plan," guests were required to pay for their meals, and to eat at a common "table d'hôte" with anyone who happened to be there, including servants traveling with their employers. Ability to pay was the only requirement for admission (unless one happened to be an unescorted female or dark-skinned), and every white patron, regardless of social background and occupation, enjoyed the kind of personal service previously available only to a privileged class. Many patrons experienced such amenities as gaslight, indoor plumbing, and steam heat for the first time in their lives. Because a large proportion of the American population stayed in hotels at one time or another—a privilege that was, in Europe, reserved for the elite—foreigners inferred that there was widespread prosperity and a much greater "equality of condition" than existed in Europe.

The hotel culture also revealed some of the limitations of the new era of democratic ideals and aspirations. African Americans, Native Americans, and women were excluded or discriminated against, just as they were denied suffrage at a time when it was being extended to all white males. The genuinely poor—of whom there were more than met the eye of most European visitors—simply could not afford to patronize the hotels and were consigned to squalid rooming houses. If the social equality *within* the hotel reflected a decline in traditional rigid class lines, the broad gulf between potential patrons and those who could not pay the rates signaled the growth of inequality based squarely on wealth rather than inherited status.

The hotel life also reflected the emergence of democratic politics. Professional politicians of a new breed, pursuing the votes of a mass electorate, spent much of their time in hotels as they traveled about. Those elected to Congress or a state legislature often stayed in hotels during the session, and the political deals and bargains required for effective party organization or legislative success were sometimes concluded in these establishments.

When Andrew Jackson arrived in Washington to prepare for his administration in 1829, he took residence at the new National Hotel. After a horde of well-wishers had made a shambles of the White House during his inaugural reception, Jackson retreated to the National for peace and quiet. The hotel was more than a public and "democratic" gathering place; it could also serve as a haven where the rising men of politics and business could find rest and privacy. In its lobbies, salons, and private rooms the spirit of an age was expressing itself.

DEMOCRACY IN THEORY AND PRACTICE

During the 1820s and 1830s, the term *democracy* first became a generally accepted term to describe how American institutions were supposed to work. The Founders had defined democracy as direct rule by the masses; most of them rejected this concept of a democratic approach to government because it was at odds with their conception of a well-balanced republic led by a "natural aristocracy." For champions of popular government in the Jacksonian period, however, the "people" were truly sovereign and could do no wrong. "The voice of the people is the voice of God" was their clearest expression of this principle. Conservatives were less certain of the wisdom of the common folk. But even they were coming to recognize that public opinion had to be won over before major policy decisions could be made.

Besides evoking a heightened sense of "popular sovereignty," the democratic impulse seemed to stimulate a process of social leveling. Earlier Americans had usually assumed the rich and well-born should be treated with special respect and recognized as natural leaders of the community and guardians of its culture and values. By the 1830s, the disappearance of inherited social ranks and clearly defined aristocracies or privileged groups struck European visitors like Alexis de Tocqueville as the most radical feature of democracy in America. Historians have described this development as a decline of the spirit of "deference."

The decline of deference meant that "self-made men" of lowly origins could now rise more readily to positions of power and influence and that exclusiveness and aristocratic pretensions were likely to provoke popular hostility or scorn. But economic equality, in the sense of an equitable

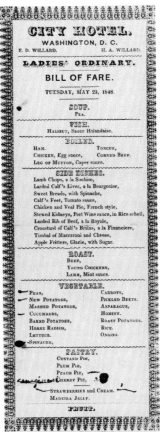

The democratic mingling of social classes was especially apparent in the dining rooms of major hotels that sprang up during the early nineteenth century. Under the "American plan," guests paid for each meal and chose their food from hearty menus like the ladies' ordinary menu from the City Hotel in Washington, D.C. in 1848 (left). Of course, dining at long tables with strangers of uncertain breeding and table manners did have its hazards, as illustrated by the contemporary cartoon, "Pass the Mustard."

sharing of wealth, was not part of the mainstream agenda of the Jacksonian period. This was, after all, a competitive capitalistic society. The watchword was equality of *opportunity* not equality of *reward*. Life was a race, and so long as white males appeared to have an equal start, there could be no reason for complaint if some were winners and some were losers. Historians now generally agree that economic inequality—the gap between rich and poor Americans—was actually increasing during this period of political and social democratization.

The Democratic Ferment

The supremacy of democracy was most obvious in the new politics of universal white manhood suffrage and mass political parties. By the 1820s, most states had removed the last remaining barriers to voting participation by all white males. This change was not as radical or controversial as it would be later in nineteenth-century Europe; ownership of land was so common in the United States that a general suffrage did not mean men without property became a voting majority.

Accompanying this broadening of the electorate was a rise in the proportion of public officials who were elected rather than appointed. More and more judges, as well as legislative and executive officeholders, were chosen by "the people." A new style of politicking developed. Politicians had to get out and campaign, demonstrating in their speeches on the stump that they could mirror the fears and concerns of the voters. Electoral politics began to assume a more festive and dramatic quality.

Skillful and farsighted politicians—like Martin Van Buren in New York—began in the 1820s to build stable statewide political organizations out of what had been loosely organized factions. Before the rise of effective national parties, politicians created true party organizations on the state level by dispensing government jobs to friends and supporters, and by attacking rivals as enemies of popular aspirations. Earlier politicians had regarded parties as a threat to republican virtue and had embraced them only as a temporary expedient, but Van Buren regarded a permanent two-party system as essential to democratic government. In his opinion, parties were an effective check on the temptation to abuse power, a tendency deeply planted in the human heart. The major break-

through in American political thought during the 1820s and 1830s was the idea of a "loyal opposition," ready to capitalize politically on the mistakes or excesses of the "ins," without denying the right of the "ins" to act in the same way when they became the "outs."

Changes in the method of nominating and electing a president fostered the growth of a two-party system on the national level. By 1828, presidential electors were chosen by popular vote rather than by state legislatures in all but two of the twenty-four states. The new need to mobilize grass-roots voters behind particular candidates required national organization. Coalitions of state parties that could agree on a single standard-bearer gradually evolved into the great national parties of the Jacksonian era—the Democrats and the Whigs. When national nominating conventions made their appearance in 1831, candidate selection became a matter to be taken up by representative party assemblies, not congressional caucuses or ad hoc political alliances.

New political institutions and practices encouraged a great upsurge of popular interest and participation. In the presidential election of 1824, the proportion of adult white males voting was less than 27 percent. In 1828, it rose sharply to 55 percent, held at about the same level for the elections of 1832 and 1836, and then shot up to 78 percent in 1840—the first election in which two fully organized national parties each nominated a single candidate and campaigned for their choices in every state in the Union.

Economic questions dominated the political controversies of the 1820s and 1830s. The panic of 1819 and the subsequent depression heightened popular interest in government economic policy, first on the state and then on the national level. No one really knew how to solve the problems of a market economy that went through cycles of boom and bust, but many people thought they had the answer. Some, especially small farmers, favored a return to a simpler and more "honest" economy without banks, paper money, and the easy credit that encouraged speculation. Others, particularly emerging entrepreneurs, saw salvation in government aid and protection for venture capital. Entrepreneurs appealed to state governments for charters that granted special privileges to banks, transportation enterprises, and manufacturing corporations. Politicians attempted to respond to these conflicting views about the best way to restore and maintain prosperity. Out of the economic distress of the early 1820s came rapid growth of state-level political activity and organization that foreshadowed the rise of national parties, which would be organized around economic programs.

The party disputes that arose over corporations, tariffs, banks, and internal improvements involved more than the direct economic concerns of particular interest groups. The republican ideology of the revolutionary period survived in the form of widespread fears of conspiracy against American liberty and equality. Whenever any group appeared to be exerting decisive influence over public policy, people who did not identify with that group's aspirations were quick to charge them with corruption and the unscrupulous pursuit of power.

The notion that the American experiment was a fragile one, constantly threatened by power-hungry conspirators, eventually took two principal forms. Jacksonians believed "the money power" endangered the survival of republicanism; their opponents feared that populist politicians like Jackson himself—alleged "rabble-rousers"—would gull the electorate into ratifying high-handed and tyrannical actions contrary to the true interests of the nation.

An object of increasing concern for both sides was the role of the federal government. Should it take positive steps to foster economic growth, as the National Republicans and later the Whigs contended, or should it simply attempt to destroy what Jacksonians decried as "special privilege" or "corporate monopoly"? Almost everyone favored equality of opportunity, but there was serious disagreement over whether this goal could best be achieved by active governmental support of commerce and industry or by divorcing the government from the economy in the name of laissez-faire and free competition.

For one group of dissenters, democracy took on a more radical meaning. Workingmen's parties and trade unions emerged in eastern cities during the late 1820s and early 1830s. Their leaders condemned the growing gap between the rich and the poor resulting from early industrialization and the growth of a market economy. They argued that an expansion of low-paying labor was putting working people under the dominance of their employers to such an extent that the American tradition of "equal rights" was in grave danger. Society, in their view, was divided between "producers"—laborers, artisans, farmers, and small business owners who ran their own enterprises—and nonproducing "parasites"—bankers, speculators, and merchant capitalists. Their aim was to give the producers greater control over the fruits of their labor.

These radicals called for a number of reforms to achieve their goal of equal rights. Thomas Skidmore, a founder of the New York Working Men's party, advocated the abolition of inheritance and a redistribution of property. Champions of the rights of labor also demanded greatly extended and improved systems of public education. But educational reform, however radical or extensive, could only provide equal opportunities to future generations. To relieve the plight of adult artisans and craftspeople at a time when their economic and social status was deteriorating, labor reformers and trade unionists experimented with cooperative production and called for a ten-hour workday, abolition of imprisonment for debt, and a currency system based exclusively on hard money so workers could no longer be paid in depreciated bank notes.

Philadelphia was an especially active center of labor politics and trade union activity. In 1827, the city's skilled artisans formed the Mechanics Union of Trade Associations, the nation's first metropolitan labor movement, and shortly thereafter launched the Working Men's party to compete in local elections. In 1834, fifty craft associations incorporated into the General Trades' Union of the City and County of Philadelphia, and within a year took the leading role in the first general strike in American history. The strike was successful in getting the ten-hour day accepted in most Philadelphia industries, but the depression that began in 1837 destroyed the General Trades' Union and nullified most of its gains. The same pattern of temporary success and ultimate defeat was repeated in other major cities. Nevertheless, American labor had set a precedent for the use of mass action aimed at the achievement of better working conditions.

In the 1830s and 1840s, northern abolitionists and early proponents of women's rights made other efforts to extend the meaning and scope of democracy. Radical abolitionists sought an immediate end to southern slavery and supported extension of the franchise and other civil rights to free blacks. A women's rights movement also

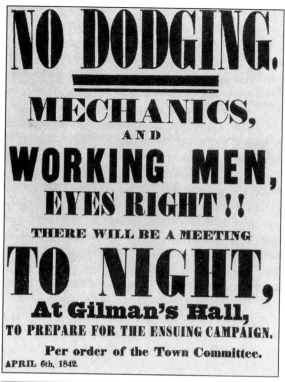

NO DODGING.

MECHANICS,

AND

WORKING MEN,

EYES RIGHT!!

THERE WILL BE A MEETING

TO NIGHT,

At Gilman's Hall,

TO PREPARE FOR THE ENSUING CAMPAIGN.

Per order of the Town Committee.

APRIL 6th, 1842.

Working Men's parties of the late 1820s and 1830s sought to close the widening gap between the rich and the poor and acted to improve working conditions.

developed, partially out of women's involvement in the abolitionist crusade and the enlarged conception of equal rights that their experiences had fostered. But Jacksonian America was too permeated with racism and male chauvinism to give much heed to claims that the equal rights prescribed by the Declaration of Independence should be extended to blacks and women. Most of those who advocated democratization explicitly limited its application to white males, and in some ways the civil and political status of blacks and women actually deteriorated during "the age of the common *man*." (See Chapter 11 for a more detailed discussion of these movements.)

Democracy and Society

Although some types of inequality persisted or even grew during the age of democracy, they did so in the face of a growing belief that equality was the governing principle of American society. What this meant in practice was that no one could expect special privileges because of family connections. The plain folk, who in an earlier period would have known their place and deferred to their betters, were now likely to greet claims for special treatment with indifference or scorn. High-status Europeans who traveled in America were constantly affronted by democratic attitudes and manners. One aristocrat was rudely rebuffed when he tried to hire an entire stage-coach for himself and his valet. On other occasions these blue-blooded tourists were forced to eat at the same table as teamsters and stagecoach drivers or share rooms in country inns with rough characters of all kinds. Another irritation to European visitors was the absence of special first-class accommodations on steamboats and railroads.

With the exception of slaveholders, wealthy Americans could not depend on a distinctive social class for domestic service. Instead of keeping "servants," they hired "help"—household workers who refused to wear livery, agreed to work for only short periods of time, and sometimes insisted on eating at the same table as their employers. As noted in the maid's comments quoted in Chapter 8, no true American was willing to be considered as a member of a servant class, and those who engaged in domestic work regarded it as a temporary stopgap. Except as a euphemistic substitute for the word *slave,* the term *servant* virtually disappeared from the American vocabulary.

The decline of distinctive modes of dress for upper and lower classes conveyed the principle of equality in yet another way. The elaborate peri-wigs and knee breeches worn by eighteenth-century gentlemen gave way to short hair and pantaloons, a style that was adopted by men of all social classes. Fashionable dress among women also ceased to be a sure index of gentility; serving girls on their day off wore the same kind of finery as the wives and daughters of the wealthy. Those with a good eye for detail might detect subtle differences in taste or in quality of materials, but the casual observer of crowds in a large city could easily conclude that all Americans belonged to a single social class.

Of course Americans were not all of one social class. In fact, inequality based on control of productive resources was increasing during the Jacksonian period. A growing percentage of the population, especially in urban areas, possessed no real estate and little other property. The rise of industrialization was creating a permanent class of low-paid, unorganized wage earners. In rural areas, there was a significant division between successful commercial farmers and smallholders or tenants who subsisted on marginal land, as well as enormous inequality of status between southern planters and their black slaves. But most foreign observers overlooked the widening gap between the propertied middle class and the laboring population; their attention was riveted on the fact that all white males were equal before the law and at the polls, a situation that was genuinely radical by European standards.

Traditional forms of privilege and elitism were also under strong attack, as evidenced by changes in the organization and status of the learned professions. Under Jacksonian pressure, state legislatures abolished the licensing requirements for physicians previously administered by local medical societies. As a result, practitioners of unorthodox modes of healing were permitted to compete freely with established medical doctors. One popular therapy was Thomsonianism, a form of treatment based entirely on the use of common herbs and roots. Thomsonians argued that their own form of medicine would make every man his own physician. The democratic tide also struck the legal profession. Local bar associations continued to set the qualifications for practicing attorneys, but in many places they lowered standards and admitted persons with little or no formal training and only the most rudimentary knowledge of the law.

For the clergy, "popular sovereignty" meant they were increasingly under the thumb of the laity. The growing dependence of ministers on the support and approval of their congregations forced them to develop a more popular and emotional style of preaching. Ministers had ceased to command respect merely because of their office. To succeed in their calling, they had to please the public, in much the same way a politician had to satisfy the electorate.

Democratic Culture

The democratic spirit also found expression in the rise of new forms of literature and art directed at a mass audience. The intentions of individual artists and writers varied considerably. Some sought success by pandering to popular taste in defiance of traditional standards of high culture. Others tried to capture the spirit of the age by portraying the everyday life of ordinary Americans rather than the traditional subjects of "aristocratic" art. A notable few hoped to use literature and art as a way of improving popular taste and instilling deeper moral and spiritual values. But all of them were aware their audience was the broad citizenry of a democratic nation rather than a refined elite.

The romantic movement in literature, which came to the fore in the early nineteenth century in both Europe and America, valued strong feeling and mystical intuition over the calm rationality and appeal to common experience that had prevailed in the writing of the eighteenth century. Romanticism was not necessarily connected with democracy; in Europe it sometimes went along with a reaffirmation of feudalism and the right of a superior few to rule over the masses. In the American setting, however, romanticism often appealed to the feelings and intuitions of ordinary people: the innate love of goodness, truth, and beauty that all people were thought to possess. Writers in search of popularity and economic success, however, often deserted the high plane of romantic art for crass sentimentalism—a willingness to pull out all emotional stops to thrill readers or bring tears to their eyes.

A mass market for popular literature was made possible by a rise in literacy and a revolution in the technology of printing. An increase in potential readers and a decrease in publishing costs led to a flood of lurid and sentimental novels, some of which became the first American best-sellers. By the 1840s and 1850s, writers like George Lippard, Mrs. Southworth, and Augusta Jane Evans had perfected the formulas that led to commercial success. Gothic horror and the perils of virtuous heroines threatened by dastardly villains were among the ingredients that readers came to expect from popular fiction. Many of the new sentimental novels were written by and for women. Some women writers implicitly protested against their situation by portraying men in general as tyrannical, unreliable, or vicious, and the women they abandoned or failed to support as resourceful individualists capable of making their own way in a man's world. But the standard happy endings sustained the convention that a woman's place was in the home, for a virtuous and protec-

James Fenimore Cooper's descriptions of the frontier shoreline of Lake Ontario in The Pathfinder *are examples of the romantic style in literature.*

134 people were killed in disorders stemming from hostility toward an English actor who was the rival of Edwin Forrest, the most popular American thespian of the time.

The spirit of "popular sovereignty" expressed itself less dramatically in the visual arts, but its influence was felt nonetheless. Beginning in the 1830s, painters turned from portraying great events and famous people to the depiction of scenes from everyday life. Democratic genre painters like William S. Mount and George Caleb Bingham captured the lives of plain folk with great skill and understanding. Mount, who painted lively rural scenes, expressed the credo of the democratic artist: "Paint pictures that will take with the public—never paint for the few but the many." Bingham was noted for his graphic images of Americans voting, carrying goods on riverboats, and engaging in other everyday activities.

Architecture and sculpture reflected the democratic spirit in a different way; they were viewed as civic art forms meant to glorify the achievements of the republic. In the 1820s and 1830s, the Greek style with its columned facades not only predominated in the architecture of public buildings but was also favored for banks, hotels, and private dwellings. Besides symbolizing an identification of the United States with the democracy of ancient Greece, it achieved monumental impressiveness at a fairly low cost. Even in newly settled frontier communities, it was relatively easy and inexpensive to put up a functional square building and then add a classical facade. Not everyone could live in structures that looked like Greek temples, but almost everyone could admire them from the outside or conduct business within their walls.

Sculpture was intended strictly for public admiration or inspiration, and its principal subjects were the heroes of the republic. The sculptors who accepted public commissions had to make sure their work met the expectations of politicians and taxpayers, who favored stately, idealized images. Horatio Greenough, the greatest sculptor of the pre–Civil War era, got into trouble when he unveiled a seated George Washington, dressed in classical garb and nude from the waist up. Much more acceptable was the equestrian figure of Andrew Jackson executed for the federal government by Clark Mills and unveiled in 1853.

tive man usually turned up and saved the heroine from independence.

In the theater, melodrama became the dominant genre. Despite religious objections, theatergoing was a popular recreation in the cities during the Jacksonian era. The standard fare involved the inevitable trio of beleaguered heroine, mustachioed villain, and a hero who asserted himself in the nick of time. Patriotic comedies extolling the common sense of the rustic Yankee who foiled the foppish European aristocrat were also popular and served to arouse the democratic sympathies of the audience. Men and women of all classes went to the theater, and those in the cheap seats often behaved raucously and even violently when they did not like what they saw. Unpopular actors or plays could even provoke serious riots. In an 1849 incident in New York,

William Sidney Mount, Rustic Dance After a Sleigh Ride, *1830. Mount's portrayals of country folk dancing, gambling, playing music, or horse-trading were pieces that appealed strongly to contemporaries, but art historians have found much to praise in his use of architecture, particularly that of the common barn, to achieve striking compositional effects.*

What most impressed the public was that Mills had succeeded in balancing the horse on two legs.

Serious exponents of a higher culture and a more refined sensibility sought to reach the new public in the hope of enlightening or uplifting it. The "Brahmin poets" of New England—Henry Wadsworth Longfellow, James Russell Lowell, and Oliver Wendell Holmes—offered lofty sentiments and moral messages to a receptive middle class; Ralph Waldo Emerson carried his philosophy of spiritual self-reliance to lyceums and lecture halls across the country, and great novelists like Nathaniel Hawthorne and Herman Melville experimented with the popular romantic genres. But Hawthorne and Melville failed to gain a large readership. The ironic and pessimistic view of life that pervaded their work clashed with the optimism of the age. For later generations of American critics, however, the works of Melville and Hawthorne became centerpieces of the American literary "renaissance" of the mid-nineteenth century. Hawthorne's *The Scarlet Letter* (1850) and Melville's *Moby-Dick* (1851) are now commonly regarded as masterworks of American fiction.

The great landscape painters of the period—Thomas Cole, Asher Durand, and Frederic Edwin Church—believed their representations of untamed nature would elevate popular taste and convey moral truths. The modern ideal of art for art's sake was utterly alien to the instructional spirit of mid-nineteenth-century American culture. The responsibility of the artist in a democratic society, it was generally assumed, was to contribute to the general welfare by encouraging virtue and proper sentiments. Only Edgar Allan Poe seemed to fit the European image of romantic genius, rebelling against middle-class pieties. But in his own way, Poe exploited the popular fascination with death in his verse and used the conventions of Gothic horror in his tales. The most original of the antebellum poets, Walt Whitman, sought to be a direct mouthpiece for the rising democratic spirit, but his abandonment of traditional verse forms and his freedom in dealing with the sexual side of human nature left him isolated and unappreciated during his most creative years.

JACKSON AND THE POLITICS OF DEMOCRACY

The public figure who came to symbolize the triumph of democracy was Andrew Jackson, who came out a loser in the presidential election of 1824. His victory four years later, his actions as

Asher Durand's paintings, such as In the Catskills *(1859), helped establish an image of a young and optimistic republic, as noble as its wilderness.*

president, and the great political party that formed around him refashioned national politics in a more democratic mold.

The Election of 1824 and J. Q. Adams's Administration

As Monroe's second term ended, the ruling Republican party was in disarray and could not agree on who should succeed to the presidency. The party's congressional caucus chose William Crawford of Georgia, an old-line Jeffersonian. But a majority of congressmen showed their disapproval of this outmoded method of nominating candidates by refusing to attend the caucus. Monroe himself favored John Quincy Adams of Massachusetts. This gave the New England statesman an important boost but did not discourage others from entering the contest. Supporters of Henry Clay and John C. Calhoun mounted campaigns for their favorites, and a group of local leaders in his home state of Tennessee tossed Jackson's hat into the ring.

Initially, Jackson was not given much of a chance. Unlike other aspirants, he had not played a conspicuous role in national politics; his sole claim to fame was as a military hero, and not even his original supporters believed this would be sufficient to catapult him into the White House. But after testing the waters, Calhoun withdrew and chose instead to run for vice president. Then Crawford suffered a debilitating stroke that weakened his chances. With one Southerner out of the race and another disabled, Jackson began to pick up support in slaveholding states. He also found favor among those in the North and West who were disenchanted with the economic nationalism of Clay and Adams.

In the election, Jackson won a plurality of the electoral votes, but lacked the necessary majority. The contest was thrown into the House of Representatives, where the legislators were to choose from among the three top candidates. Here Adams emerged victorious over Jackson and Crawford. Clay, who had just missed making the final three, provided the winning margin by persuading his supporters to vote for Adams. When Adams proceeded to appoint Clay as his secretary of state, the Jacksonians charged that a "corrupt bargain" had deprived their favorite of the presidency. Although there was no evidence Clay had bartered votes for the promise of a high office, the corrupt bargain charge was widely believed. As a result, Adams assumed office under a cloud of suspicion.

Adams had a difficult and frustrating presidency. The political winds were blowing against nationalistic programs, partly because the country was just recovering from a depression that many thought had been caused or worsened by federal banking and tariff policies. Adams refused to bow to public opinion and called for an expansion of federal activity. Advocates of states' rights and a strict construction of the Constitution were aghast, and the opposition that developed in Congress turned the administration's domestic program into a pipe dream.

The new Congress elected in 1826 was clearly under the control of men hostile to the administration and favorable to the presidential aspirations of Andrew Jackson. The tariff issue was the main business on their agenda. Pressure for greater protection came not only from manufacturers but also from many farmers, especially wool and hemp growers, who would supply critical votes in the upcoming presidential election. The cotton-growing South—the only section

The Election of 1824

Candidate	Party	Popular Vote	Electoral Vote*
J. Q. Adams	No party	113,122	84
Jackson	designations	151,271	99
Clay		47,531	37
Crawford		40,856	41

No candidate received a majority of the electoral votes. Adams was elected by the House of Representatives.

where tariffs of all kinds were unpopular—was assumed to be safely in the general's camp regardless of his stand on the tariff. Therefore, promoters of Jackson's candidacy felt safe in supporting a high tariff to swing critical votes in Jackson's direction. Jackson himself had never categorically opposed protective tariffs so long as they were "judicious."

As it turned out, the resulting tariff law was anything but judicious. Congress had operated on a give-and-take principle, trying to provide something for everybody. Those favoring protection for farmers agreed to protection for manufacturers and vice versa. The substantial across-the-board increase in duties that resulted, however, angered southern free traders and became known as the "tariff of abominations." Historians long erred in explaining the 1828 tariff as a complex Jacksonian plot that backfired; it was in fact an early example of how special interest groups can achieve their goals in democratic politics through the process of legislative bargaining known as logrolling.

Jackson Comes to Power

The campaign of 1828 actually began with Adams's election in 1824. Rallying around the charge of a corrupt bargain between Adams and Clay, Jackson's supporters began to organize on the state and local level with an eye to reversing the outcome of the election. By late 1827, a Jackson committee was functioning in virtually every county and important town or city in the nation. Influential state or regional leaders who had supported other candidates in 1824 now rallied behind the Tennessean to create a formidable coalition.

The most significant of these were Vice President Calhoun, who now spoke for the militant states' rights sentiment of the South; Senator Martin Van Buren, who dominated New York politics through the political machine known as the Albany Regency; and two Kentucky editors, Francis P. Blair and Amos Kendall, who worked in the West to mobilize opposition to Henry Clay and his "American system" (a plan for government-sponsored economic development emphasizing protective tariffs and internal improvements). As they prepared themselves for the canvass of 1828, these leaders and their many local followers laid the foundations for the first modern American political party—the Democrats. The fact that the Democratic party was founded to promote the cause of a particular presidential candidate revealed a central characteristic of the emerging two-party system. From this time on, according to historian Richard P. McCormick, national parties existed primarily "to engage in a contest for the presidency." Without this great prize, there would have been little incentive to create national organizations out of the parties and factions developing in the several states.

The election of 1828 saw the birth of a new era of mass democracy. The mighty effort on behalf of Jackson featured the widespread use of such electioneering techniques as huge public rallies, torchlight parades, and lavish barbecues or picnics paid for by the candidate's supporters. Personalities and mudslinging dominated the campaign. The Democratic party press and a legion of pamphleteers bombarded the public with vicious personal attacks on Adams and praise of "Old Hickory" as Jackson was called. The supporters of Adams responded in kind; they even sunk to the level of accusing Jackson's wife Rachel of bigamy and adultery because she had unwittingly married Jackson before being officially divorced from her first husband. The Democrats then came up with the utterly false charge that Adams's wife was born out of wedlock!

What gave Jacksonians the edge was their success in portraying their candidate as an authentic man of the people, despite his substantial fortune in land and slaves. His backwoods upbringing, his record as a popular military hero and Indian fighter, and even his lack of education were touted as evidence that he was a true representative of the common people, especially the plain folk of the South and the West. In the words of one of

When it was clear that he would not win the presidency in 1824, Henry Clay, shown here in an 1822 portrait by Charles Bird King, threw his support to John Quincy Adams.

An 1835 painting of Andrew Jackson in the heroic style by Thomas Sully. The painting shows Jackson as the common people saw him.

his supporters, Jackson had "a judgment unclouded by the visionary speculations of the academician." Adams, according to Democratic propagandists, was the exact opposite—an over-educated aristocrat, more at home in the salon and the study than among plain people. Nature's nobleman was pitted against the aloof New England intellectual, and Adams never really had a chance.

Jackson won by a popular vote margin of 150,000 and by more than 2 to 1 in the electoral college. Clearly Jackson's organization had been more effective and his popular appeal substantially greater. He had piled up massive majorities in the Deep South, but the voters elsewhere divided fairly evenly. Adams, in fact, won a majority of the electoral vote in the northern states. Furthermore, it was not clear what kind of a mandate Jackson had won. Most of the politicians in his camp favored states' rights and limited government as against the nationalism of Adams and Clay, but the general himself had never taken a clear public stand on such issues as banks, tariffs, and internal improvements. He did, however, stand for the removal of Indians

from the Gulf states, and this was the key to his immense popularity in that region.

Jackson turned out to be one of the most forceful and domineering of American presidents. His most striking character traits were an indomitable will, an intolerance of opposition, and a prickly pride that would not permit him to forgive or forget an insult or supposed act of betrayal. It is sometimes hard to determine whether his political actions were motivated by principle or personal spite. As a young man on his own in a frontier environment, he had learned to fight his own battles. Somewhat violent in temper and action, he fought a number of duels and served in wars against the British, the Spanish, and the Indians with a zeal his critics found excessive. His experiences had made him tough and resourceful but had also deprived him of the

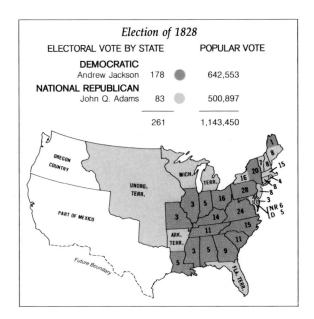

Election of 1828

ELECTORAL VOTE BY STATE · POPULAR VOTE

DEMOCRATIC
Andrew Jackson   178   642,553

NATIONAL REPUBLICAN
John Q. Adams   83   500,897

261   1,143,450

Jackson's resigning cabinet members were, according to this cartoon, rats deserting a crumbling house.

flexibility normally associated with successful politicians. Yet he generally got what he wanted.

Jackson's presidency commenced with his open endorsement of rotation of officeholders or what his critics called "the spoils system." Although he did not actually depart radically from his predecessors in the extent to which he removed federal officeholders and replaced them with his supporters, he was the first president to defend this practice as a legitimate application of democratic doctrine. He proclaimed in his first annual message that "the duties of all public officers are . . . so plain and simple that men of intelligence may readily qualify themselves for their performance" and that "no man has any more intrinsic claim to office than another."

Midway through his first administration Jackson completely reorganized his cabinet, replacing almost all of his original appointees. At the root of this upheaval was a growing feud between Jackson and Vice President Calhoun, but the incident that brought it to a head was the Peggy Eaton affair. Peggy O'Neale Eaton was the daughter of a Washington tavern owner who married Secretary of War John Eaton in 1829. Because of gossip about her moral character, the wives of other cabinet members refused to receive her socially. Jackson became her fervent champion, partly because he found the charges against her reminiscent of the slanders against his late wife Rachel. When he raised the issue of Mrs. Eaton's social status at a cabinet meeting, only

Secretary of State Van Buren, a widower, supported his stand. This seemingly trivial incident led to the resignation of all but one of the cabinet members, and the president was able to begin again with a fresh slate. Although Van Buren resigned with the rest to promote a thorough reorganization, his loyalty was rewarded by his appointment as minister to England and strong prospects of future favor.

Indian Removal

The first major policy question facing the Jackson administration concerned the fate of Native Americans. Jackson had long favored removing eastern Indians to lands beyond the Mississippi. In his military service on the southern frontier, he had been directly involved in persuading and coercing tribal groups to emigrate. Jackson's support of removal was no different from the policy of previous administrations. The only real issues to be determined were how rapidly and thoroughly the process should be carried out and by what means. At the time of Jackson's election, the states of Georgia, Alabama, and Mississippi, distressed by the federal government's failure to eliminate the substantial Indian enclaves remaining within their boundaries, were clamoring for quick action. Since Adams seemed to have dragged his feet on the issue, voters in these states turned overwhelmingly to Jackson, who promised to expel the Indians without delay.

The greatest obstacle to voluntary relocation was the Cherokee nation, which held lands in Georgia, Alabama, North Carolina, and Tennessee. The Cherokees refused to move. They had instituted a republican form of government for themselves, achieved literacy in their own language, and made considerable progress toward adopting a settled agrarian way of life similar to that of southern whites. The professed aim of the government's Indian policy was the "civilization" of the Indians, and the official reason given for removal was that this aim could not be accomplished in areas surrounded by white settlements, subject to demoralizing frontier influences. Missionaries and northeastern philanthropists argued the Cherokees were a major exception and should be allowed to remain where they were.

The southern states disagreed. Immediately after Jackson's election, Georgia extended its state laws over the Cherokees. Before his inauguration, Alabama and Mississippi took similar action by asserting state authority over the tribes in their own states. This legislation defied provisions of the Constitution giving the federal government exclusive jurisdiction over Indian affairs and also violated specific treaties. As anticipated, Jackson quickly gave his endorsement to the state actions. His own attitude toward Indians was that they were children when they did the white man's bidding and savage beasts when they resisted. He was also keenly aware of his political debt to the land-hungry states of the South. Consequently, in his December 1829 message to Congress, he advocated a new and more coercive removal policy. He denied Cherokee autonomy, asserted the primacy of states' rights over Indian rights, and called for the speedy and thorough

Sequoyah's invention of the Cherokee alphabet enabled thousands of Cherokees to read and write primers and newspapers published in their own language.

removal of all eastern Indians to designated areas beyond the Mississippi.

Early in 1830, the president's congressional supporters introduced a bill to implement this policy. The ensuing debate was vigorous and heated. Opponents took up the cause of the Cherokees in particular and charged that the president had defied the Constitution by removing federal protection from the southeastern tribes. But Jackson and his supporters were determined to ride roughshod over humanitarian or constitutional objections to Indian dispossession. With strong support from the South and the western border states, the removal bill passed the Senate by a vote of 28 to 19 and the House by the narrow margin of 102 to 97.

Jackson then moved quickly to conclude the necessary treaties, using the threat of unilateral state action to bludgeon the tribes into submission. In 1832, he condoned Georgia's defiance of a Supreme Court decision (*Worcester* v. *Georgia*) that denied the right of a state to extend its jurisdiction over tribal lands. By 1833, all the southeastern tribes except the Cherokees had agreed to evacuate their ancestral homes. In 1838, a stubbornly resisting majority faction of the Cherokees were rounded up by federal troops and forcibly marched to Oklahoma. This trek—known as the "Trail of Tears"—was made under such harsh conditions that almost 4,000 of approximately 13,000 marchers died on the way. The Cherokee removal exposed the prejudiced and greedy side of Jacksonian democracy.

The Nullification Crisis

During the 1820s, Southerners became increasingly fearful of federal encroachment on the rights of the states. Behind this concern, in South Carolina at least, was a strengthened commitment to the preservation of slavery and a resulting anxiety about possible uses of federal power to strike at the "peculiar institution." Hoping to keep the explosive slavery issue out of the political limelight, South Carolinians seized on another genuine grievance—the protective tariff—as the issue on which to take their stand in favor of a state veto power over federal actions they viewed as contrary to their interests. As a staple-producing and exporting region, the South had sound economic reasons for favoring free trade. Tariffs increased the prices that southern agriculturalists paid for manufactured goods and threatened to undermine their foreign markets by inciting counterprotection. An economic crisis in the South Carolina upcountry during the 1820s made that state particularly receptive to extreme positions on the tariff and states' rights.

Vice President John C. Calhoun emerged as the leader of the states' rights insurgency in South Carolina, abandoning his earlier support of nationalism and the American system. After the passage of the tariff of abominations in 1828, the state legislature declared the new duties unconstitutional and endorsed a lengthy statement—written anonymously by Calhoun—that affirmed the right of an individual state to nullify federal law. Calhoun supported Jackson in 1828 and planned to serve amicably as his vice president, expecting Jackson would support his native region on questions involving the tariff and states' rights. He also entertained hopes of succeeding Jackson as president.

Early in his administration, Jackson appeared well attuned to the southern slave-holding position on state versus federal authority. Besides acquiescing in Georgia's de facto nullification of

federal treaties upholding Indian tribal rights, he vetoed a major internal improvements bill in 1830, invoking a strict construction of the Constitution to deny federal funds for the building of the Maysville Road in Kentucky.

In the meantime, however, a bitter personal feud developed between Jackson and Calhoun. The vice president and his wife were viewed by Jackson as prime movers in the ostracism of Peggy Eaton. Furthermore, evidence came to light that Calhoun, as secretary of war in Monroe's cabinet in 1818, had privately advocated punishing Jackson for his incursion into Florida. As Calhoun lost favor with Jackson, it became clear that Van Buren rather than the vice president would be Jackson's designated successor. The personal breach between Jackson and Calhoun colored and intensified their confrontation over nullification and the tariff.

The two men differed on matters of principle as well. Although generally a defender of states' rights and strict construction of the Constitution, Jackson opposed the theory of nullification as a threat to the survival of the Union. In his view, federal power should be held in check, but this did not mean the states were truly sovereign. His nationalism was that of a military man who had fought for the United States against foreign enemies and was not about to permit the nation's disintegration at the hands of domestic dissidents. The differences between Jackson and Calhoun came into the open at the Jefferson Day Dinner in 1830, when Jackson offered the toast "Our Union: It must be preserved"; to which Calhoun responded: "The Union next to Liberty most dear. May we always remember that it can only be preserved by distributing equally the benefits and the burdens of the Union."

In 1830 and 1831, the movement against the tariff gained strength in South Carolina. Calhoun openly took the lead, elaborating further on his view that states had the right to set aside federal laws. In 1832, Congress passed a new tariff that lowered the rates slightly but retained the principle of protection. Supporters of nullification argued that the new law simply demonstrated that no genuine relief could be expected from Washington. They then succeeded in persuading the South Carolina state legislature to call a special convention. When the convention met in

Robert Lindneux, The Trail of Tears *(1942). Cherokees, carrying their few possessions, are prodded along by U. S. soldiers on the "Trail of Tears." Several thousand Native Americans died on the ruthless, forced march from their homelands in the East to the newly established Indian Territory in Oklahoma.*

November 1832, the members voted overwhelmingly to nullify the tariffs of 1828 and 1832 and to forbid the collection of customs duties within the state.

Jackson reacted with characteristic decisiveness. He alerted the secretary of war to prepare for possible military action, issued a proclamation denouncing nullification as a treasonous attack on the Union, and asked Congress to vote him the authority to use the army to enforce the tariff. At the same time, he sought to pacify the nullifiers somewhat by recommending a lower tariff. Congress responded by enacting the Force Bill—which gave the president the military powers he sought—and the compromise tariff of 1833. The latter was primarily the work of Jackson's political enemy Henry Clay, but the president signed it anyway. Faced with Jackson's clear intention to use force if necessary and somewhat appeased by the prospect of a lower tariff, South Carolina suspended the nullification ordinance in late January 1833 and formally rescinded it in March, after the new tariff had been enacted. To demonstrate they had not conceded their constitutional position, the convention delegates concluded their deliberations by nullifying the Force Bill.

The nullification crisis revealed South Carolinians would not tolerate any federal action that seemed contrary to their interests or raised doubts about the institution of slavery. The nullifiers' philosophy implied the right of secession as well as the right to declare laws of Congress null and void. As subsequent events would show, a fear of northern meddling with slavery was the main spur to the growth of a militant doctrine of state sovereignty in the South. At the time of the nullification crisis, the other slave states had not yet developed such strong anxieties about the future of the "peculiar institution" and had not embraced South Carolina's radical conception of state sovereignty. Jackson was himself a Southerner and a slaveholder, a man who detested abolitionists and everything they stood for. In general, he was a proslavery president; later he would use his executive power to stop antislavery literature from being carried by the U. S. mails.

Some far-sighted southern loyalists, however, were alarmed by the Unionist doctrines Jackson propounded in his proclamation against nullification. More strongly than any previous president, he had asserted the federal government was supreme over the states and that the Union was indivisible. What was more, he had justified the

Vice President John C. Calhoun emerged as a champion of states' rights during the nullification crisis, a time when cartoons depicted the emaciated South burdened by tariffs while the North grew fat at southern expense.

use of force against states that denied federal authority.

THE BANK WAR AND THE SECOND PARTY SYSTEM

Jackson's most important and controversial use of executive power was his successful attack on the Bank of the United States. "The Bank War" revealed some of the deepest concerns of Jackson and his supporters and dramatically expressed their concept of democracy. It also aroused intense opposition to the president and his policies, an opposition that crystallized in a new national party—the Whigs. The destruction of the Bank and the economic disruption that followed brought to the forefront the issue of the government's relationship to the nation's financial system. Differences on this question helped to sustain the new two-party system.

Mr. Biddle's Bank

The Bank of the United States had long been embroiled in public controversy. Its role in precipitating the panic of 1819 by first extending credit freely and then suddenly calling in its loans had led many, especially in the South and the West, to blame the Bank for the subsequent depression. But after Nicholas Biddle took over the Bank's presidency in 1823, it regained public confidence. Biddle was an able manager who probably understood the mysteries of banking

and currency better than any other American of his generation. A Philadelphia gentleman of broad culture, extensive education, and some political experience, his major faults were his arrogance and his vanity. He was inclined to rely too much on his own judgment and refused to admit his mistakes until it was too late to correct them. But his record prior to the confrontation with Jackson was a good one. In 1825 and again in 1828, he acted decisively to curb an overextension of credit by state banks and helped avert a recurrence of the boom-and-bust cycle.

The actual performance of the Bank was not the only target of criticism about it. Old-line Jeffersonians had always opposed it on principle, both because they viewed its establishment as unconstitutional and because it placed too much power in the hands of a small, privileged group. The Bank was a chartered monopoly, an essentially private corporation that performed public services in return for exclusive economic rights. "In 1828," according to historian Robert Remini, "the Bank was a financial colossus, entrenched in the nation's economy, possessing the means of draining specie from state banks at will and regulating the currency according to its own estimate of the nation's needs."

Because of the Bank's great influence, it was easy to blame it for anything that went wrong with the economy. For those who had misgivings about the rise of the national market, it epitomized the forces threatening the independence and prosperity of small producers. In an era of rising white men's democracy, an obvious and telling objection to the Bank was simply that it possessed great power and privilege without being under popular control.

The Bank Veto and the Election of 1832

Jackson came into office with strong reservations about banking and paper money in general—in part as a result of his own brushes with bankruptcy after accepting promissory notes that depreciated in value. He also harbored suspicions that branches of the Bank of the United States had illicitly used their influence on behalf of his opponent in the presidential election. In his annual messages in 1829 and 1830, Jackson called on Congress to begin discussing "possible modification of a system which cannot continue to exist in its present form without . . . perpetual apprehensions and discontent on the part of the States and the People."

Biddle began to worry about the fate of the Bank's charter when it came up for renewal in 1836. At the same time, Jackson was listening to the advice of close friends and unofficial advisers—members of his "Kitchen Cabinet"—especially Amos Kendall and Francis P. Blair, who thought an attack on the Bank would provide a good party issue for the election of 1832. Biddle then made a fateful blunder. Panicked by the presidential messages and the anti-Bank oratory of congressional Jacksonians like Senator Thomas Hart Benton of Missouri, he determined to seek recharter by Congress in 1832, four years ahead of schedule. Senator Henry Clay, leader of the antiadministration forces on Capitol Hill, encouraged this move because he was convinced Jackson had chosen the unpopular side of the issue and would be embarrassed or even discredited by a congressional endorsement of the Bank.

The bill to recharter, which was introduced in the House and Senate in early 1832, aroused Jackson and unified his administration and party against renewal. The bill found many supporters in Congress, however. A number of legislators had received loans from the Bank, and the economy seemed to be prospering under the Bank's guidance. As a result, the bill to recharter passed Congress with ease.

The next move was Jackson's, and he made the most of the opportunity. He vetoed the bill and defended his action with ringing statements of principle. After repeating his opinion that the Bank was unconstitutional, notwithstanding the Supreme Court's ruling on the issue, he went on to argue that it violated the fundamental rights of the people in a democratic society: "In the full enjoyment of the gifts of Heaven and the fruits of superior industry, economy, and virtue, every man is equally entitled to protection by law; but when the laws undertake to add to those natural and just advantages artificial distinctions, to grant . . . exclusive privileges, the humble members of society—the farmers, mechanics, and laborers—who have neither the time nor the means of securing like favors to themselves, have a right to complain of the injustice of their government." Government, he added, should "confine itself to equal protection."

Jackson thus called on the common people to join him in fighting the "monster" corporation. His veto message was the first ever to use more than strictly constitutional arguments and to deal directly with social and economic issues. Congressional attempts to override the veto failed, and Jackson resolved to take the entire issue to the people in the upcoming presidential election.

The 1832 election, the first in which candidates were chosen by national nominating conventions, pitted Jackson against Henry Clay, standard-bearer of the National Republicans. Although the Democrats did not adopt a formal platform, the party stood firmly behind Jackson in his opposition to rechartering the Bank. Clay and the National Republicans attempted to marshal the pro-Bank sentiment that was strong in many parts of the country. But Jackson won a great personal triumph, garnering 219 electoral votes to 49 for Clay. His share of the popular vote was not quite as high as it was in 1828, but it was substantial enough to be interpreted as a mandate for continuing the war against the Bank.

Killing the Bank

Not content with preventing the Bank from getting a new charter, the victorious Jackson now resolved to attack it directly by removing federal deposits from Biddle's vaults. Jackson told Van Buren, "The bank . . . is trying to kill me, but I will kill it." The Bank had indeed used all the political influence it could muster in an attempt to prevent Jackson's reelection, in an act of self-defense. Old Hickory regarded Biddle's actions as a personal attack, part of a devious plot to destroy the president's reputation and deny him the popular approval he deserved. Although he presided over the first modern American political party, Jackson did not really share Van Buren's belief in the legitimacy of a competitive party system. In his view, his opponents were not merely wrong, they were evil and deserved to be destroyed. Furthermore, the election results convinced him he was the people's chosen instrument in the struggle against corruption and privilege, the only man who could save the pure republicanism of Jefferson and the Founders from the "monster bank."

In order to remove the deposits from the Bank, Jackson had to overcome strong resistance in his own cabinet. When one secretary of the treasury refused to support the policy, he was shifted to another cabinet post. When a second balked at carrying out removal, he was replaced by Roger B. Taney, a Jackson loyalist and dedicated opponent of the Bank. Beginning in late September

Aided by Van Buren (center), Jackson wields his veto rod against the Bank, whose heads represent the directors of the state branches. Biddle is wearing the top hat.

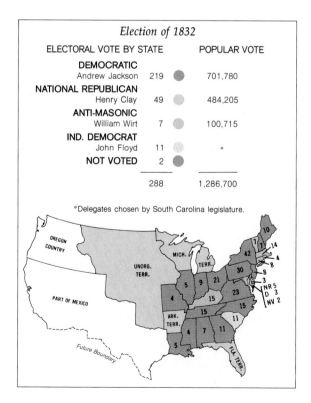

Election of 1832

ELECTORAL VOTE BY STATE		POPULAR VOTE
DEMOCRATIC		
Andrew Jackson	219	701,780
NATIONAL REPUBLICAN		
Henry Clay	49	484,205
ANTI-MASONIC		
William Wirt	7	100,715
IND. DEMOCRAT		
John Floyd	11	*
NOT VOTED	2	
	288	1,286,700

*Delegates chosen by South Carolina legislature.

1833, Taney ceased depositing government money in the Bank of the United States and began to withdraw the funds already there. Although Jackson had earlier suggested the government keep its money in some kind of public bank, he had never worked out the details and made a specific proposal to Congress. The problem of how to dispose of the funds was therefore resolved by an ill-advised decision to place them in selected state banks. By the end of 1833, twenty-three state banks had been chosen as depositories. Opponents charged the banks had been selected for political rather than fiscal reasons and dubbed them Jackson's "pet banks." Since Congress refused to approve administration proposals to regulate the credit policies of these banks, Jackson's effort to shift to a hard-money economy was quickly nullified by the use the state banks made of these new deposits. They extended credit more recklessly than before and increased the amount of paper money in circulation.

The Bank of the United States counterattacked by calling in outstanding loans and instituting a policy of credit contraction that helped bring on an economic recession. Biddle hoped to win support for recharter by demonstrating that weakening the Bank's position would be disastrous for the economy. With some justice, the president's supporters accused Biddle of deliberately and unnecessarily causing economic distress out of personal resentment and a desire to maintain his unchecked powers and privileges. The Bank never did regain its charter.

Strong opposition to Jackson's fiscal policies developed in Congress. Henry Clay and his supporters contended that the president had violated the Bank's charter and exceeded his constitutional authority when he removed the deposits. They eventually persuaded the Senate to approve a motion of censure. Jacksonians in the House were able to block such action, but the president was further humiliated when the Senate refused to confirm Taney as secretary of the treasury. Not all of this criticism and obstructionism can be attributed to sour grapes on the part of pro-Bank politicians. Some congressmen who originally defended Jackson's veto now became disenchanted with the president because they thought he had gone too far in asserting the powers of his office.

The Emergence of the Whigs

The coalition that passed the censure resolution in the Senate provided the nucleus for a new national party—the Whigs. The leadership of the new party and a majority of its support came from National Republicans associated with Clay and New England ex-Federalists led by Senator Daniel Webster of Massachusetts. The Whigs also picked up critical support from southern proponents of states' rights who had been upset by the political nationalism of Jackson's stand on nullification and now saw an unconstitutional abuse of power in his withdrawal of federal deposits from the Bank of the United States. Even Calhoun and his nullifiers occasionally cooperated with the Whig camp. The initial rallying cry for this diverse anti-Jackson coalition was "executive usurpation." The Whig label was chosen because of its associations with both English and American Revolutionary opposition to royal power and prerogatives. In their propaganda, the Whigs portrayed the tyrannical designs of "King Andrew" and his court.

The Whigs also gradually absorbed the Anti-Masonic party, a surprisingly strong political movement that had arisen in the northeastern states in the late 1820s and early 1830s.

Capitalizing on the hysteria aroused by the 1826 disappearance and apparent murder of a New Yorker who had threatened to reveal the secrets of the Masonic order, the Anti-Masons exploited traditional American fears of secret societies and conspiracies. They also appealed successfully to the moral concerns of the northern middle class under the sway of an emerging evangelical Protestantism. (For more on the evangelical movement, see Chapter 11.) Anti-Masons detested Jacksonianism mainly because it stood for a toleration of diverse lifestyles. Democrats did not think government should be concerned about people who drank, gambled, or found better things to do than go to church on Sundays. Their opponents from the Anti-Masonic tradition believed government should restrict such "sinful" behavior. This desire for moral and religious uniformity contributed an important cultural dimension to northern Whiggery.

As the election of 1836 approached, the government's fiscal policies also provoked a localized rebellion among the urban working-class elements of the Democratic coalition. In New York City, a dissident faction broke with the regular Democratic organization mainly over issues involving banking and currency. These radicals—called "Loco-Focos" after the matches they used for illumination when their opponents turned off the gaslights at a party meeting—favored a strict hard-money policy and condemned Jackson's transfer of federal deposits to the state banks as inflationary. Because they wanted working people to be paid in specie rather than bank notes, the Loco-Focos went beyond opposition to the Bank of the United States and attacked state banks as well. Seeing no basis for cooperation with the Whigs, they established the independent Equal Rights Party and nominated a separate state ticket for 1836.

Jackson himself had hard-money sentiments and regarded the "pet bank" solution as a stopgap measure rather than a final solution to the money problem. Somewhat reluctantly, he surrendered to congressional pressure in early 1836 and signed legislation allocating surplus federal revenues to the deposit banks, increasing their numbers, and weakening federal controls over them. The result was runaway inflation. State banks in the South and West responded to demands from land-speculating interests by issuing a new flood of paper money. Reacting some-what belatedly to the speculative mania he had inadvertently helped to create, Jackson pricked the bubble on July 11, 1836. He issued his "specie circular," requiring that after August 15 only gold and silver would be accepted in payment for public lands. This action served to curb inflation and land speculation but did so in such a sudden and drastic way that it helped precipitate the financial panic of 1837.

The Rise and Fall of Van Buren

As his successor, Jackson chose Martin Van Buren, who had served him loyally as vice president during his second term. Van Buren was the greatest master of practical politics in the Democratic party, and the Democratic National Convention of 1835 unanimously confirmed Jackson's choice. In accepting the nomination, Van Buren promised to "tread generally in the footsteps of General Jackson."

The newly created Whig party, reflecting the diversity of its constituency, did not try to decide on a single standard-bearer. Instead, each region chose candidates—Daniel Webster in the East, William Henry Harrison of Ohio (also the Anti-Masonic nominee) in the Old Northwest, and Hugh Lawson White of Tennessee (a former Jackson supporter) in the South. Whigs hoped to deprive Van Buren of enough electoral votes to throw the election into the House of Representatives where one of the Whigs might stand a chance.

This stratagem proved unsuccessful. Van Buren carried fifteen of the twenty-six states and won a clear majority in the electoral college. But the election foreshadowed future trouble for the Democrats, particularly in the South. There the Whigs ran virtually even, erasing the enormous majorities that Jackson had run up in 1828 and 1832. The emergence of a two-party system in the previously solid Deep South resulted from two factors—opposition to some of Jackson's policies and the image of Van Buren as an unreliable Yankee politician. The division did not reflect basic disagreement on the slavery issue. Whigs and Democrats shared a commitment to protecting slavery, and each tried to persuade the electorate they could do the job better than the opposition.

An adroit politician and a loyal vice president to Jackson, Martin Van Buren was Jackson's choice and the Democratic party's nominee for president in 1836.

As he took office Van Buren was immediately faced with a catastrophic depression. The price of cotton fell by almost 50 percent, banks all over the nation suspended specie payments, many businesses went bankrupt, and unemployed persons demonstrated in several cities. The sale of public lands fell off so drastically that the federal surplus, earmarked in 1836 for distribution to the states, now became a deficit.

The panic of 1837, economic historians have concluded, was not exclusively, or even primarily, the result of government policies. It was in fact international in scope and reflected some complex changes in the world economy that were beyond the control of American policymakers. But the Whigs were quick to blame the state of the economy on Jacksonian finance, and the administration had to make a politically effective response. Since Van Buren and his party were committed to a policy of laissez-faire on the federal level, there was little or nothing they could do to relieve economic distress through subsidies or relief measures. But Van Buren could at least try to salvage the federal funds deposited in shaky state banks and devise a new system of public finance that would not contribute to future panics by fueling speculation and credit expansion.

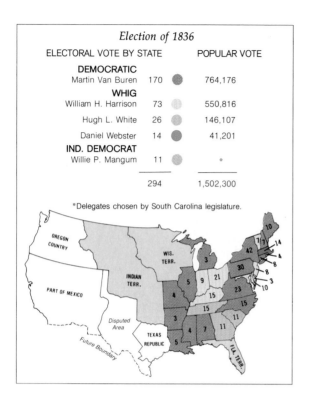

Election of 1836

ELECTORAL VOTE BY STATE		POPULAR VOTE
DEMOCRATIC		
Martin Van Buren	170	764,176
WHIG		
William H. Harrison	73	550,816
Hugh L. White	26	146,107
Daniel Webster	14	41,201
IND. DEMOCRAT		
Willie P. Mangum	11	*
	294	1,502,300

*Delegates chosen by South Carolina legislature.

Van Buren's solution was to establish a public depository for government funds with no connections whatsoever to commercial banking. His proposal for such an "independent subtreasury" aroused intense opposition from the congressional Whigs, who strongly favored the reestablishment of a national bank as the only way to restore economic stability. Whig resistance stalled the subtreasury bill for three years; it was not until 1840 that it was enacted into law. In the meantime, the economy had temporarily revived in 1838 only to sink again into a deeper depression the following year.

Van Buren's chances for reelection in 1840 were undoubtedly hurt by the state of the economy. But the fact that he lacked the popular appeal and personal charisma of Jackson left him vulnerable to a Whig campaign based on personalities and symbolism. In 1836, the Whigs had been disorganized and had not fully mastered the new democratic politics. But in 1840, they settled on a single nominee and outdid the Democrats in grass-roots organization and popular electioneering. The Whigs passed over the true leader of their party, Henry Clay, because he was identified with too many controversial positions. Instead they found their own Jackson in William Henry Harrison, a military hero of advanced age who was associated in the public mind with the battle of Tippecanoe and the winning of the West.

Harrison's views on public issues were little known, and the Whigs ran him without a platform to void distracting the electorate from his personal qualities. They pretended Harrison had been born in a log cabin—actually it was a pillared mansion—and that he preferred hard cider to more effete beverages. To balance the ticket and increase its appeal in the South they chose John Tyler of Virginia, a converted states' rights Democrat, to be Harrison's running mate.

Using the slogan, "Tippecanoe and Tyler, Too," the Whigs pulled out all stops in their bid for the White House. Rallies and parades were organized in every locality, complete with posters, placards, campaign hats and emblems, special songs, and even movable log cabins filled with coonskin caps and barrels of cider for the faithful. Imitating the Jacksonian propaganda against Adams in 1828, they portrayed Van Buren as a luxury-loving aristocrat and compared him with their own homespun candidate. The Democrats countered by using many of the same methods, but they simply could not project an image of Van Buren that rivaled Harrison's grass-roots appeal. There was an enormous turnout on election day—78 percent of those eligible to vote. When it was over, Harrison had parlayed a narrow edge in the popular vote into a landslide in the electoral college. He carried 19 of the 26 states and won 234 electoral votes to 60 for Van Buren. Buoyed by the electorate's belief that their policies might revive the economy, the Whigs also won control of both houses of Congress.

HEYDAY OF THE SECOND PARTY SYSTEM

America's "second party system" came of age in the election of 1840. Unlike the earlier competition between Federalists and Jeffersonian Republicans, the rivalry of Democrats and Whigs made the two-party pattern a normal feature of electoral politics in the United States. During the 1840s, the two national parties competed on fair-

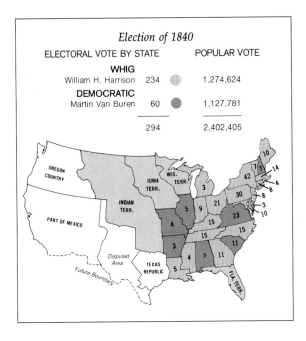

Election of 1840

ELECTORAL VOTE BY STATE **POPULAR VOTE**

WHIG
William H. Harrison 234 1,274,624

DEMOCRATIC
Martin Van Buren 60 1,127,781

294 2,402,405

ly equal terms for the support of the electorate. Allegiance to one party or the other became an important source of personal identity for many Americans and increased their interest and participation in politics.

In addition to drama and entertainment, the parties offered the voters a real choice of programs and ideologies. Whigs stood for a "positive liberal state"—which meant government had the right and duty to subsidize or protect enterprises that could contribute to general prosperity and economic growth. Democrats normally advocated a "negative liberal state." According to them, government should keep its hands off the economy; only by doing nothing could it avoid favoring special interests and interfering with free competition. They charged that granting subsidies or special charters to any group would create pockets of privilege or monopoly and put ordinary citizens under the thumb of the rich and powerful.

Conflict over economic issues helped determine each party's base of support. In the Whig camp were most industrialists and merchants, plus a majority of those farmers and planters who had adapted successfully to a market economy. Democrats appealed mainly to smaller farmers,

workers, declining gentry, and emerging entrepreneurs who were excluded from the established commercial groups that stood to benefit most from Whig programs. Democratic rhetoric about monopoly and privilege appealed to those who had mixed or negative feelings about the rise of a national market economy. To some extent, this division pitted richer and more privileged Americans against those who were poorer and less economically or socially secure. But it did not follow class lines in any simple or direct way. Many businessmen were Democrats, and large numbers of wage earners voted Whig. Merchants engaged in the import trade had no use for Whiggish high tariffs, whereas workers in industries clamoring for protection often concluded that their jobs depended on such duties.

Economic interest and ideology was not the only factor behind the choice of parties. Lifestyles and ethnic or religious identities strongly affected party loyalties during this period. In the northern states, one way to tell the typical Whig from the typical Democrat was to see what each did on Sunday. A person who went to one of the evangelical Protestant churches was very likely to be a Whig. On the other hand, the person who attended a ritualized service—Catholic, Lutheran, or Episcopalian—or did not go to church at all was most probably a Democrat.

The Democrats were the favored party of immigrants, Catholics, freethinkers, backwoods farmers, and those of all classes who enjoyed traditional amusements condemned by the new breed of moral reformers. One thing all these groups had in common was a desire to be left alone, free of restrictions on their freedom to think and behave as they liked. The Whigs enjoyed particularly strong support among Protestants of old stock living in smaller cities, towns, and prosperous rural areas devoted to market farming. In general, the Whigs welcomed a market economy but wished to restrain the individualism and disorder it created by enforcing cultural and moral values derived from the Puritan tradition. Most of those who sought to be "their brothers' keepers" were Whigs. Some of the roots of party allegiance can be found in local divisions between old stock Americans and immigrants over such matters as temperance, keeping the Sabbath, and reading the Protestant Bible in public schools.

On the Hustings in Michigan

Political candidates of the Jacksonian era traveled from town to town giving stump speeches. The political gatherings at which they spoke provided entertainment as well as an excellent source of political news. The sketch is by George Caleb Bingham, one of the most prolific of the democratic genre painters.

In 1838, Martin Van Buren's cousin Ephriam, a farmer in western Michigan, marched to the polls in rank with some seventy or eighty other Democrats, each carrying a hickory stick in honor of Andrew Jackson. An enthusiastic supporter of the Whig party fearlessly attempted to break the line. Ephriam Van Buren was called on to restrain him, which

he did. A few days after this event, an old Democrat told the Whig that if he wished to succeed in politics, he must vote with them. "What, I join you?" he exclaimed. "Sooner than vote the Democratic ticket, I would crawl on my hands and knees from Battle Creek to Detroit, and be struck by lightning every other mile." Others told a similar story of the old Democrat who once voted the Whig ticket, and the next day, goaded by his sins, bought half a dozen candles and took them home "to light them and sit up and hate himself by them." Politics was very serious business for the common voter in the age of Jackson, full of important ritual; it was also the best show in town.

As did revivalistic "camp meetings," political gatherings brought crowds and speakers into direct contact with the speakers working to entertain, inform, and convert the crowd. Between the first of July and the autumn election day, wandering political orators and local candidates would go from village to township, speaking to ready audiences on the topics of the day. An old tree stump or "husting" would often be the only stage, leading citizens to call all small-town political orators "stump" speakers. These "hustings" visits would inform the voters of each party's stance on the issues of the day; before the era of the telegraph, stump

speakers were the best source of political news.

Party workers organized parades and barbeques to boost the size and enthusiasm of the crowds. The parades would begin in the morning, at first informally as people arrived in groups from surrounding areas, and then with great pageantry, with brass bands, and wagons full of farmers and artisans joining in. A Michigan college student in 1851 recalled a time eleven years earlier, in "those glorious days of Tippecanoe and Tyler, too," when a nine-year-old from Troy, Michigan, a boy who had earnestly declared himself a Whig, was seen "on the fourth of July of that eventful year, seated upon the reach of a double wagon 45 feet long, in company with some fifty others of his party, on his way to assist in the ceremonies of the day." The informant added that "our youthful politician, in his zeal, inflicted a severe castigation upon a young gentleman of about his age because he had the audacity to mar the solemnity of the occasion, by shouting for 'Young Hickory.'" The youthful Whig, it seems, had become "gloriously fuddled" by a combination of partisan spirit and hard cider.

Such festivities would lead into the speeches. Candidates for office would either speak on their own or debate their opponents. Before and after speaking, the politicians would mix with the crowd. A Michigan schoolteacher described a favorite politician "familiarly mingling among the Democrats at their meetings, taking seat with them before the speaking began, and as one of them, talking freely on the subjects incident to the occasion. I used to think that here was where [he] got his power with the masses." That practice of elbow rubbing closed the distance between audience and speaker, between the leader and the led.

The audiences did their part to fill the gap, typically responding generously during the stump speech and filling the air with political songs between addresses. A conservative observer from Michigan noted in 1845 that prior to a typical political speech the "miserable rabble" would greet the prospective speaker with "unmeaning and bacchana-lian cries." The hurrahs of the audience (and songs with lyrics such as "Van, Van, he's a used-up man," and "The mustang colt has a killing pace/he's bound to win in the White House race") would inspire the orator. "It is well known that unless heartily cheered the 'stump orator' can do nothing," the sanctimonious onlooker continued. "It has therefore been supposed that in this kind of oratory the elements of eloquence are latently contained in cheers and are then conveyed through some unknown medium, perhaps animal magnetism, to the speaker."

Good stump speakers possessed a dramatic ability to communicate to the audience its own fears and concerns. The nearly mystic communication between speaker and hearer comes through in the following depiction of a Michigan Whig's elo-quence and sincerity on the stump: "In whatever crowd or assembly he might be his mind would catch with marvelous facility the general tendency of the mind of the audience, and a chemical process, as it were, would take place within his mind. How could he fail then to force attention of those to whom he returned their own thoughts strengthened, broadened, and adorned with superb flights of eloquence."

In retrospect, these spectacular stump-speaking trips to where the voters lived helped to affirm the democratic nature of Jacksonian politics. Politicians in the era were typically far more educated and wealthy than their constituents, but were supposed to represent faithfully the concerns of the common citizens. Mutual participation in the ritual of the hustings celebrated the people's significance in a manner that no faraway convention or latter-day press release could.

In a later era, popular politics would be less critical to a politician's election. The post–Civil War period was an era of stenography and telegraph, of industrialism and class strife. Political speeches would be widely reported, and constituencies were more economically heterogeneous. Those conditions forced politicians to become far more cautious about what they would say, when, and to whom. To a large degree the technology of the industrial age put an end to the stump speeches of Jacksonian America, and to a certain extent that same technology severed—for better or worse—the intimate bond between America's politicians and the rural electorate.

Political gatherings like that shown here in First State Election in Detroit *(1837) by Thomas Mickell Burnham gave candidates and their constituents the opportunity to meet and generated a high voter turnout on election day.*

Nevertheless, party conflict in Congress continued to center on national economic policy. Whigs stood firm for a loose construction of the Constitution and federal support for business and economic development. The Democrats persisted in their defense of strict construction, states' rights, and laissez-faire. Debates over tariffs, banking, and internal improvements remained vital and vigorous during the 1840s.

True believers in both parties saw a deep ideological or moral meaning in the clash over economic issues. Whigs and Democrats had conflicting views of the good society, and their policy positions reflected these differences. The Democrats were the party of white male equality and personal liberty. They perceived the American people as a collection of independent and self-sufficient white males. The role of government was to see to it that the individual was not interfered with—in his economic activity, in his personal habits, and in his religion (or lack of it). Democrats were ambivalent about the rise of the market economy because of the ways it threatened individual independence. The Whigs, on the other hand, were the party of orderly progress under the guidance of an enlightened elite. They believed the propertied, the well-educated, and the pious were responsible for guiding the masses toward the common good. Believing sincerely a market economy would benefit everyone in the long run, they had no qualms about the rise of a commercial and industrial capitalism.

De Tocqueville's Wisdom

The French traveler Alexis de Tocqueville, author of the most influential account ever written of the emergence of American democracy, visited the United States in 1831 and 1832. He departed well before the presidential election and had relatively little to say about national politics and the formation of political parties. For him, the essence of American democracy was local self-government, such as he observed in the town meetings of New England. The participation of ordinary citizens in the affairs of their communities impressed him greatly, and he praised Americans for not conceding their liberties to a centralized state, as he believed the French had done.

CHRONOLOGY

1824   House of Representatives elects John Quincy Adams president

1828   Congress passes "tariff of abominations" • Jackson elected president over J. Q. Adams

1830   Jackson vetoes the Maysville Road bill • Congress passes Indian Removal Act

1831   Jackson reorganizes his cabinet • First national nominating conventions meet

1832   Jackson vetoes the bill rechartering the Bank of the United States • Jackson reelected, defeating Henry Clay (National Republican candidate)

1832–1833   Crisis erupts over South Carolina's attempt to nullify the tariff of 1832

1833   Jackson removes federal deposits from the Bank of the United States

1834   Whig party comes into existence

1836   Jackson issues "specie circular" • Martin Van Buren elected president

1837   Financial panic occurs, followed by depression lasting until 1843

1840   Congress passes the Independent Subtreasury Bill • Harrison (Whig) defeats Van Buren (Democrat) for the presidency

Despite his generally favorable view of the American experiment, Tocqueville was acutely aware of the limitations of American democracy and of the dangers facing the republic. He believed the nullification crisis foreshadowed destruction of the Union and predicted the problem of slavery would lead eventually to civil war and racial conflict. He also noted the power of white supremacy, providing an unforgettable firsthand description of the sufferings of an Indian community in the course of forced migration to the West, as well as a graphic account of the way free blacks were segregated and driven from the polls in northern cities like Philadelphia. White Americans, he believed, were deeply prejudiced against people of color, and he doubted it was possible "for a whole people to rise . . . above itself." Perhaps a despot could force the equality and mingling of the races, but "while American democracy remains at the head of affairs, no one would dare attempt any such thing, and it is possible to forsee [sic] that the freer the whites in America are, the more they will seek to isolate themselves." Tocqueville was equally sure the kind of democracy men were practicing was not meant for women. Observing how women were strictly assigned to a separate domestic sphere, he concluded that Americans had never supposed "that democratic principles should undermine the husband's authority and make it doubtful who is in charge of the family." His observations have value because of their clearsighted insistence that the democracy and equality of the Jacksonian era were meant for only some of the people. The democratic idea could not be so limited; it would soon begin to burst the boundaries of white male supremacy.

Recommended Reading

Arthur M. Schlesinger, Jr., *The Age of Jackson* (1945), sees Jacksonian Democracy as a progressive protest against big business and stresses the participation of urban workers. Marvin Meyers, *The Jacksonian Persuasion: Politics and Belief* (1960), argues that Jacksonians appealed to nostalgia for an older America—"an idealized ancestral way" they believed was threatened by commercialization. Lee Benson, *The Concept of Jacksonian Democracy: New York as a Test Case* (1964), finds an ethnocultural basis for democratic allegiance. A sharply critical view of Jacksonian leadership—one that stresses opportunism, greed, and demagoguery—can be found in Edward Pessen, *Jacksonian America: Society, Personality, and Politics*, rev. ed. (1979). This work also offers a comprehensive survey of the social, economic, and political developments of the period. An excellent recent survey of Jacksonian politics is Harry L. Watson, *Liberty and Power* (1990). It stresses the crisis of "republicanism" at a time of "market revolution." Development of the view that Jacksonianism was a negative reaction to the rise of market capitalism can be found in Charles Sellers, *The Market Revolution* (1991).

The classic study of the new party system is Richard P. McCormick, *The Second Party System: Party Formation in the Jacksonian Era* (1966). On what the anti-Jacksonians stood for, see especially Daniel Walker Howe, *The Political Culture of the American Whigs* (1979). James C. Curtis, *Andrew Jackson and the Search for Vindication* (1976), provides a good introduction to Jackson's career and personality. On Jackson's popular image, see John William Ward, *Andrew Jackson: Symbol for an Age* (1955). On the other towering political figures of the period, see Merrill D. Peterson, *The Great Triumvirate: Webster, Clay, and Calhoun* (1987). The culture of the period is well-surveyed in Russel B. Nye, *Society and Culture in America, 1830–1860* (1960). Alexis de Tocqueville, *Democracy in America*, 2 vols. (1945), is a foreign visitor's wise and insightful analysis of American life in the 1830s.

Additional Bibliography

On the hotel as a symbolic institution, see Doris Elizabeth King, "The First Class Hotel and the Age of the Common Man," *Journal of Southern History* 23 (1957): 173–188. On the new politics, see Chilton Williamson, *American Suffrage from Property to Democracy* (1960), Richard Hofstadter, *The Idea of a Party System* (1970), and Harry D. Watson, *Jacksonian Politics and Community Conflict* (1981). On Jacksonian ideology and political culture, see John Ashworth, "*Aristocrats and Agrarians*" (1982) and Lawrence Kohl, *The Politics of Individualism: Parties and the American Character in the Jacksonian Era* (1989). On radical working-class movements, see Edward Pessen, *Most Uncommon Jacksonians: The Radical Leaders of the Early Labor Movement* (1967); Bruce Laurie, *Working People of Philadelphia, 1800–1850* (1980); and Sean Wilentz, *Chants Democratic: New York City and the Rise of the American Working Class, 1788–1850* (1984). Social manifestations of the democratic character are covered in Douglas T. Miller, *Jacksonian Aristocracy: Class and Democracy in New York, 1830–1860* (1967); Joseph F. Kett, *The Formation of the American Medical Profession* (1968); Daniel H. Calhoun, *Professional Lives in America: Structure and Aspiration, 1750–1850* (1965); and Donald M. Scott, *From Office to Profession: The New England Ministry, 1750–1850* (1978). On democratic culture, see E. Douglas Branch, *The Sentimental Years, 1836–1860* (1934); David Grimstad, *Melodrama Unveiled: American Theater and Culture, 1800–1850* (1968); Oliver W. Larkin, *Art and Life in America* (1960); Neil Harris, *The Artist in American Society: The Formative Years, 1790–1860* (1966); and Henry Nash Smith, *Democracy and the Novel: Popular Resistance to Classic American Writers* (1978).

The emergence of Andrew Jackson and the Democratic party is described in Samuel F. Bemis, *John Quincy Adams and the Union* (1956) and in several works by Robert V. Remini: *Martin Van Buren and the Making of the Democratic Party* (1959); *Andrew*

Jackson and the Course of American Empire, 1767–1821 (1977); *Andrew Jackson and the Course of American Freedom, 1822–1832* (1981); and *Andrew Jackson and the Course of American Democracy, 1833–1845* (1984). Jackson's presidency is also examined in Richard B. Latner, *The Presidency of Andrew Jackson: White House Politics, 1829–1837* (1979). On Jackson's Indian policy, see Bernard W. Sheehan, *The Seeds of Extinction: Jeffersonian Philanthropy and the American Indian* (1973); Michael Paul Rogin, *Fathers and Children: Andrew Jackson and the Subjugation of the American Indian* (1975); and Ronald N. Satz, *American Indian Policy in the Jacksonian Era* (1975). On nullification, see William W. Freehling, *Prelude to Civil War: The Nullification Controversy in South Carolina, 1816–1836* (1966), and Richard B. Ellis, *The Union at Risk: Jacksonian Democracy, States' Rights, and the Nullification Crisis* (1987).

The Bank War is discussed in Bray Hammond, *Banks and Politics in America from the Revolution to the Civil War* (1957); Thomas P. Govan, *Nicholas Biddle* (1959); and John M. Paul, *The Politics of Jacksonian Finance* (1972). On Van Buren, see James C. Curtis, *The Fox at Bay: Martin Van Buren and the Presidency* (1970); and Donald B. Cole, *Martin Van Buren and the American Political System* (1984).

For more on the rise of the Whigs, see two biographies of their principal leaders: Robert V. Remini, *Henry Clay: Statesman for the Union* (1991), and Maurice G. Baxter, *One and Inseparable: Daniel Webster and the Union* (1984). The growth of a two-party system in the South is described in William J. Cooper, Jr., *The South and the Politics of Slavery* (1978). The politics of the 1840s is surveyed in William R. Brock, *Parties and Political Conscience, 1840–1850* (1979). See also Ronald P. Formisano, *The Birth of Mass Political Parties: Michigan, 1827–1861* (1971).

The Pursuit of Perfection

*I*n the winter of 1830 to 1831 a wave of religious revivals swept the northern states. The most dramatic and successful took place in Rochester, New York. Large audiences, composed mostly of respectable and prosperous citizens, heard evangelist Charles G. Finney preach that every man or woman had the power to choose Christ and a godly life. For six months, Finney held prayer meetings almost daily, putting intense pressure on those who had not experienced salvation. Hundreds came forth to declare their faith, and church membership doubled during his stay. The newly awakened Christians of Rochester were urged to convert relatives, neighbors, and employees. If enough people enlisted in the evangelical crusade, Finney proclaimed, the millennium would be achieved within months.

Finney's call for religious and moral renewal fell on fertile ground in Rochester. This bustling boomtown on the Erie Canal was suffering from severe growing pains and tensions arising from rapid economic development. Leading families were divided into quarreling factions, and workers were threatening to break free from the control their employers had previously exerted over their daily lives. Most of the early converts were from the middle class. Businessmen who had been heavy drinkers and irregular churchgoers now abstained from alcohol and went to church at least twice a week. They also pressured the employees in their workshops, mills, and stores to do likewise. More rigorous standards of proper behavior and religious conformity unified Rochester's elite and increased its ability to control the rest of the community. As in other cities swept by the revival, evangelical Protestantism provided the middle class with a stronger sense of identity and purpose.

But the war on sin was not always so unifying. Among those converted in Rochester and elsewhere were some who could not rest easy until the nation as a whole conformed to the pure Christianity of the Sermon on the Mount. Finney expressed such a hope himself, but he concentrated on religious conversion and moral uplift of the individual, trusting that the purification of American society and politics would automatically follow. Other religious and moral reformers were inspired to crusade against those social and politi-cal institutions that failed to measure up to the standards of Christian perfection. They proceeded to attack such collective "sins" as the liquor traffic, war, slavery, and even government. Religiously inspired reformism cut two ways. On the one hand, it imposed a new order and cultural unity to previously divided and troubled communities like Rochester. But it also inspired a variety of more radical movements or experiments that threatened to undermine established institutions that failed to live up to the principles of the more idealistic reformers. One of these movements—abolitionism—challenged the central social and economic institution of the southern states and helped trigger political upheaval and civil war.

According to some historians, evangelical revival and the reform movements it inspired reflected the same spirit as the new democratic politics. In a sense this is true: Jacksonian politicians and evangelists both sought popular favor and assumed individuals were free agents capable of self-direction and self-improvement. But leaders of the two types of movements made different kinds of demands on ordinary people. Jacksonians idealized common folk pretty much as they found them and saw no danger to the community if individuals pursued their worldly interests. Evangelical reformers, who tended to support the Whigs or to reject both parties, believed the common people needed to be redeemed and uplifted—committed to a higher goal than self-interest. They did not trust a democracy of unbelievers and sinners. The republic would be safe, they insisted, only if a right-minded minority preached, taught, and agitated until the mass of ordinary citizens was reborn into a higher life.

THE RISE OF EVANGELICALISM

American Protestantism was in a state of constant ferment during the early nineteenth century. The separation of church and state, a process that began during the Revolution, was now complete. Government sponsorship and funding had ended, or would soon end, for the established churches of the colonial era, such as the Congregationalists of New England and the Episcopalians of the South. Dissenting groups, such as Baptists and

Graphic portrayals of good and evil like this 1862 lithograph, Way of Good and Evil, *reminded people of the message of some evangelists that wicked ways would lead to everlasting punishment.*

The Second Great Awakening: The Frontier Phase

The Second Great Awakening began in earnest on the southern frontier around the turn of the century. In 1801, a crowd estimated at nearly fifty thousand gathered at Cane Ridge, Kentucky. According to a contemporary observer:

> *The noise was like the roar of Niagara. The vast sea of human beings seemed to be agitated as if by a storm. I counted seven ministers all preaching at once. . . . Some of the people were singing, others praying, some crying for mercy . . . while others were shouting most vociferously. . . .At one time I saw at least five hundred swept down in a moment, as if a battery of a thousand guns had been opened upon them, and then followed immediately shrieks and shouts that rent the heavens.*

Methodists, welcomed full religious freedom because it offered a better chance to win new converts. All pious Protestants, however, were concerned about the spread of "infidelity"—their word for secular-humanistic beliefs. Some of the Founders of the nation had set a troubling example by their casual or even unfriendly attitude toward religious orthodoxy. Secular ideas drawn from the Enlightenment (see Chapter 4) had achieved wide acceptance as a basis for the establishment of a democratic republic, and opposition to mixing religion with public life remained strong during the age of Jackson.

Revivalism provided the best way to extend religious values and build up church membership. The Great Awakening of the mid-eighteenth century had shown the wonders that evangelists could accomplish, and new revivalists repeated this success by greatly increasing the proportion of the population that belonged to Protestant churches. They also capitalized on the growing willingness of Americans to form voluntary organizations. Spiritual renewals were often followed by mobilization of the faithful into associations to spread the gospel and reform American morals.

Highly emotional camp meetings, organized usually by Methodists or Baptists but sometimes by Presbyterians, became a regular feature of religious life in the South and the lower Midwest (see the illustration on p. 315). On the frontier, the camp meeting met social as well as religious needs. In the sparsely settled southern backcountry, it was difficult to sustain local churches with regular ministers. Methodists solved part of the problem by sending out circuit riders. Baptists licensed uneducated farmers to preach to their neighbors. But for many people the only way to get baptized, married, or have a communal religious experience was to attend a camp meeting.

Rowdies and scoffers also attended, drinking whiskey, carousing, and fornicating on the fringes of the small city of tents and wagons. Sometimes they were "struck down" by a mighty blast from the pulpit. Evangelists loved to tell stories of such conversions or near conversions. According to Methodist preacher Peter Cartwright, one scoffer was seized by the "jerks"—a set of involuntary bodily movements often observed at camp meetings. Normally such an exercise would lead to conversion, but this particular sinner was so hard-hearted that he refused to surrender to God.

The result was that he kept jerking until his neck was broken.

Camp meetings obviously provided an emotional outlet for rural people whose everyday lives were often lonely and tedious. They could also promote a sense of community and social discipline. Conversion at a camp meeting could be a rite of passage, signifying that a young man or woman had outgrown wild or antisocial behavior and was now ready to become a respectable member of the community.

In the southern states, Baptists and Presbyterians eventually deemphasized camp meetings in favor of "protracted meetings" in local churches, which featured guest preachers holding forth day after day for up to two weeks. Southern evangelical churches, especially Baptist and Methodist, grew rapidly in membership and influence during the first half of the nineteenth century and became the focus of community life in rural areas. Although they fostered societies to improve morals—to encourage temperance and discourage dueling, for example—they generally shied away from social reform. The conservatism of a slave-holding society discouraged radical efforts to change the world.

The Second Great Awakening in the North

Reformist tendencies were more evident in the distinctive kind of revivalism that originated in New England and western New York. Northern evangelists were mostly Congregationalists and Presbyterians, strongly influenced by New England Puritan traditions. Their greatest successes were not in rural or frontier areas but in small- to medium-sized towns and cities. Their revivals could be stirring affairs but were less extravagantly emotional than the camp meetings of the South. The northern brand of evangelism resulted in formation of societies devoted to the redemption of the human race in general and American society in particular.

The reform movement in New England began as an effort to defend Calvinism against the liberal views of religion fostered by the Enlightenment. The Reverend Timothy Dwight, who became president of Yale College in 1795, was alarmed by the younger generation's growing acceptance of the belief that the Deity was the benevolent master architect of a rational universe rather than an all-powerful, mysterious God. Dwight was particularly disturbed by those religious liberals whose rationalism reached the point of denying the doctrine of the Trinity and who proclaimed themselves to be "Unitarians."

To Dwight's horror, Unitarians captured some fashionable and sophisticated New England congregations and even won control of the Harvard Divinity School. He fought back by preaching to Yale undergraduates that they were "dead in sin" and succeeded in provoking a series of campus revivals. But the harshness and pessimism of orthodox Calvinist doctrine, with its stress on original sin and predestination, had limited appeal in a republic committed to human freedom and progress.

A younger generation of Congregational ministers reshaped New England Puritanism to increase its appeal to people who shared the prevailing optimism about human capabilities. The main theologian of early nineteenth-century neo-Calvinism was Nathaniel Taylor, a disciple of Dwight, who also held forth at Yale. Taylor softened the doctrine of predestination almost out of existence by contending that every individual was a free agent who had the ability to overcome a natural inclination to sin.

The first great practitioner of the new evangelical Calvinism was Lyman Beecher, another of Dwight's pupils. In the period just before and after the War of 1812, Beecher helped promote a series of revivals in the Congregational churches of New England. Using his own homespun version of Taylor's doctrine of free agency, Beecher induced thousands—in his home church in Litchfield, Connecticut, and in other churches that offered him their pulpits—to acknowledge their sinfulness and surrender to God.

During the late 1820s, Beecher was forced to confront the new and more radical form of revivalism being practiced in western New York by Charles G. Finney. Upstate New York was a seedbed for religious enthusiasms of various kinds. A majority of its population were transplanted New Englanders who had left behind their close-knit village communities and ancestral churches but not their Puritan consciences. Troubled by rapid economic changes and the social dislocations that went with them, they were ripe for a new faith and a fresh moral direction.

The Beecher family, shown here in a photograph by Matthew Brady, contributed four influential members to the reform movement. Lyman Beecher (seated center) was a successful preacher and a master strategist in the organized campaign against sin and infidelity. His eldest daughter, Catharine (on his right) was a leader in the movement supporting higher education for women. Another daughter, Harriet (seated far right) wrote the novel Uncle Tom's Cabin. *Lyman's son, Henry Ward Beecher (standing far right) was an ardent antislavery advocate and later became one of the most celebrated preachers of the post–Civil War era. He also became involved in a notorious scandal and trial; see the essay* The Beecher–Tilton Adultery Trial: Public Image Versus Private Conduct *on pp. 430–435.*

Although he worked within Congregational and Presbyterian churches (which were then cooperating under a plan of union established in 1804), Finney departed radically from Calvinist doctrines. In his hands, free agency became unqualified free will. One of his sermons was entitled "Sinners Bound to Change Their Own Hearts." Finney was relatively indifferent to theological issues. His appeal was to emotion or to the heart rather than to doctrine or reason. He wanted converts to feel the power of Christ and become new men and women. He eventually adopted the extreme view that redeemed Christians could be totally free of sin—as perfect as their Father in Heaven.

Beginning in 1823, Finney conducted a series of highly successful revivals in towns and cities of western New York, culminating in the aforementioned triumph in Rochester in 1830–1831. Even more controversial than his freewheeling approach to theology were the means he used to win converts. Finney sought instantaneous conversions through a variety of new methods. These included protracted meetings lasting all night or several days in a row, the placing of an "anxious bench" in front of the congregation where those in the process of repentance could receive special atten-

tion, and encouraging women to pray publicly for the souls of male relatives.

The results could be dramatic. Sometimes listeners fell to the floor in fits of excitement. "If I had had a sword in my hand," Finney recalled, "I could not have cut them off as fast as they fell." Although he appealed to emotion, Finney had a practical, almost manipulative, attitude toward the conversion process: It "is not a miracle or dependent on a miracle in any sense. . . . It is purely a philosophical result of the right use of constituted means."

Lyman Beecher and eastern evangelicals were disturbed by Finney's new methods and by the emotionalism that accompanied them. They were also upset because he violated long-standing Christian tradition by allowing women to pray aloud in church. An evangelical summit meeting between Beecher and Finney, held at New Lebanon, New York, in 1827, failed to reach agreement on this and other issues. Beecher even threatened to stand on the state line if Finney attempted to bring his crusade into Connecticut. But it soon became clear that Finney was not merely stirring people to temporary peaks of excitement; he was also leaving strong and active churches behind him, and eastern opposition gradually weakened.

Finney eventually founded a tabernacle in New York City that became a rallying point for evangelical efforts to reach the urban masses.

From Revivalism to Reform

The northern wing of the Second Great Awakening, unlike the southern, inspired a great movement for social reform. Converts were organized into voluntary associations that sought to stamp out sin and social evil and win the world for Christ. An activist and outgoing Christianity was being advanced, not one that called for withdrawal from a sinful world. Most of the converts of northern revivalism were middle-class citizens already active in the lives of their communities. They were seeking to adjust to the bustling world of the market revolution in ways that would not violate their traditional moral and social values. Their generally optimistic and forward-looking attitudes led to hopes that a wave of conversions would save the nation and the world.

In New England, Beecher and his evangelical associates were behind the establishment of a great network of missionary and benevolent societies. In 1810, Presbyterians and Congregationalists founded a Board of Commissioners for Foreign Missions and soon dispatched two missionaries to India. In 1816, the Reverend Samuel John Mills took the leading role in organizing the American Bible Society. By 1821, the society had distributed 140,000 Bibles, mostly in parts of the West where there was a scarcity of churches and clergymen.

Another major effort went into publication and distribution of religious tracts, mainly by the American Tract Society, founded in 1825. Groups beyond the reach of regular churches were the target of special societies, such as missions to seamen, Native Americans, and the urban poor. In 1816 to 1817, middle-class women in New York, Philadelphia, Charleston, and Boston formed societies to spread the gospel in lower-class wards—where, as one of their missionaries put it, there was "a great mass of people beyond the restraints of religion."

Evangelicals founded moral reform societies as well as missions. Some of these aimed at curbing irreligious activity on the Sabbath; others sought to stamp out dueling, gambling, and prostitution. In New York in 1831, a zealous young clergyman published a sensational report claiming there were ten thousand prostitutes in the city laying their snares for innocent young men. As a result of this exposé, an asylum was established for the redemption of "abandoned women." When middle-class women became involved in this crusade, they shifted its focus to the men who patronized prostitutes, and proposed that teams of observers record and publish the names of those seen entering brothels. This plan was abandoned because it offended those who thought the cause of virtue would be better served by suppressing public discussion and investigation of sexual vices.

Beecher was especially influential in the temperance crusade, the most successful of the reform movements; his published sermons against drink were the most important and widely distributed of the early tracts calling for total abstinence from "demon rum." The temperance movement was directed at a real social evil. Since the Revolution, whiskey had become the most popular American beverage. Made from corn by individual farmers or, by the 1820s, in commercial distilleries, it was cheaper than milk or beer and safer than water (which was often contaminated). In some parts of the country, rum and brandy were also popular. Hard liquor was frequently consumed with food as a table beverage, even at breakfast, and children sometimes imbibed along with adults. Per capita annual consumption of distilled beverages in the 1820s was almost triple what it is today, and alcoholism had reached epidemic proportions.

The temperance reformers viewed indulgence in alcohol as a threat to public morality. Drunkenness was seen as a loss of self-control and moral responsibility that spawned crime, vice, and disorder. Above all, it threatened the family. Drinking was mainly a male vice, and the main target of temperance propaganda was the husband and father who abused, neglected, or abandoned his wife and children because he was a slave to the bottle. Women played a vital role in the movement and were instrumental in making it a crusade for the protection of the home. The drinking habits of the poor or laboring classes also aroused great concern. Particularly in urban areas, the "respectable" and propertied elements lived in fear that lower-class mobs, crazed with drink, would attack private property and destroy the social order.

Many evangelical reformers regarded intemperance as the greatest single obstacle to a repub-

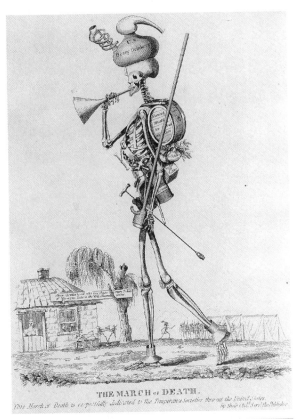

THE MARCH OF DEATH.
*This March of Death is respectfully dedicated to the Temperance Societies throu out the United States,
by their obd.t Serv.t the Publisher.*

Temperance propaganda, like this broadside, warned that "demon rum" would lead the drinker down the direct path to poverty and wretchedness and would bring about the ruin of his entire family.

in altering the drinking habits of middle-class American males by making temperance a mark of respectability. Per capita consumption of hard liquor declined more than 50 percent during the 1830s.

Cooperating missionary and reform societies—collectively known as "the benevolent empire"—were a major force in American culture by the early 1830s. Efforts to modify American attitudes and institutions seemed to be bearing fruit. A new ethic of self-control and self-discipline was being instilled in the middle class, equipping individuals to confront a new world of economic growth and social mobility without losing their cultural and moral bearings.

DOMESTICITY AND CHANGES IN THE AMERICAN FAMILY

The evangelical culture of the 1820s and 1830s influenced the family as an institution and inspired new conceptions of its role in American society. For many parents, child rearing was viewed as essential preparation for self-disciplined Christian life, and they performed their nurturing duties with great seriousness and self-consciousness. Women—regarded as particularly susceptible to religious and moral influences—were increasingly confined to the domestic circle, but assumed a greater importance within it.

Marriage and Sex Roles

The white middle-class American family underwent major changes in the decades between the revolution and the mid-nineteenth century. One was the triumph of marriage for love. Parents now exercised even less control over their children's selection of mates than they had in the colonial period. The desire to protect family property and maintain social status remained strong, but mutual affection was now considered absolutely essential to a proper union. Beginning in the late eighteenth century, romantic novels popularized the idea that marriage should be based exclusively on the promptings of the heart. It became easier for sons to marry while their fathers were still alive and for younger daughters to wed before their oldest sisters—trends that reflected a weakening of the traditional parental role.

lic of God-fearing, self-disciplined citizens. In 1826, a group of clergymen previously active in mission work organized the American Temperance Society to coordinate and extend the work already begun by local churches and moral reform societies. The original aim was to encourage abstinence from "ardent spirits" or hard liquor; there was no agreement on the evils of beer and wine. The society sent out lecturers, issued a flood of literature, and sponsored essay contests. Its agents organized revival meetings and called on those in attendance to sign a pledge promising abstinence from spirits.

The campaign was enormously effective. By 1834, there were five thousand local branches with more than a million members, a large proportion of them women. Although it may be doubted whether huge numbers of confirmed drunkards were cured, the movement did succeed

The Shakers

Ritualized dances were part of the Shakers' spiritual preparation for the Second Coming. The dancers in this nineteenth-century etching exemplify the mixed heritage of the Shaker community.

One of the communitarian religious movements that sprang up in the pre–Civil War period had a special fascination for outsiders. The Shakers—officially known as the Millennial Church or the United Society of Believers—welcomed curious travelers to their settlements, and many of the visitors reported in great detail on the unusual way of life they observed.

The Shakers were descended from a small English sect of the same name that appeared in the early to mid-eighteenth century. The English Shakers were radical millennialists, which meant they expected Christ's Second Coming to occur momentarily. Their name was derived from the

fact that they expressed their religious fervor through vigorous bodily movements, which eventually took the form of a ritualized dance. Most of the Shakers were from the working class, and one of their converts was a woman named Ann Lee, who joined the sect in 1758.

After she had been jailed several times for preaching strange and unorthodox doctrines in public places, Lee immigrated to America in 1774. Mother Ann, as she was known to her followers, came to believe she was the one sent by God to save the world. It would not be farfetched to call her the great feminist of Christian millennialism. She preached that God was both

masculine and feminine and that Christ had incarnated only the masculine side. It was her vocation to bring on the millennium by embodying the feminine attributes of the Almighty. Hence the American Shakers venerated Ann Lee and expressed belief in a new theology based squarely on the principle of sexual equality.

Mother Ann died in 1784, but not before she had made enough American converts to establish a permanent sect. Taking advantage of the great availability of land in America, the Shakers drew apart from the rest of society and established communities where they could practice their own version of Christian perfectionism free of harassment. The mother colony was at Mount Lebanon, New York, but other Shaker communities were established in the New England states before 1800 and in Ohio and Kentucky thereafter. By the 1830s, twenty settlements in seven states had a combined membership of approximately six thousand.

In the Shaker communities all property was owned in common and political authority was vested in a self-perpetuating group of ministers. Hence the Shakers practiced a form of "theocratic communism." Reflecting their belief in sexual equality, they required that the ministry of each community be composed of an equal number of elders and elderesses. What most attracted the interest of outsiders, however, was the fact that Shakers banned sexual intercourse and marriage, requiring strict celibacy of all members. To enforce this rule they segregated men and women in most social and economic activities. This novel arrangement resulted from a belief that the end of the world was at hand; thus there was no need to reproduce the human race, and those anticipating salvation should begin to live in the pure spiritual state that would arrive with the millennium. The rule of chastity obviously limited the growth of the Shaker communities, but a willingness to adopt orphans and to accept converts allowed some of them to survive well into the twentieth century.

Visitors to the Shaker settlements were, for the most part, impressed with the order, decorum, cleanliness, and quiet prosperity that prevailed. But beginning in 1837 religious services in the communities suddenly became wildly ecstatic. Relatively formalized dancing was replaced by spontaneous and violent "shaking and turning exercizes." Shakers had always believed in spiritualism, or direct communication with departed souls, but now there was an epidemic of spiritual possession. In almost every service, members fell into trances, conveyed messages from the spirit world, and spoke in what were thought to be foreign tongues. Some observers concluded that the Shakers had literally gone mad, and for a time the ministers thought it advisable to close their services to the public.

At a time when religious revivalism had recently swept the country as a whole, the Shakers were simply having their own outburst of enthusiasm, showing perhaps that they were not completely cut off from the outside world. Since Shakers were already intensely religious, their revivals were even more violent and frantic than those taking place elsewhere. Modern psychologists might attribute this frenzy to sexual frustration, but such an interpretation would not explain why the Shaker ecstatic revival ended about 1845. After that time, the calm and sober spirit of earlier years again prevailed.

The Shakers, despite their isolation and singularity, made some important contributions to American culture. They valued simplicity in all things, and this ideal became a basis for creative achievement. The virtue of simplicity was expressed in the words of the hauntingly beautiful Shaker hymn (which later became the theme for Aaron Copland's twentieth-century symphonic work *Appalachian Spring*), "'Tis a gift to be simple." Their aesthetic ideal of simplicity inspired Shaker artisans to design buildings and furnishings that were purely functional and without ornamentation. In the eyes of modern art critics and historians, Shaker handiwork achieved an elegance and purity of form that ranks it among the most beautiful ever produced in America. The Tree of Life emblem (opposite page) is from a Shaker spirit drawing that was received as a vision and recorded by Sister Hannah Cohoon in 1854.

Wives now began to behave more like the companions of their husbands and less like their servants or children. In the main, eighteenth-century correspondence between spouses had been formal and distant in tone. The husband often assumed a patriarchal role, even using such salutations as "my dear child" and rarely confessing that he missed his wife or craved her company. Letters from women to their husbands were highly deferential and did not usually give advice or express disapproval.

By the early nineteenth century first names, pet names, and terms of endearment like "honey" or "darling" were increasingly used by both sexes, and absent husbands frequently confessed they felt lost without their mates. In their replies, wives assumed a more egalitarian tone and offered counsel on a wide range of subjects. One wrote to a husband who had admitted to flirting with pretty women that she was more than "a little jealous." She asked him angrily how he would feel if she made a similar confession—"would it be more immoral in me than in you?"

The change in middle- and upper-class marriage should not be exaggerated or romanticized. In law, and in cases of conflict between spouses, the husband remained the unchallenged head of the household. True independence or equality for women was impossible at a time when men held exclusive legal authority over a couple's property and children. Divorce was difficult for everyone, but the double standard made it easier for husbands than wives to dissolve a marriage on grounds of adultery.

Such power as women exerted within the home came from their ability to affect the decisions of men who had learned to respect their moral qualities and good sense. The evangelical movement encouraged this quiet expression of feminine influence. The revivals not only gave women a role in converting men but made a Christ with stereotypical feminine characteristics the main object of worship. A nurturing, loving, merciful saviour, mediating between a stern father and his erring children, provided the model for woman's new role as spiritual head of the home. Membership in evangelical church-based associations inspired and prepared women for new roles as civilizers of men and guardians of domestic culture and morality. Female reform societies taught them the strict ethical code they were to instill in other family members; organized mothers' groups gave instruction in how to build character and encourage piety in children.

Historians have described the new conception of woman's role as the "Cult of True Womanhood" or the "ideology of domesticity." In the view of most men, a woman's place was in the home and on a pedestal. The ideal wife and mother was "an angel in the house," a model of piety and virtue who exerted a wholesome moral and religious influence over members of the coarser sex. A masculine view of the true woman was well expressed in a poem published in 1846:

I would have her as pure as the snow on the mount—
As true as the smile that to infancy's given—
As pure as the wave of the crystalline fount,
Yet as warm in the heart as the sunlight of heaven.

The sociological reality behind the Cult of True Womanhood was an increasing division between the working lives of men and women. In the eighteenth century and earlier, most economic activity had been centered in and near the home, and husbands and wives often worked together in a common enterprise. By the early to mid-nineteenth century this way of life was declining, especially in the Northeast. In towns and cities, the rise of factories and countinghouses severed the home from the workplace. Men went forth every morning to their places of labor, leaving their wives at home to tend the house and the children. Married women were therefore increasingly deprived of a productive economic role. The cult of domesticity made a virtue of the fact that men were solely responsible for running the affairs of the world and building up the economy.

A new conception of sex roles justified and glorified this pattern. The "doctrine of two spheres"—as set forth in novels, advice literature, and the new ladies' magazines—sentimentalized the woman who kept a spotless house, nurtured her children, and offered her husband a refuge from the heartless world of commerce and industry. From a modern point of view, it is easy to condemn the cult of domesticity as a rationalization for male dominance; to a considerable extent

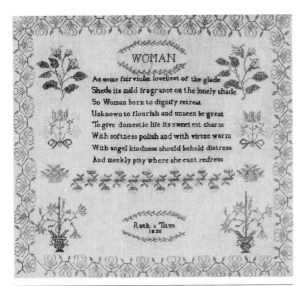

The sentiment on this sampler, stitched in 1820 by Ruth Titus, typifies beliefs about woman's proper role, according to the Cult of True Womanhood.

it was. But many women of the early to mid-nineteenth century do not seem to have felt oppressed or degraded by the new arrangement. The earlier pattern of cooperation had not implied sexual equality—normally men had been very much in charge of farms or home industries and had often treated their wives more like servants than partners. The new norm of confinement to the home did not necessarily imply women were inferior. By the standards of evangelical culture, women in the domestic sphere could be viewed as superior to men, since women were in a good position to cultivate the "feminine" virtues of love and self-sacrifice and thus act as official guardians of religious and moral values.

The domestic ideology had real meaning only for relatively affluent women. Working-class wives were not usually employed outside the home during this period, but they labored long and hard within the household. Besides cleaning, cooking, and taking care of large numbers of children, they often took in washing or piecework to supplement a meager family income. Their endless domestic drudgery made a sham of the notion that women had the time and energy for the "higher things of life."

In urban areas, unmarried working-class women often lived on their own and toiled as household servants, in the sweatshops of the garment industry, and in factories. Barely able to support themselves and at the mercy of male sexual predators, they were in no position to identify with the middle-class ideal of elevated, protected womanhood. For some of them, the relatively well-paid and gregarious life of the prostitute seemed to offer an attractive alternative to a life of loneliness and privation.

For middle-class women whose husbands or fathers earned a good income, freedom from industrial or farm labor offered some tangible benefits. They now had the leisure to read extensively in the new literature directed primarily at housewives, to participate in female-dominated charitable activities, and to cultivate deep and lasting friendships with other women. The result was a distinctively feminine subculture emphasizing "sisterhood" or "sorority." This growing sense of solidarity with other women and of the importance of sexual identity could transcend the private home and even the barriers of social class. Beginning in the 1820s, urban women of the middle and upper classes organized societies for the relief and rehabilitation of poor or "fallen women." The aim of these organizations was not economic and political equality with men but the elevation of all females to true womanhood.

For some women, the domestic ideal even sanctioned efforts to extend their sphere until it conquered the masculine world outside the home. This domestic feminism was reflected in women's involvement in crusades to stamp out such masculine sins as intemperance, gambling, and sexual vice.

In the benevolent societies and reform movements of the Jacksonian era, especially those designated as female organizations, women handled money, organized meetings and public appeals, made contracts, and sometimes even gave orders to male subordinates—activities they could not usually perform in their own households. The desire to extend the feminine sphere was the motivating force behind Catharine Beecher's campaign to make schoolteaching a woman's occupation. A prolific and influential writer on the theory and practice of domesticity, this unmarried daughter of Lyman Beecher saw the spinster-teacher as equivalent to a mother. By instilling in young males the virtues that only women could teach, the schoolmarm could help liberate America from corruption and materialism.

But Beecher and other domestic feminists continued to emphasize the role of married women who stayed home and did their part simply by being wives and mothers. Reforming husbands was difficult: they were away much of the time and tended to be preoccupied with business. But this very fact gave women primary responsibility for the rearing of children—an activity to which nineteenth-century Americans attached almost cosmic significance. Since women were considered particularly well qualified to transmit piety and morality to future citizens of the republic, the cult of domesticity exalted motherhood and encouraged a new concern with childhood as the time of life when "character" was formed.

The Discovery of Childhood

The nineteenth century has been called "the century of the child." More than before, childhood was seen as a distinct stage of life requiring the special and sustained attention of adults. The family now became "child-centered," which meant the care, nurture, and rearing of children was viewed as the family's main function. In earlier times, adults treated children in a more casual way, often sending them away from home for education or apprenticeship at a very early age. Among the well-to-do, children spent more time with servants or tutors than with their parents.

By the early decades of the nineteenth century, however, children were staying at home longer and receiving much more attention from parents, especially mothers. Almost completely abandoned was the colonial custom—nearly inconceivable today—of naming a living child after a sibling who had died in infancy. Each child was now looked on as a unique and irreplaceable individual.

New customs and fashions heralded the "discovery" of childhood. Books aimed specifically at juveniles began to roll off the presses. Parents became more self-conscious about their responsibilities and sought help from a new literature providing expert advice on child rearing. One early nineteenth-century mother wrote, "There is scarcely any subject concerning which I feel more anxiety than the proper education of my children. It is a difficult and delicate subject, the more I feel how much is to be learnt by myself."

The new concern for children resulted in more intimate relations between parents and children.

The ideal family described in the advice manuals and sentimental literature was bound together by affection rather than authority. Firm discipline remained at the core of "family government," but there was a change in the preferred method of enforcing good behavior. Corporal punishment declined, partially displaced by shaming or withholding of affection. Disobedient middle-class children were now more likely to be confined to their rooms to reflect on their sins than to receive a good thrashing. Discipline could no longer be justified as the constant application of physical force over naturally wayward beings. In an age of moral perfectionism, the role of discipline was to induce repentance and change basic attitudes. The intended result was often described as "self-government"; to achieve it parents used guilt, rather than fear, as their main source of leverage. A mother's sorrow or a father's stern and prolonged silence was deemed more effective in forming character than blows or angry words.

Child-centered families also meant smaller families. If nineteenth-century families had remained as large as those of earlier times, it would have been impossible to lavish so much care and attention on individual offspring. For reasons that are still not completely understood, the average number of children born to each woman during her fertile years dropped from 7.04 in 1800 to 5.42 in 1850. As a result, average family size declined about 25 percent, beginning a long-range trend lasting to the present day.

The practice of various forms of birth control undoubtedly contributed to this demographic revolution. Ancestors of the modern condom and diaphragm were openly advertised and sold during the pre–Civil War period, but it was likely most couples controlled family size by practicing the withdrawal method or limiting the frequency of intercourse. Abortion was also surprisingly common and was on the rise. One historian has estimated that by 1850 there was one abortion for every five or six live births.

Parents seemed to understand that having fewer children meant they could provide their offspring with a better start in life. Such attitudes were appropriate to a society that was beginning to shift from agriculture to commerce and industry. For rural households short of labor, large families were an economic asset. For urban couples who hoped to send their children into a competitive world that demanded special talents and training, they were a liability.

INSTITUTIONAL REFORM

The family could not carry the whole burden of socializing and reforming individuals. Children needed schooling as well as parental nurturing, and many lacked the advantage of a real home environment. Some adults, too, seemed to require special kinds of attention and treatment. Seeking to extend the advantages of "family government" beyond the domestic circle, reformers worked to establish or improve public institutions that were designed to shape individual character and instill a capacity for self-discipline.

The Extension of Education

The period from 1820 to 1850 saw an enormous expansion of free public schools. The new resolve to put more children in school for longer periods reflected many of the same values that exalted the child-centered family. Up to a certain age children could be effectively nurtured and educated at home. But after that they needed formal training at a character-molding institution that would prepare them to make a living and bear the burdens of republican citizenship. Purely intellectual training at school was regarded as less important than moral indoctrination.

Sometimes more than just an extension of the family, the school served as a substitute for it. Educational reformers were alarmed at the masses of poor and immigrant children who allegedly lacked a proper home environment. It was up to schools to make up for this disadvantage. Otherwise, the republic would be in danger from masses of people "incapable of self-government."

Before the 1820s, schooling in the United States was a haphazard affair. The wealthy sent their children to private schools, and some of the poor sent their children to charity or "pauper" schools that were usually financed in part by local governments. Public education was most highly developed in New England states, where towns were required by law to support elementary schools. It was weakest in the South where almost all education was private.

The agitation for expanded public education began in the 1820s and early 1830s as a central demand of the workingmen's movements in eastern cities. These hard-pressed artisans viewed free schools open to all as a way of countering the growing gap between rich and poor. Initially, strong opposition came from more affluent taxpayers who did not see why they should pay for the education of other people's children. But middle-class reformers soon seized the initiative, shaped educational reform to their own end of social discipline, and provided the momentum needed for legislative success.

The most influential spokesman for the common school movement was Horace Mann of Massachusetts. As a lawyer and member of the state legislature, Mann worked tirelessly to establish a state board of education and adequate tax support for local schools. In 1837, he persuaded the legislature to enact his proposals, and he subsequently resigned his seat to become the first secretary of the new board, an office he held with great distinction until 1848. He believed children were clay in the hands of teachers and school officials and could be molded to a state of perfection. Like advocates of child rearing through moral influence rather than physical force, he discouraged corporal punishment except as a last resort. His position on this issue led to a bitter controversy with Boston schoolmasters who retained a Calvinist sense of original sin and favored a freer use of the rod.

Against those who argued that school taxes violated property rights, Mann contended private property was actually held in trust for the good of the community. "The property of this commonwealth," he wrote, "is pledged for the education of all its youth up to such a point as will save them from poverty and vice, and prepare them for the adequate performance of their social and civil duties." Mann's conception of public education as a means of social discipline converted the middle and upper classes to the cause. By teaching middle-class morality and respect for order, the schools could turn potential rowdies and revolutionaries into law-abiding citizens. They could also encourage social mobility by opening doors for lower-class children who were determined to do better than their parents.

In practice, new or improved public schools often alienated working-class pupils and their families rather than reforming them. Compulsory attendance laws in Massachusetts and other states deprived poor families of needed wage earners without guaranteeing new occupational opportunities for those with an elementary education. As the laboring class became increasingly immigrant and Catholic in the 1840s and 1850s, dissatisfaction arose over the evangelical Protestant tone of "moral instruction" in the schools. Quite consciously, Mann and his disciples were trying to impose a uniform culture on people who valued differing traditions.

In addition to the "three Rs," reading, writing, and arithmetic, the public schools of the mid-nineteenth century taught the "Protestant ethic"—industry, punctuality, sobriety, and frugality. These were the virtues stressed in the famous McGuffey readers, which first appeared in 1836. Millions of children learned to read by digesting McGuffey's parables about the terrible fate of those who gave in to sloth, drunkenness, or wastefulness. Such moral indoctrination helped produce generations of Americans with personalities and beliefs adapted to the needs of an industrializing society—people who could be depended on to adjust to the precise and regular routines of the factory or the office. But as an education for self-government—in the sense of learning to think for oneself—it left much to be desired.

Fortunately, however, education was not limited to the schools nor devoted solely to children. Every city and almost every town or village had a lyceum, debating society, or mechanics' institute where adults of all social classes could broaden their intellectual horizons. Lyceums featured discourses on such subjects as "self-reliance" or "the conduct of life" by creative thinkers such as Ralph Waldo Emerson, explanations and demonstrations of the latest scientific discoveries, and debates among members on controversial issues.

Young Abraham Lincoln, who had received less than two years of formal schooling as a child in backwoods Indiana, sharpened his intellect in the early 1830s as a member of the New Salem (Illinois) debating society. In 1838, after moving to Springfield, he set forth his political principles when he spoke at the local lyceum on "The Perpetuation of Our Political Institutions." Unlike public schools, the lyceums and debating societies fostered independent thought and encouraged new ideas.

LESSON XXI.

1. IN'DO-LENT; *adj.* lazy; idle.
2. COM-MER'CIAL; *adj.* trading.
3. COM'IC-AL; *adj.* amusing.
3. DRONE; *n.* an idler.
4. NAV'I-GA-BLE; *adj.* in which boats can sail.

THE IDLE SCHOOL-BOY.

PRONOUNCE correctly. Do not say *indorlunt* for in-do-lent; *creepin* for creep-ing; *sylubble* for syl-la-ble; *colud* for col-ored; *scarlit* for scar-let; *ignerunt* for ig-no-rant.

1. I WILL tell you about the †laziest boy you ever heard of. He was indolent about every thing. When he played, the boys said he played as if the teacher told him to. When he went to school, he went creep-ing along like a snail. The boy had sense enough; but he was too lazy to learn any thing.

2. When he spelled a word, he †drawled out one syllable after another, as if he were afraid the †sylla-bles would quarrel, if he did not keep them a great way apart.

3. Once when he was †reciting, the teacher asked him, "What is said of †Hartford?" He answered, "Hartford is a †flourishing *comical* town." He meant that it was a "flourishing *commercial* town;" but he was such a drone, that he never knew what he was about.

4. When asked how far the River †Kennebec was navigable, he said, "it was navigable for *boots* as far as †Waterville." The boys all laughed, and the teacher could not help laughing, too. The idle boy †colored like scarlet.

5. "I say it is so in my book," said he. When one of the boys showed him the book, and pointed to the

The lessons and examples in McGuffey's Readers upheld the basic virtues of thrift, honesty, and charity, and taught that evil deeds never went unpunished.

Discovering the Asylum

Some segments of the population were obviously beyond the reach of family government and character training provided in homes and schools. In the 1820s and 1830s, reformers became acutely aware of the danger to society posed by an apparently increasing number of criminals, lunatics, and paupers. Their answer was to establish special institutions to house those deemed incapable of self-discipline. Their goals were humanitarian; they believed reform and rehabilitation were possible in a carefully controlled environment.

In earlier times, the existence of paupers, law-breakers, and insane persons had been taken for

In this 1876 woodcut, prisoners—in hand-on-shoulder lockstep—march into the dining room at Sing Sing Prison in New York. Rigid discipline and extensive rules restricting the inmates' movements, speech, and actions were thought to reform criminals. In most prisons, a strict silence was enforced at all times to allow the prisoners to reflect on the error of their ways.

granted. Their presence was viewed as the consequence of divine judgment or original sin. For the most part these people were dealt with in ways that did not isolate them from local communities. The insane were allowed to wander about if harmless and were confined at home if they were dangerous; the poor were supported by private charity or the dole provided by towns or counties; convicted criminals were whipped, held for limited periods in local jails, or—in the case of very serious offenses—executed.

By the early nineteenth century these traditional methods had come to seem both inadequate and inhumane. Dealing with deviants in a neighborly way broke down as economic development and urbanization made communities less cohesive. At the same time, reformers were concluding that all defects of mind and character were correctable—the insane could be cured, criminals reformed, and paupers taught to pull themselves out of destitution. The result was what historian David Rothman termed "the discovery of the asylum"—the invention and establishment of special institutions for the confinement and reformation of deviants.

The 1820s and 1830s saw the emergence of state-supported prisons, insane asylums, and poorhouses. New York and Pennsylvania led the way in prison reform. Institutions at Auburn, New York, and Philadelphia attracted international attention as model penitentiaries, mainly because of their experiments in isolating inmates

from one another. Solitary confinement was viewed as a humanitarian and therapeutic policy because it gave inmates a chance to reflect on their sins, free from the corrupting influence of other convicts. In theory, prisons and asylums substituted for the family. Custodians were meant to act as parents, providing moral advice and training.

In practice, these institutions were far different from the affectionate families idealized by the cult of domesticity. Most accommodated only a single sex or maintained a strict segregation of male and female inmates. Their most prominent feature was the imposition of a rigid daily routine. The early superintendents and wardens believed the enforcement of a rigorous set of rules and procedures would encourage self-discipline. The French observers Alexis de Tocqueville and Gustave de Beaumont summed up these practical expectations after a tour of American prisons in 1831 and 1832: "The habits or order to which the prisoner is subjected for several years . . . the obedience of every moment to inflexible rules, the regularity of a uniform life . . . are calculated to produce a deep impression upon his mind. Perhaps, leaving the prison he is not an honest man, but he has contracted honest habits. . . ."

Prisons, asylums, and poorhouses did not achieve the aims of their founders. Public support was inadequate to meet the needs of a growing inmate population and the personnel of these institutions often lacked the training needed to help the incarcerated. The results were overcrowding and the use of brutality to keep order. For the most part, prisons failed to reform hardened criminals, and the primitive psychotherapy known as "moral treatment" failed to cure most asylum patients. Poorhouses rapidly degenerated into sinkholes of despair. A combination of naive theories and poor performance doomed these institutions to a custodial rather than a reformatory role.

Conditions would have been even worse had it not been for Dorothea Dix. Between 1838 and the Civil War, this remarkable woman devoted her energies and skills to publicizing the inhumane treatment prevailing in prisons, almshouses, and insane asylums and lobbying for corrective action. As a direct result of her activities fifteen states opened new hospitals for the insane and others improved their supervision of penitentiaries, asylums, and poorhouses. Dix ranks as one of the most practical and effective of all the reformers of the pre–Civil War era.

REFORM TURNS RADICAL

During the 1830s, internal dissension split the great reform movement spawned by the Second Great Awakening. Efforts to promote evangelical piety, improve personal and public morality, and shape character through familial or institutional discipline continued and even flourished. But bolder spirits went beyond such goals and set their sights on the total liberation and perfection of the individual.

Divisions in the Benevolent Empire

Early nineteenth-century reformers were, for the most part, committed to changing existing attitudes and practices gradually and in ways that would not invite conflict or disrupt the society. But by the mid-1830s a new mood of impatience and perfectionism surfaced within the benevolent societies. In 1836, for example, the Temperance Society split over two issues—whether the abstinence pledge should be extended to include beer and wine and whether pressure should be applied to producers and sellers of alcoholic beverages as well as to consumers. Radicals insisted on a total commitment to "cold water" and were prepared to clash head on with an important economic interest. Moderates held back from such goals and tactics because they wished to avoid hostility from prominent citizens who drank wine or had money invested in the liquor industry.

A similar rift occurred in the American Peace Society, an antiwar organization founded in 1828 by clergymen seeking to promote Christian concern for world peace. Most of the founders admitted the propriety of "defensive wars" and were shocked when some members of the society began to denounce all use of force as a violation of the Sermon on the Mount. Dissidents, who called themselves "nonresistants," withdrew from the organization in 1838. Led by Henry C. Wright, they formed the New England Non-Resistance Society to promote an absolute pacifism, which denied the right of self-defense to nations or individuals and repudiated all forms of governmental coercion.

Dorothea Dix (1802–1887). Her efforts on behalf of the mentally ill led to the building of more than thirty institutions in the United States and the reform and restaffing— with well-trained personnel—of already existing hospitals. She died in Trenton, New Jersey, in 1887, in a hospital that she had founded.

The new perfectionism realized its most dramatic and important success within the antislavery movement. Before the 1830s, most people who expressed religious and moral concern over slavery were affiliated with the American Colonization Society, a benevolent organization founded in 1817. Most colonizationists admitted slavery was an evil, but they also viewed it as a deeply rooted social and economic institution that could only be eliminated very gradually and with the cooperation of slaveholders. Reflecting the power of racial prejudice, they proposed to transport freed blacks to Africa as a way of relieving southern fears that a race war would erupt if slaves were simply released from bondage and allowed to remain in America. In 1821, the society established the colony of Liberia in West Africa, and during the next decade a few thousand African Americans were settled there.

Colonization proved to be grossly inadequate as a step toward the elimination of slavery. Many of the blacks taken to Africa were already free, and those liberated by masters influenced by the movement represented only a tiny percentage of the natural increase of the southern slave population. Northern blacks denounced this enterprise because it denied the prospect of racial equality in America. Black opposition to colonizationism helped persuade William Lloyd Garrison and other white abolitionists to repudiate the Colonization Society and support immediate emancipation without emigration.

Garrison launched a new and more radical antislavery movement in 1831 when he began to publish a journal called the *Liberator* in Boston. Most of the small number of early subscribers to Garrison's *Liberator* were free blacks, and radical abolitionists depended heavily on black support from then on. Black orators, especially escaped slaves like Frederick Douglass, were featured at antislavery meetings, and some African Americans became officers of antislavery societies.

Besides calling for immediate and unconditional emancipation, Garrison denounced colonization as a slaveholder's plot to remove troublesome free blacks and an ignoble surrender to un-Christian prejudices. His rhetoric was as severe as his proposals were radical. As he wrote in the first issue of the *Liberator,* "I will be as harsh as truth and as uncompromising as justice. . . . I am in earnest—I will not equivocate—I will

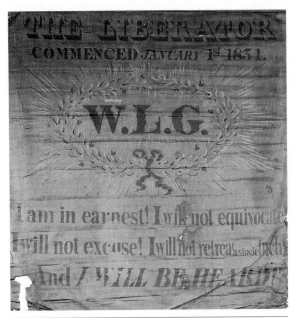

In the inaugural issue of his antislavery weekly the Liberator, *William Lloyd Garrison announced that he was launching a militant battle against the evil and sin of slavery. The stirring words that appeared in that first issue are repeated on the* Liberator's *banner.*

not excuse—I will not retreat a single inch—AND I WILL BE HEARD."

Heard he was. In 1833, Garrison and other abolitionists founded the American Anti-Slavery Society. "We shall send forth agents to lift up the voice of remonstrance, of warning, of entreaty, and of rebuke," its Declaration of Sentiments proclaimed. The colonization movement was placed on the defensive, and during the 1830s many of its most active northern supporters became abolitionists.

The Abolitionist Enterprise

The abolitionist movement, like the temperance crusade, was a direct outgrowth of the Second Great Awakening. Many leading abolitionists had undergone conversion experiences in the 1820s and were already committed to a life of Christian activism before they dedicated themselves to freeing the slaves. Several were ministers or divinity students seeking a mission in life that would fulfill spiritual and professional ambitions.

The career of Theodore Dwight Weld exemplified the connection between revivalism and abolitionism. Weld came from a long line of New England ministers. After dropping out of divinity school because of a combination of physical and spiritual ailments, he migrated to western New York. There he fell under the influence of Charles G. Finney and, after a long struggle, underwent a conversion experience in 1826. He then became an itinerant lecturer for various reform causes. By the early 1830s, he focused his attention on the moral issues raised by the institution of slavery. After a brief flirtation with the colonization movement, Weld was converted to abolitionism in 1832, recognizing that colonizationists did not really accept blacks as equals or "brothers-in-Christ." In 1834, he instigated what amounted to a series of abolitionist revivals at Lane Theological Seminary in Cincinnati. When the trustees of the seminary attempted to suppress further discussion of the case for immediate emancipation, Weld led a mass walkout of most students. "The Lane rebels" subsequently founded Oberlin College as a center for abolitionist activity.

In 1835 and 1836, Weld toured Ohio and western New York preaching abolitionism. He also supervised and trained other agents and orators as part of a campaign to convert the entire region to immediate emancipation. The tried and true methods of the revival—fervent preaching, protracted meetings, and the call for individuals to come forth and announce their redemption—were put at the service of the antislavery movement. Weld and his associates often had to face angry mobs, but they left behind them tens of thousands of new abolitionists and hundreds of local antislavery societies. As a result of their efforts, northern Ohio and western New York became hotbeds of abolitionist sentiment.

Antislavery orators and organizers tended to have their greatest successes in the small- to medium-sized towns of the upper North. The typical convert came from an upwardly mobile family engaged in small business, the skilled trades, or market farming. In larger towns and cities, or when they ventured close to the Mason-Dixon line, abolitionists were more likely to encounter fierce and effective opposition. In 1835, Garrison was mobbed in the streets of Boston and almost lynched. In New York City, the Tappan brothers—Lewis and Arthur—were frequent objects of threats and violence. These two successful merchants were key figures in the movement because they used their substantial wealth to finance antislavery activities. In 1835–1836, they supported a massive effort to print antislavery pamphlets and distribute them through the U. S. mails. But they made relatively few converts in their own city; most New Yorkers regarded them as dangerous radicals.

Abolitionists who thought of taking their message to the fringes of the South had reason to pause, given the fate of the antislavery editor Elijah Lovejoy. In 1837, while attempting to defend himself and his printing press from a mob in Alton, Illinois, just across the Mississippi River from slaveholding Missouri, Lovejoy was shot and killed.

Racism was a major cause of antiabolitionist violence in the North. Rumors that abolitionists advocated or practiced interracial marriage could easily incite an urban crowd. If it could not find white abolitionists, the mob was likely to turn on local blacks. Working-class whites tended to fear that economic and social competition with blacks would increase if abolitionists succeeded in freeing slaves and making them citizens. But a striking feature of many of the mobs was that they were dominated by "gentlemen of property and standing." Solid citizens resorted to violence, it would appear, because abolitionism threatened their conservative notions of social order and hierarchy.

By the end of the 1830s, the abolitionist movement was under great stress. Besides the burden of external repression, there was dissension within the movement. Becoming an abolitionist required an exacting conscience and an unwillingness to compromise on matters of principle. These character traits also made it difficult for abolitionists to work together and maintain a united front. Relations between black and white abolitionists were, for the most part, tense and uneasy. Blacks protested that they did not have a fair share of leadership positions or influence over policy. Not even abolitionists were entirely free of the prejudices rife in the larger white society, and blacks resented the paternalism and condescension that often resulted.

During the late 1830s, Garrison, the most visible spokesman for the cause, began to adopt positions that some other abolitionists found extreme and divisive. He embraced the nonresistant or "no-government" philosophy of Henry C. Wright and urged abolitionists to abstain from voting or otherwise participating in a corrupt political system. He also attacked the clergy and the churches for refusing to take a strong antislavery stand and

African American leaders in the abolitionist movement included Frederick Douglass (right) and William Whipper (left). Douglass, who escaped from slavery in 1838, became one of the most effective voices in the crusade against slavery. In 1837, twelve years before Thoreau's essay "Civil Disobedience," Whipper published an article entitled "An Address on Non-Resistance to Offensive Aggression." Whipper was also one of the founders of the American Moral Reform Society, an African American abolitionist organization.

encouraged his followers to "come out" of the established denominations rather than continuing to work within them.

These positions alienated those members of the Anti-Slavery Society who continued to hope that organized religion and the existing political system could be influenced or even taken over by abolitionists. But it was Garrison's stand on women's rights that led to an open break at the national convention of 1840. Following their leader's principle that women should be equal partners in the crusade, a Garrison-led majority elected a female abolitionist to the executive committee of the Anti-Slavery Society. A minority, led by Lewis Tappan, then withdrew to form a competing organization—the American and Foreign Anti-Slavery Society.

The new organization never amounted to much, but the schism did weaken Garrison's influence within the movement. When he later repudiated the U. S. Constitution as a proslavery document and called for northern secession from the Union, few antislavery people in the mid-Atlantic or midwestern states went along. Outside of New England, most abolitionists worked *within* the churches and avoided controversial side issues like women's rights and nonresistant pacifism. Some antislavery advocates chose the path of political action. The Liberty party, organized in 1840, was their first attempt to enter the electoral arena under their own banner; it signaled a new effort to turn antislavery sentiment into political power.

Historians have debated the question of whether the abolitionist movement of the 1830s and early 1840s was a success or failure. It obviously failed to convert a majority of Americans to its position that slavery was a sinful institution that should be abolished immediately. Since that position implied that blacks should be granted equality as American citizens, it ran up against the powerful conviction of white supremacy prevailing in all parts of the country. In the South, abolitionism caused a strong counterreaction and helped inspire a more militant and uncompromising defense of slavery. The belief that peaceful agitation, or what abolitionists called "moral suasion," would convert slaveholders and their northern sympathizers to abolition was obviously unrealistic.

But in another sense the crusade was successful. It brought the slavery issue to the forefront of public consciousness and convinced a substantial and growing segment of the northern population that the South's peculiar institution was morally wrong and potentially dangerous to the American way of life. The South helped the antislavery cause in the North by responding hysterically and repressively to abolitionist agitation. In 1836, Southerners in Congress forced adoption of a "gag rule" requiring that abolitionist petitions be tabled without being read; at about the same time, the Post Office refused to carry antislavery literature into the slave states. Prominent Northerners who had not been moved to action by abolitionist depictions of slave suffering became more responsive to the movement when it appeared their own civil liberties might be threatened. The politicians who later mobilized the North against the expansion of slavery into the territories drew strength from the antislavery and antisouthern sentiments that abolitionists had already called forth.

From Abolitionism to Women's Rights

Abolitionism also served as a catalyst for the women's rights movement. From the beginning women were active participants in the abolitionist crusade. Between 1835 and 1838, the American Anti-Slavery Society bombarded Congress with petitions, mostly calling for abolition of slavery in the District of Columbia. Over half of the thousands of antislavery petitions sent to Washington had women's signatures on them.

Some antislavery women went further and defied conventional ideas of their proper sphere by becoming public speakers and demanding an equal role in the leadership of antislavery societies. The most famous of these were the Grimké sisters, Sarah and Angelina, who attracted enormous attention because they were the rebellious daughters of a South Carolina slaveholder. When some male abolitionists objected to their speaking in public to mixed audiences of men and women, Garrison came to their defense and helped forge a link between black and female struggles for equality.

The battle to participate equally in the antislavery crusade made a number of female abolitionists acutely aware of male dominance and oppression. For them, the same principles that justified the liberation of the slaves also applied to the emancipation of women from all restrictions on their rights as citizens. In 1840, Garrison's American followers withdrew from the first World's Anti-Slavery Convention in London because the sponsors refused to seat the female members of their delegation. Among the women thus excluded were Lucretia Mott and Elizabeth Cady Stanton.

Wounded by male reluctance to extend the cause of emancipation to include women, Stanton and Mott organized a new and independent movement for women's rights. The high point of their campaign was the famous convention at Seneca Falls, New York, in 1848. The "Declaration of Sentiments" issued by this first national gathering of feminists charged that "the history of mankind is a history of repeated injuries and usurpations on the part of man toward woman, having in direct object the establishment of an absolute

Elizabeth Cady Stanton, a leader of the women's rights movement, reared seven children. In addition to her pioneering work, especially for women's suffrage, she also lectured frequently on family life and child care.

tyranny over her." It went on to demand that all women be given the right to vote and that married women be freed from unjust laws giving husbands control of their property, persons, and children. Rejecting the cult of domesticity with its doctrine of separate spheres, these women and their male supporters launched the modern movement for gender equality.

Radical Ideas and Experiments

Hopes for individual or social perfection were not limited to reformers inspired by evangelicalism. Between the 1820s and 1850s, a great variety of schemes for human redemption came from those who had rejected orthodox Protestantism. Some were secular humanists carrying on the freethinking tradition of the Enlightenment, but most were seeking new paths to spiritual or religious fulfillment. These philosophical and religious radicals attacked established institutions, prescribed new modes of living, and founded utopian communities to put their ideas into practice.

A radical movement of foreign origin that gained a toehold in Jacksonian America was utopian socialism. In 1825–1826, the British manufacturer and reformer Robert Owen visited the United States and founded a community based on common and equal ownership of property at New Harmony, Indiana. About the same time, Owen's associate Frances Wright gathered a group of slaves at Nashoba, Tennessee, and set them to work earning their freedom in an atmosphere of "rational cooperation." The rapid demise of both of these model communities suggested that utopian socialism did not easily take root in American soil.

But the impulse survived. In the 1840s, a number of Americans, including the prominent editor Horace Greeley, became interested in the ideas of the French utopian theorist Charles Fourier. Fourier called for cooperative communities in which everyone did a fair share of the work and tasks were allotted to make use of the natural abilities and instincts of the members. Between 1842 and 1852, about thirty Fourierist "phalanxes" were established in the northeastern and midwestern states, and approximately a hundred thousand people lived for a time in these communities or otherwise supported the movement. The phalanxes were not purely socialistic; in fact they were organized as joint-stock companies. But they did give the members an opportunity to live and work in a communal atmosphere. Like the Owenite communities, they were short-lived, surviving for an average of only two years. The common complaint of the founders was that Americans were too individualistic to cooperate in the ways that Fourier's theories required.

The most successful and long-lived of the pre–Civil War utopias was established in 1848 at Oneida, New York, and was inspired by an unorthodox brand of Christian perfectionism. Its founder, John Humphrey Noyes, believed the Second Coming of Christ had already occurred; hence human beings were totally free from sin and were no longer obliged to follow the moral rules that their previously fallen state had required. At Oneida, traditional marriage was outlawed and a carefully regulated form of "free love" was put into practice.

It was a literary and philosophical movement known as transcendentalism that inspired the era's most memorable experiments in thinking and living on a higher plane. The main idea was that the individual could transcend material reality and ordinary understanding, attaining through a higher form of reason—or intuition—a oneness with the universe as a whole and with the spiritual forces that lay behind it. Transcendentalism was the major American version of the romantic and idealist thought that emerged in the early nineteenth century. Throughout the western world, romanticism was challenging the rationalism and materialism of the Enlightenment in the name of exalted feeling and cosmic spirituality. Most American transcendentalists were Unitarians or ex-Unitarians who were dissatisfied with the sober rationalism of their denomination and sought a more intense kind of spiritual experience. Unable to embrace evangelical Christianity because of intellectual resistance to its doctrines, they sought inspiration from a philosophical and literary idealism of German origin.

Their prophet was Ralph Waldo Emerson, a brilliant essayist and lecturer who preached that each individual could commune directly with a benign spiritual force that animated nature and the universe, which he called the "oversoul." Emerson was a radical individualist committed to "self-culture" and "the sufficiency of the private man." He carefully avoided all involvement in organized movements or associations because they limited the freedom of the individual to develop inner resources and find a personal path to spiritual illumination. In the vicinity of Emerson's home in Concord, Massachusetts, a group of like-minded seekers of truth and spiritual fulfillment gathered during the 1830s and 1840s. Among them for a time was Margaret Fuller, the leading female intellectual of the age. In *Woman in the Nineteenth Century* (1845), she made a strong claim for the spiritual and artistic equality of women.

One group of transcendentalists, led by the Reverend George Ripley, rejected Emerson's radical individualism and founded a cooperative community at Brook Farm, near Roxbury, Massachusetts, in 1841. For the next four years group members worked the land in common, conducted an excellent school on the principle that spontaneity rather than discipline was the key to education, and allowed ample time for conversation, meditation, communion with nature, and artistic activity of all kinds. Visitors and guest lecturers included such luminaries as Emerson, Margaret Fuller, and Theodore Parker, the Unitarian theologian and radical reformer. In 1845, Brook Farm was reconstituted as a Fourieristic phalanx, but some of the original spirit persisted until its dissolution in 1849.

Another experiment in transcendental living adhered more closely to the individualistic spirit of the movement. Between 1845 and 1847, Henry David Thoreau, a young disciple of Emerson, lived by himself in the woods along the shore of Walden Pond and carefully recorded his thoughts and impressions. In a sense, he pushed the ideal of self-culture to its logical outcome—a utopia of one. The result was *Walden* (published in 1854), one of the greatest achievements in American literature.

Fads and Fashions

Not only venturesome intellectuals experimented with new beliefs and lifestyles. Between the 1830s and 1850s, a number of fads, fashions, and medical cure-alls appeared on the scene, indicating that a large segment of the middle class was obsessed with the pursuit of personal health, happiness, and moral perfection. Dietary reformers like Sylvester Graham convinced many people to give up meat, coffee, tea, and pastries in favor of fruit, vegetables, and whole wheat bread. Some women, especially feminists, began to wear loose-fitting pantalettes, or "bloomers," popularized by Amelia Bloomer. These clothes were more convenient and less restricting than the elaborate structure of corsets, petticoats, and hooped skirts currently in fashion. A concern with understanding and improving personal character and abilities was reflected in the craze for phrenology, a popular pseudoscience that studied the shape of the skull to determine natural aptitudes and inclinations.

In an age of perfectionism, even the dead could be enlisted on the side of universal reform. In the 1850s, spiritualists like Andrew Jackson Davis and the Fox sisters—Margaret, Leah, and Catharine—convinced an extraordinary number of people that it was possible to make direct contact with the departed, who were viewed as having "passed on" to a purer state of being and a higher wisdom. Seances were held in parlors all over the

Henry David Thoreau explained that he went to live in solitude in the woods because he wished to "front only the essential facts of life." The sketch at right appeared on the title page of the first edition of Walden, *published in 1854, the remarkable record of his experiment in living.*

nation, and large crowds turned out for demonstrations of "spirit-rapping" and other psychic manifestations. Spiritualist beliefs were a logical outgrowth (some might say to the point of absurdity) of the perfectionist dream pursued so ardently by antebellum Americans.

Counterpoint on Reform

One great American writer observed at close quarters the perfectionist ferment of the age but held himself aloof, suggesting in his novels and tales that pursuit of the ideal led to a distorted sense of human nature and possibilities. Nathaniel Hawthorne lived in Concord, knew Emerson and Margaret Fuller, and even spent time at Brook Farm. But his sense of human frailty and sinfulness made him skeptical about the claims of transcendentalism and Utopianism. He satirized transcendentalism as unworldly and overoptimistic in his allegorical tale "The Celestial Railroad" and gently lampooned the denizens of Brook Farm in his novel *The Blithedale Romance* (1852). His view of the dangers of pursuing perfection too avidly came out in his tale of a father who kills his beautiful daughter trying to remove her one blemish, a birthmark. His greatest novels, *The Scarlet Letter* (1850) and *The House of Seven Gables* (1851), imaginatively probed New England's Puritan past and the shadows it cast on the present. By dwelling on the psychological reality of original sin, Hawthorne told his contemporaries that their efforts to escape from guilt and evil were futile. One simply had to accept the world as an imperfect place. Although he did not engage in polemics against humanitarian reformers and cosmic optimists, Hawthorne wrote parables and allegories that implicitly questioned the fundamental assumptions of pre–Civil War reform.

One does not have to agree with Hawthorne's antiprogressive view of the human condition to acknowledge that the dreams of perfectionist reformers promised more than they could possibly deliver. Revivals could not make all men like Christ; temperance could not solve all social problems; abolitionist agitation could not bring a peaceful end to slavery; and transcendentalism (as Emerson himself sometimes conceded) could not fully emancipate people from the limitations and frustrations of daily life. The consequences of

Known primarily for works expressing his skepticism about reform and the pursuit of perfection, Nathaniel Hawthorne also published lighter pieces of imagination and fancy. His Tanglewood Tales *(1853) was a collection of children's stories. Pictured here is the title page from the 1854 edition.*

perfectionist efforts were often far different from what their proponents expected. In defense of the reformers however, one could argue that Hawthorne's skepticism and fatalism were a prescription for doing nothing in the face of intolerable evils. If the reform impulse was long on inspirational rhetoric but somewhat short on durable, practical achievements, it did at least disturb the complacent and opportunistic surface of American life and open the way to necessary changes. Nothing could possibly change for the better unless people were willing to dream of improvement.

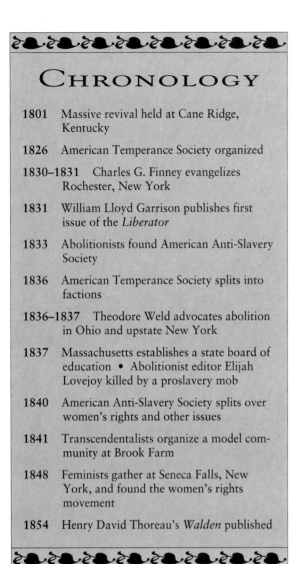

CHRONOLOGY

1801   Massive revival held at Cane Ridge, Kentucky

1826   American Temperance Society organized

1830–1831   Charles G. Finney evangelizes Rochester, New York

1831   William Lloyd Garrison publishes first issue of the *Liberator*

1833   Abolitionists found American Anti-Slavery Society

1836   American Temperance Society splits into factions

1836–1837   Theodore Weld advocates abolition in Ohio and upstate New York

1837   Massachusetts establishes a state board of education • Abolitionist editor Elijah Lovejoy killed by a proslavery mob

1840   American Anti-Slavery Society splits over women's rights and other issues

1841   Transcendentalists organize a model community at Brook Farm

1848   Feminists gather at Seneca Falls, New York, and found the women's rights movement

1854   Henry David Thoreau's *Walden* published

Recommended Reading

Alice Felt Tyler, *Freedom's Ferment: Phases of American Social History from the Colonial Period to the Outbreak of the Civil War* (1944), gives a lively overview of the varieties of pre-Civil War reform activity. Ronald G. Walters, *American Reformers, 1815–1860* (1978), provides a modern interpretation of these movements. A particularly useful selection of articles and essays is David Brion Davis, ed., *Ante-Bellum Reform* (1967). The best general work on the revivalism of the Second Great Awakening is William G. McLoughlin, *Modern Revivalism* (1959). Paul E. Johnson, *A Shopkeeper's Millennium: Society and Revivals in Rochester, New York, 1815–1837* (1978), incisively describes the impact of the revival on a single community. A good introduction to the changing roles

of women and the family in nineteenth-century America is Carl N. Degler, *At Odds: Women and the Family in America from the Revolution to the Present* (1980). On the rise of the domestic ideology see Nancy Cott, *The Bonds of Womanhood: "Woman's Sphere" in New England, 1780–1835* (1977). The condition of working-class women is incisively treated in Christine Stansell, *City of Women: Sex and Class in New York, 1789–1860* (1986).

David J. Rothman, *The Discovery of the Asylum: Social Order and Disorder in the New Republic* (1971), provides a penetrating analysis of the movement for institutional reform. For a good survey of abolitionism, see James Brewer Stewart, *Holy Warriors: The Abolitionists and American Slavery* (1976).

Additional Bibliography

The various dimensions of evangelical religion are covered in William G. McLoughlin, *Revivals, Awakenings, and Reform: An Essay on Religion and Social Change in America, 1607–1977* (1978); John B. Boles, *The Great Revival* (1972); Donald G. Mathews, *Religion in the Old South* (1977); Anne C. Loveland, *Southern Evangelicals and the Social Order, 1800–1860* (1980); Charles A. Johnson, *The Frontier Camp Meeting* (1955); Whitney R. Cross, *The Burned-Over District* (1950); Perry Miller, *The Life of the Mind in America from the Revolution to the Civil War* (1965); and Charles C. Cole, *The Social Ideas of the Northern Evangelists* (1954). The connection between revivalism and organized benevolence is treated in Clifford Griffen, *Their Brothers' Keepers: Moral Stewardship in the United States, 1800–1865* (1960); Charles I. Foster, *An Errand of Mercy: The Evangelical United Front* (1960); John R. Bodo, *The Protestant Clergy and Public Issues, 1812–1848* (1954); and Timothy L. Smith, *Revivalism and Social Reform in Mid-Nineteenth-Century America* (1957). On the temperance movement, see John A. Krout, *The Origins of Prohibition* (1925); Joseph R. Gusfield, *Symbolic Crusade: Status, Politics, and the American Temperance Movement* (1963); W. J. Rorabaugh, *The Alcoholic Republic: An American Tradition* (1979); and Ian R. Tyrrell, *Sobering Up: From Temperance to Prohibition in Antebellum America, 1800–1860* (1979).

The cult of domesticity and the status of women are the subjects of Barbara Welter, "The Cult of True Womanhood," *American Quarterly*, 18 (1966): 217–240; Kathryn Kish Sklar, *Catharine Beecher: A Study in American Domesticity* (1973); Mary Ryan, *The Cradle of the Middle Class: The Family in Oneida County New York, 1790–1865* (1981); and Suzanne Lebsock, *The Free Women of Petersburg* (1984). On women's reform activities, see Lori D. Ginzberg, *Women and the Work of Benevolence* (1990). Bernard Wishy, *The Child and the Republic: The Dawn of Modern American Child Nurture* (1968), treats childhood and child rearing. Light is shed on the limitation of family size in James Reed, *From Private Vice to Public Virtue: The Birth Control Movement and American Society Since 1830* (1978) and James C. Mohr, *Abortion in America: The Origins and Evolution of National Policy, 1800–1900* (1978). On educational reform, see Lawrence Cremin, *American Education: The National Experience, 1783–1876* (1980); Rush Welter, *Popular Education and Democratic Thought* (1962); and Michael B. Katz, *The Irony of Early School Reform: Educational Innovation in Mid-Nineteenth-Century Massachusetts* (1968). The emergence of modern prisons is described in Blake McKelvy, *American Prisons* (1936) and W. David Lewis, *From Newgate to Dannemora: The Rise of the Penitentiary in New York* (1965). On the rise of asylums, see Gerald N. Grob, *Mental Institutions in America: Social Policy to 1875* (1973).

There is a vast literature on the abolitionist movement. Among the most significant works are Gilbert H. Barnes, *The Antislavery Impulse* (1934); John L. Thomas, *The Liberator: William Lloyd Garrison* (1963); Aileen S. Kraditor, *Means and Ends in American Abolitionism: Garrison and His Critics on Strategy and Tactics* (1967); Bertram Wyatt-Brown, *Lewis Tappan and the Evangelical War Against Slavery* (1969); Lewis Perry, *Radical Abolitionism: Anarchy and the Government of God in Antislavery Thought* (1973); Ronald G. Walters, *The Antislavery Appeal: American Abolitionists After 1830* (1976); Robert H. Abzug, *Passionate Liberator: Theodore Dwight Weld and the Dilemma of Reform* (1980); Lawrence J. Friedman, *Gregarious Saints: Self and Community in American Abolitionism* (1982); Louis S. Gerteis, *Morality and Utility in Antislavery Reform* (1987); and William S. McFeely, *Frederick Douglass* (1991). Leonard L. Richards, *"Gentlemen of Property and Standing": Anti-Abolition Mobs in Jacksonian America* (1970), interprets violence against the abolitionists. On the connection between abolition and women's rights, see Gerda Lerner, *The Grimké Sisters from South Carolina: Rebels Against Slavery* (1967); Blanche Glassman Hersh, *The Slavery of Sex: Feminist Abolitionists in America* (1978); and Shirley J. Yee, *Black Women Abolitionists* (1992).

The utopian impulse is the subject of Arthur Bestor, *Backwoods Utopias* (1950); Michael Fellman, *The Unbounded Frame: Freedom and Community in Nineteenth-Century Utopianism* (1973); and Carl Guarneri, *The Utopian Alternative: Fourierism in Nineteenth-Century America* (1991). On the transcendentalists, see Anne C. Rose, *Transcendentalism as a Social Movement, 1830–1850* (1981). R. Laurence Moore, *In Search of White Crows: Spiritualism, Parapsychology, and American Culture* (1977), is the best study of spiritualism.

An Age of Expansionism

In the 1840s and early 1850s politicians, journalists, writers, and entrepreneurs frequently proclaimed themselves champions of "Young America." One of the first to use the phrase was Ralph Waldo Emerson, who told an audience of merchants and manufacturers in 1844 that the nation was entering a new era of commercial development, technological progress (as exemplified in the railroads just beginning to crisscross the landscape), and territorial expansion. Emerson suggested that a progressive new generation—the "Young Americans"—would lead this surge of physical development. More than a slogan and less than an organized movement, Young America stood for a positive attitude toward the market economy and industrial growth, a more aggressive and belligerent foreign policy, and a celebration of America's unique strengths and virtues. The idea of a young country led by young men into new paths of prosperity and greatness was bound to appeal to many. It did, however, have its opponents—cautious, tradition-minded people who had doubts about where "progress" and expansionism might lead. The Young Americans had no patience with such "old fogeys." "The spirit of young America," noted a Boston newspaper in 1844, "will not be satisfied with what has been attained but plumes its wings for more glorious flight. . . . The steam is up, the young overpowering spirit of the country will press onward."

Although the Young America ideal attracted support across party lines, it came to be identified mainly with young Democrats who sought to purge their party of its traditional fear of the expansion of commerce and industry. Unlike old-line Jeffersonians and Jacksonians, Young Americans had no qualms about the market economy and the speculative, materialistic spirit it called forth.

Furthermore, the Young Americans favored enlarging the national market by acquiring new territory. They called in turn for annexation of Texas, assertion of an American claim to all of Oregon, and the appropriation of vast new territories from Mexico. They also celebrated the technological advances that would knit this new empire together, especially the telegraph and the railroad. Telegraphs, according to one writer,

would "flash sensation and volition . . . and to and from towns and provinces as if they were organs and limbs of a single organism"; railroads would provide "a vast system of iron muscles which, as it were, move the limbs of the mighty organism."

Young America was a cultural and intellectual as well as an economic and political movement. In 1845, a Washington journal hailed the election of the relatively young James K. Polk to the presidency as a sign that youth will "dare to take antiquity by the beard, and tear the cloak from hoary-headed hypocrisy. Too young to be corrupt . . . it is Young America, awakened to a sense of her own intellectual greatness by her soaring spirit. It stands in strength, the voice of the majority." During the Polk administration, "Young American" writers and critics—mostly based in New York—called for a new and distinctive national literature, free of subservience to European themes or models and expressive of the democratic spirit. Their organ was the *Literary World*, founded in 1847, and its ideals influenced two of the greatest writers the nation has produced—Walt Whitman and Herman Melville.

Whitman captured much of the exuberance and expansionism of Young America in his "Song of the Open Road"

> *From this hour I ordain myself loos'd of limits and imaginary lines,*
> *Going where I list, my own master total and absolute,*
> . . . .
> *I inhale great draughts of space,*
> *The east and the west are mine, and the north and the south are mine.*
> *I am larger, better than I thought.*

In *Moby-Dick,* Herman Melville produced a novel sufficiently original in form and conception to more than fulfill the demand of Young Americans for "a New Literature to fit the New Man in the New Age." But Melville was too deep a thinker not to see the perils that underlay the soaring ambition and aggressiveness of the new age. The whaling captain, Ahab, who brings destruction on himself and his ship by his relentless pursuit of the white whale symbolized—among other things—the dangers facing a nation that was overreaching itself by indulging its pride and exalted sense of destiny with too little concern for moral and practical consequences.

MOVEMENT TO THE FAR WEST

In the 1830s and 1840s, the westward movement of population left the valley of the Mississippi behind and penetrated the Far West all the way to the Pacific. Pioneers pursued fertile land and economic opportunity beyond the existing boundaries of the United States and thus helped set the stage for the annexations and international crises of the 1840s. Some went for material gain, others for adventure, and a significant minority sought freedom from religious persecution. Whatever their reasons, they brought American attitudes into regions that were already occupied or claimed by Mexico or Great Britain.

Borderlands of the 1830s

U.S. expansionists directed their ambitions to the north, west, and southwest. For a time it seemed that both Canada and Mexico might be frontiers

New York native Herman Melville, shown here in an 1870 portrait by Joseph Oriel Eaton, shaped the knowledge he gained as a merchant sailor into Moby-Dick, *a cautionary saga about the dark side of human ambition.*

Walt Whitman in the "carpenter portrait" that appeared in the first edition of his great work, Leaves of Grass, *in 1855. The poet's rough clothes and slouch hat signify his identification with the common people.*

for expansionism. Conflicts over the border between the United States and British North America led periodically to calls for diplomatic or military action to wrest the northern half of the continent from the British; similar conflicts in Mexican territory led ultimately to the United States's capture and acquisition of much of northern Mexico.

Since the birth of the republic there had been a major dispute over the boundary between Maine and the Canadian province of New Brunswick. In 1839, fighting broke out between Canadian lumberjacks and the Maine militia. This long-festering controversy poisoned Anglo-American relations until 1842, when Secretary of State Daniel Webster concluded an agreement with the British government, represented by Lord Ashburton. The Webster-Ashburton Treaty gave over half of the disputed territory to the United States and established a definite northeastern boundary with Canada.

On the other side of the continent, the United States and Britain both laid claim to Oregon, a vast area that lay between the Rockies and the Pacific from the forty-second parallel (the northern boundary of California) to the latitude of 54°40′ (the southern boundary of Alaska). In 1818, the two nations agreed to joint occupation for ten years, an agreement that was renewed indefinitely in 1827. Meanwhile, the Americans had strengthened their claim by acquiring Spain's rights to the Pacific Northwest in the Adams-Onís Treaty (see Chapter 9), and the British had gained effective control of the northern portion of the Oregon country through the activities of the Hudson's Bay Company, a well-financed fur-trading concern. Blocking an equitable division was the reluctance on both sides to surrender access to the Columbia River basin and the adjacent territory extending north to the forty-ninth parallel (which later became the northern border of the state of Washington).

The Oregon country was scarcely populated before 1840. The same could not be said of the Mexican borderlands that lay directly west of Jacksonian America. Spanish settlements in present-day New Mexico dated from the end of the sixteenth century. By 1820, about forty thousand

people populated this province, engaging mainly in sheep-raising and mining. In 1821, Spain granted independence to Mexico, which then embraced areas that currently make up the states of Texas, New Mexico, Arizona, California, Nevada, Utah, and much of Colorado. Spain's mercantilistic policies had closed the region to outside traders, but the Republic of Mexico opted for a free trade policy. Mexico in 1821 informed its northern neighbors of the changed laws encouraging trade. This action succeeded in stimulating commercial prosperity, but also whetted expansionist appetites on the Anglo side of the border.

California was the other major northward extension of Mexico. Spanish missionaries and soldiers had taken control of the region in the late eighteenth century. In the 1820s and 1830s, this land of huge estates and enormous cattle herds was far less populous than New Mexico—only about four thousand Mexicans of Spanish origin lived in California in 1827. The region's other inhabitants were the thirty thousand Indians,

Territorial Expansion by the Mid-Nineteenth Century

Fervent nationalists identified the growth of America through territorial expansion as the divinely ordained "Manifest Destiny" of a chosen people.

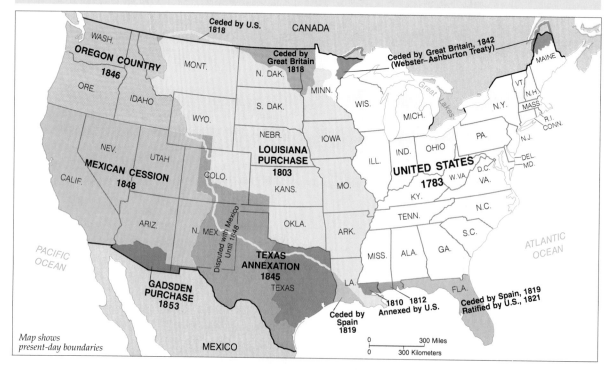

many of whom were forced to work on vast land tracts owned by Spanish missions. At the beginning of the 1830s, a chain of twenty-one mission stations, stretching from San Diego to San Francisco, controlled most of the province's land and wealth. Great as the Indian population may seem, the number represented only a small fraction of the original indigenous population; there had been a dramatic and catastrophic decline in Indian population during the previous sixty years of Spanish rule. The stresses and strains of forced labor and exposure to European diseases had taken an enormous toll.

In 1833, the Mexican Congress's "secularization act" emancipated the Indians from church control and opened the mission lands to settlement. The government awarded immense tracts of the mission land to Mexican citizens and left the Indians landless. A new class of large landowners, or *rancheros*, replaced the *padres* as rulers of Old California and masters of the province's indigenous population. Seven hundred grantees took possession of *ranchos* ranging up to nearly 50,000 acres and proceeded to subject the Indians to a new and even harsher form of servitude. During the fifteen years they held sway, the rancheros created an American legend through their lavish hospitality, extravagant dress, superb horsemanship, and taste for violent and dangerous sports. Their flamboyant lifestyle and devotion to the pursuit of pleasure captured the fancy and aroused the secret envy of many American visitors and traders.

The Americans who saw California in the 1830s were mostly merchants and sailors involved in the oceanic trade between Boston and California ports. New England clipper ships sailed around Cape Horn at the southern tip of South America to barter manufactured goods for cowhides. One Boston firm came away with over 500,000 hides in a twenty-year period. By the mid-1830s, several Yankee merchants had taken up permanent residence in towns like Monterey and San Diego in order to conduct the California end of the business. The reports they sent back about the Golden West sparked interest in eastern business circles.

The Texas Revolution

At the same time some Americans were trading with California, others were taking possession of Texas. In the early 1820s, Mexican officials encouraged settlers from the United States to settle in Texas. Newly independent Mexico granted Stephen F. Austin, son of a one-time Spanish citizen, a huge piece of land in hopes he would help attract and settle new colonists from the United States. Some fifteen other Anglo-American *empresarios* were similarly granted land in the 1820s. In 1823, three hundred families from the United States were settled on the Austin grant, and within a year the colony's population had swelled to 2,021. American immigrants were drawn by the offer of fertile and inexpensive land.

An extravagantly dressed ranchero directs his Indian overseer in this 1839 lithograph. With their thrilling lifestyles and exotic costumes, these hacienda owners contributed to the vivid images associated with California in the 1830s.

Friction soon developed between the Mexican government and the Anglo-American colonists over slavery's status and the Catholic church's authority. At its core, the dispute was a misunderstanding about whether the settlers were Anglo-Americans or Mexicans. Under the terms of settlement, all people living in Texas adopted Mexican citizenship and the Roman Catholic faith. Slavery presented a problem, for in 1829 Mexico freed all slaves under its jurisdiction. Slaveholders in Texas were given a special exemption that allowed them to emancipate their slaves and then sign them to lifelong contracts as indentured servants, but many refused to limit their ownership rights in any way. Settlers similarly either converted to Catholicism only superficially or ignored the requirement entirely.

A Mexican government commission reported in 1829 that Americans were the great majority of the Texas population and were flagrantly violating Mexican law—refusing to emancipate their slaves, evading import duties on goods from the United States, and failing to convert to Catholicism. The following year the Mexican Congress prohibited further American immigration and importation of slaves to Texas.

Enforcement of the new law was feeble, and the flow of settlers, slaves, and smuggled goods continued virtually unabated. A long-standing complaint of the Texans was the failure of the Mexican constitution to grant them local self-government. Under the Mexican federal system, Texas was joined to the state of Coahuila, and Texan representatives were outnumbered three to one in the state legislature. In 1832, the colonists showed their displeasure with Mexican rule by rioting in protest against the arrest of several Anglo-Americans by a Mexican commander.

Stephen F. Austin went to Mexico City in 1833 to present the Texans' grievances and seek concessions from the central government. He succeeded in having the ban against American immigration lifted, but got only vague promises about tariff relief, and failed to win agreement to the separation of Texas from Coahuila. As he was about to return to Texas, Austin was arrested and imprisoned for writing a letter recommending that Texans set up a state government without Mexico City's consent.

In 1835, some Texans revolted against Mexico's central government. The insurrectionists claimed they were fighting for freedom against a long experience of oppression. Actually, Mexican rule had not been harsh; the worst that can be said was that it was inefficient, inconsistent, and sometimes corrupt. Furthermore, the Texans' devotion to "liberty" did not prevent them from defending slavery against Mexico's attempt to abolish it. Texans had done pretty much what they pleased, despite laws to the contrary and angry rumblings from south of the Río Grande.

Developments in 1834 had threatened their status as "tolerated guests." In that year, General Antonio López de Santa Anna made himself dictator of Mexico and abolished the federal system of government. When news of these developments reached Texas late in the year, it was accompanied by rumors of the impending disfranchisement and even expulsion of American immigrants. The rebels, already aroused by earlier restrictive policies, were influenced by these rumors and prepared to resist Santa Anna's effort to enforce tariff regulations by military force.

When he learned that Texans were resisting customs collections, Santa Anna sent reinforcements. On June 30, 1835, before any additional troops could arrive, a band of settlers led by W. B. Travis captured the Mexican garrison at Anahuac without firing a shot. The settlers first engaged Mexican troops at Gonzales in October and forced the retreat of a cavalry detachment. Shortly thereafter, Stephen F. Austin laid siege to San Antonio with a force of five hundred men and after six weeks forced its surrender, thereby capturing most of the Mexican troops then in Texas.

The Republic of Texas

While this early fighting was going on, delegates from the American communities in Texas met in convention and after some hesitation voted overwhelmingly to declare their independence on March 2, 1836. A constitution, based closely on that of the United States, was adopted for the new Republic of Texas, and a temporary government was installed to carry on the military struggle. Although the ensuing conflict was largely one of Americans against Mexicans, some Texas-Mexicans, or *Tejanos*, joined the fray on the side of the Anglo rebels. They too wanted to be free of

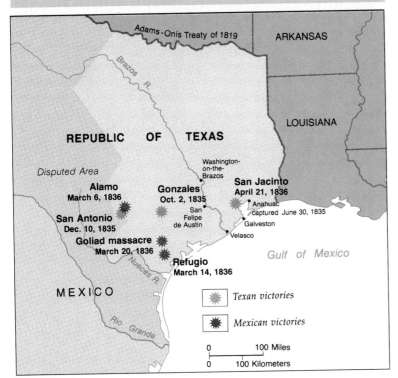

Texas Revolution
Major battles of the Texas Revolution. The Texans suffered severe losses at the Alamo and Goliad, but they scored a stunning victory at San Jacinto.

Santa Anna's heavy-handed rule. (Most of the Tejanos would become victims of the same anti-Mexican prejudice that spurred the revolt. Tejano leader Juan Seguin, who served as captain in the Texas army and became a hero of the independence struggle, was driven off his land by Anglo-Texans in 1841.)

Within days after Texas declared itself a republic, rebels and Mexican troops in San Antonio fought the famous battle of the Alamo. Myths about that battle have magnified the Anglo rebels' valor at the Mexicans' expense. The folklore is based on fact—only 187 rebels fought off a far larger number of Mexican soldiers for more than a week before eventually capitulating—but it is not true that all rebels, including the folk hero Davy Crockett, fought to the death. Crockett and seven other survivors were captured and then executed. Moreover, the rebels fought from inside a strong fortress with superior weapons against march-weary Mexican conscripts. Nevertheless, a tale that combined actual and mythical bravery inside the Alamo gave the

insurrection new inspiration, moral sanction, outside support, and the rallying cry "Remember the Alamo."

The revolt ended with an exchange of slaughters. A few days after the Alamo battle, another Texas detachment was surrounded and captured in an open plain near the San Antonio River and was marched to the town of Goliad, where most of its 350 members were executed. The next month, on April 21, 1836, the main Texas army, under General Sam Houston, assaulted Santa Anna's troops at an encampment near the San Jacinto River during the siesta hour. The final count showed that 630 Mexicans and only a handful of Texans had been killed. Santa Anna was captured and marched to Velasco, the meeting place of the Texas government, where he was forced to sign treaties recognizing the independence of Texas and its claim to territory all the way to the Río Grande. The Mexican Congress immediately repudiated the treaty, but their argument was in vain; although a strip of land between the Nueces and the Río Grande rivers

William H. Huddle, Surrender of Santa Anna at the Battle of San Jacinto, *ca. 1900. After the battle of San Jacinto, its hero Sam Houston, lying wounded under a tree, accepts the surrender of Santa Anna, at left in white breeches. The man cupping his ear at right is Erastus "Deaf" Smith, a famous scout and important man in Houston's army.*

would be disputed during the next decade, Mexico failed to impose its authority on the victorious Texas rebels.

Sam Houston, the hero of San Jacinto, became the first president of Texas. His platform sought annexation to the United States, and one of his first acts in office was to send an emissary to Washington to test the waters. Houston's agent found much sympathy for Texas independence but was told by Andrew Jackson and others that domestic politics and fear of a war with Mexico made immediate annexation impossible. The most that he could win from Congress and the Jackson administration was formal recognition of Texas sovereignty.

In its ten-year career as the "Lone Star Republic," Texas drew settlers from the United States at an accelerating rate. The panic of 1837 impelled many debt-ridden and land-hungry farmers to take advantage of the free grants of 1,280 acres that Texas offered to immigrating heads of white families. In the decade after independence, the population of Texas soared, from 30,000 to 142,000. Most of the newcomers assumed, as did the old settlers, that they would soon be annexed and restored to American citizenship.

Trails of Trade and Settlement

After New Mexico opened its trade to American merchants, a thriving commerce developed along the trail that ran from Missouri to Santa Fe. The first of these merchants to reach the New Mexican capital was William Becknell, who arrived with his train of goods late in 1821. Others followed rapidly. To protect themselves from the hostile Indians whose territory they had to cross, the traders traveled in large caravans, one or two of which would arrive in Santa Fe every summer. The federal government assisted them by providing troops when necessary and by appropriating money to purchase rights of passage from various tribes. Even so, the trip across the Cimarron desert and the southern Rockies was often difficult and hazardous. But profits from the exchange of textiles and other manufactured goods for furs, mules, and precious metals were substantial enough to make the risk worth taking.

Relations between the United States and Mexico soured following the Texas revolution, and this had a devastating effect on the Santa Fe trade. Much of the ill feeling was caused by further Anglo-American aggressions. An expedition of Texas businessmen and soldiers to Santa Fe in 1841 alarmed the Mexican authorities, and they arrested its members. In retaliation, a volunteer force of Texas avengers attacked Mexican troops along the Santa Fe Trail. The Mexican government then moved to curtail the Santa Fe trade. In April 1842, it passed a new tariff banning the importation of many of the goods sold by American merchants and prohibiting the export of gold and silver. Further restrictions in 1843 denied American traders full access to the Santa Fe market.

The famous Oregon Trail was the great overland route that brought the wagon trains of American migrants to the West Coast during the 1840s. Extending for 2,000 miles, across the northern Great Plains and the mountains beyond, it crossed the Rockies at the South Pass and then forked; the main northern route led to the Willamette Valley of Oregon, but various alternative trails were opened during the decade for overlanders heading for California. The journey from Missouri to the West Coast took about six months; most parties departed in May, hoping to arrive in November before the great snows hit the last mountain barriers.

After small groups had made their way to both Oregon and California in 1841 and 1842, a mass migration—mostly to Oregon—began in 1843. Within two years, five thousand Americans, living in the Willamette Valley south of the Columbia River, were demanding the extension of full American sovereignty over the Oregon country.

The Mormon Trek

An important and distinctive group of pioneers followed the Oregon Trail as far as the South Pass and then veered southwestward to establish a thriving colony in the region of the Great Salt Lake. These were Mormons, members of the largest religious denomination founded on American soil—the Church of Jesus Christ of Latter Day Saints.

The background of the Mormon trek was a history of persecution in the eastern states. Joseph Smith, founder of Mormonism, encountered strong opposition from the time he announced in Palmyra, New York, in 1830 that he had received a new divine revelation. According to this new revelation, the lost tribes of Israel had come to the New World in ancient times. One group had founded a Christian civilization, only to be exterminated by the heathen tribes that were the ancestors of the Indian peoples now being encountered by American settlers. Smith and those he converted to his new faith were committed to restoring the pure religion that had once thrived on American soil by founding a western Zion where they could practice their faith unmolested and carry out their special mission to convert the Native Americans.

In the 1830s, the Mormons established communities in Ohio and Missouri, but the former went bankrupt in the panic of 1837 and the latter was the target of angry mobs and vigilante violence. After the Mormons lost the "war" they fought against the Missourians in 1839, Smith led his followers back across the Mississippi to Illinois, where he received a liberal charter from the state legislature to found a town at Nauvoo. Here the Mormons had a temporary measure of security and self-government, but Smith soon reported new revelations that engendered dissension among his followers and hostility from neighboring "gentiles." Most controversial was his authorization of polygamy, or plural marriage. In 1844, Smith was killed by a mob while being held in jail in Carthage, Illinois, on a charge stemming from his quarrels with dissident Mormons who objected to his new policies.

The death of Smith confirmed the growing conviction of the Mormon leadership that they needed to move beyond the borders of the United States to establish their Zion in the wilderness. In late 1845, Smith's successor, Brigham Young, decided to send a party of fifteen hundred men to assess the chances of a colony in the vicinity of the Great Salt Lake (then part of Mexico). Nauvoo was quickly depopulated as twelve thousand Mormons took to the trail in 1846. The following year Young himself arrived in Utah and sent back word to the thousands encamped along the trail that he had found the promised land.

Among the greatest hazards faced by those migrating to the West was the rough and unfamiliar terrain over which their wagon trains traveled.

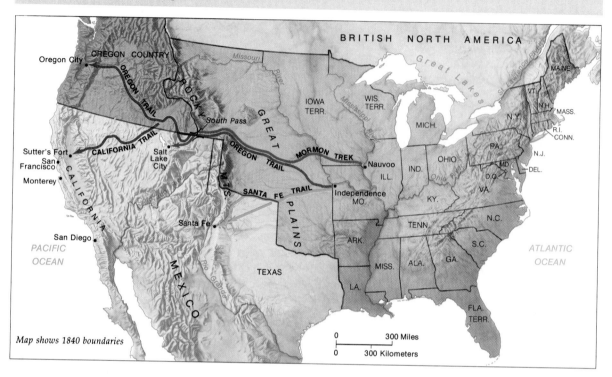

Map shows 1840 boundaries

The Mormon community that Young established in Utah is one of the great success stories of western settlement. In contrast to the rugged individualism and disorder that often characterized mining camps and other new communities, "the state of Deseret" (as Utah was originally called) was a model of discipline and cooperation. Because of its communitarian form of social organization, its centralized government, and the religious dedication of its inhabitants, this frontier society was able to expand settlement in a planned and efficient way and develop a system of irrigation that "made the desert bloom."

Utah's main problem was the determination of its political status. When the Mormons first arrived, they were encroaching illegally into Mexican territory. After Utah came under American sovereignty in 1848, the state of Deseret fought to maintain its autonomy and its custom of polygamy against the efforts of the federal government to extend American law and set up the usual type of territorial administration. In 1857, President Buchanan sent a military force to

bring Utah to heel, and the Mormons prepared to repel this "invasion." But after a heavy snow prevented the army from crossing the Rockies, Buchanan offered an olive branch in the form of a general pardon for Mormons who had violated federal law but agreed to cooperate with U. S. authorities in the future. The Mormons accepted, and in return, Brigham Young called off his plan to resist the army by force and accepted the nominal authority of an appointed territorial governor.

MANIFEST DESTINY AND THE MEXICAN WAR

The rush of settlers beyond the nation's borders in the 1830s and 1840s inspired politicians and propagandists to call for annexation of those areas occupied by migrants. Some went further and proclaimed it was the "Manifest Destiny" of the United States to expand until it had absorbed all of North America, including Canada and

Carl Christian Anton Christensen, Handcart, ca. 1840. Lacking funds to buy sufficient wagons and oxen, the Mormon colonists made their trek to Deseret on foot, hauling their possessions in handcarts and working together as families to move their heavy loads.

Mexico. Such ambitions—and the policies they inspired—led to a major diplomatic confrontation with Great Britain and a war with Mexico.

Tyler and Texas

President John Tyler initiated the politics of Manifest Destiny. He was vice president when William Henry Harrison died in office in 1841 after serving scarcely a month. The first of America's "accidental presidents," Tyler was a states' rights, proslavery Virginian who had been picked as Harrison's running mate to broaden the appeal of the Whig ticket. Profoundly out of sympathy with the mainstream of his own party, he soon broke with the Whigs in Congress, who had united behind Henry Clay's nationalistic economic program. Although he lacked a base in either of the major parties, Tyler hoped to be elected president in his own right in 1844. To accomplish this difficult feat, he needed a new issue around which he could build a following that would cut across established party lines.

In 1843, Tyler decided to put the full weight of his administration behind the annexation of Texas. He anticipated that incorporation of the Lone Star Republic would be a popular move, especially in the South where it would feed the appetite for additional slave states. With the South solidly behind him, Tyler expected to have a good chance in the election of 1844.

To achieve his objective, Tyler enlisted the support of John C. Calhoun, the leading political defender of slavery and southern rights. Calhoun saw the annexation issue as a way of uniting the South and taking the offensive against the abolitionists. Success or failure in this effort would constitute a decisive test of whether the North was willing to give the southern states a fair share of national power and adequate assurances for the future of their way of life. If antislavery sentiment succeeded in blocking the acquisition of Texas, the Southerners would at least know where they stood and could begin to "calculate the value of the union."

To prepare the public mind for an annexation, the Tyler administration launched a propaganda campaign in the summer of 1843 based on reports of British designs on Texas. According to information supplied by Duff Green, an unofficial American agent in England, the British were preparing to guarantee Texas independence and make a loan to the financially troubled republic in return for the abolition of slavery. It is doubtful the British had such intentions, but the stories were believed and used to give urgency to the annexation cause.

Secretary of State Abel Upshur, a proslavery Virginian and protégé of Calhoun, began negotiating an annexation treaty. After Upshur was killed in an accident, Calhoun replaced him and carried the negotiations to a successful conclusion. When the treaty was brought before the Senate in 1844, Calhoun denounced the British for attempting to subvert the South's essential system of labor and racial control by using Texas as a base for abolitionist operations. According to the supporters of Tyler and Calhoun, the South's security and well-being—and by extension that of the nation—required the immediate incorporation of Texas into the Union.

The strategy of linking annexation explicitly to the interests of the South and slavery led northern antislavery Whigs to charge the whole scheme was a proslavery plot meant to advance the interest of one section of the nation against the other. Consequently, the Senate rejected the treaty by a decisive vote of 35 to 16 in June 1844. Tyler then attempted to bring Texas into the Union through an alternative means—a joint resolution of both houses of Congress admitting it as a state—but Congress adjourned before the issue came to a vote, and the whole question hung fire in anticipation of the election of 1844.

The Triumph of Polk and Annexation

Tyler's initiative made the future of Texas the central issue in the 1844 campaign. But party lines held firm, and the president himself was unable to capitalize on the issue because his stand was not in line with the views of either party. Tyler tried to run as an independent, but his failure to gain significant support eventually forced him to withdraw from the race.

If the Democratic party convention had been held in 1843—as originally scheduled—ex-President Martin Van Buren would have won the nomination easily. But postponement of the Democratic conclave until May 1844 weakened his chances. In the meantime the annexation question came to the fore, and Van Buren was forced to take a stand on it. He persisted in the view he had held as president—that incorporation of Texas would risk war with Mexico, arouse sectional strife, and destroy the unity of the Democratic party. Fears of sectional and party division seemed confirmed in 1844 when the dominant party faction in Van Buren's home state of New York came out against Tyler's Texas policy. In an effort to keep the issue out of the campaign, Van Buren struck a gentleman's agreement with Henry Clay, the overwhelming favorite for the Whig nomination, that both of them would publicly oppose immediate annexation.

Van Buren's letter opposing annexation appeared shortly before the Democratic convention and it cost him the nomination. Angry southern delegates secured a rule requiring approval by a two-thirds vote to block Van Buren's nomination. After several ballots, a dark horse candidate—James K. Polk of Tennessee—emerged triumphant. Polk, a protégé of Andrew Jackson, had been Speaker of the House of Representatives and governor of Tennessee.

Polk was an avowed expansionist, and he ran on a platform calling for the simultaneous annexation of Texas and assertion of American claims to all of Oregon. He identified himself and his party with the popular cause of turning the United States into a continental nation, an aspiration that attracted support from all parts of the country. His was a much more astute political strategy than the overtly prosouthern expansionism advocated by Tyler and Calhoun. The Whig nominee, Henry Clay, was basically antiexpansionist, but his sense of the growing popularity of Texas annexation among southern Whigs caused him to waffle on the issue during the campaign. This in turn cost Clay the support of a small but crucial group of northern antislavery Whigs, who defected to the abolitionist Liberty party.

Polk won the fall election by a relatively narrow popular margin. His triumph in the electoral college—170 votes to 105—was secured by victories in New York and Michigan, where the Liberty party candidate, James G. Birney, had taken away enough votes from Clay to affect the outcome. (See the charts of the election of 1844 on the opposite page.) The closeness of the election meant the Democrats had something less than a clear mandate to implement their expan-

The Liberty Party Swings an Election

Candidate	Party	Actual Vote in New York	National Electoral Vote	If Liberty Voters Had Voted Whig	Projected Electoral Vote
Polk	Democrat	237,588	170	237,588	134
Clay	Whig	232,482	105	248,294	141
Birney	Liberty	15,812	0	—	—

The Election of 1844

Candidate	Party	Popular Vote	Electoral Vote
Polk	Democrat	1,338,464	170
Clay	Whig	1,300,097	105
Birney	Liberty	62,300	—

sionist policies, but this did not prevent them from claiming that the people had backed an aggressive campaign to extend the borders of the United States.

After the election, Congress reconvened to consider the annexation of Texas. The mood had changed as a result of Polk's victory, and some leading senators from both parties who had initially opposed Tyler's scheme for annexation by joint resolution of Congress now changed their position. As a result, annexation was approved a few days before Polk took office.

The Doctrine of Manifest Destiny

The expansionist mood that accompanied Polk's election and the annexation of Texas was given a name and a rationale in the summer of 1845. John L. O'Sullivan, a proponent of the Young America movement and editor of the influential *United States Magazine and Democratic Review* charged that foreign governments were conspiring to block the annexation of Texas in an effort to thwart "the fulfillment of our manifest destiny to overspread the continent allotted by providence for the free development of our yearly multiplying millions."

Besides coining the phrase *Manifest Destiny*, O'Sullivan pointed to the three main ideas that lay behind it. One was that God was on the side of American expansionism. This notion came naturally out of the long tradition, going back to the New England Puritans, that identified the growth of America with the divinely ordained success of a chosen people. A second idea, implied in the phrase *free development*, was that the spread of American rule meant what other propagandists for expansion described as "extending the area of freedom." Democratic institutions and local self-government would follow the flag if areas claimed by autocratic foreign governments were annexed to the United States. O'Sullivan's third premise was that population growth required the outlet that territorial acquisitions would provide. Behind this notion lurked a fear that growing numbers would lead to diminished opportunity and a European-type polarization of social classes if the restless and the ambitious were not given new lands to settle and exploit.

In its most extreme form, Manifest Destiny meant the United States would someday occupy the entire North American continent, that nothing less would appease its land-hungry population. "Make way, I say, for the young American Buffalo," bellowed a Democratic orator in 1844"—he has not yet got land enough. . . . I tell you we will give him Oregon for his summer shade, and the region of Texas as his winter pasture. (Applause) Like all of his race, he wants salt, too. Well, he shall have the use of two oceans—the mighty Pacific and the turbulent

Atlantic.... He shall not stop his career until he slakes his thirst in the frozen ocean. (Cheers)"

Polk and the Oregon Question

In 1845 and 1846, the United States came closer to armed conflict with Great Britian than at any time since the War of 1812. The willingness of some Americans to go to war over Oregon was expressed in the rallying cry "fifty-four forty or fight" (referring to the latitude of the northern boundary of the desired territory). This slogan was actually coined by Whigs seeking to ridicule Democratic expansionists, but Democrats later took it over as a vivid expression of their demand for what is now British Columbia. Polk fed this expansionist fever by laying claim in his inaugural address to all of the Oregon country, then jointly occupied by Britain and the United States. Privately, however, he was willing to accept the forty-ninth parallel as a dividing line. What made the situation so tense was that Polk was dedicated to an aggressive diplomacy of bluff and bluster. As historian David M. Pletcher has put it, Polk "set forth on a foreign policy of strong stands, over-stated arguments, and menacing public announcements, not because he wanted war but because he felt that this was the only policy which his foreign adversaries would understand."

In July 1845, Polk authorized Secretary of State James Buchanan to reply to the latest British request for terms by offering a boundary along the forty-ninth parallel. Because this did not meet the British demand for all of Vancouver Island and free navigation of the Columbia River, the British ambassador rejected the proposal out of hand. This rebuff infuriated Polk; in his view the offer was a generous and conciliatory retreat from his public position. He subsequently withdrew it and refused a British request of December 1845 that he renew the offer and submit the dispute to international arbitration. Instead he called on Congress to terminate the agreement for joint occupation of the Pacific Northwest. Congress complied in April 1846, and Polk submitted the required year's notice to the British on May 21.

Since abrogation of the joint agreement implied that the United States would attempt to extend its jurisdiction north to 54°40, the British government decided to take the diplomatic initia-tive in an effort to avert war, while at the same time dispatching warships to the Western Hemisphere in case conciliation failed. Their new proposal accepted the forty-ninth parallel as the border to a point where the boundary would veer south so that Britain could retain Vancouver Island. It also provided for British navigation rights on the Columbia River. When the draft treaty was received in June, Polk refused either to endorse or reject it and took the unusual step of submitting it directly to the Senate for advice. The Senate recommended the treaty be accepted with the single change that British rights to navigate the Columbia be made temporary. It was ratified in that form on June 15.

Polk was prompted to settle the Oregon question because he now had a war with Mexico on his hands. His reckless and aggressive diplomacy had brought the nation within an eyelash of being involved in two wars at the same time. American policymakers got what they wanted from the Oregon treaty, namely Puget Sound and the strait that led into it south of Vancouver Island. Acquisition of this splendid natural harbor gave the United States its first deep-water port on the Pacific. Polk's initial demand for all of Oregon was made partly for domestic political consumption and partly to bluff the British into making more concessions. It was a dangerous game on both fronts. When Polk finally agreed to the solution, he alienated expansionist advocates in the Old Northwest who had supported his call for "all of Oregon."

For many Northerners, the promise of new acquisitions in the Pacific Northwest was the only thing that made annexation of Texas palatable. They hoped new free states could be created to counterbalance the admission of slave-holding Texas to the Union. As this prospect receded, the charge of antislavery advocates that Texas annexation was a southern plot became more believable; to Northerners Polk began to look more and more like a president concerned mainly with furthering the interests of his native region.

War with Mexico

While the United States was avoiding a war with Great Britain, it was getting into one with Mexico. Although they had recognized Texas independence in 1845, the Mexicans rejected the Lone Star Republic's dubious claim to the unset-

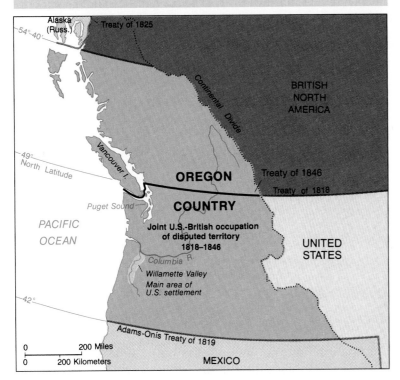

Northwest Boundary Dispute
President Polk's policy of bluff and bluster nearly involved the United States in a war with Great Britain over the disputed boundary in Oregon.

tled territory between the Nueces River and the Río Grande. When the United States annexed Texas and assumed its claim to the disputed area, Mexico broke off diplomatic relations and prepared for armed conflict.

Polk responded by placing troops in Louisiana on the alert and by dispatching John Slidell as an emissary to Mexico City in the hope he could resolve the boundary dispute and also persuade the Mexicans to sell New Mexico and California to the United States. The Mexican government refused to receive Slidell because the nature of his appointment ignored the fact that regular diplomatic relations were suspended. While Slidell was cooling his heels in Mexico City in January 1846, Polk ordered General Zachary Taylor, commander of American forces in the Southwest, to advance well beyond the Nueces and proceed toward the Río Grande, thus invading territory claimed by both sides.

By April, Taylor had taken up a position near Matamoros on the Río Grande. On the opposite bank of the river, Mexican forces had assembled and erected a fort. On April 24, sixteen hundred Mexican soldiers crossed the river and the following day met and attacked a small American detachment, killing eleven and capturing the rest. After learning of the incident, Taylor sent word to the president: "Hostilities," he reported, "may now be considered as commenced."

This news was neither unexpected nor unwelcome. Polk in fact was already preparing his war message to Congress when he learned of the fighting on the Río Grande. A short and decisive war, he had concluded, would force the cession of California and New Mexico to the United States. When Congress declared war on May 13, American agents and an "exploring expedition" under John C. Frémont were already in California stirring up dissension against Mexican rule, and ships of the U.S. Navy lay waiting expectantly off the shore. Two days later, Polk ordered a force under Colonel Stephen Kearny to march to Santa Fe and take possession of New Mexico.

This 1846 cartoon entitled "This Is the House That Polk Built" shows President Polk sitting forlornly in a house of cards, which represents the delicately balanced issues facing him.

The war lasted much longer than expected because the Mexicans refused to make peace despite a succession of military defeats. In the first major campaign of the conflict, Taylor followed up his victory in two battles fought north of the Río Grande by crossing the river, taking Matamoros and marching on Monterrey. In September, his forces assaulted and captured this major city of northern Mexico after overcoming fierce resistance.

Taylor's controversial decision to allow the Mexican garrison to go free and his unwillingness or inability to advance further into Mexico angered Polk and led him to adopt a new strategy for winning the war and a new commander to implement it. General Winfield Scott was ordered to prepare an amphibious attack on Vera Cruz with the aim of placing an American army within striking distance of Mexico City itself. With half his forces detached for the new invasion, Taylor was left to hold his position in northern Mexico.

But this did not deprive him of a final moment of glory. At Buena Vista, in February 1847, he claimed victory over a sizable Mexican army sent northward to dislodge him. Despite his unpopularity with the administration, Taylor was hailed as a national hero and a possible candidate for president

Meanwhile, the Kearny expedition captured Santa Fe, proclaimed the annexation of New Mexico by the United States, and set off for California. There they found that American settlers, in cooperation with John C. Frémont's exploring expedition, had revolted against Mexican authorities and declared their independence as the "Bear Flag Republic." The navy had also captured the port of Monterey. With the addition of Kearny's troops, a relatively small number of Americans were able to take possession of California against scattered and disorganized Mexican opposition, a process that was completed by the beginning of 1847.

The decisive Veracruz campaign was slow to develop because of the massive and careful preparations required. But in March 1847, the main American army under General Scott finally landed near that crucial port city and laid siege to it. Veracruz fell after eighteen days, and then Scott began his advance on Mexico City. In the most important single battle of the war, Scott met forces under General Santa Anna at Cerro Gordo on April 17 and 18. The Mexicans occupied an apparently impregnable position on high ground blocking the way to Mexico City. A daring flanking maneuver that required soldiers to scramble up the mountainsides enabled Scott to win the decisive victory that opened the road to the Mexican capital. By August American troops were drawn up in front of Mexico City. After a temporary armistice, a brief respite that was actually used by the Mexicans to regroup and improve their defenses, Scott ordered the massive assault that captured the city on September 14.

Settlement of the Mexican War

Accompanying Scott's army was a diplomat, Nicholas P. Trist, who was authorized to negotiate a peace treaty whenever the Mexicans decided they had had enough. Despite a sequence of American victories and the imminent fall of Mexico City, Trist made little progress. No

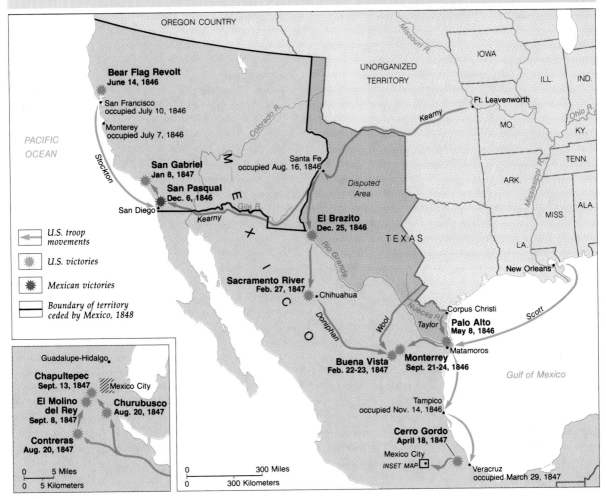

The Mexican War

The Mexican War added half a million square miles of territory to the United States, but the cost was high: $100 million and 13,000 lives.

Mexican leader was willing to invite the wrath of an intensely proud and patriotic citizenry by agreeing to the kind of terms that Polk wanted to impose. Even after the United States had achieved an overwhelming military victory, Trist found it difficult to exact an acceptable treaty from the Mexican government. In November, Polk ordered Trist to return to Washington. Radical adherents of Manifest Destiny were now clamoring for the annexation of all Mexico, and Polk himself may have been momentarily tempted by the chance to move from military occupation to outright annexation.

Trist ignored Polk's instructions and lingered in Mexico City. On February 2, 1848, he signed a treaty that gained all the concessions he had been commissioned to obtain. The Treaty of Guadalupe Hidalgo ceded New Mexico and California to the United States for $15 million, established the Río Grande as the border between Texas and Mexico, and promised that the U. S. government would assume the substantial claims of American citizens against Mexico. The treaty also provided that the Mexican residents of the new territories would become U. S. citizens. When the agreement reached Washington, Polk censured Trist for disobeying orders but approved most of his treaty, which he sent to the Senate for ratification. Senate approval by a vote of 38 to 14 came on March 10.

When popular hero Zachary Taylor (left) displeased President Polk with his actions in the capture of Monterrey, he was replaced by Winfield Scott. Scott carried out Polk's plans for the attack on the port city of Veracruz (right), which led to the capture of Mexico City.

As a result of the Mexican War, the United States gained 500,000 square miles of territory. The treaty of 1848 enlarged the size of the nation by about 20 percent, adding to its domain the present states of California, Utah, New Mexico, Nevada, and Arizona, and parts of Colorado and Wyoming. Soon those interested in a southern route for a transcontinental railroad pressed for even more territory along the southern border of the cession. That pressure led in 1853 to the Gadsden Purchase, through which the United States acquired the southernmost parts of present-day Arizona and New Mexico. But one intriguing question remains. Why, given the expansionist spirit of the age, did the campaign to acquire *all* of Mexico fail?

According to the historian Frederick Merk, a major factor was the peculiar combination of racism and anticolonialism that dominated American opinion. It was one thing to acquire thinly populated areas that could be settled by "Anglo-Saxon" pioneers. It was something else again to incorporate a large population that was mainly of mixed Spanish and Indian origin. These "mongrels," charged racist opponents of the "All Mexico" movement, could never be fit citizens of a self-governing republic. They would have to be ruled in the way the British governed India, and the possession of colonial dependencies was contrary to American ideals and traditions.

Merk's thesis sheds light on why the general public had little appetite for swallowing all of Mexico, but those actually making policy had more mundane and practical reasons for being satisfied with what was obtained at Guadalupe Hidalgo. What they had really wanted all along, historian Norman Graebner contends, were the great California harbors of San Francisco and San Diego. From these ports Americans could trade directly with the Orient and dominate the commerce of the Pacific. Once acquisition of California had been assured, policymakers had little incentive to press for more Mexican territory.

The war with Mexico divided the American public and provoked political dissension. A majority of the Whig party opposed the war in principle, arguing that the United States had no valid claims to the area south of the Nueces. Whig congressmen voted for military appropriations while the conflict was going on, but they constantly criticized the president for starting it. More ominous was the charge of some Northerners from both parties that the real purpose of the war was to spread the institution of slavery and increase the political power of the southern states. While battles were being fought in Mexico, Congress was debating the Wilmot Proviso, a proposal to prohibit slavery in any territories that might be acquired from Mexico. A bitter sectional quarrel over the status of slavery in new areas was a major legacy of the Mexican War (see Chapter 14).

The domestic controversies aroused by the war and the propaganda of Manifest Destiny revealed the limits of mid-nineteenth-century American expansionism and put a damper on additional efforts to extend the nation's boundaries. Concerns about slavery and race impeded acquisition of new territory in Latin America and the Caribbean. Resolution of the Oregon dispute clearly indicated that the United States was not willing to go to war with a powerful adversary to obtain large chunks of British North America, and the old ambition of incorporating Canada faded. From 1848 until the revival of expansionism in the late nineteenth century, American growth usually took the form of populating and developing the vast territory already acquired.

INTERNAL EXPANSIONISM

Young American expansionists saw a clear link between acquisition of new territory and other forms of material growth and development. In 1844, Samuel F. B. Morse perfected and demonstrated his electric telegraph, a device that would make it possible to communicate rapidly over the expanse of a continental nation. Simultaneously, the railroad was becoming increasingly important as a means of moving people and goods over the same great distances. Improvements in manufacturing and agricultural methods led to an upsurge in the volume and range of internal trade, and the beginnings of mass immigration were providing human resources for the exploitation of new areas and economic opportunities.

After gold was discovered in newly acquired California in 1848, a flood of emigrants from the East and several foreign nations arrived by ship or wagon train, their appetites whetted by the thought of striking it rich. The gold they unearthed spurred the national economy, and the rapid growth of population centers on the Pacific Coast inspired projects for transcontinental telegraph lines and railroad tracks.

Despite the best efforts of the Young Americans, the spirit of Manifest Destiny, and the thirst for acquiring new territory waned after the Mexican War, and the expansionist impulse was channeled mainly into internal development. Although the nation ceased to grow in size, the technological advances and population increase of the 1840s continued during the 1850s. The result was an acceleration of economic growth, a substantial increase in industrialization and urbanization, and the emergence of a new American working class.

The Triumph of the Railroad

More than anything else, the rise of the railroad transformed the American economy during the 1840s and 1850s. The technology came from England, where steam locomotives were first used to haul cars along tracks at the beginning of the century. In 1830 and 1831 two American railroads began commercial operation—the Charleston and Hamburg in South Carolina and the Baltimore and Ohio in Maryland. After these pioneer lines had shown that steam locomotion was practical and profitable, several other railroads were built and began to carry passengers and freight during the 1830s.

Canals, however, proved to be strong competitors, especially for the freight business. By 1840, railroads had 2,818 miles of track—a figure almost equal to the combined length of all canals—but the latter still carried a much larger volume of goods. Passengers might prefer the speed of trains, which reached astonishing velocities of 20 to 30 miles an hour, but the lower unit cost of transporting freight on the canal boats prevented most shippers from changing their habits. Furthermore, states like New York and Pennsylvania had invested heavily in canals and resisted chartering a competitive form of transportation. Most of the early railroads reached out from port cities, such as Boston and Baltimore, that did not have good canal routes to the interior. Steam locomotion provided them a chance to cut into the enormous commerce that flowed along the Erie Canal and gave New York an advantage in the scramble for western trade.

During the 1840s, rails extended beyond the northeastern and Middle Atlantic states, and mileage increased more than threefold, reaching a

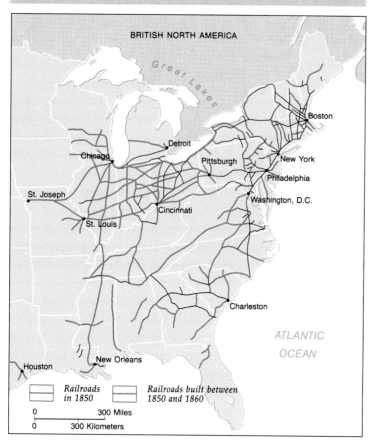

Railroads, 1850 and 1860
During the 1840s and 1850s, railroad lines moved rapidly westward. By 1860, more than 30,000 miles of track had been laid.

BRITISH NORTH AMERICA

Great Lakes

Boston

Detroit

Chicago

Pittsburgh

New York

Philadelphia

Washington, D.C.

St. Joseph

Cincinnati

St. Louis

Charleston

ATLANTIC OCEAN

Houston

New Orleans

Railroads in 1850   Railroads built between 1850 and 1860

0   300 Miles
0   300 Kilometers

total of more than 9,000 miles by 1850. Expansion, fueled by massive European investment, was even greater in the following decade when about 20,000 miles of additional track were laid. By 1860, all the states east of the Mississippi had rail service, and a traveler could go by train from New York to Chicago and return by way of Memphis. Throughout the 1840s and 1850s, railroads cut deeply into the freight business of the canals and succeeded in driving many of them out of business. The cost of hauling goods by rail decreased dramatically because of improved track construction and the introduction of powerful locomotives that could haul more cars. New York and Pennsylvania were slow to encourage rail transportation because of their early commitment to canals, but by the 1850s both states had accepted the

inevitable and were promoting massive railroad building.

The development of railroads had an enormous effect on the economy as a whole. Although the burgeoning demand for iron rails was initially met mainly by importation from England, it eventually spurred development of the domestic iron industry. Since railroads required an enormous outlay of capital, their promoters pioneered new methods for financing business enterprise. At a time when most manufacturing and mercantile concerns were still owned by families or partnerships, the railroad companies sold stock to the general public and helped to set the pattern for the separation of ownership and control that characterizes the modern corporation. They also developed new types of securities, such as "preferred stock" with no voting rights but the assur-

Railroad Mileage, ca. 1860	
Area	Miles
New England	3,660
Middle Atlantic	6,353
Old Northwest	9,592
Southeast	5,463
Southwest	4,072
Far West	1,495
Total	30,636

Source: Adapted from George R. Taylor and Irene D. Neu, *The American Railroad Network, 1861 to 1890 (1956; reprint ed., Salem, N.H.: Arno, 1981).*

ance of a fixed rate of return, and long-term bonds at a set rate of interest.

The gathering and control of private capital did not fully meet the desires of the early railroad barons. State and local governments, convinced that railroads were the key to their future prosperity, loaned the railroads money, bought their stock, and guaranteed their bonds. Despite the dominant philosophy of laissez-faire, the federal government became involved by surveying the routes of projected lines and providing land grants. In 1850, for example, several million acres of public land were granted to the Illinois Central. In all, forty companies received such aid before 1860, and a precedent was set for the massive land grants of the post–Civil War era.

The Industrial Revolution Takes Off

While railroads were initiating a revolution in transportation, American industry was entering a new phase of rapid and sustained growth. The factory mode of production, which had originated before 1840 in the cotton mills of New England, was extended to a variety of other products (see Chapter 9). Woolen manufacturing was concentrated in single production units beginning in the 1830s, and by 1860 some of the largest textile mills in the country were producing wool cloth. In the coal and iron regions of eastern Pennsylvania, iron was being forged and rolled in

factories by 1850. Among the other industries that adopted the factory system during this period were those producing firearms, clocks, and sewing machines.

The essential features of the emerging mode of production were the gathering of a supervised work force in a single place, the payment of cash wages to workers, the use of interchangeable parts, and manufacture by "continuous process." Within a factory setting, standardized parts, manufactured separately and in bulk, could be efficiently and rapidly assembled into a final product by an ordered sequence of continuously repeated operations. Mass production, which involved the division of labor into a series of relatively simple and repetitive tasks, contrasted sharply with the traditional craft mode of production, in which a single worker produced the entire product out of raw materials. The bulk of American manufacturing of the 1840s and 1850s, however, was still carried on by traditional methods. Small workshops continued to predominate in most industries and some relatively large factories were not yet mechanized. But mass production was clearly the wave of the future. The transformation of a craft into a modern industry is well illustrated by the evolution of shoemaking. The independent cobbler producing shoes for order was first challenged by a putting-out system involving the assignment of various tasks to physically separated workers, and then was virtually displaced by the great shoe factories that by the 1860s were operating in cities like Lynn, Massachusetts.

New technology often played an important role in the transition to mass production. Just as power looms and spinning machinery had made textile mills possible, the development of new and more reliable machines or industrial techniques revolutionized other industries. Elias Howe's invention of the sewing machine in 1846 laid the basis for the ready-to-wear clothing industry and also contributed to the mechanization of shoemaking. During the 1840s, iron manufacturers adopted the British practice of using coal rather than charcoal for smelting and thus produced a metal better suited to industrial needs. Charles Goodyear's discovery in 1839 of the process for the vulcanization of rubber made a new range of manufactured items available to the American consumer, most notably the overshoe.

The Age of Practical Invention

(Dates refer to patent or first successful use)

Year	Inventor	Contribution	Importance/Description
1787	John Fitch	Steamboat	First successful American steamboat
1793	Eli Whitney	Cotton gin	Simplified process of separating fiber from seeds; helped make cotton a profitable staple of southern agriculture
1798	Eli Whitney	Jig for guiding tools	Facilitated manufacture of interchangeable parts
1802	Oliver Evans	Steam engine	First American steam engine; led to manufacture of high-pressure engines used throughout eastern United States
1813	Richard B. Chenaworth	Cast-iron plow	First iron plow to be made in three separate pieces, thus making possible replacement of parts
1830	Peter Cooper	Railroad locomotive	First steam locomotive built in America
1831	Cyrus McCormick	Reaper	Mechanized harvesting; early model could cut six acres of grain a day
1836	Samuel Colt	Revolver	First successful repeating pistol
1837	John Deere	Steel plow	Steel surface kept soil from sticking; farming thus made easier on rich prairies of Midwest
1839	Charles Goodyear	Vulcanization of rubber	Made rubber much more useful by preventing it from sticking and melting in hot weather
1842	Crawford W. Long	First administered ether in surgery	Reduced pain and risk of shock in surgery during operations
1844	Samuel F. B. Morse	Telegraph	Made long-distance communication almost instantaneous
1846	Elias Howe	Sewing machine	First practical machine for automatic sewing
1846	Norbert Rillieux	Vacuum evaporator	Improved method of removing water from sugar cane; revolutionized sugar industry and was later applied to many other products
1847	Richard M. Hoe	Rotary printing press	Printed an entire sheet in one motion; vastly speeded up printing process
1851	William Kelly	"Air-boiling process"	Improved method of converting iron into steel (usually known as Bessemer process because English inventor Bessemer had more advantageous patent and financial arrangements)
1853	Elisha G. Otis	Passenger elevator	Improved movement in buildings; when later electrified, stimulated development of skyscrapers
1859	Edwin L. Drake	First American oil well	Initiated oil industry in the United States
1859	George M. Pullman	Pullman car	First sleeping car suitable for long-distance travel

Source: From *Freedom and Crisis: An American History,* Third Edition, by Allen Weinstein and Frank Otto Gatell. Copyright © 1974, 1978, 1981 by Random House, Inc. Reprinted by permission of Random House, Inc.

Perhaps the greatest triumph of American technology during the mid-nineteenth century was the development of the world's most sophisticated and reliable machine tools. Such advances as the invention of the extraordinarily accurate measuring device known as the *vernier caliper* in 1851 and the first production of turret lathes in 1854 were signs of a special American aptitude for the kind of precision toolmaking that was essential to efficient industrialization.

Progress in industrial technology and organization did not mean the United States had become an industrial society by 1860. Factory workers remained a small fraction of the work force, and agriculture retained first place both as a source of livelihood for individuals and as a contributor to the gross national product. Nearly 60 percent of the gainfully employed still worked on the land. But farming itself, at least in the North, was undergoing a technological revolution of its own. John Deere's steel plow, invented in 1837 and mass produced by the 1850s, enabled midwestern farmers to cultivate the tough prairie soils that had resisted cast-iron implements. The mechanical reaper, patented by Cyrus McCormick in 1834, offered an enormous saving in the labor required for harvesting grain; by 1851, McCormick was producing more than a thousand reapers a year in his Chicago plant. Other new farm implements that came into widespread use before 1860 included seed drills, cultivators, and threshing machines.

A dynamic interaction between advances in transportation, industry, and agriculture gave great strength and resiliency to the economy of the northern states during the 1850s. Railroads offered western farmers better access to eastern markets. After Chicago and New York were linked by rail in 1853, the flow of most midwestern farm commodities shifted from the north-south direction based on river-borne traffic that had still predominated in the 1830s and 1840s, to an east-west pattern.

The mechanization of agriculture did more than lead to more efficient and profitable commercial farming; it also provided an additional impetus to industrialization, and its labor-saving features released manpower for other economic activities. The growth of industry and the modernization of agriculture can thus be seen as mutually reinforcing aspects of a single process of economic growth.

Mass Immigration Begins

The original incentive to mechanize northern industry and agriculture came in part from a shortage of

A revolution in farming followed the introduction of new farm implements like Cyrus McCormick's reaper, which could do ten times the work of a single person. The lithograph, by an anonymous artist, is entitled The Testing of the First Reaping Machine near Steele's Tavern, Virginia, 1831.

cheap labor. Compared with that of industrializing nations of Europe, the economy of the United States in the early nineteenth century was labor-scarce. Since it was difficult to attract able-bodied men to work for low wages in factories or on farms, women and children were used extensively in the early textile mills, and commercial farmers had to rely heavily on the labor of their family members. In the face of such limited and uncertain labor supplies, producers were greatly tempted to experiment with labor-saving machinery. By the 1840s and 1850s, however, even the newly industrialized operations were ready to absorb a new influx of unskilled workers. Factories required increasing numbers of operatives, and railroad builders needed construction gangs. The growth of industrial work opportunities helped attract a multitude of European immigrants during the two decades before the Civil War.

Between 1820 and 1840, an estimated 700,000 immigrants arrived in the United States, mainly from the British Isles and German-speaking areas of continental Europe. During the 1840s, this substantial flow suddenly became a flood. No less than 4.2 million crossed the Atlantic between 1840 and 1860, and about 3 million of these arrived in the single decade between 1845 and 1855. This was the greatest influx in proportion to total population—then about 20 million—that the nation has ever experienced. The largest single source of the new mass immigration was Ireland, but Germany was not far behind. Smaller contingents came from Switzerland, Norway, Sweden, and the Netherlands.

This massive transatlantic movement had many causes; some people were "pushed" out of their homes, while others were "pulled" toward America. The great push factor that caused 1.5 million Irish to forsake the Emerald Isle between 1845 and 1854 was the great potato famine. Escape to America was made possible by the low fares then prevailing on sailing ships bound from England to North America. Ships involved in the timber trade carried their bulky cargoes from Boston or Halifax to Liverpool; as an alternative to returning to America partly in ballast, they packed Irish immigrants into their holds. The squalor and misery in these steerage accommodations were almost beyond belief.

Because of the ports involved in the lumber trade—Boston, Halifax, Saint John's, and Saint Andrews—the Irish usually arrived in Canada or the northeastern states. Immobilized by poverty and a lack of the skills required for pioneering in

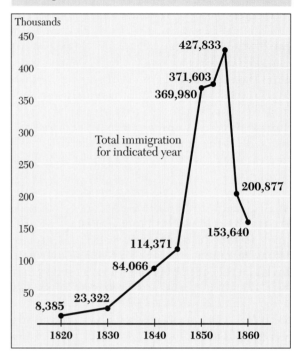

Immigration to the United States, 1820–1860

Thousands

427,833
371,603
369,980

Total immigration for indicated year

200,877

153,640

114,371

84,066

23,322

8,385

1820   1830   1840   1850   1860

the West, most of them remained in the northeast. By the 1850s, they constituted a substantial portion of the total population of Boston, New York, Philadelphia, and many smaller cities of the New England and Middle Atlantic states (see "The Irish in Boston," pp. 370–371). Forced to subsist on low-paid menial labor and crowded into festering urban slums, they were looked down on by most native-born Americans. Their devotion to Catholicism aroused Protestant resentment and mob violence (see Chapter 14 for a discussion of the growth of nativism and anti-Catholicism).

The million or so Germans who also came in the late 1840s and early 1850s were somewhat more fortunate. Most of them were also peasants, but they had fled hard times rather than outright catastrophe. Changes in German landholding patterns and a fluctuating market for grain crops put pressure on small operators. Those whose mortgages were foreclosed—or who could no longer make the regular payments to landlords that were the price of emancipation from feudal obligations—frequently opted for immigration to America. Unlike the Irish, they often escaped with

The German community in Weaverville, California, celebrates May Day, 1860, with a parade.

a small amount of capital with which to make a fresh start in the New World.

Many German immigrants were artisans and sought to ply their trades in cities like New York, St. Louis, Cincinnati, and Milwaukee—all of which became centers of German-American population. But a large portion of those with peasant backgrounds went back to the land. The possession of diversified agricultural skills and small amounts of capital enabled many Germans to become successful midwestern farmers. In general, they encountered less prejudice and discrimination than the Irish. For those who were Protestant, religious affinity with their American neighbors made for relative tolerance. But even Germans who were Catholic normally escaped the virulent scorn heaped on the Irish, perhaps because they were not so poverty stricken and did not carry the added burden of being members of an ethnic group Anglo-Americans had learned to despise from their English ancestors and cousins.

What attracted most of the Irish, German, and other European immigrants to America was the promise of economic opportunity. A minority, like some of the German revolutionaries of 1848, chose the United States because they admired its democratic political system. But most immigrants were more interested in the chance to make a decent living than in voting or running for office. The force of the economic motive can be seen in the fact that peak periods of immigration—1845

to 1854 is a prime example—coincided very closely with times of domestic prosperity and high demand for labor. During depressed periods, such as 1837 to 1842 and the mid-to-late 1850s, immigration dropped off significantly.

The arrival of large numbers of immigrants exacerbated the already serious problems of America's rapidly growing cities. The old "walking city" in which rich and poor lived in close proximity near the center of town was changing to a more segregated environment. The advent of railroads and horse-drawn streetcars enabled the affluent to move to the first American suburbs, while areas nearer commercial and industrial centers became the congested abode of newcomers from Europe. Emerging slums, such as the notorious "Five Points" district in New York City, were characterized by overcrowding, poverty, disease, and crime. Recognizing that these conditions created potential dangers for the entire urban population, middle-class reformers worked for the professionalization of police forces, introduction of sanitary water and sewage disposal systems, and the upgrading of housing standards. They made some progress in these endeavors in the period before the Civil War, but the lot of the urban poor, mainly immigrants, was not dramatically improved. Except to the extent that their own communal activities—especially those sponsored by churches and mutual aid societies—provided a sense of security and solidarity, the exis-

The Irish in Boston, 1845–1865

For the city of Boston, the period between 1845 and 1865 was an era of great change. Events half a world away rudely plucked more than fifty thousand Irish Catholic peasants from their homeland and transplanted them to a city that had hitherto been a homogeneous bastion of old-stock New England Puritanism. Some Bostonians viewed this mass of poor immigrants as an urban calamity. But the "invasion" was also a blessing, reinvigorating Boston with a substantial—and inimitable—Irish-American contribution to its social, economic, and political life.

The Irish came to America because they had no other choice. By the early nineteenth century, large landowners on the "isle of wondrous beauty"—mainly of English descent—were masters over impoverished tenant farmers who had been forced by their wretched circumstances to live on a diet consisting mostly of potatoes. When a blight caused the potato crop to rot in the mid-1840s, Ireland entered a period known as the Great Hunger. During this "state of social decomposition" between 1845 and 1851, the only alternative to starvation was emigration for most Irish peasants. One million people emigrated and another million died of starvation or disease.

The immigrants disembarked at the large northeastern seaboard cities. Although the newcomers were of rural origins, they were too poor and sick to continue westward to America's rich agricultural regions; they settled where they were dropped. Boston's population nearly doubled, growing from 93,000 to 177,000 between 1840 and 1860. In part this increase reflected the movement of a burgeoning native population

---

The corner saloon was the Irish workingman's version of a men's club. Irishmen gathered regularly, not only to partake of food and drink, but more important, to meet with friends, discuss politics, tell stories, or play cards.

from the country to the cities, but mainly it was the product of Ireland's Great Hunger.

Penniless and unskilled, the immigrants crowded into old buildings and warehouses that Boston's Yankees had abandoned—dark, unheated, unventilated, and unsanitary tenements. But as a social worker observed of the people living in Boston's Irish ghettos, "The Hibernian is first, last, and always a social being." In Ireland, poor tenant farmers had found comfort in lively conversation, sometimes made even more spirited by a convivial round of distilled refreshment, and nothing the immigrants found in Boston altered these customs. Talk came naturally to the Irish. They talked in the streets, in the shops, in the churches, in their homes—and in their saloons.

For men, by far the most popular locus of sociability was the corner saloon—where it was said a working man could not die of thirst. The Irish bar in Boston was devoid of frills. It featured wooden chairs, a long wooden bar with brass railings, card tables, sawdust-covered floors, and a philosophical bartender, who extended beer, whiskey, credit, and advice, in roughly equal doses. Irishmen sang, told stories, talked politics, or reminisced about the green fields and deep blue lakes of the Emerald Isle. In 1846, there were 850 liquor dealers in Boston, but by 1850 fully 1,500 saloons catered to the residents of the changing city.

Fortunately for Boston's capitalists and large-scale entrepreneurs, the most immediate need of the immigrants was employment—of any kind. At first the newcomers, who had been peasants in the "Ould Country," became street or yard laborers, but as it became apparent that the Irish were a potential pool of long-term proletarians—a large supply of workers who would remain in the least desirable jobs for low pay—capitalists responded by accelerating the Industrial Revolution in the Boston area. The number of industrial employees in Boston doubled in the decade of 1845 to 1855, and doubled again in the following decade. Moreover, Irish immigrants replaced much of the labor force from the early industrial era (see Chapter 9), especially in the textile mills of Boston's outlying suburbs. Irish men and unmarried women were willing to work for lower wages than those paid to Yankees and were not so insistent on decent working conditions.

Although reluctant to work outside the home for wages, married Irish-American women—who were usually raising a large family—often found themselves taking in lodgers, sewing at home for piece work rates on men's shirts and women's millinery, and doing other people's laundry. Their lot was frequently made more difficult by the long absences of their "rail-roading" husbands (Irishmen contracted out for months at a time to build and lay rails).

A large proportion of the Great Hunger immigrants from Ireland were unmarried women who, like their male counterparts, were desperate for employment. Some replaced Yankee "mill girls" but a larger number relieved an acute shortage of domestics in New England. Few native-born American women would do household work for pay, not only because the job carried the stigma of servanthood, but also because New Englanders were not willing to pay good wages for what was sometimes a 24-hour responsibility. Many maids and cooks suffered from "shattered health." But for the single Irish-American woman, the life of a domestic was often the best of a narrow range of alternatives..

Few of the first generation of Boston Irish escaped from the ranks of low-paid manual labor. The discriminatory attitudes of Yankee employers contributed significantly to this relative lack of mobility. (Many good jobs were advertised with the qualification that "no Irish need apply.") But occupational mobility was also inhibited to some extent by the tendency of the Irish immigrants to save up for the purchase of land and houses rather than starting small businesses or investing in the acquisition of education and skills. They also tended to place group security above individual advancement. They used strong communal activities and neighborhood organizations to their advantage in politics and union-building; success in local political clubs and the labor movement meant Irish politicians and labor leaders in Boston channeled several generations of Irish-Americans into secure but dead-end municipal and industrial jobs.

Although they were slow to rise out of the working class, the Irish energized the economy of Boston and soon won for themselves respect and power. They were the first large immigrant group to test the notion of America as a great melting pot. More than 150,000 Irish-Americans served in the Civil War, eager to demonstrate their loyalty to their adopted country. By 1865 the Irish, through their persistent efforts, their skill at local organization, and their willingness to be Boston's reliable working class, had found a permanent place in America's most venerable Puritan stronghold.

(a)Baron Biesele, upon his arrival in America (in German): "Hey, fellow countryman, where can we find a German tavern?" Countryman (in German): "Damme. Do you think I'm a no-good like you? I am an American."

(c) Baron Biesele, two weeks after arrival (in German): "Can you tell us –Hey, beautiful Marianel, isn't that you?" Marianel (in English): "You are mistaken. I don't talk Dutch."

(b)Baron Biesele, first week after arrival (in German): "Well, Marianel, how do you like it in America?" Marianel (in German): "Oh, Baron, the language, the language. I'll never learn it in all my life."

These lithographs from the Fliegende Blatter *(Cincinnati, 1847) feature the antics of Baron Biesele, a cartoon character popular in the German prototype of this short-lived Cincinnati periodical.*

tence of most urban immigrants remained unsafe, unhealthy, and unpleasant.

The New Working Class

A majority of immigrants ended up as wage workers in factories, mines, and construction camps, or as casual day laborers doing the many unskilled tasks required for urban and commercial growth. By providing a vast pool of cheap labor, they fueled and accelerated the Industrial Revolution. During the 1850s, factory production in Boston and other port cities previously devoted to commerce grew—partly because thousands of recent Irish immigrants worked for the kind of low wages that almost guaranteed large profits for entrepreneurs.

In established industries and older mill towns of the Northeast, immigrants gradually displaced the native-born workers who had predominated in the 1830s and 1840s. The changing work force of the textile mills in Lowell, Massachusetts, provided a striking example of this process. In 1836, only 3.7 percent of the workers in one Lowell

mill were foreign born; most members of the labor force at that time were young unmarried women from New England farms. By 1860, immigrants constituted 61.7 percent of the work force. A related development was a great increase in the number of men who tended machines in textile and other factories. Irish males, employers found, were willing to perform tasks that native-born men had generally regarded as women's work.

This trend reveals much about the changing character of the American working class. In the 1830s, most male workers were artisans, and factory work was still largely the province of women and children. Both groups were predominantly of American stock. In the 1840s, the proportion of men engaged in factory work increased, although the work force in the textile industry remained predominantly female. During that decade work conditions in many mills deteriorated. Workdays of twelve to fourteen hours were not new, but the paternalism that had earlier evoked a spirit of cooperation from workers was replaced by a more impersonal and cost-

Five Points, New York City, by an anonymous artist. At the time this work was done (ca. 1829), the area was reputedly the most dangerous neighborhood in the United States. Beggars, pimps, prostitutes, and hoodlums frequented the area, a notorious center of crime, disease, and poverty.

conscious form of management. During the depression that followed the panic of 1837, bosses attempted to reduce expenses and increase productivity by cutting wages, increasing the speed of machinery, and "stretching out"—giving each worker more machinery to operate.

The result was a new upsurge of labor militancy involving female as well as male factory workers. Mill girls in Lowell, for example, formed a union of their own—the Female Labor Reform Association—and agitated for shorter working hours. On a broader front, workers' organizations petitioned state legislatures to pass laws limiting the workday to ten hours. Some such laws were actually passed, but they turned out to be ineffective because employers could still require a prospective worker to sign a special contract agreeing to longer hours.

The employment of immigrants in increasing numbers between the mid-1840s and the late 1850s made it more difficult to organize industrial workers. Impoverished fugitives from the Irish potato famine tended to have lower economic expectations and more conservative social attitudes than native-born workers. Consequently the Irish immigrants were willing to work for less and were not so prone to protest bad working conditions. Most industrial laborers remained unorganized and resisted appeals for solidarity along class lines.

But the new working class of former rural folk did not make the transition to industrial wage labor easily or without protesting in subtle and indirect ways. Tardiness, absenteeism, drunkenness, loafing on the job, and other forms of resistance to factory discipline reflected deep hostility to the unaccustomed and seemingly unnatural routines of industrial production. The adjustment to new styles and rhythms of work was painful and took time. Historians are only now beginning to examine the inner world of the early generations of industrial workers, and they are finding evidence of discontent rather than docility, cultural resistance rather than easy adaptation.

By 1860, industrial expansion and immigration had created a working class of men and women who seemed destined for a life of low-paid wage labor. This reality stood in contrast to America's self-image as a land of opportunity and upward mobility. Wage labor was popularly viewed as a temporary condition from which workers were supposed to extricate themselves by hard work and frugality. According to Abraham Lincoln, speaking in 1850 of the North's "free labor" society, "there is no such thing as a freeman being fatally fixed for life, in the condition of a hired laborer." This ideal still had some validity in rapidly developing regions of the western states, but it was mostly myth when applied to the increasingly foreign born industrial workers of the Northeast.

Both internal and external expansion had come at a heavy cost. Tensions associated with class and ethnic rivalries were only one part of the price of rapid economic development. The acquisition of new territories became politically divisive and would soon lead to a catastrophic sectional controversy. The Young America wing of the Democratic party fought vainly to prevent this from happening. Its leader in the late 1840s and early 1850s was Senator Stephen A. Douglas of Illinois, called "the little giant" because of his small stature and large public presence. More than anyone else of this period, he sought political power for himself and his party by combining an expansionist foreign policy with the encouragement of economic development within the territories already acquired. Furthermore, his youthful dynamism made him seem the very embodiment of the Young America ideal. Recognizing that the slavery question was the main obstacle to his program, he sought to neutralize it through compromise and evasion (see Chapter 14). His failure to win the presidency or even the Democratic nomination before 1860 showed the Young Americans' dream of a patriotic consensus supporting headlong expansion and economic development could not withstand the tensions and divisions that expansionist policies created or brought to light.

CHRONOLOGY

1822	Santa Fe opened to American traders
1823	Earliest American settlers arrive in Texas
1830	Mexico attempts to halt American migration to Texas
1831	American railroads begin commercial operation
1834	Cyrus McCormick patents mechanical reaper
1835	Revolution breaks out in Texas
1836	Texas becomes independent republic
1837	John Deere invents steel plow
1841	President John Tyler inaugurated
1842	Webster-Ashburton Treaty fixes border between Maine and New Brunswick
1843	Mass migration to Oregon begins • Mexico closes Santa Fe trade to Americans
1844	Samuel F. B. Morse demonstrates electric telegraph • James K. Polk elected president on platform of expansionism
1845	Mass immigration from Europe begins • United States annexes Texas • John L. O'Sullivan coins slogan *Manifest Destiny*
1846	War with Mexico breaks out • United States and Great Britain resolve diplomatic crisis over Oregon
1847	American conquest of California completed • Mormons settle Utah • American forces under Zachary Taylor defeat Mexicans at Buena Vista • Winfield Scott's army captures Veracruz and defeats Mexicans at Cerro Gordo • Mexico City falls to American invaders
1848	Treaty of Guadalupe Hidalgo consigns California and New Mexico to United States • Gold discovered in California
1849	"Forty-niners" rush to California to dig for gold
1858	War between Utah Mormons and U. S. forces averted

Recommended Reading

An overview of expansion to the Pacific is Ray A. Billington, *The Far Western Frontier, 1830–1860* (1956). The impulse behind Manifest Destiny has been variously interpreted. Albert K. Weinberg's classic *Manifest Destiny: A Study of National Expansionism in American History* (1935) describes and stresses the ideological rationale. Frederick Merk, *Manifest Destiny and Mission in American History* (1963), analyzes public opinion and shows how divided it was on the question of territorial acquisitions. Norman A. Graebner, *Empire on the Pacific: A Study in American Continental Expansionism* (1956), highlights the desire for Pacific harbors as a motive for adding new territory. The most complete and authoritative account of the diplomatic side of expansionism in this period is David M. Pletcher, *The Diplomacy of Annexation: Texas, Oregon, and the Mexican War* (1973). Charles G. Sellers, *James K. Polk: Continentalist, 1843–1846* (1966) is the definitive work on Polk's election and the expansionist policies of his administration. For a lively narrative of Manifest Destiny at its climax, see Bernard De Voto, *The Year of Decision, 1846* (1943). A very good recent account of the Mexican War is provided by John S. D. Eisenhower, *So Far from God: The U. S. War with Mexico* (1989).

Economic developments of the 1840s and 1850s are well covered in George R. Taylor, *The Transportation Revolution, 1815–1960* (1952) and Albert Fishlow, *American Railroads and the Transformation of the Ante-Bellum Economy* (1965). A good short introduction to immigration is Maldwyn Allen Jones, *American Immigration* (1960). On the Irish, see Kerby A. Miller, *Emigrants and Exiles: Ireland and the Irish Exodus to America* (1985). Oscar Handlin, *Boston Immigrants: A Study in Acculturation*, rev. ed. (1959) is a classic study of immigration to one city. A standard work on the antebellum working class is Sean Wilentz, *Chants Democratic: New York City and the Rise of the American Working Class, 1788–1850* (1984); for the new approach to labor history that emphasizes working-class culture, see Herbert G. Gutman, *Work, Culture, and Society in Industrializing America* (1976). A pathbreaking and insightful study of workers in the textile industry is Thomas Dublin, *Women at Work: The Transformation of Work and Community in Lowell, Massachusetts, 1826–1860* (1979).

Additional Bibliography

Other important works on American penetration and settlement of the Far West include William H. Goetzmann, *Exploration and Empire: The Explorer and the Scientist in the Winning of the American West* (1966); John D. Unruh, Jr., *The Plains Across: The Overland Immigrants and the Trans-Mississippi West, 1840–1860* (1979); Thomas O'Dea, *The Mormons* (1957); Wallace Stegner, *The Gathering of Zion: The Story of the Mormon Trail* (1964); and R. W. Paul, *California Gold* (1947). On the struggle for Texas independence, see W. C. Binkley, *The Texas Revolution* (1952) and Michael A. Lofaro, ed., *Davy Crockett: The Man, the Legend, the Legacy* (1983). The politics and diplomacy of expansionism are treated in two books by Frederick Merk: *Slavery and the Annexation of Texas* (1972) and *The Monroe Doctrine and American Expansion, 1843–1849* (1966). For further insight into the expansionist motives of the Tyler administration, see William J. Cooper, *The South and the Politics of Slavery, 1828–1856* (1978). On the Mexican War, see K. Jack Bauer, *The Mexican War, 1846–1848* (1974), and Otis Singletary, *The Mexican War* (1960). John H. Schroeder, *Mr. Polk's War: American Opposition and Dissent* (1973), and Robert W. Johannsen, *To the Halls of Montezuma: The Mexican War and the American Imagination* (1985), deal with the way the war was viewed on the home front. The Mexican side of the struggle for the Southwest is well presented in Rudolfo Acuña, *Occupied America: A History of Chicanos* (1988), David J. Weber, *The Mexican Frontier, 1821–1846: The American Southwest Under Mexico* (1982), and in the early chapters of David Montejano, *Anglos and Mexicans in the Making of Texas* (1988). The ideas associated with Manifest Destiny and Young America are further explored in Reginald Horsman, *Race and Manifest Destiny* (1981), and Perry Miller, *The Raven and the Whale* (1956).

Economic growth and technological development in the late antebellum period are covered in Douglass C. North, *The Economic Growth of the United States, 1790–1860* (1961); Thomas C. Cochran and William Miller, *The Age of Enterprise: A Social History of Industrial America* (1942); Robert W. Fogel, *Railroads and American Economic Growth* (1964); Stuart Bruchey, *The Roots of American Economic Growth, 1607–1861* (1965); Peter Temin, *Iron and Steel in Nineteenth Century America* (1964); and Merritt Roe Smith, *Harpers Ferry Armory and the New Technology* (1977). For further insight into immigration, see Marcus L. Hansen, *The Atlantic Migration, 1607–1860* (1940); Katherine Neils Conzen, *Immigrant Milwaukee, 1836–1860* (1976); Robert Ernst, *Immigrant Life in New York City, 1825–1863* (1949); Philip Taylor, *The Distant Magnet: European Immigration to the United States of America* (1971); and Dale T. Knobel, *Paddy and the Republic: Ethnicity and Nationality in*

Antebellum America (1986). On urban life in this period, see Edward K. Spann, *The New Metropolis: New York City, 1840–1857* (1981). Important works that deal with the working-class experience include Alan Dawley, *Class and Community: The Industrial Revolution in Lynn* (1976); Bruce Laurie, *Working People of Philadelphia, 1800–1850* (1980); and Christine Stansell, *City of Women: Sex and Class in New York* (1986).

Masters and Slaves

O n August 22, 1831, the worst nightmare of southern slaveholders became reality. A group of slaves in Southampton County, Virginia, rose in open and bloody rebellion. Their leader was Nat Turner, a preacher and prophet who believed God had given him a sign that the time was ripe to strike for freedom; a vision of black and white angels wrestling in the sky had convinced him that divine wrath was about to be visited upon the white oppressor.

Beginning with a few followers and rallying others as he went along, Turner led his band from plantation to plantation and oversaw the killing of nearly sixty whites. The rebellion was short-lived; after only forty-eight hours, white forces dispersed the rampaging slaves. The rebels were then rounded up and executed, along with dozens of other slaves who were vaguely suspected of complicity. Nat Turner was the last to be captured, and he went to the gallows unrepentant, convinced he had acted in accordance with God's will.

After the initial panic and rumors of a wider insurrection had passed, white Southerners went about the grim business of making sure such an incident would never happen again. Their anxiety and determination were strengthened by the fact that 1831 also saw the emergence of a more militant northern abolitionism. Nat Turner and William Lloyd Garrison were viewed as two prongs of a revolutionary attack on the southern way of life. Although no evidence came to light that Turner was directly influenced by abolitionist propaganda, many whites believed he must have been or that future rebels might be. Consequently, they launched a massive campaign to quarantine the slaves from possible exposure to antislavery ideas and attitudes.

A series of new laws severely restricted the rights of slaves to move about, assemble without white supervision, or learn to read and write. The wave of repression did not stop at the color line; laws and the threat of mob action prevented white dissenters from publicly criticizing or even questioning the institution of slavery. For the most part, the South became a closed society with a closed mind. Loyalty to the region was firmly identified with defense of it and proslavery agitators sought to create a mood of crisis and danger requiring absolute unity and single-mindedness among the white population. This embattled attitude lay behind the growth of a more militant sectionalism and inspired threats to secede from the Union unless the South's peculiar institution could be made safe from northern or abolitionist attack.

The campaign for repression apparently achieved its original aim. Between 1831 and the Civil War, there were no further uprisings resulting in the mass killing of whites. This fact has led some historians to conclude that African American slaves were brainwashed into a state of docility. But resistance to slavery simply took less dangerous forms than open revolt. The brute force employed in response to the Turner rebellion and the elaborate precautions taken against its recurrence provided slaves with a more realistic sense of the odds against direct confrontation with white power. As a result they sought and perfected other methods of asserting their humanity and maintaining their self-esteem. This heroic effort to endure slavery without surrendering to it gave rise to an African American culture of lasting value.

SLAVERY AND THE SOUTHERN ECONOMY

Slavery would not have lasted as long as it did—and Southerners would not have reacted so strongly to real or imagined threats to its survival—if an influential class of whites had not had a vital and growing economic interest in this form of human exploitation. Since the early colonial period, forced labor had been considered essential to the South's plantation economy. In the period between the 1790s and the Civil War, plantation agriculture expanded enormously and so did dependence on slave labor; unfree blacks were the only workers readily available to landowners who sought to profit from expanding market opportunities by raising staple crops on a large scale.

By the time of the Civil War, 90 percent of the South's 4 million slaves worked on plantations and farms. In the seven cotton-producing states of the lower South (see the map in Chapter 9, p. 272) slaves constituted close to half the total population and were responsible for producing 90 percent of the cotton and almost all of the rice and sugar. In the upper South whites outnumbered slaves by more than 3 to 1 and were less dependent on their labor. To understand southern thought and behavior, it is necessary to bear in mind these major differences between the cotton kingdom with its entrenched one-crop plantation system and the upper South, which was actually moving away from this pattern during the pre–Civil War period.

Economic Adjustment in the Upper South

Tobacco, the original plantation crop of the colonial period, continued to be the principal slave-cultivated commodity of the upper tier of southern states during the pre–Civil War era. But markets were often depressed, and profitable tobacco cultivation was hard to sustain for very long in one place because it rapidly depleted the soil. As a result, there were continual shifts in the areas of greatest production and much experimentation with new crops and methods of farming in the original tobacco-growing regions of Virginia and Maryland. By 1860 more tobacco was grown in the new western states than in the older eastern ones, and Kentucky had emerged as a major producer.

During the lengthy depression of the tobacco market that lasted from the 1820s to the 1850s, agricultural experimentation was widespread in Virginia and Maryland. Increased use of fertilizer, systematic rotation of tobacco with other crops, and the growth of diversified farming based on a mix of wheat, corn, and livestock contributed to a gradual revival of agricultural prosperity. Such changes increased the need for capital but reduced the demand for labor. Improvements were financed in part by selling surplus slaves from the upper South to regions of the lower South, where staple crop production was more profitable. The interstate slave trade, which sent hundreds of thousands of slaves in a southwesterly direction between 1815 and 1860, was thus a godsend to the slaveowners of the upper South and a key to their survival and returning prosperity.

Some economic historians have concluded that the most important crop produced in the tobacco kingdom was not the "stinking weed" but human beings cultivated for the auction block. Respectable planters did not think of themselves as raising slaves for market, but few would refuse to sell some of their "people" if they needed money to get out of debt or make expensive improvements. The economic effect was clear: the natural increase of their slaves beyond what the planters needed for their operations provided them with a crucial source of capital in a period of transition and innovation and, as a result, encouraged the export of surplus slaves from the upper South to the Deep South.

Nevertheless, the fact that slave labor was declining in importance in the upper South meant the peculiar institution had a weaker hold on public loyalty there than in the cotton states. Diversification of agriculture was accompanied by a more rapid rate of urban and industrial development than was occurring elsewhere in the South. As a result, Virginians, Marylanders, and Kentuckians were seriously divided on whether their ultimate future lay with the Deep South's plantation economy or with the industrializing free labor system that was flourishing just north of their borders.

The Rise of the Cotton Kingdom

The warmer climate and good soils of the lower tier of southern states made it possible to raise crops more naturally suited than tobacco or cereals to the plantation form of agriculture and the heavy use of slave labor. Since the colonial period, rice and a special variety of fine cotton (known as "long staple") had been grown profitably on vast estates along the coast of South Carolina and Georgia. In lower Louisiana, between New Orleans and Baton Rouge, sugar was the cash crop. As in the West Indies, sugar production required a large investment and a great deal of back-breaking labor: in other words, large, well-financed plantations and small armies of slave laborers. Cultivation of rice, long-staple cotton, and sugar was limited by natural conditions to peripheral, semitropical areas. It was the rise of "short-staple" cotton as the South's major crop that strengthened the hold of slavery and the plantation on the southern economy.

Short-staple cotton differed from the long-staple variety in two important ways: its bolls contained seeds that were much more difficult to extract by hand, and it could be grown almost anywhere south of Virginia and Kentucky—the

Lewis Miller, Slave Sale, Virginia, probably 1853. Slave auctions, such as the one depicted in this sketch from Lewis Miller's sketchbook, were an abomination and embarrassment to many Americans. To southern plantation owners dependent on slave labor, however, such activities were essential.

main requirement was a guarantee of two hundred frost-free days. Before the 1790s, the seed extraction problem had prevented short-staple cotton from becoming a major market crop. The invention of the cotton gin in 1793 resolved that difficulty, however, and the subsequent westward expansion opened vast areas for cotton cultivation. Unlike rice and sugar, cotton could be grown on small farms as well as on plantations. But large planters enjoyed certain advantages that made them the main producers. Only relatively large operators could afford their own gins or possessed the capital to acquire the fertile bottomlands that brought the highest yields. They also had lower transportation costs because they were able to monopolize land along rivers and streams that were the South's natural arteries of transportation.

Cotton was well suited to a plantation form of production. Required tasks were relatively simple and could be performed by supervised gangs of unfree workers. Furthermore, there was enough work to be done in all seasons to keep the force occupied throughout the year. Unlike cereals, which had only to be planted, allowed to grow, and then harvested rapidly, cotton required constant weeding or "chopping" during the growing season and then could be picked over an extended period. The relative absence of seasonal variations in work needs made the use of slave laborers advantageous.

The first major cotton-producing regions were inland areas of Georgia and South Carolina that were already thinly settled at the time the cotton gin was introduced. The center of production shifted rapidly westward during the nineteenth century. By the 1830s, Alabama and Mississippi had surpassed Georgia and South Carolina as cotton-growing states. By the 1850s, Arkansas, northwest Louisiana, and east Texas were the most prosperous and rapidly growing plantation regions. The rise in total production that accompanied this geographical expansion was phenomenal. Between 1792 and 1817, the South's output of cotton rose from about 13,000 bales to 461,000; by 1840, it was 1.35 million; nine years later it had risen to 2.85 million; and in 1860 production peaked at the colossal figure of 4.8 million bales. Most of this cotton went to supply the booming textile industry of Great Britain. Lesser proportions went to the manufacturers of continental Europe and the northeastern United States.

"Cotton is king!" proclaimed a southern orator in the 1850s, and he was right. By that time, three-quarters of the world's supply of cotton came from the American South, and this single commodity accounted for over half of the total dollar value of American exports. Cotton growing and the network of commercial and industrial enterprises that marketed and processed this crop constituted the most important economic interest

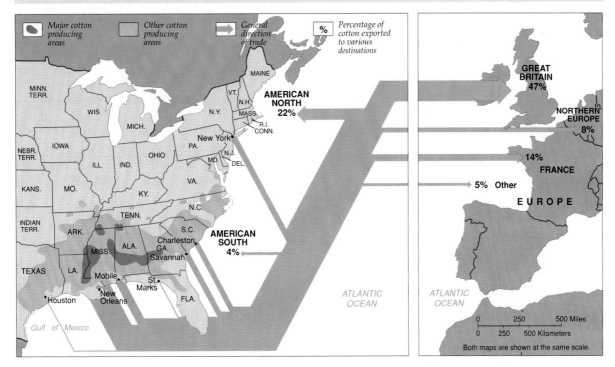

The Cotton Trade, 1857

Cotton output in the South increased rapidly as production moved westward. By the 1850s, the American South was the supplier of three-quarters of the world's cotton.

in the United States on the eve of the Civil War. Since slavery and cotton seemed inextricably linked, it appeared obvious to many Southerners that their peculiar institution was the keystone of national wealth and economic progress.

Despite its overall success, however, the rise of the cotton kingdom did not bring a uniform or steady prosperity to the lower South. Many planters worked the land until it was exhausted and then took their slaves westward to richer soils, leaving depressed and ravaged areas in their wake.

Planters were also beset and sometimes ruined by fluctuations in markets and prices. Boom periods and flush times were followed by falling prices and a wave of bankruptcies. The great periods of expansion and bonanza profits were 1815–1819, 1832–1837, and 1849–1860. The first two booms were deflated by a fall in cotton prices resulting from overproduction. During the eleven years of rising output and high prices preceding the Civil War, however, the planters gradually forgot their earlier troubles and began to imagine they were immune to future economic disasters.

Despite the insecurities associated with cotton production, most of the time this crop represented the Old South's best chance for profitable investment. Prudent planters who had not borrowed too heavily during flush times could survive periods of depression by cutting costs and making their plantations self-sufficient by shifting acreage away from cotton and planting subsistence crops. For those with worn-out land, two options existed: they could sell their land and move west or they could sell their slaves to raise capital for fertilization, crop rotation, and other improvements that could help them survive where they were. Hence planters had little incentive to seek alternatives to slavery, the plantation, and dependence on a single cash crop. From a purely economic point of view they had every reason to defend slavery and insist on their right to expand it.

Slavery and Industrialization

As the sectional quarrel with the North intensified, Southerners became increasingly alarmed by their region's lack of economic self-sufficiency. Dependence on the North for capital, marketing facilities, and manufactured goods was seen as evidence of a dangerous subservience to "external" economic interests. Southern nationalists like J. D. B. DeBow, editor of the influential *DeBow's Review*, called during the 1850s for the South to develop its own industries, commerce, and shipping. As a fervent defender of slavery, DeBow did not believe such diversification would require a massive shift to free wage labor. He saw no reason for slaves not to be used as the main work force in an industrial revolution. But his call for a diversified economy went unanswered. Men with capital were doing too well in plantation agriculture to risk their money in other ventures.

It is difficult to determine whether it was some inherent characteristic of slavery as a labor system or simply the strong market demand for cotton and the South's capacity to meet it that kept most slaves working on plantations and farms. A minority—about 5 percent during the 1850s—were, in fact, successfully employed in industrial tasks. Besides providing most of the labor for mining, lumbering, and constructing roads, canals, and railroads, slaves also worked in cotton mills and tobacco factories.

In the 1840s and 1850s, a debate raged among white capitalists over whether the South should use free whites or enslaved blacks as the labor supply for industry. William Gregg of South Carolina, the foremost promoter of cotton mills in the Old South, defended a white labor policy, arguing that factory work would provide new economic opportunities for a degraded class of poor whites. But other advocates of industrialization feared that the growth of a free working class would lead to social conflict among whites and preferred using slaves for all supervised manual labor. In practice, some factories employed slaves, others white workers, and a few even experimented with integrated work forces.

It is clear, however, that the union of slavery and cotton that was central to the South's prosperity impeded industrialization and left the region dependent on a one-crop agriculture and on the North for capital and marketing. Slaves were the only available workers who could be employed on plantations; rural whites refused to work for low wages when they had the alternative of subsistence farming on marginal lands in the southern backcountry. Industry, on the other hand, was concentrated in towns and cities where white labor was more readily available. When agriculture was booming—as it was during the 1850s—urban and industrial slaves tended to be displaced by whites and shifted to farming. So long as plantations yielded substantial profits, there could be no major movement of slaves from agriculture to industry. If anything, the trend was in the opposite direction.

The "Profitability" Issue

Some Southerners were obviously making money, and a great deal of it, using slave labor to raise cotton. The great mansions of the Alabama "black belt" and the lower Mississippi could not have been built if their owners had not been successful. But did slavery yield a good return for the great majority of slaveholders who were not large planters? Did it provide the basis for general prosperity and a relatively high standard of living for the southern population in general, or at least for the two-thirds of it who were white and free? These questions have been hotly debated by economic historians. Some knowledge of the main arguments regarding its "profitability" is helpful to an understanding of the South's attachment to slavery.

For many years historians believed slave-based agriculture was, on the average, not very lucrative. Planters' account books seemed to show at best a modest return on investment. In the 1850s, the price of slaves rose at a faster rate than the price of cotton, allegedly squeezing many operators. Some historians even concluded that slavery was a dying institution by the time of the Civil War. Profitability, they argued, depended on access to new and fertile land suitable for plantation agriculture, and virtually all such land within the limits of the United States had already been taken up by 1860. Hence slavery had allegedly reached its natural limits of expansion and was on the verge of becoming so unprofitable it would fall of its own weight in the near future.

Slaves are evident in this illustration, Baltimore Street Looking West from Calvert Street, Baltimore Maryland, ca. 1853. Only a small number of slaves worked in industry. Slaves who were not employed in agriculture worked in textile mills, tobacco factories, and ironworks; built roads and railroads; or served as dockworkers and longshoremen.

A more recent interpretation, based on modern economic theory, holds that slavery was in fact still an economically sound institution in 1860 and showed no signs of imminent decline. A reexamination of planters' records using modern accounting methods shows that during the 1850s planters could normally expect an annual return of 8 to 10 percent on capital invested. This yield was roughly equivalent to the best that could then be obtained from the most lucrative sectors of northern industry and commerce.

Furthermore, it is no longer clear that plantation agriculture had reached its natural limits of expansion by 1860. Production in Texas had not yet peaked, and construction of railroads and levees was opening up new areas for cotton growing elsewhere in the South. With the advantage of hindsight, economic historians have pointed out that improvements in transportation and flood control would enable the post-Civil War South to double its cotton acreage. Those who now argue that slavery was profitable and had an expansive future have made a strong and convincing case.

But the larger question remains: what sort of economic development did a slave plantation system foster? The system may have made slaveholders wealthy, but did the benefits trickle down to the rest of the population—to the majority of whites who owned no slaves and to the slaves themselves? Did it promote efficiency and progressive change? Economists Robert Fogel and Stanley Engerman have argued that slave plantation agriculture was more efficient than northern family farming. They came to this conclusion using a measure of productivity involving a ratio of "input"—capital, labor, and land—to "output"—the dollar value of the crop when sold. Critics have pointed out, however, that the higher efficiency rate for plantation agriculture may be due entirely to market conditions, or, in other words, to the fact that cotton was in greater demand than such northern commodities as wheat and livestock. Hence Fogel and Engerman's calculations would not prove their assertion that the plantation's success was due to an internally efficient enterprise with good managers and industrious, well-motivated workers.

Other evidence suggests that large plantation owners were the only segment of the population to profit so greatly. Small slaveholders and nonslaveholders shared only to a very limited extent in the bonanza profits of the cotton economy. Because of various insecurities—lack of credit, high transportation costs, and a greater vulnerability to market fluctuations—they had to devote a larger share of their acreage to subsistence crops, especially corn and hogs, than did the planters. They were thus able to survive, but their standard of living was lower than that of most northern farmers. Slaves benefited from planter profits only to the extent that they were better fed, housed, and clothed than they would have been

Slave Concentration, 1820

In 1820, most slaves lived in the eastern seaboard states of Virginia and South Carolina and in Louisiana on the Gulf of Mexico.

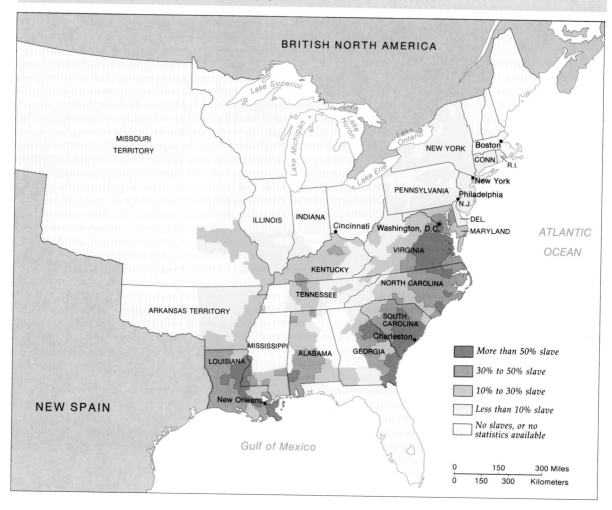

had their owners been less prosperous. But it is proslavery propaganda rather than documented fact to suggest they were better off than northern wage laborers.

The South's economic development was skewed in favor of a single route to wealth, open only to the minority possessing both a white skin and access to capital. The concentration of capital and business energies on cotton production foreclosed the kind of diversified industrial and commercial growth that would have provided wider opportunities. Thus, in comparison to the industrializing North, the South was an underdeveloped region in which much of the population had little incentive to work hard. A lack of public education for whites and the denial of even minimal literacy to slaves represented a critical failure to develop human resources. The South's economy was probably condemned to backwardness so long as it was based on slavery.

THE SLAVEHOLDING SOCIETY

If the precise effect of slavery on the South's economic life remains debatable, there is less room for disagreement concerning its impact on social arrangements and attitudes. More than any other factor, the ownership of slaves determined gradations of social prestige and influence among whites. The large planters were the dominant class, and nonslaveholders were of lower social rank. But the fact that all whites were free and

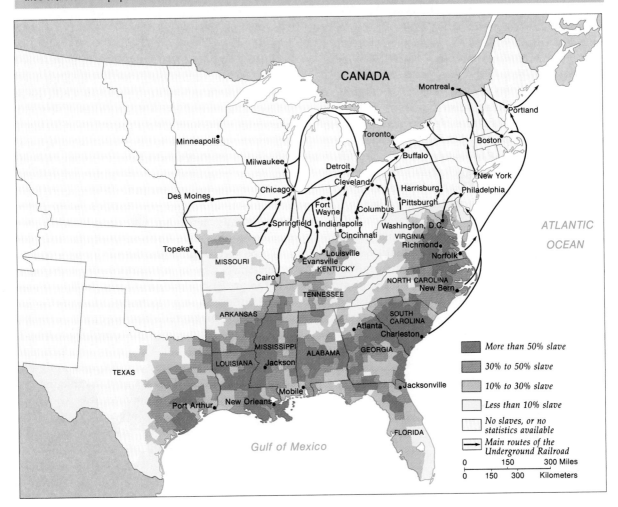

Slave Concentration, 1860

In 1860, slavery had extended throughout the southern states, with the greatest concentrations of slaves in the states of the Deep South. There were also sizable slave populations in the new states of Missouri, Arkansas, Texas, and Florida.

More than 50% slave

30% to 50% slave

10% to 30% slave

Less than 10% slave

No slaves, or no statistics available

Main routes of the Underground Railroad

most blacks were slaves created a sharp cleavage between the races that could create the impression (some would say the illusion) of a basic equality within "the master race." In the language of sociologists, inequality in the Old South was determined in two ways: by "class"—differences in status resulting from unequal access to wealth and productive resources—and by "caste"—inherited advantages or disadvantages associated with racial ancestry. Awareness of both systems of social ranking is necessary for an understanding of southern society.

The Planters' World

Those who know the Old South only from modern novels, films, and television programs are likely to envision a land filled with majestic plantations. Pillared mansions behind oak-lined carriageways are portrayed as scenes of aristocratic splendor, where courtly gentlemen and elegant ladies, attended by hordes of uniformed black servants, lived in refined luxury. It is easy to conclude from such images that the typical white Southerner was an aristocrat who belonged to a family that owned large numbers of slaves.

The great houses existed—many of them can still be seen in places like the low country of South Carolina and the lower Mississippi Valley—and some wealthy slaveholders did maintain as aristocratic a lifestyle as was ever seen in the United States. But census returns indicate that this was the world of only a small percentage of slaveowners and a minuscule portion of the total white population.

In 1850, only 30 percent of all white Southerners belonged to families owning slaves; by 1860, the proportion had shrunk to 25 percent. Even in the cotton belt of the Deep South, slaveholders were a minority of whites on the eve of the Civil War—about 40 percent. Planters, defined by the census takers as agriculturalists owning twenty or more slaves, were the minority of a minority. In 1860, planters and their families constituted about 12 percent of all slaveholders and less than 4 percent of the total white population of the South. Even the master of twenty to fifty slaves could rarely live up to the popular image of aristocratic grandeur. To build a great house and entertain lavishly, a planter had to own at least fifty slaves. In 1860, these substantial planters comprised less than 3 percent of all slaveholders and less than 1 percent of all whites.

Although few in numbers, the great planters had a weighty influence on southern life. They set the tone and values for much of the rest of society, especially for the less wealthy slaveowners who sought to imitate the planters' style of living to the extent that resources allowed. Although many of them were too busy tending to their plantations to become openly involved in politics, wealthy planters held more than their share of high offices and often exerted a decisive influence on public policy. Within those regions of the South in which plantation agriculture predominated, they were a ruling class in every sense of the term.

Contrary to legend, a majority of the great planters of the pre-Civil War period were self-made rather than descendants of the old colonial gentry. Some were ambitious young men who married planters' daughters. Others started as lawyers and used their fees and connections to acquire plantations.

As the cotton kingdom spread westward from South Carolina and Georgia to Alabama, Mississippi, and Louisiana, the men who became the largest slaveholders were less and less likely to have come from old and well-established planter families. A large proportion of them began as hard-driving businessmen who built up capital from commerce, land speculation, banking, and even slave-trading. They then used their profits to buy plantations. The highly competitive, boom-or-bust economy of the western Gulf states put a greater premium on sharp dealing and business skills than on genealogy. Stephen Duncan of Mississippi, probably the most prosperous cotton planter in the South during the 1850s (he owned eight plantations and 1,018 slaves), had invested the profits from his banking operations. Among the largest sugar planters of southern Louisiana at this time were Maunsel White and John Burnside, Irish immigrants who had prospered as New Orleans merchants, and Isaac Franklin, former king of the slave traders.

To be successful, a planter had to be a shrewd businessman who kept a careful eye on the market, the prices of slaves and land, and the extent of his indebtedness. Reliable "factors"—the agents who marketed the crop and provided advances against future sales—could assist him in making decisions, but a planter who failed to spend a good deal of time with his account books could end up in serious trouble. Managing the slaves and plantation production was also difficult and time consuming, even when overseers were available to supervise day-to-day activities. Hence few planters could be the men of leisure featured in the popular image of the Old South. Likewise, the responsibility of running an extended household that produced much of its own food and clothing kept plantation mistresses from being the idle ladies of legend.

Some of the richest and most secure plantation families did aspire to live in the manner of a traditional landed aristocracy. A few were so successful that they were accepted as equals by visiting English nobility. Big houses, elegant carriages, fancy-dress balls, and excessive numbers of house servants all reflected aristocratic aspirations. The romantic cult of chivalry, described in the popular novels of Sir Walter Scott, was in vogue in some circles and even led to the nonviolent reenactment of medieval tournaments. Dueling, despite efforts to repress it, remained the standard way to settle "affairs of honor" among gentlemen. Another sign of gentility was the tenden-

Ration Day on the Plantation, *an illustration by A. R. Waud for* Harper's Weekly, *February 2, 1867. The planter's need to keep track of all expenses was evident on ration day, when field slaves received their weekly food allotment—usually cornmeal and three to four pounds of meat, frequently bacon.*

cy of planters' sons to avoid "trade" as a primary or secondary career in favor of law or the military. Planters' daughters were trained from girlhood to play the piano, speak French, dress in the latest fashions, and sparkle in the drawing room or on the dance floor. The aristocratic style originated among the older gentry of the seaboard slave states, but by the 1840s and 1850s it had spread southwest as a second generation of wealthy planters began to displace the rough-hewn pioneers of the cotton kingdom.

Planters and Slaves

No assessment of the planters' outlook or "worldview" can be made without considering their relations with their slaves. Planters, by the census definition, owned more than half of all the slaves in the South and set standards for treatment and management. Most planters, it is clear from their private letters and journals, as well as from proslavery propaganda, liked to think of themselves as kindly and paternalistic. Often they referred to their slaves as if they were members of an extended patriarchal family—a favorite phrase was "our people." Blacks in general were described as a race of perpetual children requiring constant care and supervision by superior whites. Paternalistic rhetoric increased greatly after aboli-

tionists began to charge that most slaveholders were sadistic monsters. To some extent, the planters' response was part of a defensive effort to redeem the South's reputation and self-respect.

There was, nevertheless, a grain of truth in the planters' claim that their slaves were relatively well provided for. Recent comparative studies have suggested that North American slaves of the pre–Civil War period enjoyed a somewhat higher standard of living than those in other New World slave societies, such as Brazil and the West Indian sugar islands. Their food, clothing, and shelter were normally sufficient to sustain life and labor at slightly above a bare subsistence level and the rapid increase of the slave population in the Old South stands in sharp contrast to the usual failure of slave populations to reproduce themselves.

The concern of many planters for slave health and nutrition does not prove they put ethical considerations ahead of self-interest. The ban on the transatlantic slave trade in 1808 was effective enough to make the domestic reproduction of the slave force an economic necessity if the system was to be perpetuated. Rising slave prices thereafter inhibited extreme physical abuse and deprivation. Slaves were valuable property and the main tools of production for a booming economy, and it was in the interest of masters to see that their property remained in good enough condition to work hard and bear large numbers of children. Furthermore, a good return on their investment enabled southern planters to divert a significant portion of their profits to slave maintenance, a luxury not available to masters in less prosperous plantation economies. But some planters did not behave rationally. They failed to control their tempers or tried to work more slaves than they could afford to maintain. Consequently, there were more cases of physical abuse and undernourishment than a purely economic calculation would lead us to expect.

The testimony of slaves themselves and of some independent white observers suggests that masters of large plantations generally did not have close and intimate relationships with the mass of field slaves. The kind of affection and concern associated with a father figure appears to have been limited mainly to relationships with a few favored house servants or other elite slaves, such as drivers and highly skilled artisans. The field hands on large estates dealt mostly with

Slave cabins, such as these on a prosperous plantation, were small and crude, but still were better than many that had only a doorway leading into a dirt-floored hovel.

overseers who were hired or fired on their ability to meet production quotas.

When they were being most realistic, planters conceded that the ultimate basis of their authority was the slaves' fear of force and intimidation, rather than the natural obedience resulting from a loving parent-child relationship. Scattered among their statements are admissions that they relied on the "principle of fear," "more and more on the power of fear," or—most graphically—that it was necessary "to make them stand in fear." Devices for inspiring fear including whipping—a common practice on most plantations—and the threat of sale away from family and friends. Planters' manuals and instructions to overseers reveal that certain and swift punishment for any infraction of the rules or even for a surly attitude was the preferred method for maintaining order and productivity.

When some masters inevitably yielded to the temptations of power or to their bad tempers and tortured or killed their slaves or raped slave women, the slaves had little recourse. Slaves had little legal protection against such abuse because slave testimony was not accepted in court. Abolitionists were correct in condemning slavery on principle because it gave one human being nearly absolute power over another. Human nature being what it is, such a situation was bound to result in atrocities. Even Harriet Beecher Stowe acknowledged in *Uncle Tom's Cabin,* her celebrated anti-slavery novel of 1852, that most slaveholders were not as sadistic and brutish as Simon Legree. But—and this was her real point—there was something terribly wrong with an institution that made a Simon Legree possible.

The World of the Plain Folk

As we have seen, 88 percent of all slaveholders in 1860 owned fewer than twenty slaves and thus were not planters in the usual sense of the term. Of these, the great majority had fewer than ten.

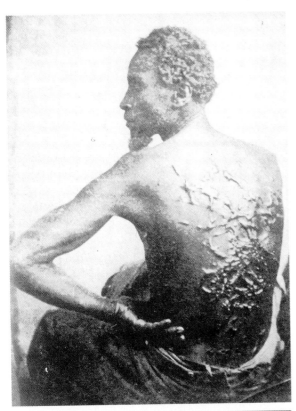

Not all slaves and masters had the benevolent relationship often cited in defense of slavery. Whippings that could produce scars like these were common on most plantations.

acter and disposition of the master. Given a choice, most slaves preferred to live on plantations because they offered the sociability, culture, and kinship of the quarters, as well as better prospects for adequate food, clothing, and shelter. Marginal slaveholders often sank into poverty and were forced either to sell their slaves or give them short rations.

Just below the small slaveholders on the social scale was a substantial class of yeoman farmers who owned land they worked themselves. Contrary to another myth about the Old South, most of these people did not fit the image of the degraded, shiftless poor white. Such poor whites did exist, mainly as squatters on stretches of barren or sandy soil that no one else wanted. In parts of the South, a significant proportion of those working the land were tenants; some of these were "shiftless poor whites," but others were ambitious young men seeking to accumulate the capital to become landowners. The majority of the nonslaveholding rural population were proud, self-reliant farmers whose way of life did not differ markedly from that of family farmers in the Midwest during the early stages of settlement. If they were disadvantaged in comparison with farmers elsewhere in the United States, it was because the lack of economic development and urban growth perpetuated frontier conditions and denied them the opportunity to produce a substantial surplus for market.

The yeomen were mostly concentrated in the backcountry where slaves and plantations were rarely seen. In every southern state, there were hilly sections unsuitable for plantation agriculture. The foothills or interior valleys of the Appalachians and the Ozarks offered reasonably good soils for mixed farming, and long stretches of piney barrens along the Gulf Coast were suitable for raising livestock. In such regions slaveless farmers concentrated, giving rise to the "white counties" that complicated southern politics. A somewhat distinct group were the genuine mountaineers, who lived too high up to succeed at farming and relied heavily on hunting, lumbering, and distilling whiskey.

The lack of transportation facilities, more than some failure of energy or character, limited the prosperity of the yeomen. A large part of their effort was devoted to growing subsistence crops, mainly corn. They raised a small percentage of

Some of the small slaveholders were urban merchants or professional men who needed slaves only for domestic service, but more typical were farmers who used one or two slave families to ease the burden of their own labor. Relatively little is known about life on these small slaveholding farms; unlike the planters, the owners left few records behind. We do know that life was relatively spartan. Masters lived in log cabins or small frame cottages and slaves lived in lofts or sheds that were not usually up to plantation housing standards.

For better or worse, relations between owners and their slaves were more intimate than on larger estates. Unlike planters, these farmers often worked in the fields alongside their slaves and sometimes ate at the same table or slept under the same roof. But such closeness did not necessarily result in better treatment. Slave testimony reveals that both the best and the worst of slavery could be found on these farms, depending on the char-

Plantation Women—White and Black

Fanny Cannady, a former slave girl, had mixed recollections of her mistress. Miss Sally was always kind, except when her husband Jordan was around. Her mother, Fanny recalled, had once spilled some coffee, and Jordan had ordered Miss Sally to slap her. Sally did so, but not hard enough to satisfy Master Jordan. "Hit her, Sally, hit the black bitch like she deserves to be hit," he told his wife. Then Miss Sally slapped her again—hard. After Master Jordan left the room, Sally began to cry, and she hugged Fanny's mother. "I loved Miss Sally when Marse Jordan wasn't around," Fanny said.

Fanny's memories illustrate that planters ruled their wives and children as well as their slaves. The planter's wife, in accordance with the conventions of the time, was supposed to exercise a softening influence on her lord and husband. As the lady of the manor, she was to provide a delicate and pure feminine presence within the big family of the plantation. This could lead planters' wives to have sympathy for their fellow subjects. But ultimately, the planter's wife was still a white lady and lived in a world apart from her enslaved counterparts.

Although they supervised the operations of the household and were actually kept very busy making sure everyone on the plantation was fed and clothed, women of the planter's family were supposed to be ladies. They had servants to wait on them, so they could give the impression to visitors they had nothing to do. Ladies could identify each other—and, just as important, townspeople could identify ladies—by their manners, their dress, and the number, behavior, and dress of their personal servants. Unmarried ladies were pure (if sometimes flirtatious), and married ladies demure. Their honor was reinforced by the wealth and weapons of their male relatives. If someone were so unwise as to insult a lady's honor, a duel with her brother, father, or husband would most likely follow.

Plantation women were able to be ladies at social functions. They made social calls on each other, to gossip and to confirm their status, which was defined by their husbands' wealth and honor. They also made charity calls on the less fortunate, thus fulfilling their religious and social obligations to help the poor of their community. Sometimes, they nursed sick slaves and supervised the lying-in of preg-

This satiric illustration, in which a slave woman kneels before and attends to her white mistress, appeared in The Life and Adventure of Jonathan Jefferson Whitlaw, or Scenes in Mississippi, *by Frances Trollope, an English author of novels and travel books and mother of the English novelist Anthony Trollope.*

nant slave women. In the evenings came the balls, which were the underpinning of plantation society and the chief opportunity for ladies to flash their finery among respectable company. The unmarried ladies reigned at the balls, attracting as many suitors as they could handle.

Ladies often expressed themselves privately in writing, or even, in rare cases, in print. One such lady was Mary Boykin Chesnut. In her journal of the Civil War years, she often commented caustically on the customs of southern slave society. She wrote about the evils she believed slavery caused, how it made violence a perpetual presence in society and corrupted the character of the slaveholder. She also equated the institution of slavery with the constraints placed on southern women: "There is no slave, after all, like a wife," she wrote. Still, even though she apparently felt sympathy for mistreated slaves and wives, she could never bring herself to believe either ought to liberate themselves.

Trapped though southern ladies were, theirs was a gilded cage, a prison decked with lace and perfumed with magnolia. Everything they strove to be stood out in stark contrast against the lives of their counterparts on the plantation: women slaves. While white women on plantations tried to uphold the standards of ladyhood, black women had to struggle to maintain some semblance of womanhood. Sojourner Truth escaped slavery to become a prominent spokesperson for abolition and gave voice to the plight of black women by demanding of a northern audience, "Ar'n't I a woman?"

Black women had the worst of two important prejudices: as blacks, they could be owned as slaves, and as owned women, they could be sexually exploited. The guilt caused by sex between masters and slaves helped create polarized stereotypes of black women's sexuality: on the one hand there was the Jezebel, the woman who was all sexuality, and on the other, Mammy, who had none. A mammy took care of the white children and often exercised considerable authority in household matters, especially if a young mistress had earlier been in her charge. But she often lacked the time to pay adequate attention to her own slave family.

Masters' control over the bodies of female slaves extended to their wombs. It was in the master's interest to promote procreation among slaves. As Thomas Jefferson said, "I consider a woman who brings a child every two years as more profitable than the best man of the farm. What she produces is an addition to the capital, while his labors disappear in mere consumption." For a black woman to be owned as a slave meant that her womb was owned and her children were owned.

Black women nevertheless managed to create private lives and communities. Most lived in two-parent slave families in which husbands and wives normally shared responsibilities in a more equitable way than was the case with their owners. But labor gangs were often separated into men and women, and the sort of work women did usually allowed them to be with each other. This was probably the beginning of a sense of female community. The persistence of African traditions of spirituality and healing helped as well. Women acting as midwives, or known to have an understanding of folk medicine, had a certain authority.

Perhaps most important in terms of rebelling against the master, women in the slave quarters sometimes worked together to avoid bringing more children into slavery by the use of contraceptives, abortifacients, and even infanticide. More often, however, they valued their children and sought to teach them how to survive under slavery.

Slave women also resisted in smaller ways, particularly against their mistresses. When the master was not about, they were that much more likely to shirk work, to talk back to the mistress, and to play tricks, for they knew the master would invariably put it down to his wife's weakness as a woman and inability to wield authority effectively.

Black women were subject to special hardships because they were women, but unlike white ladies, they were not entitled to special treatment because of their gender. This was especially graphic when masters punished slaves. White men who would consider it unthinkable to strike a white lady had no qualms about whipping slave women. An extreme and illustrative example is that of the man who shot a slave named Lydia while she was running away from punishment. The Supreme Court of North Carolina held that the master had a right to do so because "The Power of the master must be absolute to render the submission of the slave perfect."

Power was the first and final fact of life under slavery. The southern economy had made slavery indispensable. White Southerners had to ensure their dominion over blacks. This kept plantation ladies and female slaves from finding their potential solidarity as women.

the South's cotton and tobacco, but production was severely limited by the difficulty of market-ing. Their main source of cash was livestock, especially hogs. Hogs could be walked to market over long distances, and massive droves from the backcountry to urban markets were common-place. But southern livestock, which was general-ly allowed to forage in the woods rather than being fattened on grain, was of poor quality and did not bring high prices or big profits to raisers.

Although they did not benefit directly from the peculiar institution, most yeomen and other non-slaveholders tolerated slavery and were fiercely opposed to abolitionism in any form. A few anti-slavery Southerners, most notably Hinton R. Helper of North Carolina, tried to convince the yeomen they were victimized by planter domi-nance and should work for its overthrow. These dissenters presented a plausible set of arguments, emphasizing that slavery and the plantation sys-tem created a privileged class and severely limited the economic opportunities of the nonslavehold-ing white majority.

Most yeomen were staunch Jacksonians who resented aristocratic pretensions and feared con-centrations of power and wealth in the hands of the few. When asked about the gentry, they com-monly voiced their disdain of "cotton snobs" and rich planters generally. In state and local politics, they sometimes expressed these feelings by voting against planter interests on issues involving repre-sentation, banking, and internal improvements. Why, then, did they fail to respond to antislavery appeals that called on them to strike at the real source of planter power and privilege?

One reason was that some nonslaveholders hoped to get ahead in the world, and in the South this meant acquiring slaves of their own. Just enough of the more prosperous yeomen broke into the slaveholding classes to make this dream seem believable. Planters, anxious to ensure the loyalty of nonslaveholders, strenuously encour-aged the notion that every white man was a potential master.

Even if they did not aspire to own slaves, white farmers often viewed black servitude as providing a guarantee of their own liberty and indepen-dence. A society that gave them the right to vote and the chance to be self-sufficient on land of their own encouraged the feeling they were fun-damentally equal to the largest slaveholders.

Although they had no natural love of planters and slavery, they believed—or could be induced to believe—that abolition would threaten their liberty and independence. In part their anxieties were economic; freed slaves would compete with them for land or jobs. But an intense racism deep-ened their fears and made their opposition to black freedom implacable. "Now suppose they was free," a nonslaveholder told a northern trav-eler, "you see they'd think themselves just as good as we . . . just suppose you had a family of children, how would [you] like to hev a niggar feeling just as good as a white man? how'd you like to hev a niggar steppin' up to your darter?" Emancipation was unthinkable because it would remove the pride and status that automatically went along with a white skin in this acutely race-conscious society. Slavery, despite its drawbacks, served to keep blacks "in their place" and to make all whites, however poor and uneducated they might be, feel they were free and equal mem-bers of a master race.

A Closed Mind and a Closed Society

Despite the tacit assent of most nonslaveholders, the dominant planters never lost their fear that lower-class whites would turn against slavery. They felt threatened from two sides: from the slave quarters where a new Nat Turner might be gathering his forces, and from the backcountry where yeomen and poor whites might heed the call of abolitionists and rise up against planter domination. Beginning in the 1830s, the ruling element tightened the screws of slavery and used their control of government and communications to create a mood of impending catastrophe designed to ensure that all southern whites were of a single mind on the slavery issue.

Before the 1830s, open discussion of the rights or wrongs of slavery had been possible in many parts of the South. Apologists commonly described the institution as "a necessary evil." In the upper South, as late as the 1820s, there had been significant support for the American Colonization Society, with its program of gradual voluntary emancipation accompanied by deporta-tion of the freedmen. In 1831 and 1832—in the wake of the Nat Turner uprising—the Virginia state legislature debated a gradual emancipation plan. Major support for ensuring white safety by getting rid of both slavery and blacks came from representatives of the yeoman farmers living west of the Blue Ridge Mountains. But the defeat of the proposal effectively ended the discussion. The argument that slavery was "a positive good"—rather than an evil slated for gradual elimination—won the day.

The positive good defense of slavery was an answer to the abolitionist charge that the institution was inherently sinful. The message was carried in a host of books, pamphlets, and newspaper editorials published between the 1830s and the Civil War. Who, historians have asked, was it meant to persuade? Partly, the argument was aimed at the North, as a way of bolstering the strong current of antiabolitionist sentiment. But Southerners themselves were a prime target; the message was clearly calculated to resolve the kind of doubts and misgivings that had been freely expressed before the 1830s. Much of the message may have been over the heads of nonslaveholders, many of whom were semiliterate, but some of the arguments, in popularized form, were used to arouse racial anxieties that tended to neutralize antislavery sentiment among the lower classes.

The proslavery argument was based on three main propositions. The first and foremost was that enslavement was the natural and proper status for people of African descent. Blacks, it was alleged, were innately inferior to whites and suited only for slavery. Biased scientific and historical evidence was presented to support this claim. Secondly, slavery was held to be sanctioned by the Bible and Christianity—a position made necessary by the abolitionist appeal to Christian ethics. Ancient Hebrew slavery was held up as a divinely sanctioned model, and Saint Paul was quoted endlessly on the duty of servants to obey their masters. Southern churchmen took the lead in reconciling slavery with religion and also made renewed efforts to convert the slaves as a way of showing that enslavement could be a means for spreading the gospel.

Finally, efforts were made to show that slavery was consistent with the humanitarian spirit of the nineteenth century. The premise that blacks were naturally dependent led to the notion they needed some kind of "family government" or special regime equivalent to the asylums that existed for the small numbers of whites who were also inca-pable of caring for themselves. The plantation allegedly provided such an environment, as benevolent masters guided and ruled this race of "perpetual children."

By the 1850s, the proslavery argument had gone beyond mere apology for the South and its peculiar institution and featured an ingenious attack on the free labor system of the North. According to the Virginian George Fitzhugh, the master-slave relationship was *more* humane than the one prevailing between employers and wage laborers in the North. Slaves had security against unemployment and a guarantee of care in old age, whereas free workers might face destitution and even starvation at any time. Worker insecurity in free societies led inevitably to strikes, bitter class conflicts, and the rise of socialism; slave societies, on the other hand, could more effectively protect property rights and maintain other traditional values because its laboring class was both better treated, and at the same time, more firmly controlled.

In addition to arguing against the abolitionists, proslavery Southerners attempted to seal off their region from antislavery ideas and influences. Whites who were bold enough to criticize slavery publicly were mobbed or persecuted. One of the last and bravest of the southern abolitionists, Cassius M. Clay of Kentucky, armed himself with a brace of pistols when he gave speeches, until the threat of mob violence finally forced him across the Ohio. In 1856, a University of North Carolina professor was fired because he admitted he would vote for the moderately antislavery Republican party if he had a chance. Clergymen who questioned the morality of slavery were driven from their pulpits, and northern travelers suspected of being abolitionist agents were tarred and feathered. When abolitionists tried to send their literature through the mails during the 1830s, it was seized in southern post offices and publicly burned.

Such flagrant denials of free speech and civil liberties were inspired in part by fears that nonslaveholding whites and slaves would get subversive ideas about slavery. Hinton R. Helper's book, *The Impending Crisis of the South,* an 1857 appeal to nonslaveholders to resist the planter regime, was suppressed with particular vigor; those found with copies were beaten up or even lynched. But the deepest fear was that slaves

This proslavery cartoon of 1841 contends that the slave in America had a better life than did the working-class white in England. Supposedly, the grateful slaves were clothed, fed, and cared for in their old age by kindly and sympathetic masters, while starving English workers were mercilessly exploited by factory owners.

would hear the abolitionist talk or read antislavery literature and be inspired to rebel. Such anxieties rose to panic pitch after the Nat Turner rebellion. Consequently, new laws were passed making it a crime to teach slaves to read and write. Other repressive legislation aimed at slaves banned meetings unless a white man was present, severely restricted the activities of black preachers, and suppressed independent black churches. Free blacks, thought to be possible instigators of slave revolt, were denied basic civil liberties and were the object of growing surveillance and harassment.

All these efforts at thought control and internal security did not allay the fears of abolitionist subversion, lower-class white dissent, and, above all, slave revolt. The persistent barrage of proslavery propaganda and the course of national events in the 1850s created a mood of panic and despera-

tion. By this time an increasing number of Southerners had become convinced that safety from abolitionism and its associated terrors required a formal withdrawal from the Union—secession.

THE BLACK EXPERIENCE UNDER SLAVERY

Most African Americans of the early to mid-nineteenth century experienced slavery on plantations; the majority of slaves lived on units owned by planters who had twenty or more slaves. The masters of these agrarian communities sought to ensure their personal safety and the profitability of their enterprises by using all the means—physical and psychological—at their command to make slaves docile and obedient. By word and deed, they tried to convince the slaves that whites were superior and had a right to rule over blacks. Masters also drew constant attention to their awesome power and ability to deal harshly with rebels and malcontents. As increasing numbers of slaves were converted to Christianity and attended white-supervised services, they were forced to hear, over and over again, that God had commanded slaves to serve and obey their masters.

It is a great tribute to the resourcefulness and spirit of African Americans that most of them resisted these pressures and managed to retain an inner sense of their own worth and dignity. When conditions were right, they openly asserted their desire for freedom and equality and showed their disdain for white claims that slavery was a positive good. But the struggle for freedom involved more than the confrontation between master and slave; free blacks, in both the North and the South, did what they could to speed the day when all African Americans would be free.

This woman is believed to be the granddaughter of Marie Therese, a freed slave who married a Frenchman and built Melrose Plantation in Louisiana. Despite its slave heritage, even this planter family owned slaves.

Forms of Slave Resistance

Open rebellion, the bearing of arms against the oppressors by organized groups of slaves, was the most dramatic and clear-cut form of slave resistance. In the period between 1800 and 1831, a number of slaves participated in revolts that showed their willingness to risk their lives in a desperate bid for liberation. In 1800, a Virginia slave named Gabriel Prosser mobilized a large band of his fellows to march on Richmond. But a violent storm dispersed "Gabriel's army" and enabled whites to suppress the uprising without any loss of white life.

In 1811, several hundred Louisiana slaves marched on New Orleans brandishing guns, waving flags, and beating drums. It took three hundred soldiers of the U.S. Army, aided by armed planters and militiamen, to stop the advance and to end the rebellion. In 1822, whites in Charleston, South Carolina, uncovered an extensive and well-planned conspiracy, organized by a free black man named Denmark Vesey, to seize local armories, arm the slave population, and take possession of the city. Although the Vesey conspiracy was nipped in the bud, it convinced South Carolinians that blacks were "the Jacobins of the country [a reference to the militants of the French Revolution] against whom we should always be on guard."

Only a year after the Vesey affair, whites in Norfolk County, Virginia, complained of the activities of a marauding band of runaway slaves that had killed several whites. The militia was sent out and captured the alleged leader—a fugitive of several years' standing named Bob Ferebee. Groups of runaways, who hid for years in places like the Great Dismal Swamp of Virginia, continued to raid plantations throughout the antebellum period and were inclined to fight to the death rather than be recaptured.

As we have already seen, the most bloody and terrifying of all slave revolts was the Nat Turner insurrection of 1831. Although it was the last slave rebellion of this kind during the pre-Civil War period, armed resistance had not ended. Indeed, the most sustained and successful effort of slaves to win their freedom by force of arms took place in Florida between 1835 and 1842 when hundreds of black fugitives fought in the Second Seminole War alongside the Indians who had given them a haven. The Seminoles were resisting removal to Oklahoma, but for the blacks who took part, the war was a struggle for their own freedom, and when it ended most of them were allowed to accompany their Indian allies to the trans-Mississippi West.

Only a tiny fraction of all slaves ever took part in organized acts of violent resistance against white power. Most realized the odds against a successful revolt were very high, and bitter experience had shown them that the usual outcome was death to the rebels. As a consequence, they characteristically devised safer or more ingenious ways to resist white dominance.

One way of protesting against slavery was to run away, and thousands of slaves showed their discontent and desire for freedom in this fashion. Most fugitives never got beyond the neighborhood of the plantation; after "lying out" for a time, they would return, often after negotiating immunity from punishment. But many escapees remained free for years by hiding in swamps or other remote areas, and a fraction made it to freedom in the North or Mexico. Some fugitives stowed away aboard ships heading to northern ports; others traveled overland for hundreds of miles, avoiding patrols and inquisitive whites by staying off the roads and moving only at night. Light-skinned blacks sometimes made it to freedom by passing for whites, and one resourceful slave even had himself packed in a box and shipped to the North.

The typical fugitive was a young, unmarried male from the upper South. For the majority of slaves, however, flight was not a real option. Either they lived too deep in the South to have any chance of reaching free soil, or they were reluctant to leave family and friends behind. Slaves who did not or could not leave the plantation had to register their opposition to the masters' regime while remaining under the yoke of bondage.

The normal way of expressing discontent was engaging in a kind of indirect or passive resistance. Many slaves worked slowly and inefficiently, not because they were naturally lazy (as whites supposed), but as a gesture of protest or alienation as conveyed in the words of a popular slave song, "You may think I'm working/But I ain't." Others withheld labor by feigning illness or

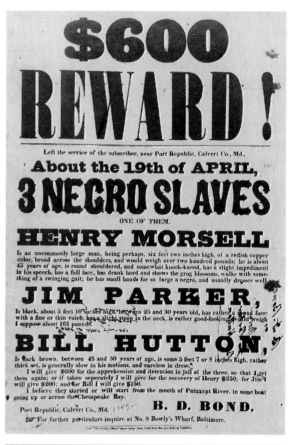

Running away was one way to escape slavery, but for most slaves, flight was impossible. Instead, they sought other means by which to improve their condition as slaves.

injury. Stealing provisions—a very common activity on most plantations—was another way to show contempt for authority. According to the code of ethics prevailing in the slave quarters, theft from the master was no sin; it was simply a way for slaves to get a larger share of the fruits of their own labors.

Substantial numbers of slaves committed acts of sabotage. Tools and agricultural implements were deliberately broken, animals were willfully neglected or mistreated, and barns or other outbuildings were set afire. Often masters could not identify the culprits because slaves did not readily inform on one another. The ultimate act of clandestine resistance was poisoning the master's food. Some slaves, especially the "conjure" men and women who practiced a combination of folk medicine and witchcraft, knew how to mix rare, virtually untraceable poisons; and a suspiciously large number of plantation whites became suddenly and mysteriously ill. Sometimes whole families died from obscure "diseases" that did not infect the slave quarters.

The basic attitude behind such actions was revealed in the folk-tales that slaves passed down from generation to generation. The famous Brer Rabbit stories showed how a small, apparently defenseless animal could overcome a bigger and stronger one through cunning and deceit. Although these tales often had an African origin, they also served as an allegory for the black view of the master-slave relationship. Other stories—which were not told in front of whites—openly portrayed the slave as a clever trickster outwitting the master. In one such tale a slave reports to his master that seven hogs have died of "malitis." Thinking this is a dread disease, the master agrees to let the slaves have all the meat. What really happened, so the story goes, was that "One of the strongest Negroes got up early in the morning" and "skitted to the hog pen with a heavy mallet in his hand. When he tapped Mister Hog 'tween the eyes with that mallet, 'malitis' set in mighty quick."

The Struggles of Free Blacks

In addition to the 4 million blacks in bondage, there were approximately 500,000 free African Americans in 1860, about half of them living in slave states. Whether they were in the North or in the South, "free Negroes" were treated as social outcasts and denied legal and political equality with whites. Public facilities were strictly segregated, and after the 1830s blacks in the United States could vote only in four New England states. Nowhere but in Massachusetts could they testify in court cases involving whites.

Free blacks had difficulty finding decent jobs; most employers preferred immigrants or other whites over blacks, and the latter were usually relegated to menial and poorly paid occupations: casual day labor or domestic service. Many states excluded blacks entirely from public schools, and the federal government barred them from serving in the militia, working for the postal service, and laying claim to public lands. Free blacks were even denied U. S. passports; in effect they were stateless persons even before the 1857 Supreme Court ruling that no Negro could claim American citizenship.

In the South, free blacks were subject to a set of direct controls that tended to make them semi-slaves. They were often forced to register or have white guardians who were responsible for their behavior. Invariably they were required to carry papers proving their free status, and in some states they had to obtain official permission to move from one county to another. Licensing laws were invoked to exclude blacks from several occupations, and attempts by blacks to hold meetings or form organizations were frequently blocked by the authorities. Sometimes vagrancy and apprenticeship laws were used to force free blacks into a state of economic dependency barely distinguishable from outright slavery. Just before the outbreak of the Civil War, a campaign developed in some southern states to carry this pattern of repression and discrimination to its logical conclusion: several state legislatures proposed laws giving free Negroes the choice of emigrating from the state or being enslaved.

Although beset by special problems of their own, most free blacks identified with the suffering of the slaves; when circumstances allowed, they protested against the peculiar institution and worked for its abolition. Many of them had once been slaves themselves or were the children of slaves; often they had close relatives who were still in bondage. Furthermore, they knew the discrimination from which they suffered was rooted in slavery and the racial attitudes that accompanied it. So long as slavery existed, their own rights were likely to be denied and even their freedom was at risk; former slaves who could not prove they had been legally freed were subject to reenslavement. This threat existed even in the North: under federal fugitive slave laws, escaped slaves could be returned to bondage. Even blacks who were born free were not perfectly safe. Kidnapping or fraudulent seizure by slave-catchers was always a possibility.

Because of the elaborate system of control and surveillance, free blacks in the South were in a relatively weak position to work against slavery. The case of Denmark Vesey showed that a prosperous and well-situated free black might make a stand in the struggle for freedom, but it also revealed the dangers of revolutionary activity and the odds against success. The wave of repression against the free black population that followed the Vesey conspiracy heightened the dangers and increased the odds. Consequently, most free blacks found that survival depended on creating the impression of loyalty to the planter regime. In some parts of the lower South, groups of relatively privileged free Negroes, mostly of racially mixed origin, were sometimes persuaded it was to their advantage to preserve the status quo. As skilled craftsmen and small businessmen dependent on white favors and patronage, they had little incentive to risk everything by taking the side of the slaves. In southern Louisiana, there was even a small group of mulatto planters who lived in luxury, supported by the labor of other African Americans.

Free blacks in the North were in a better position to join the struggle for freedom. Despite all the prejudice and discrimination they faced, they still enjoyed some basic civil liberties denied to southern blacks. They could protest publicly against slavery or white supremacy and could form associations for the advancement and liberation of African Americans. Frederick Douglass, the escaped slave who became an abolitionist orator, was their most eloquent spokesman. Among the other leading black male abolitionists were Charles Remond, William Wells Brown, Robert Purvis, and Henry Highland Garnet. Outspoken women like Sojourner Truth, Maria Stewart, and Frances Harper also played a significant role in black antislavery activity. The Negro Convention movement, which sponsored national meetings of black leaders beginning in 1830, provided an important forum for independent black expression. Their most eloquent statement came in 1854, when black leaders met in Cleveland to declare their faith in a separate racial identity, proclaiming, "We pledge our integrity to use all honorable means, to unite us, as one people, on this continent."

Black newspapers, such as *Freedom's Journal*, first published in 1827, and *The North Star*, founded by Douglass in 1847, gave black writers a chance to preach their gospel of liberation to black readers. African American authors also produced a stream of books and pamphlets attacking slavery, refuting racism, and advocating various forms of resistance. One of the most influential publications was David Walker's *Appeal . . . to the Colored Citizens of the World*, which appeared in 1829. Walker denounced slavery in the most vigorous language possible and called for a black revolt against white tyranny.

Free blacks in the North did more than make verbal protests against racial injustice. They were also the main conductors on the fabled underground railroad that opened a path for fugitives from slavery. It has been supposed that benevolent whites were primarily responsible for organized efforts to guide and assist fugitive slaves, but modern research has shown that the underground railroad was largely a black-operated enterprise. Courageous ex-slaves like Harriet Tubman and Josiah Henson made regular forays into the slave states to lead other blacks to freedom, and many of the "stations" along the way were manned by free Negroes. In northern towns and cities, free blacks organized "vigilance committees" to protect fugitives and thwart the slave catchers. Groups of blacks even used force to rescue recaptured fugitives from the authorities. In Boston in 1851, one such group seized a slave named Shadrack from a U. S. marshal who was in the process of returning him to bondage. In deeds as well as words, free blacks showed their unyielding hostility to slavery and racism.

African American Religion

African Americans could not have resisted or even endured slavery if they had been utterly demoralized by its oppressiveness. What made the struggle for freedom possible were inner resources and patterns of thought that gave some dignity to their lives and inspired hopes for a brighter future. From the realm of culture and fundamental beliefs African Americans drew the strength to hold their heads high and look beyond their immediate condition.

Religion was the cornerstone of this emerging African American culture. Black Christianity may have owed its original existence to the efforts of white missionaries, but it was far from a mere imitation of white religious forms and beliefs. This distinctive variant of evangelical Protestantism incorporated elements of African religion and stressed those portions of the Bible that spoke to the aspirations of an enslaved people thirsting for freedom.

Harriet Tubman, on the extreme left, is shown here with some of the slaves she helped escape on the underground railroad. Born a slave in Maryland, she escaped to Philadelphia in 1849. She is said to have helped as many as three hundred African Americans flee slavery. She led many of them all the way to Canada, where they would be beyond the reach of the Fugitive Slave Law.

Free blacks formed the first independent black churches by seceding from white congregations that discriminated against them in seating and church governance. Out of these secessions came a variety of autonomous Baptist groups and the highly successful African Methodist Episcopal (AME) church, organized as a national denomination under the leadership of Reverend Richard Allen of Philadelphia in 1816. But the mass of blacks did not have access to these independent churches. These churches mainly served free blacks and urban slaves with indulgent masters. In the deep South, whites regarded AME churches with suspicion and sometimes suppressed them; a thriving congregation in Charleston was forced to close its doors in 1822 after some of its members had been implicated in the Vesey conspiracy.

Plantation slaves who were exposed to Christianity either attended neighboring white churches or worshiped at home. On large estates masters or white missionaries often conducted Sunday services. But the narratives and recollections of ex-slaves reveal that white-sanctioned religious activity was only a superficial part of the slaves' spiritual life. The true slave religion was practiced at night, often secretly, and was led by black preachers. Historian Albert J. Raboteau has described this underground black Christianity as "the invisible institution."

This covert slave religion was a highly emotional affair that featured singing, shouting, and dancing. In some ways the atmosphere resembled a backwoods revival meeting. But much of what went on was actually an adaptation of African religious beliefs and customs. The chanting mode of preaching—with the congregation responding at regular intervals—and the expression of religious feelings through rhythmical movements, especially the counterclockwise movement known as "the ring shout," were clearly African in origin. The black conversion experience was normally a state of ecstasy more akin to possession by spirits—a major form of African religious expression—than to the agony of those "struck down" at white revivals. The emphasis on sinfulness and fear of damnation that were core themes of white evangelicalism played a lesser role among blacks. For them, religion was more an affirmation of the joy of life than a rejection of worldly pleasures and temptations.

Slave sermons and religious songs spoke directly to the plight of a people in bondage and implicitly asserted their right to be free. The most popular of all biblical subjects was the deliverance of the children of Israel from slavery in Egypt. The book of Exodus provided more than its share of texts for sermons and images for songs. In one moving spiritual, God commands Moses to "tell Old Pharaoh" to "let my people

Go." In another, Mary is told she can stop weeping and begin to rejoice because "Pharaoh's army got drownded" trying to cross the Red Sea. Many sermons and songs referred to the crossing of Jordan and the arrival in the Promised Land. "Oh Canaan, sweet Canaan, I am bound for the land of Canaan" and "Oh brothers, don't get weary . . . . We'll land on Canaan's shore" are typical of lines from spirituals known to have been sung by slaves. Other songs invoked the liberation theme in different ways. One recalled that Jesus had "set poor sinners free," and another prophesied that "We'll soon be free, when the Lord will call us home."

Most of the songs of freedom and deliverance can be interpreted as referring exclusively to religious salvation and the afterlife—and this was undoubtedly how slaves hoped their masters would understand them. But the slaves did not forget that God had once freed a people from slavery in this life and punished their masters. The Bible thus gave African Americans the hope that they, as a people, would repeat the experience of the Israelites and be delivered from bondage. During the Civil War, observers noted that freed slaves seemed to regard their emancipation as something that had been preordained and were inclined to view Lincoln as the reincarnation of Moses.

Besides being the basis for a deep-rooted hope for eventual freedom, religion helped the slaves endure bondage without losing their sense of inner worth. Unless their masters were unusually pious, religious slaves could regard themselves as superior to their owners. Some slaves even believed all whites were damned because of their unjust treatment of blacks, while all slaves would be saved because any sins they committed were the involuntary result of their condition.

More important, "the invisible institution" of the church gave African Americans a chance to create and control a world of their own. Preachers, elders, and other leaders of slave congregations could acquire a sense of status within their own community that had not been conferred by whites; the singers who improvised the spirituals found an outlet for independent artistic expression. Although religion seldom inspired slaves to open rebellion, it must be regarded as a prime source of resistance to the dehumanizing effects of enslavement. It helped create a sense of community, solidarity, and self-esteem among slaves by giving them something of their own that they found infinitely precious.

The Slave Family

The African American family was the other institution that prevented slavery from becoming utterly demoralizing. Contrary to what historians and sociologists used to believe, the majority of slaves lived in two-parent households. Although slave marriages were not legally binding, many masters encouraged stable unions, and the slaves themselves apparently preferred monogamy to more casual or promiscuous relationships. Plantation registers reveal that many slave marriages lasted for as long as twenty or thirty years and were more often broken by death or sale than by voluntary dissolution of the union. The breakup of marriages and families by sale occurred frequently enough to introduce an element of desperation and instability into slave family relationships. Nevertheless, the black family ethic valued marital fidelity and a sense of responsibility for children, attitudes strongly influenced by Christian teachings. Relations between spouses and between parents and children were normally close and affectionate. Slave husbands and fathers did not, of course, have the same power and authority as free heads of families; they could not play the role of breadwinner or even protect their wives and children from harsh punishment or sexual abuse by masters or overseers. But they usually did what they could, and this included supplementing the family diet by hunting, fishing, or pilfering plantation stores. Husbands and wives tried to relieve each other's burdens; together they taught their children how to survive slavery and plantation life.

The terrible anguish that usually accompanied the breakup of families through sale showed the depth of kinship feelings. Masters knew the first place to look for a fugitive was in the neighborhood of a family member who had been sold away. After emancipation, thousands of freed slaves wandered about looking for spouses, children, or parents from whom they had been forcibly separated years before. The famous spiritual, "Sometime I feel like a motherless child," was far more than an expression of religious need; it also reflected the family anxieties and personal tragedies of many slaves.

John Antrobus, Plantation Burial, *ca. 1860. The painting depicts slaves gathering in a forest to bury a fellow slave. Many spirituals sung by the slaves on such occasions portrayed death as a welcome release from bondage and created an image of an afterlife where the trials and cares of this life were unknown.*

Feelings of kinship and mutual obligation extended beyond the nuclear family. Grandparents, uncles, aunts, and even cousins were often known to slaves through direct contact or family lore. A sense of family continuity over three or more generations was revealed in the names that slaves gave to their children or took for themselves. Infants were frequently named after grandparents, and those slaves who assumed surnames often chose that of an ancestor's owner rather than the family name of a current master.

Kinship ties were not limited to blood relations. When families were broken up by sale, individual members who found themselves on plantations far from home were likely to be "adopted" into new kinship networks. Orphans or children without responsible parents were quickly absorbed without prejudice into new families.

What becomes apparent from studies of the slave family is that kinship provided a model for personal relationships and the basis for a sense of community. For some purposes, all the slaves on a plantation were in reality members of a single extended family, as their forms of address clearly reveal. Elderly slaves were addressed by everyone else as "uncle" and "aunty," and younger unre-

An invoice of ten negroes sent this day to John B Williamson by Geo Kremer named & cost as follows —

To wit · Bitsey Kackley . . . . $ 410 . 00
Nancy Aulick . . . . . .515 . 00
Harry & Helen Miller . . . 1200 . 00
Mary Kootz . . . . . 600 . 00
Bitsey Ott? . . . . 560 . 00
Isaac & Fanny Brent . . . 992 . 00
Lucinda Luckett . . . . . 467 . 50
George Smith . . . . . . 510 . 00
Amount of my traveling expences & boarding 5 254 . 50
of lot No 9 not included in the other bills . 39 . 50
Kremers expences transporting lot N3 to Richd 51 . 00
Carryall hire . . 6 . 00
                            $ 5351 . 00

I have this day delivered the above named negroes costing including my expences and other expences five thousand three hundred & fifty dollars this May 26th 1835

                            John W. Pittman

I did intend to leave Nancy child but she made such a damned fuss I had to let her take it I could of got fifty Dollars for so you must add forty Dollars to the above

Some slave families managed to stay together, as shown by the footnote to this 1835 bill of sale: "I did intend to leave Nancy['s] child but she made such a damned fuss I had to let her take it. . . ."

lated slaves commonly called each other "brother" or "sister." Slave culture was a family culture, and this was one of its greatest sources of strength and cohesion. Strong kinship ties, whether real or fictive, meant slaves could depend on one another in times of trouble. The kinship network also provided a vehicle for the transmission of African American folk traditions from one generation to the next. Together with slave religion, kinship gave African Americans some sense they were members of a community, not just a collection of individuals victimized by oppression.

Some historians have argued that a stress on the strength of slave culture obscures the harshness and cruelty of the system and its damaging effect on the African American personality. Slavery was of course often a demoralizing and even brutalizing experience, and it provided little opportunity for learning about the world outside the plantation, developing mental skills, and exercising individual initiative. Compared with serfs in Russia or even with slaves on some of the large sugar plantations of the Caribbean, bondspeople on the relatively small southern plantations or farms with their high turnover of personnel had less chance to develop communal ties of the kind associated with peasant villages. Nevertheless, their sense of being part of a distinctive group with its own beliefs and ways of doing things, fragile and precarious though it may have been, made *psychic survival* possible and helped engender an African American ethnicity that would be a source of strength in future struggles. Although slave culture did not normally provoke violent resistance to the slaveholders' regime, the inner world that slaves made for themselves gave them the spiritual strength to thwart the masters' efforts to take over their hearts and minds. After emancipation, this resilient cultural heritage would combine with the tradition of open protest created by rebellious slaves and free black abolitionists to inspire and sustain new struggles for equality.

If slaves lived to some extent in a separate and distinctive world of their own, so did planters, less affluent whites, and even free blacks. The Old South was thus a deeply divided society. The northern traveler Frederick Law Olmsted, who made three journeys through the slave states in the 1850s, gives us a vivid sense of how diverse in outlook and circumstances southern people could be. Visiting a great plantation, he watched the slaves stop working as soon as the overseer turned away; on a small farm he saw a slave and his owner working in the fields together. Treatment of slaves, he found, ranged from humane paternalism to flagrant cruelty. Olmsted heard nonslaveholding whites damn the planters as "cotton snobs" but also talk about blacks as "niggars" and express fear of interracial marriages if slaves were freed. He received hospitality from poor whites living in crowded one-room cabins as well as from fabulously wealthy planters in pillared mansions and found life in the "backcountry" radically different than in the plantation belts. In short, he showed that the South was a kaleidoscope of groups divided by class, race, culture, and geography. What held it together and provided some measure of unity was a booming plantation economy and a web of customary relationships and loyalties that could obscure the underlying cleavages and antagonisms. The fractured and fragile nature of this society would soon become apparent when it was subjected to the pressures of civil war.

Recommended Reading

Major works that take a broad view of slavery are Kenneth M. Stampp, *The Peculiar Institution: Slavery in the Antebellum South* (1956), which stresses its coercive features; John W. Blassingame, *The Slave Community: Plantation Life in the Antebellum South* (1972), which focuses on slave culture and psychology; and Eugene D. Genovese, *Roll, Jordan, Roll: The World the Slaves Made* (1974), which probes the paternalistic character of the institution and the way in which slaves made a world for themselves within its bounds.

On the economics of slavery, see Gavin Wright, *The Political Economy of the Cotton South: Households, Markets, and Wealth in the Nineteenth Century* (1978). Clement Eaton, *The Growth of Southern Civilization, 1790–1860* (1961), provides a good introduction to life in the Old South. A more recent and insightful interpretation of antebellum southern society is James Oakes, *Slavery and Freedom* (1990). On the effect of slavery and the plantation on women, see Elizabeth Fox-Genovese, *Within the Plantation Household* (1988), and Deborah Gray White, *Ar'n't I a Woman: Female Slaves in the Plantation South* (1985).

Black resistance to slavery is described in Vincent Harding, *There Is a River: The Black Struggle for Freedom in America* (1981). Slave culture is examined in Albert J. Raboteau, *Slave Religion* (1978); Herbert G. Gutman, *The Black Family in Slavery and Freedom, 1750–1925* (1976); Lawrence W. Levine, *Black Culture and Consciousness: Afro-American Folk Thought from Slavery to Freedom* (1977); and Sterling Stuckey, *Slave Culture: Nationalist Theory and the Foundations of Black America* (1987).

Additional Bibliography

The classic account of southern agriculture is Lewis C. Gray, *History of Agriculture in the Southern United States to 1860*, 2 vols. (1941). On the economics of slavery, see Eugene D. Genovese, *The Political Economy of Slavery: Studies in the Economy and Society of the Slave South* (1965); Robert William Fogel and Stanley L. Engerman, *Time on the Cross: The Economics of American Negro Slavery*, 2 vols. (1974); and Paul A. David et al., *Reckoning with Slavery: A Critical Study of the Quantitative History of American Negro Slavery* (1976). Unsurpassed as a contemporary account of the economic and social aspects of slavery is Frederick L. Olmsted, *The Cotton Kingdom* (1962).

Nonagricultural slavery is examined in Robert S. Starobin, *Industrial Slavery in the Old South* (1970); Richard C. Wade, *Slavery in the Cities* (1964); and Claudia Dale Goldin, *Urban Slavery in the American South, 1820–1860: A Quantitative History* (1976).

On the slave trade, see Michael Tadman, *Speculators and Slaves* (1989). For comparisons with slavery elsewhere, see Frank Tannebaum, *Slave and*

Citizen: The Negro in the Americas (1946), Carl N. Degler, *Neither Black Nor White: Slavery and Race Relations in Brazil and the United States* (1971); George M. Fredrickson, *White Supremacy: A Comparative Study in American and South African History* (1981), Peter Kolchin, *Unfree Labor: American Slavery and Russian Serfdom* (1987); and Shearer Davis Bowman, *Masters and Lords: Mid-19th Century U.S. Planters and Prussian Junkers* (1993).

On the society and culture of the southern white population, see W. J. Cash, *The Mind of the South* (1941); Dickson D. Bruce, Jr., *Violence and Culture in the Antebellum South* (1979); Clement Eaton, *The Mind of the Old South* (1964); Drew Gilpin Faust, *A Sacred Circle: The Dilemma of the Intellectual in the Old South, 1840–1860* (1977); Bertram Wyatt-Brown, *Southern Honor: Ethics and Behavior in the Old South* (1982); John McCardell, *The Idea of a Southern Nation: Southern Nationalists and Southern Nationalism, 1830–1860* (1979); James Oakes, *The Ruling Race: A History of American Slaveholders* (1982); Steven M. Stowe, *Intimacy and Power: Ritual in the Lives of the Planters* (1987), and Kenneth S. Greenberg, *Masters and Statemen: The Political Culture of American Slavery* (1985). On the relation of white society and culture to political attitudes and behavior, see two excellent studies: J. Mills Thorton, *Politics and Power in a Slave Society: Alabama, 1800–1860* (1978); and Lacy K. Ford, *The Origins of Southern Radicalism: The South Carolina Upcountry, 1800–1860* (1988).

Proslavery consciousness is treated in William Sumner Jenkins, *Pro-Slavery Thought in the Old South* (1935); George M. Fredrickson, *The Black Image in the White Mind: The Debate on Afro-American Character and Destiny, 1817–1914* (1971); Eugene D. Genovese, *The World the Slaveholders Made: Two Essays in Interpretation* (1969); and H. Shelton Smith, *In His Image, But . . . : Racism in Southern Religion, 1780–1910* (1972). Southern dissent and efforts to repress it are well covered in Carl N. Degler, *The Other South: Southern Dissenters in the Nineteenth Century* (1974).

On slave revolts, see Herbert Aptheker, *American Negro Slave Revolts* (1943), and Eugene D. Genovese, *From Rebellion to Revolution: Afro-American Slave Revolts in the Making of the Modern World* (1979). The plight of southern free blacks is covered in Ira Berlin, *Slaves Without Masters: The Free Negro in the Antebellum South* (1974), and Michael P. Johnson and James L. Roark, *Black Masters: A Free Family of Color in the Old South* (1984), while racial discrimination in the North is described in Leon Litwack, *North of Slavery: The Free Negro in the Free States, 1790–1860* (1961). On the antislavery activities of northern blacks, see Benjamin Quarles, *Black Abolitionists* (1969); Jane H. Pease and William H. Pease, *They Who Would Be Free* (1974); William S. McFeely, *Frederick Douglass* (1991), and Shirley Yee, *Black Women Abolitionists* (1992). On life in the slave quarters, see George P. Rawick, *From Sundown to Sunup: The Making of the Black Community* (1972), and Thomas L. Webber, *Deep Like Rivers: Education in the Slave Quarters, 1831–1865* (1978). Further insight into the family life of both races in the Old South can be found in Orville Vernon Burton, *In My Father's House Are Many Mansions: Family and Community in Edgefield, South Carolina* (1983).

The Sectional Crisis

On May 22, 1856, Representative Preston Brooks of South Carolina erupted onto the floor of the Senate with a cane in his hand. He approached Charles Sumner, the antislavery senator from Massachusetts who had recently given a fiery oration condemning the South for plotting to extend slavery to the Kansas Territory. What was worse, the speech had included insulting references to Senator Andrew Butler of South Carolina, a kinsman of Brooks. When he found Sumner seated at his desk, Brooks proceeded to batter him over the head. Amazed and stunned, Sumner made a desperate effort to rise and ripped his bolted desk from the floor. He then collapsed under a continued torrent of blows.

Sumner was so badly injured by the assault that he did not return to the Senate for three years. But his home state reelected him in 1857 and kept his seat vacant as testimony against southern brutality and "barbarism." In parts of the North that were up in arms against the expansion of slavery, Sumner was hailed as a martyr to the cause of "free soil." Brooks, denounced in the North as a bully, was lionized by his fellow Southerners. When he resigned from the House after a vote of censure had narrowly failed because of solid southern opposition, his constituents reelected him unanimously.

These contrasting reactions show how bitter sectional antagonism had become by 1856. Sumner spoke for the radical wing of the new Republican party, which was making a bid for national power by mobilizing the North against the alleged aggressions of "the slave power." Southerners viewed the very existence of this party as an insult to their section of the country and a threat to its vital interests. Sumner came closer to being an abolitionist than any other member of Congress, and nothing created greater fear and anxiety among Southerners than their belief that antislavery forces were plotting against their way of life. To many Northerners, "bully Brooks" stood for all the arrogant and violent slaveholders who were allegedly conspiring to extend their barbaric labor system. By 1856, therefore, the sectional cleavage that would lead to the Civil War had already undermined the foundations of national unity.

The crisis of the mid-1850s came only a few years after the elaborate compromise of 1850 had seemingly resolved the dispute over the future of slavery in the territories acquired as a result of the Mexican War. The renewed agitation over the extension of slavery that led to Brooks's attack on Sumner was set in motion by the Kansas-Nebraska Act of 1854. This legislation revived the sectional conflict and led to the emergence of the Republican party. From that point on, a dramatic series of events increased sectional confrontation and destroyed the prospects for a new compromise. The caning of Charles Sumner was one of these events, and violence on the Senate floor foreshadowed violence on the battlefield.

THE COMPROMISE OF 1850

The "irrepressible conflict" over slavery in the territories began in the late 1840s. The positions taken on this issue between 1846 and 1850 established the range of options that would reemerge after 1854. But during this earlier phase of the sectional controversy, the leaders of two strong national parties, each with substantial followings in both the North and the South, had a vested interest in resolving the crisis. Efforts to create uncompromising sectional parties failed to disrupt what historians call the second party system—the vigorous competition between Whigs and Democrats that had characterized elections since the 1830s. Furthermore, the less tangible features of sectionalism—emotion and ideology—were not as divisive as they would later become. Hence a fragile compromise was achieved through a kind of give-and-take that would not be possible in the changed environment of the mid-1850s.

The Problem of Slavery in the Mexican Cession

As the price of union between states committed to slavery and those in the process of abolishing it, the Founders had attempted to limit the role of the slavery issue in national politics. The Constitution gave the federal government the right to abolish the international slave trade but no definite authority to regulate or destroy the institution where it existed under state law. Although many of the Founders hoped for the

eventual demise of slavery, they provided no direct means to achieve this end except voluntary state action. These ground rules limited the effect of northern attacks on the South's peculiar institution. It was easy to condemn slavery in principle but very difficult to develop a practical program to eliminate it without defying the Constitution.

Radical abolitionists saw this problem clearly and resolved it by rejecting the law of the land in favor of a "higher law" prohibiting human bondage. In 1844, William Lloyd Garrison publicly burned the Constitution, condemning it as "A Covenant with Death, an Agreement with Hell." But Garrison spoke for a small minority dedicated to freeing the North, at whatever cost, from the sin of condoning slavery.

During the 1840s, the majority of Northerners showed that while they disliked slavery, they also detested abolitionism. They were inclined to view slavery as a backward and unwholesome institution, much inferior to their own free labor system, and could be persuaded that slaveholders were power-hungry aristocrats seeking more than their share of national political influence. But they regarded the Constitution as a binding contract between slave and free states and were likely to be prejudiced against blacks and reluctant to accept large numbers of them as free citizens. Consequently, they saw no legal or desirable way to bring about emancipation within the southern states.

But the Constitution had not predetermined the status of slavery in *future* states. Since Congress had the power to admit new states to the Union under any conditions it wished to impose, a majority could arguably require the abolition of slavery as the price of admission. An effort to use this power had led to the Missouri crisis of 1819–1820 (see Chapter 9). The resulting compromise was designed to decide future cases by drawing a line between slave and free states and extending it westward through the unsettled portions of what was then American soil. When specific territories were settled, organized, and prepared for statehood, slavery would be permitted south of the line and prohibited north of it.

This tradition of providing both the free North and the slave South with opportunities for expansion and the creation of new states broke down when new territories were wrested from Mexico in the 1840s. When Texas was admitted as a slave state, northern expansionists could still look forward to the admission of Oregon as a counterbalancing free state. But the Mexican War raised the prospect that California and New Mexico, both south of the Missouri Compromise line, would also be acquired. Since it was generally assumed in the North that Congress had the power to prohibit slavery in new territories, a movement developed in Congress to do just that.

The Wilmot Proviso Launches the Free-Soil Movement

The "Free-Soil" crusade began in August 1846, only three months after the start of the Mexican

War, when Congressman David Wilmot, a Pennsylvania Democrat, proposed an amendment to the military appropriations bill that would ban slavery in any territory that might be acquired from Mexico.

Wilmot spoke for the large number of northern Democrats who felt neglected and betrayed by the party's choice of Polk over Van Buren in 1844 and by the "pro-southern" policies of the Polk administration. Pennsylvanians like Wilmot were upset because the tariff of 1846 reduced duties to a level unacceptable to the manufacturing interests of their state. Others, especially midwesterners, were annoyed that Polk had vetoed a bill to provide federal funds for the improvement of rivers and harbors. Democratic expansionists also felt betrayed because Polk had gone back on his pledge to obtain "all of Oregon" up to 54°40´ and then had proceeded to wage war to win all of Texas. This twist in the course of Manifest Destiny convinced them that the South and its interests were dominating the party and the administration. David Wilmot spoke for many when he wrote that he was "jealous of the power of the South."

These pioneer Free-Soilers had a genuine interest in the issue actually at hand—the question of who would control and settle the new territories. Combining an appeal to racial prejudice with opposition to slavery as an institution, Wilmot defined his cause as involving the "rights of white freemen" to go to areas where they could live "without the disgrace which association with negro slavery brings on white labor." Wilmot proposed that slavery as well as settlement by free African Americans be prohibited in the territory obtained in the Mexican cession, thus giving the common folk of the North a fair chance by preventing job competition from slaves and free blacks. By linking racism with resistance to the spread of slavery, Wilmot appealed to a broad spectrum of northern opinion.

Northern Whigs backed Wilmot's Proviso because they shared his concern about the outcome of an unregulated competition between slave and free labor in the territories. Furthermore, voting for the measure provided a good outlet for their frustration at being unable to halt the annexation of Texas and the Mexican War. The preferred position of some Whig leaders was no expansion at all, but when expansion could not be avoided the northern wing of the party endorsed the view that acquisition of Mexican territory should not be used to increase the power of the slave states.

In the first House vote on the Wilmot Proviso, party lines crumbled and were replaced by a sharp sectional cleavage. Every northern congressman with the exception of two Democrats voted for the amendment, and every Southerner except two Whigs went on record against it. After passing the House, the Proviso was blocked in the Senate by a combination of southern influence and Democratic loyalty to the administration. When the appropriation bill went back to the House without the Proviso, the administration's arm-twisting succeeded in changing enough northern Democratic votes to pass the bill and thus send the Proviso down to defeat.

Reactions to the Proviso on the state and local level provided further evidence of the polarizing effect of the territorial issue. Northern state legislatures, with one exception, endorsed the Proviso, while southern orators proclaimed that its passage would insult their section and violate the principle of equality among the states by denying slaveholding citizens access to federal territories.

The end of the Mexican War, the formal acquisition of New Mexico and California, and the approaching election of 1848 gave new urgency to a search for politically feasible solutions to the crisis. The extreme alternatives—the Proviso policy of free soil and the radical southern response that slavery could be extended to any territory—threatened to destroy the national parties because there was no bisectional support for either of them.

Squatter Sovereignty and the Election of 1848

After a futile attempt was made to extend the Missouri Compromise line to the Pacific—a proposal that was unacceptable to Northerners because most of the Mexican cession lay south of the line—a new approach was devised that appealed especially to Democrats. Its main proponent was Senator Lewis Cass of Michigan, an aspirant for the party's presidential nomination. Cass, who described his formula as "squatter sovereignty," would leave the determination of the status of slavery in a territory to the actual settlers. From the beginning this proposal contained an ambiguity that allowed it to be interpreted differently in the North and the South. For northern Democrats squatter sovereignty—or "popular sovereignty" as it was later called—meant the settlers could vote slavery up or down at the first meeting of a territorial legislature. For the southern wing of the party, it meant a decision would only be made at the time a convention drew up a constitution and applied for statehood. It was in the interest of national Democratic leaders to leave this ambiguity unresolved for as long as possible.

Congress failed to resolve the future of slavery in the Mexican cession in time for the election of 1848, and the issue entered the arena of presidential politics. The Democrats nominated Cass on a platform of squatter sovereignty. The Whigs evaded the question by running General Zachary Taylor—the hero of the battle of Buena Vista—without a platform. Taylor refused to commit himself on the status of slavery in the territories, but northern Whigs favoring restriction took heart from the general's promise not to veto any territorial legislation passed by Congress. Southern Whigs went along with Taylor mainly because he was a Southerner who owned slaves and would presumably defend the interests of his native region.

Northerners who strongly supported the Wilmot Proviso—and felt betrayed that neither the Whigs nor the Democrats were supporting it—were attracted by a third party movement. In August a tumultuous convention in Buffalo nominated former president Van Buren to carry the banner of the Free-Soil party. Support for the Free-Soilers came from antislavery Whigs dismayed by their party's nomination of a slaveholder and its evasiveness on the territorial issue, disgruntled Democrats who had backed the Proviso and resented southern influence in their party, and some of the former adherents of the abolitionist Liberty party. Van Buren himself was motivated less by antislavery zeal than by bitterness at being denied the Democratic nomination in 1844 because of southern obstructionism. The founding of the Free-Soil party was the first significant effort to create a broadly based sectional party addressing itself to voters' concerns about the extension of slavery.

After a noisy and confusing campaign, Taylor came out on top, winning a majority of the elec-

The Election of 1848			
Candidate	Party	Popular Vote	Electoral Vote
Taylor	Whig	1,360,967	163
Cass	Democratic	1,222,342	127
Van Buren	Free Soil	291,263	—

toral votes in both the North and the South and a total of 1,361,000 popular votes to 1,222,000 for Cass and 291,000 for Van Buren. The Free-Soilers failed to carry a single state but did quite well in the North, coming in second behind Taylor in New York, Massachusetts, and Vermont.

Taylor Takes Charge

Once in office, Taylor devised a bold plan to decide the fate of slavery in the Mexican cession. A brusque military man who disdained political give-and-take, he tried to engineer the immediate admission of California and New Mexico to the Union as states, thus bypassing the territorial stage entirely and avoiding a congressional debate on the status of slavery in the federal domain. Under the administration's urging, California, which was filling up rapidly with settlers drawn by the lust for gold, convened a constitutional convention and applied for admission to the Union as a free state.

Instead of resolving the crisis, President Taylor's initiative only worsened it. Once it was clear that California was going to be a free state, the administration's plan aroused intense opposition in the South. Fearing that New Mexico would also be free because Mexican law had prohibited slavery there, Southerners of both parties accused the president of trying to impose the Wilmot Proviso in a new form. The prospect that only free states would emerge from the entire Mexican cession inspired serious talk of secession.

In Congress, Senator John C. Calhoun of South Carolina saw a chance to achieve his longstanding goal of creating a southern voting bloc that would cut across regular party lines. State legislatures and conventions throughout the South denounced

In this cartoon, Democrats Lewis Cass and John C. Calhoun and antislavery radicals Horace Greeley, William Lloyd Garrison, and Abby Folsom look on as Martin Van Buren, the Free-Soil party candidate in the election of 1848, attempts to bridge the chasm between the Democratic platform and that of the antislavery Whigs. The Free-Soil influence was decisive in the election; it split the New York Democratic vote, thus allowing Whig candidate Zachary Taylor to win New York and the presidency.

"northern aggression" against the rights of the slave states. As signs of southern fury increased, Calhoun rejoiced that the South had never been so "united . . . bold, and decided." In the fall and winter of 1849–1850 several southern states agreed to participate in a convention, to be held in Nashville in June, where grievances could be aired and demands made. For an increasing number of southern political leaders the survival of the Union would depend on the North's response to the demands of the southern rights movement.

Forging a Compromise

When it became clear that the president would not abandon or modify his plan in order to appease the South, independent efforts began in Congress to arrange a compromise. Hoping that he could again play the role of "great pacificator" as he had in the Missouri Compromise of 1820, Senator Henry Clay of Kentucky offered a series of resolutions meant to restore sectional harmony. He hoped to reduce tension by providing mutual concessions on a range of divisive issues. On the critical territorial question, his solution was to admit California as a free state and organize the rest of the Mexican cession with no explicit prohibition of slavery—in other words, without the Wilmot Proviso. Noting that Mexican law had already abolished slavery there, he also pointed to the arid climate of the New Mexico region, which made it unsuitable for cotton culture and slavery. He also sought to resolve

a major boundary dispute between New Mexico and Texas by granting the disputed region to New Mexico while compensating Texas through federal assumption of its state debt. As a concession to the North on another issue—the existence of slavery in the District of Columbia—he recommended prohibiting the buying and selling of slaves at auction and permitting the abolition of slavery itself with the consent of the District's white inhabitants. He also called for a more effective fugitive slave law.

The compromise plan, which was proposed in February 1850, took several months to get through Congress. One obstacle was President Taylor's firm resistance to the proposal; another was the difficulty of getting congressmen to vote for it in the form of a single package or "omnibus bill." Few politicians from either section were willing to go on record as supporting the key concessions to the *other* section. The logjam was broken in July by two crucial developments: President Taylor died and was succeeded by Millard Fillmore, who favored the compromise; and a decision was made to abandon the omnibus strategy in favor of a series of measures that could be voted on separately. After the breakup of the omnibus bill, Democrats replaced the original Whig sponsors as leaders of the compromise movement and some of Clay's proposals were modified to make them more acceptable to the South and the Democrats. Senator Stephen A. Douglas, a Democrat from Illinois, was particularly influential in maneuvering the separate provisions of the plan through Congress.

As the price of Democratic support, the popular sovereignty principle was included in the bills organizing New Mexico and Utah. Territorial legislatures in the Mexican cession were explicitly granted power over "all rightful subjects of legislation," which might include slavery. Half of the compensation to Texas for giving up its claims to New Mexico was paid directly to holders of Texas bonds, a decision that reflected intense lobbying by interested parties.

Abolition of slave auctions and depots in the District of Columbia and a new fugitive slave law were also enacted. The latter was a particularly outrageous piece of legislation. As the result of southern pressures and amendments, suspected fugitives were now denied a jury trial, the right to testify in their own behalf, and other basic constitutional rights. As a result, there were no effective safeguards against false identification by accusers or against the kidnapping of blacks who were legally free.

The compromise passed because its key measures were supported by northern Democrats, southern Whigs, and representatives of both parties from the border states. No single bill was backed by a majority of the congressmen from both sections, and few senators or representatives actually voted for the entire package. Many northern Whigs and southern Democrats thought the end result conceded too much to the other section. Doubts therefore persisted over the value of workability of a "compromise" that was really more like an armistice or a cease-fire.

Yet the Compromise of 1850 did serve for a short time as a basis for sectional peace. In southern state elections during 1850–1851 moderate coalitions won out over the radicals who viewed the compromise as a sellout to the North. But this emerging "unionism" was conditional. Southerners demanded strict northern adherence to the compromise, especially to the Fugitive Slave Law, as the price for suppressing threats of secession. In the North, the compromise was backed by virtually the entire Democratic party and by one faction of the Whigs.

The Fugitive Slave Law was unpopular in areas where abolitionism was particularly strong because it required Northerners to enforce slavery, and there were a few sensational rescues or attempted rescues of escaped slaves. In Boston in 1854, an antislavery mob led by armed abolition-ists tried to free fugitive Anthony Burns from the courthouse where his extradition hearing was to take place. One of the men guarding Burns was killed but the fugitive himself could not be reached. After the hearing had declared Burns an escaped slave, he was escorted by units of the U. S. Army through a hissing and groaning crowd of twenty thousand to a waiting ship. Despite such abolitionist resistance, the Fugitive Slave Law was enforced fairly successfully in the early 1850s. Other parts of the compromise were less troublesome. In 1852, when the Democrats endorsed the compromise in their platform and the Whigs failed to condemn it in theirs, it seemed that sharp differences on the slavery issue had once again been banished from national politics.

POLITICAL UPHEAVAL, 1852–1856

The second party system—Democrats versus Whigs—survived the crisis over slavery in the Mexican cession, but in the long run the Compromise of 1850 may have weakened it. Although both national parties had been careful during the 1840s not to take stands on the slavery issue that would alienate their supporters in either section of the country, they had in fact offered voters alternative ways of dealing with the question. Democrats had endorsed headlong territorial expansion with the promise of a fair division of the spoils between slave and free states. Whigs had generally opposed annexations or acquisitions, because they were likely to bring the slavery question to the fore and threaten sectional harmony. With some shifts of emphasis and interpretation, each strategy could be presented to southern voters as a good way to protect slavery and to Northerners as a good way to contain it.

The consensus of 1852 meant the parties had to find other issues on which to base their distinctive appeals. Their failure to do so encouraged voter apathy and a disenchantment with the major parties. When the Democrats sought to revive the Manifest Destiny issue in 1854, they reopened the explosive issue of slavery in the territories. By this time, the Whigs were too weak and divided to respond with a policy of their own, and a purely sectional Free-Soil party—the Republicans—gained prominence. The collapse of the second party system released sectional agitation from the earlier constraints imposed by the competition of strong national parties.

The Compromise of 1850

The Kansas–Nebraska Act of 1854 repudiated the compromise that had been agreed upon in 1820. One tragic result was the fighting that erupted in "Bleeding" Kansas.

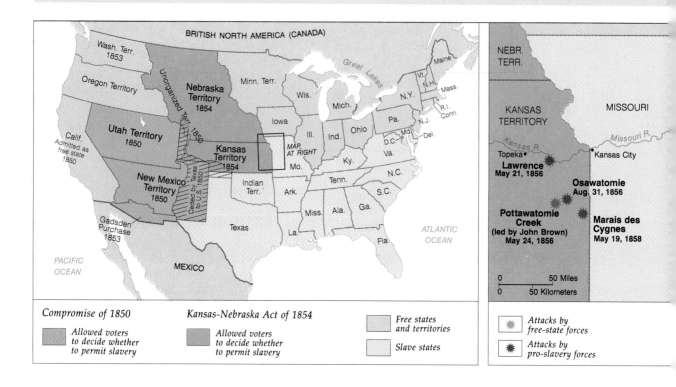

Compromise of 1850
Allowed voters to decide whether to permit slavery

Kansas-Nebraska Act of 1854
Allowed voters to decide whether to permit slavery

Free states and territories

Slave states

Attacks by free-state forces

Attacks by pro-slavery forces

The Party System in Crisis

The presidential campaign of 1852 was singularly devoid of major issues. With the slavery question under wraps, some Whigs tried to revive interest in the nationalistic economic policies that were the traditional hallmarks of their party. But convincing arguments in favor of a protective tariff, a national bank, and internal improvements were hard to make in a period of sustained prosperity. Business was thriving under the Democratic program of virtual laissez-faire.

Another tempting issue was immigration. Many Whigs were upset by the massive influx from Europe, partly because most of the new arrivals were Catholics, and the Whig following was largely evangelical Protestant. For office-seeking Whig politicians a more urgent problem was the fact that immigrants voted overwhelmingly for their Democratic opponents. The Whig leadership was divided on whether to compete with the Democrats for the immigrant vote or respond to the prejudices of the party rank and file by calling for restrictions on immigrant voting rights.

The Whigs nominated General Winfield Scott of Mexican War fame who supported the faction that resisted nativism and sought to broaden the appeal of the party. The fact that Scott's daughters were being raised as Catholics was publicized to demonstrate his good intentions toward immigrant communities. This strategy backfired and contributed to disaster at the polls. For the most part, Catholic immigrants retained their Democratic allegiance, and some nativist Whigs apparently sat out the election to protest their party's disregard of their cultural prejudices.

But the main cause for Scott's crushing defeat was the support he lost in the South when he allied himself with the dominant northern antislavery wing of the party, led by Senator William Seward of New York. The Democratic candidate, Franklin Pierce of New Hampshire, was a color-

CAUTION!!

COLORED PEOPLE

OF BOSTON, ONE & ALL,

You are hereby respectfully CAUTIONED and advised, to avoid conversing with the

Watchmen and Police Officers of Boston,

For since the recent ORDER OF THE MAYOR & ALDERMEN, they are empowered to act as

KIDNAPPERS

AND

Slave Catchers,

And they have already been actually employed in KIDNAPPING, CATCHING, AND KEEPING SLAVES. Therefore, if you value your LIBERTY, and the *Welfare of the Fugitives* among you, *Shun* them in every possible manner, as so many *HOUNDS* on the track of the most unfortunate of your race.

Keep a Sharp Look Out for KIDNAPPERS, and have TOP EYE open.

APRIL 24, 1851.

THEODORE PARKER'S PLACARD

Placard written by Theodore Parker and printed and posted by the Vigilance Committee of Boston after the rendition of Thomas Sims to slavery in April, 1851.

This abolitionist broadside was printed in response to a ruling that fugitive slave Thomas Sims must be returned to his master in Georgia.

The Election of 1852

Candidate	Party	Popular Vote	Electoral Vote
Pierce	Democratic	1,601,117	254
Scott	Whig	1,385,453	42
Hale	Free Soil	155,825	

less nonentity compared to his rival, but he ran up huge majorities in the Deep South where Whigs stayed home in massive numbers. He also edged out Scott in most of the free states. In the most one-sided election since 1820, Pierce received 254 electoral votes from 27 states while Scott carried only 4 states with 42 electoral votes. This outcome revealed the Whig party was in deep trouble because it lacked a program that would distinguish it from the Democrats and would appeal to voters in both sections of the country.

Despite their overwhelming victory in 1852, the Democrats had reasons for anxiety about the loyalty of their supporters. Because the major parties had ceased to offer clear-cut alternatives to the electorate, voter apathy or alienation was a growing trend in the early 1850s. The Democrats won majorities in both North and South in 1852 primarily because the public viewed them as the most reliable supporters of the Compromise of 1850, not because of long-term party allegiance.

The Kansas-Nebraska Act Raises a Storm

In January 1854, Senator Stephen A. Douglas proposed a bill to organize the territory west of Missouri and Iowa. Since this region fell within the area where slavery had been banned by the Missouri Compromise, Douglas anticipated objections from Southerners concerned about the creation of more free states. To head off this opposition and keep the Democratic party united, Douglas disregarded the compromise line and sought to set up the territorial government in Kansas and Nebraska on the basis of popular sovereignty, relying on the alleged precedent set in the Compromise of 1850.

Douglas wanted to organize the Kansas-Nebraska area quickly because he was a strong supporter of the expansion of settlement and commerce. Along with other midwestern promoters of the economic development of the frontier, he hoped a railroad would soon be built to the Pacific with Chicago (or another midwestern city) as its eastern terminus. A long controversy over the status of slavery there would slow down the process of organization and settlement and might hinder the building of the railroad through the territory in question. As a leader of the Democratic party, Douglas also hoped his Kansas-Nebraska bill would revive the spirit of Manifest Destiny that had given the party cohesion and electoral success in the mid-1840s (see Chapter 12). As the main spokesman for a new expansionism, he expected to win the Democratic nomination and the presidency.

The price of southern support, Douglas soon discovered, was the addition of an amendment explicitly repealing the Missouri Compromise. Although he realized this would "raise a hell of a storm," he reluctantly agreed. In this more provocative form, the bill made its way through Congress, passing the Senate by a large margin and the House by a narrow one. The vote in the House showed that Douglas had split his party rather than uniting it; exactly half of the northern Democrats voted against the legislation.

The Democrats who broke ranks created the storm Douglas had predicted but underestimated. A manifesto of "independent Democrats" denounced the bill as "a gross violation of a sacred pledge." A memorial from three thousand New England ministers described it as a craven and sinful surrender to the slave power. For many Northerners, probably a majority, the Kansas-Nebraska Act was an abomination because it permitted the possibility of slavery in an area where it had previously been prohibited. Except for an aggressive minority, Southerners had not pushed for such legislation or even shown much interest in it, but now they felt obligated to support it. Their support provided deadly ammunition to those who were seeking to convince the northern public that there was a conspiracy to extend slavery.

Douglas's bill had a catastrophic effect on sectional harmony. It repudiated a compromise that many in the North regarded as a binding sectional compact, almost as sacred and necessary to the survival of the Union as the Constitution itself. In defiance of the whole compromise tradition, it made a concession to the South on the issue of slavery extension without providing an equivalent concession to the North. It also shattered the fragile sectional accommodation of 1850 and made future compromises less likely. From now on, northern sectionalists would be fighting to regain what they had lost, while Southerners would battle to maintain rights already conceded.

The act also destroyed what was left of the second party system. The already weakened and tottering Whig party totally disintegrated when its congressional representation split cleanly along sectional lines on the Kansas-Nebraska issue. The Democratic party survived, but its ability to act as a unifying national force was seriously impaired. Northern desertions and southern gains (resulting from the recruitment of proslavery Whigs) combined to destroy the sectional balance within the party and place it under firm southern control.

The congressional elections of 1854 revealed the political chaos Douglas had created. In the North, "anti-Nebraska" coalitions of Whigs, dissident Democrats, and Free-Soilers swept regular Democrats out of office. Most congressmen who had voted for the act were decisively defeated, and sixty-six of the ninety-one House seats held by northern Democrats were lost to opponents running under various labels. In some states, these anti-Democratic coalitions would evolve directly into a new and stronger Free-Soil party— the Republicans. In the Deep South, however, the Democrats routed the remaining Whigs and came close to ending two-party competition on the state level.

The furor over Kansas-Nebraska also doomed the efforts of the Pierce administration to revive an expansionist foreign policy. Pierce and Secretary of State William Marcy were committed to acquiring Cuba from Spain. In October 1854, the American ministers to England, France, and Spain met in Ostend, Belgium, and drew up a memorandum for the administration urging acquisition of Cuba by any means necessary—including force, if Spain refused to sell the island. The "Ostend Manifesto" became public in the midst of the controversy resulting from the Kansas-Nebraska Act, and those Northerners who were convinced that the administration was trying to extend slavery to the Great Plains were enraged to discover it was also scheming to fulfill the southern expansionist dream of a "Caribbean slave empire." The resulting storm of protest forced Pierce and his cohorts to abandon their scheme.

An Appeal to Nativism: The Know-Nothing Episode

The collapse of the Whigs created the opening for a new political party. The anti-Nebraska coalitions of 1854 suggested that such a party might be organized on the basis of northern opposition to the extension of slavery to the territories. Before such a prospect could be realized, however, an alternative emerged in the form of a major political movement based on hostility to immi-

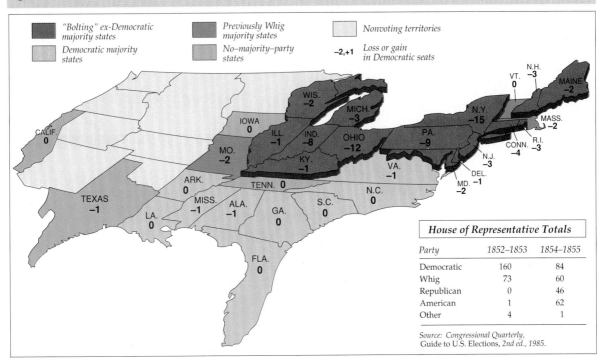

Congressional Election of 1854

The impact of the Kansas–Nebraska Act was immediately felt in the election of 1854. "Anti-Nebraska" coalitions and the fledgling Republican party made gains in the North; the Democrats remained dominant in the South.

Legend	
"Bolting" ex-Democratic majority states	
Democratic majority states	
Previously Whig majority states	
No–majority–party states	
Nonvoting territories	
-2,+1 Loss or gain in Democratic seats	

State seat changes: N.H. -3, VT. 0, MAINE -2, WIS. -2, MICH. -3, IOWA 0, N.Y. -15, MASS. -2, ILL. -1, IND. -8, OHIO -12, PA. -9, R.I. -3, CONN. -4, CALIF. 0, MO. -2, KY. -1, N.J. -3, VA. -1, DEL. -1, ARK. 0, TENN. 0, N.C. 0, MD. -2, TEXAS -1, MISS. -1, ALA. -1, GA. 0, S.C. 0, LA. 0, FLA. 0

House of Representative Totals

Party	1852–1853	1854–1855
Democratic	160	84
Whig	73	60
Republican	0	46
American	1	62
Other	4	1

Source: *Congressional Quarterly, Guide to U.S. Elections,* 2nd ed., 1985.

grants. For a time, it appeared that the Whigs would be replaced by a nativist party rather than an antislavery one.

Massive immigration of Irish and Germans (see Chapter 12), most of whom were Catholic, led to increasing tension between ethnic groups during the 1840s and early 1850s. The fact that most of these new arrivals clustered in their own separate communities or neighborhoods helped arouse the suspicion and distrust of older-stock Americans. Native-born and even immigrant Protestants viewed the newcomers as bearers of an alien culture. Their fears were demonstrated in bloody anti-Catholic riots, church and convent burnings, and in a barrage of propaganda and lurid literature trumpeting the menace of "popery" to the American way of life. Nativist agitators charged that immigrants were agents of a foreign despotism, based in Rome, that was bent on overthrowing the American republic.

Political nativism first emerged during the 1840s in the form of local "American" parties protesting immigrant influence in cities like New York and Philadelphia. In 1849, a secret fraternal organization, the Order of the Star-Spangled Banner, was founded in New York as a vehicle for anti-immigrant attitudes. When members were asked about the organization, they were instructed to reply, "I know nothing." The order grew rapidly in size, and in 1854 it had a membership of somewhere between 800,000 and 1,500,000. The political objective of the Know-Nothings was to extend the period of naturalization in order to undercut immigrant voting strength and to keep aliens in their place.

From 1854 to 1855 the movement surfaced as a major political force, calling itself the American party. Much of its backing came from Whigs looking for a new home, but the party also attracted some ex-Democrats. Know-Nothingism also appealed to native-born workers fearful of competition from low-paid immigrants. Many others supported the American party simply because it was an alternative for those who wanted to vote against the Democrats. In the North, Know-Nothing candidates generally opposed the

Know-Nothings often charged that immigrant voters were stealing American elections. In the cartoon above, German and Irish immigrants, represented by German beer and Irish whiskey, steal a ballot box. An anti-Know-Nothing cartoon (left) portrays the Know-Nothings as gun-wielding ruffians.

Kansas-Nebraska Act, and some of their support came from voters who were more anxious about the expansion of slavery than about the evils of immigration.

The success of the new party was so dramatic that it was compared to a hurricane. In 1854, it won complete control in Massachusetts, capturing the governorship, most of the seats in the legislature, and the entire congressional delegation. In 1855, the Know-Nothings took power in three more New England states, swept Maryland, Kentucky, and Texas, and emerged as the principal opposition to the Democrats everywhere else, except in the Midwest. By late 1855, the Know-Nothings showed every sign of displacing the Whigs as the nation's second party.

Yet, almost as rapidly as it had risen, the Know-Nothing movement collapsed. Its demise in 1856 is one of the great mysteries of American political history. As an intersectional party, its failure is understandable enough. When the Know-Nothings attempted to hold a national convention in 1856, northern and southern delegates split on the question of slavery in the territories, showing that former Whigs were still at

odds over the same issue that had destroyed their old party.

Less clear is why the Know-Nothings failed to become the major opposition party to the Democrats in the North. The most persuasive explanation is that their Free-Soil Republican rivals, who were seeking to build a party committed to the containment of slavery, had an issue with wider appeal. In 1855 and 1856, the rate of immigration declined noticeably, and the conflict in Kansas heightened the concern about slavery. Consequently, voters who opposed both the expansion of slavery and unrestricted immigration were inclined to give priority to the former threat.

But the movement's peculiar "antipolitical" character also contributed to its rapid disintegration. Besides being a manifestation of real ethnic tensions, Know-Nothingism was a grass-roots protest against the professional politicians who had led the Whig and Democratic parties. Concern about the effects of immigration on American culture and society would not have generated a mass political movement with the initial appeal of the Know-Nothings had it not been for the belief that political bosses were recruiting immigrant voters for their own corrupt purposes. As a result of the Know-Nothing party's distrust of conventional politics, most of its spokesmen and elected officials were neither professional politicians nor established community leaders. The very inexperience that was a major source of voter attraction to the party may have made it hard for it to develop organizational discipline. With inexperienced leaders and a lack of cohesion, the Know-Nothings were unable to make effective use of power once they had it. When voters discovered the Know-Nothings also *did* nothing, or at least failed to do anything that a more conventional party could not do better, they looked for more competent and experienced leadership.

Kansas and the Rise of the Republicans

The new Republican party was an outgrowth of the anti-Nebraska coalition of 1854. The Republican name was first used in midwestern states like Wisconsin and Michigan where Know-Nothingism failed to win a mass following. A new political label was required because Free-Soil Democrats—who were an especially important element in the midwestern coalitions—refused to march under the Whig banner or even support any candidate for high office who called himself a Whig.

When the Know-Nothing party split over the Kansas-Nebraska issue in 1856, most of the northern nativists went over to the Republicans. The Republican argument that "the slave power conspiracy" was a greater threat to American liberty and equality than an alleged "popish plot" proved to be persuasive. But nativists did not have to abandon their ethnic and religious prejudices to become Republicans. Although Republican leaders generally avoided taking anti-immigrant positions—some out of strong principle and others with an eye to the votes of the foreign born—the party showed a clear commitment to the values of native-born evangelical Protestants. On the local level Republicans generally supported causes that reflected an anti-immigrant or anti-Catholic bias—such as prohibition of the sale of alcoholic beverages, observance of the Sabbath, defense of Protestant Bible-reading in schools, and opposition to state aid for parochial education.

Unlike the Know-Nothings, the Republican party was led by seasoned professional politicians, men who had earlier been prominent Whigs or Democrats. Adept at organizing the grass roots, building durable coalitions, and employing all the techniques of popular campaigning, they built up an effective party apparatus in an amazingly short time. By late 1855, the party had won the adherence of two-thirds of the anti-Nebraska congressmen elected in 1854. One of these, Nathaniel Banks of Massachusetts, was elected Speaker of the House after a lengthy struggle. By early 1856, the new party was well established throughout the North and was preparing to make a serious bid for the presidency.

Underlying the rapid growth of the Republican party was the strong and growing appeal of its position on slavery in the territories. Republicans viewed the unsettled West as a land of opportunities, a place to which the ambitious and hardworking could migrate in the hope of improving their social and economic position. Free soil would serve as a guarantee of free competition or "the right to rise." But if slavery was permitted to expand, the rights of "free labor" would be denied. Slaveholders would monopolize the best land, use their slaves to compete unfairly with free white workers, and block efforts at commercial and industrial development. They could also use their political control of new western states to dominate the federal government in the interest of the "slave power." Some Republicans also pandered to race prejudice: they presented their policy as a way to keep African Americans out of the territories, thus preserving the new lands for exclusive white occupancy.

Although passage of the Kansas-Nebraska Act raised the territorial issue and gave birth to the Republican party, it was the turmoil associated with attempts to implement popular sovereignty in Kansas that kept the issue alive and enabled the Republicans to increase their following throughout the North. When Kansas was organized in the fall of 1854, a bitter contest began for control of the territorial government. New Englanders founded an Immigrant Aid Society to encourage antislavery settlement in Kansas, but the earliest arrivals came from slaveholding Missouri. In the first territorial elections, proslavery settlers were joined at the polls by thousands

FREE STATE CONVENTION!

All persons who are favorable to a union of effort, and a permanent organization of all the Free State elements of Kansas Territory, and who wish to secure upon the broadest platform the co-operation of all who agree upon this point, are requested to meet at several places of holding elections, in their respective districts on the 25th of August, instant, at one o'clock, P. M, and appoint five delegates to each representative to which they were entitled in the Legislature Assembly, who shall meet in general Convention at

Big Springs, Wednesday, Sept. 5th '55,

at 10 o'clock A. M., for the purpose of adopting a Platform upon which all may act harmoniously who prefer Freedom to Slavery.

The nomination of a Delegate to Congress, will also come up before the General Convention.

Let no sectional or party issue distract or prevent the perfect co-operation of Free State men. Union and harmony are absolutely necessary to success. The pro-slavery party are fully and effectually organized. No party nor minor issue divide them. And to contend against them successfully, we also must be united—Without prudence and harmony of action we are certain to fail. Let every man then do his duty and we are certain of victory.

All Free State men, without distinction, are earnestly requested to take immediate and effective steps to insure a full and correct representation for every District in the Territory. "Union we stand; divided we fall."

By order of the Executive Committee of the Free State Party of the Territory of Kansas, as per resolution of the Mass Convention in session at Lawrence.

Aug 13th and 14th, 1855.

J. K. GOODIN, Sec'y.   C. ROBINSON, Chairman.

Herald of Freedom, Print.

Free-Soil settlers in Kansas, outraged by the manner in which the proslavery forces had seized control of the territorial legislature, called for a new state convention to draw up a constitution outlawing slavery.

of Missouri residents who crossed the border to vote illegally. The result was a decisive victory for the slave-state forces. The legislature then proceeded to pass laws that not only legalized slavery but made it a crime to speak or act against it.

Settlers favoring free soil, most of whom came from the Midwest, were already a majority of the actual residents of the territory when the fraudulently elected legislature stripped them of their civil liberties. To defend themselves and their convictions, they took up arms and established a rival territorial government under a constitution that outlawed slavery. The Pierce administration and its appointed local agents refused to recognize this "free-state" initiative, but Republicans in Congress defended it.

A small-scale civil war then broke out between the rival regimes, culminating in May 1856 when proslavery adherents raided the free-state capital at Lawrence. Portrayed in Republican propaganda as "the sack of Lawrence," this incursion resulted in substantial property damage but no loss of life. More bloody was the reprisal carried out by the antislavery zealot John Brown. Upon hearing of the attack on Lawrence, Brown and a few followers murdered five proslavery settlers in cold blood. During the next few months—until a truce was arranged by an effective territorial governor in the fall of 1856—a hit-and-run guerrilla war raged between free-state and slave-state factions. (See the map of "Bleeding Kansas" on p. 408.)

The national Republican press had a field day with the events in Kansas, exaggerating the extent of the violence but correctly pointing out that the federal government was favoring rule by a proslavery minority over a Free-Soil majority. Since the "sack of Lawrence" occurred at about the same time that Charles Sumner was assaulted on the Senate floor, the Republicans launched their 1856 campaign under the twin slogans, "Bleeding Kansas and Bleeding Sumner." The image of an evil and aggressive "slave power," using violence to deny constitutional rights to its opponents, was a potent device for arousing northern sympathies and winning votes.

Sectional Division in the Election of 1856

The Republican nominating convention revealed the strictly sectional nature of the new party. Only a handful of the delegates from the slave states attended, and all of these were from the upper South. The platform called for liberation of Kansas from the slave power and congressional prohibition of slavery in all territories. The nominee was John C. Frémont, explorer of the West and participant in the conquest of California during the Mexican War.

The Democratic convention dumped the ineffectual Pierce, passed over Stephen A. Douglas, and nominated James Buchanan of Pennsylvania who had a long career in public service. The Democrats' platform endorsed popular sovereignty in the territories. The American party, a Know-Nothing remnant that survived mainly as the rallying point for anti-Democratic conservatives in the border states and parts of the South, chose ex-President Millard Fillmore as its standard-bearer and received the backing of those northern Whigs who resisted the Republicans and hoped to revive the tradition of sectional compromise.

The election was really two separate races—one in the North, where the main contest was between Frémont and Buchanan, and the other in the South, which pitted Fillmore against Buchanan. The Pennsylvania Democrat emerged victorious because he outpolled Fillmore in all but one of the slave states (Maryland) and edged out Frémont in four crucial northern states—Pennsylvania, New Jersey, Indiana, and Illinois. But the Republicans did remarkably well for a party that was scarcely more than a year old. Frémont won eleven of the sixteen free states,

The Election of 1856			
Candidate	Party	Popular Vote	Electoral Vote
Buchanan	Democratic	1,832,955	174
Frémont	Republican	1,339,932	114
Fillmore	American (Know-Nothing)	871,731	8

sweeping the upper North with substantial majorities and winning a larger proportion of the northern popular vote than either of his opponents. Since the free states had a substantial majority in the electoral college, a future Republican candidate could win the presidency simply by overcoming a slim Democratic edge in the lower North.

In the South, where the possibility of a Frémont victory had revived talk of secession, the results of the election brought a momentary sense of relief tinged with deep anxiety about the future. The very existence of a sectional party committed to restricting the expansion of slavery constituted an insult to the Southerners' way of life. That such a party was genuinely popular in the North was profoundly alarming and raised grave doubts about the security of slavery within the Union. The continued success of a unified Democratic party under southern control was widely viewed as the last hope for the maintenance of sectional balance and "southern rights."

THE HOUSE DIVIDED, 1857–1860

The sectional quarrel deepened and became virtually "irreconcilable" in the years between the election of Buchanan in 1856 and Lincoln's victory in 1860. A series of incidents provoked one side or the other, heightened the tension, and ultimately brought the crisis to a head. Behind the panicky reaction to public events lay a growing sense that the North and South were so different in culture and so opposed in basic interests that they could no longer coexist in the same nation.

Cultural Sectionalism

Signs of cultural and intellectual cleavage had appeared well before the triumph of sectional politics. In the mid-1840s, the Methodist and Baptist churches split into northern and southern denominations because of differing attitudes toward slaveholding. Presbyterians remained formally united, but had informal northern and southern factions that went their separate ways on the slavery issue. Instead of unifying Americans around a common Protestant faith, the churches became nurseries of sectional discord. Increasingly, northern preachers and congregations denounced slaveholding as a sin, while most southern church leaders rallied to a biblical defense of the peculiar institution and became influential apologists for the southern way of life. Prominent religious leaders—such as Henry Ward Bseecher, George B. Cheever, and Theodore Parker in the North, and James H. Thornwell, Leonidas Polk, and Bishop Stephen Elliott in the South, were in the forefront of sectional mobilization. As men of God, they helped to turn political questions into moral issues and reduced the prospects for a compromise.

American literature also became sectionalized during the 1840s and 1850s. Southern men of letters, including such notable figures as the novelist William Gilmore Simms and Edgar Allan Poe, wrote proslavery polemics. Popular novelists produced a flood of "plantation romances" that seemed to glorify southern civilization and sneer at that of the North. The notion that planter "cavaliers" were superior to money-grubbing Yankees was the message that most Southerners derived from the homegrown literature they read. In the North, prominent men of letters—Emerson, Thoreau, James Russell Lowell, and Herman Melville—expressed strong antislavery sentiments in prose and poetry, particularly after the outbreak of the Mexican War.

Literary abolitionism reached a climax in 1852 when Harriet Beecher Stowe published *Uncle Tom's Cabin,* an enormously successful novel (it sold more than 300,000 copies in a single year) that fixed in the northern mind the image of the slaveholder as a brutal Simon Legree. Much of its emotional impact came from the book's portrayal of slavery as a threat to the family and the cult of domesticity. When the saintly Uncle Tom was sold away from his adoring wife and children,

The Webb family, pictured here, toured the northern states giving dramatic readings from Uncle Tom's Cabin.

Northerners shuddered with horror and some Southerners felt a painful twinge of conscience.

Southern defensiveness gradually hardened into cultural and economic nationalism. Northern textbooks were banished from southern schools in favor of those with a prosouthern slant; young men of the planter class were induced to stay in the South for higher education rather than going North (as had been the custom); and a movement developed to encourage southern industry and commerce as a way of reducing dependence on the North. Almost without exception, prominent southern educators and intellectuals of the late 1850s rallied behind southern sectionalism, and many even endorsed the idea of a southern nation.

The Dred Scott Case

When James Buchanan was inaugurated on March 4, 1857, the dispute over the legal status of slavery in the territories was an open door through which sectional fears and hatreds could enter the political arena. Buchanan hoped to close that door by encouraging the Supreme Court to resolve the constitutional issue once and for all.

The Court was then about to render its decision in the case of *Dred Scott* v. *Sandford*. The plaintiff in this case was a Missouri slave whose owner had taken him to the Wisconsin Territory for a time during the 1830s. After his master's death, Dred Scott sued for his freedom on the grounds that he had lived for many years in an area where slavery had been outlawed by the Missouri Compromise. The Supreme Court could have decided the issue on the narrow ground that a slave was not a citizen and therefore had no right to sue in federal courts. But President-elect Buchanan, in the days just before the inauguration, encouraged the Court to render a broader decision that would settle the slavery issue.

On March 6, Chief Justice Roger B. Taney announced that the majority had ruled against Scott. One argument on which the Court based its decision was that Scott could not sue because he was not a citizen. Taney, in fact, argued further that *no* African American—slave or free—could be a citizen of the United States. But the real bombshell in the decision was the ruling that Dred Scott would not have won his case even if he had been a legal plaintiff. His residence in the Wisconsin Territory established no right to freedom because Congress had no power to prohibit slavery there. The Missouri Compromise was thus declared unconstitutional and so, implicitly, was the main plank in the Republican platform.

If Buchanan expected the decision to reduce sectional tension, he was quickly proved wrong. In the North, and especially among Republicans, the Court's verdict was viewed as the latest diabolical act of the "slave power conspiracy." The charge that the decision was a political maneuver rather than a disinterested interpretation of the Constitution was supported by strong circumstantial evidence. Five of the six judges who voted in the majority were proslavery Southerners, and their resolution of the territorial issue was close to the extreme southern rights position long advocated by John C. Calhoun.

Republicans denounced the decision as "a wicked and false judgment" and as "the greatest crime in the annals of the republic"; but they stopped short of openly defying the Court's authority. Instead, they argued on narrow technical grounds that the decision as written was not binding on Congress and that a ban on slavery in the territories could still be enacted. The decision actually helped the Republicans build support; it lent credence to their claim that an aggressive slave power was dominating all branches of the federal government and attempting to use the Constitution to achieve its own ends.

The Lecompton Controversy

While the Dred Scott case was being decided, leaders of the proslavery faction in Kansas concluded that the time was ripe to draft a constitution and seek admission to the Union as a slave state. Since settlers with free-state views were now an overwhelming majority in the territory, the success of the plan required a rigged, gerrymandered election for convention delegates. When it became clear the election was fixed, the free-staters boycotted it, and the proslavery forces won complete control. The resulting constitution, drawn up at Lecompton, was certain to be voted down if submitted to the voters in a fair election, and sure to be rejected by Congress if no referendum of any kind was held.

To resolve this dilemma, supporters of the constitution decided to permit a vote on the slavery provision alone, giving the electorate the narrow choice of allowing or forbidding the future importation of slaves. Since there was no way to vote for total abolition, the free-state majority again resorted to a boycott, thus allowing ratification of a constitution that protected existing slave property and placed no restriction on importations. Meanwhile, however, the free-staters had finally gained control of the territorial legislature, and they authorized a second referendum on the constitution as a whole. This time, the proslavery party boycotted the election, and the Lecompton constitution was overwhelmingly rejected.

The Lecompton constitution was such an obvious perversion of popular sovereignty that Stephen A. Douglas spoke out against it. But the Buchanan administration, bowing to southern pressure, tried to push it through Congress in early 1858, despite overwhelming evidence that the people of Kansas did not wish to enter the Union as a slave state. The resulting debate in Congress became so bitter and impassioned that it provoked fistfights between northern and southern members. Buchanan, using all the political muscle he could command, scored a victory in the Senate, which voted to admit Kansas under the Lecompton constitution on March 23. But on April 1, a coalition of Republicans and Douglas Democrats defeated the bill in the House. A face-saving compromise was then devised. It allowed resubmission of the constitution to the Kansas voters on the pretext that a change in the provisions for a federal land grant was required. Finally, in August 1858, the people of Kansas killed the Lecompton constitution when they voted it down by a margin of 6 to 1.

The Lecompton controversy aggravated the sectional quarrel and made it truly "irreconcilable," if it had not been before. For Republicans, the administration's frantic efforts to admit Kansas as a slave state exposed southern dominance of the Democratic party and the lengths to which proslavery conspirators would go to achieve their ends. Among Democrats, the affair opened a deep rift between the followers of Douglas and the backers of the Buchanan administration. Because of his anti-Lecompton stand, Douglas gained popularity in the North, and some Republicans even flirted with the idea of joining forces with him against the "doughfaces"—prosouthern Democrats—who stood with Buchanan.

For Douglas himself, however, the affair was a disaster; it destroyed his hopes of uniting the Democratic party and defusing the slavery issue through the application of popular sovereignty. What had happened in Kansas suggested that popular sovereignty in practice was an invitation to civil war. Furthermore, the Dred Scott decision implied that the voters of a territory could not legally decide the fate of slavery at any time before the constitution-making stage. Hence, the interpretation of popular sovereignty favored in the North was undermined, and Southerners could insist on full protection of their right to own human property in all federal territories. For his stand against Lecompton, Douglas was denounced as a traitor in the South, and his hopes of being elected president were seriously diminished.

Debating the Morality of Slavery

Douglas's more immediate problem was to win reelection to the Senate from Illinois in 1858. Here he faced surprisingly tough opposition from

The Case of Dred and Harriet Scott

Dred Scott and his wife Harriet both wanted to be free; the North and South both wanted to find a way to end the crisis over slavery in the territories. On March 6, 1857, the U. S. Supreme Court handed down a decision that fulfilled neither the Scotts's nor the nation's hopes. The case began when the Scotts brought suit against the widow of Dred's owner, an army doctor who had taken Dred from the slave state of Missouri to Fort Snelling in the Wisconsin Territory, where slavery was prohibited by the Missouri Compromise. It was there that Dred and Harriet Scott met and married. Two daughters were born to the couple. In their suit, filed after they had been brought back to Missouri, the Scotts argued that the doctor, now the master of Harriet as well, had made them permanently free by taking them into free territory. Ten years after it was filed, the case made its way to the Supreme Court.

The first question faced by the Court was whether or not Dred Scott was a citizen. Until 1857, neither the wording of the Constitution nor the legal system of the young nation had addressed the question of black citizenship. It was clear enough that slaves were denied the rights of citizenship, including the right to sue in court, but the status of free blacks had not been estab-

The case of Dred and Harriet Scott resulted in a Supreme Court ruling that has been called the "most overturned decision in history."

lished. Although lower courts considered Dred Scott at least a potential citizen by allowing his case to proceed, the Supreme Court attempted to make such a future eventuality impossible by ruling that all blacks, free or slave, were barred from citizenship.

Chief Justice Roger B. Taney's opinion stated that at the time the Constitution was framed, blacks were "so far inferior" to whites "that they had no rights which the white man was bound to respect; and . . . might justly and lawfully be reduced to slavery for their benefit." Although he did not say so, Taney implied that such racist judgments still prevailed. Astute contemporaries agreed. "Judge Taney's decision, infamous as it is," said Susan B. Anthony, "is but the reflection of the spirit and practice of the American people, North as well as South." One scholar concluded that the Scott decision contained "an argument weak in its law, logic, history, and factual accuracy"; but that in its ruling on black citizenship the Taney Court interpreted the Constitution with its finger on the public pulse. Only when the Civil War had helped them consolidate power did Republicans begin the process of giving blacks the legal basis for full citizenship that culminated in the Fourteenth Amendment to the Constitution.

A second constitutional question rising out of the Dred Scott case was whether Congress had the authority to prohibit slavery in the federal territories. Because Dred Scott had lived in a territory for four years, his suit for freedom rested in part on the contention that residency in a territory where slavery was outlawed by the Missouri Compromise had rendered him legally free. In response, the Court ruled that Congress had *unconstitutionally* restricted slavery when it enacted the Missouri Compromise. Although the Constitution authorized Congress "to dispose of and make all needful rules and regulations respecting the territory or other property belonging to the United States," Chief Justice Taney argued that this passage

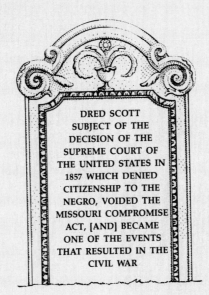

DRED SCOTT SUBJECT OF THE DECISION OF THE SUPREME COURT OF THE UNITED STATES IN 1857 WHICH DENIED CITIZENSHIP TO THE NEGRO, VOIDED THE MISSOURI COMPROMISE ACT, [AND] BECAME ONE OF THE EVENTS THAT RESULTED IN THE CIVIL WAR

allowed Congress to set rules for the disposal of federally owned land, not to determine the rights of those who settled there. Furthermore, Taney maintained, the clause affected only land already owned or claimed when the Constitution was signed in 1789. If the first construction is somewhat flimsy, the second argument verges on the absurd. (Taney found authority elsewhere in the Constitution for Congress to govern the territories—namely in the power to admit new states.) Such was the questionable logic that the Supreme Court used in 1857 to invalidate the Missouri Compromise.

A third major constitutional issue raised by the case pertained to the limits of judicial sovereignty, and, unlike the other issues, it has never been fully resolved. In its famous *Marbury v. Madison* ruling in 1803, the Court under Chief Justice John

Marshall effectively claimed the role of final arbiter of constitutional questions. But in *Dred Scott* the Court went much further. For the first time, it actually invalidated a major piece of legislation. The Court could have voided Scott's suit, resolved the immediate question of Scott's status, and left the territorial issue to the politicians. But tremendous pressure was brought to bear on the justices to convince them that they had the duty and the authority to settle the most stubborn and divisive political problem of the time. It turned out that they did not settle it; the Dred Scott ruling has been called the "most overturned decision in history." Nonetheless, it forced the country to confront great constitutional issues and marked the beginning of a dynamic movement toward judicial activism.

Ironically, Dred and Harriet Scott were freed by a later master soon after the Court handed down its decision. They remained in St. Louis, where Dred worked as a hotel porter and Harriet as a laundress. They both died of natural causes on the eve of the Civil War.

Several of the descendents of their daughter Lizzie, including Dred Scott Madison, a great-grandson of Dred and Harriet, attended a centennial observation in 1957 during which Dred Scott's grave was at long last marked with a headstone. The inscription on the stone, shown above, notes the political and constitutional importance of the case.

Stephen Douglas, the "Little Giant" from Illinois, won election to Congress when he was just thirty years old. Four years later he was elected to the Senate.

a Republican candidate who, in defiance of precedent, was nominated by a party convention. (At this time senators were elected by state legislatures.) Douglas's rival, former Whig Congressman Abraham Lincoln, set out to convince the voters that Douglas could not be relied on to oppose the extension of slavery, even though he had opposed the admission of Kansas under a proslavery constitution.

In the famous speech that opened his campaign, Lincoln tried to distance himself from his opponent by taking a more radical position. He argued that the nation had reached the crisis point in the struggle between slavery and freedom: "'A house divided against itself cannot stand.' I believe this government cannot endure, permanently half *slave* and half *free*." He then described the chain of events between the Kansas-Nebraska Act and the Dred Scott decision as evi-

dence of a plot to extend and nationalize slavery and called for defensive actions to stop the spread of slavery and place it "where the public mind shall rest in the belief that it is in the course of ultimate extinction." He tried to link Douglas to this proslavery conspiracy by pointing to his rival's unwillingness to take a stand on the morality of slavery, to his professed indifference about whether slavery was voted up or down in the territories. For Lincoln, the only security against the triumph of slavery and the slave power was moral opposition to human bondage. Neutrality on the moral issue would lull the public into accepting the expansion of slavery until it was legal everywhere.

In the subsequent series of debates that focused national attention on the Illinois senatorial contest, Lincoln hammered away at the theme that Douglas was a covert defender of slavery because he was not a principled opponent of it. Douglas responded by accusing Lincoln of endangering the Union by his talk of putting slavery on the path to extinction. Denying that he was an abolitionist, Lincoln made a distinction between tolerating slavery in the South, where it was protected by the Constitution, and allowing it to expand to places where it could legally be prohibited. Restriction of slavery, he argued, had been the policy of the Founders, and it was Douglas and the Democrats who had departed from the great tradition of containing an evil that could not be immediately eliminated.

In the debate at Freeport, Illinois, Lincoln questioned Douglas on how he could reconcile popular sovereignty with the Dred Scott decision. The Little Giant, as Douglas was called by his admirers, responded that slavery could not exist without supportive legislation to sustain it and that territorial legislatures could simply refrain from passing a slave code if they wanted to keep it out. Historians formerly believed that Douglas's "Freeport doctrine" suddenly alienated his southern supporters. In truth, Douglas's anti-Lecompton stand had already undermined his popularity in the slave states. But the Freeport speech undoubtedly hardened southern opposition to his presidential ambitions.

Douglas's most effective debating point was to charge that Lincoln's moral opposition to slavery implied a belief in racial equality. Lincoln, facing an intensely racist electorate, vigorously denied

Abraham Lincoln, shown here in his first full-length portrait. Although Lincoln lost the contest for the Senate seat in 1858, the Lincoln–Douglas debates established his reputation as a rising star of the Republican party.

this charge and affirmed his commitment to white supremacy. He would grant blacks the right to the fruits of their own labor while denying them the "privileges" of citizenship. This was an inherently contradictory position, and Douglas made the most of it.

Although Republican candidates for the state legislature won a majority of the popular votes, the Democrats carried more counties and thus were able to send Douglas back to the Senate. Lincoln lost an office, but he won respect in Republican circles throughout the country. By stressing the moral dimension of the slavery question and undercutting any possibility of fusion between Republicans and Douglas Democrats, he had sharpened his party's ideological focus and had stiffened its backbone against any temptation to compromise its Free-Soil position.

The South's Crisis of Fear

After Kansas became a free territory instead of a slave state in August 1858, the issue of slavery in the territories lost some of its immediacy, although it continued to carry great emotional and symbolic meaning. The remaining unorganized areas, which were in the Rockies and northern Great Plains, were unlikely to attract slaveholding settlers. Southern expansionists still dreamed of annexations in the Caribbean and Central America but had little hope of winning congressional approval. Nevertheless, Southerners continued to demand the "right" to take their slaves into the territories, and Republicans persisted in denying it to them. Although the Republicans repeatedly promised they would not interfere with slavery where it already existed, Southerners refused to believe them and interpreted their unyielding stand against the extension of slavery as a threat to southern rights and security.

A chain of events in late 1859 and early 1860 turned southern anxiety about northern attitudes and policies into a "crisis of fear." These events alarmed slaveholders because they appeared to threaten their safety and dominance in a new and direct way.

The first of these incidents was John Brown's raid on Harpers Ferry, Virginia, in October 1859. Brown had shown in Kansas that he was prepared to use violence against the enemies of black freedom. He had the appearance and manner of an Old Testament prophet and thought of himself as God's chosen instrument "to purge this land with blood" and eradicate the sin of slaveholding. On October 16, he led eighteen men from his band of twenty-two (which included five free blacks) across the Potomac River from his base in Maryland and seized the federal arsenal and armory in Harpers Ferry.

Brown's aim was to arm the local slave population to commence a guerrilla war from havens in the Appalachians that would eventually extend to the plantation regions of the lower South. But the neighboring slaves did not rise up to join him, and Brown's raiders were driven out of the armory and arsenal by the local militia and forced to take refuge in a fire-engine house. There they held out until their bastion was stormed by a force of U. S. Marines commanded by Colonel Robert E. Lee. In the course of the fighting, ten of Brown's men were killed or mortally wounded, along with seven of the townspeople and soldiers who opposed them.

The wounded Brown and his remaining followers were put on trial for treason against the state of Virginia. The subsequent investigation produced evidence that several prominent north-ern abolitionists had approved of Brown's plan—to the extent they understood it—and had raised money for his preparations. This seemed to confirm southern fears that abolitionists were actively engaged in fomenting slave insurrection.

After Brown was sentenced to be hanged, Southerners were further stunned by the outpouring of sympathy and admiration that his impending fate aroused in the North. As Ralph Waldo Emerson expressed it, Brown "would make the gallows as glorious as the cross." His actual execution on December 2 completed Brown's elevation to the status of a martyred saint of the antislavery cause. The day of his death was marked in parts of the North by the tolling of bells, the firing of cannons, and the holding of memorial services.

Although Republican politicians were quick to denounce John Brown for his violent methods, Southerners interpreted the wave of northern sympathy as an expression of the majority opinion and the Republicans' "real" attitude. According to historian James McPherson, "They identified Brown with the abolitionists, the abolitionists with Republicans, and Republicans with the whole North." Within the South, the raid and its aftermath touched off a frenzy of fear, repres-

John Brown, shown here barricaded at Harpers Ferry with his followers and hostages, looked on his fight against slavery as a holy campaign ordained by God. In his last speech to the court before his execution for conviction of murder, promoting slave insurrection, and treason, Brown proclaimed, "Now, if it is deemed necessary that I should forfeit my life for the furtherance of the ends of justice and mingle my blood further with the blood of my children and with the blood of millions in this slave country whose rights are disregarded by wicked, cruel, and unjust enactments—I say, let it be done!"

sion, and mobilization. Witch-hunts searched for the agents of a vast imagined conspiracy to stir up slave rebellion; vigilance committees were organized in many localities to resist subversion and ensure control of slaves, and orators pointed increasingly to secession as the only way to protect southern interests.

Brown was scarcely in his grave when another set of events put southern nerves on edge once more. Next to abolitionist-abetted rebellions, the slaveholding South's greatest fear was that the nonslaveholding majority would turn against the master class and the solidarity of southern whites behind the peculiar institution would crumble. When Congress met to elect a Speaker of the House on December 5, the Republican candidate—John Sherman of Ohio—was bitterly denounced by Southerners because he had endorsed as a campaign document Hinton R. Helper's *Impending Crisis of the South*. Helper's book, which called on lower-class whites to resist planter dominance and abolish slavery in their own interest, was regarded by slaveholders as even more seditious than *Uncle Tom's Cabin*, and they feared the spread of "Helperism" among poor whites almost as much as they feared the effect of "John Brownism" on the slaves.

The ensuing contest over the speaker's office lasted almost two months. As the balloting went on, southern congressmen threatened secession if Sherman was elected, and feelings became so heated that some representatives began to carry weapons on the floor of the House. Since the Republicans did not have an absolute majority and needed the votes of a few members of the American party, it eventually became clear that Sherman could not be elected, and his name was withdrawn in favor of a moderate Republican who had refrained from endorsing Helper's book. The impasse over the speakership was thus resolved, but the contest helped persuade Southerners that the Republicans were committed to stirring up class conflict among southern whites.

Republicans' identification with Helper's ideas may have been decisive in convincing many conservative planters that a Republican victory in the presidential election of 1860 would be intolerable. Anxiety about the future allegiance of nonslaveholding whites had been growing during the 1850s because of changes in the pattern of slave ownership. A dramatic rise in the price of slaves was undermining the ambition of slaveless farmers to join the slaveholding ranks. During the decade, the proportion of white heads of families owning slaves had shrunk from 30 to 25 percent in all the slave states and from 50 to 40 percent in the cotton belt of the lower South. Perceiving in this trend the seeds of class conflict, proslavery extremists had called for the reopening of the Atlantic slave trade as a way to reduce the price of slaves and make them more widely available. Although the interest of large owners in preserving the appreciated value of their human property had helped prevent this "proslavery crusade" from gaining broad support, many slaveholders were concerned about the social and political consequences of their status as a shrinking minority. Even those most strongly committed to the Union were terrified by the prospect that a Republican party in control of the federal government would use its power to foster "Helperism" among the South's nonslaveholding majority.

The Election of 1860

The Republicans, sniffing victory and generally insensitive to the depth of southern feeling against them, met in Chicago on May 16 to nominate a presidential candidate. The initial frontrunner, Senator William H. Seward of New York, had two strikes against him: he had a reputation for radicalism and a long record of strong opposition to the nativist movement. What a majority of the delegates wanted was a less controversial nominee who could win two or three of the northern states that had been in the Democratic column in 1856. Abraham Lincoln met their specifications: he was from Illinois, a state the Republicans needed to win, he had a more moderate image than Seward, and he had kept his personal distaste for Know-Nothingism to himself. In addition, he was a self-made man, whose rise from frontier poverty to legal and political prominence embodied the Republican ideal of equal opportunity for all. After trailing Seward by a large margin on the first ballot, Lincoln picked up enough strength on the second to pull virtually even and was nominated on the third.

The platform, like the nominee, was meant to broaden the party's appeal in the North. Although a commitment to halt the expansion of

NATIONAL

slavery remained, economic matters received more attention than they had in 1856. With an eye on Pennsylvania, the delegates called for a high protective tariff; other planks included endorsement of free homesteads, which was popular in the Midwest and among working men, and federal aid for internal improvements, especially a transcontinental railroad. The platform was cleverly designed to bring most ex-Whigs into the Republican camp while also accommodating enough renegade Democrats to give the party a solid majority in the northern states.

The Democrats failed to present a united front against this formidable challenge. When the party first met in the sweltering heat of Charleston in late April, Douglas commanded a majority of the delegates but was unable to win the two-thirds required for nomination because of unyielding southern opposition. He did succeed in getting the convention to endorse popular sovereignty as its slavery platform, but the price was a walkout by Deep South delegates who favored a federal slave code for the territories.

Unable to agree on a nominee, the convention adjourned to reconvene in Baltimore in June. The next time around, a fight developed over whether to seat newly selected pro-Douglas delegations from some Deep South states in place of the bolters from the first convention. When the Douglas forces won most of the contested seats, another and more massive southern walkout took place. The result was a fracture of the Democratic party. The delegates who remained nominated Douglas and reaffirmed the party's commitment to popular sovereignty, while the bolters convened elsewhere to nominate John Breckinridge of Kentucky on a platform of federal protection for slavery in the territories.

By the time the campaign was underway, four parties were running presidential candidates. In addition to the Republicans, the Douglas Democrats, and the "Southern Rights" Democrats, a remnant of conservative Whigs and Know-Nothings nominated John Bell of Tennessee under the banner of the Constitutional Union party. Taking no explicit stand on the issue of slavery in the territories, the Constitutional Unionists tried to represent the spirit of sectional accommodation that had led to compromise in 1820 and 1850. In effect, the race became a separate two-party contest in each section: in the North the real choice was between Lincoln and Douglas, and in the South the only candidates with a fighting chance were Breckinridge and Bell. Douglas alone tried to carry on a national campaign, gaining some support in every state, but actually winning only in Missouri.

When the results came in, the Republicans had achieved a stunning victory. By gaining the electoral votes of all the free states except a fraction of New Jersey's, Lincoln won a decisive majority—180 to 123 over his combined opponents. In the North, his 54 percent of the popular vote annihilated Douglas. In the South, where Lincoln

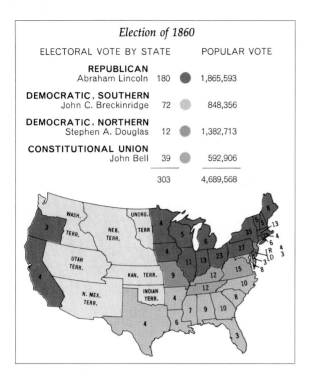

Election of 1860

ELECTORAL VOTE BY STATE		POPULAR VOTE
REPUBLICAN Abraham Lincoln	180	1,865,593
DEMOCRATIC, SOUTHERN John C. Breckinridge	72	848,356
DEMOCRATIC, NORTHERN Stephen A. Douglas	12	1,382,713
CONSTITUTIONAL UNION John Bell	39	592,906
	303	4,689,568

Generations of historians have searched for the underlying causes of the crisis leading to disruption of the Union but have failed to agree on exactly what they were. Some have stressed the clash of economic interests between agrarian and industrializing regions. But this interpretation does not reflect the way people at the time expressed their concerns. The main issues in the sectional debates of the 1850s were whether slavery was right or wrong and whether it should be extended or contained. Disagreements over protective tariffs and other economic measures benefiting one section or the other were clearly secondary. Furthermore, it has never been clear why the interests of northern industry and those of the South's commercial agriculture were irreconcilable. From a purely economic point of view, there was no necessity for producers of raw materials to go to war with those who marketed or processed them.

Another group of historians have blamed the crisis on "irresponsible" politicians and agitators on both sides of the Mason-Dixon line. Public opinion, they argue, was whipped into a frenzy over issues that competent statesmen could have resolved. But this viewpoint has been sharply criticized for failing to acknowledge the depths of feeling that could be aroused by the slavery question and for underestimating the obstacles to a peaceful solution.

The dominant modern view is that the crisis was rooted in profound ideological differences over the morality and utility of slavery as an institution. Most interpreters are now agreed that the roots of the conflict lay in the fact that the South was a slave society and determined to stay that way, while the North was equally committed to a free labor system. In the words of historian David Potter, "slavery really had a polarizing effect, for the North had no slaveholders—at least not of resident slaves—and the South had virtually no abolitionists." No other differences divided the regions in this decisive way, and it is hard to imagine that secessionism would have developed if the South had followed the North's example and abolished slavery in the postrevolutionary period.

Nevertheless, the existence or nonexistence of slavery will not explain why the crisis came when it did and in the way that it did. Why did the con-

was not even on the ballot, Breckinridge triumphed everywhere except in Virginia, Kentucky, and Tennessee, which went for Bell and the Constitutional Unionists. The Republican strategy of seeking power by trying to win decisively in the majority section was brilliantly successful. Although less than 40 percent of those who went to the polls throughout the nation actually voted for Lincoln, his support in the North was so solid that he would have won in the electoral college even if his opponents had been unified behind a single candidate.

Most Southerners saw the result of the election as a catastrophe. A candidate and a party with no support in their own section had won the presidency on a platform viewed as insulting to southern honor and hostile to vital southern interests. Since the birth of the republic, Southerners had either sat in the White House or exerted considerable influence over those who did. Those days might now be gone forever. Rather than accepting permanent minority status in American politics and facing the resulting dangers to black slavery and white "liberty," the political leaders of the lower South launched a movement for immediate secession from the Union.

A "Wide-Awakes" torchlight parade in New York City, 1860. In the presidential campaign of 1860, the Republicans organized their supporters into "Wide-Awake Clubs," whose uniformed members marched in small towns and large cities to drum up support for Lincoln and a Republican victory.

flict become "irreconcilable" in the 1850s and not earlier or later? Why did it take the form of a political struggle over the future of slavery in the territories? Adequate answers to both questions require an understanding of political developments that were not directly caused by tensions over slavery.

By the 1850s, the established Whig and Democratic parties were in trouble partly because they no longer offered the voters clear-cut alternatives on the economic issues that had been the bread and butter of politics during the heyday of the second party system. This situation created an opening for new parties and issues. After the Know-Nothings failed to make attitudes toward immigrants the basis for a political realignment, the Republicans used the issue of slavery in the territories to build the first successful sectional party in American history. They called for "free

soil" rather than freedom for blacks because abolitionism conflicted with the northern majority's commitment to white supremacy and its respect for the original constitutional compromise that established a hands-off policy toward slavery in the southern states. For Southerners, the Republican party now became the main issue, and they fought against it from within the Democratic party until it ceased to function as a national organization in 1860.

If politicians seeking new ways to mobilize an apathetic electorate are seen as the main instigators of sectional crisis, the reasons that certain appeals were more effective than others must still be uncovered. Why did the slavery extension issue arouse such strong feelings in the two sections during the 1850s? The same issue had arisen earlier and had proved adjustable, even in 1820 when the second party system—with its vested interest in compromise—had not yet emerged. If the expansion of slavery had been as vital and emotional a question in 1820 as it was in the 1850s, the declining Federalist party would presumably have revived in the form of a northern sectional party adamantly opposed to the admission of slave states to the Union.

Ultimately, therefore, the crisis of the 1850s must be understood as having a deep social and cultural dimension as well as a purely political one. In *Uncle Tom's Cabin,* Harriet Beecher Stowe personified the cultural conflict in her depiction of two brothers with similar personalities, one of whom settled in Vermont "to rule over rocks and stones" and the other in Louisiana "to rule over men and women." The first became a deacon in the church, a member of the local abolition society, and, despite his natural authoritarianism, the adherent of "a democratic theory." The second became indifferent to religion, openly aristocratic, a staunch defender of slavery, and an extreme racist—"he considered the negro, through all possible gradations of color, as the intermediate link between man and animals." Stowe's comparison may have been biased, but she showed a good understanding of how the contrasting environments of slavery and freedom could lead very similar men to have sharply conflicting views of the world.

This divergence in basic beliefs and values had increased and become less manageable between the 1820s and the 1850s. Both sections continued to profess allegiance to the traditional "republican" ideals of individual liberty and independence, and both were strongly influenced by evangelical religion. But differences in the way each region developed economically and socially transformed a common culture into two conflicting cultures. In the North a rising middle class adapted to the new market economy with the help of an evangelical Christianity that sanctioned self-discipline and social reform (see Chapter 11). The South, on the other hand, embraced slavery as a foundation for the liberty and independence of whites. Its evangelicalism encouraged personal piety but not social reform and gave only limited attention to building the kind of personal character that made for commercial success. The notion that white liberty and equality depended on resistance to social and economic change and—to get to the heart of the

CHRONOLOGY

1846   David Wilmot introduces proviso banning slavery in the Mexican cession

1848   Free-Soil party is founded • Zachary Taylor (Whig) elected president, defeating Lewis Cass (Democrat) and Martin Van Buren (Free-Soil)

1849   California seeks admission to the Union as a free state

1850   Congress debates sectional issues and enacts Compromise of 1850

1852   Harriet Beecher Stowe publishes *Uncle Tom's Cabin* • Franklin Pierce (Democrat) elected president by a large majority over Winfield Scott (Whig)

1854   Congress passes Kansas-Nebraska Act, repealing Missouri Compromise • Republican party founded in several northern states • Anti-Nebraska coalitions score victories in congressional elections in the North

1854–1855   Know-Nothing party achieves stunning successes in state politics

1854–1856   Free-state and slave-state forces struggle for control of Kansas Territory

1856   Preston Brooks assaults Charles Sumner on Senate floor • James Buchanan wins presidency despite strong challenge in the North from John C. Frémont.

1857   Supreme Court decides Dred Scott case and legalizes slavery in all territories

1858   Congress refuses to admit Kansas to Union under the proslavery Lecompton constitution • Lincoln and Douglas debate slavery issue in Illinois

1859   John Brown raids Harpers Ferry, is captured and executed

1859–1860   Fierce struggle takes place over election of a Republican as Speaker of the House (December–February)

1860   Republicans nominate Abraham Lincoln for presidency (May) • Democratic party splits into northern and southern factions with separate candidates and platforms (June) • Lincoln wins the presidency over Douglas, Breckinridge, and Bell.

matter—on continuing to have enslaved blacks to do menial labor became more deeply entrenched.

When politicians appealed to sectionalism during the 1850s, therefore, they could evoke conflicting views of what constituted the good society. The South—with its allegedly idle masters, degraded unfree workers, and shiftless poor whites—seemed to a majority of Northerners to be in flagrant violation of the Protestant work ethic and the ideal of open competition in "the race of life." From the dominant southern point of view, the North was a land of hypocritical money-grubbers who denied the obvious fact that the virtue, independence, and liberty of free citizens was only possible when dependent laboring classes—especially racially inferior ones—were kept under the kind of rigid control that only slavery could provide. According to the ideology of northern Republicans, the freedom of the individual depended on equality of opportunity for everyone; in the minds of southern sectionalists, it required that part of the population be enslaved. Once these contrary views of the world had become the main themes of political discourse, sectional compromise was no longer possible.

Recommended Reading

The best general account of the politics of the sectional crisis is David M. Potter, *The Impending Crisis, 1848–1861* (1976). This well-written and authoritative work combines a vivid and detailed narrative of events with a shrewd and detailed interpretation of them. A provocative analysis of the party system in crisis is Michael F. Holt, *The Political Crisis of the 1850s* (1978). Holt incorporates the social-scientific approaches and methods of the "new political history." The most important studies of northern political sectionalism are Eric Foner, *Free Soil, Free Labor, Free Men: The Ideology of the Republican Party Before the Civil War* (1970), and William E. Gienapp, *The Origins of the Republican Party, 1852–1856* (1987), on the Republican party generally, and Don E. Fehrenbacher, *Prelude to Greatness: Lincoln in the 1850s* (1962), on Lincoln's rise to prominence. On the background of southern separatism, see William W. Freehling, *The Road to Disunion: Secessionists at Bay, 1776–1854* (1990); and William L. Barney, *The Road to Secession: A New Perspective on the Old South* (1972).

Additional Bibliography

The most detailed and thorough discussion of the events leading up to the Civil War is Allan Nevins, *The Ordeal of the Union*, vols. 1–4 (1947–1950). More concise efforts to cover the same ground are Avery Craven, *The Coming of the Civil War*, 2d ed. (1957); John Niven, *The Coming of the Civil War, 1837–1861* (1990); and Bruce Levine, *Half Slave and Half Free: The Roots of the Civil War* (1992). Craven has also produced an extensive study of southern responses to the events of the crisis period in *The Growth of Southern Nationalism, 1848–1861* (1953).

There are good books on most of the specific political events and personalities of the period. On developments between 1846 and 1850, see Chaplain W. Morrison, *Democratic Politics and Sectionalism: The Wilmot Proviso Controversy* (1967), and Holman Hamilton, *Prologue to Conflict: The Crisis and Compromise of 1850* (1964). Enforcement of the fugitive slave law is the subject of Stanley W. Campbell, *The Slave Catchers* (1970). The rise of antislavery politics in the 1840s and 1850s is well described in Richard H. Sewell, *Ballots for Freedom: Antislavery Politics in the United States, 1837–1860* (1976). Eugene H. Berwanger, *The Frontier Against Slavery: Western Anti-Negro Prejudice in the Slavery Extension Controversy* (1967), stresses the role of racial attitudes in the Free-Soil movement. Insights into the origin and nature of the Republican party—specifically its relation to nativism—can be derived from Ronald P. Formisano, *The Birth of Mass Political Parties: Michigan, 1827–1861* (1971); Michael F. Holt, *Forging a New Majority: The Formation of the Republican Party in Pittsburgh, 1848–1860* (1969); and Dale Baum, *The Civil War Party System: The Case of Massachusetts, 1848–1876* (1984). On nativism generally, see Ray Allen Billington, *The Protestant Crusade, 1800–1860* (1938). The best treatment of the Know-Nothing movement is Tyler Anbinder, *Nativism and Slavery: The Northern Know-Nothings and the Politics of the 1850s* (1992). James A. Rawley, *Race and Politics: "Bleeding Kansas" and the Coming of the Civil War* (1969), deals with the struggle over slavery in the Kansas Territory. Stephen A. Douglas, a key participant in the crisis of the 1850s, is the subject of a major biography by Robert W. Johannsen: *Stephen A. Douglas* (1973). David Donald, *Charles Sumner and the Coming of the Civil War* (1960), puts another important political figure into context. Don E. Fehrenbacher, *The Dred Scott Case: Its Significance in American Law and Politics* (1978), is the definitive work on the subject. The best treatment of the Lecompton controversy and its significance can be found in Kenneth M. Stampp, *America in 1857: A*

Nation on the Brink (1990). An incisive analysis of the "great debates" is Harry V. Jaffa, *Crisis of the House Divided: An Interpretation of the Lincoln-Douglas Debates* (1959). A stimulating psychoanalytic interpretation of the Lincoln-Douglas rivalry is George B. Forgie, *Patricide in the House Divided: A Psychological Interpretation of Lincoln and His Age* (1979). Roy Franklin Nichols, *The Disruption of American Democracy* (1948), treats the breakdown of the Democratic party between 1856 and 1860. On John Brown and his raid, see Stephen B. Oates, *To Purge This Land with Blood: A Biography of John Brown* (1970). Stephen A. Channing, *Crisis of Fear: Secession in South Carolina,* (1970), details the hysteria that seized one southern state after Brown's raid. On the controversy over Helper's inflammatory book, see the introduction to Hinton R. Helper, *The Impending Crisis of the South: How to Meet It,* edited by George M. Fredrickson (1968).

Perspectives on the intellectual, social, and cultural aspects of the sectional conflict can be derived from William R. Taylor, *Cavalier and Yankee: The Old South and American National Character* (1961); John McCardell, *The Idea of a Southern Nation: Southern Nationalists and Southern Nationalism, 1830–1860* (1979); Major L. Wilson, *Space and Freedom: The Quest for Nationality and the Irrepressible Conflict* (1974); Paul C. Nagel, *One Nation Indivisible: The Union in American Thought* (1964); Donald G. Mathews, *Slavery and Methodism: A Chapter in American Morality, 1780–1845* (1965); and Ronald T. Takaki, *A Pro-Slavery Crusade: The Agitation to Reopen the African Slave Trade* (1971). See also works cited in the bibliographies of earlier chapters dealing with evangelicalism, abolitionism, and proslavery arguments.

LAW & SOCIETY II

The Beecher-Tilton Adultery Trial

Public Image Versus Private Conduct

There were no tickets left for the trial. City policemen guarded the door to the Brooklyn city courthouse. Citizens of Brooklyn and New York thronged against the cordon, clamoring to be allowed in. Every now and then someone would wend his or her way to the front of the crowd, show a harried policeman a ticket, and the officers would part just enough to let the ticketholder through.

Inside the courtroom, the judge was preparing to allow the opening arguments to commence. He sternly warned the still-settling audience that he would not tolerate outbursts or demonstrations of sentiment from them. Nevertheless, the trial, which lasted from January through June of 1875, was repeatedly interrupted, especially by applause when the defendant, the Reverend Mr. Henry Ward Beecher, ridiculed the charges brought against him—charges of adultery. Theodore Tilton, one of Beecher's old friends and a member of his congregation, was suing the minister for having an illicit affair with his wife, Mrs. Elizabeth Tilton.

Beecher, of the famous Beecher family, was then the most prominent minister in the country. The father of the family, Lyman Beecher, had been an influential minister during the early part of the nineteenth century, leading a wing of the revivalist movement to bring religion to the mass of Americans. Henry's sister Catharine wrote tremendously popular tracts advocating expanded roles for women. Another sister Harriet, who wrote under her married name of Stowe, was, in President Lincoln's words, "the little lady who started this big war," with her antislavery novel *Uncle Tom's Cabin.* Henry Ward Beecher was himself something of an antislavery activist, popular for having held auctions at which benevolent Northerners could buy slaves into freedom. His published sermons sold by the thousands. But he

was most famous for simply playing his role as the outspoken, charismatic, and ever-popular preacher and public personality, Henry Ward Beecher. Following in his father's footsteps (in method if not in doctrine), Beecher tried to adapt religion to the changing times.

At the time of the trial, only ten years had passed since the end of the Civil War. Middle-class white Northerners—the members of Beecher's congregation and readership—had difficulty reconciling themselves to the drastic changes that were afoot. There were new amendments to the Constitution, reshaping the language of the rights of citizens of the United States. Some people argued that those rights ought to apply not only to the newly freed class of black Americans, but also to the much larger class of free white women, who as yet could not vote or own property as easily as men. In addition to those problems, on the eve of the war Charles Darwin's book *On the Origin of Species* had made its first appearance, sending shock waves through the literate circles of Britain and America, and undermining religious authority on both sides of the Atlantic.

Beecher addressed these issues within the familiar and comfortable language of liberal Protestant Christianity. He presented Darwinian evolution as a benevolent metaphor for the advance of Christian civilization. Evolution thus became progress. He advocated women's rights in a relatively conservative way: like his sister Catharine, he believed women's virtues should be strengthened in order to make the home and the family stronger, not so women could become independent of men and the family.

In the middle of the nineteenth century, Brooklyn was still a separate city from New York. No bridge yet spanned the East River. When Beecher came to Brooklyn, he dedicated himself to reaching as wide an audience as possible. He wanted to bring all the community into his church. He believed he could do that by making himself into a public personality, making the congregation feel they knew him and could trust him. Consequently Beecher always phrased his sermons in colloquial language, and he had Plymouth Church constructed so the audience could sit all around the pulpit. This made the church "perfect," as Beecher said, "because it was built on a principle,—the principle of social and personal magnetism, which emanates reciprocally from a speaker and a close throng of hearers." To achieve his effect, he needed to be near his audience, and his audience needed to be near him, so they could see his whole body, and feel his "magnetic influence."

Beecher made himself into a public figure, a kind of modern celebrity. He acted as the moral and intellectual voice of a large urban community. It was Beecher's prominence and importance that made the trial such a public event. Furthermore, the trial occurred during the last years of the Grant administration, in which the president's personal secretary and some members of his cabinet had already been implicated in scandalous dealings. The war hero president stood accused of surrounding himself with scoundrels and of being unable to govern effectively. Would Beecher become another great man laid low?

Theodore Tilton edited a leading religious newspaper and was a liberal activist, working in the women's rights and abolition movements. He was an old friend and ally of Beecher's; the minister had presided at the marriage of Tilton and his wife Elizabeth. During the Civil War, Beecher and Tilton worked together to join antislavery forces and women's rights advocates into a single organization, the American Equal Rights Association. At a speech in 1866 Beecher linked the two groups, saying "suffrage is the inherent right of mankind" (which, in his mind, included women as well). As Reconstruction wore on, however, some reformers began to argue that those who stood for equal rights ought to focus first on the newly freed slaves, because this was, after all, "the Negro's hour."

This argument occasioned a split in the women's movement. Some women's activists believed they ought to put off their hopes for female suffrage until black suffrage had been secured. Others believed women should not wait, but must push forward with their own agenda. The split became permanent when Congress passed the Fifteenth Amendment, which read "The right of citizens of the United States to vote shall not be denied or abridged by the United States or by any State on account of race, color, or previous condition of servitude." The criterion of sex was conspicuously absent. Elizabeth Cady Stanton and a large group of her supporters opposed the amendment. Soon after, Stanton and Susan B. Anthony withdrew from the Equal Rights Association to form the National Woman Suffrage Association (NWSA). Women who supported the Fifteenth Amendment (including Julia Ward Howe, author of the "Battle Hymn of the Republic") formed the American Woman Suffrage Association (AWSA). The fissure in the feminist movement led to the split between Tilton and Beecher; by 1870, Tilton had become president of the NWSA and Beecher of the rival AWSA.

Tilton's association with the NWSA brought him into contact with the more radical activists of the women's movement. Chief among these was Victoria C. Woodhull, who in 1870 became the first woman to address Congress when she presented the national legislature with a petition on behalf of woman suffrage. Woodhull and her sister, Tennie C. (sometimes "Tennessee") Claflin, founded the first all-female brokerage on Wall Street. They also started the publication *Woodhull and Claflin's Weekly*, in which they advocated the philosophy of free love. Free love, Woodhull said, meant she came into the world "with an inalienable, constitutional, and natural right to love whom I may, to love as long or as short a period as I can, to change that love everyday if I please!" In the postwar period, free love, like socialism, was widely regarded as a threat to American institutions. Woodhull was doubly notorious because she was also a radical socialist; she served a term as leader of the New York division of the Marxist Second International and also published the first English translation of Marx and Engel's *Communist Manifesto*.

Tilton apparently chose Woodhull as a confidant for his troubles. He was having difficulties with his marriage. His wife found him difficult to live with. Elizabeth Tilton had sought out her minister—Beecher—as a sympathetic ear for her unhappiness. Beecher may have advised her to separate from her husband. But Tilton was suspicious of their intimacy for other reasons as well. When he confronted his wife, she confessed—in writing—to having entertained "improper proposals" from Beecher. Tilton took the confession to a conference with Beecher and Frank Moulton, a mutual friend, who could be trusted to act as a neutral party. Beecher and Moulton persuaded Tilton that what had happened was unclear and it was in nobody's best interest to pursue the matter. Tilton tore up the confession.

Beecher visited Elizabeth Tilton, who was in her sickbed. (She had suffered a miscarriage, but she seems not to have told anyone this at the time.) Distraught at the trouble her confession seemed to have caused, she agreed to write out a retraction to quell any possible rumors. "Wearied by importunity and weakened by sickness," she wrote,

> I gave a letter inculpating my friend Henry Ward Beecher, under assurances that would remove all difficulties between me and my husband. That letter I now revoke. I was persuaded—almost forced—when I was in a weakened state of mind. I regret it and recall all of its statements. . . . I desire to say explicitly, Mr. Beecher has never offered any improper solicitations, but has always treated me in a manner becoming a Christian gentleman.

When Tilton learned his wife had given such a letter to Beecher, he immediately worried it might be used against him. So he persuaded his wife to write yet another letter expressing this concern to Beecher. Beecher was now upset. There seemed no way to reassure Tilton. Moulton suggested that Beecher write out an apology. The minister agreed, but was too shaken to write the document himself. Moulton composed the letter, addressed to himself, which Beecher then signed:

> My Dear Friend Moulton:
>
> I ask through you Theodore Tilton's forgiveness, and I humble myself before him as I do before my God. He would have been a better man in my circumstances than I have been. I can ask nothing except that he will remember all the other hearts that will ache. I will not

plead for myself. I even wish I were dead, but others must live and suffer.

> I will die before any one but myself shall be implicated. All my thoughts are running toward my friends, toward the poor child lying there and praying with her folded hands. She is guiltless, sinned against, bearing the transgression of another. Her forgiveness I have. I humbly pray to God that he may put it into the heart of her husband to forgive me. I have trusted this to Moulton in confidence.

Things seemed to quiet down after that, but then Victoria Woodhull published a lurid account of the affair in her *Weekly*. She hoped that by exposing Beecher, the spokesman for decent traditional institutions, especially marriage, as an adulterer and thus a hypocrite, she could advance the credibility of her cause. In this, if in nothing else, she was mistaken; she and her sister were soon arrested under the Comstock Laws, which prohibited distributing obscene materials through the mails, and held in jail until Woodhull's health broke down and she had to be released.

The two letters—Mrs. Tilton's retraction and Beecher's apology—constituted the bulk of the real evidence in the trial. Given that Mrs. Tilton had written first a confession and then a retraction and then a conditional statement regarding the retraction—and all under some coercion—and that Beecher hadn't even written his apology himself, the flimsy evidence hardly seem to prove anything. Nevertheless, as prosecuting attorney Samuel B. Morris noted in his opening remarks, "Adultery is peculiarly a crime of darkness and secrecy. Parties are rarely surprised in it, and so it not only may, but ordinarily must, be established by circumstantial evidence." If Beecher were innocent, then what exactly was he apologizing so abjectly for? What did the note mean to say when it suggested that Mrs. Tilton (the "poor child") had borne the sin of another?

The affair would never have become public knowledge had Victoria Woodhull not chosen to publish it, believing she could implicate Beecher as a free lover and thus advance her own beliefs. Even after she printed her account of the scandal, the case might never have gone to trial. But Woodhull cited Tilton as her source, and Tilton fanned the flames of scandal even as they began to die by publishing a suggestive letter in the newspapers. The leaders of Plymouth Church had had enough and called a meeting to drop Tilton from the roll of the congregation. They had a ready pretext; Tilton had not attended church in four years. Tilton, outraged, carried on an argument in print with various members of the church, all the while hinting that Beecher was guilty of illicit behavior. Finally, Beecher called an examining committee from the congregation to clear his name. Tilton appeared before the committee to accuse Beecher of "criminal intimacy" with his wife. Beecher testified to deny the charges. When Mrs. Tilton came to the stand, the committee asked her just what was the sin of which she and Beecher were so apologetic? "I do not think," she said, "that I felt that it was anything more than giving to another what was due my husband." The committee pressed her further: "When you speak of what was due to him, what do you refer to?" Mrs. Tilton replied, "Why, the all of my nature; I do not think I feel any great sin about it now. . . . I harmed [Theodore] in his pride by allowing any one else into my life at all; I think that was [the] sin."

After hearing all the testimony, the investigating committee reported that "It is proper . . . to state that the offence as alleged by Mr. Tilton during some four years and until recently to numerous persons, in writing and otherwise, was an improper suggestion or solicitation by Mr. Beecher to Mrs. Tilton. But as time passed and purposes matured, this charge passed and matured into another form and substance. . . . The charge, in effect, is that Mr. Beecher . . . committed adultery with Elizabeth R. Tilton."

Did the gradual escalation of the charge from impropriety to adultery reflect Tilton's increasingly outraged imagination, or did it reflect his initial unwillingness to level so monstrous an accusation at such a public figure? Elizabeth Tilton believed her husband was jealous because Beecher had become a closer friend to his wife than he. She never even mentioned adultery. Beecher claimed that the apology, which he had not written himself, referred only to his sorrow at the apparent bad feeling. The committee acquitted him. Tilton, in order to preserve what remained of his dignity, felt he had to sue Beecher for adultery.

The evidence the court would hear was the same as that presented to the church committee—the letters and Mrs. Tilton's and Beecher's respective denials. There was again the confusion over what the charge had actually been—improper suggestions or actual adultery. Public interest in the scandal soared. The court, in order to ensure there would be room for the participants and the jury, limited audience admission by issuing tick-

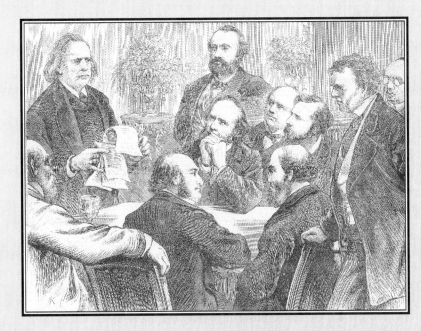

The members of the examining committee from the Plymouth Church congregation listen intently as Reverend Henry Ward Beecher reads his statement concerning his affair with Elizabeth Tilton. The committee, appointed by Beecher and composed mainly of his close friends and staunch supporters, completely exonerated Beecher.

MR. MOULTON ANSWERS AN EASY QUESTION.   MRS. TILTON GAZES AT HER HUSBAND.   MR. TILTON CATCHES A MOMENTARY GLIMPSE OF HIS WIFE.

THE TILTON-BEECHER SCANDAL CASE.—See Page 343.

The popular media of the day carried detailed accounts—complete with illustrations—of the Tilton-Beecher scandal case, as it was called. The sketches shown here of three of the principal figures in the trial, Frank Moulton, Elizabeth Tilton, and Theodore Tilton, are from a pictorial history of the trial.

ets. On the streets of New York and in cities throughout the country, Americans purchased various accounts of the infamous "Brooklyn scandal," each of which included reprints of the correspondence, profiles of the participants, and, after discussing the details of the case for many pages, a comment regretting the whole affair had come before the public. One concluded, "Ten thousand immoral and obscene novels could not have done the harm which this case has done, in teaching the science of wrong to thousands of quick-witted and curious boys and girls." Benjamin F. Butler, who had been a Union general during the Civil War and was an acquaintance of both Beecher and Tilton, summed up this sentiment when he declared, "I don't care who is right and who is wrong. This exposure will work harm. . . . The thing to be advised in the case was to keep it hidden."

Butler believed, as did others, that the country did not need to have its moral authority challenged. It was a time of crisis economically as well as politically; the country had been in a depression for two years. Beecher represented the moral rectitude of the new nation that had emerged from the Civil War. To have his authority challenged could only hurt the whole country.

Beecher apparently thought in such public terms as well. At the trial, he testified grandly that he cared but little for the damage done to him personally and spoke of "the intensity with which I [have] expressed my sorrow to lie in the sorrow of other people." Beecher probably exaggerated his unselfishness a bit, but it is true he was more concerned with the well-being of his

public persona than the truth of his own behavior. When the prosecutor asked him why he did not step forth immediately to quell the rumors that surrounded him, Beecher said he was only aware of a few suspicions.

PROSECUTOR.   *Well, suspicion of what?*

BEECHER.   *Suspicion of moral conduct and character.*

PROSECUTOR.   *Well, Sir, did you not want to clear up that suspicion?*

BEECHER.   *I wanted to have it [his "moral conduct and character"] unquestioned.*

(Beecher would have preferred the affair to remain private and his public character to remain unstained.)

Butler's and Beecher's instincts appear to have been correct. The trial did nobody any good, and it probably harmed some worthy causes. Beecher was acquitted, but he never again commanded the same moral authority once his character had been questioned. Tilton had lost his job as editor of the religious newspaper and alienated his wife. Elizabeth Tilton had been forced to defend her character in public. Victoria Woodhull nearly died in jail, and free love came no closer to respectability.

The feminist movement suffered by having two of its leading figures quarreling in court over a sex scandal. In a broader sense, the cause of reform overall was hurt: the Beecher case added to the list of scandals that beset the country during the Grant administration and fueled public skepticism regarding the ability of government, institutions, and prominent leaders to act in the public interest.

For a time, the Plymouth Church community took care of Elizabeth Tilton. She earned money by privately tutoring children of the congregation. On April 16, 1878, however, the *New York Times* printed this letter, from Mrs. Tilton to her lawyer, on its front page:

> *A few weeks since, after long months of mental anguish, I told, as you know, a few friends, whom I had bitterly deceived, that the charge brought by my husband, of adultery between myself and the Rev. Henry Ward Beecher, was true, and that the lie I had lived as well the last four years had become intolerable to me . . . . I know full well the explanations that will be sought by many for this acknowledgment; a desire to return to my husband, insanity, malice, everything except the true and only one—my quickened conscience, and the sense of what is due to the cause of truth and justice.*

In the next column the *Times* printed this letter:

> *I confront Mrs. Tilton's confession with complete and absolute denial. The testimony to her own innocence and to mine which, for four years, she has made to hundreds in private and in public, before the court, in writing and orally, I declare to be true. And the allegations now made in contradiction of her uniform, solemn, and unvarying statements hitherto I utterly deny.*
>
> *I declare her to be innocent of the great transgression.*
>
> *Henry Ward Beecher*

The public's taste for the scandal appeared to have long gone, and no great consequence came of this new twist on the case. The story was replaced in the *Times* after two days by the description of Boss Tweed's funeral. Plymouth Church removed Elizabeth Tilton from its rolls four years after it had dropped her husband.

The case raises several intriguing legal questions. Most obviously, was Beecher innocent or guilty of the charges against him? The jury seems to have reached a sensible verdict given the evidence presented to them. But if Elizabeth Tilton's later confession had been before them, they might have come to a different conclusion—or would they? A second question is whether or not a jury could fairly judge a famous public figure about whom they already held strong feelings of approval or disapproval. Would a panel of middle-class Protestant males have believed the testimony of an apparently overwrought woman against a man like Beecher? Finally, what does the affair tell us about American efforts to extend the law into the most private and most intimate areas of life? Adultery was a crime, but—as this case suggests—it was rarely prosecuted successfully. Virtually unenforceable laws concerning private moral conduct are still on the books in many states. The real function of such laws may be to discourage people from violating community norms rather than to punish them for their transgressions.

Secession and the Civil War

The man elected to the White House in 1860 was striking in appearance—he was 6 feet 4 inches in height and seemed even taller because of his disproportionately long legs and his habit of wearing a high silk "stovepipe" hat. But Abraham Lincoln's previous career provided no guarantee he would tower over most of our other presidents in more than physical height. When Lincoln sketched the main events of his life for a campaign biographer in June 1860, he was modest almost to the point of self-deprecation. Especially regretting his "want of education," he assured the biographer that "he does what he can to supply the want."

Born to poor and illiterate parents on the Kentucky frontier in 1809, Lincoln received a few months of formal schooling in Indiana after the family moved there in 1816. But mostly he educated himself, reading and rereading a few treasured books by firelight. In 1831, when the family migrated to Illinois, he left home to make a living for himself in the struggling settlement of New Salem, where he worked as a surveyor, shopkeeper, and local postmaster. His brief career as a merchant was disastrous: he went bankrupt and was saddled with debt for years to come. But he eventually found a path to success in law and politics. While studying law on his own in New Salem, he managed to get elected to the state legislature. In 1837, he moved to Springfield, a growing town that offered bright prospects for a young lawyer-politician. Lincoln combined exceptional political and legal skills with a down-to-earth, humorous way of addressing jurors and voters. Consequently, he became a leader of the Whig party in Illinois and one of the most sought after of the lawyers who rode the central Illinois judicial circuit.

The high point of his political career as a Whig was one term in Congress (1847–1849). Lincoln did not seek reelection, but he would have faced certain defeat had he done so. His strong stand against the Mexican War alienated much of his constituency, and the voters expressed their disaffection in 1848 by electing a Democrat over the Whig who tried to succeed Lincoln. In 1849, President Zachary Taylor, for whom Lincoln had campaigned vigorously and effectively, failed to appoint him to a patronage job he coveted. Having been repudiated by the electorate and

ignored by the national leadership of a party he had served loyally and well, Lincoln concentrated on building his law practice.

The Kansas-Nebraska Act of 1854, with its advocacy of popular sovereignty, provided Lincoln with a heaven-sent opportunity to return to politics with a stronger base of support. For the first time, his driving ambition for political success and his personal convictions about what was best for the country were easy to reconcile. Lincoln had long believed slavery was an unjust institution that should be tolerated only to the extent the Constitution and the tradition of sectional compromise required. He attacked Douglas's plan of popular sovereignty because it broke with precedents for federal containment or control of the growth of slavery. After trying in vain to rally free-soilers around the Whig standard, Lincoln threw in his lot with the Republicans, assumed leadership of the new party in Illinois, attracted national attention in his bid for Douglas's Senate seat in 1858, and turned out to have the right qualifications when the Republicans chose a presidential nominee in 1860.

After Lincoln's election provoked southern secession and plunged the nation into the greatest crisis in its history, there was understandable skepticism about him in many quarters: was the former rail-splitter from Illinois up to the responsibilities he faced? Lincoln had less experience relevant to a wartime presidency than any previous chief executive, never having been a governor, senator, cabinet officer, vice president, or high-ranking military officer. But some of his training as a prairie politician would prove extremely useful in the years ahead.

Lincoln had shown himself adept at the art of party leadership; he was able to accommodate various factions and define party issues and principles in a way that would encourage unity and dedication to the cause. Since the Republican party would serve during the war as the main vehicle for mobilizing and maintaining devotion to the Union effort, these political skills assumed crucial importance. When a majority of the party came around to the view that freeing the slaves was necessary to the war effort, Lincoln found a way to comply with their wishes while minimizing the disenchantment of the conservative minority. Lincoln held the party together by persuasion,

This Matthew Brady photograph of Abraham Lincoln was taken when Lincoln arrived in Washington for his inauguration. In his inaugural address, Lincoln appealed for preservation of the Union.

patronage, and flexible policy making; this cohesiveness was essential to Lincoln's success in unifying the nation by force.

Another reason for Lincoln's effectiveness as a war leader was that he identified wholeheartedly with the northern cause and could inspire others to make sacrifices for it. In his view, the issue in the conflict was nothing less than the survival of the kind of political system that gave men like himself a chance for high office. In addressing a special session of Congress in 1861, Lincoln provided a powerful statement of what the war was all about.

And this issue embraces more than the fate of these United States. It presents to the whole family of man, the question of whether a constitutional republic, or a democracy—a government of the people

by the same people—can or cannot, maintain its territorial integrity against its own domestic foes.

The Civil War put on trial the very principle of democracy at a time when most European nations had rejected political liberalism and accepted the conservative view that popular government would inevitably collapse into anarchy. It also showed the shortcomings of a purely white man's democracy and brought the first hesitant steps toward black citizenship. As Lincoln put it in the Gettysburg Address, the only cause great enough to justify the enormous sacrifice of life on the battlefields was the struggle to preserve and extend the democratic ideal, or to ensure that "government of the people, by the people, for the people, shall not perish from the earth."

THE STORM GATHERS

Lincoln's election provoked the secession of seven states of the Deep South but did not lead immediately to armed conflict. Before the sectional quarrel would turn from a cold war into a hot one, two things had to happen: a final effort to defuse the conflict by compromise and conciliation had to fail, and the North needed to develop a firm resolve to maintain the Union by military action. Both of these developments may seem inevitable in retrospect, but for most of those living at the time it was not clear until the guns blazed at Fort Sumter that the sectional crisis would have to be resolved on the battlefield.

The Deep South Secedes

South Carolina, which had long been in the forefront of southern rights and proslavery agitation, was the first state to secede. On December 20, 1860, a convention meeting in Charleston declared unanimously that "the union now subsisting between South Carolina and other states, under the name of the 'United States of America,' is hereby dissolved." The constitutional theory behind secession was that the Union was a "compact" among sovereign states, each of which could withdraw from the Union by the vote of a

CHARLESTON
MERCURY
EXTRA:

Passed unanimously at 1.15 o'clock, P. M., December 20th, 1860.

AN ORDINANCE

To dissolve the Union between the State of South Carolina and other States united with her under the compact entitled "The Constitution of the United States of America."

We, the People of the State of South Carolina, in Convention assembled, do declare and ordain, and it is hereby declared and ordained,

That the Ordinance adopted by us in Convention, on the twenty-third day of May, in the year of our Lord one thousand seven hundred and eighty-eight, whereby the Constitution of the United States of America was ratified, and also, all Acts and parts of Acts of the General Assembly of this State, ratifying amendments of the said Constitution, are hereby repealed; and that the union now subsisting between South Carolina and other States, under the name of "The United States of America," is hereby dissolved.

THE
UNION
IS
DISSOLVED!

A South Carolina newspaper announces the dissolution of the Union. South Carolina's secession was celebrated in the South with bonfires, parades, and fireworks.

convention similar to the one that had ratified the Constitution in the first place. The South Carolinians justified seceding at this time by charging that "a sectional party" had elected a president "whose opinions and purposes are hostile to slavery."

In other states of the cotton kingdom there was similar outrage at Lincoln's election but less certainty about how to respond to it. Those who advocated immediate secession by each state individually were opposed by the "cooperationists," who believed the slave states should act as a unit. If the cooperationists had triumphed, secession

would have been delayed until a southern convention had agreed on it. Some of these moderates hoped a delay would provide time to extort major concessions from the North and thus remove the need for dissolving the Union. But South Carolina's unilateral action set a precedent that weakened the cooperationists' cause.

Elections for delegates to secession conventions in six other Deep South states were hotly contested. Cooperationists did especially well in Georgia, Louisiana, and Texas. But nowhere did they stop secessionists from winning a majority. By February 1, seven states had removed themselves from the Union—South Carolina, Alabama, Mississippi, Florida, Georgia, Louisiana, and Texas. In the upper South, however, calls for immediate secession were unsuccessful; majority opinion in Virginia, North Carolina, Tennessee, and Arkansas did not subscribe to the view that Lincoln's election was a sufficient reason for breaking up the Union. In these states, a moderate unionist element, deriving mainly from the old Whig party, had maintained its strength and cohesion despite the sectional crisis. Economic diversification had increased the importance of free labor and ties to the northern economy. Consequently, leaders in the border slave states were more willing than those in the lower South to seek a sectional compromise.

Without waiting for their sister slave states to the north, delegates from the Deep South met in Montgomery, Alabama, on February 4 to establish the Confederate States of America. The convention acted as a provisional government while at the same time drafting a permanent constitution. Relatively moderate leaders, most of whom had not supported secession until *after* Lincoln's election, dominated the proceedings and defeated or modified some of the pet schemes of a radical faction composed of extreme southern nationalists. Voted down were proposals to reopen the Atlantic slave trade, to abolish the three-fifths clause (in favor of counting all slaves in determining congressional representation), and to prohibit the admission of free states to the new Confederacy.

The resulting constitution was surprisingly similar to that of the United States. Most of the differences merely spelled out traditional southern interpretations of the federal charter: the central government was denied the authority to impose protective tariffs, subsidize internal improvements, or interfere with slavery in the states, and was required to pass laws protecting slavery in the territories. As provisional president and vice president, the convention chose Jefferson Davis of Mississippi and Alexander Stephens of Georgia, men who had resisted secessionist agitation. Stephens, in fact, had led the cooperationist forces in his home state. Radical "fire eaters" like William Yancey of Alabama and Robert Barnwell Rhett of South Carolina were denied positions of authority in the new government.

The moderation shown in Montgomery resulted in part from a desire to win support for the cause of secessionism in the reluctant states of the upper South, where such radical measures as reopening the slave trade were unpopular. But it also revealed something important about the nature of the separatist impulse even in the lower South. Proslavery reactionaries, who were totally lacking in reverence for the Union and wished to found an aristocratic nation very different from the democratic United States, had never succeeded in getting a majority behind them. Most Southerners had been opposed to dissolving the Union and repudiating their traditional patriotic loyalties so long as there had been good reasons to believe slavery was safe from northern interference.

Lincoln's election and the panic that ensued gave Southerners cause to fear that Northerners would no longer keep their "hands off" southern slavery; but it was clear from the actions of the Montgomery convention that the goal of the new converts to secessionism was not to establish a slaveholder's reactionary utopia. What they really wanted was to recreate the Union as it had been before the rise of the new Republican party, and they opted for secession only when it seemed clear that separation was the only way to achieve their aim. The decision to allow free states to join the Confederacy reflected a hope that much of the old Union could be reconstituted under southern direction. Some optimists even predicted that all of the North except New England would eventually transfer their loyalty to the new government.

Secession and the formation of the Confederacy thus amounted to a very conservative and defensive kind of "revolution." The only justification for southern independence on which a majority could agree was the need for greater security for the "peculiar institution." Vice President Stephens spoke for all the founders of the Confederacy when he described the cornerstone of the new government as "the great truth that the negro is not equal to the white man—that slavery—subordination to the superior race—is his natural condition."

The Failure of Compromise

While the Deep South was opting for independence, moderates in the North and border slave states were trying to devise a compromise that would stem the secessionist tide before it could engulf the entire South. When the lame-duck Congress reconvened in December 1860, strong sentiment existed, even among some Republicans, to seek an adjustment of sectional differences. Senator John Crittenden of Kentucky presented a plan that served as the focus for discussion. Crittenden's proposal, which resembled Henry Clay's earlier compromises, advocated extending the Missouri Compromise line to the Pacific to guarantee the protection of slavery in the southwestern territories and in any territories south of the line that might be acquired in the future. It also recommended federal compensation to the owners of escaped slaves and a constitutional amendment that would forever prohibit the federal government from abolishing or regulating slavery in the states.

Initially, congressional Republicans showed some willingness to give ground and take these proposals seriously. At one point William Seward of New York, the leading Republican in the Senate, leaned toward supporting a version of the Crittenden plan. Somewhat confused about how firmly they should support the party position that slavery must be banned in all territories, Republicans in Congress turned for guidance to the president-elect, who had remained in Springfield and was refusing to make public statements on the secession crisis. An emissary brought back word that Lincoln was adamantly opposed to the extension of the compromise line. In the words of one of his fellow Republicans, he stood "firm as an oak."

This resounding "no" to the central provision of the Crittenden plan and other similar compromise proposals stiffened the backbone of congressional Republicans, and they voted against compromise in committee. Also voting against it, and thereby ensuring its defeat, were the remaining senators and congressmen of the seceding states, who had vowed in advance to support no compromise unless the majority of Republicans also endorsed it. Their purpose in taking this stand was to obtain guarantees that the northern sectional party would end its attacks on "southern rights." The Republicans did in the end agree to support Crittenden's "unamendable" amendment guaranteeing that slavery would be immune from future federal action. This action was not really a concession to the South, because Republicans had always acknowledged that the federal government had no constitutional authority to meddle with slavery in the states.

Some historians have blamed Lincoln and the Republicans for causing an unnecessary war by rejecting a compromise that would have appeased southern pride without providing any immediate practical opportunities for the expansion of slavery. But it is questionable whether approval of the compromise would have halted secession of the Deep South. If we take the secessionists at their word, they would have been satisfied with nothing less than federal protection of slavery in *all* territories and the active suppression of antislavery agitation in the North.

Furthermore, Lincoln and those who took his advice had what they considered to be very good reasons for not making territorial concessions. One of these derived from the mistaken northern notion that the secession movement was a conspiracy that reflected the will of only a minority of Southerners. Concessions would allegedly demoralize southern Unionists and moderates by showing that the "rule-or-ruin" attitude of the radical sectionalists paid dividends. It is doubtful, however, that Lincoln and the dedicated free-soilers for whom he spoke would have given ground even if they had realized the secession movement was genuinely popular in the Deep South. In their view, extending the Missouri Compromise line of 36° 30′ to the Pacific would not halt agitation for extending slavery to new areas. South of the line were Cuba and Central America, long the target of southern expansionists who dreamed of a Caribbean slave empire. The only way to resolve the crisis over the future of slavery and to reunite "the house divided" was to remove any chance that slaveholders could enlarge their domain.

Lincoln was also convinced that backing down in the face of secessionist threats would fatally undermine the democratic principle of majority rule. In his inaugural address of March 4, 1861, he recalled that during the winter many "patriotic men" had urged him to accept a compromise that would "shift the ground" on which he had been elected. But to do so would have signified that a victorious presidential candidate "cannot be inaugurated till he betrays those who elected him by breaking his pledges, and surrendering to those who tried and failed to defeat him at the polls." Making such a concession would mean that "this government and all popular government is already at an end."

And the War Came

By the time of Lincoln's inauguration, seven states had seceded, formed an independent confederacy, and seized most federal forts and other installations in the Deep South without firing a shot. Lincoln's predecessor, James Buchanan, had denied the right of secession but had also refused to use "coercion" to maintain federal authority. In January, he sent an unarmed merchant ship, the *Star of the West,* to reinforce the federal garrison in Charleston Harbor, but the vessel turned back after being fired upon. Buchanan's doubts about whether a Union held together by force was worth keeping were, for a time, widely shared in the North. Besides the business community, which was fearful of breaking commercial links with the cotton-producing South, some antislavery Republicans and abolitionists opposed coercive action because they thought the nation might be better off if "the erring sisters" of the Deep South were allowed "to depart in peace."

The collapse of compromise efforts eliminated the option of peaceful maintenance of the Union and narrowed the choices to peaceful separation or war between the sections. By early March, the tide of public opinion was beginning to shift in favor of strong action to preserve the Union. Once the business community realized conciliation would not keep the cotton states in the Union, it put most of its weight behind coercive measures, reasoning that a temporary disruption of commerce was better than the permanent loss of the South as a market and source of raw materials.

In his inaugural address, Lincoln called for a cautious and limited use of force. He would defend federal forts and installations not yet in Confederate hands but would not attempt to recapture the ones already taken. He thus tried to shift the burden for beginning hostilities to the Confederacy, which would have to attack before it would be attacked.

As Lincoln spoke, only four military installations within the seceded states were still held by U. S. forces. Two of these were in the remote Florida Keys and thus attracted little attention. The others were Fort Pickens in northern Florida, which was located in a defensible position on an island outside of the port of Pensacola, and Fort Sumter inside Charleston Harbor. Attention focused on Sumter because the Confederacy, egged on by South Carolina, was demanding the surrender of a garrison that was within easy reach of shore batteries and running low on supplies. Shortly after taking office, Lincoln was informed Sumter could not hold out much longer and that he would have to decide whether to reinforce it or let it fall.

Initially, the majority of Lincoln's cabinet opposed efforts to reinforce or provision Sumter on the grounds that it was indefensible anyway. Secretary of State Seward was so certain this would be the ultimate decision that he so advised representatives of the Confederacy. Lincoln kept his options open in regard to Sumter. On April 4, he ordered that an expedition be prepared to bring food and other provisions to the beleaguered troops in Charleston Harbor. Two days later, he discovered his orders to reinforce Fort Pickens had not been carried out. Later that same day, he sent word to the governor of South Carolina that the relief expedition was being sent.

The expedition sailed on April 8 and 9; but before it arrived, Confederate authorities decided the sending of provisions was a hostile act and proceeded to attack the fort. Early on the morning of April 12, shore batteries opened fire; the bombardment continued for forty hours without loss of life but with heavy damage to the walls of the fort. Finally, on April 13, the Union forces under Major Robert Anderson surrendered, and the Confederate flag was raised over Fort Sumter. The South had won a victory but had also assumed responsibility for firing the first shot. Lincoln had taken pains to ensure that if the South was really determined to fight for its independence, it would have to begin by taking an aggressive action.

On April 15, Lincoln proclaimed that an insurrection against federal authority existed in the Deep South and called on the militia of the loyal states to provide 75,000 troops for short-term service to put it down. Two days later, a sitting Virginia convention, which had earlier rejected secession, reversed itself and voted to join the Confederacy. Within the next five weeks, Arkansas, Tennessee, and North Carolina followed suit. These slave states of the upper South had been unwilling to secede just because Lincoln was elected, but when he called on them to provide troops to "coerce" other southern states, they had to choose sides. Believing secession was a constitutional right, they were quick to cut their ties with a government that opted for the use of force to maintain the Union and called on them to join in the effort.

In the North, the firing on Sumter evoked strong feelings of patriotism and dedication to the Union. "It seems as if we were never alive till now; never had a country till now," wrote a New Yorker; and a Bostonian noted that "I never before knew what a popular excitement can be." Stephen A. Douglas, Lincoln's former political rival, pledged his full support for the crusade against secession and literally worked himself to death rallying midwestern Democrats behind the government. By firing on the flag, the Confederacy united the North. Everyone assumed the war would be short and not very bloody. It remained to be seen whether Unionist fervor could be sustained through a long and costly struggle.

The entire Confederacy, which now moved its capital from Montgomery to Richmond, Virginia, contained only eleven of the fifteen states in which slavery was lawful. In the border slave states of Maryland, Delaware, Kentucky, and Missouri, secession was thwarted by a combination of local Unionism and federal intervention. Kentucky, the most crucial of these states, greeted the outbreak of war by proclaiming its neutrality. Kentucky eventually sided with the Union, mainly because Lincoln, who was careful to respect this tenuous neutrality, provoked the South into violating neutrality first by sending regular troops into the state. Maryland, which surrounded the nation's capital and provided it with access to the free states, was kept in the Union by more ruthless methods, which included the use of martial law to suppress Confederate sympathizers. In Missouri, the presence of regular troops, aided significantly by a staunchly pro-Union German immigrant population, stymied the secession

Secession

The fall of Fort Sumter was a watershed for the secessionist movement. With no room left for compromise, slave states of the upper South chose to join the Confederacy.

movement. But pro-Union forces failed to establish order in this deeply divided frontier state. Brutal guerrilla fighting made wartime Missouri an unsafe and bloody place.

Hence the Civil War was not, strictly speaking, a struggle between slave and free states. Nor did it simply pit states that could not tolerate Lincoln's election against those that could. More than anything else, conflicting views on the right of secession determined the ultimate division of states and the choices of individuals in areas where sentiment was divided. General Robert E. Lee, for example, was neither a defender of slavery nor a southern nationalist. But he followed Virginia out of the Union because he was the loyal son of a "sovereign state." General George Thomas, another Virginian, chose the Union because he believed it was indissoluble. Although concern about the future of slavery had driven the Deep South to secede in the first place, the actual lineup of states and supporters meant the two sides would define the war less as a struggle over slavery than as a contest to determine whether the Union was indivisible.

ADJUSTING TO TOTAL WAR

The Civil War was a "total war" involving every aspect of society because the North could achieve its aim of restoring the Union only by defeating the South so thoroughly that its separatist government would be overthrown. It was a long war because the Confederacy put up "a hell of a fight" before it would agree to be put to death. Total war is a test of societies, economies, and political systems, as well as a battle of wits between generals and military strategists—and the Civil War was no exception.

Prospects, Plans, and Expectations

If the war was to be decided by sheer physical strength, then the North had an enormous edge in population, industrial capacity, and railroad mileage. Nevertheless, the South had some advantages that went a long way toward counterbalancing the North's demographic and industrial superiority. It could do more with less, because its armies faced an easier task. To achieve its aim

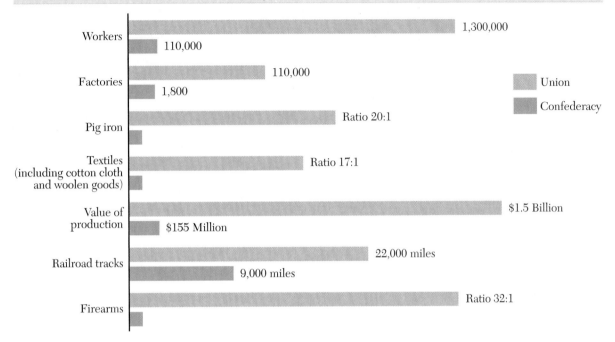

Resources of the Union and the Confederacy, 1861

Workers — Union: 1,300,000 / Confederacy: 110,000

Factories — Union: 110,000 / Confederacy: 1,800

Pig iron — Ratio 20:1

Textiles (including cotton cloth and woolen goods) — Ratio 17:1

Value of production — Union: $1.5 Billion / Confederacy: $155 Million

Railroad tracks — Union: 22,000 miles / Confederacy: 9,000 miles

Firearms — Ratio 32:1

Legend: Union / Confederacy

of independence, the Confederacy needed only to defend its own territory successfully. The North, on the other hand, had to invade and conquer the South. Consequently, the Confederacy faced a less serious supply problem, had a greater capacity to choose the time and place of combat, and could take advantage of familiar terrain and a friendly civilian population.

The nature of the war meant southern leaders could define their cause as defense of their homeland against an alien invader and thus appeal to the fervid patriotism of a white population that viewed Yankee domination as a form of slavery. The northern cause, however, was not nearly as clear cut as that of the South. It seemed doubtful in 1861 that Northerners would be willing to give equally fervent support to a war fought for the seemingly abstract principle that the Union was sacred and perpetual.

Confederate optimism on the eve of the war was also fed by other—and more dubious—calculations. It was widely assumed that Southerners would make better fighting men than Yankees. Farm boys used to riding and shooting could allegedly whip several times their number among the clerks and factory workers (many of them immigrants) who, it was anticipated, would make up a large part of the Union Army. (Actually a majority of northern soldiers would also be farm boys.) When most of the large proportion of

Confederate volunteers at the start of the war.

high-ranking officers in the U.S. Army who were of southern origin resigned to accept Confederate commands, Southerners confidently expected that their armies would be better led. If external help was needed, such major foreign powers as England and France might come to the aid of the Confederacy because the industrial economies of those European nations depended on southern cotton.

As they thought about strategy in the weeks and months after Fort Sumter, the leaders of both sides tried to find the best way to capitalize on their advantages and compensate for their limitations. The choice before President Davis, who assumed personal direction of the Confederate military effort, was whether to stay on the defensive or seek a sudden and dramatic victory by invading the North. He chose to wage a mainly defensive war in the hope he could make the Union pay so dearly for its incursions into the South that the northern populace would soon tire of the effort. But this plan did not preclude invading the North for psychological or military effect when good opportunities presented themselves. Nor did it inhibit Confederate aggressiveness against exposed northern forces within the South. Although their primary strategic orientation was defensive, it was an "offensive defense" that southern commanders put into effect.

Northern military planners had greater difficulty in working out a basic strategy, and it took a good deal of trial and error (mostly error) before there was a clear sense of what had to be done. Some optimists believed the war could be won quickly and easily by sending an army to capture the Confederate capital of Richmond, scarcely 100 miles from Washington. The "On to Richmond" solution died on the battlefields of Virginia when it soon became clear that difficult terrain and an ably led, hard-fighting Confederate army blocked the way. Aware of the costs of invading the South at points where its forces were concentrated, the aged General Winfield Scott—who commanded the Union Army during the early months of the war—recommended an "anaconda policy." Like a great boa constrictor, the North would squeeze the South into submission by blockading the southern coasts, seizing control of the Mississippi, and cutting off supplies of food and other essential commodities. This plan pointed to the West as the main locus of military operations.

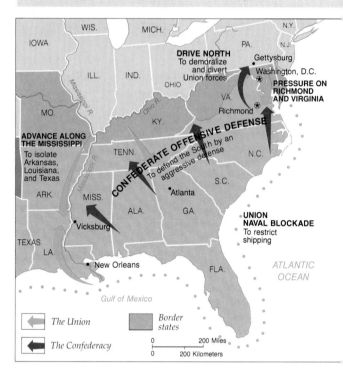

Overview of Civil War Strategy
Confederate military leaders were convinced the South could not be defended unless they took the initiative to determine where critical battles would be fought.

Eventually Lincoln decided on a two-front war. He would keep the pressure on Virginia in the hope a breakthrough would occur there, while at the same time, he would authorize an advance down the Mississippi Valley with the aim of isolating Texas, Arkansas, and Louisiana. Lincoln also attached great importance to the coastal blockade and expected naval operations to seize the ports through which goods entered and left the Confederacy. His basic plan of applying pressure and probing for weaknesses at several points simultaneously was a good one because it took maximum advantage of the North's superiority in manpower and matériel. But it required better military leadership than the North possessed at the beginning of the war and took a painfully long time to put into effect.

Mobilizing the Home Fronts

The North and South faced similar problems in trying to create the vast support systems needed by armies in the field. At the beginning of the conflict, both sides had more volunteers than could be armed and outfitted. The South was forced to reject about 200,000 men in the first year of the war, and the North could commit only a fraction of its forces to battle. Further confusion resulted from the fact that recruiting was done primarily by the states, which were reluctant to surrender control of the forces they had raised. Both Lincoln and Davis had to deal with governors who resisted centralized direction of the military effort.

As it became clear that hopes for a short and easy war were false, the pool of volunteers began to dry up. Many of the early recruits, who had been enrolled for short terms, showed a reluctance to reenlist. To resolve this problem, the Confederacy passed a conscription law in April 1862, and the Union edged toward a draft in July when Congress gave Lincoln the power to assign manpower quotas to each state and resort to conscription if they were not met (see "Soldiering in the Civil War," pp. 448–449).

To produce the materials of war, both governments relied mainly on private industry. In the North, especially, the system of contracting with private firms and individuals to supply the army resulted in much corruption and inefficiency. The government at times bought shoddy uniforms that disintegrated in a heavy rain, defective rifles, and broken-down horses unfit for service. But the North's economy was strong at the core, and by 1863 its factories and farms were producing more than enough to provision the troops without significantly lowering the living standards of the civilian population.

The southern economy was much less adaptable to the needs of a total war. Because of the weakness of its industrial base, the South of 1861 depended on the outside world for most of its manufactured goods. As the Union blockade became more effective, the Confederacy had to rely increasingly on a government-sponsored crash program to produce war materials. In addition to encouraging and promoting private initiative, the government built its own munitions plants, including a gigantic powder factory at Augusta, Georgia. Astonishingly, the Confederate Ordnance Bureau, under the able direction of General Josiah Gorgas, succeeded in producing or procuring sufficient armaments to keep southern armies well supplied throughout the conflict.

Southern agriculture, however, failed to meet the challenge. Planters were reluctant to shift from staples that could no longer be readily exported to foodstuffs that were urgently needed. But more significant was the inadequacy of the South's internal transportation system. Its limited rail network was designed to link plantation regions to port cities rather than to connect food-producing areas with centers of population, as was the pattern in the North. New railroad construction during the war did not resolve the problem; most of the new lines were aimed to facilitate the movement of troops rather than the distribution of food.

When northern forces penetrated parts of the South, they created new gaps in the system. As a result, much of the corn or livestock that was raised could not reach the people who needed it. Although well armed, Confederate soldiers were increasingly undernourished, and by 1863 civilians in urban areas were rioting to protest shortages of food. To supply the troops, the Confederate commissary resorted to the impressment of available agricultural produce at below the market price, a policy resisted so vigorously by farmers and local politicians that it eventually had to be abandoned.

Another challenge faced by both sides was how to finance an enormously costly struggle. Although special war taxes were imposed, neither side was willing to resort to the heavy taxation that was needed to maintain fiscal integrity. Americans, it seems, were more willing to die for their government than to pay for it. Besides floating loans and selling bonds, both treasuries deliberately inflated the currency by printing large quantities of paper money that could not be redeemed in gold and silver. In August 1861, the Confederacy issued $100 million of such currency, and the Union followed suit by printing $150 million in early 1862. The presses rolled throughout the war, and runaway inflation was the inevitable result. The problem was much less severe in the North because of the overall strength of its economy. War taxes on income were more readily collectable than in the South, and bond issues were more successful.

The Confederacy was hampered from the outset by a severe shortage of readily disposable wealth that could be tapped for public purposes. Land and cotton could not easily be turned into rifles and cannons, and the southern treasury had to accept payments "in kind." As a result, Confederate "assets" eventually consisted mainly

Soldiering in the Civil War

Early in the Civil War, William Tecumseh Sherman told an audience of fresh-faced recruits that "There's many a boy here today who looks on war as all glory, but, boys, it is all hell." Letters from Civil War soldiers reveal that Sherman's lesson was painfully learned by young men in both armies over the four years of conflict. At the outset, the firing on Fort Sumter infected both North and South with war fever. What later became a national nightmare began as a glorious defense of home and country. Young men rushed to join up in great numbers, taxing the ability of the authorities to process enlistments.

Initially, the creation and supply of Union and Confederate army units was in the hands of local communities. A leading citizen—or politician—would advertise for men to fill a company or regiment. Once a unit was assembled, it elected its own officers and chose a commander—usually the man who had led the recruiting drive. The entire procedure, with its solicitation of votes and promises of patronage, was much like a peacetime local election.

Early Union defeats and a strategic stalemate not only ended talk on both sides of a "short engagement filled with glory" but also revealed how undisciplined the troops were. Of the more than 3 million Civil War servicemen, two-thirds were younger than twenty-three years of age and came from rural areas. They were not accustomed to the regimentation necessary to military life; as a young recruit from Illinois put it, "It comes rather hard at first to be deprived of liberty." Inadequate leadership, as well as the beginnings of war weariness and the arrival of letters from home pleading for help with the harvest, led to a degree of military anarchy. The early battles were contests between armed mobs that might break and run with little provocation. Moreover, the long casualty lists from these early battles discouraged new waves of enlistments.

Both governments hit on similar methods of recruiting and disciplining troops. Enlistment and reenlistment bounties were instituted, and the nation's first conscription laws were passed. The dual aim was to maintain the ranks of the original volunteers, while at the same time stimulating more enlistments. Terms of service were lengthened, in most cases to three years, and all nonenlisted men of military age were registered and called on either to volunteer or be faced with the disgrace of being drafted. Although some Southerners were exempted to oversee their large numbers of slaves, and Northerners could escape military duty by paying a $300 fee, the laws did spur enlistments. Between 1861 and 1865, more than half of the nation's 5.5 million men of military age were mustered into service.

The solution to the problem of training the troops was the army training camp. With its "50,000 pup tents and wigwams," the camp was the volunteer's way station between home and battlefield. It was the place the raw recruit received his first bitter taste of the tedium, hardship, and deprivation of soldiering. "A soldier is not his own man," a Louisiana recruit wrote, astonished at how markedly camp routines differed from civilian life. "He has given up all claim on himself. . . . I will give you a little information concerning evry day business. consider youreself a private soldier and in camp . . . the drum beats for drill. you fall in and start. you here feel youre inferirority. even the Sargeants is hollering at you close up; Ketch step. dress to the right, and sutch like."

Professional noncommissioned officers from the peacetime army were used, most effectively by the Union, to turn men into soldiers who could fire a rifle and understand simple commands. The liberal use of the court martial and the board of review enabled the professional soldiers to rid the army of its most incompetent officer-politicians and instill discipline in the ranks. Many recruits spent their entire terms of service within these tent cities, forming a reserve on which field commanders could call to replace casualties.

The camps were themselves the sites of hundreds of thousands of Civil War casualties. Fewer men died of battle wounds than of dysentery, typhoid fever, and other water-borne diseases contracted in the camps, which were often located on swampy land without adequate fresh water. The army food was always the butt of soldier humor—one soldier complained

the beef issued to him must have been carved from a bull "too old for the conscript law"—but it was also the source of its own set of diseases, particularly scurvy. Men in the field were condemned to a diet of "hardtack and half-cooked beans," and no soldier could expect to receive fresh fruits or vegetables. But food became steadily more plentiful in the Union camps; and doctors, officers, and agents of the U. S. Sanitary Commission teamed up to improve camp cleanliness. "Johnny Reb," however, had to survive under steadily worsening conditions. The Confederate supply system did not improve significantly during the course of the war and grew worse wherever the North invaded or blockaded. Nevertheless, the battlefield performance of fighting men on the two sides remained roughly on a par throughout the war.

Camp lessons were often forgotten in the heat of battle, particularly by green troops who "saw the elephant" (went into battle for the first time) and ran from it. Like the youth in Stephen Crane's *The Red Badge of Courage*, a Mississippian anxiously admitted after his first fight that "though i did not run i

mite have if i had thought of it in time." The Union's ability to call more new men into service may have guaranteed ultimate victory, but it meant that battle-hardened Confederate veterans faced large numbers of raw northern recruits in every major battle. Since experience often counted for more than basic training and equipment, southern troops could expect to engage the enemy on fairly equal terms.

The Civil War was the most costly and brutal struggle in which American soldiers have ever been engaged. More American servicemen died in that war (618,000) than in the two world wars and Vietnam combined. Contests were decided by deadly charges in which muskets were exploded at such close range as to sear the faces of the contestants. The survivors, in their letters home, attempted to describe the inhuman events but, as a Maine soldier wrote to his parents after the battle of Gettysburg: "You can form no idea of a battlefield. . . . no pen can describe it. No tongue can tell its horror[.] I hope none of my brothers will ever have to go into a fight."

Fresh recruits cannot avoid seeing battle casualties and field amputations as they wait to join the battle of Fredericksburg in this painting The Battle of Fredericksburg (1862) *by John Richards, based on an engraving that appeared in* Harper's *shortly after the battle.*

of bales of cotton that were unexportable because of the blockade. As the Confederate government fell deeper and deeper into debt and printed more and more paper money, its rate of inflation soared out of sight. By August 1863, a Confederate dollar was worth only eight cents in gold. Late in the war, it could be said with little exaggeration that it took a wheelbarrow full of money to buy a purse full of goods.

Political Leadership: Northern Success and Southern Failure

Total war also forced political adjustments, and both the Union and the Confederacy had to face the question of how much democracy and individual freedom could be permitted when military success required an unprecedented exercise of governmental authority. Since both constitutions made the president commander in chief of the army and navy, Lincoln and Davis took actions that would have been regarded as arbitrary or even tyrannical in peacetime. Nevertheless, "politics as usual"—in the form of free elections, public political controversy, and the maneuverings of parties, factions, and interest groups—persisted to a surprising degree.

Lincoln was especially bold in assuming new executive powers. After the fighting started at Fort Sumter, he expanded the regular army and advanced public money to private individuals without authorization by Congress. On April 27, 1861, he declared martial law, which enabled the military to arrest civilians suspected of aiding the enemy, and suspended the writ of habeas corpus in the area between Philadelphia and Washington, an action deemed necessary because of mob attacks on Union troops passing through Baltimore. Suspension of the writ enabled the government to arrest Confederate sympathizers and hold them without trial, and in September 1862 Lincoln extended this authority to all parts of the United States where "disloyal" elements were active. Such willingness to interfere with civil liberties was unprecedented and possibly unconstitutional, but Lincoln argued that "necessity" justified a flexible interpretation of his war powers. For critics of suspension he had a question: "are all the laws, *but one,* to go unexecuted, and the government itself to go to pieces, lest that one be violated?" In fact, however, most of the

thousands of civilians arrested by military authorities were not exercising their right to criticize the government but were suspected deserters and draft dodgers, refugees, smugglers, or people who were simply found wandering in areas under military control.

For the most part, the Lincoln administration showed restraint and tolerated a broad spectrum of political dissent. Although the government closed down a few newspapers for brief periods when they allegedly published false information or military secrets, antiadministration journals were allowed to criticize the president and his party at will. A few politicians, including an Ohio Congressman, were arrested for proconfederate activity, but a large number of "Peace Democrats"—who called for restoration of the Union by negotiation rather than force—ran for office, sat in Congress and in state legislatures, and thus had ample opportunity to present their views to the public. Lincoln's hand was in fact strengthened by the persistence of vigorous two-party competition in the North during the Civil War. Since his war policies were also the platform of his party,

Jefferson Davis, inaugurated as president of the Confederacy on February 18, 1861, was a West Point graduate and had served as secretary of war under President Franklin Pierce.

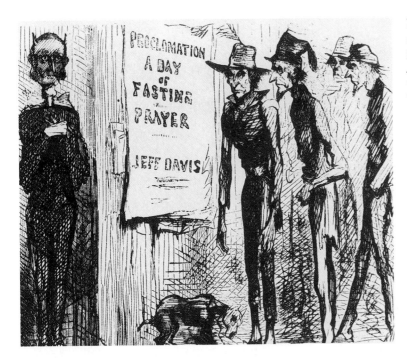

Gaunt southern citizens stare unbeliev-ingly at a poster announcing a day of fasting proclaimed by a horned Jefferson Davis. Davis's insistent demands for his army aroused the hard-pressed Southerners' anger.

he could usually rely on unified partisan backing for the most controversial of his decisions.

Jefferson Davis, most historians agree, was a less effective war leader than Lincoln. He defined his powers as commander in chief narrowly and literally, which meant he assumed personal direction of the armed forces but left policy making for the mobilization and control of the civilian population primarily to the Confederate Congress. Unfortunately, he overestimated his capacities as a strategist and lacked the tact to handle field commanders who were as proud and testy as he was. Two of the South's best generals—Joseph E. Johnston and P. G. T. Beauregard—were denied the commands they deserved because they could not get along with Davis. One of the worst—Braxton E. Bragg—happened to be a personal favorite of the president and was allowed to keep a major command even after he had clearly demonstrated his incompetence.

Davis's greatest failing, however, was his lack of initiative and leadership in dealing with the problems of the home front. He devoted little attention to a deteriorating economic situation that caused great hardship and sapped Confederate morale. Although the South had a much more serious problem of internal division and disloyalty than the North, he refrained from declaring martial law on his own authority. The

Confederate Congress grudgingly voted him such power when he asked for it but allowed it to be applied only in limited areas and for short periods.

As the war dragged on, Davis's political and popular support eroded. He was opposed and obstructed by state governors—such as Joseph E. Brown of Georgia and Zebulon Vance of North Carolina—who resisted conscription and other Confederate policies that violated the tradition of states' rights. The Confederate Congress served as a forum for bitter attacks on the administration's conduct of the war, and by 1863 a majority of southern newspapers were taking an anti-Davis stand. Even if he had been a more able and inspiring leader, Davis would have had difficulty maintaining his authority and credibility. Unlike Lincoln, he did not have an organized party behind him, for the Confederacy never developed a two-party system. As a result, it was difficult to mobilize the support required for hard decisions and controversial policies.

Early Campaigns and Battles

The war's first major battle was a disaster for northern arms. Against his better judgment, General Winfield Scott responded to the "On to Richmond" clamor and ordered poorly trained Union troops under General Irvin McDowell to

The battle of the ironclads between the huge Merrimack *and the smaller* Monitor *ended in the* Merrimack *being forced into port. Both ships were later lost; the* Merrimack *was blown up in Norfolk harbor in May 1862 and the* Monitor *went down in a gale in December.*

advance against the Confederate forces gathered at Manassas Junction, Virginia. They attacked the enemy position near Bull Run Creek on July 21, 1861, and seemed on their way to victory until Confederate reinforcements arrived from the Shenandoah Valley. After Confederate General Thomas J. Jackson had earned the nickname "Stonewall" for holding the line against the northern assault, the augmented southern army counterattacked and routed the invading force. As they retreated toward Washington, the raw Union troops gave in to panic and broke ranks in their stampede to safety.

The humiliating defeat at Bull Run led to a shake-up of the northern high command. The man of the hour was George McClellan, who first replaced McDowell as commander of troops in the Washington area and then became general-in-chief when Scott was eased into retirement. A cautious disciplinarian, McClellan spent the fall and winter drilling his troops and whipping them into shape. President Lincoln, who could not understand why McClellan was taking so long to go into the field, became increasingly impatient and finally tried to order the army into action.

Before McClellan made his move, Union forces in the West won some important victories. In February 1862, a joint military-naval operation, commanded by General Ulysses S. Grant, captured Fort Henry on the Tennessee River and Fort Donelson on the Cumberland. Fourteen thousand prisoners were taken at Donelson, and the Confederate Army was forced to withdraw from Kentucky and middle Tennessee. Southern forces in the West then massed at Corinth, Mississippi, just across the border from Tennessee. When a slow-moving Union Army arrived just north of the Mississippi state line, the South launched a surprise attack on April 6. In the battle of Shiloh, one of the bloodiest of the war, only the timely arrival of reinforcements prevented the annihilation of Union troops backed up against the Tennessee River. After a second day of fierce fighting, the Confederates retreated to Corinth, leaving the enemy forces battered and exhausted.

Although the Union's military effort to seize control of the Mississippi Valley was temporarily halted at Shiloh, the Union Navy soon contributed dramatically to the pursuit of that objec-

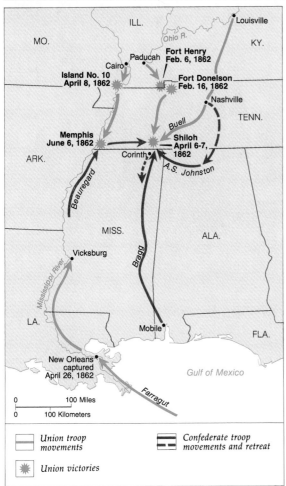

ILL.

Louisville

MO.

KY.

Ohio R.

Paducah

Fort Henry
Feb. 6, 1862

Cairo

Island No. 10
April 8, 1862

Fort Donelson
Feb. 16, 1862

Nashville

TENN.

Buell

Memphis
June 6, 1862

Shiloh
April 6-7,
1862

Corinth

A. S. Johnston

ARK.

Beauregard

MISS.

ALA.

Vicksburg

Mississippi River

Bragg

LA.

Mobile

FLA.

New Orleans
captured
April 26, 1862

Gulf of Mexico

Farragut

| 0 | 100 Miles |
| 0 | 100 Kilometers |

Union troop movements

Confederate troop movements and retreat

Union victories

repulsed by the *Monitor,* an armored and turreted Union gunship.

Successes around the edges of the Confederacy did not relieve northern frustration at the inactivity or failure of Union forces on the eastern front. Only after Lincoln had relieved him of supreme command and ordered him to take the offensive at the head of the Army of the Potomac did McClellan start campaigning. Spurning the treacherous overland route to Richmond, he moved his forces by water to the peninsula southeast of the Confederate capital. After landing at Fortress Monroe, which had remained in Union hands, McClellan began moving up the peninsula in early April 1862. For a month he was bogged down before Yorktown, which he chose to besiege rather than assault directly. After Yorktown fell on May 4, he pushed ahead to a point 20 miles from Richmond, where he awaited the additional troops that he expected Lincoln to send.

These reinforcements were not forthcoming. While McClellan was inching his way up the peninsula, a relatively small southern force under Stonewall Jackson was on the rampage in the Shenandoah Valley, where it succeeded in pinning down a much larger Union Army and defeating its detached units in a series of lightning moves. When it appeared by late May that Jackson might be poised to march east and attack the Union capital, Lincoln decided to withhold troops from McClellan so they would be available to defend Washington.

If McClellan had moved more boldly and decisively, he probably could have captured Richmond with the forces he had. But a combination of faulty intelligence reports and his own natural caution led him to falter in the face of what he wrongly believed to be superior numbers. At the end of May, the Confederates under Joseph E. Johnston took the offensive when they discovered McClellan's army was divided into two segments by the Chickahominy River. In the battle of Seven Pines, McClellan was barely able to hold his ground on the side of the river under attack until a corps from the other side crossed over just in time to save the day. During the battle, General Johnston was severely wounded; succeeding him in command of the Confederate Army of Northern Virginia was native Virginian and West Point graduate Robert E. Lee.

tive. On April 26 a fleet under Flag Officer David Farragut, coming up from the Gulf, captured the port of New Orleans after boldly running past the forts below the city. The occupation of New Orleans, besides securing the mouth of the Mississippi, climaxed a series of naval and amphibious operations around the edges of the Confederacy that had already succeeded in capturing South Carolina's Sea Islands and North Carolina's Roanoke Island. Strategically located bases were thus available to enforce a blockade of the southern coast. The last serious challenge to the North's naval supremacy ended on March 9, 1862, when the Confederate ironclad vessel *Virginia* (originally the USS *Merrimack*)—which had demolished wooden-hulled northern ships in the vicinity of Hampton Roads, Virginia—was

After Antietam, Lincoln visited McClellan's headquarters to urge the general to take action. McClellan is on the left facing the President.

Toward the end of June, Lee began an all-out effort to expel McClellan from the outskirts of Richmond. In a series of battles that lasted for seven days, the two armies clawed at each other indecisively. Although McClellan repulsed Lee's final assaults at Malvern Hill, the Union general decided to retreat down the peninsula to a more secure base. This backward step convinced Lincoln that the peninsula campaign was an exercise in futility.

On July 11 Lincoln appointed General Henry W. Halleck, who had been in overall command in the western theater, to be the new general-in-chief and through Halleck ordered McClellan to withdraw his army from the peninsula to join a force under General John Pope that was preparing to move on Richmond by the overland route. As usual, McClellan was slow in responding, and the Confederates got to Pope before he did. At the end of August, in the second battle fought near Bull Run, Lee established his reputation for brilliant generalship; he sent Stonewall Jackson to Pope's rear, provoked the rash Union general to attack Jackson with full force, and then threw the main Confederate Army against the Union's flank. Badly beaten, Pope retreated to the defens-

es of Washington, where he was stripped of command. Out of sheer desperation, Lincoln reappointed McClellan to head the Army of the Potomac.

Lee proceeded to lead his exuberant troops on an invasion of Maryland, in the hope of isolating Washington from the rest of the North. McClellan caught up with him near Sharpsburg, and the bloodiest one-day battle of the war ensued. When the smoke cleared at Antietam on September 17, almost five thousand men had been killed on the two sides and more than eighteen thousand were wounded. The result was a draw, but Lee was forced to fall back south of the Potomac to protect his dangerously extended supply lines. McClellan was slow in pursuit, and Lincoln blamed him for letting the enemy escape.

Convinced that McClellan was fatally infected with "the slows," Lincoln once again sought a more aggressive general and put Ambrose E. Burnside in command of the Army of the Potomac. Burnside was aggressive enough, but he was also rather dense. His limitations were disastrously revealed at the battle of Fredericksburg, Virginia, on December 13, 1862, when he launched a direct assault to try to capture an entrenched and elevated position. Throughout the Civil War such uphill charges almost invariably failed because of the range and deadly accuracy of small arms fire when concentrated on exposed troops. The debacle at Fredericksburg, where Union forces suffered more than twice as many casualties as their opponents, ended a year of bitter failure for the North on the eastern front.

The Diplomatic Struggle

The critical period of Civil War diplomacy was 1861 to 1862, when the South was making every effort to induce major foreign powers to recognize its independence and break the Union blockade. The hope that England and France could be persuaded to intervene on the Confederate side stemmed from the fact that these nations depended on the South for three-quarters of their cotton supply. In the case of Britain, the uninterrupted production of cotton textiles appeared essential to economic prosperity; an estimated 20 to 25 percent of its entire population was supported either directly or indirectly by this single industry.

The Confederate commissioners sent to England and France in May 1861 succeeded in gaining recognition of southern "belligerency," which meant the new government could claim some international rights of a nation at war. The North protested vigorously, but by declaring a blockade of southern ports, it had undermined its official position that the rebellion was merely a domestic insurrection. The main advantage of belligerent status was that it permitted the South to purchase and outfit privateers in neutral ports. As a result, Confederate raiders, built and armed in British shipyards, like the *Alabama*—which single-handedly sank sixty-two vessels—devastated northern shipping to such an extent that insurance costs eventually forced most of the American merchant marine off the high seas for the duration of the war.

In the fall of 1861 the Confederate government dispatched James M. Mason and John Slidell to be its permanent envoys to England and France, respectively, and instructed them to push for full recognition of the Confederacy. They took passage on the British steamer *Trent,* which was stopped and boarded in international waters by a U. S. warship. Mason and Slidell were taken into custody by the Union captain, causing a diplo-

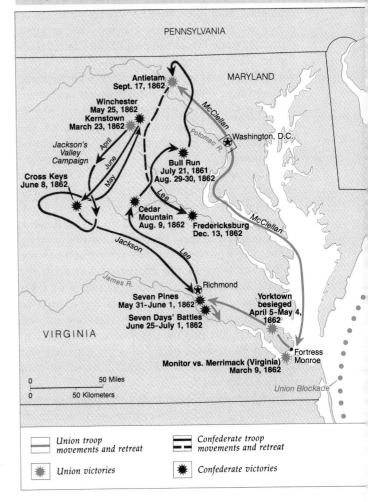

Eastern Theater of War, 1861–1862
Defeats on the battlefield forced a change in the Union's initial military campaign of capturing Richmond, the Confederate capital.

matic crisis that nearly led to war between England and the United States. Refusing to tolerate this flagrant violation of its maritime rights, Britain threatened war if the Confederate emissaries were not released. After a few weeks of ferocious posturing by both sides, Lincoln and Secretary of State Seward made the prudent decision to allow Mason and Slidell to proceed to their destinations.

These envoys may as well have stayed at home; they failed in their mission to obtain full recognition of the Confederacy from either England or France. The anticipated cotton shortage was slow to develop, for the bumper crop of 1860 had created a large surplus in British and French ware-houses. Recognition did seem likely for a brief period in the fall of 1862. Napoleon III, the emperor of France, personally favored the south-ern cause, mainly because he was trying to set up a puppet government in Mexico and saw the chance to trade French support of the Confederacy for an acceptance of his regime south of the bor-der. But he was unwilling to risk war with the United States unless the British would cosponsor his plan to offer European mediation of the American conflict and then recognize the Confederacy if—as expected—the North refused to go along.

British opinion, both official and public, was seriously divided on how to respond to the American conflict. In 1861 and 1862, Lord Palmerston, the prime minister, and Lord Russell, the foreign secretary, played a cautious waiting game. Their government was sympathetic to the South but wary of the danger of war with the United States if they acted in support of their preference. Northern diplomats knew how to play on these fears: Secretary of State Seward and Charles Francis Adams, the American minister to Great Britain, could be relied on to threaten war at any hint of British recognition or support of the Confederacy.

In September 1862, the British cabinet debated mediation and recognition as serious possibilities. Lord Russell pressed for a pro-Confederate policy because he was convinced the South was now strong enough to secure its independence. But when word arrived that Lee had failed to win a clear victory at Antietam and was retreating, Lord Palmerston overruled the foreign secretary and decided to maintain a hands-off policy. The British would intervene, his decision suggested, only if the South won decisively on the battle-field.

The cotton famine finally hit in late 1862, causing massive unemployment in the British tex-tile industry. But, contrary to southern hopes, public opinion did not compel the government to abandon its neutrality and use force to break the Union blockade. Historians used to believe that unselfish pro-Union sympathy among the suffer-ing mill workers was a main cause of restraint, but the British working class still lacked the right to vote and thus had relatively little influence over policy.

Lord Punch: "That was Jeff Davis. . . . Don't you recog-nize him?" Lord [Palmerston]: "Not exactly—may have to do so one of these days." Britain never recognized the Confederacy.

Influential interest groups, which actually ben-efited from the famine, provided the crucial sup-port for continuing a policy of nonintervention. Among these groups were owners of large cotton mills who had made bonanza profits on their existing stocks and were happy to see weaker competitors go under while they awaited new sources of supply. By early 1863, cotton from Egypt and India put the industry back on the track toward full production. Other obvious ben-eficiaries of nonintervention were manufacturers of wool and linen textiles, munition makers who supplied both sides, and shipping interests that profited from the decline of American competi-tion on the world's sea lanes. Since the British economy as a whole gained more than it lost from neutrality, it is not surprising that there was little effective pressure for a change in policy.

By early 1863, when it was clear that "King Cotton Diplomacy" had failed, the Confederacy broke off formal relations with Great Britain. Its hopes for foreign intervention came to nothing because the European powers acted out of self-interest and calculated that the advantages of getting involved were not worth the risk of a long and costly war with the United States. Only a decisive military victory would have gained recognition for southern independence, and if the Confederacy had actually won such a victory, it would not have needed foreign backing.

FIGHT TO THE FINISH

The last two and a half years of the struggle saw the implementation of more radical war measures. The most dramatic and important of these was the North's effort to follow through on Lincoln's decision to free the slaves and bring the black population into the war on the Union side. The tide of battle turned in the summer of 1863, but the South continued to resist valiantly for two more years, until finally overcome by the sheer weight of the North's advantages in manpower and resources.

The Coming of Emancipation

At the beginning of the war, when the North still hoped for a quick and easy victory, only dedicated abolitionists favored turning the struggle for the Union into a crusade against slavery. In the summer of 1861 Congress voted almost unanimously for a resolution affirming that the war was being fought only to preserve the Union and not to change the domestic institutions of any state. But as it became clear how hard it was going to be to subdue the "rebels," sentiment developed for striking a blow at the South's economic and social system by freeing its slaves. In a tentative move toward emancipation, Congress in July 1862 authorized the government to confiscate the slaves of masters who supported the Confederacy. By this time, the actions of the slaves themselves were influencing policy making. They were voting for freedom with their feet by deserting their plantations in areas where the Union forces were close enough to offer a haven. In this way, they put pressure on the government to determine their status and, in effect, offered themselves as a source of manpower to the Union on the condition that they be made free.

Although Lincoln favored freedom for blacks as an ultimate goal, he was reluctant to commit his administration to a policy of immediate emancipation. In the fall of 1861 and again in the spring of 1862, he had disallowed the orders of field commanders who sought to free slaves in areas occupied by their forces, thus angering abolitionists and the strongly antislavery Republicans known as "Radicals." Lincoln's caution stemmed from a fear of alienating Unionist elements in the border slave states and from his own preference for a gradual, compensated form of emancipation. He hoped that such a plan could be put into effect in loyal slaveholding areas and then extended to the rebellious states as the basis for a voluntary restoration of the Union.

Lincoln was also aware that one of the main obstacles to any program leading to emancipation was the strong racial prejudice of most whites in both the North and the South. Although personally more tolerant than most, Lincoln was pessimistic about prospects of equality for blacks in the United States. He therefore coupled moderate proposals with a plea for government subsidies to support the voluntary "colonization" of freed blacks outside of the United States, and he actively sought places that would accept them.

But the slaveholding states that remained loyal to the Union refused to endorse Lincoln's gradual plan, and the failure of Union arms in the spring and summer of 1862 increased the public clamor for striking directly at the South's peculiar institution. The Lincoln administration also realized emancipation would win sympathy for the Union cause in England and France and thus might counter the growing threat that these nations would come to the aid of the Confederacy. In July Lincoln drafted an emancipation proclamation and read it to his cabinet but was persuaded by Secretary of State Seward not to issue it until the North had won a victory and could not be accused of acting out of desperation. Later in the summer Lincoln responded publicly to critics of his cautious policy, indicating that he would take any action in regard to slavery that would further the Union cause.

Finally, on September 22, 1862, Lincoln issued his preliminary Emancipation Proclamation. McClellan's success in stopping Lee at Antietam provided the occasion, but the president was also responding to growing political pressures. Most Republican politicians were now firmly committed to an emancipation policy, and many were on the verge of repudiating the administration for its

The Emancipation Proclamation, here being read to slaves on a Carolina Sea Island plantation, committed the Union to the abolition of slavery as a war aim.

inaction. Had Lincoln failed to act, his party would have been badly split, and he would have been in the minority faction. The proclamation gave the Confederate states one hundred days to give up the struggle without losing their slaves. There was little chance they would do so, but in offering them the chance, Lincoln left the door open for a more conservative and peaceful way of ending slavery than sudden emancipation at the point of a gun. In December Lincoln proposed to Congress that it approve a series of constitutional amendments providing for gradual, compensated emancipation and subsidized colonization.

Since there was no response from the South and little enthusiasm in Congress for Lincoln's gradual plan, the president went ahead on January 1, 1863, and declared that all slaves in those areas under Confederate control "shall be . . . thenceforward, and forever free." He justified the final proclamation as an act of "military necessity" sanctioned by the war powers of the president and authorized the enlistment of freed slaves in the Union Army. The language and tone of the document—one historian has described it as having "all the moral grandeur of a bill of lading"—made it clear that blacks were being freed for reasons of state and not out of humanitarian conviction.

Despite its uninspiring origin and limited appli-

cation—it did not extend to slave states loyal to the Union or to occupied areas and thus did not immediately free a single slave—the proclamation did commit the Union to the abolition of slavery as a war aim. It also accelerated the breakdown of slavery as a labor system, a process that was already well under way by early 1863. The blacks who had remained in captured areas or deserted their masters to cross Union lines before 1863 had been kept in a kind of way station between slavery and freedom, in accordance with the theory that they were "contraband of war." As word spread among the slaves that emancipation was now official policy, larger numbers of them were inspired to run off and seek the protection of approaching northern armies. One slave who crossed the Union lines summed up their motives: "I wants to be free. I came in from the plantation and don't want to go back;. . . I don't want to be a slave again." Approximately one-quarter of the slave population gained freedom during the war under the terms of the Emancipation Proclamation and thus deprived the South of an important part of its agricultural work force.

African Americans and the War

Almost 200,000 African Americans, most of them newly freed slaves, eventually served in the

Union armed forces and made a vital contribution to the North's victory. Although they were enrolled in segregated units under white officers, were initially paid less than their white counterparts, and were used disproportionately for garrison duty or heavy labor behind the lines, "blacks in blue" fought heroically in several major battles during the last two years of the war. The assistant secretary of war observed them in action at Millikin's Bend on the Mississippi in June 1863 and reported that "the bravery of blacks in the battle . . . completely revolutionized the sentiment of the army with regard to the employment of Negro troops."

Those freed during the war who did not serve in the military were often conscripted to serve as contract wage laborers on cotton plantations owned or leased by "loyal" white planters within the occupied areas of the Deep South. Abolitionists protested that the coercion used by military authorities to get blacks back into the cotton fields amounted to slavery in a new form, but those in power argued that the necessities of war and the northern economy required such "temporary" arrangements. To some extent, regimentation of the freedmen within the South was a way of assuring racially prejudiced Northerners, especially in the Midwest, that emancipation would not result in a massive migration of black refugees to their region of the country.

The heroic performance of African American troops and the easing of northern fears of being swamped by black migrants led to a deepening commitment to emancipation as a permanent and comprehensive policy.

Realizing his proclamation had a shaky constitutional foundation and might apply only to slaves actually freed while the war was going on, Lincoln sought to organize and recognize loyal state governments in southern areas under Union control on condition that they abolish slavery in their constitutions. He also encouraged local

This 1890 lithograph by Kurz and Allison commemorates the 54th Massachusetts Colored Regiment charging Fort Wagner, South Carolina, in July 1863. The 54th was the first African American unit recruited during the war. Charles and Lewis Douglass, sons of Frederick Douglass, served with this regiment.

campaigns to emancipate the slaves in the border states and saw these programs triumph in Maryland and Missouri in 1864.

Finally, Lincoln pressed for an amendment to the federal constitution outlawing involuntary servitude. After supporting its inclusion as a central plank in the Republican platform of 1864, Lincoln used all his influence to win congressional approval for the new Thirteenth Amendment. On January 31, 1865, the House approved the amendment by a narrow margin. There was an explosion of joy on the floor and in the galleries, and then the House voted to adjourn for the rest of the day "in honor of this immortal and sublime event." The cause of freedom for blacks and the cause of the Union had at last become one and the same. Lincoln, despite his earlier hesitations and misgivings, had earned the right to go down in history as "the great emancipator."

The Tide Turns

By early 1863, the Confederate economy was in shambles and its diplomacy had collapsed. The social order of the South was also showing signs of severe strain. Masters were losing control of their slaves, and nonslaveholding whites were becoming disillusioned with the hardships of a war that some of them described as a "rich man's war and a poor man's fight." As slaves fled from the plantations, increasing numbers of lower-class whites deserted the army or refused to be drafted in the first place. Whole counties in the southern backcountry became "deserter havens," which Confederate officials could enter only at the risk of their lives. Appalachian mountaineers, who had remained loyal to the Union, resisted the Confederacy more directly by enlisting in the Union Army or joining guerrilla units operating behind southern lines.

Yet the North was slow to capitalize on the South's internal weaknesses because it had its own serious morale problems. The long series of defeats on the eastern front had engendered war weariness, and the new policies that "military necessity" forced the government to adopt encountered fierce opposition.

Although popular with Republicans, emancipation was viewed by most Democrats as a betrayal of northern war aims. Racism was a main ingredient in their opposition to freeing blacks. According to one Democratic senator, "We mean that the United States . . . shall be the white man's home . . . and the nigger shall never be his equal." Riding a backlash against the preliminary proclamation, Democrats made significant gains in the congressional elections of 1862, especially in the Midwest, where they also captured several state legislatures.

The Enrollment Act of March 1863, which provided for outright conscription of white males, but permitted men of wealth to hire substitutes or pay a fee to avoid military service, provoked a violent response from those unable to buy their way out of service and unwilling to "fight for the niggers." A series of antidraft riots broke out, culminating in one of the bloodiest domestic disorders in American history—the New York riot of July 1863. The New York mob, composed mainly of Irish-American laborers, burned the draft offices, the homes of leading Republicans, and an orphanage for black children. They also lynched more than a dozen defenseless blacks who fell into their hands. At least 120 people died before federal troops restored order. Besides racial prejudice, the draft riots also reflected working-class anger at the wartime privileges and prosperity of the middle and upper classes; they showed how divided the North really was on the administration's conduct of the war.

To fight dissension and "disloyalty," the government used its martial law authority to arrest a few alleged ringleaders, including one prominent Democratic congressman—Clement Vallandigham of Ohio. Private patriotic organizations also issued a barrage of propaganda aimed at what they believed was a vast secret conspiracy to undermine the northern war effort. Historians disagree about the real extent of covert and illegal antiwar activity. No vast conspiracy existed, but militant advocates of "peace at any price"—popularly known as Copperheads—were certainly active in some areas, especially among the immigrant working classes of large cities and in southern Ohio, Indiana, and Illinois. Many Copperheads presented themselves as Jeffersonian believers in limited government who feared a war-induced growth of federal power. But it was opposition to emancipation on racial grounds rather than anxiety about big government that gave the movement most of its emotional force.

The only effective way to overcome the disillu-

The prison camps of the North (like Point Lookout, Maryland, above) and the South (like Andersonville, Georgia, right) were both deadly, but Andersonville was worse because the South ran out of food. Nearly 50,000 prisoners died in the camps during the war.

sionment that fed the peace movement was to start winning battles and thus convince the northern public that victory was assured. Before this could happen, the North suffered one more humiliating defeat on the eastern front. In early May 1863, Union forces under General Joseph Hooker were routed at Chancellorsville, Virginia, by a Confederate Army less than half its size. Once again, Robert E. Lee demonstrated his superior generalship, this time by dividing his forces and sending Stonewall Jackson to make a devastating surprise attack on the Union right. The Confederacy prevailed, but it did suffer one major loss: Jackson himself died as a result of wounds he received in the battle.

In the West, however, a major Union triumph was taking shape. For over a year, General Ulysses S. Grant had been trying to put his forces in position to capture Vicksburg, Mississippi, the almost inaccessible Confederate bastion that stood between the North and control of the Mississippi River. Finally, in late March 1863, he crossed to the west bank north of the city and moved his forces to a point south of it, where he joined up with naval forces that had run the Confederate batteries mounted on Vicksburg's high bluffs. In one of the boldest campaigns of the war, Grant crossed the river, deliberately cutting himself off from his sources of supply, and marched into the interior of Mississippi. Living off the land and out of communication with an anxious and perplexed Lincoln, his troops won a series of victories over two separate Confederate Armies and advanced on Vicksburg from the east. After unsuccessfully assaulting the city's defenses, Grant settled down for a siege on May 22.

The Confederate government considered and rejected proposals to mount a major offensive

An 1863 draft call in New York first provoked violence against African Americans, viewed by the rioters as the cause of an unnecessary war, and rage against the rich men who had been able to buy exemptions from the draft.

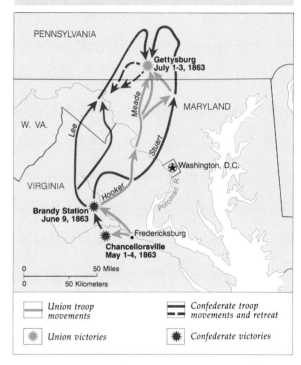

Eastern Theater of War, 1863
After the hard-won Union victory at Gettysburg, the South never again invaded the North.

into Tennessee and Kentucky in the hope of drawing Grant away from Vicksburg. Instead, President Davis approved Robert E. Lee's plan for an all-out invasion of the Northeast. Although this option provided no hope for relieving Vicksburg, it might lead to a dramatic victory that would more than compensate for the probable loss of the Mississippi stronghold. Lee's army crossed the Potomac in June and kept going until it reached Gettysburg, Pennsylvania. There Lee confronted a Union Army that had taken up strong defensive positions on Cemetery Ridge and Culp's Hill. This was one of the few occasions in the war when the North could capitalize on the tactical advantage of choosing its ground and then defending it against an enemy whose supply lines were extended.

On July 2 a series of Confederate attacks failed to dislodge General George Meade's troops from the high ground they occupied. The following day, Lee faced the choice of retreating to protect his lines of communication or launching a final, desperate assault. With more boldness than wisdom, he chose to make a direct attack on the strongest part of the Union line. The resulting charge on Cemetery Ridge was disastrous; advancing Confederate soldiers dropped like flies under the barrage of Union artillery and rifle fire. Only a few made it to the top of the ridge, and they were killed or captured.

Retreat was now inevitable, and Lee withdrew his battered troops to the Potomac, only to find that the river was at flood stage and could not be crossed for several days. But Meade failed to follow up his victory with a vigorous pursuit, and Lee was allowed to escape a predicament that could have resulted in his annihilation. Vicksburg fell to Grant on July 4, the same day Lee began his withdrawal, and Northerners rejoiced at the simultaneous Independence Day victories that turned the tide of the war. The Union had secured control of the Mississippi and had at last

Bold and decisive, Confederate General Robert E. Lee (left) often faced an enemy army that greatly outnumbered his own troops. Union General Ulysses S. Grant (right) demonstrated a relentless determination that eventually triumphed.

Western Theater of War, 1863
Grant's victories at Port Gibson, Champion's Hill, and Jackson cleared the way for his siege of Vicksburg.

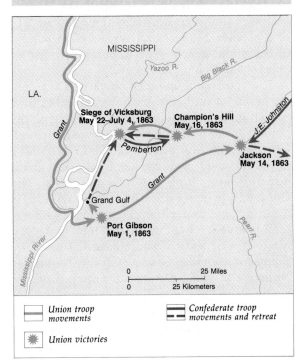

Western Theater of War, 1863
Grant's victories at Port Gibson, Champion's Hill, and Jackson cleared the way for his siege of Vicksburg.

won a major battle in the East. But Lincoln's joy turned to frustration when he learned his generals had missed the chance to capture Lee's army and bring a quick end to the war.

Last Stages of the Conflict

Later in 1863 the North finally gained control of the middle South, an area where indecisive fighting had been going on since the beginning of the conflict. The main Union target was Chattanooga, "the gateway to the Southeast." In September, troops under General William Rosecrans managed to maneuver the Confederates out of the city only to be outfought and driven back at Chickamauga. The Union Army then retreated into Chattanooga, where it was surrounded and besieged by southern forces. After Grant arrived from Vicksburg to take command, the encirclement was broken by daring assaults on the Confederate positions on Lookout Mountain and Missionary Ridge. As a result of its success in the battle of Chattanooga, the North was poised for an invasion of Georgia.

Grant's victories in the West earned him promotion to general-in-chief of all the Union armies. After assuming that position in March 1864, he ordered a multipronged offensive to finish off the Confederacy. The offensive's main movements were a march on Richmond under Grant's personal command and a thrust by the western armies, now led by General William T. Sherman, to Atlanta and the heart of Georgia.

In May and early June, Grant and Lee fought a series of bloody battles in northern Virginia that tended to follow a set pattern. Lee would take up an entrenched position in the path of the invading force, and Grant would attack it, sustaining heavy losses but also inflicting casualties the shrinking Confederate Army could ill afford. When his direct assault had failed, Grant would move to his left, hoping in vain to maneuver Lee into a less defensible position. In the battles of the Wilderness, Spotsylvania, and Cold Harbor, the Union lost about sixty thousand men—more than twice the number of Confederate casualties—without defeating Lee or opening the road to Richmond. After losing twelve thousand men in a single day at Cold Harbor, Grant decided to change his tactics and moved his army to the south of Richmond. There he drew up before Petersburg, a rail center that linked Richmond to the rest of the Confederacy; after failing to take it by assault, he settled down for a siege.

The siege of Petersburg was a long, drawn-out affair, and the resulting stalemate in the East caused northern morale to plummet during the summer of 1864. Lincoln was facing reelection, and his failure to end the war dimmed his prospects. Although nominated with ease in June—with Andrew Johnson, a proadministration Democrat from Tennessee, as his running mate—Lincoln confronted growing opposition within his own party, especially from Radicals who disagreed with his apparently lenient approach to the future restoration of seceded states to the Union. After Lincoln vetoed a Radical-supported congressional reconstruction plan in July, some Radicals began to call for a new convention to nominate another candidate.

The Democrats seemed to be in a good position to capitalize on Republican divisions and make a strong bid for the White House. Their platform appealed to war weariness by calling for a cease-fire followed by negotiations to reestablish the Union. The party's nominee, General George McClellan, announced he would not be bound by the peace plank and would pursue the war. But he promised to end the conflict sooner than Lincoln could because he would not insist on emancipation as a condition for reconstruction. By late summer Lincoln confessed privately that he would probably be defeated.

But northern military successes changed the political outlook. Sherman's invasion of Georgia went well; between May and September he employed a series of skillful flanking movements to force the Confederates to retreat to the outskirts of Atlanta. On September 2, the city fell, and northern forces occupied the hub of the Deep South. The news unified the Republican party behind Lincoln and improved his chances for defeating McClellan in November. The election itself was almost an anticlimax: Lincoln won 212 of a possible 233 electoral votes and 55 percent of the popular vote. The Republican cause of "liberty and Union" was secure.

The concluding military operations revealed the futility of further southern resistance. Cutting himself off from his supply lines and living off the land, Sherman marched unopposed through Georgia to the sea, destroying almost everything of possible military or economic value in a corridor 300 miles long and 60 miles wide. The Confederate Army that had opposed him at Atlanta, now under the command of General John B. Hood, moved northward into Tennessee, where it was defeated and almost destroyed by Union forces under General George Thomas at Nashville in mid-December. Sherman captured Savannah on December 22 and presented the city to Lincoln as a Christmas present. He then turned north and marched through the Carolinas with

The Election of 1864			
Candidate	Party	Popular Vote	Electoral Vote*
Lincoln	Republican	2,218,388	212
McClellan	Democrat	1,812,807	21

*Out of a total of 233 electoral votes. The eleven secessionist states—Alabama, Arkansas, Florida, Georgia, Louisiana, Mississippi, North Carolina, South Carolina, Tennessee, Texas, and Virginia—did not vote.

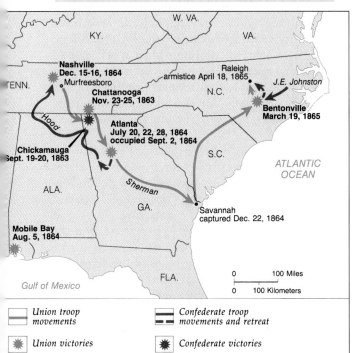

Sherman's March to the Sea
Leaving Atlanta in flames, Sherman marched to the Georgia coast, took Savannah, then moved his troops north through the Carolinas.

W. VA.
KY.
VA.
TENN.
Nashville
Dec. 15-16, 1864
Murfreesboro
Chattanooga
Nov. 23-25, 1863
Raleigh
armistice April 18, 1865
J.E. Johnston
N.C.
Bentonville
March 19, 1865
Hood
Atlanta
July 20, 22, 28, 1864
occupied Sept. 2, 1864
Chickamauga
Sept. 19-20, 1863
S.C.
ATLANTIC
OCEAN
ALA.
Sherman
GA.
Savannah
captured Dec. 22, 1864
Mobile Bay
Aug. 5, 1864
FLA.
Gulf of Mexico

0   100 Miles
0   100 Kilometers

◻ Union troop movements
◼ Confederate troop movements and retreat
✹ Union victories
✹ Confederate victories

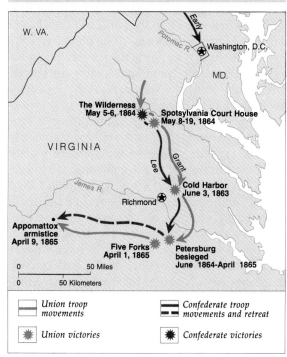

The Road to Appomattox
Grant's terms of surrender were generous, allowing the Confederate soldiers to take home their horses and mules so that they might "put in a crop."

W. VA.
Potomac R.
Early
Washington, D.C.
MD.
The Wilderness
May 5-6, 1864
Spotsylvania Court House
May 8-19, 1864
VIRGINIA
Lee
Grant
James R.
Cold Harbor
June 3, 1863
Richmond
Appomattox
armistice
April 9, 1865
Five Forks
April 1, 1865
Petersburg
besieged
June 1864-April 1865

0   50 Miles
0   50 Kilometers

◻ Union troop movements
◼ Confederate troop movements and retreat
✹ Union victories
✹ Confederate victories

the aim of joining up with Grant at Petersburg near Richmond.

While Sherman was bringing the war to the Carolinas, Grant finally ended the stalemate at Petersburg. When Lee's starving and exhausted army tried to break through the Union lines, Grant renewed his attack and forced the Confederates to abandon Petersburg and Richmond on April 2, 1865. He then pursued them westward for 100 miles, placing his forces in position to cut off their line of retreat to the south. Recognizing the hopelessness of further resistance, Lee surrendered his army at Appomattox Courthouse on April 9.

But the joy of the victorious North turned to sorrow and anger when John Wilkes Booth, a pro-Confederate actor, assassinated Abraham Lincoln as the president watched a play at Ford's Theater in Washington on April 14. Although Booth had a few accomplices—one of whom attempted to murder Secretary of State Seward—popular theories that the assassination was the result of a vast conspiracy involving Confederate leaders or (according to another version) Radical Republicans have never been substantiated and are extremely implausible.

The man who had spoken of the need to sacrifice for the Union cause at Gettysburg had himself given "the last full measure of devotion" to the cause of "government of the people, by the people, for the people." Four days after Lincoln's death, the only remaining Confederate force of any significance (the troops under Joseph E. Johnston who had been opposing Sherman in North Carolina) laid down its arms. The Union was saved.

Effects of the War

The nation that emerged from four years of total war was not the same America that had split apart in 1861. The 618,000 young men who were in their graves, victims of enemy fire or the diseases that spread rapidly in military encampments in this era before modern medicine and sanitation, would otherwise have married, raised families, and contributed their talents to building up the country. The widows and sweethearts they left behind temporarily increased the proportion of unmarried women in the population, and some members of this generation of involuntary "spinsters" sought new opportunities for making a living or serving the community that went beyond the purely domestic roles previously prescribed for women. The large number who had served as nurses or volunteer workers during the war were especially responsive to calls for broadening "the woman's sphere." Some of the northern women who were prominent in wartime service organizations—like Louise Lee Schuyler, Josephine Shaw Lowell, and Mary Livermore—became leaders of postwar philanthropic and reform movements.

At enormous human and economic cost, the nation had emancipated four million African Americans from slavery, but it had not yet resolved that they would be equal citizens. At the time of Lincoln's assassination, most northern states still denied blacks equality under the law and the right to vote. Whether the North would extend more rights to southern freedmen than it had granted to "free Negroes" was an open question.

The impact of the war on white working people was also unclear. Those in the industrializing parts of the North had suffered and lost ground economically because prices had risen much faster than wages during the conflict. But Republican rhetoric stressing "equal opportunity" and the "dignity of labor" raised hopes that the crusade against slavery could be broadened into a movement to improve the lot of working people in general. Foreign-born workers had additional reason to be optimistic; the fact that so many immigrants had fought and died for the Union cause had—for the moment—weakened nativist sentiment and encouraged ethnic tolerance.

What the war definitely decided was that the federal government was supreme over the states and had a broad grant of constitutional authority to act on matters affecting "the general welfare." The southern principle of state sovereignty and strict construction died at Appomattox, and the United States was on its way to becoming a true nation-state with an effective central government. But it retained a federal structure; although states could no longer claim the right to secede or nullify federal law, they still had primary responsibility for most functions of government. Everyone agreed that the Constitution placed limits on what the national government could do, and questions would continue to arise about where federal authority ended and states' rights began.

A broadened definition of federal powers had

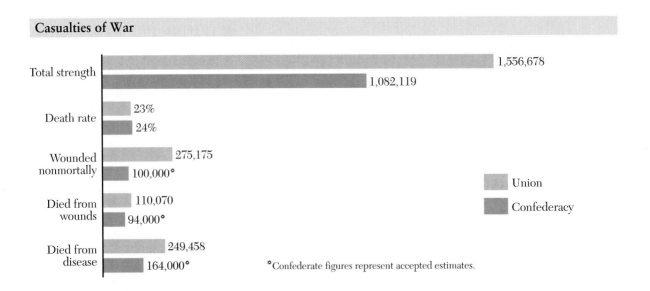

Casualties of War

	Union	Confederacy
Total strength	1,556,678	1,082,119
Death rate	23%	24%
Wounded nonmortally	275,175	100,000*
Died from wounds	110,070	94,000*
Died from disease	249,458	164,000*

*Confederate figures represent accepted estimates.

During the war, many women replaced skilled male workers in the manufacturing labor force. These women are filling cartridges in the United States Arsenal at Watertown, New York.

its greatest impact in the realm of economic policy. During the war, Republican-dominated Congresses passed a rash of legislation designed to give encouragement and direction to the nation's economic development. Taking advantage of the absence of southern opposition, Republicans rejected the pre–Civil War tradition of virtual laissez-faire and enacted a Whiggish program of active support for business and agriculture. In 1862, Congress passed a high protective tariff, approved a homestead act intended to encourage settlement of the West by providing free land to settlers, granted huge tracts of public land to railroad companies to support the building of a transcontinental railroad, and gave the states land for the establishment of agricultural colleges. The following year, Congress set up a national banking system that required member banks to keep adequate reserves and invest one-third of their capital in government securities. The notes the national banks issued became the country's first standardized and reliable circulating currency.

These wartime achievements added up to a decisive shift in the relationship between the federal government and private enterprise. The Republicans took a limited government that did little more than seek to protect the marketplace from the threat of monopoly and changed it into an activist state that promoted and subsidized the efforts of the economically industrious.

The most pervasive effect of the war on northern society was to encourage an "organizational revolution." Aided by government policies, venturesome businessmen took advantage of the new national market created by military procurement to build larger firms that could operate across state lines; some of the huge corporate enterprises of the postwar era began to take shape. Philanthropists also developed more effective national associations; the most notable of these were the Sanitary and Christian Commissions that ministered to the physical and spiritual needs of the troops. Efforts to care for the wounded influenced the development of the modern hospital and the rise of nursing as a female profession. Both the men who served in the army and those men and women who supported them on the home front or behind the lines became accustomed to working in large, bureaucratic organizations of a kind that had scarcely existed before the war.

Ralph Waldo Emerson, the era's most prominent man of letters, revealed in his wartime writ-

CHRONOLOGY

1860   South Carolina secedes from the Union (December)

1861   Rest of Deep South secedes: Confederacy is founded (January–February) • Fort Sumter is fired upon and surrenders to Confederate forces (April) • Upper South secedes (April–May). South wins first battle of Bull Run (July)

1862   Grant captures forts Henry and Donelson (February) • Farragut captures New Orleans for the Union (April) • McClellan leads unsuccessful campaign on the peninsula southeast of Richmond (March–July) • South wins second battle of Bull Run (August) • McClellan stops Lee at battle of Antietam (September) • Lincoln issues preliminary Emancipation Proclamation (September) • Lee defeats Union Army at Fredericksburg (December)

1863   Lincoln issues final Emancipation Proclamation (January) • Lee is victorious at Chancellorsville (May) • North gains major victories at Gettysburg and Vicksburg (July) • Grant defeats Confederate forces at Chattanooga (November)

1864   Grant and Lee battle in northern Virginia (May–June) • Atlanta falls to Sherman (September) • Lincoln is reelected president, defeating McClellan (November) • Sherman marches through Georgia (November–December)

1865   Congress passes Thirteenth Amendment abolishing slavery (January) • Grant captures Petersburg and Richmond; Lee surrenders at Appomattox (April) • Lincoln assassinated by John Wilkes Booth (April) • Remaining Confederate forces surrender (April–May)

ment in an inner world of imagination and cosmic intuition. During the conflict, he began to exalt the claims of organization, government, and "civilization" over the endeavors of "the private man" to find fulfillment through "self-culture." He even extolled military discipline and became an official visitor to West Point. In 1837, he had said of young men who aspired to political office: "Wake them up and they shall quit the false good and leap to the true, and leave governments to clerks and desks." Now he affirmed almost the opposite: "Government must not be a parish clerk, a justice of the peace. It has, of necessity, in any crisis of the state, the absolute powers of a dictator." In purging his thoughts of extreme individualism and hailing the need to accept social discipline and participate in organized, cooperative activity, Emerson epitomized the way the war affected American thought and patterns of behavior.

The North won the war mainly because it had shown a greater capacity than the South to organize, innovate, and "modernize." Its victory meant the nation as a whole would now be ready to embrace the conception of progress that the North had affirmed in its war effort—not only advances in science and technology, but also in bringing together and managing large numbers of men and women for economic and social goals. The Civil War was thus a catalyst for the great transformation of American society from an individualistic society of small producers into the more highly organized and "incorporated" America of the late nineteenth century.

Recommended Reading

The best one-volume history of the Civil War is James M. McPherson, *Battle Cry of Freedom: The Civil War Era* (1988). Other valuable surveys of the war and its aftermath are J. G. Randall and David Herbert Donald, *The Civil War and Reconstruction*, 2d ed. (1969); and James M. McPherson, *Ordeal by Fire: The Civil War and Reconstruction* (1981). An excellent shorter account is David Herbert Donald, *Liberty and Union* (1978). The Confederate experience is well covered in Clement Eaton, *A History of the Southern Confederacy* (1954), and Emory M. Thomas, *The Confederate Nation: 1861–1865* (1979). Eaton stresses internal problems and weaknesses; Thomas highlights achievements under adversity. On the North's war effort, see Phillip Paludan, *"A People's Contest: The Union and the Civil War, 1861–1865"* (1988). The best one-vol-

ings that the conflict encouraged a dramatic shift in American thought about the relationship between the individual and society. Before the war, Emerson had generally championed "the transcendent individual," who stood apart from institutions and organizations and sought fulfill-

ume introduction to the military side of the conflict is still Bruce Catton, *This Hallowed Ground* (1956).

Lincoln's career and wartime leadership are treated in two competent biographies: Benjamin P. Thomas, *Abraham Lincoln* (1954), and Stephen B. Oates, *With Malice Toward None: The Life of Abraham Lincoln* (1977). A penetrating analysis of events immediately preceding the fighting is Kenneth M. Stampp, *And the War Came: The North and the Sectional Crisis* (1950). John Hope Franklin, *The Emancipation Proclamation* (1963) is a good short account of the North's decision to free the slaves. An incisive account of the transition from slavery to freedom is Barbara Jeanne Fields, *Slavery and Freedom on the Middle Ground: Maryland in the Nineteenth Century* (1985). Five leading historians offer conflicting interpretations in their attempts to explain the South's defeat in *Why the North Won the Civil War,* edited by David Donald (1960). A brilliant study of the writings of those who experienced the war is Edmund Wilson, *Patriotic Gore: Studies in the Literature of the American Civil War* (1962). On the intellectual impact see George M. Fredrickson, *The Inner Civil War: Northern Intellectuals and the Crisis of the Union,* 2d ed. (1993).

Additional Bibliography

The most thorough modern history of the Civil War is Allan Nevins, *The War for the Union,* 4 vols. (1959–1971). Bruce Catton, *Centennial History of the Civil War,* 3 vols. (1961–1965) is the most detailed account of the military aspects of the conflict. The day-to-day drama of the war is well conveyed in Shelby Foote, *The Civil War: A Narrative,* 3 vols. (1958–1974). Among the many collections of essays that deal with general issues of the period are Allan Nevins, *The Statesmanship of the Civil War* (1962); David Donald, *Lincoln Reconsidered: Essays on the Civil War Era* (1956); Eric Foner, *Politics and Ideology in the Age of the Civil War* (1980); and David M. Potter, *The South and the Sectional Conflict* (1968).

Further insight into the Confederate side of the struggle can be derived from Charles P. Roland, *The Confederacy* (1960); Frank E. Vandiver, *Their Tattered Flags: The Epic of the Confederacy* (1970); Emory M. Thomas, *The Confederacy as a Revolutionary Experience* (1971); and Bell I. Wiley, *The Road to Appomattox* (1956). Jefferson Davis's leadership is assessed in Paul D. Escott, *After Secession: Jefferson Davis and the Failure of Confederate Nationalism* (1978); Hudson Strode, *Jefferson Davis,* 3 vols. (1955–1964); Clement Eaton, *Jefferson Davis* (1977); and Frank E. Vandiver, *Jefferson Davis and the Confederate States* (1964). The most detailed works on Lincoln's stewardship of the Union cause are James G. Randall, *Lincoln the President,* 4 vols. (1945–1955,

vol. 4 completed by Richard N. Current), and Carl Sandburg's less reliable *Abraham Lincoln: The War Years,* 4 vols. (1939). For illuminating essays on Lincoln's leadership, see Don E. Fehrenbacher, *Lincoln in Text and Context* (1987). On Lincoln's most notable speech, see Garry Wills, *Lincoln at Gettysburg* (1992).

Events leading up to the outbreak of hostilities are covered in Dwight L. Dumond, *The Secession Movement* (1931); Ralph Wooster, *The Secession Conventions of the South* (1962); Daniel W. Crofts, *Reluctant Confederates: Upper South Unionists in the Secession Crisis* (1989); Charles R. Lee, *The Confederate Constitutions* (1963); David M. Potter, *Lincoln and His Party in the Secession Crisis,* 2d ed. (1962); and Richard N. Current, *Lincoln and the First Shot* (1963).

The literature on military commanders, campaigns, and battles is enormous, but mention must be made of Douglas Southall Freeman's outstanding works on southern generalship: *R. E. Lee: A Biography,* 4 vols. (1934–1935) and *Lee's Lieutenants,* 3 vols. (1942–1944). Also of exceptional merit is Bruce Catton's trilogy on the Army of the Potomac: *Mr. Lincoln's Army* (1951), *Glory Road* (1952), and *A Stillness at Appomattox* (1953). See also T. Harry Williams, *Lincoln and His Generals* (1952). A provocative interpretation of the ethos of total war is Charles B. Royster, *The Destructive War: William Tecumseh Sherman and the Americans* (1991). On the guerilla war in Missouri see Michael Fellman, *Inside War* (1989). On the common soldier's experience of the war, see two books by Bell I. Wiley: *The Life of Johnny Reb* (1943) and *The Life of Billy Yank* (1952), as well as Reid Mitchell, *The Northern Soldier Leaves Home* (1993).

Major works on northern politics during the war are William B. Hesseltine, *Lincoln and the War Governors* (1948); T. Harry Williams, *Lincoln and the Radicals* (1941); Hans Trefousse, *The Radical Republicans: Lincoln's Vanguard for Racial Justice* (1969); David Donald, *Charles Sumner and the Rights of Man* (1970); Allan G. Bogue, *The Earnest Men: Republicans of the Civil War Senate* (1981); Joel Silbey, *A Respectable Minority: The Democratic Party in the Civil War Era* (1977); Wood Gray, *The Hidden Civil War: The Story of the Copperheads* (1942); Frank L. Klement, *Copperheads in the Middle West* (1960); and Leonard P. Curry, *Blueprint for Modern America: Non-Military Legislation of the First Civil War Congress* (1968). On legal and constitutional issues, see James G. Randall, *Constitutional Problems Under Lincoln,* rev. ed. (1961); Harold M. Hyman, *A More Perfect Union: The Impact of the Civil War and Reconstruction on the Constitution* (1973); Phillip S. Paludan, *A Covenant with Death: The Constitution, the Law, and Equality in the Civil War Era* (1975);

and Mark E. Neely, Jr., *The Fate of Liberty: Abraham Lincoln and Civil Liberties* (1991).

Other aspects of northern life during the war are treated in Paul W. Gates, *Agriculture and the Civil War* (1965); Iver Bernstein, *The New York Draft Riots* (1990); Lori D. Ginzberg, *Women and the Work of Benevolence* (1990); Daniel Aaron, *The Unwritten War: American Writers and the Civil War* (1973); and James H. Morehead, *American Apocalypse: Yankee Protestants and the Civil War* (1978).

For an understanding of the South's internal problems, see Frank Owsley, *States' Rights in the Confederacy* (1925); Curtis A. Amlund, *Federalism in the Southern Confederacy* (1966); Wilfred B. Yearns, *The Confederate Congress* (1960); Richard C. Todd, *Confederate Finance* (1954); Bell I. Wiley, *The Plain People of the Confederacy* (1943); and J. William Harris, *Plain Folk and Gentry in a Slave Society* (1985).

Emancipation and the role of blacks in the war are the subject of a number of excellent studies, including Benjamin Quarles, *The Negro in the Civil War* (1953) and *Lincoln and the Negro* (1962); Bell I. Wiley, *Southern Negroes, 1861–1865* (1938); James M. McPherson, *The Struggle for Equality: Abolitionists and the Negro in the Civil War and Reconstruction* (1964); LaWanda Cox, *Lincoln and Black Freedom* (1981); V. Jacque Voegeli, *Free But Not Equal: The Midwest and the Negro During the Civil War;* Forrest G. Wood, *Black Scare: The Racist Response to the Civil War and Reconstruction* (1968); Louis Gerteis, *From Contraband to Freedman: Federal Policy Toward Southern Blacks 1861–1865* (1973); Willie Lee Rose, *Rehearsal for Reconstruction: The Port Royal Experiment* (1964); Herman Belz, *A New Birth of Freedom: The Republican Party and Freedmen's Rights, 1861–1866* (1976); Robert F. Durden, *The Gray and the Black: The Confederate Debate on Emancipation* (1972).

On wartime diplomacy, see David P. Crook, *The North, the South and the Powers, 1861–1865* (1974); Frank Owsley, *King Cotton Diplomacy,* rev. ed. (1959); Brian Jenkins, *Britain and the War for the Union* (1974); and Mary Ellison, *Support for Secession: Lancashire and the American Civil War* (1972).

The Agony of Reconstruction

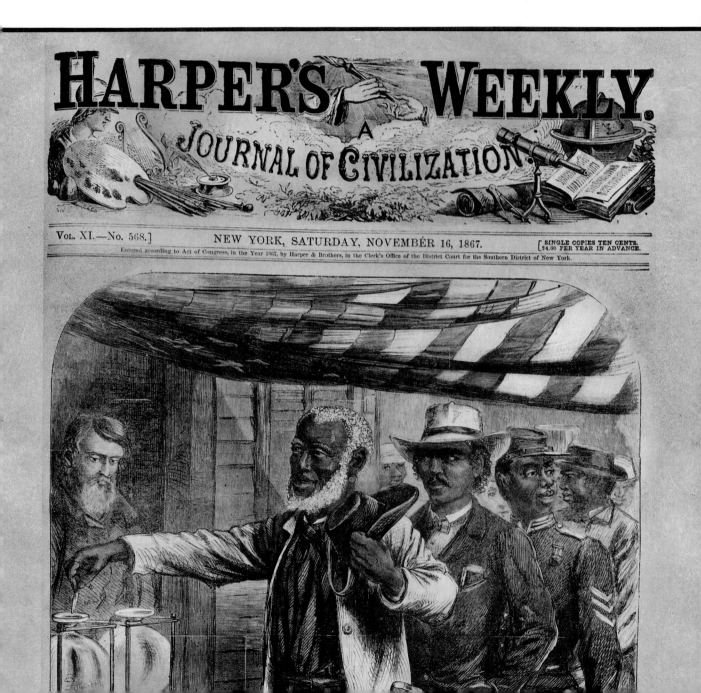

HARPER'S WEEKLY.

A JOURNAL OF CIVILIZATION.

Vol. XI.—No. 568.]   NEW YORK, SATURDAY, NOVEMBER 16, 1867.   [SINGLE COPIES TEN CENTS.
$4.00 PER YEAR IN ADVANCE.

Entered according to Act of Congress, in the Year 1867, by Harper & Brothers, in the Clerk's Office of the District Court for the Southern District of New York.

During the Reconstruction period immediately following the Civil War, African Americans struggled to become equal citizens of a democratic republic. They produced a number of remarkable leaders who showed that blacks were as capable as other Americans of voting, holding office, and legislating for a complex and rapidly changing society. Among these leaders was Robert Smalls of South Carolina. Although virtually forgotten by the time of his death in 1915, Smalls was perhaps the most famous and widely respected southern black leader of the Civil War and Reconstruction era. His career reveals some of the main features of the African American experience during that crucial period.

Born a slave in 1839, Smalls had a white father whose identity has never been clearly established. But his white ancestry apparently gained him some advantages, and as a young man he was allowed to live and work independently, hiring his own time from a master who may have been his half-brother. Smalls worked as a sailor and trained himself to be a pilot in Charleston Harbor. When the Union Navy blockaded Charleston in 1862, Smalls, who was then working in a Confederate steamship called the *Planter,* saw a chance to win his freedom in a particularly dramatic way. At three o'clock in the morning on May 13, 1862, when the white officers of the *Planter* were ashore, he took command of the vessel and its slave crew, sailed it out of the heavily fortified harbor, and surrendered it to the Union Navy. Smalls immediately became a hero to those antislavery Northerners who were seeking evidence that the slaves were willing and able to serve the Union. The *Planter* was turned into a Union transport and Smalls was made its captain after being commissioned as an officer in the Armed Forces of the United States. During the remainder of the war, he rendered conspicuous and gallant service as captain and pilot of Union vessels off the coast of South Carolina.

Like a number of other African Americans who had fought valiantly for the Union, Smalls went on to a distinguished political career during Reconstruction, serving in the South Carolina constitutional convention, the state legislature, and for several terms in the U.S. Congress. He was also a shrewd businessman and became the owner of extensive properties in Beaufort, South Carolina, and its vicinity. (His first purchase was the house of his former master where he had spent his early years as a slave.) As the leading citizen of Beaufort during Reconstruction and for some years thereafter, he acted like many successful white Americans, combining the acquisition of wealth with the exercise of political power. The electoral organization he established resembled in some ways the well-oiled "machines" being established in northern towns and cities. It was so effective that Smalls was able to control local government and get himself elected to Congress even after the election of 1876 had placed the state under the control of white conservatives bent on depriving blacks of political power. Organized mob violence defeated him in 1878, but he bounced back to win by decision of Congress a contested congressional election in 1880. He did not leave the House of Representatives for good until 1886, when he lost another contested election that had to be decided by Congress. It revealed the changing mood of the country that his white challenger was seated despite evidence of violence and intimidation against black voters.

In their efforts to defeat him, Smalls's white opponents frequently charged that he had a hand in the corruption that was allegedly rampant in South Carolina during Reconstruction. But careful historical investigation shows that he was, by the standards of the time, an honest and responsible public servant. In the South Carolina convention of 1868 and later in the state legislature, he was a conspicuous champion of free and compulsory public education. In Congress, he fought for the enactment and enforcement of federal civil rights laws. Not especially radical on social questions, he sometimes bent over backward to accommodate what he regarded as the legitimate interests and sensibilities of South Carolina whites. Like other middle-class black political leaders in Reconstruction-era South Carolina, he can perhaps be faulted in hindsight for not doing more to help poor blacks gain access to land of their own. But in 1875 he sponsored congressional legislation that opened for purchase at low prices the land in his own district that had been confiscated by the federal government during the war. As a result, blacks were able to buy most of

Robert Smalls (1839–1915) in an engraving from an 1862 newspaper. Smalls, who commandeered the frigate Planter and delivered it to the Union, later served in congress.

it, and they soon owned three-fourths of the land in Beaufort and its vicinity.

Smalls spent the later years of his life as U. S. collector of customs for the port of Beaufort, a beneficiary of the patronage that the Republican party continued to provide for a few loyal southern blacks. But the loss of real political clout for Smalls and men like him was one of the tragic consequences of the fall of Reconstruction.

THE PRESIDENT VERSUS CONGRESS

The problem of how to reconstruct the Union in the wake of the South's military defeat was one of the most difficult and perplexing challenges ever faced by American policymakers. The Constitution provided no firm guidelines, for the framers had not anticipated a division of the country into warring sections. Once emancipation became a northern war aim, the problem was compounded by a new issue: how far should

the federal government go to secure freedom and civil rights for 4 million former slaves?

The debate that evolved led to a major political crisis. Advocates of a minimal Reconstruction policy favored quick restoration of the Union with no protection for the freed slaves beyond the prohibition of slavery. Proponents of a more radical policy wanted readmission of the southern states to be dependent on guarantees that "loyal" men would displace the Confederate elite in positions of power, and that blacks would acquire basic rights of American citizenship. The White House favored the minimal approach, whereas Congress came to endorse the more radical and thoroughgoing form of Reconstruction. The resulting struggle between Congress and the chief executive was the most serious clash between two branches of government in the nation's history.

Wartime Reconstruction

Tension between the president and Congress over how to reconstruct the Union began during the war. Occupied mainly with achieving victory, Lincoln never set forth a final and comprehensive plan for bringing rebellious states back into the fold. But he did take initiatives that indicated he favored a lenient and conciliatory policy toward Southerners who would give up the struggle and repudiate slavery. In December 1863, he issued a Proclamation of Amnesty and Reconstruction; it offered a full pardon to all Southerners (with the exception of certain classes of Confederate leaders) who would take an oath of allegiance to the Union and acknowledge the legality of emancipation. Once 10 percent or more of the voting population of any occupied state had taken the oath, they were authorized to set up a loyal government. Efforts to establish such regimes were quickly undertaken in states that were wholly or partially occupied by Union troops; by 1864 Louisiana and Arkansas had fully functioning Unionist governments.

Lincoln's policy was meant to shorten the war. The president hoped that granting pardons and political recognition to oath-taking minorities would weaken the southern cause by making it easy for disillusioned or lukewarm Confederates to switch sides. He also hoped to further his emancipation policy by insisting the new governments abolish slavery, an action that might prove crucial if—as seemed possible before Lincoln's reelection in 1864 and Congress's subsequent passage of the Thirteenth Amendment—the courts or a future Democratic administration were to disallow or revoke the Emancipation Proclamation. When constitutional conventions operating under the 10 percent plan in Louisiana and Arkansas dutifully abolished slavery in 1864, emancipation came closer to being irreversible.

Congress was unhappy with the president's reconstruction experiments and in 1864 refused to seat the Unionists elected to the House and Senate from Louisiana and Arkansas. A minority of congressional Republicans—the strongly anti-slavery Radicals—favored protection for black rights as a precondition for the readmission of southern states. These Republican militants were upset because Lincoln had not insisted the constitution makers provide for black male suffrage. But a larger group in Congress was not yet prepared to implement civil and political equality for blacks. Many of these moderates also opposed Lincoln's plan, but they did so primarily because they did not trust the repentant Confederates who would play a major role in the new governments. No matter what their position on black rights, most congressional Republicans feared that hypocritical oath taking would allow the old ruling class to return to power and cheat the North of the full fruits of its impending victory.

Congress also felt the president was exceeding his authority by using executive powers to restore the Union. Lincoln operated on the theory that secession, being illegal, did not place the Confederate states outside the Union in a constitutional sense. Since individuals and not states had defied federal authority, the president could use his pardoning power to certify a loyal electorate, which could then function as the legitimate state government.

The dominant view in Congress, on the other hand, was that the southern states had forfeited their place in the Union and that it was up to Congress to decide when and how they would be readmitted. The most popular justification for congressional responsibility was based on the clause of the Constitution providing that "the United States shall guarantee to every State in this Union a Republican Form of Government." By seceding, Radicals argued, the Confederate states had ceased to be republican, and Congress must set the conditions to be met before they could be readmitted.

After refusing to recognize Lincoln's 10 percent governments, Congress passed a Reconstruction bill of its own in July 1864. Known as the Wade-Davis bill, this legislation required that 50 percent of the voters must take an oath of future loyalty before the restoration process could begin. Once this had occurred, those who could swear they had never willingly supported the Confederacy could vote in an election for delegates to a constitutional convention. The bill in its final form did not require black suffrage, but it did give federal courts the power to enforce emancipation. Faced with this attempt to nullify his own program, Lincoln exercised a pocket veto by refusing to sign the bill before Congress adjourned. He justified his action by announcing he did not wish to be committed to any single Reconstruction plan. The sponsors of the bill responded with an angry manifesto, and Lincoln's relations with Congress reached their low.

Congress and the president remained stalemated on the Reconstruction issue for the rest of the war. During his last months in office, however, Lincoln showed some willingness to compromise. He persisted in his efforts to obtain full recognition for the governments he had nurtured in Louisiana and Arkansas but seemed receptive to the setting of other conditions—perhaps including black suffrage—for readmission of those states where wartime conditions had prevented execution of his plan. However, he died without clarifying his intentions, leaving historians to speculate on whether his quarrel with Congress would have worsened or been resolved. Given Lincoln's past record of political flexibility, the best bet is that he would have come to terms with the majority of his party.

Andrew Johnson at the Helm

Andrew Johnson, the man suddenly made president by an assassin's bullet, attempted to put the Union back together on his own authority in 1865. But his policies eventually set him at odds with Congress and the Republican party and provoked the most serious crisis in the history of relations between the executive and legislative branches of the federal government.

Nearly insurmountable problems with a Congress determined to enact its own Reconstruction policy plagued Andrew Johnson through his presidency. Impeached in 1868, he escaped conviction by a single vote.

Johnson's background shaped his approach to Reconstruction. Born in dire poverty in North Carolina, he migrated as a young man to eastern Tennessee, where he made his living as a tailor. Lacking formal schooling, he did not learn to read and write until adult life. Entering politics as a Jacksonian Democrat, he became known as an effective stump speaker. His railing against the planter aristocracy made him the spokesman for Tennessee's nonslaveholding whites and the most successful politician in the state. He advanced from state legislator to congressman to governor and in 1857 was elected to the U. S. Senate.

When Tennessee seceded in 1861, Johnson was the only senator from a Confederate state who remained loyal to the Union and continued to serve in Washington. But his Unionism and defense of the common people did not include antislavery sentiments. Nor was he friendly to blacks. While campaigning in Tennessee, he had objected only to the fact that slaveholding was the privilege of a wealthy minority. He revealed his attitude when he wished that "every head of family in the United States had one slave to take the drudgery and menial service of his family."

During the war, while acting as military governor of Tennessee, Johnson endorsed Lincoln's emancipation policy and carried it into effect. But he viewed it primarily as a means of destroying the power of the hated planter class rather than as a recognition of black humanity. He was chosen as Lincoln's running mate in 1864 because it was thought that a proadministration Democrat, who was a southern Unionist in the bargain, would strengthen the ticket. No one expected Johnson to succeed to the presidency; it is one of the strange accidents of American history that a southern Democrat, a fervent white supremacist, came to preside over a Republican administration immediately after the Civil War.

Some Radical Republicans initially welcomed Johnson's ascent to the nation's highest office. Their hopes make sense in the light of Johnson's record of fierce loyalty to the Union and his apparent agreement with the Radicals that ex-Confederates should be severely treated. More than Lincoln, who had spoken of "malice toward none and charity for all," Johnson seemed likely to punish southern "traitors" and prevent them from regaining political influence. Only gradually did the deep disagreement between the president and the Republican majority in Congress become evident.

The Reconstruction policy that Johnson initiated on May 29, 1865, created some uneasiness among the Radicals, but most Republicans were willing to give it a chance. Johnson placed North Carolina and eventually other states under appointed provisional governors chosen mostly from among prominent southern politicians who had opposed the secession movement and had rendered no conspicuous service to the Confederacy. The governors were responsible for calling constitutional conventions and ensuring that only "loyal" whites were permitted to vote for delegates. Participation required taking the oath of allegiance that Lincoln had prescribed earlier. Once again Confederate leaders and former officeholders who had participated in the rebellion were excluded. To regain their political and property rights, those in the exempted categories had to apply for individual presidential pardons. Johnson made one significant addition to the list of the excluded: all those possessing taxable property exceeding $20,000 in value. In this fashion, he sought to prevent his longtime adversaries—the wealthy planters—from participating in the Reconstruction of southern state governments.

Once the conventions met, Johnson urged them to do three things: declare the ordinances of secession illegal, repudiate the Confederate debt, and ratify the Thirteenth Amendment abolishing slavery. After governments had been reestablished under constitutions meeting these conditions, the president assumed the Reconstruction process would be complete and that the ex-Confederate states could regain their full rights under the Constitution.

The conventions, dominated by prewar Unionists and representatives of backcountry yeoman farmers, did their work in a way satisfactory to the president but troubling to many congressional Republicans. Rather than quickly accepting Johnson's recommendations, delegates in several states approved them begrudgingly or with qualifications. Furthermore, all the resulting constitutions limited suffrage to whites, disappointing the large number of Northerners who hoped, as Lincoln had, that at least some African Americans—perhaps those who were educated or had served in the Union army—would be given the vote. Johnson on the whole seemed eager to give southern white majorities a free hand in determining the civil and political status of the freed slaves.

Republican uneasiness turned to disillusionment and anger when the state legislatures elected under the new constitutions proceeded to pass "Black Codes" subjecting former slaves to a variety of special regulations and restrictions on their freedom. Especially troubling were vagrancy and apprenticeship laws that forced African Americans to work and denied them a free choice of employers. Blacks in some states were also prevented from testifying in court on the same basis as whites and were subject to a separate penal code. To Radicals, the Black Codes looked suspiciously like slavery under a new guise. More upsetting to northern public opinion in general, a number of prominent ex-Confederate leaders were elected to Congress in the fall of 1865.

Johnson himself was partly responsible for this turn of events. Despite his lifelong feud with the planter class, he was generous in granting pardons to members of the old elite who came to him, hat in hand, and asked for them. When for-

mer Confederate Vice President Alexander Stephens and other proscribed ex-rebels were elected to Congress although they had not been pardoned, Johnson granted them special amnesty so they could serve.

The growing rift between the president and Congress came into the open in December when the House and Senate refused to seat the recently elected southern delegation. Instead of endorsing Johnson's work and recognizing the state governments he had called into being, Congress established a joint committee, chaired by Senator William Pitt Fessenden of Maine, to review Reconstruction policy and set further conditions for readmission of the seceded states.

Congress Takes the Initiative

The struggle over how to reconstruct the Union ended with Congress doing the job of setting policy all over again. The clash between Johnson and Congress was a matter of principle and could not be reconciled. Johnson's personality—his prickly pride, sharp tongue, intolerance of opposition, and stubborn refusal to give an inch—did not help his political cause. But the root of the problem was that he disagreed with the majority of Congress on what Reconstruction was supposed to accomplish. An heir of the Democratic states' rights tradition, he wanted to restore the prewar federal system as quickly as possible and without change except that states would no longer have the right to legalize slavery or to secede.

Most Republicans wanted firm guarantees that the old southern ruling class would not regain regional power and national influence by devising new ways to subjugate blacks. Since emancipation had nullified the three-fifths clause of the Constitution by which slaves had been counted as three-fifths of a person, all blacks were now to be counted in determining representation. Consequently, Republicans worried about increased southern strength in Congress and the electoral college. The current Congress favored a Reconstruction policy that would give the federal government authority to limit the political role of ex-Confederates and provide some protection for black citizenship.

Republican leaders—with the exception of a few extreme Radicals like Charles Sumner—

lacked any firm conviction that blacks were inherently equal to whites. They *did* believe, however, that in a modern democratic state, all citizens must have the same basic rights and opportunities, regardless of natural abilities. Principle coincided easily with political expediency; southern blacks, whatever their alleged shortcomings, were likely to be loyal to the Republican party that had emancipated them. They could be used, if necessary, to counteract the influence of resurgent ex-Confederates, thus preventing the Democrats from returning to national dominance through control of the South.

The disagreement between the president and Congress became irreconcilable in early 1866 when Johnson vetoed two bills that had passed with overwhelming Republican support. The first extended the life of the Freedmen's Bureau—a temporary agency set up to aid the former slaves by providing relief, education, legal help, and assistance in obtaining land or employment. The second was a civil rights bill meant to nullify the Black Codes and guarantee to freedmen "full and equal benefit of all laws and proceedings for the security of person and property as is enjoyed by white citizens."

Johnson's vetoes shocked moderate Republicans who had expected the president to accept these relatively modest measures as a way of heading off more radical proposals, such as black suffrage and a prolonged denial of political rights to ex-Confederates. Presidential opposition to policies that represented the bare minimum of Republican demands on the South alienated moderates in the party and ensured a wide opposition to Johnson's plan of Reconstruction. Johnson succeeded in blocking the Freedmen's Bureau bill, although a modified version later passed. But the Civil Rights Act won the two-thirds majority necessary to override his veto, signifying that the president was now hopelessly at odds with most of the congressmen from what was supposed to be his own party. Never before had Congress overridden a presidential veto.

Johnson soon revealed that he intended to abandon the Republicans and place himself at the head of a new conservative party uniting the small minority of Republicans who supported him with a reviving Democratic party that was rallying behind his Reconstruction policy. In

THE RECONSTRUCTION DOSE.

According to this 1867 cartoon from Frank Leslie's Illustrated Newspaper, *Congress's program for Reconstruction was a bitter dose for the South, and President "Naughty Andy" urged Southerners not to accept the plan. Mrs. Columbus insisted, however, that Dr. Congress knew what was best.*

preparation for the elections of 1866, Johnson helped found the National Union movement to promote his plan to readmit the southern states to the Union without further qualifications. A National Union convention meeting in Philadelphia in August 1866 called for the election to Congress of men who endorsed the presidential plan for Reconstruction.

Meanwhile, the Republican majority on Capitol Hill, fearing that Johnson would not enforce civil rights legislation or that the courts would declare such federal laws unconstitutional, passed the Fourteenth Amendment. This, perhaps the most important of all our constitutional amendments, gave the federal government responsibility for guaranteeing equal rights under the law to all Americans. The first section defined national citizenship for the first time as extending to "all persons born or naturalized in the United States." The states were prohibited from abridg-

Amendment	Main Provisions	Congressional Passage (2/3 majority in each house required)	Ratification Process (3/4 of all states including ex-Confederate states required)
13	Slavery prohibited in United States	January 1865	December 1865 (twenty-seven states, including eight southern states)
14	1. National citizenship 2. State representation in Congress reduced proportionally to number of voters disfranchised 3. Former Confederates denied right to hold office 4. Confederate debt repudiated	June 1866	Rejected by twelve southern and border states, February 1867 Radicals make readmission of southern states hinge on ratification Ratified July 1868
15	Denial of franchise because of race, color, or past servitude explicitly prohibited	February 1869	Ratification required for readmission of Virginia, Texas, Mississippi, Georgia Ratified March 1870

ing the rights of American citizens and could not "deprive any person of life, liberty, or property, without due process of law; nor deny to any person . . . equal protection of the laws."

The other sections of the amendment were important in the context of the time but had fewer long-term implications. Section two sought to penalize the South for denying voting rights to black males by reducing the congressional representation of any state that formally deprived a portion of its male citizens of the right to vote. The third section denied federal office to those who had taken an oath of office to support the U. S. Constitution and then had supported the Confederacy, and the fourth repudiated the Confederate debt. The amendment was sent to the states with the understanding that Southerners would have no chance of being readmitted to Congress unless their states ratified it.

The congressional elections of 1866 served as a referendum on the Fourteenth Amendment. Johnson opposed the amendment on the grounds that it created a "centralized" government and denied states the right to manage their own affairs; he also counseled southern state legislatures to reject it, and all except Tennessee followed his advice. But the president's case for state autonomy was weakened by the publicity resulting from bloody race riots in New Orleans and Memphis. These and other reported atrocities against blacks made it clear that the existing southern state governments were failing abysmally to protect the "life, liberty, or property" of the ex-slaves.

Johnson further weakened his cause by taking the stump on behalf of candidates who supported his policies. In his notorious "swing around the circle," he toured the nation, slandering his opponents in crude language and engaging in undignified exchanges with hecklers. Enraged by southern inflexibility and the antics of a president who acted as if he were still campaigning in the backwoods of Tennessee, northern voters repudiated the administration. The Republican majority in Congress increased to a solid two-thirds in both houses, and the Radical wing of the party gained strength at the expense of moderates and conservatives.

Congressional Reconstruction Plan Enacted

Congress was now in a position to implement its own plan of Reconstruction. In 1867 and 1868 it passed a series of acts that nullified the president's initiatives and reorganized the South on a new basis. Generally referred to as "Radical Reconstruction," these measures actually represented a compromise between genuine Radicals and more moderate elements within the party.

Consistent Radicals like Senator Charles Sumner of Massachusetts and Congressmen Thaddeus Stevens of Pennsylvania and George Julian of Indiana wanted to reshape southern society before readmitting ex-Confederates to the Union. Their program of "regeneration before reconstruction" required an extended period of military rule, confiscation and redistribution of large landholdings among the freedmen, and federal aid for schools to educate blacks and whites for citizenship. But the majority of Republican congressmen found such a program unacceptable because it broke too sharply with American traditions of federalism and regard for property rights and might mean that decades would pass before the Union was back in working order.

The First Reconstruction Act, passed over Johnson's veto on March 2, 1867, did place the South under the rule of the army by reorganizing the region into five military districts. But military rule would last for only a short time. Subsequent acts of 1867 and 1868 opened the way for the quick readmission of any state that framed and ratified a new constitution providing for black suffrage. Ex-Confederates disqualified from holding federal office under the Fourteenth Amendment were prohibited from voting for delegates to the constitutional conventions or in the elections to ratify the conventions' work. Since blacks were allowed to participate in this process, Republicans thought they had found a way to ensure that "loyal" men would dominate the new governments. Speed was essential because some Republican leaders anticipated they would need votes from the reconstructed South in order to retain control of Congress and the White House in 1868.

"Radical Reconstruction" was based on the dubious assumption that once blacks had the vote, they would have the power to protect themselves against white supremacists' efforts to deny them their rights. The Reconstruction Acts thus signaled a retreat from the true Radical position that a sustained use of federal authority was needed to complete the transition from slavery to

This cartoon of Columbia (the personification of a united America) and Robert E. Lee, which appeared in the August 5, 1865, issue of Harper's Weekly, depicts the Radical Republicans' demand for signs of "regeneration" before readmitting Confederate states to the Union.

freedom and prevent the resurgence of the South's old ruling class. (Troops were used in the South after 1868 but only in a very limited and sporadic way.) The majority of Republicans were unwilling to embrace centralized government and an extended period of military rule over civilians. Such drastic steps went beyond the popular northern consensus on necessary and proper Reconstruction measures. Thus, despite strong reservations, Radicals like Thaddeus Stevens supported the plan of readmitting the southern states on the basis of black suffrage, recognizing this was as far as the party and the northern public were willing to go.

Even so, congressional Reconstruction did have a radical aspect. Although the program won

Among the most influential of the radicals was Congressman Thaddeus Stevens of Pennsylvania. He advocated seizing land from southern planters and distributing it among the freed slaves.

Republican support partly because it promised practical political advantages, a genuine spirit of democratic idealism gave legitimacy and fervor to the cause of black male suffrage. Enabling people who were so poor and downtrodden to have access to the ballot box was a bold and innovative application of the principle of government by the consent of the governed. The problem was finding a way to enforce equal suffrage under conditions then existing in the postwar South.

The Impeachment Crisis

The first obstacle to enforcement of congressional Reconstruction was resistance from the White House. Johnson thoroughly disapproved of the new policy and sought to thwart the will of Congress by administering the plan in his own obstructive fashion. He immediately began to dismiss officeholders who sympathized with Radical

Reconstruction, and he countermanded the orders of generals in charge of southern military districts who were zealous in their enforcement of the new legislation. Some Radical generals were transferred and replaced by conservative Democrats. Congress responded by passing laws designed to limit presidential authority over Reconstruction matters. One of these measures was the Tenure of Office Act, requiring Senate approval for the removal of cabinet officers and other officials whose appointment had needed the consent of the Senate. Another measure—a rider to an army appropriations bill—sought to limit Johnson's authority to issue orders to military commanders.

Johnson objected vigorously to these restrictions on the grounds, that they violated the constitutional doctrine of the separation of powers. When it became clear that the president was resolute in fighting for his powers and using them to resist the establishment of Radical regimes in the southern states, some congressmen began to call for his impeachment. A preliminary effort foundered in 1867, but when Johnson tried to discharge Secretary of War Edwin Stanton—the only Radical in the cabinet—and persisted in his efforts despite the disapproval of the Senate, the proimpeachment forces gained in strength.

In January 1868, Johnson ordered General Grant, who already commanded the army, to replace Stanton as head of the War Department. But Grant had his eye on the Republican presidential nomination and refused to defy Congress. Johnson subsequently appointed General Lorenzo Thomas, who agreed to serve. Faced with this apparent violation of the Tenure of Office Act, the House voted overwhelmingly to impeach the president on February 24, and he was placed on trial before the Senate.

Because seven Republican senators broke with the party leadership and voted for acquittal, the effort to convict Johnson and remove him from office fell one vote short of the necessary two-thirds. This outcome resulted in part from a skillful defense. Attorneys for the president argued for a narrow interpretation of the constitutional provision that a president could be impeached only for a "high crime and misdemeanor," asserting that this referred only to an indictable crime. Responding to the charge that Johnson had delib-

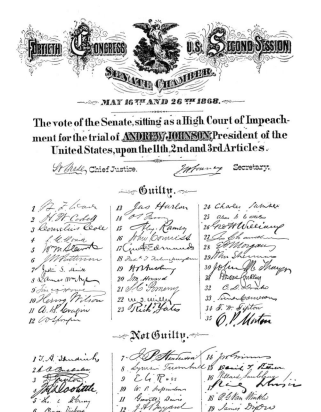

The record of the Senate vote on Andrew Johnson's impeachment trial. Charles Sumner, one of the leaders of the pro-impeachment forces, spoke of the trial as "one of the last great battles with slavery" and urged that "every sentiment, every conviction, every vow against slavery must now be directed against him [Johnson]." James Grimes, who spoke for Johnson's acquittal, argued that "This government can only be preserved and the liberty of the people maintained by preserved intact the coordinate branches of it—legislative, executive, judicial—alike. I am no convert to any doctrine of the omnipotence of Congress."

erately violated the Tenure of Office Act, the defense contended that the law did not apply to the removal of Stanton because he had been appointed by Lincoln, not Johnson.

The prosecution countered with a different interpretation of the Tenure of Office Act, but the core of their case was that Johnson had abused the powers of his office in an effort to sabotage the congressional Reconstruction policy. Obstructing the will of the legislative branch, they claimed, was sufficient grounds for conviction even if no crime had been committed. The Republicans who broke ranks to vote for acquit-

tal could not endorse such a broad view of the impeachment power. They feared that removal of a president for essentially political reasons would threaten the constitutional balance of powers and open the way to legislative supremacy over the executive. In addition, the man who would have succeeded Johnson—Senator Benjamin Wade of Ohio, the president pro tem of the Senate—was unpopular with conservative Republicans because of his radical position on labor and currency questions.

Although Johnson's acquittal by the narrowest of margins protected the American presidency from congressional domination, the impeachment episode helped create an impression in the public mind that the Radicals were ready to turn the Constitution to their own use to gain their objectives. Conservatives were again alarmed when Congress took action in 1868 to deny the Supreme Court's appellate jurisdiction in cases involving the military arrest and imprisonment of anti-Reconstruction activists in the South. But the evidence of congressional ruthlessness and illegality is not as strong as most historians used to think. Modern legal scholars have found merit in the Radicals' claim that their actions did not violate the Constitution.

Failure to remove Johnson from office was an embarrassment to congressional Republicans, but the episode did ensure that Reconstruction in the South would proceed as the majority in Congress intended. During the trial, Johnson helped influence the verdict by pledging to enforce the Reconstruction Acts, and he held to this promise during his remaining months in office. Unable to depose the president, the Radicals had at least succeeded in neutralizing his opposition to their program.

RECONSTRUCTION IN THE SOUTH

The Civil War left the South devastated, demoralized, and destitute. Slavery was dead, but what this meant for future relationships between whites and blacks was still in doubt. The overwhelming majority of southern whites wanted to keep blacks adrift between slavery and freedom—without rights, in a status resembling that of the "free Negroes" of the Old South. Blacks sought to be independent of their former masters and viewed the acquisition of land, education, and the vote as the best means of achieving this goal. The thousands of Northerners who went south after the war for materialistic or humanitarian reasons hoped to extend Yankee "civilization" to what they viewed as an unenlightened and barbarous region. For most of them this reformation required the aid of the freedmen; not enough southern whites were willing to accept the new order and embrace northern middle-class values.

The struggle of these groups to achieve their conflicting goals bred chaos, violence, and instability. Unsettled conditions created many opportunities for corruption, crime, and terrorism. This was scarcely an ideal setting for an experiment in interracial democracy, but one was attempted nonetheless. Its success depended on massive and sustained support from the federal government. To the extent that this was forthcoming, progressive reform could be achieved. When it faltered, the forces of reaction and white supremacy were unleashed.

Social and Economic Adjustments

The Civil War scarred the southern landscape and wrecked its economy. One devastated area—central South Carolina—looked to an 1865 observer "like a broad black streak of ruin and desolation—the fences are gone; lonesome smokestacks, surrounded by dark heaps of ashes and cinders, marking the spots where human habitations had stood; the fields all along the roads widely overgrown with weeds, with here and there a sickly patch of cotton or corn cultivated by negro squatters." Other areas through which the armies had passed were similarly ravaged. Several major cities—including Atlanta, Columbia, and Richmond—were gutted by fire. Most factories were dismantled or destroyed, and long stretches of railroad were torn up.

Physical ruin would not have been so disastrous if investment capital had been available for rebuilding. But the substantial wealth represented by Confederate currency and bonds had melted away, and emancipation of the slaves had divested the propertied classes of their most valuable and productive assets. According to some estimates, the South's per capita wealth in 1865 was only about half what it had been in 1860.

Recovery could not even begin until a new labor system replaced slavery. It was widely assumed in both the North and the South that southern prosperity would continue to depend on cotton and that the plantation was the most efficient unit for producing the crop. Hindering efforts to rebuild the plantation economy were lack of capital, the deep-rooted belief of southern whites that blacks would work only under compulsion, and the freedmen's resistance to labor conditions that recalled slavery.

Blacks strongly preferred to be small independent farmers rather than plantation laborers, and for a time they had reason to hope the federal government would support their ambitions. General Sherman, hampered by the huge numbers of black fugitives that followed his army on its famous march, issued an order in January 1865 that set aside the islands and coastal areas of Georgia and South Carolina for exclusive black occupancy on 40-acre plots. Furthermore, the Freedmen's Bureau, as one of its many responsibilities, was given control of hundreds of thousands of acres of abandoned or confiscated land and was authorized to make 40-acre grants to black settlers for three-year periods, after which they would have the option to buy at low prices. By June 1865, forty thousand black farmers were at work on 300,000 acres of what they thought would be their own land.

But for most of them the dream of "forty acres and a mule" was not to be realized. President Johnson pardoned the owners of most of the land consigned to the ex-slaves by Sherman and the Freedmen's Bureau, and proposals for an effective program of land confiscation and redistribution failed to get through Congress. Among the considerations prompting most congressmen to oppose land reform were a tenderness for property rights, fears of sapping the freedmen's initiative by giving them something they allegedly had not earned, and the desire to restore cotton production as quickly as possible to increase agricultural exports and stabilize the economy. Consequently, most blacks in physical possession of small farms failed to acquire title, and the mass of freedmen were left with little or no prospect of becoming landowners. Recalling the plight of southern blacks in 1865, an ex-slave later wrote that "they were set free without a dollar, without a foot of land, and without the wherewithal to get the next meal even."

Painting of a sharecropper's cabin, by William Aiken Walker. Too often freed slaves discovered that sharecropping led to a new form of economic servitude.

Despite their poverty and landlessness, ex-slaves were reluctant to settle down and commit themselves to wage labor for their former masters. Many took to the road, hoping to find something better. Some were still expecting grants of land, but others were simply trying to increase their bargaining power. "One ob de rights ob bein free," one freedman later recalled, "wuz dat we could move around en change bosses." As the end of 1865 approached, many freedmen had still not signed up for the coming season; anxious planters feared they were plotting to seize the land by force. Within a few weeks, however, most holdouts signed for the best terms they could get.

One common form of agricultural employment in 1866 was a contract labor system. Under this system, workers committed themselves for a year in return for fixed wages, a substantial portion of which was withheld until after the harvest. Since many planters were inclined to drive hard bargains, abuse their workers, or cheat them at the end of the year, the Freedmen's Bureau assumed the role of reviewing the contracts and enforcing them. But bureau officials had differing notions of what it meant to protect African Americans from exploitation. Some stood up strongly for the

rights of the freedmen; others served as allies of the planters, rounding up available workers, coercing them to sign contracts for low wages, and then helping keep them in line.

The Bureau's influence waned after 1867 (it was phased out completely by 1869), and the experiment with contract wage labor was abandoned. Growing up alongside the contract system and eventually displacing it was an alternative capital-labor relationship—sharecropping. First in small groups known as "squads" and later as individual families, blacks worked a piece of land independently for a fixed share of the crop, usually one-half. The advantage of this arrangement for credit-starved landlords was that it did not require much expenditure in advance of the harvest. The system also forced the tenant to share the risks of crop failure or a fall in cotton prices. These considerations loomed larger after disastrous harvests in 1866 and 1867.

African Americans initially viewed sharecropping as a step up from wage labor in the direction of land-ownership. But during the 1870s this form of tenancy evolved into a new kind of servitude. Croppers had to live on credit until their cotton was sold, and planters or merchants seized the chance to "provision" them at high prices and exorbitant rates of interest. Creditors were entitled to deduct what was owed to them out of the tenant's share of the crop and this left most sharecroppers with no net profit at the end of the year—more often than not with a debt that had to be worked off in subsequent years. Various methods, legal and extralegal, were eventually devised in an effort to bind indebted tenants to a single landlord for extended periods, but considerable movement was still possible.

While landless African Americans in the countryside were being reduced to economic dependence, those in towns and cities found themselves living in an increasingly segregated society. The Black Codes of 1865 attempted to require separation of the races in public places and facilities; when most of the codes were set aside by federal authorities as violations of the Civil Rights Act of 1866, the same end was often achieved through private initiative and community pressure. In some cities, blacks successfully resisted being consigned to separate streetcars by appealing to the military during the brief period when it exercised authority or by organizing boycotts. But they found it almost impossible to gain admittance to most hotels, restaurants, and other privately owned establishments catering to whites. On railroads, separate black, or "Jim Crow," cars were not yet the rule, but African Americans were normally denied first-class accommodations. After 1868, black-supported Republican governments passed civil rights acts requiring equal access to public facilities, but little effort was made to enforce the legislation.

Some forms of racial separation were not openly discriminatory, and blacks accepted or even endorsed them. Freedmen who had belonged to white churches as slaves welcomed the chance to join all-black denominations like the African Methodist Episcopal church, which provided freedom from white dominance and a more congenial style of worship. The first schools for ex-slaves were all-black institutions established by the Freedmen's Bureau and various northern missionary societies. Having been denied all education during the antebellum period, most blacks viewed separate schooling as an opportunity rather than as a form of discrimination. When Radical governments set up public school systems, they condoned de facto educational segregation. Only in city schools of New Orleans and at the University of South Carolina were there

serious attempts during Reconstruction to bring white and black students together in the same classrooms.

The upshot of all forms of racial separatism—whether produced by white prejudice or black independence—was to create a divided society, one in which blacks and whites lived much of the time in separate worlds. There were two exceptions to this pattern: one was at work, where blacks necessarily dealt with white employers; the other was in the political sphere, where blacks sought to exercise their rights as citizens.

Political Reconstruction in the South

The state governments that emerged in 1865 had little or no regard for the rights of the freed slaves. Some of their codes even made black unemployment a crime, which meant blacks had to make long-term contracts with white employers or be arrested for vagrancy. Others limited the rights of African Americans to own property or engage in occupations other than those of servant or laborer. The codes were set aside by the actions of Congress, the military, and the Freedmen's Bureau, but private violence and discrimination against blacks continued on a massive scale unchecked by state authorities. Hundreds, perhaps thousands, of blacks were murdered by whites in 1865–1866, and few of the perpetrators were brought to justice.

The imposition of military rule in 1867 was designed in part to protect former slaves from violence and intimidation, but the task was beyond the capacity of the few thousand troops stationed in the South. When new constitutions were approved and states readmitted to the Union under the congressional plan in 1868, the problem became more severe. White opponents of Radical Reconstruction adopted systematic terrorism and organized mob violence to keep blacks away from the polls. Yet the military presence was progressively reduced, leaving the new Republican regimes to fight a losing battle against armed white supremacists. In the words of historian William Gillette, "there was simply no federal force large enough to give heart to black Republicans or to bridle southern white violence."

Hastily organized in 1867, the southern Republican party dominated the constitution-

At left, an African-American soldier and his sweetheart are wed by a Freedmen's Bureau chaplain. Many black soldiers asked that the unions they made in slave days be legalized so that their families would qualify for survivors' benefits when they died.

Below is a Freedmen's school, one of the more successful endeavors supported by the Freedmen's Bureau. The Bureau, working with teachers from northern abolitionist and missionary societies, founded thousands of schools for freed slaves and poor whites.

making of 1868 and the regimes that came out of it. The party was an attempted coalition of three social groups (which varied in their relative strength from state to state). One was the same class that was becoming the backbone of the Republican party in the North—businessmen with an interest in enlisting government aid for private enterprise. Many Republicans of this stripe were recent arrivals from the North—the so-called carpetbaggers—but some were scalawags, former Whig planters or merchants who were born in the South or had immigrated to the region before the war and now saw a chance to realize their dreams for commercial and industrial development.

Poor white farmers, especially those from upland areas where Unionist sentiment had been strong during the Civil War, were a second element in the original coalition. These owners of small farms expected the party to favor their interests at the expense of the wealthy landowners and to come to their aid with special legislation when—as was often the case in this period of economic upheaval—they faced the loss of their homesteads to creditors. Newly enfranchised blacks were the third group to which the Republicans appealed. Blacks formed the vast majority of the Republican rank and file in most states and were concerned mainly with education, civil rights, and land-ownership.

Under the best of conditions, these coalitions would have been difficult to maintain. Each group had its own distinct goals and did not fully support the aims of the other segments. White yeomen, for example, had a deeply rooted resistance to black equality. And for how long could one expect essentially conservative businessmen to support costly measures for the elevation or relief of the lower classes of either race? In some states, astute Democratic politicians exploited these divisions by appealing to disaffected white Republicans.

But during the relatively brief period when they were in power in the South—varying from one to nine years depending on the state—the Republicans chalked up some notable achievements. They established (on paper at least) the South's first adequate systems of public education, democratized state and local government, and appropriated funds for an enormous expansion of public services and responsibilities.

Important as these social and political reforms were, they took second place to the Republicans' major effort—to foster economic development and restore southern prosperity by subsidizing the construction of railroads and other internal improvements. But the policy of aiding railroads turned out to be disastrous, even though it addressed the region's real economic needs and was initially very popular. Extravagance, corruption, and routes laid out in response to local

political pressure rather than on sound economic considerations made for an increasing burden of public debt and taxation. The policy did not produce the promised payoff of efficient, cheap transportation. Subsidized railroads frequently went bankrupt, leaving the taxpayers holding the bag. When the panic of 1873 brought many southern state governments to the verge of bankruptcy, and railroad building came to an end, it was clear the Republicans' "gospel of prosperity" through state aid to private enterprise had failed miserably. Their political opponents, many of whom had originally favored such policies, now saw an opportunity to take advantage of the situation by charging that Republicans had ruined the southern economy.

In general, the Radical regimes failed to conduct public business honestly and efficiently. Embezzlement of public funds and bribery of state lawmakers or officials were common occurrences. State debts and tax burdens rose enormously, mainly because governments had undertaken heavy new responsibilities, but partly because of waste and graft. The situation varied from state to state; ruling cliques in Louisiana and South Carolina were guilty of much wrongdoing, yet Mississippi had a relatively honest and frugal regime.

Furthermore, southern corruption was not exceptional, nor was it a special result of the extension of suffrage to uneducated African Americans, as critics of Radical Reconstruction have claimed. It was part of a national pattern during an era when private interests considered buying government favors to be a part of the cost of doing business, and many politicians expected to profit by obliging them.

Blacks bore only a limited responsibility for the dishonesty of the Radical governments. Although sixteen African Americans served in Congress—two in the Senate—between 1869 and 1880, only in South Carolina did blacks constitute a majority of even one house of the state legislature. Furthermore, no black governors were elected during Reconstruction (although P. B. S. Pinchback served for a time as acting governor of Louisiana). The biggest grafters were opportunistic whites. Some of the most notorious were carpetbaggers but others were native Southerners. Businessmen offering bribes included members of the prewar gentry who were staunch opponents

Although African Americans represented a majority in many of the former slave states in the Deep South, they constituted a majority only in the South Carolina state legislature (above right). A small number of African Americans were elected to Congress. Among them was Senator Blanche K. Bruce (left) who championed the causes of citizenship for Native Americans and improvement of the Mississippi River.

of Radical programs. Some black legislators went with the tide and accepted "loans" from those railroad lobbyists who would pay most for their votes, but the same men could usually be depended on to vote the will of their constituents on civil rights or educational issues.

If blacks served or supported corrupt and wasteful regimes it was because they had no alternative. Although the Democrats, or "Conservatives" as they called themselves in some states, made sporadic efforts to attract African American voters, it was clear that if they won control they would attempt to strip blacks of their civil and political rights. But opponents of Radical Reconstruction were able to capitalize on racial prejudice and persuade many Americans that "good government" was synonymous with white supremacy.

Contrary to myth, the small number of African Americans elected to state or national office during Reconstruction demonstrated on the average more integrity and competence than their white counterparts. Most were fairly well educated,

having been free Negroes or unusually privileged slaves before the war. Among the most capable were Robert Smalls (whose career was described earlier); Senator Blanche K. Bruce of Mississippi, elected to the Senate in 1874 after rising to deserved prominence in the Republican party of his home state; Congressman Robert Brown Elliott of South Carolina, an adroit politician who was also a consistent champion of civil rights; and Congressman James T. Rapier of Alabama, who stirred Congress and the nation in 1873 with his eloquent appeals for federal aid to southern education and new laws to enforce equal rights for African Americans.

THE AGE OF GRANT

Ulysses S. Grant was the only president between Jackson and Wilson to serve two full and consecutive terms. But unlike other chief executives so favored by the electorate, Grant is commonly regarded as a failure. Historians used to blame him mainly for the corruption that surfaced in his administration. More recently he also has been condemned for the inconsistency and ultimate failure of his southern policy. The charges have some validity, and no one is likely to make the case that he was a great statesman. At times Grant's highest priority seemed to be loyalty to old friends and to politicians who supported him. But the problems he faced were certainly difficult. A president with a clearer sense of duty might have done little better.

Rise of the Money Question

The impeachment crisis of 1868 represented the high point of popular interest in Reconstruction issues. Already competing for public attention was the question of how to manage the nation's currency, and more specifically, what to do about greenbacks—paper money issued during the war. Hugh McCulloch, secretary of the treasury under Johnson, favored a return to "sound" money, and in 1866 he had initiated a policy of withdrawing greenbacks from circulation. Opposition to this hard-money policy and the resulting deflation came from a number of groups. In general, the "greenbackers" were strongest in the credit-hungry West and among expansion-minded manufacturers. Defenders of hard money were mostly the commercial and financial interests in the East; they received crucial support from intellectuals who regarded government-sponsored inflation as immoral or contrary to the natural laws of classical economics.

In 1868, the money question surged briefly to the forefront of national politics. Faced with a business recession blamed on McCulloch's policy of contracting the currency, Congress voted to stop the retirement of greenbacks. The Democratic party, responding to midwestern pressure, included in its platform a plan calling for the redemption of much of the Civil War debt in greenbacks rather than the gold that bondholders had been anticipating. But divisions within the parties prevented the money question from becoming a central issue in the presidential campaign. The Democrats nominated Governor Horatio Seymour of New York, a sound-money supporter, thus nullifying their pro-greenback platform. Republicans based their campaign mainly on a defense of their Reconstruction policy and a celebration of their popular candidate. With the help of votes from the Republican-dominated southern states, Grant won a decisive victory.

In 1869 and 1870, a Republican-controlled Congress passed laws that assured payment in gold to most bondholders but eased the burden of the huge Civil War debt by exchanging bonds soon coming due for those that would not be payable for ten, fifteen, or thirty years. In this way the public credit was protected.

Still unresolved was the problem of what to do about the $356 million in greenbacks that remained in circulation. Hard-money proponents wanted to retire them quickly; inflationists thought more should be issued to stimulate the economy. The Grant administration followed the middle course of allowing the greenbacks to float until economic expansion would bring them to a par with gold, thus permitting a painless return to specie payments. But the panic of 1873, which brought much of the economy to its knees, led to a revival of agitation to inflate the currency. Debt-ridden farmers, who would be the backbone of the greenback movement for years to come, now joined the soft-money clamor for the first time.

Responding to the money and credit crunch, Congress moved in 1874 to authorize a modest issue of new greenbacks. But Grant, influenced by the opinions of hard-money financiers, vetoed the bill. In 1875, Congress, led by Senator John Sherman of Ohio, enacted the Specie Resumption Act, which provided for a limited reduction of greenbacks leading to full resumption of specie payments by January 1, 1879. Its action was widely interpreted as deflation in the midst of depression. Farmers and workers, who were already suffering acutely from deflation, reacted with dismay and anger.

The Democratic party could not capitalize adequately on these sentiments because of the influence of its own hard-money faction, and in 1876 an independent Greenback party entered the national political arena. The party's nominee for president, Peter Cooper, received an insignificant number of votes, but in 1878 the Greenback Labor party polled more than a million votes and

Shown seated at the table are feminist leaders Elizabeth Cady Stanton and Susan B. Anthony. They and their adherents split with Lucy Stone (right) and her followers over the Fifteenth Amendment and its failure to extend the vote to women.

The Election of 1868

Candidate	Party	Popular Vote	Electoral Vote
Grant	Republican	3,013,421	214
Seymour	Democratic	2,706,829	80
Not voted*			23

Unreconstructed states did not participate in the election.

elected fourteen congressmen. The Greenbackers were able to keep the money issue alive into the following decade.

Retreat from Reconstruction

The Republican effort to make equal rights for blacks the law of the land culminated in the Fifteenth Amendment. Passed by Congress in 1869 and ratified by the states in 1870, the amendment prohibited any state from denying a citizen the right to vote because of race, color, or previous condition of servitude. A more radical version, requiring universal manhood suffrage, was rejected partly because it departed too sharply from traditional views of federal-state relations. States therefore could still limit the suffrage by imposing literacy tests, property qualifications, or poll taxes allegedly applying to all racial groups; such devices would eventually be used to strip southern blacks of the right to vote. But the makers of the amendment did not foresee this result. They believed their action would prevent future Congresses or southern constitutional conventions from repealing or nullifying the provisions for black male suffrage included in the Reconstruction Acts. A secondary aim was to enfranchise African Americans in those northern states that still denied them the vote.

Many feminists were bitterly disappointed that the amendment did not extend the vote to women as well as freedmen. A militant wing of the woman's rights movement led by Elizabeth Cady Stanton and Susan B. Anthony was so angered that the Constitution was being amended to make gender an explicit qualification for voting that they campaigned against ratification of the Fifteenth Amendment. Another group of feminists led by Lucy Stone supported the amendment on the grounds that this was "the Negro's hour" and that women could afford to wait a few years for the vote. This disagreement divided the women's suffrage movement for a generation to come.

The Grant administration was charged with enforcing the amendment and protecting black voting rights in the reconstructed states. Since survival of the Republican regimes depended on African American support, political partisanship dictated federal action, even though the North's emotional and ideological commitment to black citizenship was waning.

Changing Views of Reconstruction

A central issue of Reconstruction was the place of blacks in American life after slavery. Changing attitudes on this question strongly influenced later representations of the Reconstruction era, whether in historical writing or in the popular media. Indeed, what later generations imagined had happened in the South in the years immediately after the Civil War is a fairly reliable index of how they viewed black/white relations in their own time.

In the early twentieth century, when white supremacists were in control in the South and northern public opinion was learning to tolerate southern policies of rigid segregation and disfranchisement of blacks, historians played a major role in rationalizing the new order in southern race relations. According to historians like Professor John W. Burgess of Columbia University, writing in 1902, Reconstruction governments represented an unholy alliance of corrupt northern "carpetbaggers" seeking to profit at the expense of the "prostrate South"; southern white opportunists of mean origins, known as "scalawags"; and black demagogues who sought power by putting false and dangerous aspirations for equality into the heads of newly freed slaves. What made this orgy of misrule possible, said Burgess, was the colossal blunder that Congress made when it extended

the vote to "ignorant and vicious" blacks. In the eyes of Burgess and a whole school of historians, Reconstruction was "the most soul-sickening spectacle that Americans have ever been called upon to behold . . . here was government by the most ignorant and vicious part of the population for the vulgar, materialistic, brutal benefit of the governing set."

In 1915 the most ambitious film yet made by the fledgling American movie industry— D. W. Griffith's *Birth of a Nation*—popularized this image of Reconstruction and made its racism more lurid and explicit. To underscore the message of this technically brilliant film, words flashed on the screen describing Reconstruction as a callous attempt to "<u>put the white South under the heel of the black South.</u>" In the film, leering blacks carry signs advocating interracial marriage. Mainly responsible for this state of affairs is a vengeful Congressman meant to represent Thaddeus Stevens, who hatches a devilish plot to oppress and humiliate the white South. One famous scene portrays the South Carolina state legislature as a mob of grinning barefoot blacks, carousing at the taxpayers' expense. The film's melodramatic plot features the suicide of one southern white maiden to escape the embraces of a black pursuer and the Ku Klux Klan's epic res-

cue of another damsel from a forced marriage to a mulatto politician.

Birth of a Nation's depiction of the Klan as saving white civilization from bestial blacks inspired vigorous protests from the recently founded National Association for the Advancement of Colored People (NAACP), and censors in a few northern cities deleted some of the more blatantly racist scenes. But President Woodrow Wilson endorsed the film. "My only regret is that it is all so terribly true," he is reported to have said. Most white moviegoers seemed to agree with the president rather than with the NAACP. Millions of Americans saw and applauded this cinematic triumph.

During the period between 1915 and the 1940s, most historians echoed the judgment of

Birth of a Nation that efforts to enforce equal rights for blacks after the Civil War had been a grave mistake. One popular work of that era was entitled *The Tragic Era,* and another summed up Reconstruction as "the blackout of honest government." The biases of mainstream historiography served to justify the Jim Crow system of the South by portraying blacks as unqualified for citizenship.

A few black historians of the 1920s and 1930s advanced the contrary view that Reconstruction was a noble effort to achieve a color-blind democracy that failed because of the strength of white racism and conservative economic interests. The most powerful example of this early revisionism was W. E. B. DuBois's *Black Reconstruction in America* (1935).

During the 1950s and 1960s another image of Reconstruction emerged. The majority of historians writing about the era finally rejected the exaggerations, distortions, and racist assumptions of the traditional view. The triumph of "revisionism" was evident in 1965 when Kenneth M. Stampp published his *Era of Reconstruction.* As influential northern opinion shifted from tolerance of segregation to support for the black struggle for equality in the South, a more favorable view of earlier efforts on behalf of civil rights became acceptable. White liberal historians like Stampp concentrated on rehabilitating the Radical Republicans by stressing their idealism, while black scholars like John Hope Franklin highlighted the constructive policies and positive achievements of the much maligned black leaders of the Reconstruction South.

A scene from Birth of a Nation. *Note that the role of the black man at right is played by a white actor in dark makeup.*

Previous moral judgments thus tended to be reversed; white and black Republicans became the heroes, and the southern whites who resisted and eventually overthrew Reconstruction became the villains. The analogy between these earlier adversaries and the civil rights activists and southern segregationists of the 1960s was clear.

During the 1970s and early 1980s, a "postrevisionism" began to develop. As it became apparent that the dream of equality for blacks was still unrealized, historians responded to the changing perceptions and complex crosscurrents of black/white relations in their own time by taking another look at Reconstruction. They found, among other things, that those in charge of efforts to make blacks equal citizens in the late 1860s had views that were quite moderate by the standards of the post–civil rights era of the 1970s and early 1980s. "Radical Reconstruction" no longer seemed very radical. The reputations of carpetbaggers and upper-class scalawags went down again as historians emphasized their opportunism and probusiness economic policies at

the expense of social justice. Black politicians, too, came in for critical reassessment. It was argued that many worked more for their own interests as members of a black middle class than for the kinds of policies—such as land reform—that would have met the vital needs of their impoverished constituents.

The postrevisionists seem to be agreed that Reconstruction failed because it was inadequately motivated, conceived, and enforced. But the causes of this failure remain in doubt. Some recent historians explain it in terms of an underlying racism that prevented white Republicans from identifying fully with the cause of black equality. Others stress the gulf between the class interests of those in charge of implementing and managing Reconstruction and the poor people of the South who were supposed to be its beneficiaries.

The basic issue raised by Reconstruction—how to achieve racial equality in America—has not yet been resolved. So long as this is the case, we will continue to look at our first effort in this direction for whatever guideposts it provides.

Between 1868 and 1872, the main threat to southern Republican regimes came from the Ku Klux Klan and other secret societies bent on restoring white supremacy by intimidating blacks who sought to exercise their political rights. First organized in Tennessee in 1866, the Klan spread rapidly to other states, adopting increasingly lawless and brutal tactics. A grass-roots vigilante movement and not a centralized conspiracy, the Klan thrived on local initiative and gained support from whites of all social classes. Its secrecy, decentralization, popular support, and utter ruthlessness made it very difficult to suppress. As soon as blacks had been granted the right to vote, hooded night riders began to visit the cabins of those who were known to be active Republicans; some victims were only threatened, but others were whipped or even murdered. A typical incident was related by a black Georgian: "They broke my door open, took me out of bed, took me to the woods and whipped me three hours or more and left me for dead. They said to me, 'Do you think you will vote for another damned radical ticket?'"

These methods were first used effectively in the presidential election of 1868. Grant lost in Louisiana and Georgia mainly because the Klan—or the Knights of the White Camelia as the Louisiana variant was called—launched a reign of terror to prevent prospective black voters from exercising their right. In Louisiana political violence claimed more than a thousand lives, and in Arkansas, which Grant managed to carry, more than two hundred Republicans, including a congressman, were assassinated.

Thereafter, Klan terrorism was directed mainly at Republican state governments. Virtual insurrections broke out in Arkansas, Tennessee, North Carolina, and parts of South Carolina. Republican governors called out the state militia to fight the Klan, but only the Arkansas militia succeeded in bringing it to heel. In Tennessee, North Carolina, and Georgia, Klan activities helped undermine Republican control, thus allowing the Democrats to come to power in all of these states by 1870.

Faced with the violent overthrow of the southern Republican party, Congress and the Grant administration were forced to act. A series of laws passed in 1870–1871 sought to enforce the Fifteenth Amendment by providing federal protection for black suffrage and authorizing use of the army against the Klan. These "Ku Klux Klan" or "Force" Acts made interference with voting rights a federal crime and established provisions for government supervision of elections. In addition, the legislation empowered the president to call out troops and suspend the writ of habeas corpus to quell insurrection. In 1871–1872, thousands of suspected Klansmen were arrested by the military or U. S. marshals, and the writ was suspended in nine counties of South Carolina that had been virtually taken over by the secret order. Although most of the accused Klansmen were never brought to trial, were acquitted, or received suspended sentences, the enforcement effort was vigorous enough to put a damper on hooded terrorism and ensure relatively fair and peaceful elections in 1872.

In these elections, a heavy black turnout enabled the Republicans to hold on to power in most states of the Deep South, despite efforts of the Democratic-Conservative opposition to cut into the Republican vote by taking moderate positions on racial and economic issues. As a result of this setback, the Democratic-Conservatives made a significant change in their strategy and ideology. No longer did they try to take votes away from the Republicans by proclaiming their support of black suffrage and government aid to business. They began instead to appeal openly to white supremacy and to the traditional Democratic and agrarian hostility to governmental promotion of economic development. Consequently, they were able to bring back to the polls a portion of the white electorate, mostly small farmers, who had not been turning out because they were alienated by the leadership's apparent concessions to Yankee ideas.

This new and more effective electoral strategy dovetailed with a resurgence of violence meant to reduce Republican, especially black Republican, voting. The new reign of terror differed from the previous Klan episode; its agents no longer wore masks but acted quite openly. They were effective because the northern public was increasingly disenchanted with federal intervention on behalf of what were widely viewed as corrupt and tottering Republican regimes. Grant used force in the South for the last time in 1874 when an overt paramilitary organization in Louisiana, known as the White League, tried to overthrow a Republican government accused of stealing an election. When another unofficial militia—in Mississippi—insti-

Members of the Ku Klux Klan, a secret white supremacist organization, in typical regalia. Before elections, hooded Klansmen terrorized AfricanAmericans to discourage them from voting.

By 1876, Republicans held on to only three southern states: South Carolina, Louisiana, and Florida. Partly because of Grant's hesitant and inconsistent use of presidential power but mainly because the northern electorate would no longer tolerate military action to sustain Republican governments and black voting rights, Radical Reconstruction was falling into total eclipse.

Spoilsmen Versus Reformers

One reason Grant found it increasingly difficult to take strong action to protect southern Republicans was the bad odor surrounding his stewardship of the federal government and the Republican party. Reformers charged that a corrupt national administration was propping up bad governments in the South for personal and partisan advantage. An apparent case in point was Grant's intervention in Louisiana in 1872 on behalf of an ill-reputed Republican faction headed by his wife's brother-in-law, who controlled federal patronage as collector of customs in New Orleans.

The Republican party in the Grant era was losing the idealism and high purpose associated with the crusade against slavery. By the beginning of the 1870s, the men who had been the conscience of the party—old-line radicals like Thaddeus Stevens, Charles Sumner, and Benjamin Wade—were either dead, out of office, or at odds with the administration. New leaders of a different stamp, whom historians have dubbed "spoilsmen" or "politicos," were taking their place. When he made common cause with hard-boiled manipulators like senators Roscoe Conkling of New York and James G. Blaine of Maine, Grant lost credibility with reform-minded Republicans.

During Grant's first administration, an aura of scandal surrounded the White House but did not directly implicate the president. In 1869, the financial buccaneer Jay Gould enlisted the aid of a brother-in-law of Grant to further his fantastic scheme to corner the gold market. Gould failed in the attempt, but he did manage to save himself and come away with a huge profit.

Grant's first-term vice president, Schuyler Colfax of Indiana, was directly involved in the notorious Crédit Mobilier scandal. Crédit

gated a series of bloody race riots prior to the state elections of 1875, Grant refused the governor's request for federal troops. As a result, black voters were successfully intimidated—one county registered only seven Republican votes where there had been a black majority of two thousand, and Mississippi fell to the Democratic-Conservatives. According to one account, Grant decided to withhold troops because he had been warned that intervention might cost the Republicans the crucial state of Ohio in the same off-year elections.

Mobilier was a construction company that actually served as a fraudulent device for siphoning off profits that should have gone to the stockholders of the Union Pacific Railroad, which was the beneficiary of massive federal land grants. In order to forestall government inquiry into this arrangement, Crédit Mobilier stock was distributed to influential congressmen, including Colfax (who was Speaker of the House before he was elected vice president). The whole business came to light just before the campaign of 1872.

Republicans who could not tolerate such corruption or had other grievances against the administration broke with Grant in 1872 and formed a third party committed to "honest government" and "reconciliation" between the North and the South. Led initially by high-minded reformers like Senator Carl Schurz of Missouri, the "Liberal Republicans" endorsed reform of the civil service to curb the corruption-breeding patronage system and advocated laissez-faire economic policies—which meant low tariffs, an end to government subsidies for railroads, and hard money. Despite their rhetoric of idealism and reform, the Liberal Republicans were extremely conservative in their notions of what government should do to assure justice for blacks and other underprivileged Americans.

The Liberal Republicans' national convention nominated Horace Greeley, editor of the respected New York *Tribune*. This was a curious and divisive choice, since Greeley was at odds with the founders of the movement on the tariff question and was indifferent to civil service reform. The Democrats also endorsed Greeley, mainly because he promised to end Radical Reconstruction by restoring "self-government" to the South.

But the journalist turned out to be a poor campaigner who failed to inspire enthusiasm from lifelong supporters of either party. Most Republicans stuck with Grant, despite the corruption issue, because they still could not stomach the idea of ex-rebels returning to power in the South. Many Democrats, recalling Greeley's previous record as a staunch Republican, simply stayed away from the polls. The result was a decisive victory for Grant, whose 56 percent of the popular vote was the highest percentage won by any candidate between Andrew Jackson and Theodore Roosevelt.

The Election of 1872			
Candidate	Party	Popular Vote	Electoral Vote*
Grant	Republican	3,598,235	286
Greeley	Democrat and Liberal Republican	2,834,761	Greeley died before the electoral college voted.

*Out of a total of 366 electoral votes. Greeley's votes were divided among the four minor candidates.

Grant's second administration seemed to bear out the reformers' worst suspicions about corruption in high places. In 1875, the public learned that federal revenue officials had conspired with distillers to defraud the government of millions of dollars in liquor taxes. Grant's private secretary, Orville E. Babcock, was indicted as a member of the "Whiskey Ring" and was saved from conviction only by the president's personal intercession. The next year, Grant's secretary of war, William E. Belknap, was impeached by the House after an investigation revealed he had taken bribes for the sale of Indian trading posts. He avoided conviction in the Senate only by resigning from office before his trial. Grant fought hard to protect Belknap, to the point of participating in what a later generation might call a "cover-up."

There is no evidence that Grant profited personally from any of the misdeeds of his subordinates. Yet he is not entirely without blame for the corruption in his administration. He failed to take firm action against the malefactors, and even after their guilt had been clearly established, he sometimes tried to shield them from justice.

REUNION AND THE NEW SOUTH

Congressional Reconstruction prolonged the sense of sectional division and conflict for a dozen years after the guns had fallen silent. Its final liquidation in 1877 opened the way to a reconciliation of North and South. But the costs of reunion were high for less privileged groups in the South. The civil and political rights of African

In this Puck cartoon, U. S. Grant clutches the Whiskey and Navy rings and supports an assortment of bosses, profiteers, and scandals associated with the Grant administration.

Americans, left unprotected, were progressively and relentlessly stripped away by white supremacist regimes. Lower-class whites saw their interests sacrificed to those of capitalists and landlords. Despite the rhetoric hailing a prosperous "New South," the region remained poor and open to exploitation by northern business interests.

The Compromise of 1877

The election of 1876 pitted Rutherford B. Hayes of Ohio, a Republican governor untainted by the scandals of the Grant era, against Governor Samuel J. Tilden of New York, a Democratic reformer who had battled against Tammany Hall and the Tweed Ring. Honest government was apparently the electorate's highest priority. When the returns came in, Tilden had clearly won the popular vote and seemed likely to win a narrow

victory in the electoral college. But the result was placed in doubt when the returns from the three southern states still controlled by the Republicans—South Carolina, Florida, and Louisiana—were contested. If Hayes were to be awarded these three states, plus one contested electoral vote in Oregon, Republican strategists realized, he would triumph in the electoral college by a single vote.

The outcome of the election remained undecided for months, plunging the nation into a major political crisis. To resolve the impasse, Congress appointed a special electoral commission of fifteen members to determine who would receive the votes of the disputed states. Originally composed of seven Democrats, seven Republicans, and an independent, the commission fell under Republican control when the independent member resigned to run for the Senate and a Republican was appointed to take his place. The commission split along party lines and voted 8 to 7 to award Hayes all of the disputed votes. But this decision still had to be ratified by both houses of Congress. The Republican-dominated Senate readily approved it, but Democrats in the House planned a filibuster to delay the final counting of the electoral votes until after inauguration day. If the filibuster succeeded, neither candidate would have a majority and, as provided in the Constitution, the election would be decided by the House, where the Democrats controlled enough states to elect Tilden.

To ensure Hayes's election, Republican leaders negotiated secretly with conservative southern Democrats, some of whom seemed willing to abandon the filibuster if the last troops were withdrawn and "home rule" was restored to the South. Eventually an informal bargain was struck, which historians have dubbed "the Compromise of 1877." What precisely was agreed to and by whom remains a matter of dispute; but one thing at least was understood by both sides—Hayes would be president and southern blacks would be abandoned to their fate. In a sense, Hayes did not concede anything, because he had already decided to end federal support for the crumbling Radical regimes. But southern negotiators were heartened by firm assurances that this would indeed be the policy. Some were also influenced by vaguer promises involving federal support for southern railroads and internal improvements.

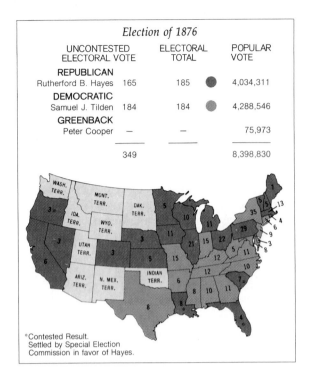

Election of 1876

	UNCONTESTED ELECTORAL VOTE	ELECTORAL TOTAL		POPULAR VOTE
REPUBLICAN				
Rutherford B. Hayes	165	185	●	4,034,311
DEMOCRATIC				
Samuel J. Tilden	184	184	●	4,288,546
GREENBACK				
Peter Cooper	–	–		75,973
		349		8,398,830

*Contested Result.
Settled by Special Election
Commission in favor of Hayes.

With southern Democratic acquiescence, the filibuster was broken and Hayes took the oath of office. He immediately ordered the army not to resist a Democratic takeover of state governments in South Carolina and Louisiana. Thus fell the last of the Radical governments, and the entire South was firmly under the control of white Democrats. The trauma of the war and Reconstruction had destroyed the chances for a renewal of two-party competition among white Southerners.

Northern Republicans soon reverted to denouncing the South for its suppression of black suffrage. But this "waving of the bloody shirt," which also served as a reminder of the war and northern casualties, quickly degenerated into a campaign ritual aimed at northern voters who could still be moved by sectional antagonism.

The New South

The men who came to power after Radical Reconstruction fell in one southern state after another are usually referred to as the "Redeemers." They had differing backgrounds and previous loyalties. Some were members of the Old South's ruling planter class who had warmly supported secession and now sought to reestablish the old order with as few changes as possible. Others, of middle-class origin or outlook, favored commer-

cial and industrial interests over agrarian groups and called for a "New South," committed to diversified economic development. A third group were professional politicians bending with the prevailing winds—like Joseph E. Brown of Georgia who had been a secessionist, a wartime governor, and a leading scalawag Republican, before becoming a Democratic "Redeemer."

Although historians have tried to assign the Redeemers a single coherent ideology or view of the world and have debated whether it was Old South agrarianism or New South industrialism they endorsed, these leaders can perhaps best be understood as power brokers mediating among the dominant interest groups of the South in ways that served their own political advantage. In many ways, the "rings" that they established on the state and county level were analogous to the political machines developing at the same time in northern cities.

They did, however, agree on and endorse two basic principles: laissez-faire and white supremacy. Laissez-faire—the notion that government should be limited and should not intervene openly and directly in the economy—could unite planters, frustrated at seeing direct state support going to businessmen, and capitalist promoters who had come to realize that low taxes and freedom from government regulation were even more advantageous than state subsidies. It soon became clear that the Redeemers responded only to privileged and entrenched interest groups, especially landlords, merchants, and industrialists, and offered little or nothing to tenants, small farmers, and working people. As industrialization began to gather steam in the 1880s, Democratic regimes became increasingly accommodating to manufacturing interests and hospitable to agents of northern capital who were gaining control of the South's transportation system and its extractive industries.

White supremacy was the principal rallying cry that brought the Redeemers to power in the first place. Once in office, they found they could stay there by charging that opponents of ruling Democratic cliques were trying to divide "the white man's party" and open the way for a return to "black domination." Appeals to racism could also deflect attention away from the economic grievances of groups without political clout.

The new governments were more economical than those of Reconstruction, mainly because

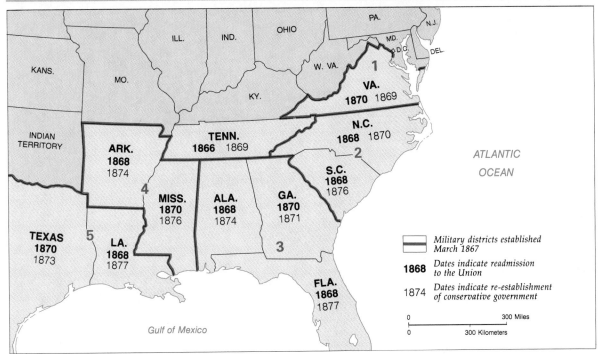

Reconstruction

During the Reconstruction era, the southern state governments passed through three phases: control by white ex-Confederates; domination by Republican legislators, both white and black; and, finally, the regain of control by conservative white Democrats.

Legend:
- Military districts established March 1867
- **1868** Dates indicate readmission to the Union
- 1874 Dates indicate re-establishment of conservative government

0 — 300 Miles
0 — 300 Kilometers

they cut back drastically on appropriations for schools and other needed public services. But they were scarcely more honest—embezzlement of funds and bribery of officials continued to occur to an alarming extent. Louisiana, for example, suffered for decades from the flagrant corruption associated with a state-chartered lottery.

The Redeemer regimes of the late 1870s and 1880s badly neglected the interests of small white farmers. Whites, as well as blacks, were suffering from the notorious "crop lien" system, which gave local merchants who advanced credit at high rates of interest during the growing season the right to take possession of the harvested crop on terms that buried farmers deeper and deeper in debt. As a result, increasing numbers of whites lost title to their homesteads and were reduced to tenancy. When a depression of world cotton prices added to the burden of a ruinous credit system, agrarian protesters began to challenge the ruling elite, first through the Southern Farmers' Alliance of the late 1880s and then by supporting its political descendant—the Populist party of the 1890s (see Chapter 20).

But the greatest hardships imposed by the new order were reserved for African Americans. The Redeemers promised, as part of the understanding that led to the end of federal intervention in 1877, that they would respect the rights of blacks as set forth in the Fourteenth and Fifteenth amendments. Governor Wade Hampton of South Carolina was especially vocal in pledging that African Americans would not be reduced to second-class citizenship by the new regimes. But when blacks tried to vote Republican in the "redeemed" states, they encountered renewed violence and intimidation. "Bulldozing" African American voters remained common practice in state elections during the late 1870s and early 1880s; those blacks who withstood the threat of losing their jobs or being evicted from tenant farms if they voted for the party of Lincoln were visited at night and literally whipped into line. The message was clear: vote Democratic or vote not at all.

Furthermore, white Democrats now controlled the electoral machinery and were able to manipulate the black vote by stuffing ballot boxes, dis-

The first industries of the New South were usually processing plants for the agricultural products of the region. In this 1871 drawing by A. R. Waud for Harper's Weekly, *African American laborers on a sugar plantation in Gretna, Louisiana, across the river from New Orleans, are cutting sugarcane to be processed in the plantation's refinery.*

carding unwanted votes, or reporting fraudulent totals. Some states also imposed complicated new voting requirements to discourage black participation. Full-scale disfranchisement did not occur until literacy tests and other legalized obstacles to voting were imposed in the period from 1890 to 1910, but by that time less formal and comprehensive methods had already made a mockery of the Fifteenth Amendment.

Nevertheless, blacks continued to vote freely in some localities until the 1890s; a few districts, like the one Robert Smalls represented, even elected black Republicans to Congress during the immediate post-Reconstruction period. The last of these, Representative George H. White of North Carolina, served until 1901. His farewell address eloquently conveyed the agony of southern blacks in the era of Jim Crow (strict segregation).

These parting words are in behalf of an outraged, heart-broken, bruised, and bleeding but God-fearing people, faithful, industrious, loyal people—rising people, full of potential force. . . . The only apology that I have to make for the earnestness with which I have spoken is that I am pleading for the life, the liberty, the future happiness, and manhood suffrage of one-eighth of the entire population of the United States.

The dark night of racism that fell on the South after Reconstruction seemed to unleash all the baser impulses of human nature. Between 1889 and 1899, an average of 187 blacks were lynched every year for alleged offenses against white supremacy. Those convicted of petty crimes against property were often little better off; many

Lynching accounted for more than 3,000 deaths between 1899 and 1918, and lynchings were not confined to the South. During that period, only seven states reported no lynchings.

Henry M. Turner, who was born in freedom, became a bishop of the African Methodist Episcopal Church and was elected to the Georgia legislature.

were condemned to be leased out to private contractors whose brutality rivaled that of the most sadistic slaveholders. (Annual death rates in the convict camps ranged as high as 25 percent.) Finally, the dignity of blacks was cruelly affronted by the wave of segregation laws passed around the turn of the century, which served to remind them constantly that they were deemed unfit to associate with whites on any basis that implied equality. To some extent, the segregation laws were a white reaction to the refusal of many blacks to submit to voluntary segregation of railroads, streetcars, and other public facilities.

The North and the federal government did little or nothing to stem the tide of racial oppression in the South. A series of Supreme Court decisions between 1875 and 1896 gutted the Reconstruction amendments and the legislation passed to enforce them, leaving blacks virtually defenseless against political and social discrimination.

The career of Henry McNeal Turner sums up the bitter side of the black experience in the South during and after Reconstruction. Born free in South Carolina in 1834, Turner became a minister of the African Methodist Episcopal church (AME) just before the outbreak of the Civil War.

During the war, he recruited African Americans for the Union Army and later served as chaplain for black troops. After the fighting was over, he went to Georgia to work for the Freedmen's Bureau but encountered racial discrimination from white Bureau officers and left government service for church work and Reconstruction politics. Elected to the 1867 Georgia constitutional convention and to the state legislature in 1868, he was one of a number of black clergymen who assumed leadership roles among the freedmen. But whites won control of the Georgia legislature and expelled all the black members. Turner's reaction was an angry speech in which he proclaimed that white men were never to be trusted. As the inhabitant of a state in which blacks never gained the degree of power that they achieved in some other parts of the South, Turner was one of the first black leaders to see the failure of

Hall v. *DeCuir* (1878)	Struck down Louisiana law prohibiting racial discrimination by "common carriers" (railroads, steamboats, buses). Court declared the law a "burden" on interstate commerce, over which states had no authority.
United States v. *Harris* (1882)	Declared federal laws to punish crimes such as murder and assault unconstitutional. Such crimes declared to be the sole concern of local government. Court ignored the frequent racial motivation behind such crimes in the South.
Civil Rights Cases (1883)	Struck down Civil Rights Act of 1875. Congress may not legislate on civil rights unless a *state* passes a discriminatory law. Court declared the Fourteenth Amendment silent on racial discrimination by private citizens.
Plessy v. *Ferguson* (1896)	Upheld Louisiana statute requiring "separate but equal" accommodations on railroads. Court declared that segregation is *not* necessarily discrimination.
Williams v. *Mississippi* (1898)	Upheld state law requiring a literacy test to qualify for voting. Court refused to find any implication of racial discrimination in the law, although it permitted illiterate whites to vote if they "understood" the Constitution. Using such laws, southern states rapidly disenfranchised blacks.

Reconstruction as the betrayal of African American hopes for citizenship.

Becoming a bishop of the AME church in 1880, Turner emerged as the late nineteenth century's leading proponent of black emigration to Africa. Because he believed white Americans were so deeply prejudiced against blacks that they would never grant them equal rights, Turner became an early advocate of black nationalism and a total separation of the races. Emigration became a popular movement among southern blacks who were especially hard hit by terror and oppression just after the end of Reconstruction, but a majority of blacks in the nation as a whole and even in Turner's own church refused to give up on the hope of eventual equality on American soil. But Bishop Turner's anger and despair were the understandable responses of a proud man to the way that he and his fellow African Americans had been treated in the post–Civil War period.

By the late 1880s, the wounds of the Civil War were healing, and white Americans were seized by the spirit of sectional reconciliation. Union and Confederate veterans were tenting together and celebrating their common Americanism. "Reunion" was becoming a cultural as well as political reality. But whites could come back together only because Northerners had tacitly agreed to give Southerners a free hand in their efforts to reduce blacks to a new form of servitude. The "outraged, heart-broken, bruised, and bleeding" African Americans of the South paid the heaviest price for sectional reunion.

Recommended Reading

The best one-volume account of Reconstruction is Eric Foner, *Reconstruction: America's Unfinished Revolution* (1988). Two excellent short surveys are Kenneth M. Stampp, *The Era of Reconstruction, 1865–1877* (1965), and John Hope Franklin, *Reconstruction: After the Civil War* (1961). Both were early efforts to synthesize modern "revisionist" interpretations. W. E. B. DuBois, *Black Reconstruction in America, 1860–1880* (1935) remains brilliant and provocative. Reconsiderations of Reconstruction issues can be found in J. Morgan Kousser and James M. McPherson, eds., *Region, Race, and Reconstruction: Essays in Honor of C. Vann Woodward* (1982), and Eric Foner, *Nothing But Freedom: Emancipation and Its Legacy* (1983). Morton Keller, *Affairs of State: Public Life in Late Nineteenth Century America* (1977), provides an insightful analysis of American government and politics during Reconstruction and afterward. A perspective on the corruption of the period is provided by Mark Wahlgren Summers in *The Era of Good Stealings* (1993).

Formulation and implementation of northern policies on Reconstruction are covered in Eric L. McKitrick, *Andrew Johnson and Reconstruction, 1865–1867* (1960); W. R. Brock, *An American Crisis: Congress and Reconstruction, 1865–1867* (1963); and

CHRONOLOGY

1863 Lincoln sets forth 10 percent Reconstruction plan

1864 Wade-Davis Bill passes Congress but is pocket vetoed by Lincoln

1865 Johnson moves to reconstruct the South on his own initiative • Congress refuses to seat representatives and senators elected from states reestablished under presidential plan (December)

1866 Johnson vetoes Freedmen's Bureau Bill (February) • Johnson vetoes Civil Rights Act; it passes over his veto (April) • Congress passes Fourteenth Amendment (June) • Republicans increase their congressional majority in the fall elections

1867 First Reconstruction Act is passed over Johnson's veto (March)

1868 Johnson is impeached; he avoids conviction by one vote (February–May) • Southern blacks vote and serve in constitutional conventions • Grant wins presidential election, defeating Horatio Seymour

1869 Congress passes Fifteenth Amendment, granting African Americans the right to vote

1870–1871 Congress passes Ku Klux Klan Acts to protect black voting rights in the South

1872 Grant reelected president, defeating Horace Greeley, candidate of Liberal Republicans and Democrats

1873 Financial panic plunges nation into depression

1875 Congress passes Specie Resumption Act • "Whiskey Ring" scandal exposed

1876–1877 Disputed presidential election resolved in favor of Republican Hayes over Democrat Tilden

1877 "Compromise of 1877" results in end to military intervention in the South and fall of the last Radical governments

---

William Gillette, *Retreat from Reconstruction, 1869–1879* (1979). Leon F. Litwack, *Been in the Storm So Long: The Aftermath of Slavery* (1979), provides a moving portrayal of the black experience of emancipation. On what freedom meant in economic terms, see Gerald David Jaynes, *Branches Without Roots: Genesis of the Black Working Class in the American South, 1862–1882* (1986). The best overview of the postwar southern economy is Gavin Wright, *Old South, New South* (1986). The best introduction to the Grant era is William S. McFeeley, *Grant: A Biography* (1981). On the end of Reconstruction and the character of the post-Reconstruction South, see two classic works by C. Vann Woodward: *Reunion and Reaction,* rev. ed. (1956) and *Origins of the New South, 1877–1913* (1951). A good recent survey of the South after Reconstruction is Edward Ayers, *The Promise of the New South* (1992).

Additional Bibliography

The Reconstruction era is surveyed briefly but well in Michael L. Perman, *Emancipation and Reconstruction, 1862–1879* (1987). The conflict between the president and Congress is examined in David Donald, *The Politics of Reconstruction, 1863–1867* (1965); Michael Les Benedict, *A Compromise of Principle: Congressional Republicans and Reconstruction* (1974) and *The Impeachment and Trial of Andrew Johnson* (1973). On constitutional issues, Stanley I. Kutler, *Judicial Power and Reconstruction Politics* (1968), and Harold M. Hyman, *A More Perfect Union: The Impact of the Civil War and Reconstruction on the Constitution* (1973), are useful.

Presidential Reconstruction in the South is surveyed in Dan T. Carter, *When the War Was Over: Self-Reconstruction in the South* (1985). A major aspect of Radical Reconstruction is covered in Mark W. Summers, *Railroads, Reconstruction, and the Gospel of Prosperity* (1984).

Michael Perman, *Reunion Without Compromise: The South and Reconstruction, 1865–1868* (1973), and *The Road to Redemption: Southern Politics, 1869–1879* (1984), deal authoritatively with southern politics in the postwar years. On the Freedmen's Bureau, see George R. Bentley, *A History of the Freedmen's Bureau* (1965); William McFeeley, *Yankee Stepfather: General O. O. Howard and the Freedmen* (1968); and Donald G. Nieman, *To Set the Law in Motion: The Freedmen's Bureau and Legal Rights for Blacks, 1865–1869* (1979).

On carpetbaggers, see Richard N. Current, *Those Terrible Carpetbaggers: A Reinterpretation* (1989). Among the most valuable of the many state studies of Reconstruction in the South are Joel Williamson, *After Slavery: The Negro in South Carolina, 1861–77* (1965); Elizabeth Studley Nathans, *Losing the Peace: Georgia Republicans and Reconstruction, 1865–1871* (1968); and Thomas Holt, *Black over White: Negro*

Political Leadership in South Carolina During Reconstruction (1977). Essays on black leadership in several southern states can be found in Howard N. Rabinowitz, ed., *Southern Black Leaders of the Reconstruction Era* (1982). See also Okon Edet Uya, *From Slavery to Public Service: Robert Smalls, 1839–1915* (1971); and Peggy Lawson, *The Glorious Failure: Congressmen Robert Brown Elliott and Reconstruction in South Carolina* (1973).

Howard N. Rabinowitz, *Race Relations in the Urban South, 1865–1890* (1977); C. Vann Woodward, *The Strange Career of Jim Crow*, 3d rev. ed. (1974); and Joel Williamson, *The Crucible of Race: Black-White Relations in the American South Since Emancipation* (1984) cover race relations in the postwar South. Economic and social adjustments are analyzed in Lawrence N. Powell, *New Masters: Northern Planters During the Civil War and Reconstruction* (1980); Michael Wayne, *The Reshaping of Plantation Society* (1983); Roger L. Ransom and Richard Sutch, *One Kind of Freedom: The Economic Consequences of Emancipation* (1977); Daniel A. Novak, *The Wheel of Servitude: Black Forced Labor After Emancipation*

(1978); Stephen Hahn, *The Roots of Southern Populism: Yeoman Farmers and the Transformation of the Georgia Upcountry, 1850–1896* (1983); and Charles L. Flynn, Jr., *White Land, Black Labor: Caste and Class in Late Nineteenth-Century Georgia* (1983).

American labor during Reconstruction is the subject of David Montgomery, *Beyond Equality: Labor and the Radical Republicans, 1861–1872* (1967). Liberal republicanism is examined in Ari A. Hoogenboom, *Outlawing the Spoils: A History of Civil Service Reform* (1961), and John G. Sproat, *"The Best Men": Liberal Reformers in the Gilded Age* (1968).

Keith I. Polakoff, *The Politics of Inertia* (1977), challenges C. Vann Woodward's interpretation of the Compromise of 1877. Woodward's conclusions on the Redeemer period have been confirmed or disputed in Paul M. Gaston, *The New South Creed* (1970); William Cooper, *The Conservative Regime: South Carolina, 1877–1890* (1968); Jonathan M. Weiner, *Social Origins of the New South: Alabama, 1860–1885* (1978); and J. Morgan Kousser, *The Shaping of Southern Politics: Suffrage Restriction and the Establishment of the One-Party South* (1974).

APPENDIX

The Declaration of Independence

The Articles of Confederation

The Constitution of the United States of America

Amendments to the Constitution

Choosing the President

Cabinet Members

Supreme Court Justices

Admission of States into the Union

Ten Largest Cities by Population, 1700–1990

A Demographic Profile of the American People

The Declaration of Independence

In Congress, July 4, 1776

**The Unanimous Declaration
of the Thirteen United States of America,**

When, in the course of human events, it becomes necessary for one people to dissolve the political bonds which have connected them with another, and to assume, among the powers of the earth, the separate and equal station to which the laws of nature and of nature's God entitle them, a decent respect to the opinions of mankind requires that they should declare the causes which impel them to the separation.

We hold these truths to be self-evident: That all men are created equal; that they are endowed by their Creator with certain unalienable rights; that among these are life, liberty, and the pursuit of happiness; that, to secure these rights, governments are instituted among men, deriving their just powers from the consent of the governed; that whenever any form of government becomes destructive of these ends, it is the right of the people to alter or to abolish it, and to institute new government, laying its foundation on such principles, and organizing its powers in such form, as to them shall seem most likely to effect their safety and happiness. Prudence, indeed, will dictate that governments long established should not be changed for light and transient causes; and accordingly all experience hath shown that mankind are more disposed to suffer, while evils are sufferable, than to right themselves by abolishing the forms to which they are accustomed. But when a long train of abuses and usurpations, pursuing invariably the same object, evinces a design to reduce them under absolute despotism, it is their right, it is their duty, to throw off such government, and to provide new guards for their future security. Such has been the patient sufferance of these colonies; and such is now the necessity which constrains them to alter their former systems of government. The history of the present King of Great Britain is a history of repeated injuries and usurpations, all having in direct object the establishment of an absolute tyranny over these states. To prove this, let facts be submitted to a candid world.

He has refused his assent to laws, the most wholesome and necessary for the public good.

He has forbidden his governors to pass laws of immediate and pressing importance, unless suspended in their operation till his assent should be obtained; and, when so suspended, he has utterly neglected to attend to them.

He has refused to pass other laws for the accommodation of large districts of people, unless those people would relinquish the right of representation in the legislature, a right inestimable to them, and formidable to tyrants only.

He has called together legislative bodies at places unusual, uncomfortable, and distant from the depository of their public records, for the sole purpose of fatiguing them into compliance with his measures.

He has dissolved representative houses repeatedly, for opposing, with manly firmness, his invasions on the rights of the people.

He has refused for a long time, after such dissolutions, to cause others to be elected; whereby the legislative powers, incapable of annihilation, have returned to the people at large for their exercise; the state remaining, in the mean time, exposed to all the dangers of invasions from without and convulsions within.

He has endeavored to prevent the population of these states; for that purpose obstructing the laws for naturalization of foreigners; refusing to pass others to encourage their migration hither, and raising the conditions of new appropriations of lands.

He has obstructed the administration of justice, by refusing his assent to laws for establishing judiciary powers.

He has made judges dependent on his will alone, for the tenure of their offices, and the amount and payment of their salaries.

He has erected a multitude of new offices, and sent hither swarms of officers to harass our people and eat out their substance.

He has kept among us, in times of peace, standing armies, without the consent of our legislatures.

He has affected to render the military independent of, and superior to, the civil power.

He has combined with others to subject us to a jurisdiction foreign to our constitution, and unacknowledged by our laws, giving his assent to their acts of pretended legislation:

For quartering large bodies of armed troops among us;

For protecting them, by a mock trial, from punishment for any murder which they should commit on the inhabitants of these states;

For cutting off our trade with all parts of the world;

For imposing taxes on us without our consent;

For depriving us, in many cases, of the benefits of trial by jury;

For transporting us beyond seas, to be tried for pretended offenses;

For abolishing the free system of English laws in a neighboring province, establishing therein an arbitrary government, and enlarging its boundaries, so as to render it at once an example and fit instrument for introducing the same absolute rule into these colonies;

For taking away our charters abolishing our most valuable laws, and altering fundamentally the forms of our governments;

For suspending our own legislatures, and declaring themselves invested with power to legislate for us in all cases whatsoever.

He has abdicated government here, by declaring us out of his protection and waging war against us.

He has plundered our seas, ravaged our coasts, burned our towns, and destroyed the lives of our people.

He is at this time transporting large armies of foreign mercenaries to complete the works of death, desolation, and tyranny already begun with circumstances of cruelty and perfidy scarcely paralleled in the most barbarous ages, and totally unworthy the head of a civilized nation.

He has constrained our fellow-citizens, taken captive on the high seas, to bear arms against their country, to become the executioners of their friends and brethren, or to fall themselves by their hands.

He has excited domestic insurrection among us, and has endeavored to bring on the inhabitants of our frontiers the merciless Indian savages, whose known rule of warfare is an undistinguished destruction of all ages, sexes, and conditions.

In every stage of these oppressions we have petitioned for redress in the most humble terms; our repeated petitions have been answered only by repeated injury. A prince, whose character is thus marked by every act which may define a tyrant, is unfit to be the ruler of a free people.

Nor have we been wanting in our attentions to our British brethren. We have warned them, from time to time, of attempts by their legislature to extend an unwarrantable jurisdiction over us. We have reminded them of the circumstances of our emigration and settlement here. We have appealed to their native justice and magnanimity; and we have conjured them, by the ties of our common kindred, to disavow these usurpations, which would inevitably interrupt our connections and correspondence. They, too, have been deaf to the voice of justice and of consanguinity. We must, therefore, acquiesce in the necessity which denounces our separation, and hold them, as we hold the rest of mankind, enemies in war, in peace friends.

We, therefore, the representatives of the United States of America, in General Congress assembled, appealing to the Supreme Judge of the world for the rectitude of our intentions, do, in the name and by the authority of the good people of these colonies, solemnly publish and declare, that these United Colonies are, and of right ought to be, FREE AND INDEPENDENT STATES; that they are absolved from all allegiance to the British crown, and that all political connection between them and the state of Great Britain is, and ought to be, totally dissolved; and that, as free and independent states, they have full power to levy war, conclude peace, contract alliances, establish commerce, and do all other acts and things which independent states may of right do. And for the support of this declaration, with a firm reliance on the protection of Divine Providence, we mutually pledge to each other our lives, our fortunes, and our sacred honor.

JOHN HANCOCK

BUTTON GWINNETT
LYMAN HALL
GEO. WALTON
WM. HOOPER
JOSEPH HEWES
JOHN PENN
EDWARD RUTLEDGE
THOS. HEYWARD, JUNR.
THOMAS LYNCH, JUNR.
ARTHUR MIDDLETON
SAMUEL CHASE
WM. PACA
THOS. STONE
CHARLES CARROLL
  OF CARROLLTON
GEORGE WYTHE
RICHARD HENRY LEE
TH. JEFFERSON
BENJ. HARRISON

THOS. NELSON, JR.
FRANCIS LIGHTFOOT LEE
CARTER BRAXTON
ROBT. MORRIS
BENJAMIN RUSH
BENJA. FRANKLIN
JOHN MORTON
GEO. CLYMER
JAS. SMITH
GEO. TAYLOR
JAMES WILSON
GEO. ROSS
CAESAR RODNEY
GEO. READ
THO. M'KEAN
WM. FLOYD
PHIL. LIVINGSTON
FRANS. LEWIS
LEWIS MORRIS

RICHD. STOCKTON
JNO. WITHERSPOON
FRAS. HOPKINSON
JOHN HART
ABRA. CLARK
JOSIAH BARTLETT
WM. WHIPPLE
SAML. ADAMS
JOHN ADAMS
ROBT. TREAT PAINE
ELBRIDGE GERRY
STEP. HOPKINS
WILLIAM ELLERY
ROGER SHERMAN
SAM'EL HUNTINGTON
WM. WILLIAMS
OLIVER WOLCOTT
MATTHEW THORNTON

The Articles of Confederation

Between the States of New Hampshire, Massachusetts Bay, Rhode Island and Providence Plantations, Connecticut, New York, New Jersey, Pennsylvania, Delaware, Maryland, Virginia, North Carolina, South Carolina, Georgia

Article 1.

The stile of this confederacy shall be "The United States of America."

Article 2.

Each State retains its sovereignty, freedom and independence, and every power, jurisdiction, and right, which is not by this confederation expressly delegated to the United States, in Congress assembled.

Article 3.

The said states hereby severally enter into a firm league of friendship with each other for their common defence, the security of their liberties and their mutual and general welfare; binding themselves to assist each other against all force offered to, or attacks made upon them, or any of them, on account of religion, sovereignty, trade, or any other pretence whatever.

Article 4.

The better to secure and perpetuate mutual friendship and intercourse among the people of the different states in this union, the free inhabitants of each of these states, paupers, vagabonds, and fugitives from justice excepted, shall be entitled to all privileges and immunities of free citizens in the several states; and the people of each State shall have free ingress and regress to and from any other State, and shall enjoy therein all the privileges of trade and commerce, subject to the same duties, impositions, and restrictions, as the inhabitants thereof respectively; provided, that such restrictions shall not extend so far as to prevent the removal of property, imported into any State, to any other State of which the owner is an inhabitant; provided also, that no imposition, duties, or restriction, shall be laid by any State on the property of the United States, or either of them.

If any person guilty of, or charged with treason, felony, or other high misdemeanor in any State, shall flee from justice and be found in any of the United States, he shall, upon demand of the governor or executive power of the State from which he fled, be delivered up and removed to the State having jurisdiction of his offence.

Full faith and credit shall be given in each of these states to the records, acts, and judicial proceedings of the courts and magistrates of every other State.

Article 5.

For the more convenient management of the general interests of the United States, delegates shall be annually appointed, in such manner as the legislature of each State shall direct, to meet in Congress, on the 1st Monday in November in every year, with a power reserved to each State to recall its delegates, or any of them, at any time within the year, and to send others in their stead for the remainder of the year.

No State shall be represented in Congress by less than two, nor by more than seven members; and no person shall be capable of being a delegate for more than three years in any term of six years; nor shall any person, being a delegate, be capable of holding any office under the United States, for which he, or any other for his benefit, receives any salary, fees, or emolument of any kind.

Each State shall maintain its own delegates in a meeting of the states, and while they act as members of the committee of the states.

In determining questions in the United States, in Congress assembled, each State shall have one vote.

Freedom of speech and debate in Congress shall not be impeached or questioned in any court or place out of Congress: and the members of Congress shall be protected in their persons from arrests and imprisonments, during the time of their going to and from, and attendance on Congress, *except for treason,* felony, or breach of the peace.

Article 6.

No State, without the consent of the United States, in Congress assembled, shall send any embassy to, or receive any embassy from, or enter into any conference, agreement, alliance, or treaty with any king, prince, or state; nor shall any person, holding any office of profit or trust under the United States, or any of them, accept of any present, emolument, office or title, of any kind whatever, from any king, prince, or foreign state; nor shall the United States, in Congress assembled, or any of them, grant any title of nobility.

No two or more states shall enter into any treaty, confederation, or alliance, whatever, between them, without the consent of the United States, in Congress assembled, specifying accurately the purposes for which the same is to be entered into, and how long it shall continue.

No State shall lay any imposts or duties which may interfere with any stipulations in treaties entered into by the United States, in Congress assembled, with any king, prince, or state, in pursuance of any treaties already proposed by Congress to the courts of France and Spain.

No vessels of war shall be kept up in time of peace by any State, except such number only as shall be deemed necessary by the United States, in Congress assembled, for the defence of such State or its trade; nor shall any body of forces be kept up by any State, in time of peace, except such number only as, in the judgment of the United States, in Congress assembled, shall be deemed requisite to garrison the forts necessary for the defence of such State; but every State shall always keep up a well regulated and disciplined militia, sufficiently armed and accoutred, and shall provide, and constantly have ready for use, in public stores, a due number of field pieces and tents, and a proper quantity of arms, ammunition and camp equipage.

No State shall engage in any war without the consent of the United States, in Congress assembled, unless such State be actually invaded by enemies, or shall have received certain advice of a resolution being formed by some nation of Indians to invade such State, and the danger is so imminent as not to admit of a delay till the United States, in Congress assembled, can be consulted; nor shall any State grant commissions to any ships or vessels of war, nor letters of marque or reprisal, except it be after a declaration of war by the United States, in Congress assembled, and then only against the kingdom or state, and the subjects thereof, against which war has been so declared, and under such regulations as shall be established by the United States, in Congress assembled, unless such States be infested by pirates, in which case vessels of war may be fitted out for that occasion, and kept so long as the danger shall continue, or until the United States, in Congress assembled, shall determine otherwise.

Article 7.

When land forces are raised by any State for the common defence, all officers of or under the rank of colonel, shall be appointed by the legislature of each State respectively, by whom such forces shall be raised, or in such manner as such State shall direct; and all vacancies shall be filled up by the State which first made the appointment.

Article 8.

All charges of war and all other expences, that shall be incurred for the common defence or general welfare, and allowed by the United States, in Congress assembled, shall be defrayed out of a common treasury, which shall be supplied by the several states, in proportion to the value of all land within each State, granted to or surveyed for any person, as such land and the buildings and improvements thereon shall be estimated according to such mode as the United States, in Congress assembled, shall, from time to time, direct and appoint.

The taxes for paying that proportion shall be laid and levied by the authority and direction of the legislatures of the several states, within the time agreed upon by the United States, in Congress assembled.

Article 9.

The United States, in Congress assembled, shall have the sole and exclusive right and power of determining on peace and war, except in the cases mentioned in the 6th article; of sending and receiving ambassadors; entering into treaties and alliances, provided that no treaty of commerce shall be made, whereby the legislative power of the respective states shall be restrained from imposing such imposts and duties on foreigners as their own people are subjected to, or from prohibiting the exportation or importation of any species of goods or commodities whatsoever; of establishing rules for deciding, in all cases, what captures on land or water shall be legal, and in what manner prizes, taken by land or naval forces in the service of the United States, shall be divided or appropriated; of granting letters of marque and reprisal in times of peace; appointing courts for the trial of piracies and felonies committed on the high seas, and establishing courts for receiving and determining, finally, appeals in all cases of captures; provided, that no member of Congress shall be appointed a judge of any of the said courts.

The United States, in Congress assembled, shall also be the last resort on appeal in all disputes and differences now subsisting, or that hereafter may arise between two or more states concerning boundary, jurisdiction or any other cause whatever; which authority shall always be exercised in the manner following: whenever the legislative or executive authority, or lawful agent of any State, in controversy with another, shall present a petition to Congress, stating the matter in question, and praying for a hearing, notice thereof shall be given, by order of Congress, to the legislative or executive authority of the other State in controversy, and a day assigned for the appearance of the parties by their lawful agents, who shall then be directed to appoint, by joint consent, commissioners or judges to constitute a court for hearing and determining the matter in question; but, if they cannot agree, Congress shall name three persons out of each of the United States, and from the list of such persons each party shall alternately strike out one, in the petitioners beginning, until the number shall be reduced to thirteen; and from that number not less than seven, nor more than nine names, as Congress shall direct, shall, in the presence of Congress, be drawn out by lot; and the persons whose names shall be drawn, or any five of them, shall be commissioners or judges to hear and finally determine the controversy, so always as a major part of the judges who shall hear the cause shall agree in the determination; and if either party shall neglect to attend at the day appointed, without shewing reasons which Congress shall judge sufficient, or, being present, shall refuse to strike, the Congress shall proceed to nominate three persons out of each State, and the secretary of Congress shall strike in behalf of such party absent or refusing; and the judgment and sentence of the court to be appointed, in the manner before prescribed, shall be final and conclusive; and if any of the parties shall refuse to submit to the authority of such court, or to appear or defend their claim or cause, the court shall nevertheless proceed to pronounce sentence or judgment, which shall, in like manner, be final and decisive, the judgment or sentence and other proceedings being, in either case, transmitted to Congress, and lodged among the acts of Congress for the security of the parties concerned: provided, that every commissioner, before he sits in judgment, shall take an oath, to be administered by one of the judges of the supreme or superior court of the State where the cause shall be tried, "well and truly to hear and determine the matter in question, according to the best of his judgment, without favour, affection, or hope of reward": provided, also, that no State shall be deprived of territory for the benefit of the United States.

All controversies concerning the private right of soil, claimed under different grants of two or more states, whose jurisdictions, as they may respect such lands and the states which passed such grants, are adjusted, the said grants, or either of them, being at the same time claimed to have originated antecedent to such settlement of jurisdiction, shall, on the petition of either party to the Congress of the United States, be finally determined, as near as may be, in the same manner as is before prescribed for deciding disputes respecting territorial jurisdiction between different states.

The United States, in Congress assembled, shall also have the sole and exclusive right and power of regulating the alloy and value of coin struck by their own authority, or by that of the respective states; fixing the standard of weights and measures throughout the United States; regulating the trade and managing all affairs with the Indians not members of any of the states; provided that the legislative right of any State within its own limits be not infringed or violated; establishing and regulating post offices from one State to another throughout all the United States, and exacting such postage on the papers passing through the same as may be requisite to defray the expences of the said office; appointing all officers of the land forces in the service of the United States, excepting regimental officers; appointing all the officers of the naval forces, and commissioning all officers whatever in the service of the United

States; making rules for the government and regulation of the said land and naval forces, and directing their operations.

The United States, in Congress assembled, shall have authority to appoint a committee to sit in the recess of Congress, to be denominated "a Committee of the States," and to consist of one delegate from each State, and to appoint such other committees and civil officers as may be necessary for managing the general affairs of the United States, under their direction; to appoint one of their number of preside; provided that no person be allowed to serve in the office of president more than one year in any term of three years; to ascertain the necessary sums of money to be raised for the service of the United States, and to appropriate and apply the same for defraying the public expences; to borrow money or emit bills on the credit of the United States, transmitting, every half year, to the respective states, an account of the sums of money so borrowed or emitted; to build and equip a navy; to agree upon the number of land forces, and to make requisitions from each State for its quota, in proportion to the number of white inhabitants in such State; which requisitions shall be binding; and, thereupon, the legislature of each State shall appoint the regimental officers, raise the men, and cloathe, arm, and equip them in a soldier-like manner, at the expence of the United States; and the officers and men so cloathed, armed, and equipped, shall march to the place appointed and within the time agreed on by the United States, in Congress assembled; but if the United States, in Congress assembled, shall, on consideration of circumstances, judge proper that any State should not raise men, or should raise a smaller number than its quota, and that any other State should raise a greater number of men than the quota thereof, such extra number shall be raised, officered, cloathed, armed, and equipped in the same manner as the quota of such State, unless the legislature of such State shall judge that such extra number cannot be safely spared out of the same, in which case they shall raise, officer, cloathe, arm, and equip as many of such extra number as they judge can be safely spared. And the officers and men so cloathed, armed, and equipped, shall march to the place appointed and within the time agreed on by the United States, in Congress assembled.

The United States, in Congress assembled, shall never engage in a war, nor grant letters of marque and reprisal in time of peace, nor enter into any treaties or alliances, nor coin money, nor regulate the value thereof, nor ascertain the sums and expences necessary for the defence and welfare of the United States, or any of them: nor emit bills, nor borrow money on the credit of the United States, nor appropriate money, nor agree upon the number of vessels of war to be built or purchased, or the number of land or sea forces to be raised, nor appoint a commander in chief of the army or navy, unless nine states assent to the same; nor shall a question on any other point, except for adjourning from day to day, be determined, unless by the votes of a majority of the United States, in Congress assembled.

The Congress of the United States shall have power to adjourn to any time within the year, and to any place within the United States, so that no period of adjournment be for a longer duration than the space of six months, and shall publish the journal of their proceedings monthly, except such parts thereof, relating to treaties, alliances or military operations, as, in their judgment, require secrecy; and the yeas and nays of the delegates of each State on any question shall be entered on the journal, when it is desired by any delegate; and the delegates of a State, or any of them, at his, or their request, shall be furnished with a transcript of the said journal, except such parts as are above excepted, to lay before the legislatures of the several states.

Article 10.

The committee of the states, or any nine of them, shall be authorized to execute, in the recess of Congress, such of the powers of Congress as the United States, in Congress assembled, by the consent of nine states, shall, from time to time, think expedient to vest them with; provided, that no power be delegated to the said committee for the exercise of which, by the articles of confederation, the voice of nine states, in the Congress of the United States assembled, is requisite.

Article 11.

Canada acceding to this confederation, and joining in the measures of the United States, shall be admitted into and entitled to all the advantages of this union; but no other colony shall be admitted into the same, unless such admission be agreed to by nine states.

Article 12.

All bills of credit emitted, monies borrowed and debts contracted by, or under the authority of Congress before the assembling of the United States, in pursuance of the present confederation, shall be deemed and considered as a charge against the United States, for payment and satisfaction whereof the said United States and the public faith are hereby solemnly pledged.

Article 13.

Every State shall abide by the determinations of the United States, in Congress assembled, on all questions which, by this confederation, are submitted to them. And the articles of this confederation shall be inviolably observed by every State, and the union shall be perpetual; nor shall any alteration at any time hereafter be made in any of them, unless such alteration be agreed to in a Congress of the United States, and be afterwards confirmed by the legislatures of every State.

These articles shall be proposed to the legislatures of all the United States, to be considered, and if approved of by them, they are advised to authorize their delegates to ratify the same in the Congress of the United States; which being done, the same shall become conclusive.

The Constitution of the United States of America

Preamble

We the People of the United States, in Order to form a more perfect Union, establish Justice, insure domestic Tranquility, provide for the common defence, promote the general Welfare, and secure the Blessings of Liberty to ourselves and our Posterity, do ordain and establish this Constitution for the United States of America.

Article I.

Section 1   All legislative Powers herein granted shall be vested in a Congress of the United States, which shall consist of a Senate and House of Representatives.

Section 2   The House of Representatives shall be composed of Members chosen every second Year by the People of the several States, and the Electors in each State shall have the Qualifications requisite for Electors of the most numerous Branch of the State Legislature.

No Person shall be a Representative who shall not have attained to the Age of twenty five Years, and been seven Years a Citizen of the United States, and who shall not, when elected, be an inhabitant of that State in which he shall be chosen.

Representatives and direct Taxes shall be apportioned among the several States which may be included within this Union, according to their respective Numbers, *which shall be determined by adding to the whole Number of free Persons, including those bound to Service for a Term of Years, and excluding Indians not taxed, three fifths of all other Persons.* * The actual Enumeration shall be made within three Years after the first Meeting of the Congress of the United States, and within every subsequent Term of ten Years, in such Manner as they shall by Law direct. The Number of Representatives shall not exceed one for every thirty Thousand, but each State shall have at Least one Representative; *and until such enumeration shall be made, the State of New Hampshire shall be entitled to chuse three, Massachusetts eight, Rhode-Island and Providence Plantations one, Connecticut five, New York six, New Jersey four, Pennsylvania eight, Delaware one, Maryland six, Virginia ten, North Carolina five, South Carolina five, and Georgia three.*

When vacancies happen in the Representation from any State, the Executive Authority thereof shall issue Writs of Election to fill such Vacancies.

The House of Representatives shall chuse their Speaker and other Officers; and shall have the sole Power of Impeachment.

Passages no longer in effect are printed in italic type.

Section 3   The Senate of the United States shall be composed of two Senators from each State, *chosen by the Legislature thereof,* for six Years; and each Senator shall have one Vote.

Immediately after they shall be assembled in Consequence of the first Election, they shall be divided as equally as may be into three Classes. The Seats of the Senators of the first Class shall be vacated at the Expiration of the second Year, of the second Class at the Expiration of the fourth Year, and of the third Class at the Expiration of the sixth Year so that one third may be chosen every second Year; *and if Vacancies happen by Resignation, or otherwise, during the Recess of the Legislature of any state, the Executive thereof may make temporary Appointments until the next Meeting of the Legislature, which shall then fill such Vacancies.*

No Person shall be a Senator who shall not have attained to the Age of thirty Years, and been nine Years a Citizen of the United States, and who shall not, when elected, be an Inhabitant of that State for which he shall be chosen.

The Vice President of the United States shall be President of the Senate, but shall have no Vote, unless they be equally divided.

The Senate shall chuse their other Officers, and also a President *pro tempore,* in the Absence of the Vice President, or when he shall exercise the Office of President of the United States.

The Senate shall have the sole Power to try all Impeachments. When sitting for that Purpose, they shall be on Oath or Affirmation. When the President of the United States is tried the Chief Justice shall preside: And no Person shall be convicted without the Concurrence of two thirds of the Members present.

Judgment in Cases of Impeachment shall not extend further than to removal from Office, and disqualification to hold and enjoy any Office of honor, Trust or Profit under the United States: but the Party convicted shall nevertheless be liable and subject to Indictment, Trial, Judgment and Punishment, according to Law.

Section 4   The Times, Places and Manner of holding Elections for Senators and Representatives, shall be prescribed in each State by the Legislature thereof; but the Congress may at any time by Law make or alter such Regulations, except as to the Places of chusing Senators.

The Congress shall assemble at least once in every Year, and such Meeting *shall be on the first Monday in December, unless they shall by Law appoint a different Day.* *

Section 5   Each House shall be the Judge of the Elections, Returns and Qualifications of its own Members, and a Majority of each shall constitute a Quorum to do Business; but a smaller Number may adjourn from day to day, and may be authorized to compel the Attendance of absent Members, in such Manner, and under such Penalties as each House may provide.

Each House may determine the Rules of its Proceedings, punish its Members for disorderly Behaviour, and, with the Concurrence of two thirds, expel a Member.

Each House shall keep a Journal of its Proceedings, and from time to time publish the same, excepting such Parts as may in their Judgment require Secrecy; and the Yeas and Nays of the Members of either House on any question shall, at the Desire of one fifth of those Present, be entered on the Journal.

Neither House, during the Session of Congress, shall, without the Consent of the other, adjourn for more than three days, nor to any other Place than that in which the two Houses shall be sitting.

Section 6   The Senators and Representatives shall receive a Compensation for their Services, to be ascertained by Law, and paid out of the Treasury of the United States. They shall in all Cases, except Treason, Felony and Breach of the Peace, be privileged from Arrest during their Attendance at the Session of their respective Houses, and in going to and returning from the same; and for any Speech or Debate in either House, they shall not be questioned in any other Place.

No Senator or Representative shall, during the Time for which he was elected, be appointed to any civil Office under the Authority of the United States, which shall have been created, or the Emoluments whereof shall have been encreased during such time, and no Person holding any Office under the United States, shall be a Member of either House during his Continuance in Office.

Section 7   All Bills for raising Revenue shall originate in the House of Representatives; but the Senate may propose or concur with Amendments as on other Bills.

Every Bill which shall have passed the House of Representatives and the Senate, shall, before it become a Law, be presented to the President of the United States; If he approve he shall sign it, but if not he shall return it, with his Objections to the House in which it shall have originated, who shall enter the Objections at large on their Journal, and proceed to reconsider it. If after such Reconsideration two thirds of that House shall agree to pass the Bill, it shall be sent, together with the Objections, to the other House, by which it shall likewise be reconsidered, and if approved by two thirds of that House, it shall become a Law. But in all such Cases the Votes of both Houses shall be determined by yeas and Nays, and the Names of the Persons voting for and against the Bill shall be entered on the Journal of each House respectively. If any Bill shall not be returned by the President within ten Days (Sundays excepted) after it shall have been presented to him, the Same shall be a Law, in like Manner as if he had signed it, unless the Congress by their Adjournment prevent its Return, in which Case it shall not be a Law.

Every Order, Resolution, or Vote to which the Concurrence of the Senate and House of Representatives may be necessary (except on a question of Adjournment) shall be presented to the President of the United States; and before the Same shall take Effect, shall be approved by him, or being disapproved by him, shall be repassed by two thirds of the Senate and House of Representatives, according to the Rules and Limitations prescribed in the Case of a Bill.

Section 8   The Congress shall have Power To lay and collect Taxes, Duties, Imposts and Excises, to pay the Debts and provide for the common Defence and general Welfare of the United States; but all Duties, Imposts and Excises shall be uniform throughout the United States;

To borrow Money on the credit of the United States;

To regulate Commerce with foreign Nations, and among the several States, and with the Indian Tribes;

To establish an uniform Rule of Naturalization, and uniform Laws on the subject of Bankruptcies throughout the United States;

To coin Money, regulate the Value thereof, and of foreign Coin, and fix the Standard of Weights and Measures;

To provide for the Punishment of counterfeiting the Securities and current Coin of the United States;

To establish Post Offices and post Roads;

To promote the Progress of Science and useful Arts, by securing for limited Times to Authors and Inventors the exclusive Right to their respective Writings and Discoveries;

To constitute Tribunals inferior to the supreme Court;

To define and punish Piracies and Felonies committed on the high Seas, and Offences against the Law of Nations;

To declare War, grant Letters of Marque and Reprisal, and make Rules concerning Captures on Land and Water;

To raise and support Armies, but no Appropriation of Money to that Use shall be for a longer Term than two Years;

To provide and maintain a Navy;

To make Rules for the Government and Regulation of the land and naval Forces;

To provide for calling forth the Militia to execute the Laws of the Union, suppress Insurrections and repel Invasions;

To provide for organizing, arming, and disciplining, the Militia, and for governing such Part of them as may be employed in the Service of the United States, reserving to the States respectively, the Appointment of the Officers, and the Authority of training the Militia according to the discipline prescribed by Congress;

To exercise exclusive Legislation in all Cases whatsoever, over such District (not exceeding ten Miles square) as may, by Cession of particular States, and the Acceptance of Congress, become the Seat of the Government of the United States, and to exercise like Authority over all Places purchased by the Consent of the Legislature of the State in which the Same shall be, for the Erection of Forts, Magazines, Arsenals, dock-Yards, and other needful Buildings;—And

To make all Laws which shall be necessary and proper for carrying into Execution the foregoing Powers, and all other Powers vested by this Constitution in the Government of the United States, or in any Department of Officer thereof.

Section 9 *The Migration or Importation of such Persons as any of the States now existing shall think proper to admit, shall not be prohibited by the Congress prior to the Year one thousand eight hundred and eight, but a Tax or duty may be imposed on such Importation, not exceeding ten dollars for each Person.*

The Privilege of the Writ of Habeas Corpus shall not be suspended, unless when in Cases of Rebellion or Invasion the public Safety may require it.

No Bill of Attainder or ex post facto Law shall be passed.

No Capitation, or other direct, Tax shall be laid, unless in Proportion to the Census or Enumeration herein before directed to be taken.

No Capitation, or other direct, Tax shall be laid, unless in Proportion to the Census or Enumeration herein before directed to be taken.

No Tax or Duty shall be laid on Articles exported from any State.

No Preference shall be given by any Regulation of Commerce or Revenue to the Ports of one State over those of another: nor shall Vessels bound to, or from, one State, be obliged to enter, clear, or pay Duties in another.

No Money shall be drawn from the Treasury, but in Consequence of Appropriations made by Law; and a regular Statement and Account of the Receipts and Expenditures of all public Money shall be published from time to time.

No Title of Nobility shall be granted by the United States: And no Person holding any Office of Profit or Trust under them, shall, without the Consent of the Congress, accept of any present, Emolument, Office, or Title, of any kind whatever, from any King, Prince, or foreign State.

Section 10 No State shall enter into any Treaty, Alliance, or Confederation; grant Letters of Marque and Reprisal; coin Money; emit Bills of Credit; make any Thing but gold and silver Coin a Tender in Payment of Debts; pass any Bill of Attainder, ex post facto Law, or Law impairing the obligation of Contracts, or grant any Title of Nobility.

No State shall, without the Consent of the Congress, lay any Imposts or Duties on Imports or Exports, except what may be absolutely necessary for executing its inspection Laws: and the net Produce of all Duties and Imposts, laid by any State on Imports or Exports, shall be for the Use of the Treasury of the United States; and all such Laws shall be subject to the Revision and Controul of the Congress.

No State shall, without the Consent of Congress, lay any Duty of Tonnage, keep Troops, or Ships of War in time of Peace, enter into any Agreement or Compact with another State, or with a foreign Power, or engage in War, unless actually invaded, or in such imminent Danger as will not admit of delay.

Article II.

Section 1 The executive Power shall be vested in a President of the United States of America. He shall hold his Office during the Term of four Years, and, together with the Vice President, chosen for the same Term, be elected, as follows:

Each State shall appoint, in such Manner as the Legislature thereof may direct, a Number of Electors, equal to the whole Number of Senators and Representatives to which the State may be entitled in the Congress: but no Senator or Representative, or Person holding an Office of Trust or Profit under the United States, shall be appointed an Elector.

The Electors shall meet in their respective States, and vote by Ballot for two Persons, of whom one at least shall not be an Inhabitant of the same State with themselves. And they shall make a List of all the Persons voted for, and of the Number of Votes for each; which List they shall sign and certify, and transmit sealed to the Seat of the Government of the United States, directed to the President of the Senate. The President of the Senate shall, in the Presence of the Senate and House of Representatives, open all the Certificates, and the Votes shall then be counted. The Person having the greatest Number of Votes shall be the President, if such Number be a Majority of the whole number of Electors appointed; and if there be more than one who have such Majority, and have an equal Number of Votes, then the House of Representative shall immediately chuse by Ballot one of them for President; and if no Person have a Majority, then from the five highest on the List the said House shall in like Manner chuse the President. But in chusing the President, the Votes shall be taken by States, the Representation from each State having one Vote; A quorum for this Purpose shall consist of a Member or Members from two thirds of the States, and a Majority of all the States shall be necessary to a Choice. In every Case, after the Choice of the President, the Person having the greatest Number of Votes of the Electors shall be the Vice President. But if there should remain two or more who have equal Votes, the Senate shall chuse from them by Ballot the Vice President.

The Congress may determine the time of chusing the Electors, and the Day on which they shall give their Votes; which Day shall be the same throughout the United States.

No person except a natural born Citizen, *or a Citizen of the United States, at the time of the Adoption of this Constitution,* shall be eligible to the Office of President; neither shall any Person be eligible to that Office who shall not have attained to the Age of thirty five Years, and been fourteen Years a Resident within the United States.

In Case of the Removal of the President from Office, or of his Death, Resignation, or Inability to discharge the Powers and Duties of the said Office, the Same shall devolve on the Vice President, and the Congress may by Law provide for the Case of Removal, Death, Resignation or Inability, both of the President and Vice President, declaring what Officer shall then act as President, and such Officer shall act accordingly, until the Disability be removed, or a President shall be elected.

The President shall, at stated Times, receive for his Services, a Compensation, which shall neither be encreased nor diminished during the Period for which he shall have been elected, and he shall not receive within that period any other Emolument from the United States, or any of them.

Before he enter on the Execution of his Office, he shall take the following Oath or Affirmation:—"I do solemnly swear (or affirm) that I will faithfully execute the Office of President of the United States, and will to the best of my Ability, preserve, protect and defend the Constitution of the United States."

Section 2   The President shall be Commander in Chief of the Army and Navy of the United States, and of the Militia of the several States, when called into the actual Service of the United States; he may require the Opinion, in writing, of the principal Officer in each of the executive Departments, upon any Subject relating to the Duties of their respective Offices, and he shall have Power to grant Reprieves and Pardons for Offences against the United States, except in Cases of Impeachment.

He shall have Power, by and with the Advice and Consent of the Senate, to make Treaties, provided two thirds of the Senators present concur; and he shall nom-

inate, and by and with the Advice and Consent of the Senate, shall appoint Ambassadors, other public Ministers and Consuls, Judges of the supreme Court, and all other Officers of the United States, whose Appointments are not herein otherwise provided for, and which shall be established by Law: but the Congress may by Law vest the Appointment of such inferior Officers, as they think proper in the President alone, in the Courts of Law, or in the Heads of Departments.

The President shall have Power to fill up all Vacancies that may happen during the Recess of the Senate, by granting Commissions which shall expire at the End of their next Session.

Section 3   He shall from time to time give to the Congress Information of the State of the Union, and recommend to their Consideration such Measures as he shall judge necessary and expedient; he may, on extraordinary Occasions, convene both Houses, or either of them, and in Case of disagreement between them, with Respect to the Time of Adjournment, he may adjourn them to such Time as he shall think proper; he shall receive Ambassadors and other public Ministers; he shall take Care that the Laws be faithfully executed, and shall Commission all the officers of the United States.

Section 4   The President, Vice President and all civil Officers of the United States, shall be removed from Office on Impeachment for, and Conviction of, Treason, Bribery or other high Crimes and Misdemeanors.

Article III.

Section 1   The judicial Power of the United States, shall be vested in one supreme Court, and in such inferior Courts as the Congress may from time to time ordain and establish. The Judges, both of the supreme and inferior Courts, shall hold their offices during good Behaviour, and shall, at stated Times, receive for their Services, a Compensation, which shall not be diminished during their Continuance in Office.

Section 2   The judicial Power shall extend to all Cases, in Law and Equity, arising under this Constitution, the Laws of the United States, and Treaties made, or which shall be made, under their Authority;—to all Cases affecting Ambassadors, other public Ministers and Consuls;—to all Cases of admiralty and maritime Jurisdiction;—to Controversies to which the United States shall be a Party;—to Controversies between two or more States;—*between a State and Citizens of another State;*—between Citizens of different States,—between Citizens of the same State claiming Lands under Grants of different States, and between a State, or the

Citizens thereof, and foreign States, Citizens or Subjects.

In all Cases affecting Ambassadors, other public Ministers and Consuls, and those in which a State shall be Party, the supreme Court shall have original Jurisdiction. In all the other Cases before mentioned, the supreme Court shall have appellate Jurisdiction, both as to Law and Fact, with such Exceptions, and under such Regulations as the Congress shall make.

The Trial of all Crimes, except in Cases of Impeachment, shall be by Jury; and such Trial shall be held in the State where the said Crimes shall have been committed, but when not committed within any State, the Trial shall be at such Place or Places as the Congress may by Law have directed.

Section 3   Treason against the United States, shall consist only in levying War against them, or in adhering to their Enemies, giving them Aid and Comfort. No person shall be convicted of Treason unless on the Testimony of two Witnesses to the same overt Act, or on Confession in open Court.

The Congress shall have Power to declare the Punishment of Treason, but no Attainder of Treason shall work Corruption of Blood, or Forfeiture except during the Life of the Person attainted.

Article IV.

Section 1   Full Faith and Credit shall be given in each State to the public Acts, Records, and judicial Proceedings of every other State. And the Congress may be general Laws prescribe the Manner in which such Acts, Records and Proceedings shall be proved, and the Effect thereof.

Section 2   The Citizens of each State shall be entitled to all Privileges and Immunities of Citizens in the several States.

A Person charged in any State with Treason, Felony, or other Crime, who shall flee from Justice, and be found in another State, shall on Demand of the executive Authority of the State from which he fled, be delivered up, to be removed to the State having Jurisdiction of the Crime.

No Person held to Service or Labour in one State, under the Laws thereof, escaping into another, shall, in Consequence of any Law or Regulation therein, be discharged from such Service or Labour, but shall be delivered up on Claim of the Party to whom such Service or Labour may be due.*

Section 3   New States may be admitted by the Congress into this Union; but no new State shall be formed or erected within the Jurisdiction of any other State; nor any State be formed by the Junction of two or more States, or Parts of States, without the Consent of the Legislatures of the States concerned as well as of the Congress.

The Congress shall have Power to dispose of and make all needful Rules and Regulations respecting the Territory or other Property belonging to the United States; and nothing in this Constitution shall be so construed as to Prejudice any Claims of the United States, or of any particular States.

Section 4   The United States shall guarantee to every State in this Union a Republican Form of Government, and shall protect each of them against Invasion; and on Application of the Legislature, or of the Executive (when the Legislature cannot be convened) against domestic violence.

Article V.

The Congress, whenever two thirds of both Houses shall deem it necessary, shall propose Amendments to this Constitution, or, on the Application of the Legislatures of two thirds of the several States, shall call a Convention for proposing Amendments, which, in either Case, shall be valid to all Intents and Purposes, as Part of this Constitution, when ratified by the Legislatures of three fourths of the several States, or by Conventions in three fourths thereof, as the one or the other Mode of Ratification may be proposed by the Congress; Provided *that no Amendment which may be made prior to the Year One thousand eight hundred and eight shall in any Manner affect the first and fourth Clauses in the Ninth Section of the first Article;* and that no State without its Consent, shall be deprived of its equal Suffrage in the Senate.

Article VI.

All Debts contracted and Engagements entered into, before the Adoption of this Constitution, shall be as valid against the United States under this Constitution, as under the Confederation.

This Constitution, and Laws of the United States which shall be made in Pursuance thereof; and all Treaties made, or which shall be made, under the Authority of the United States, shall be the supreme Law of the Land; and the Judges in every State shall be bound thereby, any Thing in the Constitution or Laws of any State to the Contrary notwithstanding.

The Senators and Representatives before mentioned, and the Members of the several State Legislatures, and all executive and Judicial Officers, both of the United States and of the several States, shall be bound by Oath or Affirmation, to support this Constitution; but no religious Test shall ever be required as a Qualification to any Office of public Trust under the United States.

Article VII.

The Ratification of the Conventions of nine States, shall be sufficient for the Establishment of this Constitution-between the States so ratifying the Same.

Done in Convention by the Unanimous Consent of the States present the Seventeenth Day of September in the Year of our Lord one thousand seven hundred and Eighty seven and of the Independence of the United States of America the Twelfth* IN WITNESS whereof We have hereunto subscribed our Names,

George Washington
President and Deputy from Virginia

New Hampshire
JOHN LANGDON
NICHOLAS GILMAN

Massachusetts
NATHANIEL GORHAM
RUFUS KING

Connecticut
WILLIAM S. JOHNSON
ROGER SHERMAN

New York
ALEXANDER HAMILTON
New Jersey
WILLIAM LIVINGSTON
DAVID BREARLEY
WILLIAM PATERSON
JONATHAN DAYTON

Pennsylvania
BENJAMIN FRANKLIN
THOMAS MIFFLIN
ROBERT MORRIS
GEORGE CLYMER
THOMAS FITZSIMONS
JARED INGERSOLL
JAMES WILSON
GOUVERNEUR MORRIS

Delaware
GEORGE READ
GUNNING BEDFORD, JR.
JOHN DICKINSON
RICHARD BASSETT
JACOB BROOM

Maryland
JAMES MCHENRY
DANIEL OF ST. THOMAS JENIFER
DANIEL CARROLL

Virginia
JOHN BLAIR
JAMES MADISON, JR.

North Carolina
WILLIAM BLOUNT
RICHARD DOBBS SPRAIGHT
HU WILLIAMSON

South Carolina
J. RUTLEDGE
CHARLES G. PINCKNEY
PIERCE BUTLER

Georgia
WILLIAM FEW
ABRAHAM BALDWIN

The Constitution was submitted on September 17, 1787, by the Constitutional Convention, was ratified by the conventions of several states at various dates up to May 29, 1790, and became effective on March 4, 1789.

Amendments to the Constitution

Amendment I

Congress shall make no law respecting an establishment of religion, or prohibiting the free exercise thereof; or abridging the freedom of speech, or of the press; or the right of the people peaceably to assemble, and to petition the Government for a redress of grievances.

Amendment II

A well regulated Militia being necessary to the security of a free State, the right of the people to keep and bear Arms, shall not be infringed.

Amendment III

No Soldier shall, in time of peace be quartered in any house, without the consent of the Owner, nor in time of war, but in a manner to be prescribed by law.

Amendment IV

The right of the people to be secure in their persons, houses, papers, and effects, against unreasonable searches and seizures, shall not be violated, and no Warrants shall issue, but upon probable cause, supported by Oath or affirmation, and particularly describing the place to be searched, and the persons or things to be seized.

Amendment V

No person shall be held to answer for a capital, or otherwise infamous crime, unless on a presentment or indictment of a Grand Jury, except in cases arising in the land or naval forces, or in the Militia, when in actual service in time of War or public danger; nor shall any person be subject for the same offense to be twice put in jeopardy of life or limb; nor shall be compelled in any criminal case to be a witness against himself, nor be deprived of life, liberty, or property, without due process of law; nor shall private property be taken for public use, without just compensation.

Amendment VI

In all criminal prosecutions, the accused shall enjoy the right to a speedy and public trial, by an impartial jury of the State and district wherein the crime shall have been committed, which district shall have been previously ascertained by law, and to be informed of the nature and cause of the accusation; to be confronted with the witnesses against him; to have compulsory process for obtaining witnesses in his favor, and to have the Assistance of Counsel for his defence.

Amendment VII

In Suits at common law, where the value in controversy shall exceed twenty dollars, the right of trial by jury shall be preserved, and no fact trial by a jury, shall be otherwise re-examined in any Court of the United States, than according to the rules of the common law.

Amendment VIII

Excessive bail shall not be required, nor excessive fines imposed, nor cruel and unusual punishments inflicted.

Amendment IX

The enumeration in the Constitution, of certain rights, shall not be construed to deny or disparage others retained by the people.

Amendment X*

The powers not delegated to the United States by the Constitution, nor prohibited by it to the States, are reserved to the States respectively, or to the people.

Amendment XI
[Adopted 1798]

The Judicial power of the United States shall not be construed to extend to any suit in law or equity, commenced or prosecuted against one of the United States by Citizens of another State, or by Citizens or Subjects of any Foreign State.

Amendment XII
[Adopted 1804]

The Electors shall meet in their respective states, and vote by ballot for President and Vice-President, one of whom, at least, shall not be an inhabitant of the same state with themselves; they shall name in their ballots the person voted for as President, and in distinct ballots the person voted for as Vice-President, and they shall make distinct lists of all persons voted for as President, and of all persons voted for as Vice-President, and of the number of votes for each, which lists they shall sign and certify, and transmit sealed to the seat of the government of the United States, directed to the President of the Senate;—The President of the Senate shall, in the presence of the Senate and House of Representatives,

---

The first ten amendments (the Bill of Rights) were ratified and adoption certified on December 15, 1791.

open all the certificates and the votes shall then be counted;—The person having the greatest number of votes for President, shall be the President, if such number be a majority of the whole number of Electors appointed; and if no person have such majority, then from the persons having the highest numbers not exceeding three on the list of those voted for as President, the House of Representatives shall choose immediately, by ballot, the President. But in choosing the President, the votes shall be taken by states, the representation from each state having one vote; a quorum for this purpose shall consist of a member or members from two-thirds of the states, and a majority of all the states shall be necessary to a choice. And if the House of Representatives shall not choose a President whenever the right of choice shall devolve upon them, before *the fourth day of March* next following, then the Vice-President shall act as President, as in the case of the death or other constitutional disability of the President.—The person having the greatest number of votes as Vice-President, shall be the Vice-President, if such number be a majority of the whole number of Electors appointed, and if no person have a majority, then from the two highest numbers on the list, the Senate shall choose the Vice-President; a quorum for the purpose shall consist of two-thirds of the whole number of Senators, and a majority of the whole number shall be necessary to a choice. But no person constitutionally ineligible to the office of President shall be eligible to that of Vice President of the United States.

Amendment XIII [Adopted 1865]

Section 1   Neither slavery nor involuntary servitude, except as a punishment for crime whereof the party shall have been duly convicted, shall exist within the United States, or any place subject to their jurisdiction.

Section 2   Congress shall have power to enforce this article by appropriate legislation.

Amendment XIV [Adopted 1868]

Section 1   All persons born or naturalized in the United States, and subject to the jurisdiction thereof, are citizens of the United States and of the State wherein they reside. No State shall make or enforce any law which shall abridge the privileges or immunities of citizens of the United States; nor shall any State deprive any person of life, liberty, or property, without due process of law; nor deny to any person within its jurisdiction the equal protection of the laws.

Section 2   Representatives shall be apportioned among the several States according to their respective numbers, counting the whole number of persons in each State, excluding Indians not taxed. But when the right to vote at any election for the choice of electors for President and Vice-President of the United States, Representatives in Congress, the Executive and Judicial officers of a State, or the members of the Legislature thereof, is denied to any of the male inhabitants of such State, being twenty-one years of age, and citizens of the United States, or in any way abridged, except for participation in rebellion, or other crime, the basis of representation therein shall be reduced in the proportion which the number of such male citizens shall bear to the whole number of male citizens twenty-one years of age in such State.

Section 3   No person shall be a Senator or Representative in Congress, or elector of President and Vice President, or hold any office, civil or military, under the United States, or under any State, who, having previously taken an oath, as a member of Congress, or as an officer of the United States, or as a member of any State legislature, or as an executive or judicial officer of any State, to support the Constitution of the United States, shall have engaged in insurrection or rebellion against the same, or given aid or comfort to the enemies thereof. But Congress may be a vote of two-thirds of each House, remove such disability.

Section 4   The validity of the public debt of the United States, authorized by law, including debts incurred for payment of pensions and bounties for services in suppressing insurrection or rebellion, shall not be questioned. But neither the United States nor any State shall assume or pay any debt or obligation incurred in aid of insurrection or rebellion against the United States, or any claim for the loss or emancipation of any slave; but all such debts, obligations and claims shall be held illegal and void.

Section 5   The Congress shall have power to enforce, by appropriate legislation, the provisions of this article.

Amendment XV [Adopted 1870]

Section 1   The right of citizens of the United States to vote shall not be denied or abridged by the United States or by any State on account of race, color, or previous condition of servitude.

Section 2   The Congress shall have power to enforce this article by appropriate legislation.

Amendment XVI
[Adopted 1913]

The Congress shall have power to lay and collect taxes on incomes, from whatever source derived, without apportionment among the several States, and without regard to any census or enumeration.

Amendment XVII
[Adopted 1913]

The Senate of the United States shall be composed of two Senators from each State, elected by the people thereof, for six years; and each Senator shall have one vote. The electors in each State shall have the qualifications requisite for electors of the most numerous branch of the State legislatures.

When vacancies happen in the representation of any State in the Senate, the executive authority of such State shall issue writs of election to fill such vacancies: *Provided,* That the legislature of any State may empower the executive thereof to make temporary appointments until the people fill the vacancies by election as the legislature may direct.

This amendment shall not be so construed as to affect the election or term of any Senator chosen before it becomes valid as part of the Constitution.

Amendment XVIII
[Adopted 1919, repealed 1933]

Section 1   *After one year from the ratification of this article the manufacture, sale, or transportation of intoxicating liquors within, the importation thereof into, or the exportation thereof from the United States and all territory subject to the jurisdiction thereof for beverage purposes is hereby prohibited.**

Section 2   *The Congress and the several States shall have concurrent power to enforce this article by appropriate legislation.*

Section 3   *This article shall be inoperative unless it shall have been ratified as an amendment to the Constitution by the legislatures of the several States, as provided in the Constitution, within seven years from the date of the submission hereof to the States by the Congress.*

Amendment XIX
[Adopted 1920]

The right of citizens of the United States to vote shall not be denied or abridged by the United States or by any State on account of sex.

---

*Passages no longer in effect are printed in italic type.

Congress shall have power to enforce this article by appropriate legislation.

Amendment XX
[Adopted 1933]

Section 1   The terms of the President and Vice President shall end at noon on the 20th day of January, and the terms of Senators and Representatives at noon on the 3d day of January, of the years in which such terms would have ended if this article had not been ratified and the terms of their successors shall then begin.

Section 2   The Congress shall assemble at least once in every year, and such meeting shall begin at noon on the 3d day of January, unless they shall by law appoint a different day.

Section 3   If, at the time fixed for the beginning of the term of the President, the President elect shall have died, the Vice President elect shall become President. If a President shall not have been chosen before the time fixed for the beginning of his term, or if the President elect shall have failed to qualify, then the Vice President elect shall act as President until a President shall have qualified; and the Congress may by law provide for the case wherein neither a President elect nor a Vice President elect shall have qualified, declaring who shall then act as President, or the manner in which one who is to act shall be selected, and such person shall act accordingly until a President or Vice President shall have qualified.

Section 4   The Congress may by law provide for the case of the death of any of the persons from whom the House of Representatives may choose a President whenever the right of choice shall have devolved upon them, and for the case of the death of any of the persons from whom the Senate may choose a Vice President whenever the right of choice shall have devolved upon them.

Section 5   Sections 1 and 2 shall take effect on the 15th day of October following the ratification of this article.

Section 6   This article shall be inoperative unless it shall have been ratified as an amendment to the Constitution by the legislatures of three fourths of the several States within seven years from the date of its submission.

Amendment XXI [Adopted 1933]

Section 1   The eighteenth article of amendment to the Constitution of the United States is hereby repealed.

Section 2 The transportation or importation into any State, Territory, or possession of the United States for delivery or use therein of intoxicating liquors in violation of the laws thereof, is hereby prohibited.

Section 3 This article shall be inoperative unless it shall have been ratified as an amendment to the Constitution by conventions in the several States, as provided in the Constitution, within seven years from the date of the submission hereof to the States by the Congress.

Amendment XXII [Adopted 1951]

Section 1 No person shall be elected to the office of the President more than twice, and no person who has held the office of President, or acted as President, for more than two years of a term to which some other person was elected President shall be elected to the office of the President more than once. But this Article shall not apply to any person holding the office of President when this Article was proposed by the Congress, and shall not prevent any person who may be holding the office of President, or acting as President, during the term within which this Article becomes operative from holding the office of President or acting as President during the remainder of such term.

Section 2 This article shall be inoperative unless it shall have been ratified as an amendment to the Constitution by the legislatures of three-fourths of the several States within several years from the date of its submission to the States within seven years from the date of its submission to the States by the Congress.

Amendment XXIII [Adopted 1961]

Section 1 The District constituting the seat of Government of the United States shall appoint in such manner as the Congress shall direct:

A number of electors of President and Vice President equal to the whole number of Senators and Representatives in Congress to which the District would be entitled if it were a State, but in no event more than the least populous State; they shall be in addition to those appointed by the States, but they shall be considered, for the purposes of the election of President and Vice President, to be electors appointed by a State; and they shall meet in the District and perform such duties as provided by the twelfth article of amendment.

Section 2 The Congress shall have power to enforce this article by appropriate legislation.

Amendment XXIV [Adopted 1964]

Section 1 The right of citizens of the United States to vote in any primary or other election for President or Vice President, for electors for President or Vice President, or for Senator or Representative in Congress, shall not be denied or abridged by the United States or any state by reason of failure to pay any poll tax or other tax.

Section 2 The Congress shall have the power to enforce this article by appropriate legislation.

Amendment XXV [Adopted 1967]

Section 1 In case of the removal of the President from office or his death or resignation, the Vice President shall become President.

Section 2 Whenever there is a vacancy in the office of the Vice President, the President shall nominate a Vice President who shall take the office upon confirmation by a majority vote of both houses of Congress.

Section 3 Whenever the President transmits to the President pro tempore of the Senate and the Speaker of the House of Representatives his written declaration that he is unable to discharge the powers and duties of his office, and until he transmits to them a written declaration to the contrary, such powers and duties shall be discharged by the Vice President as Acting President.

Section 4 Whenever the Vice President and a majority of either the principal officers of the executive departments or of such other body as Congress may by law provide, transmit to the President pro tempore of the Senate and the Speaker of the House of Representatives their written declaration that the President is unable to discharge the powers and duties of his office, the Vice President shall immediately assume the powers and duties of the office as Acting President.

Thereafter, when the President transmits to the President pro tempore of the Senate and the Speaker of the House of Representatives his written declaration that no inability exists, he shall resume the powers and duties of his office unless the Vice President and a majority of either the principal officers of the executive department or of such other body as Congress may by law provide, transmit within four days to the President pro tempore of the Senate and the Speaker of the House of Representatives their written declaration that the President is unable to discharge the powers and duties of his office.

Thereupon Congress shall decide the issue, assembling within 48 hours for that purpose if not in session. If the Congress, within 21 days after receipt of the latter written declaration, or, if Congress is not in session, within 21 days after Congress is required to assemble, determines by two-thirds vote of both houses that the President is unable to discharge the powers and duties of his office, the Vice President shall continue to discharge the same as Acting President; otherwise, the President shall resume the powers and duties of his office.

Amendment XXVI [Adopted 1971]

Section 1 The right of citizens of the United States, who are 18 years of age or older, to vote shall not be de

nied or abridged by the United States or any state on account of age.

Section 2 The Congress shall have the power to enforce this article by appropriate legislation.

Amendment XXVII [Adopted 1992]

No law, varying the compensation for the services of the Senators and Representatives shall take effect, until an election of Representatives shall have intervened.

Choosing the President

Presidential Election Year	Elected to Office			
	President	Party	Vice President	Party
1789	George Washington		John Adams	Parties not yet established
1792	George Washington		John Adams	Federalist
1796	John Adams	Federalist	Thomas Jefferson	Democratic-Republican
1800	Thomas Jefferson	Democratic-Republican	Aaron Burr	Democratic-Republican
1804	Thomas Jefferson	Democratic-Republican	George Clinton	Democratic-Republican
1808	James Madison	Democratic-Republican	George Clinton	Democratic-Republican
1812	James Madison	Democratic-Republican	Elbridge Gerry	Democratic-Republican
1816	James Monroe	Democratic-Republican	Daniel D. Tompkins	Democratic-Republican
1820	James Monroe	Democratic-Republican	Daniel D. Tompkins	Democratic-Republican
1824	John Quincy Adams Elected by House of Representatives because no candidate received a majority of electoral votes.	National Republican	John C. Calhoun	Democratic
1828	Andrew Jackson	Democratic	John C. Calhoun	Democratic
1832	Andrew Jackson	Democratic	Martin Van Buren	Democratic
1836	Martin Van Buren	Democratic	Richard M. Johnson First and only vice president elected by the Senate (1837), having failed to receive a majority of electoral votes.	Democratic

Major Opponents		Electoral Vote		Popular Vote
For President	*Party*			
		Washington	69	Electors selected
		J. Adams	34	by state legislatures
George Clinton	Democratic-Republican	Washington	132	Electors selected
		J. Adams	77	by state legislatures
		Clinton	50	
Thomas Pinckney	Federalist	J. Adams	71	Electors selected
Aaron Burr	Democratic-Republican	Jefferson	68	by state legislatures
		Pinckney	59	
John Adams	Federalist	Jefferson	73	Electors selected
Charles Cotesworth Pinckney	Federalist	J. Adams	65	by state legislatures
Charles Cotesworth Pinckney	Federalist	Jefferson	162	Electors selected
		Pinckney	14	by state legislatures
Charles Cotesworth Pinckney	Federalist	Madison	122	Electors selected
		Pinckney	47	by state legislatures
George Clinton	Eastern Republican			
De Witt Clinton	Democratic-Republican (antiwar faction) and Federalist	Madison	128	Electors selected
		Clinton	89	by state legislatures
Rufus King	Federalist	Monroe	183	Electors selected
		King	34	by state legislatures
		Monroe	231	Electors selected
		J. Q. Adams	1	by state legislatures
Andrew Jackson	Democratic	J. Q. Adams	84	113,122
Henry Clay	Democratic-Republican	Jackson	99	151,271
		Clay	37	47,531
William H. Crawford	Democratic-Republican	Crawford	41	40,856
John Quincy Adams	National Republican	Jackson	178	642,553
		J. Q. Adams	83	500,897
Henry Clay	National Republican	Jackson	219	701,780
		Clay	49	482,205
William Wirt	Anti-Masonic	Wirt	7	100,715
		Floyd (Ind. Dem.)	11	
		Delegates chosen by South Carolina legislature		
Daniel Webster	Whig	Van Buren	170	764,176
Hugh L. White	Whig	W. Harrison	73	550,816
William Henry Harrison	Anti-Masonic	White	26	146,107
		Webster	14	41,201
		Mangum (Ind. Dem.)	11	
		Delegates chosen by South Carolina legislature		

Presidential Election Year	Elected to Office			
	President	Party	Vice President	Party
1840	William Henry Harrison	Whig	John Tyler	Whig
1844	James K. Polk	Democratic	George M. Dallas	Democratic
1848	Zachary Taylor	Whig	Millard Fillmore	Whig
1852	Franklin Pierce	Democratic	William R. King	Democratic
1856	James Buchanan	Democratic	John C. Breckinridge	Democratic
1860	Abraham Lincoln	Republican	Hannibal Hamlin	Republican
1864	Abraham Lincoln	National Union Republican	Andrew Johnson	National Union/ Democratic
1868	Ulysses S. Grant	Republican	Schuyler Colfax	Republican
1872	Ulysses S. Grant	Republican	Henry Wilson	Republican
1876	Rutherford B. Hayes Contested result settled by special election commission in favor of Hayes	Republican	William A. Wheeler	Republican
1880	James A. Garfield	Republican	Chester A. Arthur	Republican
1884	Grover Cleveland	Democratic	Thomas A. Hendricks	Democratic
1888	Benjamin Harrison	Republican	Levi P. Morton	Republican

Major Opponents		Electoral Vote		Popular Vote
For President	*Party*			
Martin Van Buren	Democratic	W. Harrison	234	1,274,624
James G. Birney	Liberty	Van Buren	60	1,127,781
Henry Clay	Whig	Polk	170	1,338,624
James G. Birney	Liberty	Clay	105	1,300,097
		Birney	—	62,300
Lewis Cass	Democratic	Taylor	163	1,360,967
Martin Van Buren	Free-Soil	Cass	127	1,222,342
		Van Buren	—	291,263
Winfield Scott	Whig	Pierce	254	1,601,117
John P. Hale	Free-Soil	Scott	42	1,385,453
		Hale	—	155,825
John C. Frémont	Republican	Buchanan	174	1,832,955
Millard Fillmore	American (Know-Nothing)	Frémont	114	1,339,932
		Fillmore	8	871,731
John Bell	Constitutional Union	Lincoln	180	1,865,593
Stephen A. Douglas	Democratic	Breckinridge	72	848,356
John C. Breckinridge	Democratic	Douglas	12	1,382,713
		Bell	39	592,906
George B. McClellan	Democratic	Lincoln	212	2,218,388
		McClellan	21	1,812,807
		Eleven secessionist states did not participate		
Horatio Seymour	Democratic	Grant	286	3,598,235
		Seymour	80	2,706,829
		Texas, Mississippi, and Virginia did not participate		
Horace Greeley	Democratic and Liberal Republican	Grant	286	3,598,235
		Greeley	80	2,834,761
Charles O'Conor	Democratic	Greeley died before the electoral college met. His electoral votes were divided among the four minor candidates.		
James Black	Temperance			
Samuel J. Tilden	Democratic	Hayes	185	4,034,311
Peter Cooper	Greenback	Tilden	184	4,288,546
Green Clay Smith	Prohibition	Cooper	—	75,973
Winfield S. Hancock	Democratic	Garfield	214	4,446,158
James B. Weaver	Greenback	Hancock	155	4,444,260
Neal Dow	Prohibition	Weaver	—	305,997
James G. Blaine	Republican	Cleveland	219	4,874,621
John P. St. John	Prohibition	Blaine	182	4,848,936
Benjamin F. Butler	Greenback	Butler	—	175,096
		St. John	—	147,482
Grover Cleveland	Democratic	B. Harrison	233	5,447,129
Clinton B. Fisk	Prohibition	Cleveland	168	5,537,857
Alson J. Streeter	Union Labor			

Presidential Election Year	Elected to Office			
	President	*Party*	*Vice President*	*Party*
1892	Grover Cleveland	Democratic	Adlai E. Stevenson	Democratic
1896	William McKinley	Republican	Garret A. Hobart	Republican
1900	William McKinley	Republican	Theodore Roosevelt	Republican
1904	Theodore Roosevelt	Republican	Charles W. Fairbanks	Republican
1908	William Howard Taft	Republican	James S. Sherman	Republican
1912	Woodrow Wilson	Democratic	Thomas R. Marshall	Democratic
1916	Woodrow Wilson	Democratic	Thomas R. Marshall	Democratic
1920	Warren G. Harding	Republican	Calvin Coolidge	Republican
1924	Calvin Coolidge	Republican	Charles G. Dawes	Republican
1928	Herbert C. Hoover	Republican	Charles Curtis	Republican
1932	Franklin D. Roosevelt	Democratic	John N. Garner	Democratic
1936	Franklin D. Roosevelt	Democratic	John N. Garner	Democratic
1940	Franklin D. Roosevelt	Democratic	Henry A. Wallace	Democratic
1944	Franklin D. Roosevelt	Democrat	Harry S Truman	Democratic

Major Opponents		Electoral Vote		Popular Vote
For President	Party			
Benjamin Harrison	Republican	Cleveland	277	5,555,426
James B. Weaver	Populist	B. Harrison	145	5,182,600
John Bidwell	Prohibition	Weaver	22	1,029,846
William Jennings Bryan	Democratic, Populist, and National Silver	McKinley	271	7,102,246
Joshua Levering	Republican	Bryan	176	6,492,559
John M. Palmer	Prohibition, National Democratic			
William Jennings Bryan	Democratic and Fusion	McKinley	292	7,218,039
Wharton Barker	Populist	Bryan	155	6,358,345
Eugene V. Debs	Anti-Fusion	Woolley	—	209,004
John G. Woolley	Populist	Debs	—	86,935
	Social Democratic, Prohibition			
Alton B. Parker	Democratic	T. Roosevelt	336	7,626,593
Eugene V. Debs	Socialist	Parker	140	5,082,898
Silas C. Swallow	Prohibition	Debs	—	402,489
		Swallow	—	258,596
William Jennings Bryan	Democratic	Taft	321	7,676,258
Eugene V. Debs	Socialist	Bryan	162	6,406,801
Eugene W. Chafin	Prohibition	Debs	—	420,380
		Chafin	—	252,821
William Howard Taft	Republican	Wilson	435	6,296,547
Theodore Roosevelt	Progressive (Bull Moose)	T. Roosevelt	88	4,118,571
Eugene V. Debs	Socialist	Taft	8	3,486,720
Eugene W. Chafin	Prohibition			
Charles E. Hughes	Republican	Wilson	277	9,127,695
Allen L. Benson	Socialist	Hughes	254	8,533,507
J. Frank Hanley	Prohibition			
Charles W. Fairbanks	Republican			
James M. Cox	Democratic	Harding	404	16,133,314
Eugene V. Debs	Socialist	Cox	127	9,140,884
		Debs	—	913,664
John W. Davis	Democratic	Coolidge	382	15,717,553
Robert M. La Follette	Progressive	Davis	136	8,386,169
		La Follette	13	4,814,050
Alfred E. Smith	Democratic	Hoover	444	21,391,993
Norman Thomas	Socialist	Smith	87	15,016,169
Herbert C. Hoover	Republican	F. Roosevelt	472	22,809,638
Norman Thomas	Socialist	Hoover	59	15,758,901
Alfred M. Landon	Republican	F. Roosevelt	523	27,752,869
William Lemke	Union	Landon	8	16,674,665
Wendell L. Willkie	Republican	F. Roosevelt	449	27,263,448
		Willkie	82	22,336,260
Thomas E. Dewey	Republican	F. Roosevelt	432	25,611,936
		Dewey	99	22,013,372

Presidential Election Year	Elected to Office			
	President	Party	Vice President	Party
1948	Harry S Truman	Democratic	Alben W. Barkley	Democratic
1952	Dwight D. Eisenhower	Republican	Richard M. Nixon	Republican
1956	Dwight D. Eisenhower	Republican	Richard M. Nixon	Republican
1960	John F. Kennedy	Democratic	Lyndon B. Johnson	Democratic
1964	Lyndon B. Johnson	Democratic	Hubert H. Humphrey	Democratic
1968	Richard M. Nixon	Republican	Spiro T. Agnew	Republican
1972	Richard M. Nixon	Republican	Spiro T. Agnew	Republican
1976	Jimmy Carter	Democratic	Walter Mondale	Democratic
1980	Ronald Reagan	Republican	George Bush	Republican
1984	Ronald Reagan	Republican	George Bush	Republican
1988	George Bush	Republican	J. Danforth Quayle	Republican
1992	William Clinton	Democrat	Albert Gore, Jr.	Democrat

Major Opponents		Electoral Vote		Popular Vote
For President	Party			
Thomas E. Dewey	Republican	Truman	303	24,105,182
J. Strom Thurmond	States' Rights,	Dewey	189	21,970,065
	Democratic	Thurmond	39	1,169,063
Henry A. Wallace	Progressive	H. Wallace	—	1,157,326
Adlai E. Stevenson	Democratic	Eisenhower	442	33,936,137
		Stevenson	89	27,314,649
Adlai E. Stevenson	Democratic	Eisenhower	457	35,585,245
		Stevenson	73	26,030,172
Richard M. Nixon	Republican	Kennedy	303	34,227,096
		Nixon	219	34,108,546
		H. Byrd (Ind. Dem.)	15	—
Barry M. Goldwater	Republican	Johnson	486	43,126,584
		Goldwater	52	27,177,838
Hubert H. Humphrey	Democratic	Nixon	301	31,770,237
George C. Wallace	American Independent	Humphrey	191	31,270,533
		G. Wallace	46	9,906,141
George S. McGovern	Democratic	Nixon	520	46,740,323
		McGovern	17	28,901,598
		Hospers (Va.)	1	—
Gerald R. Ford	Republican	Carter	297	40,830,763
Eugene McCarthy	Independent	Ford	240	39,147,793
		E. McCarthy	—	756,631
Jimmy Carter	Democratic	Reagan	489	43,899,248
John B. Anderson	Independent	Carter	49	35,481,435
Ed Clark	Libertarian	Anderson	—	5,719,437
Walter Mondale	Democratic	Reagan	525	54,451,521
David Bergland	Libertarian	Mondale	13	37,565,334
Michael Dukakis	Democratic	Bush	426	47,946,422
		Dukakis	111	41,016,429
		Bentsen	1	—
George Bush	Republican	Clinton	357	43,728,275
H. Ross Perot	Independent	Bush	168	38,167,416
		Perot	—	19,237,245

Cabinet Members

The Washington Administration

Secretary of State	Thomas Jefferson	1789-1793
	Edmund Randolph	1794-1795
	Timothy Pickering	1795-1797
Secretary of Treasury	Alexander Hamilton	1789-1795
	Oliver Wolcott	1795-1797
Secretary of War	Henry Knox	1789-1794
	Timothy Pickering	1795-1796
	James McHenry	1796-1797
Attorney General	Edmund Randolph	1789-1793
	William Bradford	1794-1795
	Charles Lee	1795-1797
Postmaster General	Samuel Osgood	1789-1791
	Timothy Pickering	1791-1794
	Joseph Habersham	1795-1797

The John Adams Administration

Secretary of State	Timothy Pickering	1797-1800
	John Marshall	1800-1801
Secretary of Treasury	Oliver Wolcott	1797-1800
	Samuel Dexter	1800-1801
Secretary of War	James McHenry	1797-1800
	Samuel Dexter	1800-1801
Attorney General	Charles Lee	1797-1901
Postmaster General	Joseph Habersham	1797-1801
Secretary of Navy	Benjamin Stoddert	1798-1801

The Jefferson Administration

Secretary of State	James Madison	1801-1809
Secretary of Treasury	Samuel Dexter	1801
	Albert Gallatin	1801-1809
Secretary of War	Henry Dearborn	1801-1809
Attorney General	Levi Lincoln	1801-1805
	Robert Smith	1805
	John Breckinridge	1805-1806
	Caesar Rodney	1807-1809
Postmaster General	Joseph Habersham	1801
	Gideon Granger	1801-1809
Secretary of Navy	Robert Smith	1801-1809

The Madison Administration

Secretary of State	Robert Smith	1809-1811
	James Monroe	1811-1817
Secretary of Treasury	Albert Gallatin	1809-1813
	George Campbell	1814
	Alexander Dallas	1814-1816
	William Crawford	1816-1817
Secretary of War	William Eustis	1809-1812
	John Armstrong	1813-1814
	James Monroe	1814-1815
	William Crawford	1815-1817
Attorney General	Caesar Rodney	1809-1811
	William Pinkney	1811-1814
	Richard Rush	1814-1817
Postmaster General	Gideon Granger	1809-1814
	Return Meigs	1814-1817
Secretary of Navy	Paul Hamilton	1809-1813
	William Jones	1813-1814
	Benjamin Crowninshield	1814-1817

The Monroe Administration

Secretary of State	John Quincy Adams	1817-1825
Secretary of Treasury	William Crawford	1817-1825
Secretary of War	George Graham	1817
	John C. Calhoun	1817-1825
Attorney General	Richard Rush	1817
	William Wirt	1817-1825
Postmaster General	Return Meigs	1817-1823
	John McLean	1823-1825
Secretary of Navy	Benjamin Crowninshield	1817-1818
	Smith Thompson	1818-1823
	Samuel Southard	1823-1825

The John Quincy Adams Administration

Secretary of State	Henry Clay	1825-1829
Secretary of Treasury	Richard Rush	1825-1829
Secretary of War	James Barbour	1825-1828
	Peter Porter	1828-1829
Attorney General	William Wirt	1825-1829
Postmaster General	John McLean	1825-1829
Secretary of Navy	Samuel Southard	1825-1829

The Jackson Administration

Secretary of State	Martin Van Buren	1829-1831
	Edward Livingston	1831-1833

Secretary	Louis McLane	1833-1834
of State	John Forsyth	1834-1837
Secretary	Samuel Ingham	1829-1831
of Treasury	Louis McLane	1831-1833
	William Duane	1833
	Roger B. Taney	1833-1834
	Levi Woodbury	1834-1837
Secretary	John H. Eaton	1829-1831
of War	Lewis Cass	1831-1837
	Benjamin Butler	1837
Attorney	John M. Berrien	1829-1831
General	Roger B. Taney	1831-1833
	Benjamin Butler	1833-1837
Postmaster	William Barry	1829-1835
General	Amos Kendall	1835-1837
Secretary	John Branch	1829-1831
of Navy	Levi Woodbury	1831-1834
	Mahlon Dickerson	1834-1837

The Van Buren Administration

Secretary	John Forsyth	1837-1841
of State		
Secretary	Levi Woodbury	1837-1841
of Treasury		
Secretary	Joel Poinsett	1837-1841
of War		
Attorney	Benjamin Butler	1837-1838
General	Felix Grundy	1838-1840
	Henry D. Gilpin	1840-1841
Postmaster	Amos Kendall	1837-1840
General	John M. Niles	1840-1841
Secretary	Mahlon Dickerson	1837-1838
of Navy	James Paulding	1838-1841

The William Harrison Administration

Secretary	Daniel Webster	1841
of State		
Secretary	Thomas Ewing	1841
of Treasury		
Secretary	John Bell	1841
of War		
Attorney	John J. Crittenden	1841
General		
Postmaster	Francis Granger	1841
General		
Secretary	George Badger	1841
of Navy		

The Tyler Administration

Secretary	Daniel Webster	1841-1843
of State	Hugh S. Legaré	1843
	Abel P. Upshur	1843-1844
	John C. Calhoun	1844-1845
Secretary	Thomas Ewing	1841
of Treasury	Walter Forward	1841-1843

	John C. Spencer	1843-1844
	George Bibb	1844-1845
Secretary	John Bell	1841
of War	John C. Spencer	1841-1843
	James M. Porter	1843-1844
	William Wilkins	1844-1845
Attorney	John J. Crittenden	1841
General	Hugh S. Legaré	1841-1843
	John Nelson	1843-1845
Postmaster	Francis Granger	1841
General	Charles Wickliffe	1841
Secretary	George Badger	1841
of Navy	Abel P. Upshur	1841
	David Henshaw	1843-1844
	Thomas Gilmer	1844
	John Y. Mason	1844-1845

The Polk Administration

Secretary	James Buchanan	1845-1849
of State		
Secretary	Robert J. Walker	1845-1849
of Treasury		
Secretary	William L. Marcy	1845-1849
of War		
Attorney	John Y. Mason	1845-1846
General	Nathan Clifford	1846-1848
	Isaac Toucey	1848-1849
Postmaster	Cave Johnson	1845-1849
General		
Secretary	George Bancroft	1845-1846
of Navy	John Y. Mason	1846-1849

The Taylor Administration

Secretary	John M. Clayton	1849-1850
of State		
Secretary	William Meredith	1849-1850
of Treasury		
Secretary	George Crawford	1849-1850
of War		
Attorney	Reverdy Johnson	1849-1850
General		
Postmaster	Jacob Collamer	1849-1850
General		
Secretary	William Preston	1849-1850
of Navy		
Secretary	Thomas Ewing	1849-1850
of Interior		

The Fillmore Administration

Secretary	Daniel Webster	1850-1852
of State	Edward Everett	1852-1853
Secretary	Thomas Corwin	1850-1853
of Treasury		

Secretary of War	Charles Conrad	1850-1853
Attorney General	John J. Crittenden	1850-1853
Postmaster General	Nathan Hall	1850-1852
	Sam D. Hubbard	1852-1853
Secretary of Navy	William A. Graham	1850-1852
	John P. Kennedy	1852-1853
Secretary of Interior	Thomas McKennan	1850
	Alexander Stuart	1850-1853

The Pierce Administration

Secretary of State	William L. Marcy	1853-1857
Secretary of Treasury	James Guthrie	1853-1857
Secretary of War	Jefferson Davis	1853-1857
Attorney General	Caleb Cushing	1853-1857
Postmaster General	James Campbell	1853-1857
Secretary of Navy	James C. Dobbin	1853-1857
Secretary of Interior	Robert McClelland	1853-1857

The Buchanan Administration

Secretary of State	Lewis Cass	1857-1860
	Jeremiah S. Black	1860-1861
Secretary of Treasury	Howell Cobb	1857-1860
	Philip Thomas	1860-1861
	John A. Dix	1861
Secretary of War	John B. Floyd	1857-1861
	Joseph Holt	1861
Attorney General	Jeremiah S. Black	1857-1860
	Edwin M. Stanton	1860-1861
Postmaster General	Aaron V. Brown	1857-1859
	Joseph Holt	1859-1861
	Horatio King	1861
Secretary of Navy	Isaac Toucey	1857-1861
Secretary of Interior	Jacob Thompson	1857-1861

The Lincoln Administration

Secretary of State	William H. Seward	1861-1865
Secretary of Treasury	Salmon P. Chase	1861-1864
	William P. Fessenden	1864-1865
	Hugh McCulloch	1865
Secretary of War	Simon Cameron	1861-1862
	Edwin M. Stanton	1862-1865
Attorney General	Edward Bates	1861-1864
	James Speed	1864-1865
Postmaster General	Horatio King	1861
	Montgomery Blair	1861-1864
	William Dennison	1864-1865
Secretary of Navy	Gideon Welles	1861-1865
Secretary of Interior	Caleb B. Smith	1861-1863
	John P. Usher	1863-1865

The Andrew Johnson Administration

Secretary of State	William H. Seward	1865-1869
Secretary of Treasury	Hugh McCulloch	1865-1869
Secretary of War	Edwin M. Stanton	1865-1867
	Ulysses S. Grant	1867-1868
	Lorenzo Thomas	1868
	John M. Schofield	1868-1869
Attorney General	James Speed	1865-1866
	Henry Stanbery	1866-1868
	William M. Evarts	1868-1869
Postmaster General	William Dennison	1865-1866
	Alexander Randall	1866-1869
Secretary of Navy	Gideon Welles	1865-1869
Secretary of Interior	John P. Usher	1865
	James Harlan	1865-1866
	Orville H. Browning	1866-1869

The Grant Administration

Secretary of State	Elihu B. Washburne	1869
	Hamilton Fish	1869-1877
Secretary of Treasury	George S. Boutwell	1869-1873
	William Richardson	1873-1874
	Benjamin Bristow	1874-1876
	Lot M. Morrill	1876-1877
Secretary of War	John A. Rawlins	1869
	William T. Sherman	1869
	William W. Belknap	1869-1876
	Alphonso Taft	1876
	James D. Cameron	1876-1877
Attorney General	Ebenezer Hoar	1869-1870
	Amos T. Ackerman	1870-1871
	G. H. Williams	1871-1875
	Edwards Pierrepont	1875-1876
	Alphonso Taft	1876-1877
Postmaster General	John A. Creswell	1869-1874
	James W. Marshall	1874
	Marshall Jewell	1874-1876
	James N. Tyner	1876-1877
Secretary of Navy	Adolph E. Borie	1869
	George M. Robeson	1869-1877
Secretary of Interior	Jacob D. Cox	1869-1870
	Columbus Delano	1870-1875

Secretary of Interior	Zachariah Chandler	1875-1877

The Hayes Administration

Secretary of State	William B. Evarts	1877-1881
Secretary of Treasury	John Sherman	1877-1881
Secretary of War	George W. McCrary Alex Ramsey	1877-1879 1879-1881
Attorney General	Charles Devens	1877-1881
Postmaster General	David M. Key Horace Maynard	1877-1880 1880-1881
Secretary of Navy	Richard W. Thompson Nathan Goff, Jr.	1877-1880 1881
Secretary of Interior	Carl Shurz	1877-1881

The Garfield Administration

Secretary of State	James G. Blaine	1881
Secretary of Treasury	William Windom	1881
Secretary of War	Robert T. Lincoln	1881
Attorney General	Wayne MacVeagh	1881
Postmaster General	Thomas L. James	1881
Secretary of Navy	William H. Hunt	1881
Secretary of Interior	Samuel J. Kirkwood	1881

The Arthur Administration

Secretary of State	F. T. Frelinghuysen	1881-1885
Secretary of Treasury	Charles J. Folger Walter Q. Gresham Hugh McCulloch	1881-1884 1884 1884-1885
Secretary of War	Robert T. Lincoln	1881-1885
Attorney General	Benjamin H. Brewster	1881-1885
Postmaster General	Timothy O. Howe Walter Q. Gresham Frank Hatton	1881-1883 1883-1884 1884-1885
Secretary of Navy	William H. Hunt William E. Chandler	1881-1882 1882-1885
Secretary of Interior	Samuel J. Kirkwood Henry M. Teller	1881-1882 1882-1885

The Cleveland Administration (first)

Secretary of State	Thomas F. Bayard	1885-1889
Secretary of Treasury	Daniel Manning Charles S. Fairchild	1885-1887 1887-1889
Secretary of War	William C. Endicott	1885-1889
Attorney General	Augustus H. Garland	1885-1889
Postmaster General	William F. Vilas Don M. Dickinson	1885-1888 1888-1889
Secretary of Navy	William C. Whitney	1885-1889
Secretary of Interior	Lucius Q. C. Lamar William F. Vilas	1885-1889 1888-1889
Secretary of Agriculture	Norman J. Colman	1889

The Benjamin Harrison Administration

Secretary of State	James G. Blaine John W. Foster	1889-1892 1892-1893
Secretary of Treasury	William Windom Charles Foster	1889-1891 1891-1893
Secretary of War	Redfield Proctor Stephen B. Elkins	1889-1891 1891-1893
Attorney General	William H. H. Miller	1889-1891
Postmaster General	John Wanamaker	1889-1893
Secretary of Navy	Benjamin F. Tracy	1889-1893
Secretary of Interior	John W. Noble	1889-1893
Secretary of Agriculture	Jeremiah M. Rusk	1889-1893

The Cleveland Administration (second)

Secretary of State	Walter Q. Gresham Richard Olney	1893-1895 1895-1897
Secretary of Treasury	John G. Carlisle	1893-1897
Secretary of War	Daniel S. Lamont	1893-1897
Attorney General	Richard Olney James Harmon	1893-1895 1895-1897
Postmaster General	Wilson S. Bissell William L. Wilson	1893-1895 1895-1897
Secretary of Navy	Hilary A. Herbert	1893-1897
Secretary of Interior	Hoke Smith David R. Francis	1893-1896 1896-1897

Secretary of Agriculture	Julius S. Morton	1893-1897

The McKinley Administration

Secretary of State	John Sherman	1897-1898
	William R. Day	1898
	John Hay	1898-1901
Secretary of Treasury	Lyman J. Gage	1897-1901
Secretary of War	Russell A. Alger	1897-1899
	Elihu Root	1899-1901
Attorney General	Joseph McKenna	1897-1898
	John W. Griggs	1898-1901
	Philander C. Knox	1901
Postmaster General	James A. Gary	1897-1898
	Charles E. Smith	1898-1901
Secretary of Navy	John D. Long	1897-1901
Secretary of Interior	Cornelius N. Bliss	1897-1899
	Ethan A. Hitchcock	1899-1901
Secretary of Agriculture	James Wilson	1897-1901

The Theodore Roosevelt Administration

Secretary of State	John Hay	1901-1905
	Elihu Root	1905-1909
	Robert Bacon	1909
Secretary of Treasury	Lyman J. Gage	1901-1902
	Leslie M. Shaw	1902-1907
	George B. Cortelyou	1907-1909
Secretary of War	Elihu Root	1901-1904
	William H. Taft	1904-1908
	Luke E. Wright	1908-1909
Attorney General	Philander C. Knox	1901-1904
	William H. Moody	1904-1906
	Charles J. Bonaparte	1906-1909
Postmaster General	Charles E. Smith	1901-1902
	Henry C. Payne	1902-1904
	Robert J. Wynne	1904-1905
	George B. Cortelyou	1905-1907
	George von L. Meyer	1907-1909
Secretary of Navy	John D. Long	1901-1902
	William H. Moody	1902-1904
	Paul Morton	1904-1905
	Charles J. Bonaparte	1905-1906
	Victor H. Metcalf	1906-1908
	Truman N. Newberry	1908-1909
Secretary of Interior	Ethan A. Hitchcock	1901-1907
	James R. Garfield	1907-1909
Secretary of Agriculture	James Wilson	1901-1909
Secretary of Labor and Commerce	George B. Cortelyou	1903-1904
	Victor H. Metcalf	1904-1906
	Oscar S. Straus	1906-1909
	Charles Nagel	1909

The Taft Administration

Secretary of State	Philander C. Knox	1909-1913
Secretary of Treasury	Franklin MacVeagh	1909-1913
Secretary of War	Jacob M. Dickinson	1909-1911
	Henry L. Stimson	1911-1913
Attorney General	George W. Wickersham	1909-1913
Postmaster General	Frank H. Hitchcock	1909-1913
Secretary of Navy	George von L. Meyer	1909-1913
Secretary of Interior	Richard A. Ballinger	1909-1911
	Walter L. Fisher	1911-1913
Secretary of Agriculture	James Wilson	1909-1913
Secretary of Labor and Commerce	Charles Nagel	1909-1913

The Wilson Administration

Secretary of State	William J. Bryan	1913-1915
	Robert Lansing	1915-1920
	Bainbridge Colby	1920-1921
Secretary of Treasury	William G. McAdoo	1913-1918
	Carter Glass	1918-1920
	David F. Houston	1920-1921
Secretary of War	Lindley M. Garrison	1913-1916
	Newton D. Baker	1916-1921
Attorney General	James C. McReynolds	1913-1914
	Thomas W. Gregory	1914-1919
	A. Mitchell Palmer	1919-1921
Postmaster General	Albert S. Burleson	1913-1921
Secretary of Navy	Josephus Daniels	1913-1921
Secretary of Interior	Franklin K. Lane	1913-1920
	John B. Payne	1920-1921
Secretary of Agriculture	David F. Houston	1913-1919
	Edwin T. Meredith	1919-1921
Secretary of Commerce	William C. Redfield	1913-1919
	Joshua W. Alexander	1919-1921
Secretary of Labor	William B. Wilson	1913-1921

The Harding Administration

Secretary of State	Charles E. Hughes	1921-1923
Secretary of Treasury	Andrew Mellon	1921-1923
Secretary of War	John W. Weeks	1921-1923

Attorney General	Harry M. Daugherty	1921-1923
Postmaster General	Will H. Hays	1921-1922
	Hubert Work	1922-1923
	Harry S. New	1923
Secretary of Navy	Edwin Denby	1921-1923
Secretary of Interior	Albert B. Fall	1921-1923
	Hubert Work	1923
Secretary of Agriculture	Henry C. Wallace	1921-1923
Secretary of Commerce	Herbert C. Hoover	1921-1923
Secretary of Labor	James J. Davis	1921-1923

The Coolidge Administration

Secretary of State	Charles B. Hughes	1923-1925
	Frank B. Kellogg	1925-1929
Secretary of Treasury	Andrew Mellon	1923-1929
Secretary of War	John W. Weeks	1923-1925
	Dwight F. Davis	1925-1929
Attorney General	Henry M. Daugherty	1923-1924
	Harlan F. Stone	1924-1925
	John G. Sargent	1925-1929
Postmaster General	Harry S. New	1923-1929
Secretary of Navy	Edwin Denby	1923-1924
	Curtis D. Wilbur	1924-1929
Secretary of Interior	Hubert Work	1923-1928
	Roy O. West	1928-1929
Secretary of Agriculture	Henry C. Wallace	1923-1924
	Howard M. Gore	1924-1925
	William M. Jardine	1925-1929
Secretary of Commerce	Herbert C. Hoover	1923-1928
	William F. Whiting	1928-1929
Secretary of Labor	James J. Davis	1923-1929

The Hoover Administration

Secretary of State	Henry L. Stimson	1929-1933
Secretary of Treasury	Andrew Mellon	1929-1932
	Ogden L. Mills	1932-1933
Secretary of War	James W. Good	1929
	Patrick J. Hurley	1929-1933
Attorney General	William D. Mitchell	1929-1933
Postmaster General	Walter F. Brown	1929-1933
Secretary of Navy	Charles F. Adams	1929-1933

Secretary of Interior	Ray L. Wilbur	1929-1933
Secretary of Agriculture	Arthur M. Hyde	1929-1933
Secretary of Commerce	Robert P. Lamont	1929-1932
	Roy D. Chapin	1932-1933
Secretary of Labor	James J. Davis	1929-1930
	William N. Doak	1930-1933

The Franklin D. Roosevelt Administration

Secretary of State	Cordell Hull	1933-1944
	E. R. Stettinius, Jr.	1944-1945
Secretary of Treasury	William H. Woodin	1933-1934
	Henry Morgenthau, Jr.	1934-1945
Secretary of War	George H. Dern	1933-1936
	Henry A. Woodring	1936-1940
	Henry L. Stimson	1940-1945
Attorney General	Homer S. Cummings	1933-1939
	Frank Murphy	1939-1940
	Robert H. Jackson	1940-1941
	Francis Biddle	1941-1945
Postmaster General	James A. Farley	1933-1940
	Frank C. Walker	1940-1945
Secretary of Navy	Claude A. Swanson	1933-1940
	Charles Edison	1940
	Frank Knox	1940-1944
	James V. Forrestal	1944-1945
Secretary of Interior	Harold L. Ickes	1933-1945
Secretary of Agriculture	Henry A. Wallace	1933-1940
	Claude R. Wickard	1940-1945
Secretary of Commerce	Daniel C. Roper	1933-1939
	Harry L. Hopkins	1939-1940
	Jesse Jones	1940-1945
	Henry A. Wallace	1945
Secretary of Labor	Frances Perkins	1933-1945

The Truman Administration

Secretary of State	James F. Byrnes	1945-1947
	George C. Marshall	1947-1949
	Dean G. Acheson	1949-1953
Secretary of Treasury	Fred M. Vinson	1945-1946
	John W. Snyder	1946-1953
Secretary of War	Robert P. Patterson	1945-1947
	Kenneth C. Royall	1947
Attorney General	Tom C. Clark	1945-1949
	J. Howard McGrath	1949-1952
	James P. McGranery	1952-1953
Postmaster General	Frank C. Walker	1945
	Robert E. Hannegan	1945-1947
	Jessee M. Donaldson	1947-1953
Secretary of Navy	James V. Forrestal	1945-1947

Secretary of Interior	Harold L. Ickes	1945-1946
	Julius A. Krug	1946-1949
	Oscar I. Chapman	1949-1953
Secretary of Agriculture	Clinton P. Anderson	1945-1948
	Charles F. Brannan	1948-1953
Secretary of Commerce	Henry A. Wallace	1945-1946
	W. Averell Harriman	1946-1948
	Charles W. Sawyer	1948-1953
Secretary of Labor	Lewis B. Schwellenbach	1945-1948
	Maurice J. Tobin	1948-1953
Secretary of Defense	James V. Forrestal	1947-1949
	Louis A. Johnson	1949-1950
	George C. Marshall	1950-1951
	Robert A. Lovett	1951-1953

The Eisenhower Administration

Secretary of State	John Foster Dulles	1953-1959
	Christian A. Herter	1959-1961
Secretary of Treasury	George M. Humphrey	1953-1957
	Robert B. Anderson	1957-1961
Attorney General	Herbert Brownell, Jr.	1953-1958
	William P. Rogers	1958-1961
Postmaster General	Arthur E. Summerfield	1953-1961
Secretary of Interior	Douglas McKay	1953-1956
	Fred A. Seaton	1956-1961
Secretary of Agriculture	Ezra T. Benson	1953-1961
Secretary of Commerce	Sinclair Weeks	1953-1958
	Lewis L. Strauss	1958-1959
	Frederick H. Mueller	1959-1961
Secretary of Labor	Martin P. Durkin	1953
	James P. Mitchell	1953-1961
Secretary of Defense	Charles E. Wilson	1953-1957
	Neil H. McElroy	1957-1959
	Thomas S. Gates, Jr.	1959-1961
Secretary of Health, Education and Welfare	Oveta Culp Hobby	1953-1955
	Marion B. Folsom	1955-1958
	Arthur S. Flemming	1958-1961

The Kennedy Administration

Secretary of State	Dean Rusk	1961-1963
Secretary of Treasury	C. Douglas Dillon	1961-1963
Attorney General	Robert F. Kennedy	1961-1963
Postmaster General	J. Edward Day	1961-1963
	John A. Gronouski	1963
Secretary of Interior	Stewart L. Udall	
Secretary of Agriculture	Orville L. Freeman	1961-1963

Secretary of Commerce	Luther H. Hodges	1961-1963
Secretary of Labor	Arthur J. Goldberg	1961-1962
	W. Williard Wirtz	1962-1963
Secretary of Defense	Robert F. McNamara	1961-1963
Secretary of Health, Education and Welfare	Abraham A. Ribicoff	1961-1962
	Anthony J. Celebrezze	1962-1963

The Lyndon Johnson Administration

Secretary of State	Dean Rusk	1963-1969
Secretary of Treasury	C. Douglas Dillon	1963-1965
	Henry H. Fowler	1965-1969
Attorney General	Robert F. Kennedy	1963-1964
	Nicholas Katzenbach	1965-1966
	Ramsey Clark	1967-1969
Postmaster General	John A. Gronouski	1963-1965
	Lawrence F. O'Brien	1965-1968
	Marvin Watson	1968-1969
Secretary of Interior	Stewart L. Udall	1963-1969
Secretary of Agriculture	Orville L. Freeman	1963-1969
Secretary of Commerce	Luther H. Hodges	1963-1964
	John T. Connor	1964-1967
	Alexander B. Trowbridge	1967-1968
	Cyrus R. Smith	1968-1969
Secretary of Labor	W. Willard Wirtz	1963-1969
Secretary of Defense	Robert F. McNamara	1963-1968
	Clark Clifford	1968-1969
Secretary of Health, Education and Welfare	Anthony J. Celebrezze	1962-1963
	John W. Gardner	1965-1968
	Wilbur J. Cohen	1968-1969
Secretary of Housing and Urban Development	Robert C. Weaver	1966-1969
	Robert C. Wood	1969
Secretary of Transportation	Alan S. Boyd	1967-1969

The Nixon Administration

Secretary of State	William P. Rogers	1969-1973
	Henry A. Kissinger	1973-1974
Secretary of Treasury	David M. Kennedy	1969-1970
	John B. Connally	1971-1972
	George P. Shultz	1972-1974
	William E. Smon	1974
Attorney General	John N. Mitchell	1969-1972
	Richard G. Kleindienst	1972-1973

	Elliot L. Richardson	1973
	William B. Saxbe	1973-1974
Postmaster General	Winton M. Blount	1969-1971
Secretary of Interior	Walter J. Hickel	1969-1970
	Rogers Morton	1971-1974
Secretary of Agriculture	Clifford M. Hardin	1969-1971
	Earl L. Butz	1971-1974
Secretary of Commerce	Maurice H. Stans	1969-1972
	Peter G. Peterson	1972-1973
	Frederick B. Dent	1973-1974
Secretary of Labor	George P. Shultz	1969-1970
	James D. Hodgson	1970-1973
	Peter J. Brennan	1973-1974
Secretary of Defense	Melvin R. Laird	1969-1973
	Elliot L. Richardson	1973
	James R. Schlesinger	1973-1974
Secretary of Health, Education and Welfare	Robert H. Finch	1969-1970
	Elliot L. Richardson	1970-1973
	Caspar W. Weinberger	1973-1974
Secretary of Housing and Urban Development	George Romney	1969-1973
	James T. Lynn	1973-1974
Secretary of Transportation	John A. Volpe	1969-1973
	Claude S. Brinegar	1973-1974

The Ford Administration

Secretary of State	Henry A. Kissinger	1974-1977
Secretary of Treasury	William E. Simon	1974-1977
Attorney General	William B. Saxbe	1974-1975
	Edward Levi	1975-1977
Secretary of Interior	Rogers Morton	1974-1975
	Stanley K. Hathaway	1975
	Thomas Kleppe	1975-1977
Secretary of Agriculture	Earl L. Butz	1974-1976
	John A. Knebel	1976-1977
Secretary of Commerce	Frederick B. Dent	1974-1975
	Rogers Morton	1975-1976
	Elliot L. Richardson	1976-1977
Secretary of Labor	Peter J. Brennan	1974-1975
	John T. Dunlop	1975-1976
	W. J. Usery	1976-1977
Secretary of Defense	James R. Schlesinger	1974-1975
	Donald Rumsfeld	1975-1977
Secretary of Health, Education and Welfare	Caspar Weinberger	1974-1975
	Forrest D. Mathews	1975-1977
Secretary of Housing and Urban Development	James T. Lynn	1973-1974
	Carla A. Hills	1975-1977

Secretary of Transportation	Claude S. Brinegar	1974-1975
	William T. Coleman	1975-1977

The Carter Administration

Secretary of State	Cyrus R. Vance	1977-1980
	Edmund Muskie	1980-1981
Secretary of Treasury	W. Michael Blumenthal	1977-1979
	G. William Miller	1979-1981
Attorney General	Griffin Bell	1977-1979
	Benjamin R. Civiletti	1979-1981
Secretary of Interior	Cecil D. Andrus	1977-1981
Secretary of Agriculture	Robert Bergland	1977-1981
Secretary of Commerce	Juanita M. Kreps	1977-1979
	Philip M. Klutznick	1979-1981
Secretary of Labor	F. Ray Marshall	1977-1981
Secretary of Defense	Harold Brown	1977-1981
Secretary of Health, Education and Welfare	Joseph A. Califano	1977-1979
	Patricia R. Harris	1979
Secretary of Health and Human Services	Patricia R. Harris	1979-1981
Secretary of Education	Shirley M. Hufstedler	1979-1981
Secretary of Housing and Urban Development	Patricia R. Harris	1977-1979
	Moon Landrieu	1979-1981
Secretary of Transportation	Brock Adams	1977-1979
	Neil E. Goldschmidt	1979-1981
Secretary of Energy	James R. Schlesinger	1977-1979
	Charles W. Duncan	1979-1981

The Reagan Administration

Secretary of State	Alexander M. Haig	1981-1982
	George P. Shultz	1982-1989
Secretary of Treasury	Donald T. Regan	1981-1985
	James A. Baker	1985-1988
	Nicholas Brady	1988-1989
Attorney General	William French Smith	1981-1985
	Edwin Meese	1985-1988
	Richard Thornburgh	1988-1989
Secretary of Interior	James Watt	1981-1983
	William P. Clark	1983-1985
	Donald Hodel	1985-1989
Secretary of Agriculture	John R. Block	1981-1985
	Richard E. Lyng	1985-1989
Secretary of Commerce	Malcolm Baldrige	1981-1987
	C. William Verity	1987-1989

Secretary of Labor	Raymond J. Donovan	1981-1985
	William E. Brock	1985-1988
	Ann Dore McLaughlin	1988-1989
Secretary of Defense	Caspar W. Weinberger	1981-1988
	Frank C. Carlucci	1988-1989
Secretary of Health and Human Services	Richard S. Schweiker	1981-1983
	Margaret M. Heckler	1983-1985
	Otis R. Bowen	1985-1989
Secretary of Education	Terrel H. Bell	1981-1985
	William J. Bennett	1985-1988
	Lauro F. Cavazos	1988-1989
Secretary of Housing and Urban Development	Samuel R. Pierce, Jr.	1981-1989
Secretary of Transportation	Drew Lewis	1981-1983
	Elizabeth H. Dole	1983-1987
	James L. Burnely	1987-1989
Secretary of Energy	James B. Edwards	1981-1982
	Donald P. Hodel	1982-1985
	John S. Herrington	1985-1989

The Bush Administration

Secretary of State	James A. Baker	1989-1992
	Lawrence S. Eagleburger	1992-1993
Secretary of Treasury	Nicholas F. Brady	1989-1993
Attorney General	Richard Thornburgh	1989-1992
	William P. Barr	1992-1993
Secretary of Interior	Manuel Lujan	1989-1993
Secretary of Agriculture	Clayton Yeutter	1989-1991
	Edward Madigan	1991-1993
Secretary of Commerce	Robert Mosbacher	1989-1992
	Barbara H. Franklin	1992-1993
Secretary of Labor	Elizabeth H. Dole	1989-1991
	Lynn Martin	1991-1993
Secretary of Defense	Richard B. Cheney	1989-1993
Secretary of Health and Human Services	Louis W. Sullivan	1989-1993
Secretary of Housing and Urban Development	Jack F. Kemp	1989-1993

Secretary of Transportation	Samuel Skinner	1989-1992
	Andrew Card	1992-1993
Secretary of Energy	James D. Watkins	1989-1993
Secretary of Education	Lauro F. Cavazos	1989-1991
	Lamar Alexander	1991-1993
Secretary of Veterans Affairs	Edward J. Derwinski	1989-1993

The Clinton Administration

Secretary of State	Warren M. Christopher	1993-
Secretary of Treasury	Lloyd Bentsen	1993-
Attorney General	Janet Reno	1993-
Secretary of Interior	Bruce Babbitt	1993-
Secretary of Agriculture	Mike Espy	1993-1994
Secretary of Commerce	Ronald Brown	1993-
Secretary of Labor	Robert R. Reich	1993-
Secretary of Defense	Les Aspin	1993-1994
	William Perry	1994-
Secretary of Health and Human Services	Donna Shalala	1993-
Secretary of Housing and Urban Development	Henry G. Cisneros	1993-
Secretary of Transportation	Federico F. Peña	1993-
Secretary of Energy	Hazel R. O'Leary	1993-
Secretary of Education	Richard W. Riley	1993-
Secretary of Veterans Affairs	Jesse Brown	1993-

Supreme Court Justices

Name	Terms of Service[1]	Appointed by	Name	Terms of Service[1]	Appointed by
John Jay	1789–1795	Washington	Rufus W. Peckham	1896–1909	Cleveland
James Wilson	1789–1798	Washington	Joseph McKenna	1898–1925	McKinley
John Rutledge	1790–1791	Washington	Oliver W. Holmes	1902–1932	T. Roosevelt
William Cushing	1790–1810	Washington	William R. Day	1903–1922	T. Roosevelt
John Blair	1790–1796	Washington	William H. Moody	1906–1910	T. Roosevelt
James Iredell	1790–1799	Washington	Horace H. Lurton	1910–1914	Taft
Thomas Johnson	1792–1793	Washington	Charles E. Hughes	1910–1916	Taft
William Paterson	1793–1806	Washington	Willis Van Devanter	1911–1937	Taft
John Rutledge[1]	1795	Washington	Joseph R. Lamar	1911–1916	Taft
Samuel Chase	1796–1811	Washington	**Edward D. White**	1910–1921	Taft
Oliver Ellsworth	1796–1800	Washington	Mahlon Pitney	1912–1922	Taft
Bushrod Washington	1799–1829	J. Adams	James C. McReynolds	1914–1941	Wilson
Alfred Moore	1800–1804	J. Adams	Louis D. Brandeis	1916–1939	Wilson
John Marshall	1801–1835	J. Adams	John H. Clarke	1916–1922	Wilson
William Johnson	1804–1834	Jefferson	**William H. Taft**	1921–1930	Harding
William Johnson	1804–1834	Jefferson	George Sutherland	1922–1938	Harding
Brockholst Livingston	1807–1823	Jefferson	Pierce Butler	1923–1939	Harding
Thomas Todd	1807–1826	Jefferson	Edward T. Sanford	1923–1930	Harding
Gabriel Duval	1811–1835	Madison	Harlan F. Stone	1925–1941	Coolidge
Joseph Story	1812–1845	Madison	**Charles E. Hughes**	1930–1941	Hoover
Smith Thompson	1823–1843	Monroe	Owen J. Roberts	1930–1945	Hoover
Robert Trimble	1826–1828	J. Q. Adams	Benjamin N. Cardozo	1932–1938	Hoover
John McLean	1830–1861	Jackson	Hugo L. Black	1937–1971	F. Roosevelt
Henry Baldwin	1830–1844	Jackson	Stanley F. Reed	1938–1957	F. Roosevelt
James M. Wayne	1835–1867	Jackson	Felix Frankfurter	1939–1962	F. Roosevelt
Roger B. Taney	1836–1864	Jackson	William O. Douglas	1939–1975	F. Roosevelt
Philip P. Barbour	1836–1841	Jackson	Frank Murphy	1940–1949	F. Roosevelt
John Cartron	1837–1865	Van Buren	**Harlan F. Stone**	1941–1946	F. Roosevelt
John McKinley	1838–1852	Van Buren	James F. Byrnes	1941–1942	F. Roosevelt
Peter V. Daniel	1842–1860	Van Buren	Robert H. Jackson	1941–1954	F. Roosevelt
Samuel Nelson	1845–1872	Tyler	Wiley B. Rutledge	1943–1949	F. Roosevelt
Levi Woodbury	1845–1851	Polk	Harold H. Burton	1945–1958	Truman
Robert C. Grier	1846–1870	Polk	**Frederick M. Vinson**	1946–1953	Truman
Benjamin R. Curtis	1851–1857	Fillmore	Tom C. Clark	1949–1967	Truman
John A. Campbell	1853–1861	Pierce	Sherman Minton	1949–1956	Truman
Nathan Clifford	1858–1881	Buchanan	**Earl Warren**	1953–1969	Eisenhower
Noah H. Swayne	1862–1881	Lincoln	John Marshall Harlan	1955–1971	Eisenhower
Samuel F. Miller	1862–1890	Lincoln	William J. Brennan, Jr.	1956–1990	Eisenhower
David Davis	1862–1877	Lincoln	Charles E. Whittaker	1957–1962	Eisenhower
Stephen J. Field	1863–1897	Lincoln	Potter Stewart	1958–1981	Eisenhower
Salmon P. Chase	1864–1873	Lincoln	Byron R. White	1962–1993	Kennedy
William Strong	1870–1880	Grant	Arthur J. Goldberg	1962–1965	Kennedy
Joseph P. Bradley	1870–1892	Grant	Abe Fortas	1965–1969	Johnson
Ward Hunt	1873–1882	Grant	Thurgood Marshall	1967–1991	Johnson
Morrison R. Waite	1873–1882	Grant	**Warren E. Burger**	1969–1986	Nixon
John M. Harlan	1877–1911	Hayes	Harry A. Blackmun	1970–1994	Nixon
William B. Woods	1881–1887	Hayes	Lewis F. Powell, Jr.	1971–1987	Nixon
Stanley Matthews	1881–1889	Garfield	William H. Rehnquist	1971–1986	Nixon
Horace Gray	1882–1902	Arthur	John Paul Stevens	1975–	Ford
Samuel Blatchford	1882–1893	Arthur	Sandra Day O'Connor	1981–	Reagan
Lucius Q. C. Lamar	1888–1893	Cleveland	**William H. Rehnquist**	1986–	Reagan
Melville W. Fuller	1888–1910	Cleveland	Antonin Scalia	1986–	Reagan
David J. Brewer	1890–1910	B. Harrison	Anthony M. Kennedy	1988–	Reagan
Henry B. Brown	1891–1906	B. Harrison	David H. Souter	1990–	Bush
George Shiras, Jr.	1892–1903	B. Harrison	Clarence Thomas	1991–	Bush
Howell E. Jackson	1893–1895	B. Harrison	Ruth Bader Ginsburg	1992–	Clinton
Edward D. White	1894–1910	Cleveland	Stephen G. Breyer	1994–	Clinton

Chief Justices in bold type.

[1]The date on which the justice took his judicial oath is here used as the date of the beginning of his service, for until that oath is taken he is not vested with the prerogatives of his office. Justices, however, receive their commissions ("letters patent") before taking their oath—in some instances, in the preceding year.

[2]Acting Chief Justice; Senate refused to confirm appointment.

Admission of States into the Union

State	Date of Admission	State	Date of Admission
1. Delaware	December 7, 1787	26. Michigan	January 26, 1837
2. Pennsylvania	December 12, 1787	27. Florida	March 3, 1845
3. New Jersey	December 18, 1787	28. Texas	December 29, 1845
4. Georgia	January 2, 1788	29. Iowa	December 28, 1846
5. Connecticut	January 9, 1788	30. Wisconsin	May 29, 1848
6. Massachusetts	February 6, 1788	31. California	September 9, 1850
7. Maryland	April 28, 1788	32. Minnesota	May 11, 1858
8. South Carolina	May 23, 1788	33. Oregon	February 14, 1859
9. New Hampshire	June 21, 1788	34. Kansas	January 29, 1861
10. Virginia	June 25, 1788	35. West Virginia	June 20, 1863
11. New York	July 26, 1788	36. Nevada	October 31, 1864
12. North Carolina	November 21, 1789	37. Nebraska	March 1, 1867
13. Rhode Island	May 29, 1790	38. Colorado	August 1, 1876
14. Vermont	March 4, 1791	39. North Dakota	November 2, 1889
15. Kentucky	June 1, 1792	40. South Dakota	November 2, 1889
16. Tennessee	June 1, 1796	41. Montana	November 8, 1889
17. Ohio	March 1, 1803	42. Washington	November 11, 1889
18. Louisiana	April 30, 1812	43. Idaho	July 3, 1890
19. Indiana	December 11, 1816	44. Wyoming	July 10, 1890
20. Mississippi	December 10, 1817	45. Utah	January 4, 1896
21. Illinois	December 3, 1818	46. Oklahoma	November 16, 1907
22. Alabama	December 14, 1819	47. New Mexico	January 6, 1912
23. Maine	March 15, 1820	48. Arizona	February 14, 1912
24. Missouri	August 10, 1821	49. Alaska	January 3, 1959
25. Arkansas	June 15, 1836	50. Hawaii	August 21, 1959

Ten Largest Cities by Population, 1700–1990

	City	Population		City	Population
1700	Boston	6,700		St. Louis	687,029
	New York	4,937		Boston	670,585
	Philadelphia	4,400		Cleveland	560,663
				Baltimore	558,485
1790	Philadelphia	42,520		Pittsburgh	533,905
	New York	33,131		Detroit	465,766
	Boston	18,038		Buffalo	423,715
	Charleston, S.C.	16,359			
	Baltimore	13,503	1930	New York	6,930,446
	Salem, Mass.	7,921		Chicago	3,376,438
	Newport, R.I.	6,716		Philadelphia	1,950,961
	Providence, R.I.	6,380		Detroit	1,568,662
	Marblehead, Mass.	5,661		Los Angeles	1,238,048
	Portsmouth, N.H.	4,720		Cleveland	900,429
				St. Louis	821,960
1830	New York	197,112		Baltimore	804,874
	Philadelphia	161,410		Boston	781,188
	Baltimore	80,620		Pittsburgh	669,817
	Boston	61,392			
	Charleston, S.C.	30,289	1950	New York	7,891,957
	New Orleans	29,737		Chicago	3,620,962
	Cincinnati	24,831		Philadelphia	2,071,605
	Albany, N.Y.	24,209		Los Angeles	1,970,358
	Brooklyn, N.Y.	20,535		Detroit	1,849,568
	Washington, D.C.	18,826		Baltimore	949,708
				Cleveland	914,808
1850	New York	515,547		St. Louis	856,796
	Philadelphia	340,045		Washington, D.C.	802,178
	Baltimore	169,054		Boston	801,444
	Boston	136,881			
	New Orleans	116,375	1970	New York	7,895,563
	Cincinnati	115,435		Chicago	3,369,357
	Brooklyn, N.Y.	96,838		Los Angeles	2,811,801
	St. Louis	77,860		Philadelphia	1,949,996
	Albany, N.Y.	50,763		Detroit	1,514,063
	Pittsburgh	46,601		Houston	1,233,535
				Baltimore	905,787
1870	New York	942,292		Dallas	844,401
	Philadelphia	674,022		Washington, D.C.	756,668
	Brooklyn, N.Y.	419,921		Cleveland	750,879
	St. Louis	310,864			
	Chicago	298,977	1990	New York	7,322,564
	Baltimore	267,354		Los Angeles	3,485,398
	Boston	250,526		Chicago	2,783,726
	Cincinnati	216,239		Houston	1,630,553
	New Orleans	191,418		Philadelphia	1,585,577
	San Francisco	149,473		San Diego	1,110,549
				Detroit	1,027,974
1910	New York	4,766,883		Dallas	1,006,877
	Chicago	2,185,283		Phoenix	983,403
	Philadelphia	1,549,008		San Antonio	935,933

A Demographic Profile of the American People

Life Expectancy, 1900–1992

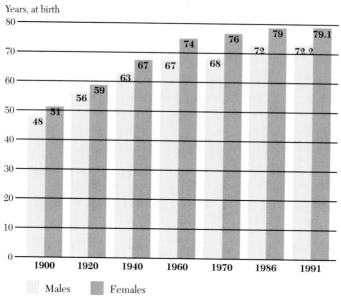

Years, at birth

Males Females

Source: U.S. Bureau of the Census, Statistical Abstract of the United States: 1993, *Washington, D.C., 1993.*

Birthrate, 1820–1992

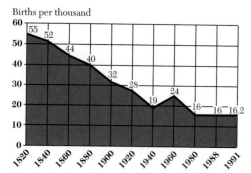

Births per thousand

Source: U.S. Bureau of the Census, Statistical Abstract of the United States: 1993, *Washington, D.C., 1993.*

Death Rate, 1900–1992

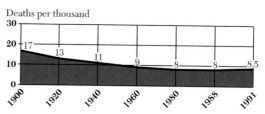

Deaths per thousand

Source: U.S. Bureau of the Census, Statistical Abstract of the United States: 1993, *Washington, D.C., 1993.*

Women in the Labor Force, 1890–1988

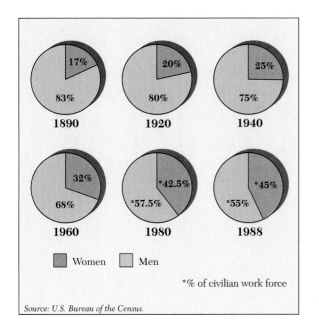

1890 — 17% / 83%
1920 — 20% / 80%
1940 — 25% / 75%
1960 — 32% / 68%
1980 — °42.5% / °57.5%
1988 — °45% / °55%

■ Women   ■ Men

°% of civilian work force

Source: U.S. Bureau of the Census.

Urban/Rural Population, 1750–1990

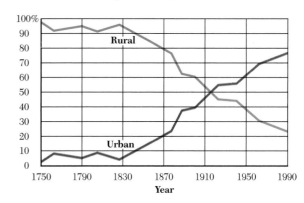

Rural

Urban

Year

Origin of Immigrants, 1820–1988

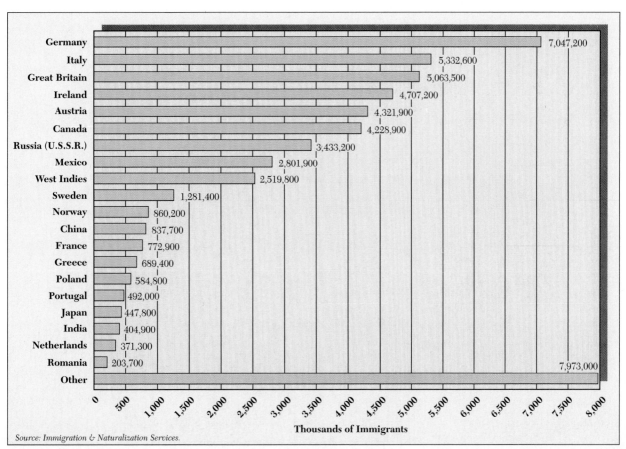

Country	Thousands of Immigrants
Germany	7,047,200
Italy	5,332,600
Great Britain	5,063,500
Ireland	4,707,200
Austria	4,321,900
Canada	4,228,900
Russia (U.S.S.R.)	3,433,200
Mexico	2,801,900
West Indies	2,519,800
Sweden	1,281,400
Norway	860,200
China	837,700
France	772,900
Greece	689,400
Poland	584,800
Portugal	492,000
Japan	447,800
India	404,900
Netherlands	371,300
Romania	203,700
Other	7,973,000

Source: Immigration & Naturalization Services.

Ethnic Diversity of the United States

The classifications on this map suggest the pluralism of American society but fail to reflect completely the nation's ethnic diversity.

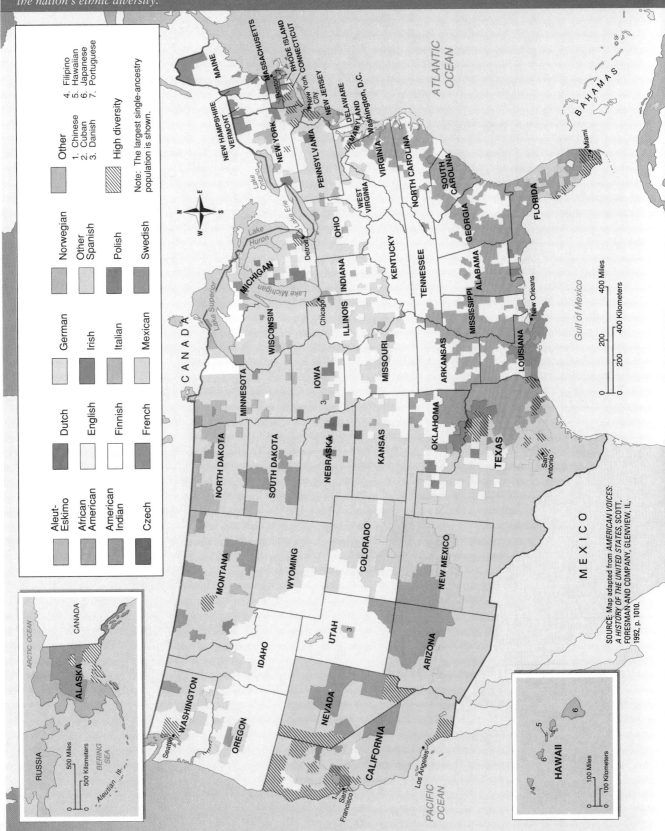

Other

1. Chinese
2. Cuban
3. Danish

4. Filipino
5. Hawaiian
6. Japanese
7. Portuguese

High diversity

Note: The largest single-ancestry population is shown.

Aleut-Eskimo
African American
American Indian
Czech
Dutch
English
Finnish
French
German
Irish
Italian
Mexican
Norwegian
Other Spanish
Polish
Swedish

SOURCE: Map adapted from *AMERICAN VOICES: A HISTORY OF THE UNITED STATES*, SCOTT, FORESMAN AND COMPANY, GLENVIEW, IL, 1992, p. 1010.

Credits

Photos

Unless otherwise acknowledged, all photographs are the property of Scott, Foresman & Company. Positions of the photographs are indicated in abbreviated forms as follows: T top, C center, B bottom, L left, R right.

viiT Print Collection, Miriam and Ira D. Wallach Division of Art, Prints, and Photography/New York Public Library, Astor, Lenox and Tilden Foundations viiB The Maryland Historical Society viiiT Courtesy American Antiquarian Society viiiC Courtesy, Virginia Historical Society viiiB Courtesy, Museum of Fine Arts, Boston ixT The New-York Historical Society, New York City ixC Lillian L. and John A. Harney Collection ixB Collection of Davenport West Jr. xT Historical Society of York County, Pennsylvania xC Century Association Company xB Library of Congress xiT St. Louis Art Museum; Purchase: The Eliza McMillan Fund xiC St. Louis Art Museum xiB The New-York Historical Society, New York City xiiT Courtesy The Museum of the Confederacy, Richmond, Va. xiiB 1867/Harper's Weekly

Chapter 1

1 Print Collection, Miriam and Ira D. Wallach Division of Art, Prints, and Photography/New York Public Library, Astor, Lenox and Tilden Foundations 3T From the Carta a Santangel Barcelona, 1493 4T Library of Congress 7 Ernest Haas 10L New York Public Library, Astor, Lenox and Tilden Foundations 10R New York Public Library, Astor, Lenox and Tilden Foundations 11T Biblioteca Medices Laurenziana/Biblioteca Medices Laurenziana 13T Bibliotheque Nationale, Paris 14 The Huntington Library and Art Gallery, San Marino, Ca. 15 Giraudon/Art Resource, New York 16 From Theodor de Bry *America* 1595/New York Public Library, Astor, Lenox and Tilden Foundations 19 Museo de America, Madrid/foto MAS 21 National Gallery of Art, Washington, D.C. 24 The Folger Shakespeare Library 27 Copyright the British Museum

Chapter 2

31 The Maryland Historical Society 36B Courtesy of the Edward E. Ayer Collection From Joan Blaeu: *Le Theatre du Monde 1646*/Courtesy of The Newberry Library, Chicago 36T New York Public Library, Astor, Lenox and Tilden Foundations 37 Ashmolean Museum, Oxford 38 National Portrait Gallery, Smithsonian Institution 39 Smithsonian Institution 41 Enoch Pratt Free Library, Baltimore 43 Peabody Essex Museum, Salem 44 Courtesy American Antiquarian Society 46 Massachusetts Historical Society 47 Historical Pictures/Stock Montage, Inc. 52 New York Public Library, Astor, Lenox and Tilden Foundations 53 New York Public Library, Astor, Lenox and Tilden Foundations 56 New York Public Library, Astor, Lenox and Tilden Foundations

Chapter 3

63 Courtesy American Antiquarian Society 65 Courtesy of the Harvard Law School Cambridge, MA 67TL New York Public Library, Astor, Lenox and Tilden Foundations 67TR New York Public Library, Astor, Lenox and Tilden Foundations 71 David Hiser/Photographers/Aspen 75 National Maritime Museum, Greenwich, England 76 Duke University Library, Durham, N. C. 78 Courtesy American Antiquarian Society 79 Abby Aldrich Rockefeller Folk Art Center 80 New York Public Library, Astor, Lenox and Tilden Foundations 84 Photograph by Ken Burris/Shelburne Museum, Shelburne, Vermont 85TL National Portrait Gallery, London 85TR National Portrait Gallery, London 87INS New York Public Library, Astor, Lenox and Tilden Foundations 87 Copyright the British Museum 91 North Wind Picture Archives 92 North Wind Picture Archives 93 Scott, Foresman

Chapter 4

98 Courtesy, Virginia Historical Society, Richmond 100 Special Collections Department/University of Virginia Library 102 Historical Society of Pennsylvania 103L National Gallery of Art, Washington, D.C. 104 The New-York Historical Society, New York City 107 Martin Rogers 108 Courtesy of Westover 110TR Library Company of Philadelphia 110TL Historical Society of Philadelphia 112ALL Library of Congress 113 Newport Historical Society 115 National Portrait Gallery, London 118 The Trustees of Sir John Soane's Museum 121 Albany Institute of History and Art 124 Copyright Yale University Art Gallery

Chapter 5

131 Courtesy, Museum of Fine Arts, Boston 133 The Colonial Williamsburg Foundation 136 Courtesy, Museum of Fine Arts, Boston 140 Bequest of Charles Allen Munn, 1924/The Metropolitan Museum of Art 143 Library of Congress 144 The New-York Historical Society, New York City 145 New York Public Library, Astor, Lenox and Tilden Foundations 148 Rare Book Division/New York Public Library, Astor, Lenox and Tilden Foundations 151 Chicago Historical Society 152TL Library of Congress 152TR National Portrait Gallery, London 153 Historical Society of Pennsylvania 156B Historical Society of Pennsylvania 162 The Connecticut Historical Society

New-York Historical Society, New York City **391** Melrose Plantation, Natchitoches, La., Photo by B. A. Cohen **392** State Historical Society of Wisconsin **395** Sophia Smith Collection, Smith College, Northampton, Ma. **397** The Historic New Orleans Collection **398** Library of Congress

Chapter 14

401 The New-York Historical Society, New York City **403** New York Public Library, Astor, Lenox and Tilden Foundations **406** Library of Congress **409** Chicago Public Library **412R** New York Public Library, Astor, Lenox and Tilden Foundations **412L** The Maryland Historical Society **414** The Kansas State Historical Society, Topeka **416** Stowe-Day Foundation **418** Frank Leslie's Illustrated Newspaper **420** Library of Congress **421** Library of Congress **422** The Ohio Historical Society **424** Library of Congress **426** Culver Pictures **433** Culver Pictures **434** Culver Pictures

Chapter 15

437 Courtesy The Museum of the Confederacy, Richmond, Va. **439** Chicago Historical Society **440** Library of Congress **445** Valentine Museum, Richmond, Virginia **447** Collection of Mrs. Nelson A. Rockefeller **448** Library of Congress **450** Library of Congress **451** Harper's Weekly **452** Chicago Historical Society **454** Library of Congress **456** From *Punch* **458** Lightfoot Collection **459** Library of Congress **461L** The Maryland Historical Society **461R** Chicago Historical Society **462L** The New-York Historical Society, New York City **463L** Library of Congress **463R** Library of Congress **467** Harper's Weekly

Chapter 16

471 1867/Harper's Weekly **473** The Granger Collection, New York **475** Library of Congress **477** Frank Leslie's Illustrated Newspaper **479** Courtesy Frank & Marie T. Wood/Print Collections, Alexandria, N. Y. **480** The National Archives **481** Historical Pictures/Stock Montage, Inc. **483** Courtesy Jay P. Altmayer **485T** The Historic New Orleans Collection **485B** Valentine Museum, Richmond, Virginia **487L** Library of Congress **487R** Bettmann Archive **489R** Bettmann Archive **489L** Culver Pictures **490** Bettmann Archive **491** Bettmann Archive **493** Rutherford B. Hayes Presidential Center, Fremont, Ohio **495** Culver Pictures **498** The Historic New Orleans Collection **499L** Brown Brothers **499R** Yale Joel © 1968/Life Magazine/Time Warner Inc.

Literary

In addition, the authors and publisher acknowledge with gratitude permission to reprint, quote from, or adapt the following materials. (The numbers shown below refer to pages of this text.)

74 (Map) Adapted from Philip D. Curtin, *Atlantic Slave Trade,* University of Wisconsin Press, 1969, pp. 88-89 **377** (Map) Adapted from Thomas Ellaison, *A Hand-Book of the Cotton Trade,* J. Woodland, Liverpool, 1838, pp. 24-25.

Index

Note: Page numbers followed by *t* designate tables; page numbers followed by *f* designate photographs.

Cape
Flattery

Puget
Sound

Olympia ★
Mt. St. Helens
8,366 ft.
(2,550 m) ▲

● Seattle

RANGE
Columbia   River

● Spokane

WASHINGTON

▲ Mt. Rainier
14,410 ft.
(4,300 m)

ROCKY

Portland ●

Columbia River

Salem ★

CASCADE

● Great Falls

Missouri   River

★ Helena   MONTANA

NORTH DAKO

● Eugene

OREGON

RANGES

COLUMBIA

IDAHO

MOUNTAINS

● Billings

Bismarck ★

Cape Blanco

● Boise ★

Cape
Mendocino

PLATEAU

Idaho Falls ●

SOUTH   DAKOTA

COAST

Snake River

● Pocatello

WYOMING

BLACK
HILLS

● Rapid City

★ Pierre

Sacramento
River

GREAT

Great
Salt
Lake

● Ogden

● Casper

North Platte River

G
R
E
A
T

NEBRASKA

Reno ●

RANGES

CENTRAL

SIERRA

Carson City ★

NEVADA

Lake Tahoe

BASIN

★ Salt Lake City

● Provo

Laramie ●

★ Cheyenne

Longs Peak
14,256 ft.
(4,344 m) ▲

South Platte River

● Grand Island

● Platte

San Francisco Bay

Oakland ●

Sacramento ●

NEVADA

UTAH

Green River

ROCKY

Colorado River

★ Denver

San Francisco ●
San Jose ●

San Joaquin River

VALLEY

Mt. Elbert
14,433 ft.
(4,400 m) ▲

COLORADO

★ Colorado Springs

KANSA

COAST

Mt. Whitney
14,500 ft.
(4,400 m) ▲

DEATH
VALLEY

● Las
Vegas

COLORADO

Pikes Peak
14,110 ft.
(4,300 m) ▲

● Pueblo

Arkansas   River

CALIFORNIA

MOJAVE
DESERT

River

PLATEAU

MOUNTAINS

PLAINS

Wic ●

RANGES

Los Angeles ●
Long Beach ●

● Anaheim

Salton
Sea

Colorado

★ Santa Fe

OKLAHO

ARIZONA

● Albuquerque

PACIFIC
OCEAN

San Diego ●

NEW MEXICO

Oklahoma Ci ●

Phoenix ★
● Mesa

Rio Grande

La ●

Tucson ●

LLANO
ESTACADO

TEXAS

Las Cruces ●

● El Paso

Rio Grande

Brazos River

22°N

155°W

180°

170°W

ARCTIC
OCEAN

KAUAI

OAHU

SOVIET
UNION

70°N

San Antonio ●

Honolulu ★

MOLOKAI

BROOKS   RANGE

Rio Grande

HAWAII

LANAI

● MAUI

PACIFIC OCEAN

160°W

Arctic Circle

Bering Strait

Nome ●

ALASKA

160°W

0   50 Miles

0   50 Kilometers

Hilo ●
HAWAII

Yukon   River

● Fairbanks

ATLA ●

19°N

60°N

MEXICO

BERING SEA

ALASKA

RANGE

CANADA

170°W

150°W

Mt. McKinley
20,320 ft.
(6,194 m) ▲

PACIFIC
OCEAN

50°N

0   250 Miles

0   250 Kilometers

● Anchorage

60°N

25°N

ALEUTIAN

KENAI
PENINSULA

Gulf of Alaska

Juneau ★

ISLANDS

KODIAK I.

130°W

CANADA

Lake Superior

MICHIGAN

Lake Huron

MINNESOTA

Duluth

WISCONSIN

St. Paul
nneapolis

Green Bay

Madison

Milwaukee

Lake Michigan

Grand Rapids

Lansing

Detroit

Lake Erie

Lake Ontario

Rochester

Buffalo

NEW YORK

ADIRONDACK MTS

MAINE

Augusta

Burlington

Lewiston

VT. N.H.

Montpelier

Portland

Concord

Manchester

Boston

Cape Cod

MASS.

Worcester

Providence

CONN.

R.I.

Hartford

Bridgeport

Albany

St. Lawrence River

Bay of Fundy

MOUNTAINS

Hudson River

New York City

LONG ISLAND

IOWA

Cedar Rapids

Rockford

Chicago

Gary

Ft. Wayne

Toledo

Cleveland

Akron

PENNSYLVANIA

Susquehanna

Harrisburg

Jersey City

Newark

NEW JERSEY

Trenton

Philadelphia

Wilmington

40°N

Moines

Davenport

Peoria

CENTRAL

INDIANA

OHIO

Columbus

Wheeling

Pittsburgh

ALLEGHENY MTS

Baltimore

DELAWARE

Dover

ATLANTIC OCEAN

ILLINOIS

Springfield

Indianapolis

Cincinnati

WEST VIRGINIA

WASHINGTON D.C.

Annapolis

MARYLAND

Missouri River

Kansas City

St. Louis

PLAINS

Frankfort

Louisville

Lexington

Ohio River

Huntington

Charleston

VIRGINIA

James River

Richmond

DELMARVA PENINSULA

Chesapeake Bay

Jefferson City

MISSOURI

OZARK PLATEAU

KENTUCKY

Nashville

Knoxville

APPALACHIAN MTS

Newport News

Norfolk

35° North Latitude

Mt. Mitchell 6,684 ft. (2,030 m)

Greensboro

Raleigh

Cape Hatteras

70° West Longitude

ARKANSAS

Fort Smith

Little Rock

TENNESSEE

Memphis

Tennessee River

BLUE RIDGE

PIEDMONT

NORTH CAROLINA

Charlotte

Pine Bluff

Mississippi River

Birmingham

Greenville

SOUTH CAROLINA

Columbia

COASTAL

PLAIN

Cape Fear

MISSISSIPPI

ALABAMA

Atlanta

GEORGIA

Columbus

Charleston

Jackson

Montgomery

Meridian

Alabama River

ATLANTIC

Savannah

Shreveport

LOUISIANA

Baton Rouge

COASTAL

PLAIN

Biloxi

Mobile

Jacksonville

Tallahassee

FLORIDA PENINSULA

Cape Canaveral

New Orleans

Mississippi Delta

90°W

85°W

FLORIDA

Tampa

St. Petersburg

Lake Okeechobee

Miami

Gulf of Mexico

20°N

ATLANTIC OCEAN

PUERTO RICO (U.S.)

San Juan

100 Miles

100 Kilometers

Florida Keys

Straits of Florida

CUBA

Tropic of Cancer

	International boundaries
	State boundaries
⊛	National capital
★	State capitals
•	Other cities
▲	Mountain peaks

0   100   200 Miles

0   100   200 Kilometers

GREENLAND
(KALAALLIT NUNAAT)
(Den.)

ICELAND

KI

IRELAND

PORTUG

ALASKA
(U.S.)

C A N A D A

UNITED STATES

ATLANTIC
OCEAN

AZORES (Port.)

MORO

CANARY IS. (Sp.)

WESTERN SAHARA
(Mor.)

Tropic of Cancer

20° N

HAWAII (U.S.)

MEXICO

BAHAMAS
DOMINICAN
REPUBLIC
HAITI
CUBA
PUERTO RICO (U.S.)
ST. KITTS AND NEVIS
JAMAICA
ANTIGUA AND BARBUDA
BELIZE
GUADELOUPE (Fr.)
DOMINICA
GUATEMALA
HONDURAS
MARTINIQUE (Fr.)
EL SALVADOR
ST. LUCIA
NICARAGUA
BARBADOS
GRENADA
COSTA RICA
TR INIDAD AND TOBAGO
PANAMA
VENEZUELA
GUYANA
SURINAME
COLOMBIA
FRENCH GUIANA (Fr.)

ST. VINCENT AND THE GRENADINES

MAURITAN

CAPE
VERDE

SENEGAL

GAMBIA

GUINEA–BISSAU
GUINEA
SIERRA LEONE
LIBERIA
CÔTE D'IVO

PACIFIC OCEAN

0° Equator

GALÁPAGOS IS.
(Ec.)

ECUADOR

PERU

BRAZIL

BURKINA

WESTERN
SAMOA
AMERICAN
SAMOA (U.S.)

TONGA

FRENCH
POLYNESIA (Fr.)

BOLIVIA

PARAGUAY

20° S Tropic of Capricorn

CHILE

URUGUAY

ATLANT

OCEAN

40° S

ARGENTINA

FALKLAND IS. (U.K.)

60° S

Antarctic Circle

80° S